THE AVRO 748

THE FULL STORY OF THE 748, ANDOVER & ATP

Richard J Church

Air-Britain

Copyright © Air-Britain Publishing 2017

Published in the United Kingdom by
Air-Britain Publishing

Regd Office:
Victoria House, Stanbridge Park,
Staplefield Lane, Staplefield,
West Sussex RH17 6AS, England

Sales Dept:
Unit 1A, Munday Works, 58-66 Morley Road,
Tonbridge, Kent TN9 1RA, England

Membership Enquiries:
Barry J. Coleman,
1 Rose Cottages, 179 Penn Road,
Hazlemere, Bucks. HP15 7NE, England

Correspondence regarding this book to:
richard_church748@hotmail.com

ISBN 978-0-85130-492-2

Printed in Poland
www.lfbookservices.co.uk

Origination by Howard Marks, France
Cover Origination by Lee Howard

CONTENTS

INTRODUCTION

It is now some fifty-six years since the first flight of the 748 airliner/military transport and fifty-four years since the Avro 748 flew its first revenue flight. During the years of manufacture of the type, the company was involved in a multiplicity of changes to the British aircraft manufacturing industry which saw mergers and contractions together with nationalisation and then denationalisation. The original A.V. Roe & Co. Ltd initially became part of the Hawker Siddeley Group, which in turn became part of British Aerospace. However, despite all of these changes the 748 has proved to be one of the most successful twin turbo-propeller airliners of its era and remained in production for twenty-eight years, during which time 350 aircraft were built, 89 of these being produced under licence in India. To be added to this figure were 31 Andover C.Mk.1s. Over the years the aircraft established a reputation for reliability, adaptability, unsurpassed ruggedness, ease of maintenance and low operating costs under the most arduous operating conditions in the world. The overall hours flown by the type have recently exceeded seven million (excluding the figures for the Andovers and Indian military aircraft).

Air-Britain (Historians) produced its original 748 Monograph in 1986 and it was thought appropriate to produce an updated version considering the multitude of changes that have taken place since that time. This new edition also incorporates the BAe ATP, a development of the 748 which never lived up to its hoped-for sales success. Although its capacity is some 50% greater than the 748 and the fuel efficiency greatly improved, the ATP has not been perceived as being as rugged as its predecessor. Only sixty-five aircraft were flown of which the last two were of the updated Jetstream 61 variety. The only two new-build Jetstream 61s to fly, did so from Prestwick rather than Woodford and were subsequently dismantled without ever seeing service. BAe sold ATPs in the Azores, Bangladesh, Denmark, Indonesia, Korea, Portugal, Turkey, the United Kingdom and the USA. However, many of the aircraft later returned to Europe with Air Europa Express taking a sizeable fleet of used aircraft. West Air Sweden, following its success with the 748 in the cargo rôle, set about adapting the ATP for a similar task. A sizeable fleet of aircraft, initially flying alongside its elder brethren, finally replaced them fully in May 2007 and gave the type a new lease of life. Some of the new fleet are fitted with large main-deck cargo doors allowing them to carry much bulkier loads. The success of the West Air Large Freight Door conversion led to BAe setting up a production line of door conversions at Romaero SA's Băneasa plant in Romania. These conversions of previously stored ATPs have seen aircraft placed with several European operators. August 2011 saw the twenty-fifth anniversary of the first flight of the ATP.

It was difficult to see what type could replace the 748 in Northern Canada where it became an established part of the scenery, although in December 2001 First Air/Bradley Air Services started to gradually replace its 748s with ATR42s, on scheduled services firstly out of its Yellowknife hub and in late 2004 its Iqaluit hub before finally withdrawing the type in February 2011. Calm Air International, Air Inuit, Air North and Air Creebec in particular have been using their aircraft for many years supplying isolated communities in the extreme north with essential supplies and providing affordable transport to markets for Inuit produced goods. Conditions can be extreme, with -40°C temperatures, snow and ice and continual dark during the winter months. Another niche the 748 created for itself in more recent years in Europe was in the night mail and parcels delivery rôle with Emerald Airways, Air Provence International and West Air Sweden. Operators in Southern, Central and East Africa have recently come to appreciate the worth of the 748 and Andover both in the scheduled rôle and in emergency relief operations, especially with former military examples as they have been retired from service.

The original text has been amended and updated considerably where appropriate, while a new selection of photographs has been included. It is very much appreciated that many of these have come from the collections of the Avro Heritage Centre Woodford (shown as WHC in the credits), Fred Barnes, Marty Boisvert, Allan

Fantham, Keith Gaskell, Ralph Harrison, Richard Hunt, George Jenks, Kurt Lang and Simon Watson (his unique Indian collection). Many of the Avro Heritage Centre images originated with the BAe Systems archive collection. The fascinating collection of items, models and paperwork contained within this Heritage Centre are a must visit for anybody interested in the history of the Chadderton and Woodford sites and is manned by an enthusiastic and dedicated team. Special thanks are due to Mike Zoeller who has kindly used his skills to put together the collection of three-view scale drawings and cabin layouts that have been collated from numerous sources.

Regrettably Fred Barnes, the co-author of the original 'Monograph', was unable to assist with this updated version due to pressure of work. However, I cannot thank him enough for all his contributions to the original book which included writing the 'General History' and 'Technical Description' sections and collating the Specification Data for the 748s.

Without the unfailing assistance of Harry Holmes, the Public Relations Manager at British Aerospace Manchester during the research for the original 'Monograph' it would have been impossible to produce this book. Mike Haslam and Adonai Agnello of BAe Systems at Toulouse together with Tony Carpenter, Kevin Haigh, Mark McLeod and Stephen Morrison from BAe Systems at Prestwick and Woodford have supplied more recent data. Many thanks are due to Ralph Harrison who has continually supplied information from his own comprehensive records over the many years I have been monitoring the progress of both the 748 and ATP. More recently George Jenks, who is deeply involved with the famed Avro Heritage Centre as its Manager, has contributed much historical data for which I am most indebted. This included much of the information in the 'Projected versions of the 748' section. Ken Haynes, also from Woodford, made available his own detailed records and has cross-checked his own data against my own. This uncovered much additional information on individual aircraft histories, especially in relation to worldwide demonstration and sales tours and first flight details with different UK and Class B registrations. Tony Blackman, the former Chief Test Pilot of A.V. Roe and Co Ltd, kindly made available his flying log books which uncovered details of previously unrecorded demonstration tours and delivery details from the early 748 days. Jim Halley's and Phil Butler's incredible specialist knowledge on the military versions of the 748 cannot go unrecorded. Their help with this section of the book could not be more appreciated.

Without the considerable assistance of Colin Carswell over many years it would have been impossible to follow the Canadian 748 scene in such detail. After working 748s with the RAF Queen's Flight at Benson, he moved to Canada and worked with Calm Air International and Wasaya Airways and was involved with the work carried out by Springer Aerospace. Similarly, Allan Fantham who has worked with 748s since 1973 until the end of their service life with Mount Cook Airlines and later with Emerald Airways, Executive Aerospace, Horizon Airlines, Aero Lanka, 748 Air Services in Nairobi and most recently Westwind Aviation also in Nairobi, has been a constant source of information. Allan still found time to repair damaged aircraft and renovate others in Nepal, Thailand and other parts of the world. Colin Kearney, after many years working 748s with First Air in Canada, was more recently deeply involved in bringing the diverse West Air Sweden fleet of aircraft up to a similar standard. His final task at West Air was to oversee the conversion to freighter configuration and the fitting and certification of the large freight door in the first of the company's new fleet of ATPs in association with BAe Systems at Prestwick. Since Colin's departure, Håkan Frylén has been a constant source of information on updating West Air's rapidly expanding fleet. Håkan, Robert Drews and Christian Lindberg (with his brilliant photographic collection) together with all the engineering team at the now-closed Lidköping engineering base have been a great source of information and assistance with the preparation of this updated book. More recently, Colin Frost has been very helpful with his specialist knowledge on ATPs. Herman Bosman, an avid 748 and Andover enthusiast, has uncovered much additional information on African operations with the aircraft, especially with regards to South Africa, while Lorne McDonald has solved many a mystery with Andovers and 748s employed in relief work in war torn Southern Sudan. More recently Gordon Reid, the Air Transport Editor of 'Australian Aviation', has been a constant source of information on 748s with an Australian connection, while Roger Thiedeman, originally with 'Airways Magazine', has uncovered much information on 748s with a Sri Lankan connection. Many thanks are also due to the QinetiQ team at Boscombe Down, especially Paul Bevis, Colin Froude, Paul Lampard and Mac Pile. Thanks are also due to Dave Whatley, the Chief Archivist at the Solent Sky Museum who came up with details of Folland's production of early 748 wing sets.

To mention everybody who assisted with information would be a monumental task since data has been collected over the past thirty-six years. I offer my apologies to those who have assisted me who are not mentioned. Special thanks are due to Jérôme Cassart, Steve Darke (Air-Britain's Thailand specialist), Jaime Escobar (for his specialist Colombian knowledge), Andy Heape, Ray Hoddinott, Derek A. King, Kurt Lang, Ruud Leeuw, Wing Commander M.D. Ratnayake & Air Commodore E.G.J.P De Silva (Sri Lanka Air Force), John Roach, Nils Rosengaard, Sandro Rota (Ecuador Aviation Photography), Dick Spurrell, Arthur Stevens, Barry Tippet, Ray Turner and Robert Urquhart for their assistance while Keith Gaskell has kindly checked the early proofs of this amended version and made various suggestions for improvements while also making available his unique collection of slides.

On the commercial and military front, thanks are due to the following for providing detailed information on their organisations' operations with the aircraft types covered in this book: - Aberdeen Airways Ltd (John Begg), Aden Airways Ltd (Dacre Watson & Peter Pickering), Africana Air (Ngenrr Senghore), Air BVI Ltd (David W. Oldbury), Air Cape (Pty) Ltd (C.F. Crocker), Air Creebec Inc (Marty Boisvert, Carl Lehto, J.A. Morrison and R. Novossiltzeff), Air Inuit (1985) Ltd (Colin Kearney and Eddie Lapointe), Air Madagascar (J.L. Rajaonarivelo), Air Malawi Ltd, Air Manitoba Ltd (R.V. Nyman), Air North Ltd (Kyle Cameron and James Connor), Air Ontario Inc (Ken Bittle), AirQuarius (Pty) Ltd (Cobus Conradie), Atlantic Airlines Ltd (Stuart Powney), Austin Airways Ltd (R.J. Deluce, H.J. McCracken & Gayle Belhumeur), Bouraq Indonesia Airlines PT (Soebadi Roeslanhadi), Bradley Air Services Ltd (John W. Crichton, M.G. Headland & Ray Patterson), British Airways plc, British Airways CitiExpress (Stuart Brawn & Andy Howard), British Independent Airways (Vincent Sharwood), Calm Air International Ltd (Chris Hughes and more recently Kevin Forbes), Cascade Airways Inc, Chieftain Airways Ltd (Finlay Cunningham), Dan-Air Engineering Ltd at Ringway (especially Alan Beeston), Eastern Provincial Airways Ltd (H.G. Robinson), Emerald Airways Ltd (Wayne Barker & Maureen Hall), Executive Aerospace (Pty) Ltd (Keith Roseveare, Peter Ovenstone and Jeff McKenzie), Fred. Olsen's Flyselskap A/S (Jan Hallin), Himalayan Aviation (Mahesh Rimal), Intensive Air (Pty) Ltd, Inter City Airways Inc (Bob Burns), International Air Parts Pty Ltd/Horizon Airlines Pty Ltd (Steve Ferris), Jersey European Airways Ltd (Paul Chapman), LIAT (1974) Ltd (P. Bird), Linhas Aéreas Regionais SA (Carlos da Roza Leal & José Sequeira Marcelino), Macavia International Inc, Mount Cook Airline, Necon Air Ltd (P.D. Bahadur), Philippine Airlines Inc (M.P. Hernaez), RF Saywell Ltd (Peter Saywell), Réunion Air Service (G. Graulich), the Royal New Zealand Air Force, Royal Tongan Airlines Ltd (P. Soakai), Nepal Army Air Wing (Col N.B. Bhandari), Ryanair Ltd (C.F. Ryan), SATA Air Açores (J. Cabral), South African Airways (J.G. Prozesky), Thai Airways Co Ltd (M.L. Ajcharaporn Na Songkhla), Thunderbird Tours Inc, TTAS/BWIA (L.L. Sing), Venture Airways Ltd (M. Hollick), Wasaya Airways Ltd (Colin Carswell and Lori Olsen), West Air Sweden, West Wind Aviation Inc (Ginette Lepage and Cory and Darcy Roussell) and Zambia Airways Corporation Ltd (E.S. Hapuhda).

Material has been compiled from official manufacturer's data where possible. Other sources have included Aeroplane, Air International, Airliner World, Air Pictorial, Ascend/Airclaims, Australian Aviation, Aviation Letter, Flight International, Propliner, Skyliner Magazine (Chris Witt), Scramble, The Aviation Safety Network, 'The Eagle Years' by David Hedges, the movement CDs of 'Ringway Through the Decades' released by Ringway Publications, 'Avro One' by Wing Commander J. A. Robinson, 'The Queen's Flight' by Michael Burns, 'Farnborough – 100 Years of British Aviation' by Peter J Cooper, 'The Spirit of Dan-Air' by Graham M. Simons, 'British Independent Airlines' by A.C. Merton Jones, the 'History of the Brazilian Air Force' by Col. Aparecido Camazano Alamino and from Rudnei Dias da Cunha on the same subject, 'The Avro 748 with Aerolíneas Argentinas' by Carlos Abella via the Latin American Aviation Historical Society, the many books written by Harry Holmes and of course the numerous Air-Britain publications, especially Air-Britain News, Digest and Aviation World and their many contributors. The 'ADF serials' web site has also proved very useful in exchanging data on the military operations of Antipodean 748s and Andovers with the co-operation of Darren Crick and Ivan Prince, while 'Bud' Oke was a great help in giving an insight into the specialist operations of the RAAF 748s. The OAG World Airways Guide and its predecessor the ABC World Airways Guide have been a constant source of detailed information on the scheduled carriers and the routes that they have flown for very many years. The publishers very kindly permitted me to carry out research in their extensive archives at Dunstable with the cooperation of Loraine Roberts. Additional information has been gleaned from the images on the 'abpic', 'airliners.net', 'jetphotos' and 'planepictures' websites.

Data for Indian produced aircraft has proved very difficult to obtain and all known information at the time of publication has been included. Group Captain Kapil Bhargava, who commanded the first flight of the HAL prototype, has been a great source of information in trying to fill this shortfall, while Bharat Rakshak's brilliant 'Indian Air Force' website is recommended for providing a wealth of information on this vast subject. Phil Camp has contributed much from his extensive records of Indian Air Force 748s, while more recently Aidan Curley has highlighted how many of the Indian Air Force aircraft are still active from his detailed reports in 2006 and 2007 and updates in 2011.

In addition to those mentioned already, the help provided by many individual Air-Britain members in the preparation and production of the book is highly appreciated, and whilst some may be omitted from this list, particular thanks go to Chris Alcock, Martin Bleasdale, Roy Blewett, John Bransbury, Chris Chatfield, Nigel Dingley, Bob Evans, Ian Hampton, Lee Howard, Howard Marks, Peter Marson, Keith Parkinson, Jenni Phillips, Colin Scarth, Tom Singfield, Terry Smith, Tony Szulc, Barrie Towey and Rich Tregear.

Over the years, a great deal of information has been published about the 748 and ATP and inevitably conflicts over dates and records have occurred. To endeavour to solve all such questions would have been a lengthy and almost impossible task. For the British built aircraft the official British Aerospace/BAe Systems record has been taken as factual. As 748s and ATPs have moved through the used aircraft market, information has become less readily available and sometimes impossible to verify. In these circumstances what is believed to be the most accurate information has been quoted.

Finally I am amazed at the tolerance of my wife Sue, who has put up with the inevitable chaos in our home during the period of time it took to prepare this book from all the paperwork that has been collected over the years. Similarly, Matthew, Clare and Ben have been a great help in assisting me with their word processing and computer skills, which have never been my forté.

A fully-searchable DVD accompanies this book and presents operator and individual production histories in tabular and linear formats which, it is hoped, readers will find useful.

Data is current up to the end of December 2016. Any additional information or corrections would be much appreciated at the address shown below or by Email to richard_church748@ hotmail.com.

31st December 2016

Richard J. Church,
44 South Street, Epsom, Surrey KT18 7PQ ENGLAND

ABBREVIATIONS

A & AEE	Aeroplane and Armament Experimental Establishment
AB	Swedish company designation
AC	Alternating Current
ADF	Airborne Direction Finding (Equipment)
AEO	Air Electronics Officer
A/F	Air Force
a/o	as of
AOC	Air Operator's Certificate
Apr	April
APU	Auxiliary Power Unit
A/S	Air Services
ASF	Aircraft Servicing Flight
Aug	August
AUW	All-up Weight
BAe	British Aerospace
BCAR	British Civil Aviation Requirements
BCF	Bromochlorodifluoromethane
b/u	Broken-up
°C	Degrees Centigrade
CA	Controller (Air) (also C(A))
CAA	Civil Aviation Authority
Cld	Cancelled
cm	Centimetres
c/o	Carried out
CofA	Certificate of Airworthiness
CofR	Certificate of Registration
config	configuration
Corp	Corporation
c/s	Colour scheme
dBA	Decibel
Dec	December
del	Delivered or delivery
demo	Demonstration
DC	Direct Current
DME	Distance Measuring Equipment
DRC	Democratic Republic of Congo
ECM	Electronic Counter Measures
EPNdB	Effective Perceived Noise Decibel
eshp	Equivalent Shaft Horse Power
EWAU	Electronic Warfare and Avionics Unit
°F	Degrees Fahrenheit
FAA	Federal Aviation Authority
Feb	February
F/F	First Flight
f/n	fleet number
Ft	Feet
GPU	Ground Power Unit
GPWS	Ground Proximity Warning System
HAL	Hindustan Aeronautics Limited
HF	High Frequency
h/o	handed over
HP	High Pressure
hr(s)	Hour(s)
HS	Hawker-Siddeley
IAS	Indicated Air Speed
ie	that is
Imp Gals	Imperial Gallons
In(s)	Inch(es)
Inc	Incorporated
IFE	In-Flight Entertainment
Int	International
Jan	January
Jul	July
Jun	June
kg	Kilogramme
km	Kilometre
kt	Knot
kVA	Kilovolt-Ampères
lb	Pound
LCN	Load Classification Number
ldgs	Landings

LFD	Large Freight Door
LP	Low Pressure
Lse/lsd	Lease/Leased
Ltd	Limited
m	Metre
maint	Maintenance
Mar	March
min	Minute
mk	Mark or Mark Number
mls	Statute Miles
MLW	Maximum Landing Weight
mm	Milimetre
'	Minute of Degree
mods	Modifications
mph	Miles Per Hour
MTOW	Maximum Take-off Weight
MU	Maintenance Unit
MZFW	Maximum Zero Fuel Weight
NACA	United States National Advisory Committee for Aeronautics (now National Aeronautics and Space Administration – NASA)
napsab	Northern Aircraft Painting Services AB
nm	Nautical Miles
Nov	November
ntu	Not Taken Up
Oct	October
pax	Passenger(s)
plc	Public limited company
psi	pounds per square inch
PWFU	Permanently withdrawn from use
RAAF	Royal Australian Air Force
RAE	Royal Aircraft Establishment
RAF	Royal Air Force
Regd	Registered
Regn	Registration
Re-regd	Re-registered
RNZAF	Royal New Zealand Air Force
r/o	Rolled out
rpm	Revolutions per Minute
rsvd	Reserved
SA	Socièta Anonima/Sociedad Anonima
Sep	September
shp	Shaft Horse Power
soc/SOC	Struck off charge
Srs	Series
TAWS	Terrain Awareness Warning System
TBO	Time Between Overhaul
TCAS	Traffic Collision and Avoidance System
TGT	Turbine Gas Temperature
TT	Total time
US Gals	United States Gallons
V	Volt
VA	Volt-Ampère
VHF	Very High Frequency
WAT	Weight Altitude Temperature
WFS	Withdrawn from service
WFU	Withdrawn from use
WHC	Woodford Heritage Centre
W/O	Written Off

Australian States

ACT	Australian Capital Territory
NSW	New South Wales
NT	Northern Territory
QLD	Queensland
SA	South Australia
TAS	Tasmania
VIC	Victoria
WA	Western Australia

Canadian States/Provinces

The Canadian states listing shows the current abbreviation (first and previous usages in brackets).

AB (Alta)	Alberta
BC	British Columbia
MB (Man)	Manitoba
NB	New Brunswick
NL (Nfld)	Newfoundland (& Labrador)
NS	Nova Scotia
NT (NWT)	Northwest Territories
NU	Nunavut
ON (Ont)	Ontario
PE (PEI)	Prince Edward Island
QC (Que/PQ)	Quebec
SK (Sask)	Saskatchewan
YK (Yuk)	Yukon Territory

United States States and Territories

AK	Alaska
AL	Alabama
AR	Arkansas
AZ	Arizona
CA	California
CO	Colorado
CT	Connecticut
DC	District of Columbia
DE	Delaware
FL	Florida
GA	Georgia
HI	Hawaii
IA	Iowa
ID	Idaho
IL	Illinois
IN	Indiana
KS	Kansas
KY	Kentucky
LA	Louisiana
MA	Massachusetts
MD	Maryland
ME	Maine
MI	Michigan
MN	Minnesota
MO	Missouri
MS	Mississippi
MT	Montana
ND	North Dakota
NE	Nebraska
NH	New Hampshire
NM	New Mexico
NJ	New Jersey
NV	Nevada
NY	New York
OH	Ohio
OK	Oklahoma
OR	Oregon
PA	Pennsylvania
PR	Puerto Rico
RI	Rhode Island
SC	South Carolina
SD	South Dakota
TN	Tennessee
TX	Texas
UT	Utah
VA	Virginia
VI	Virgin Islands
VT	Vermont
WA	Washington
WI	Wisconsin
WV	West Virginia
WY	Wyoming

748 and Andover

The two Avro 748 prototypes in flight, G-APZV c/n 1534 and G-ARAY c/n 1535.

Chapter 1
General History

The British Aerospace 748, previously known as the Avro 748 and Hawker Siddeley 748, became one of the best-selling British post-war designs and a useful number still remain in service fifty-seven years since detailed design work began in January 1959 and some fifty-six years since the first flight of the first prototype. When the 748 was introduced into service, the type offered new standards of reliability, ease of maintenance, economy, passenger appeal and flexibility of operation combined with good overall performance. The original design was improved and updated continually in the light of experience, and it was also adapted to fulfil a multiplicity of rôles, both civil and military, leading to its use worldwide.

The 748 story really began with the Duncan Sandys White Paper on Defence in 1957, which forecast that there would be no further requirement for manned military combat aircraft. During the post-war period AV Roe & Co Ltd, more commonly known as Avro, had become a predominantly military aircraft constructor and the future for new military types was looking bleak. The company decided to diversify and re-enter the civil aircraft market where their previous ventures, the Lancastrian, York and Tudor had met with only limited success. Avro reviewed the civil market to establish where their future resources should be directed. Douglas, Lockheed, Convair, Bristol and Vickers-Armstrongs were well established with viable types that were already in service. After assessing the civil aircraft requirements the company realised that there was a 'slot' with great potential in the short-haul sector for a DC-3 type replacement. At the time there were nearly 3,000 DC-3s/C-47s in both airline and military use throughout the world. Avro consequently began evaluations for a DC-3 type replacement and endeavoured to lay down the basic criteria for such an aircraft. The aircraft would be required to operate into any airfield currently used by DC-3s but with improved payload and economics.

At an early stage, it was envisaged that the aircraft would be able to operate with forty passengers from city centres, even from especially prepared roofs of railway stations. These ideas were quickly rejected as being over-ambitious. A study of DC-3 operations was undertaken and operators were asked for their requirements for a suitable replacement type. After lengthy evaluations and discussions, Avro established the following requirements for the new design:

a) A full payload/range of 400nm (740km) with the capability for flying longer distances with a reduced payload

b) Ability to operate from semi-prepared strips no longer than 4,000ft (1,220m) in hot/high conditions

c) Ability to operate from remote airfields without servicing, refuelling, navigation or communication aids

d) Good flying characteristics for operation into difficult and primitive airfields

e) Good fatigue life construction using fail-safe methods and capable of easy repair in the field

f) Simple aircraft systems using well-proven components, low maintenance costs and easy accessibility

g) Pressurisation for passenger comfort

h) Proven reliable, easy to maintain and economical civilian turbo-propeller powerplant

i) Ease of loading/unloading and option of quickly convertible passenger to cargo configuration or combination of both

j) Certification to both United Kingdom and later United States requirements

k) Low internal and external noise levels

The short-lived aircraft G-ARMV c/n 1536 of Skyways of London.   *(WHC/AV Roe & Co Ltd)*

COMPETITION

During the late 1950s, there were other types in production aimed at a similar market and Avro had to take this competition into account. Avro felt that whilst the Vickers-Armstrongs Viscount was aimed at the trunk route market, Fokker with their F.27 (to be licence-built in the USA by Fairchild as the F-27) was offering a feeder-type aircraft without the same rough-field characteristics envisaged by their own design. Handley Page was also on the scene but had lost ground when they had decided to switch powerplants from four Alvis Leonides piston engines to twin Rolls-Royce Darts in their Herald aircraft. Nevertheless, competition did not only come from the aforementioned aircraft. Consideration was also taken into account of the large numbers of Convair 240/340/440 and to a lesser degree Martin 202/404 aircraft that could be expected to move down into the second-hand market as the larger airlines replaced these types with newer equipment. Fokker was regarded as the main competitor as their F.27 Friendship was already beginning to sell. Avro remained confident that they could make a success of their proposals and decided to continue their design studies.

DESIGN STAGE

During 1958 the Avro design team in Manchester looked at the various options available to them to fulfil the above requirements. Initially, a high wing was studied, similar to the Fokker F.27, Herald and the de Havilland DH 123 proposal from Hatfield. The project was allotted the design number 748 and represented a high-wing 20-seat aircraft powered by two de Havilland Gnome or Armstrong-Siddeley P.182 turbine engines of around 1,000 shp derived from existing helicopter powerplants. Following further consultation with operators, the low wing layout proved more acceptable and the low/high wing argument was re-evaluated. The main advantages of a high wing were a better maximum co-efficient of lift, low floor level throughout the fuselage for ease of loading, good propeller/ground clearance and better passenger outlook. In comparison, the low wing advantages were ease of control, stability at low airspeeds, ease of maintenance, a short sturdy undercarriage and passenger protection in the event of a belly landing. The main disadvantage of the high wing layout was that the main spar passed through the cabin with the subsequent weight penalty of the strengthened fuselage to support the wing. After much consideration, it was concluded that overall the low wing layout was the most advantageous. Initial designs centred on an aircraft with a gross weight of 18,500lbs (8,400kgs) offering a payload of 4,500lbs (2,043kgs) over a range of 410nm (760km) using two 1,100 shp P.182 powerplants.

Further discussions with prospective customers indicated that the 7ft 6in (2.29m) wide cabin with headroom of only 5ft 10in (1.8m) was too small. By the end of 1958, the 748 design had grown to a gross weight of 29,000lbs (13,154kgs) and later to 33,000lbs (14,980kgs). The cabin width was increased to 8ft 1in (2.46m) and the height to 6ft 4in (1.92m), allowing a four-abreast layout for 36 passengers. Other changes included raising the maximum payload to 9,650lbs (4,380kgs) over a range of 580nm (1,075km) and an increase in wingspan from 71ft (21.66m) to 95ft (28.98m) with an improvement in aspect ratio from 10 to 11.35. With the

The second prototype G-ARAY c/n 1535 undertook a demonstration tour of the Middle East and India in October and November 1962. This picture shows the aircraft at Kathmandu, Nepal, with a DC-3, the aircraft it was designed to replace, in the foreground.   *(WHC/BAe)*

The second prototype 748, G-ARAY c/n 1535, on the cargo ramp at Johannesburg with C-47 O-38866 and an SAA Viscount.

increase in size and weight more powerful engines were required and it was decided to adopt the Rolls-Royce Dart, a type already proven in the Viscount and Fokker Friendship and selected for the Armstrong Whitworth AW 650 Argosy. The design team selected an engine mounting position ahead of and above the main spar, permitting the jet pipes to exhaust over the wing. The main undercarriage was designed to retract forwards into a bulbous compartment ahead of the wing and beneath the engine housings. By mounting the engines in this way a short sturdy undercarriage could be used while sufficient ground clearance could be obtained for the propellers.

The design now fulfilled the company's requirements for a new aircraft to launch Avro back into the civil aircraft market, and in January 1959 the Hawker Siddeley Group Board decided to back the project. Authorisation was received to proceed with the construction of four airframes, comprising two flying prototypes, one static test airframe and one fatigue test airframe. Unlike most post-war British designs, the Avro 748 project was launched as a private venture with no government backing or orders to help with development costs. From the outset it was company policy to keep down costs wherever possible by utilising features of existing types that had been proven already. After the Dart engine had been selected, design rights were purchased from Vickers-Armstrongs for the engine compartment forward of the fireproof bulkhead incorporating the complete nacelle and sub-frame of the Viscount 800 Series. The Dowty-Rotol accessory gearbox was a standard Viscount component and the same company's propellers used hubs similar to those of the Armstrong Whitworth Argosy. Avro's overall design was aimed at a tough durable aircraft, easy to maintain, cheap to operate, reliable in service and with good handling characteristics for safe flying for operators worldwide.

PROTOTYPES

After the project was given the "go-ahead" by the Board, detailed design work started in January 1959 and the first metal was cut the following month. The first flight was planned to take place in early 1960, but the target slipped after delays in the construction of the initial prototype. However, on the 24th June 1960 the first

prototype of the Avro 748 made its maiden flight from the company's Woodford airfield with Chief Test Pilot Jimmy Harrison and second pilot Colin Allen at the controls. Also on board were Flight Test Observers Bob Dixon-Stubbs and Mike Turner. The aircraft, registered G-APZV, was airborne for 2 hours 41 minutes, a record for the first flight of a civil airliner at the time. Two Rolls-Royce Dart RDa.6 Mk 514 engines rated at 1,600 shp were installed for this first flight. The first prototype was allotted to the certification flying programme, airframes numbers 2 and 4 were assigned for ground testing, while airframe number 3 would become the second flying prototype to assist in the certification programme and to become the company's demonstration aircraft. This last airframe was registered G-ARAY but was badly damaged in a major fire in 1960 at Avro's Chadderton factory near Manchester. Inevitably, construction of the remaining three prototype/test airframes was delayed, which led to G-ARAY not flying until 10th April 1961, by which time G-APZV had already completed some 360 of the planned 1,000 hours of certification flying.

The Avro 748 was designed using the "fail-safe" principle, whereby if a crack or structural failure occurred during the aircraft's normal operating life then other parts of the structure would take the load. By employing this principle the aircraft could remain in service until a repair could be carried out. In April 1961 static testing started using airframe number 2. During the tests, cabin pressure was increased gradually to over twice the normal working load and the complete airframe withstood loads of 103% of the ultimate design load without failure. The crack-free life of the structure and the "fail-safe" characteristics were proven by fatigue tests using airframe number 4. These tests started in August 1961 in a water tank at the Chadderton plant, where tests were carried out to simulate 100,000 flying hours giving a safety factor of three. For test purposes the loads of a typical one-and-three-quarter hour flight were simulated in each cycle. The first cracks did not appear until some 30,000 hours (57,500 test cycles) had been completed and they were easily located. The tests also demonstrated that those cracks that did appear showed a slow growth rate. Later the static and fatigue test airframes were used during subsequent design development studies and for special cases when required.

LV-HHC c/n 1541 of Aerolineas Argentinas in an early publicity shot taken over Buenos Aires docks, dated 29th April 1968, on approach to Aeroparque.
(WHC/HSA)

PRODUCTION GO-AHEAD IN THE UNITED KINGDOM AND INDIA

Towards the end of 1959, sufficient interest had been generated by the 748 design to warrant the authorisation by the Hawker Siddeley Board of the first batch of ten production aircraft. Tooling and construction of jigs started and long lead-time items for a second batch of ten aircraft were also ordered. The production facilities were set up at the Chadderton factory. The Indian Government had shown a keen interest in the 748 project and concluded an agreement for licence-manufacture of the type on 10th December 1959. A feature of the Indian agreement was that 748 aircraft would be licence-assembled and later licence-manufactured in a specially-built factory at Kanpur. Initially, components would be supplied from the Avro facilities in the United Kingdom for assembly at Kanpur. Later the Indians would manufacture the entire aircraft under licence with locally-produced components. The Indian production line would be used to supply aircraft to the Indian Air Force and later to Indian Airlines Corporation. Avro staff were sent to Kanpur to assist with the establishment of the production facilities in parallel with those at Chadderton. On 1st November 1961 the first Indian-assembled 748 made its first flight, all components having been shipped out from the United Kingdom. Hindustan Aeronautics Limited later took over the Kanpur facilities and continued licence-production of the HAL 748.

FIRST ORDERS

BKS Air Transport Ltd ordered two aircraft in September 1959 followed by a further three aircraft a year later. These orders were later cancelled when BKS ran into financial difficulties, but they did, however, operate the type in later years. Aden Airways ordered three Series 2 aircraft (of which more later) on 26th April 1960 through BOAC Associated Companies. A fuselage mock-up of the 748 in Aden Airways livery was displayed at the 1960 Farnborough Air Show. The aircraft were scheduled for delivery in June 1962 but the order was cancelled subsequently. This was due to Avro being unable to guarantee that the aircraft would be able to operate out of some of the hot and high airfields within the Protectorate in the event of an engine failure on take-off.

An important milestone for the Avro 748 took place on 25th January 1961 when Aerolíneas Argentinas signed a contract for nine aircraft for operation on their domestic and regional routes. The order was increased later to twelve aircraft in January 1963. Previously, Skyways Coach Air Ltd had stated its intention to purchase the 748, but the lease/purchase agreement for three aircraft was not finalised until 31st May 1961. The first United Kingdom production aircraft, registered G-ARMV, took to the air for the first time on 31st August 1961 in the livery of Skyways Coach Air.

CERTIFICATION

During the latter part of 1961, Avro was in the final phase of the certification flying programme and by November all of the required flight trials had been undertaken. The second prototype had undertaken hot weather and high altitude trials in Cyprus and Madrid respectively in July 1961. The two prototype aircraft had been used to fulfil the certification programme with G-APZV completing 683 and G-ARAY 367 hours of test flying. The certification programme included 160 hours of route-proving trials by Skyways Coach Air using G-ARMV between Lympne, Beauvais, Lyon and Montpellier. After all the necessary work had been completed, the Avro 748 was awarded a Transport Category Certificate of Airworthiness on 9th January 1962. The initial production aircraft were certificated at a gross weight of 36,200lbs (16,435kgs), an increase from 34,500lbs (15,663kgs) at the start of the flying programme.

Production had started during 1959 and was geared for deliveries starting in early 1962. The production aircraft differed from the two flying prototypes in having an increased wingspan of 98ft 6in (30,04m) and slightly higher-rated Dart RDa.6 Mk 514 engines of 1,740 shp. Both G-APZV and G-ARAY were modified to the 98ft 6in wing span standard prior to certification. On 18th January 1962 the first customer delivery took place when Aerolíneas Argentinas accepted its initial Avro 748 with c/n 1539. The type entered regular service with Aerolíneas on 2nd April 1962 after an ad hoc flight to Punte del Este on 15th February and Avro's DC-3 replacement design had become a commercial reality. Skyways Coach Air Ltd introduced the type into service just over a fortnight later on 17th April with G-ARMV on its short sector schedules from Lympne across the English Channel.

DEVELOPMENT

Whilst the certification programme was under way and production had started, the Avro design team had been working on a development programme for the 748 project. Rolls-Royce had developed a new variant of the Dart engine designated Dart RDa.7 with an increased power rating of 1,910 shp. This new engine enabled the Avro 748 to be operated at higher weights, thus offering increased payloads over a given range or additional range with the same payload. Furthermore, the new engines enabled improvements to be achieved with take-off weights in high temperature situations or at high altitude airfields. Avro decided to market the Dart 6 powered aircraft as the 748 Series 1 and the new Dart 7 powered aircraft as the 748 Series 2. The new Series 2 version required some structural strengthening of the wing and undercarriage to obtain higher operating weights whilst an increase in cabin pressure differential to 5.5 psi (0.39 kg/cm²) to allow operations up to 25,000 ft required some strengthening of the fuselage structure. Maximum take-off weight of the Series 2 was planned at 43,500lbs (19,750kgs).

The second prototype aircraft, G-ARAY, was converted at Woodford from a Series 1 to a Series 2 version, including the installation of the new Rolls-Royce Dart RDa.7 Mk 531 engines. On 6th November 1961 G-ARAY made its first flight as an Avro 748 Series 2. After an extensive test programme, which included tropical trials in Kenya and Nigeria during March and April 1962 and further fatigue tests, the Series 2 received its type Certification in October 1962. With the overall improved performance of the Series 2, it quickly became the most popular version with customers and became the standard production version. Only 23 Series 1 aircraft were produced, including the first four off the Kanpur production line. The first production Series 2 first flew from Woodford on 27th August 1962. This was the first of six aircraft ordered by the Força Aérea Brasileira and on 17th November 1962 was the first Series 2 to be delivered to a customer. Indian production was also changed to the Series 2 and the first Kanpur produced version first flew on 28th January 1964.

During the early 1960s, the Royal Air Force issued a requirement for a medium tactical freighter and Avro decided to offer a design to fulfil the rôle. Avro's design team began work on a project to modify the 748 Series 2 to meet the military requirements for a rear loading aircraft. The basic 748 fuselage and low wing layout were retained while the rear fuselage was upswept to incorporate a rear loading ramp with doors capable of opening in flight. Major modifications were carried out to the standard airframe, wing and landing gear and the tailplane was moved to the base of the fin. More powerful Rolls-Royce Dart RDa.12 Mk 301 engines of 3,245 shp were installed driving four-bladed propellers of 14ft 6in (4.42m) diameter, offering improved short-field performance. A unique "kneeling" undercarriage was developed whereby the landing gear could be adjusted to raise or lower the height of the rear cabin floor sill for loading and unloading. The new design was designated the Avro Type 780 but was also known as the 748MF and was effectively a new aircraft type. Handley Page was also planning a Dart Herald derivative to fulfil the RAF's requirements, competing directly with the 748MF. Both aircraft offered similar capabilities at the design stage and so a series of trials was set up by the Ministry of Defence to establish the better of the two designs. The trials took place during February 1962 at Martlesham Heath, Suffolk. Avro used the prototype Series 2 G-ARAY to demonstrate the type's capabilities. The 748 performed well and operated from unprepared surfaces including rutted mud, an exercise that Handley Page did not undertake with the Dart Herald. As a result of the trials, the RAF decided to order the Avro 748MF rather than the Dart Herald. During October 1962 detailed design work on the Avro 780 (748MF) project started and a production contract for 31 aircraft was awarded in April 1963. The RAF designated the Avro 780/748MF as the Andover C.Mk.1 while six standard Series 2 748s were ordered for Transport Command with the designation Andover CC.Mk.2. Two of the standard 748 aircraft were intended for the Queen's Flight to replace the older de Havilland Heron aircraft in service at the time. A third aircraft from that order was later allocated to the Queen's Flight and all had special interiors and avionics installed. The remaining three aircraft were VIP Andover CC.Mk.2s.

The first prototype 748 G-APZV was converted to 748MF configuration as a flying development test aircraft. Changes included a wider centre section to accommodate the larger diameter propellers, the wing tips were each reduced by 18in (46cm) to maintain the same overall wingspan and a dihedral tailplane was fitted in order to clear the propeller slipstream. G-APZV, originally allotted c/n 1534, was re-registered G-ARRV with a new c/n 1548 for its new rôle. On 21st December 1963 G-ARRV made its first flight in the 748MF configuration and was then used for the development programme.

Andover C.Mk.1 production started and the first production aircraft made its maiden flight on 9th July 1965. After gaining the Certificate of Airworthiness Release in May 1966, the Andover C.Mk.1 entered service with No.46 Squadron RAF and later aircraft were introduced into service with No.52 Squadron Far East Air Force based in Singapore and with No.84 Squadron based at Sharjah in the Middle East. All C.Mk.1s were delivered by the end of February 1968, while the CC.Mk.2s were delivered in 1964 and 1965.

NAME CHANGE

On 1st July 1963 the Hawker Siddeley Group re-organised their main aircraft manufacturing companies into one new company entitled Hawker Siddeley Aviation Limited (HSA). Well-known companies such as AV Roe, Armstrong Whitworth, Blackburn, de Havilland, Folland, Gloster and Hawker were all included in the new corporate identity and their historic separate names disappeared. Virtually overnight, the Avro 748 became the Hawker Siddeley 748 but was more commonly known as the HS 748.

Royal Air Force Andover CC.Mk.2 XS790 c/n 1562, delivered to RAF Benson on 10th July 1964 for use by the Queen's Flight.   (Fred Barnes collection)

Shown at the 1962 Farnborough Air Show, C-91 2500 c/n 1550 was delivered to the Fôrça Aérea Brasileira on 17th November 1962, the first of an initial order for six Series 2 transports.
(WHC/BAe)

1966 production line at Woodford with both Andover C.Mk.1s and 748s in view. The foremost aircraft, labelled 'Set 77', was destined to join the RAAF as a Srs.2/229 operating in the VIP rôle as A10-596. *(WHC)*

HS748 fuselage assembly at Chadderton, from where they were transported by road to Woodford for final assembly. *(BAe)*

RAAF VIP aircraft A10-595 c/n 1595, showing the cowling re-contoured to house the Rover APU aft of the starboard Dart engine..   ('Bud' Oke)

SALES

Initial sales of United Kingdom-built 748s were relatively slow after the orders from Aerolíneas Argentinas (all twelve Series 1s being delivered in 1962 and 1963) and Fôrça Aérea Brasileira (six aircraft delivered in 1962 and 1963). Skyways Coach Air took delivery of three Series 1 aircraft in 1962 and 1963, while BKS Air Transport accepted single Series 1s in 1963 and 1964. Only one non-airline Series 1 was sold from the United Kingdom production line and this went to the Aviation Division of S Smith & Sons in 1963. From 1964, sales started picking up and over the next five years airline sales were made in the Far East and Australasia to Air Ceylon (1), Thai Airways (8), Philippine Airlines (8), Mount Cook Airlines (1) and Fiji Airways (2). In the United Kingdom and Europe sales were made to Channel Airways (4), BKS Air Transport (1), Autair (2) and Austrian Airlines (2). South and Central America and the West Indies were to prove major areas for sales. Airline sales to LAV of Venezuela (6), LIAT (2), Bahamas Airways (4), Aeromaya of Mexico (2), COPA of Panama (1), LAN - Chile (9), VARIG (10) and AVIANCA (2) were concluded. The second prototype G-ARAY and the former BKS Air Transport G-ATAM (which was returned to HSA in July 1967) were demonstrated and in many cases leased to several of the above companies prior to delivery of their own aircraft. Two of Channel Airways' aircraft were also leased by HSA for similar work. Details of these leases and the many worldwide demonstration tours can be found in the 'Individual Aircraft Histories' section of this book. The LAV aircraft were the first to be fitted with an optional Auxiliary Power Unit (APU) in the form of a Rover Gas Turbines 2S/150A APU mounted immediately behind the starboard Dart power plant above the engine jet-pipes in a re-contoured housing. The second prototype and much-travelled G-ARAY was sold to Falcks Flyvetjeneste A/S of Denmark in 1967.

With the receipt of the Royal Air Force and Brazilian Air Force orders, Hawker Siddeley was in a strong position with potential military customers and further development of military rôles was undertaken. When the Australian Government ordered ten aircraft for the Royal Australian Air Force, comprising two VIP aircraft and eight navigation trainers, further military sales looked even more promising. The two VIP aircraft had standard Dart RDa.7 engines while the eight navigation trainers were fitted with Dart RDa.8 Mk 550-2 engines of 2,250 shp, to enable higher dry take-off power to be achieved and all ten were fitted with the optional APU. The standard aircraft were delivered in 1967 with the specialised aircraft following in 1968 and 1969.

Special interiors could also be installed and apart from the Queen's Flight, the Royal Thai Air Force, the Venezuela and Argentine Governments and the Zambia Air Force also ordered VIP versions. The Venezuela and Zambia purchasers also took up the APU option.

Hawker Siddeley suffered a setback in 1967 when an order for eight aircraft for LADE, the transport wing of the Fuerza Aérea Argentina, was cancelled after a disagreement at government level. The President of Argentina was due to ratify the contract when an outbreak of foot and mouth disease in the United Kingdom was blamed on imported contaminated Argentine meat. Regrettably, the statements were never substantiated and the Argentine Government retaliated by cancelling British contracts. The Argentine Government subsequently ordered the rival Fokker F.27 aircraft and later increased that order to twelve aircraft.

By far the largest military customer was the Indian Air Force, with orders totalling 55 aircraft all from the Kanpur assembly line. These are dealt with in a later section of this book.

HS 748 SERIES 2A

During 1967 the standard HS 748 Series 2 was further improved by installing new more powerful Rolls-Royce Dart RDa.7 Mk 532 engines rated at 2,230 shp. The new version was marketed as the HS 748 Series 2A and the first flight took place on 5th September by a new company demonstration aircraft c/n 1635 registered G-AVRR. On 7th September 1968 the first production Series 2A, c/n 1657 registered HK-1408, was delivered to AVIANCA of Colombia. Two different variants of the Dart RDa.7 were installed in the new version under the designations Mk 532-2L and Mk 532-2S. In-service experience with the Series 2 aircraft and continued structural and fatigue testing together with routine development had led to certification of higher maximum take-off and landing weights, offering improved payload capabilities. Most of the earlier-produced Series 2 aircraft were upgraded to Series 2A standard by modifying their Dart engines to the new standards until by 1969 the Series 2A had become the standard production version.

One of the 748's major selling points was its operating flexibility, enabling the operator to fulfil a number of rôles and thus increase utilisation. The two Austrian Airlines examples were used for scheduled passenger services during the daytime and were then converted quickly to freighters for night flights before their re-configuration to passenger aircraft the next morning. Adaptations to the basic 748 were also made for special purpose duties. Smiths' Aviation Division purchased a single Series 1 748 to be used in conjunction with several research projects until it was later sold to the Royal Aircraft Establishment at Bedford. The UK Civil Aviation Flying Unit (CAFU) ordered two aircraft for 1969 delivery for radio and navigation calibration and flight inspection duties, initially based at Stansted. Fitted with specialised equipment, these flight inspection aircraft were capable of checking and calibrating many radio and radar aids in everyday use. The aircraft also flight-checked ILS equipment up to Autoland standards and the type's good handling qualities enabled overshoots from very low heights to be carried out regularly.

Subsequent to the CAFU's order and satisfactory performance in service the West German equivalent, the Bundesanstalt für Flugsicherung (BFS), also ordered two flight-inspection 748s. The BFS aircraft were fitted with the higher-powered Rolls-Royce Dart RDa.8 engines and had a modified pressurisation system to enable high altitude sorties to be flown as well as the normal duties. After satisfactory entry into service in 1969 and 1973, a further five aircraft were purchased by the BFS for similar work for delivery in 1975 and 1976. All the BFS aircraft were fitted with the Rover APU.

FURTHER SALES

By December 1968, HS 748s had accumulated half a million flying hours with twenty operators in twenty countries and in June 1970 Hawker Siddeley won the Queen's Award to Industry for its export achievements with the 748. Further airline sales were made in 1969 and 1970 to Air Malawi (2), Midwest Airlines of Canada (1), Royal Nepal Airlines (2), SAESA of Mexico (3), Rousseau Aviation (2), Ghana Airways (2), Zambia Airlines (3) and SATA Açores (1) while repeat orders came from COPA (1), LIAT (1), Thai Airways (1), Philippine Airlines (4) and Fiji Airways (1). The first used aircraft came onto the market in the late 1960s and early 1970s. Channel Airways' fleet of four aircraft, after many overseas and domestic leases, were disposed of, with a single aeroplane going to Midwest Airlines in December 1967, two to LIAT in May and June 1968 and the last aircraft to Philippine Airlines in September 1970. Austrian Airlines' two aircraft were sold to Skyways Coach Air in November 1969 and to Philippine Airlines in September 1970. This last company had purchased an aircraft from Bahamas Airways in June of the same year.

Military sales continued with orders from the Fuerza Aérea Ecuatoriana (FAE) (3), the Brunei Government (1) and a repeat order from the Zambia Air Force (1) for an APU-equipped aircraft, following the loss of its initial aircraft. The FAE order was interesting as the 748s were for operation by TAME, the

G-ASJT c/n 1559 of Smiths' Aviation Division was used for various research projects.

(WHC/HSA)

The much-travelled second prototype G-ARAY c/n 1535 in service with Dan-Air London at Gatwick on 20th October 1989.   *(Keith Gaskell)*

Ecuadorian domestic airline operated by the Air Force to develop communications to the more remote parts of the country. Often primitive airstrips were used with little provision for any navigational facilities. After witnessing the impressive 748 service record in Ecuador, the Colombian Government later ordered four aircraft for SATENA, a similar military airline operation in that country. These were all delivered in 1972.

The 748 also found a small market as a corporate aircraft in 1969 when AMOCO (Canada) purchased c/n 1669 registered CF-AMO. Chevron Standard Oil of Canada followed suit by purchasing c/n 1679 in 1970, and in both cases the 748s were used for many years to ferry personnel and equipment to remote airstrips throughout Canada.

FURTHER USED AIRCRAFT SALES

In May 1971, Dan-Air Services took delivery of the first of what was to be a large fleet of used 748s. This first aircraft was the much-travelled second prototype G-ARAY. In October of the same year the company purchased a Series 2 from International Skyways (the former Skyways Coach Air), before taking over that company together with its four Series 1 748s in April the following year. Dan-Air also purchased a Series 2 from BOAC Associated Companies in May 1972. This was one of three aircraft to come on the used aircraft market in October 1970 after the collapse of Bahamas Airways Ltd. The others went to Mandala Airlines of Indonesia in June 1971 and to Inexco Oil of Canada in February 1973. Other used aircraft sales during this period included the two former company demonstrators G-ATAM and G-AVRR to Transgabon in October and December 1972, the latter after earlier lease to the same company from October 1972. One of Court Line's (previously Autair) aircraft was sold to LIAT in December 1971. Six of Aerolíneas Argentina's aircraft were transferred to the state oil company, Yacimientos Petrolíferos Fiscales (YPF), between 1973 and 1976 and were used for ferrying workers and officials to the various production sites throughout Argentina. From 1971 to 1974, further airline sales were made to South African Airways (3), Merpati Nusantara (2),

Polynesian Airlines (2), Air Gaspé of Canada (1), TACV (2) and Bouraq Indonesia (3) while repeat orders came from Mount Cook Airlines (2), Thai Airways (1), SATA (1), Rousseau Aviation (1) and Zambia Airways (1). The last-mentioned aircraft was leased initially to Botswana Airways Corporation. Military sales during this period included two aircraft for the Republic of Korea Air Force, a VIP aircraft for the Tanzanian Government, a second aircraft for the Royal Thai Air Force and two aircraft for the Royal Australian Navy. These last two aircraft, powered by Dart R Da.8 engines, were used initially for general transport duties and later for electronic warfare training and were fitted additionally with Rover APUs.

LARGE FREIGHT DOOR

During the early 1970s the Hawker Siddeley design team started work on the installation of a Large Freight Door in the standard Series 2A airframe. The company had received many enquiries from potential and existing customers (particularly military) for such a variant and with potential future sales at stake the cost of the venture could be justified. A military requirement was that the large door was designed in such a way that it could be opened in flight to facilitate the air dropping of paratroops and/or supplies. The Large Freight Door was designed to include a passenger entrance door that formed the rear portion of the freight door enabling the aircraft to operate in pure freighter, all passenger, mixed traffic or military rôle. When in operation the freight door is opened forwards along the fuselage. The passenger door was re-designed to open rearwards along the fuselage but not to open in flight. With both doors open the total aperture size is 8ft 9in (2.67m) wide by 5ft 8in (1.72m) high. A heavy-duty freight floor was designed with roller equipment, and an air-transportable hoist was produced for operators using airfields lacking suitable facilities. Both were offered as customer optional extras. Standard production 748 fuselages were converted to Large Freight Door configuration at the Chadderton factory and conversions were made as orders were received. The first conversions for the Força Aérea Brasileira took place at Woodford as the aircraft involved were at a late stage of construction. A standard production

C-FLIY c/n 1723 undergoing Large Freight Door conversion at Sault Ste Marie with Skyservices Ltd in June 2007. This was the last of five aircraft similarly converted in Canada. *(Marty Boisvert)*

C-FLIY c/n 1723 of Air Creebee on arrival at Timmins, Ontario, 23rd January 2008, after Large Freight Door conversion . *(Marty Boisvert)*

Series 2A aircraft, c/n 1698 registered G-AZJH, was converted to Large Freight Door configuration during 1971 and the first flight of the variant took place at Woodford on 31st December 1971. The designation HS 748 Series 2C was initially used for marketing Large Freight Door equipped versions but that was soon changed to Series 2A/LFD. During 1972, flight trials were conducted with G-AZJH to verify the new version's performance and to prove the ability of the aircraft to operate with the door open in flight. After exhaustive tests including military sorties in India during May 1972, when paratrooping and supply dropping trials were undertaken successfully, the LFD version was ready for the market. In the military rôle, the 748 LFD can accommodate 48 paratroops and dispatchers, or in the supply dropping rôle either twelve 750lb (340kg) containers or six 1,500lb (680kg) "1 ton" type containers.

FAA 748 CERTIFICATION

A major sales breakthrough came in April 1973 when Air Illinois, a third-level operator based in Carbondale, Illinois, purchased a single HS 748 Series 2A which represented the first order in the lucrative United States market. Hawker Siddeley had regarded the United States as a difficult market to penetrate, particularly as the Fairchild F-27/FH-227 were well-established and the Japanese built NAMCO YS-11 had met with limited sales success. Many older Convair 240 aircraft had been converted to turbo-propeller status in the form of the Convair 580 and 600, and the commuter industry was still at an early stage of development generally using aircraft with less than twenty seats. For companies which required larger types, many piston-engined DC-3s, Martin 404s and Convair 240/340/440s were available at attractive prices.

Air Illinois Series 2A N748LL c/n 1716 gained its FAA certification following a lakeside demonstration at Chicago-Meigs Field, from which it began operations in November 1973.

Hawker Siddeley Aviation had not applied for an FAA Type Certificate for the 748 under the earlier UK/US agreement and in order to get the 748 onto the United States register, some systems modifications were required to comply with FAA regulations. Although at the time the FAA certification programme for the 748 was costly, it bore fruit in later years. Once the FAA Type Certificate was awarded, the US version became known as the 748 Series 2A/FAA. An interesting feature of the Air Illinois order was the requirement to operate the 748 from Chicago's Meigs Field Airport on the city's waterfront. The short runway at Meigs Field had an FAA restriction placed on it for transport aircraft up to 12,500lbs (5,680kgs) and was only used for aircraft up to Twin Otter size. On 18th October 1973 a demonstration by the 748 2A/FAA c/n 1716, registration N748LL took place in

C-FLIY c/n 1723 at Timmins showing the rollerball floor at the door and the rollermat system forward and aft of this.   *(Marty Boisvert)*

front of FAA officials to prove the type's suitability for regular operations into Meigs Field. The officials were suitably impressed by the 748's performance, and approval was received for regular services, making it the largest type to use Meigs Field at the time. In November 1973 Air Illinois placed their aircraft into service on the Springfield - Chicago (Meigs Field) route with six services per day plus services to other points on their network.

Military interest soon became apparent in the Large Freight Door-equipped version of the 748, which offered even greater flexibility of operation than the standard aircraft. The first major order came from the Força Aérea Brasileira for six aircraft, all being delivered in 1975 where they joined the six earlier ordered standard Series 2s. The Fuerza Aérea Ecuatoriana ordered two aircraft with delivery in 1975 and 1976 (again a repeat order adding to standard Series 2As). The Belgian Air Force took delivery of three Large Freight Door equipped aircraft in 1976, an order that had been won against extreme competition from other European manufacturers. Later military sales of Large Freight Door equipped aircraft included the Tanzanian Peoples' Defence Force (3) in 1977 and 1978, the Cameroon Air Force (2) in 1977, the Upper Volta Air Force (1) in 1977 and the Nepal Royal Flight, which purchased the prototype conversion in early 1975.

The oil crisis of late 1973, with the subsequent increase in fuel prices, led many operators to review the economics of the turbo-propeller against jet-powered aircraft. Airlines also became interested in smaller aircraft for feeder routes as projected passenger growth was influenced negatively by the oil crisis and the economic recession that was expected to follow.

Airline sales had tailed off during the second half of the 1970s, but in 1975 British Airways took delivery of two Series 2A aircraft for operation on their Scottish Division routes. The order was significant as British Airways required an economical aircraft to replace the Viscounts which they operated with weight restrictions to some points on their Scottish network. In particular, Shetland's Sumburgh Airport with its bad weather record, difficult terrain and short runways was an important influence for the selection of the 748. Improved radar facilities

and Instrument Landing System (ILS) could only be provided on the short runway, which could not be extended. The longer runway at Sumburgh has a hill at one end. The 748 could use the short runway as the main runway with lower operating minima, reduce the number of weather diversions and improve the reliability of the Shetland services. The oil boom in the North Sea had increased business on the Aberdeen to Shetland route, and once the 748s were introduced into service they soon proved very successful and became popular with passengers and crews alike and helped improve the economics of previously loss-making routes.

In January 1975 the lead 748 aircraft completed 30,000 flying hours and by March 1975 a LIAT aircraft had completed 44,000 landings. By December 1975, 748s had amassed two million flying hours, carried out two million landings and carried over forty million passengers worldwide.

The Large Freight Door option proved attractive to several airline customers during the second half of the 1970s. Outsize cargo could be carried, including the ability to carry spare Dart engines to stranded aircraft. The first civilian customer was Williamson Diamonds Ltd of Tanzania for a single aircraft. It was purchased to ferry personnel, freight and equipment between the company's various facilities and was delivered in April 1976. New airline customers over this period were Guyana Airways (2 with an LFD), Air Liberia (1 with an LFD), Trinidad and Tobago Air Services (6 of which 2 were LFD fitted), Bahamasair (4 of which one had an LFD), Linhas Aéreas da Guiné-Bissau (1), Air Sénégal (1) and Transkei Airways (1), while repeat orders came from Línea Aeropostal Venezolana - LAV (2), Mount Cook Airlines (1), LIAT (1 with an LFD) and Royal Nepal Airlines (1 with an LFD).

MAJOR USED AIRCRAFT SALES

During the second half of the 1970s, several carriers started trading up to larger aircraft, releasing many 748s onto the used aircraft market. Dan-Air Services further expanded its fleet by

The untitled 5H-WDL c/n 1740 was owned by Williamson Diamonds Ltd in support of its mining activities in Tanzania between April 1976 and June 1995, operating with a large rear freight door in all-passenger, combi or all-freight configurations. (WHC/BAe)

British Aerospace's Coastguarder prototype, G-BCDZ c/n 1662, first flew on 18th February 1977 before undertaking demonstration tours in Africa and the Far East.   *(WHC/BAe)*

taking one Series 2 aircraft from LIAT in June 1975, a Series 2 from Fiji Airways in June 1976, a Series 2A from AVIANCA in March 1978, a Series 2 from the Civil Aviation Flying Unit in July 1978 and another from Philippine Airlines in November 1979, but by far the largest buy was the remaining fleet of aircraft with Aerolíneas Argentinas and YPF. This comprised seven Series 1 aircraft that were delivered in 1976 and 1977. This new fleet allowed Dan-Air to compete in the North Sea oil prospecting support rôle as well as increasing its scheduled network. The disposal of the VARIG fleet commenced with the sale of one aircraft to Fred Olsens Flyselskap in September 1975. This aircraft was converted for use in the airfield calibration rôle under contract to the Norwegian Government. The remaining six VARIG aircraft were sold to Bouraq Indonesia Airlines in late 1976 and/or early 1977. This last company also bought five of LAN - Chile's fleet in 1978. LAN - Chile's remaining four aircraft were sold to Austin Airways Ltd of Canada in May and July 1979. Austin Airways was to become a major purchaser of used 748s, having acquired its first aircraft from Air Gabon in May 1976, two aircraft from SAESA in December 1976 and November 1977 and a single aircraft from the Argentine Government in September 1978. Used 748s were becoming increasingly popular in Canada where the type's ruggedness and good performance were ideal for the harsh conditions present there, especially in winter. Gander-based Eastern Provincial Airways bought its first aircraft from Inexco Oil in March 1975. Additional aircraft were added in March 1976 from Air Gabon and in April 1978 a third aircraft from COPA. These aircraft were soon employed on scheduled routes throughout the Canadian Maritime provinces. Two other Canadian Airlines that began 748 operations during the same period were Bradley Air Services Ltd and Calm Air International. Bradley Air Services took its first aircraft from Bouraq Indonesia Airlines in January 1979 and its second from Philippine Airlines in October of the same year, while Calm Air acquired its first 748 from Northward Airlines of Canada in December 1979. Both airlines used their aircraft for both scheduled and charter work. Rousseau Aviation, which was integrated into Touraine Air Transport in 1976, also disposed of its fleet of 748s. The first was sold to Air Cape of South Africa in November 1974, the second to Air Services Botswana in

December 1975 and the final aircraft to Réunion Air Service in August 1977. Air Ceylon doubled its 748 fleet with the purchase of an aircraft from Transair Canada in May 1975, but following the destruction of one of its aircraft by saboteurs, the company sold its last aircraft to the Sri Lanka Air Force in September 1979. Mount Cook Airlines purchased its fifth 748 when it obtained one of Air Pacific's 748s in October 1979. The Philippine Government converted another 748 for use as a calibration aircraft in March 1979, sourcing the aircraft from Philippine Airlines.

748 COASTGUARDER

During the 1970s many governments throughout the world were becoming aware of the economic need to protect their territorial waters. As countries extended their territorial waters to the 200 nautical mile limit, forming "Exclusive Economic Zones" (EEZs) to protect their natural resources, mainly fishing and oil/gas exploration rights, the requirements for patrolling such areas became impractical for surface patrol boats. A requirement existed for an aircraft to undertake such tasks as surface surveillance, fishery protection, pollution/contraband control, search and rescue and tactical surveillance. Such tasks would be prohibitively expensive with conventional and sophisticated long-range maritime reconnaissance aircraft and a cheaper option was required. Hawker Siddeley Aviation, using the company's post-war experience with the Avro Shackleton and Nimrod aircraft, decided to produce an aeroplane for that market. The high price of jet fuel led the company towards a turbo-propeller type with sufficient capacity to accommodate the crew, observers, navigators and specialised equipment, thus making the 748 the ideal choice. Hawker Siddeley had purchased a second-hand 748 Series 2A aircraft, c/n 1662, from COPA of Panama in May 1974, and had used the aircraft subsequently for trials, undertaking performance tests in South America and Africa re-registered as G-BCDZ. When the requirement for a prototype maritime patrol aircraft had been established, this was the selected airframe, and it was flown to Hawarden to undergo conversion. Hawker Siddeley named the new aircraft the "748 Coastguarder".

Changes made to the basic 748 airframe included the addition of a radome beneath the forward fuselage to house the 3ft (0.91m) antenna of the search radar. The radar had full 360° surveillance capability. A 1ft (0.30m) diameter chute was provided in the aft fuselage for air launching five-man rescue dinghies and smoke or flame floats. Two optically flat windows were provided in the forward fuselage for high definition photography, and bubble windows on each side of the rear fuselage were installed for observation work. The standard radio, radar and navigation fit was extended to cover naval radio frequencies and to provide improved navigation aids for long over-water operations. Fuel tankage was increased to 2,210 imperial gallons (10,047 litres) to provide extended range for maritime patrols, with an endurance of up to 12 hours.

The Coastguarder was equipped with a MEL MAREC radar display and plotting board, Decca 72 Doppler, a Decca 9447 Tactical Navigation System computer (TANS) and a Marconi Omega VLF or Inertial Navigation System. With such equipment, the Coastguarder was capable of plotting surface vessels or aircraft. A camera was also offered with the optional capability of annotating individual photographs with time, date, latitude and longitude from the TANS computer. The Coastguarder was offered to customers with the level of surveillance equipment determined by how much they were prepared to pay. The cabin provided accommodation for the tactical navigator's station, two beam observers and a crew rest area with galley, essential for long over-water patrols. Two pilots would have also been included in the crew complement. In order to maintain the multi-rôle capability, the Coastguarder could be offered with the large rear freight door for the airdropping of survival equipment and even paramedical teams, though the prototype did not have such a fitment. The navigator's station was designed to be removable to enable other configurations to be utilised and the seat rails were retained in the cabin in order that seats could be installed easily for passenger duties.

It was not until November 1975 that Hawker Siddeley released details of the new aircraft. The prototype first flew on 18th February 1977 and G-BCDZ made its public debut in its new guise at the Paris Air Show in June of the same year. The aircraft was demonstrated during 1977 and 1978 in Europe, South and Central America and the Far East where it was promoted as the "BAe 748 Coastguarder". Fokker also produced a patrol version of their F.27 known as the F.27 Maritime and chalked up a few sales.

Although the Coastguarder represented a cost-effective answer to the surveillance tasks required, sadly no orders were taken for the type. G-BCDZ made its last flight as a Coastguarder on 13th November 1979 before conversion back to a standard Series 2A 748 and subsequent use for the first flight trials of the extended wing of the new Series 2B version.

BRITISH AEROSPACE

On 1st April 1977 Hawker Siddeley Aviation became part of the new British Aerospace Group when united with the British Aircraft Corporation, Scottish Aviation and Hawker Siddeley Dynamics. The UK Government had decided that a larger and more broadly-based aerospace group would be in a better position to compete successfully in the world market against foreign conglomerates. The Hawker Siddeley 748 then became known as the British Aerospace 748 or more commonly the BAe 748.

BRITISH AEROSPACE 748 SERIES 2B

In keeping with its policy of continually updating its products, British Aerospace decided to revamp the existing 748 Series 2A aircraft and offer an improved version. The 748 still had a viable future and an improved and updated version was expected to have a much improved sales potential especially in the growing commuter and feeder line market. Fuel prices were still inflated and turbo-propeller aircraft were still in demand.

Six important areas were identified for the development programme:

1) Increased operational performance
2) Reduced operating costs
3) Greater reliability
4) Incorporation of the latest technology and equipment
5) Improved passenger appeal
6) Improved environmental acceptance

The new version was designated the BAe 748 Series 2B. New features included the latest Rolls-Royce Dart RDa.7 Mk 536-2 engines offering improvements in single-engine performance. A wing-tip extension was designed to offer more lift and the wingspan was increased by 4ft (1.22m), increasing the wing area to 829ft^2 (77.01m^2) and the aspect ratio to 12.67. Control surface gaps were sealed and flap shrouds were modified to increase flap effectiveness, both factors reducing drag. Together the new engines and wing design offered improvements in cruise speed and operating altitude and made possible an approximately four per cent fuel saving on typical sectors. Single engine ceiling was also increased by 3,000ft (900m).

Three-view drawings of the Series 2A and 2B, together with 748 passenger, freight and combi configurations appear on the following three pages.

In conjunction with Rolls-Royce, British Aerospace developed a new system that provided automatic injection of water-methanol into the live engine in the event of an engine failure on take-off. The new development was entitled the "Standby Water-Methanol System". With the standby system fitted, the use of "wet" take-off power (i.e. injection of water methanol to boost power) was normally only necessary from the shortest runways and not for WAT limited operations. The use of the standby system reduced the amount of water-methanol reserves needed to be carried on board the aircraft and further reduced water-methanol consumption. Engine reliability was improved considerably as the number of "wet" take-offs was reduced. The system not only reduced operator costs but also reduced the amount of water-methanol required to be held at stations round the operator's network, and the improved take-off performance increased payload capability.

The flight deck of the 748 Series 2B was re-styled and updated. Bendix RDR 1300 three-colour weather radar was fitted as standard with an optional auto-checklist display. Sperry SPZ 500 multi-mode autopilot and automatic flight control system, Sperry RN 200 radio/navigation display and an automatic cabin pressurisation system were also fitted as standard. Improved lighting and crew seats were also features of the new flight deck.

Several changes were made in the cabin to improve passenger appeal and comfort. A widebody look interior with discrete and downwash fluorescent lighting and Concorde style overhead stowage bins improved the cabin environment. Better cabin insulation and forward acoustic bulkheads reduced internal noise and vibration levels. New lightweight seats and colour decor provided further improvements in passenger appeal.

The 748 Series 2B was marketed by British Aerospace from June 1979 and the first production example c/n 1768, registration G-BGJV, made its first flight as such on 22nd June 1979. The new 2B version was available to both civil and military markets and many of the new features could be retrofitted to earlier Series 2A aircraft. G-BGJV was used for development flying and then painted in British Aerospace livery as a company demonstrator. The aircraft was also fitted with a large rear freight door.

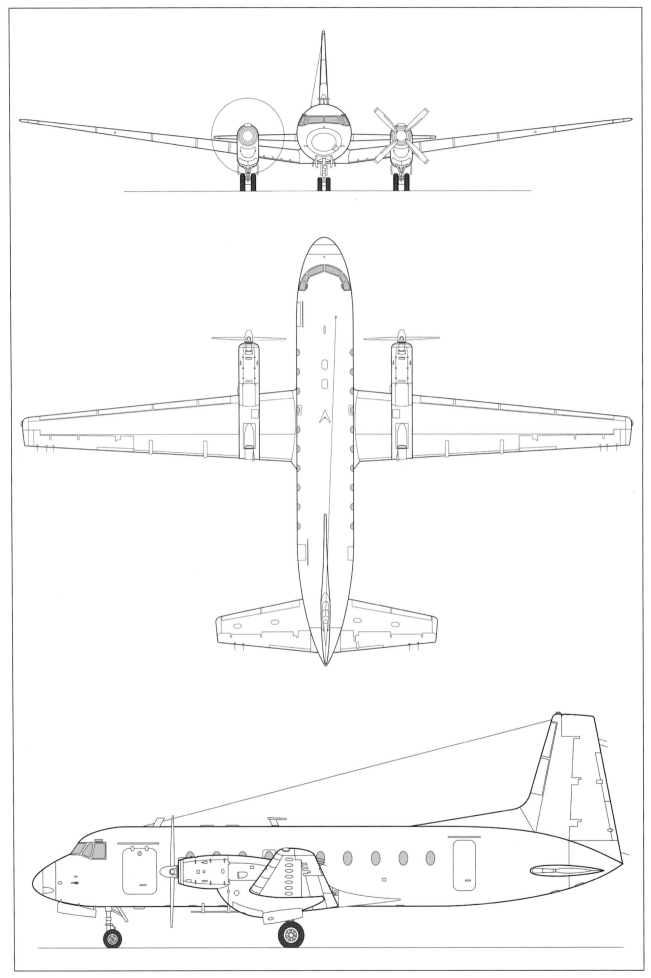

HS 748 Series 2A.

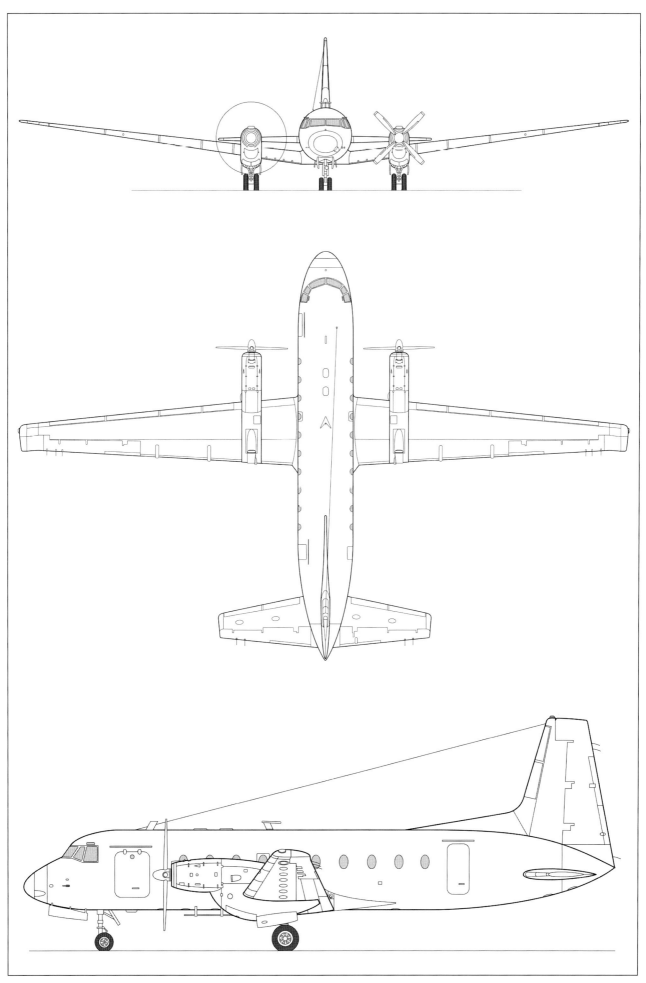

HS 748 Series 2B showing the wing-tip extensions.

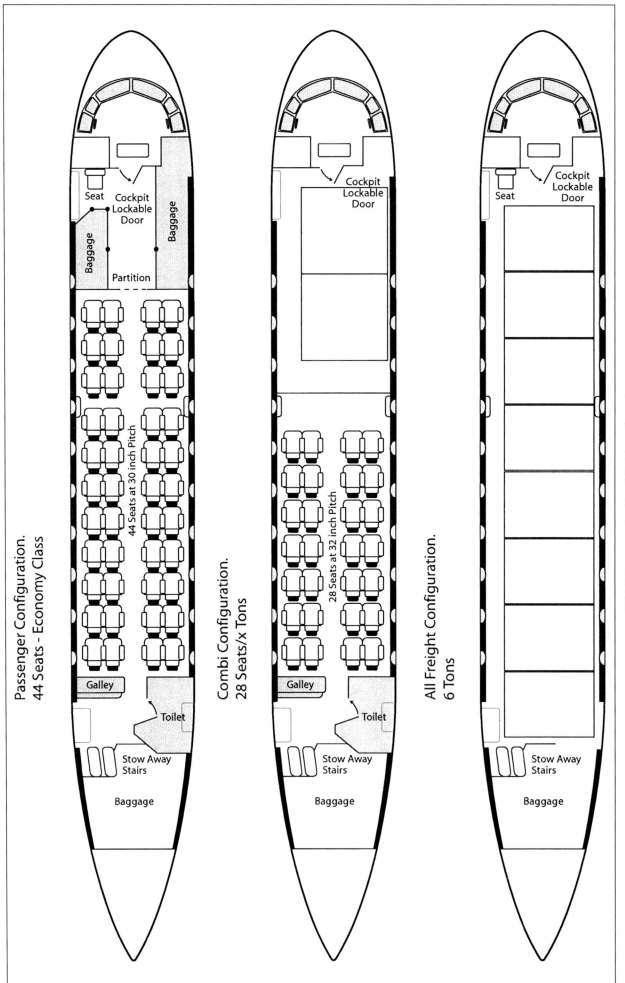

Passenger Configuration.
44 Seats - Economy Class

Combi Configuration.
28 Seats/x Tons

All Freight Configuration.
6 Tons

HS 748 Passenger, Combi and Freight configurations.

British Aerospace concentrated on selling Series 2B aircraft from 1980 onwards, using their demonstrator G-BGJV c/n 1768 for sales tours in North and South America, Yugoslavia, Greece, Libya and elsewhere.

(WHC/BAe)

Later the aircraft was also used for a North American sales tour and the livery was repainted with "Intercity 748" titles. For the United States, the aircraft was marketed as the "Intercity 748" and was fitted with Dart RDa.7 Mk 535-2 engines to FAA standards.

HUSH KIT

The 748 already met FAR Part 36 and ICAO Annex 16 noise regulations but in anticipation of the possible introduction of more stringent rules, British Aerospace and Rolls-Royce entered into a joint programme for the development of a Dart Hush Kit. Rolls-Royce produced annular acoustic linings for the engine intakes using RB 211 technology. This was tuned specially to reduce approach, taxi and ramp noise. Measured performance showed improvements of up to 11 dBA for external noise and 8 dBA at ground idle. The Hush Kit weighed only 14lbs (6.3kgs) and could be retrofitted to earlier Dart R Da.7 engines. The former Coastguarder aircraft, c/n 1662 registered G-BCDZ, after conversion back to Series 2A standard was used for the Hush Kit development/flying programme. First flight with the new Hush Kit installed took place on 4th March 1980 and Hush Kits became a customer option for all production Series 2B aircraft. Another feature under development at the time for the Series 2B was propeller dynamic balancing which reduced internal noise and vibration.

SERIES 2B SALES

After delivery of the last two new Series 2A aircraft to SATA of the Azores in May 1980 and the Force Aérienne de Haute-Volta on 5th August 1981, British Aerospace concentrated on producing Series 2B aircraft. The first customer for this new version of the aircraft was Air Madagascar. The company ordered two Large Freight Door equipped aircraft for use on their domestic network. These two aircraft were both delivered in 1980, the first in January as a Series 2A was modified up to full 2B standard after delivery. A third Series 2B with a VIP interior kit was delivered in 1981 for operation on behalf of the Madagascar Government. The first delivery of a true Series 2B was Air Madagascar's second aircraft, which was delivered on 28th November.

After a North American sales tour with G-BGJV, interest in the Series 2B looked promising. One of the major problems facing the commuter airlines that wished to trade up from twenty-seat types to larger aircraft was finance. Often new turbo-props such as 748s, Fokker F.27s or de Havilland Canada Dash 7s were just too expensive. All manufacturers were competing head on and financing arrangements were crucial to conclude sales contracts. In an effort to offset some expenditure, British Aerospace entered into an agreement with Aero Spacelines Incorporated in the United States whereby "green" aircraft would be ferried from Woodford for fitting out and painting. Aero Spacelines Inc, based in Goleta, California would fit out the aircraft to FAA standards using American equipment thus reducing costs at a time when the US Dollar was weak. Orders were received from Air Virginia and Cascade Airways for two aircraft each. All four aircraft were delivered to Goleta in 1980 and/or 1981. After completion, Cascade Airways' two aircraft were both delivered in December 1981 while Air Virginia's aircraft were delivered in October 1981 and May 1982. Tracor Aviation took over Aero Spacelines in September 1981 and continued the agreement with British Aerospace. A fifth aircraft was also fitted out and used as a company demonstrator in the United States and South America. It was later sold in Europe.

British Aerospace was well represented in the United States by its subsidiary British Aerospace Incorporated based in Washington. BAe Inc could trace its origins back to the Viscount era when Vickers-Armstrongs set up a spares facility in Washington to support US operators. The same facility was used later for BAC One-Eleven aircraft and later played a vital rôle in Jetstream, ATP and 146/RJ customer support. BAe Inc also leased aircraft to American operators and provided spares and liaison facilities.

FURTHER SALES

Other orders received for Series 2B aircraft in the first half of the 1980s came from Air Illinois (1), Air Niger (1 + 1 with LFD), Fuerza Aérea Colombiana (1 with LFD), Deutsche Luftverkehrsgesellschaft mbH - DLT (6), Bouraq Indonesia Airlines (5 + 1 with LFD), Airline of the Marshall Islands (1) and British Airways (2 + 1 with LFD).

C-GDUN c/n 1581 seen on arrival in Canada in 1981 still wearing Aeropostal colours but without titles.   *(Fred Barnes collection)*

The Air Illinois aircraft was the company's second 748 and joined an earlier delivered Series 2A. It was delivered direct from Woodford and did not go through the Aero Spacelines facility. DLT's order totalled six aircraft over a period of three years and all were built to FAA standards. British Airways' order included the freight door equipped Series 2B prototype brought up to the latest standards.

MULTI-RÔLE 748

In 1980 c/n 1746, registered G-BDVH, was designated the company Military Demonstrator. Previously, British Aerospace had employed this Large Freight Door equipped aircraft for use by customers awaiting delivery of their own new aircraft. The aircraft was painted in semi-camouflage and was used for demonstration and development flying. Later the Coastguarder-style lower forward radome, bubble observation windows and photographic windows were fitted. The removable Coastguarder tactical navigation station could also be installed if required. The aircraft was then re-designated as the Multi-Rôle 748 to demonstrate to potential customers the operational flexibility of the type. However, the last new military 748 to be delivered was that to Colombia in August 1981.

MORE USED AIRCRAFT SALES

In the first half of the 1980s many used 748 transactions took place. Once again Canada was the recipient of many aircraft. Austin Airways bought the entire Linea Aérea Venezolana - LAV fleet late in 1980. These six aircraft, which included two aircraft that had been passed on to the Venezuelan military, were purchased mainly for onward sale. One of these was sold to Northern Wings Ltd in January 1981. This last company, a subsidiary of Québecair Inc which already operated two 748s, was renamed Regionair (1981) Inc later in the same year and took delivery of a further three of the ex-Venezuelan 748s sold to Austin Airways Ltd, increasing the company fleet to six. Austin Airways had earlier leased three of its aircraft to Maersk Air Ltd of Denmark from June 1980 to July 1981. Austin Airways added another three aircraft when it purchased South African Airways' fleet of three aircraft in August and November 1983. Other Canadian operators expanded their fleets over this period. Bradley Air Services took its third aircraft, this time from Air Pacific Ltd in December 1980, while two further aircraft came

from Québecair/Regionair in September and October 1984 after that company had ceased operations. Eastern Provincial Airways purchased its fourth aircraft from Ghana Airways in May 1981 and its fifth from Austin Airways in April 1982, although from January 1982 a separate division of Eastern Provincial known as Air Maritime operated the 748 fleet. Calm Air International took delivery of the much-travelled BAe development and demonstration aircraft, c/n 1662, in October 1984, doubling the company 748 fleet. Two other new Canadian 748 operators during this period were Air Creebec, which obtained one aircraft from Austin Airways Ltd in December 1983 that was to herald a much larger fleet in later years and Ilford Riverton Airways that purchased a single aircraft from Austin Airways in January 1984. Outside Canada, Philippine Airlines sold one of its aircraft to Airfast Services of Indonesia in May 1980 for charter work, while Zambia Airways sold an aircraft to Air Sénégal in March 1980, doubling that company's fleet. Thai Airways commenced the disposal of its fleet with the sale of one aircraft to Airfast Services in May 1981, while the remaining four airworthy aircraft were sold to the Royal Thai Air Force between September 1983 and January 1984, where they joined two existing aircraft. In February 1982 Cameroon Airlines took over the two Large Freight Door equipped 748s from the Cameroon Air Force and put them into service on domestic schedules. Mount Cook Airlines increased its 748 fleet to six with the addition of the little-flown aircraft previously with the Royal Brunei Malay Regiment and Royal Brunei Airlines.

In February 1982 Dan-Air Services disposed of one of its early Series 1s to Cayman Airways Ltd for use on its inter-island routes while another went to new Spanish airline Air Condal in July 1983. In May 1981 Dan-Air took delivery of a former Polynesian Airlines Series 2A which was fitted with a Large Rear Freight Door by Dan-Air Engineering Ltd at Manchester later in the same year. This door, which had been supplied in kit form by British Aerospace, was the first to be fitted by anybody other than the manufacturer. Dan-Air also leased three aircraft to British Airways for use by the Highlands Division at the start of the summer schedules in 1982, enabling that company to withdraw the last of its Vickers Viscount fleet. Dan-Air also leased three aircraft to Philippine Airlines with effect from October and November 1984. A short-lived UK 748 operator was Venture Airways Ltd which flew schedules between Coventry and Paris with a luxuriously-appointed 33 passenger seat Series 1 aircraft that it purchased from Cayman Airways in February 1984. By August of the same year the company had ceased to exist.

BAe SUPER 748

British Aerospace continued to review the 748 Series 2B and decided on a further programme of improvements in 1983. The new version was designated the Super 748. A new advanced flight deck with state of the art technology was introduced.

Improvements included

1) A central warning light panel for all major systems which alerts the crew to any malfunction
2) Miniaturised engine instruments to give additional panel space
3) Radio controls repositioned for easier access
4) A flat glare shield coaming over the central panel to provide unobstructed forward vision and improved pilot orientation in marginal visual flight conditions
5) Colour weather radar plus optional checklist display with an automatic crew drill display in the event of a system malfunction
6) Push button selector indicators replacing switches

The push button selector indicators denoted the system status by illuminated colour coding. The colour coding system simplified checklist requirements for take-off and landing with only green or blue lights showing. Red denoted a malfunction requiring immediate action, whilst amber denoted a malfunction not requiring immediate action. Either red or amber warnings also appeared on the central warning panel. White lights represented temporary operation of a system that should not be selected for take-off or landing. New crew seats similar to those used on the BAe 146 were also introduced. The Dart Hush Kit was fitted as standard together with acoustic cabin bulkheads, while optional dynamic propeller balancing further reduced noise and vibration.

In the cabin, trim and furnishings were redesigned for the new look wide-body interior. Improved contoured lightweight passenger seats were fitted, whilst the previous lighting and overhead storage bins from the Series 2B were retained. The new cabin decor resulted in a light and spacious environment and the new trim, carpeting and tasteful fabric shading completed the cabin upgrade.

Baggage-hold capacity was increased to offer more baggage space per passenger in a 48-seat configuration. A new lightweight galley was designed for better passenger service. Up to 60 cold meals could be served and optional ovens and service trolley were available plus hot and cold drink service. The cabin attendant's seat was relocated to the rear, giving better access to the public address system and galley. An electric flushing toilet with external servicing was available as a customer option. Rolls-Royce Dart RDa.7 Mk 551 or 552 engines were due to power late production Super 748s. These would have improved fuel consumption by 12%, but although flown in c/n 1790 for the first time on 10th May 1985, no customer deliveries took place with this mark of engine fitted. However, Rolls-Royce Modification 1860 with revised and matched compressors and turbines was able to achieve a 10/11% fuel saving without installing the modified fuel control unit fitted to the Mark 551/2 engine. Super 748s were delivered with this modification incorporated, while several Series 2As and 2Bs have been similarly modified subsequently.

The Super 748 met ICAO Annex 16 Chapter 3 and FAR Part 36 Stage 3 noise certification criteria. First production Super 748 c/n 1800, registered G-BLGJ, made its first flight on 30th July 1984 and the aircraft appeared at the 1984 Farnborough Air Show in British Aerospace house livery. In December 1984 LIAT (1974) Ltd ordered two Super 748s to replace early high-cycled Series 2s. First delivery was the initial production aircraft, re-registered V2-LCQ and ferried from Woodford on 18th December 1984 in LIAT's striking new colour scheme. The airline subsequently ordered two further Super 748s and all were in service by early July 1985. Later in 1985, Cameroon Airlines took delivery of two Super 748s for which it traded in its existing two aircraft. After this order was completed only four further aircraft were built. Two of these were delivered to Makung Airlines Co Ltd of Taiwan in November 1988 and January 1989 while the remaining two airframes never entered the final assembly stage although delivered in component form to Woodford. Both fuselages were used for experimental work at Hatfield and Woodford. By the time the last 748s were delivered, the British Aerospace ATPs were rolling off the Woodford assembly line. With the first flight of c/n 1807 (the last 748 to be completed) on 2nd December 1988, no fewer than 350 748s had flown of which 89 had been built in India. Of the 261 748s completed in the United Kingdom, 20 were completed as Series 1s, 106 as Series 2s, 100 as Series 2As and the remaining 35 as Series 2B/Super 2Bs. To this total could be added 31 Andover C.Mk.1s all first flown at Woodford.

V2-LCT c/n 1803, a Super 748 of LIAT, is seen overflying a Caribbean scene in a fine publicity shot. (WHC/BAe)

CONSTRUCTION

Construction of all UK built 748s and Andovers took place at the former AV Roe factory at Chadderton in Manchester. The aircraft were normally laid down in batches of twenty and, apart from at least fourteen early wing sets and nose cones produced by Folland Aircraft Ltd at Hamble for both UK and Indian assembled Series 1 and 2 aircraft, fuselage, wings, fin and tailplane were all produced at Chadderton. At the peak of production, some batches of forty were authorised, though towards the end of production this had been reduced to ten. Set Numbers were allocated to each 748 airframe at an early production stage. This included Andover C.Mk.1s and the first 28 HAL produced aircraft, using either kits or components supplied from the British production line.

A Construction Number was allocated when the individual aircraft was identified for a particular customer. Model Numbers were also allotted to aircraft and denoted a customer's specific order. Orders from the same customer could have different Model Numbers if specifications were different for individual aircraft within that order. This applied where some aircraft had Large Freight Doors and others did not, or in some cases where one aircraft in a fleet was fitted with a VIP interior.

After basic construction, the fuselage, wings and other components were transported by road to Woodford for final assembly. This usually took place on a Sunday morning to avoid traffic congestion problems. At Woodford the fuselage and wings, which had already been painted in green primer, were mated. The fin and tailplane were added, the undercarriage fitted and the engines installed. Instrumentation was fitted and detailed fitting-out completed before the aircraft was painted in the customer's colour scheme. Flight-testing and customer acceptance were completed at Woodford. Large Freight Door equipped aircraft were modified after initial production at Chadderton by removing a section of the port rear fuselage and replacing it with the cargo door unit. Four aircraft, c/ns 1546, 1547, 1724 and 1725 were completed at the Hawarden factory when final production at Woodford was at a peak. In the slack sales period of the early 1980s some aircraft were completed at Woodford and then ferried to Prestwick in a grey and white paint scheme for storage and ultimate customer completion.

SUBSEQUENT USED AIRCRAFT SALES AND LEASES

Production of the 748 may have been completed, but demand for used examples throughout the world continued unabated. In the latter half of the 1980s, Canada was still a major player in 748 fleet changes. Air Inuit, after earlier leasing an aircraft from Austin Airways, purchased a Large Freight Door equipped Series 2A in January 1985 and added a second similarly-equipped aircraft in January 1989 before doubling its fleet with two standard Series 2As in 1989 and 1990. Another new but short-lived Canadian scheduled 748 airline was Inter City Airways, which operated two former BFS Series 2s from its base at Oshawa in Ontario between April and October 1986. Winnipeg-based Ilford Riverton Airways changed its name to Northland Air Manitoba in February 1986 at which time it added a second Series 2A, purchased in South Africa. Other aircraft added in this period were a third Series 2A from Québecair in April 1988 and two further aircraft in October 1989 and January 1990. In April 1987 the historic Austin Airways name, which had existed since 1934, was to disappear from the Canadian scene. Air Canada purchased 75% of both Austin Airways and Air Ontario and it was the latter's name that survived. Air Ontario now had a fleet of eight Series 2A 748s. The company planned to convert three aircraft to pure unpressurised freighters, and work commenced in early 1988 on the conversion of the first aircraft, the much-travelled c/n 1576 registered C-GMAA and formerly G-ATAM of BKS, one of the manufacturer's demonstrators. The aircraft had a Large

Rear Freight Door fitted and had major work carried out before completion in January 1989. The large door was designed and manufactured by ACS of Winnipeg and, unlike the Woodford produced version, was hinged and opened outwards. Further details of the conversion are given under Air Ontario in the '748 Operators' chapter of this book. However, in a December 1988 policy change, it was decided to sell the entire 748 fleet to Air Creebec Inc and only the one aircraft was converted.

Bradley Air Services, operating scheduled services as First Air, considerably expanded its fleet over the period. In September 1987 four Series 2As were obtained, two coming from Québecair and two Large Freight Door equipped aircraft coming from Trinidad. In April of the following year, Bradley Air Services bought the two former Cascade Airways Series 2Bs, its first 748s of this type. Calm Air International doubled its fleet with the addition of two Series 2As from Canadian Pacific in June 1987 and January 1988. In 1989 Springer Aerospace Ltd of Sault Ste. Marie, Ontario purchased three Series 2As from Dan-Air Services. This engineering company converted these aircraft into freighters for onward sale. One was delivered to V. Kelner Airways in August 1989 prior to its later freighter conversion, while another was fitted immediately with a Large Freight Door and sold to a subsidiary of Northland Air Manitoba named Nunasi-Northland Airways Ltd in November 1989. Springer Aerospace became a 748 specialist, converting three former BFS Series 2 aircraft to standard 2A types, fitting locally-designed large rear cargo doors to several aircraft and also fitting an Auxiliary Power Unit to an aircraft for Wasaya Airways.

In the United Kingdom, Euroair Transport commenced a scheduled service from Dundee to London-Heathrow via Carlisle in November 1985 with the former Venture Airways Series 1 aircraft on behalf of Air Écosse, later operating the service under its own name. A new airline named Chieftain Airways purchased two former West Indies based Series 2As that entered service on international schedules from Glasgow and Edinburgh in March 1987, but the airline only lasted two months before it failed. Yet another Scottish airline was created using the same two aircraft over similar routes. Named Scottish European, it commenced operations in October 1988 but like its predecessor it too failed, although not until April 1990.

British Airways modified its two owned Series 2As G-BCOE and G-BCOF to Series 2B standard at its Glasgow engineering base between January and June 1985 with kits of parts supplied by British Aerospace. These were the only such conversions carried out and raised the company's Series 2B fleet to five including G-BGJV with its Large Freight Door. The company replaced some of the leased Dan-Air Series 2As with two former Trinidad & Tobago Air Services Series 2As leased from Euroair Transport Ltd between May 1986 and April 1989. The Series 2B fleet was expanded further with the lease of three former DLT aircraft between March and June 1988, enabling the leased Series 2A aircraft to be returned to their owners. Two other new UK-based 748 operators during this period were Air Atlantique and Brymon Airways Ltd, both leasing the same Series 1 from Euroair Transport Ltd. The former flew schedules between Southampton and Jersey from May to October 1988 followed by ad hoc charters until the aircraft was returned to the lessor in March 1989. Brymon Airways used the aircraft primarily on oil-related charter work in Scotland from October 1987 to January 1988. Yet another UK based 748 operator was Aberdeen Airways, which commenced scheduled operations over the Aberdeen to East Midlands via Edinburgh route on 4th December 1989 with a leased Series 1A and a Series 2A. In November the same year Jersey European Airways commenced 748 passenger operations with a leased Euroair Transport Series 2A, adding a second the following month.

In Europe, DLT finally disposed of its last aircraft in May 1989. Apart from the earlier-mentioned three aircraft leased to British Airways, British Aerospace leased one to LIAT from December

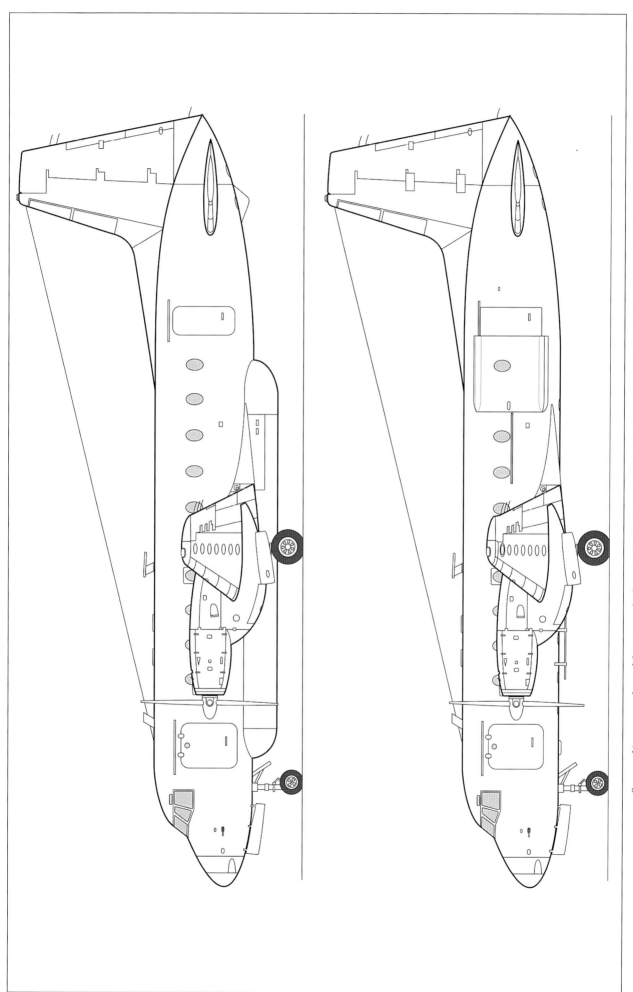

Seen on this page are the modifications to the Series 2A for fire-bombing (top) and to the Series 2B for carrying large cargoes (lower).

G-BCOF c/n 1737 of British Airways, showing the earlier livery carried by this aircraft with the airline.   *(WHC/BAe)*

1988 and another was leased to SATA from June 1989. This last company had replaced its Series 2A aircraft earlier with two Series 2Bs obtained from British Aerospace in May and June 1987. Another new European operator was Portuguese-based Linhas Aéreas Regionais (LAR) that commenced operations in April 1988. Schedules were flown from Lisbon to Faro and Oporto with two former SATA and one former Jambo Air Lines' Series 2A (the latter fitted with a Large Freight Door). A fourth aircraft was leased from September to December 1988 and another former SATA aircraft was added in October 1989.

The now well-known Ryanair Ltd began with two Series 1 748s in April and May 1986 on scheduled routes linking Luton with Dublin and Waterford and later in the year with Connaught/Knock, together with charter work. The two former Dan-Air and Air Condal aircraft were withdrawn in January 1987 and November 1988 respectively. In France, Transvalair purchased a Series 2A from South Africa in October 1988 and immediately leased it to Kel Air also based in France. The aircraft flew passenger schedules on behalf of Air Inter and Touraine Air Transport and also nightly newspaper charters within France. Kel Air also leased two former Zambia Airways Series 2As in March and June 1989 having commenced operations with their initial aircraft in December 1988.

The Sri Lanka Air Force increased its fleet with the addition of the former Multi-Rôle Military demonstrator G-BDVH. This Large Freight Door equipped Series 2A was delivered in March 1986 and later became CR-833.

Air Saint-Pierre purchased a Series 2A from Air Maritime in October 1986. This carrier, based in the Saint-Pierre and Miquelon Islands off the Canadian Atlantic coast, had earlier contracted out its scheduled services to Eastern Provincial Airways/Air Maritime. The company, which joined the 'Canadian Partner' programme in 1987, leased a second aircraft from Air Maritime in April and May 1987 and operated schedules to Halifax, Montréal and Sydney in Canada from its home base.

In Africa, Jambo Airlines of Nigeria purchased a Large Freight Door equipped Series 2A in December 1986 but it had returned to the UK for storage by October the following year. Bop-Air Ltd of Bophuthatswana obtained a former North American-operated Series 2B in February 1986 to operate on schedules from Johannesburg to Sun City and Mmabatho, while Cameroon Airlines leased a Series 2B with a Large Freight Door to Ecuato Guineana de Aviación for one year from August 1986, which was flown on passenger services from Malabo to Bata, Douala and Libreville. Exported from Africa was one of Air Malawi's two Series 2As that was sold to Air BVI Ltd of the British Virgin Islands in January 1988.

Philippine Airlines leased three additional Series 2s from British Aerospace that had been traded in by LIAT after delivery of their Super 2Bs. These aircraft were operated by Philippine Airlines (PAL) from September 1985 until June 1987, while three aircraft leased from Dan-Air were returned in February 1989. After nearly twenty-two years of service, PAL withdrew its 748 fleet at the end of May 1989. Three aircraft were sold to LBC Airways, a small-package carrier in the Philippines, with two going in May 1989 and one in September of the same year. The last two aircraft were sold to Shabair of Zaire in October and November 1989.

MACAVIA BAe 748 TURBINE TANKER

An interesting conversion was carried out on a former Canadian Series 2A which was purchased by Macavia International in March 1987. Macavia International of Santa Rosa, California was one of the major aerial fire-fighting and aerial patrol companies and maintained offices in New York, London and Paris at this time. The company also provided avionics, maintenance support, training and general fire suppression services. The company was looking for a new type, preferably turbine-powered, to supplement and eventually replace some of the existing aircraft in their fleet. Aircraft such as the DC-4, DC-6 and DC-7, although cheap to purchase, were becoming expensive to maintain as spares became increasingly difficult to obtain. Low utilisation was not a matter to be considered when using these written-down types. However, the cost of replacement turbine-engined aircraft was considerably higher and this could only be recovered by increased utilisation of the new aircraft. To achieve this, any conversion would have to have a multiplicity of capabilities in its new rôle. Any new type added to the company's fleet would need to have good handling and manoeuvring qualities at low flying speed, good airfield performance from unpaved runways, rugged durable construction and come from a long production run with good spares support, preferably worldwide. A low wing aircraft was favoured since it provided structural efficiency, excellent stability, easy access to underfloor systems, a sturdy undercarriage and safety in the event of an accident.

After studies of several aircraft types, the British Aerospace 748 was selected as the most suitable for conversion since it fitted all the basic requirements and was used by some twenty air forces and many airlines for a multiplicity of duties. The product support unit of British Aerospace supported the type worldwide and the well-proven Rolls-Royce Dart engine had already achieved some 107 million hours of operation with some operators achieving a TBO (Time Between Overhaul) of 8,000 hours.

Once the BAe 748 had been selected, the Macavia team employed its own expertise to plan the aerial tanker conversion. The British company Cranfield Aeronautical Services, the engineering affiliate of the Cranfield Institute of Technology, was contracted to undertake the design and actual conversion work jointly with Macavia. An agreement was reached with British Aerospace to supply technical data, drawings and later test pilots for the project.

A former Eastern Provincial Airways Series 2A aircraft, c/n 1594 registered C-GEPI, was purchased on 1st March 1987 and subsequently ferried to Cranfield in the United Kingdom on 4th April. The aircraft was registered to Macair International on 5th May and allocated the British marks G-BNJK for certification flying. At Cranfield the aircraft was stripped of all passenger fittings including toilet and galley and fuselage frames were strengthened and hard points installed.

The new name selected for the aircraft was the Macavia BAe 748 Turbine Tanker. The conversion comprised pannier tanks externally fitted to the lower fuselage measuring 25ft (7.62m) x 6ft (1.83m) and 2ft (0.61m) deep, with twelve permanent hard points for attachment permitting easy fitting and disconnection. Total tank capacity offered was 2,000 US gallons (7,570 litres) in eight 250 US gallon (946 litre) compartments with doors arranged in two rows of four each and having individual flow regulators. A separate 108 US gallon (409 litre) foam concentrate tank was installed, permitting nine trips without refilling and offering auto-mixing with water in the dropping compartment prior to delivery. Another feature was computer controlled door sequencing with flow regulators programming the amount, rate, velocity and length of the fire retardant drop. Two emergency dump systems were fitted, one connected automatically to the propeller auto-feather system in the event of an engine failure on take-off and the other which used nitrogen operated by an emergency handle in the cockpit to blow open the pannier tank doors.

The Macavia conversion retained the normal pressurisation system of the standard 748, enabling freight and passengers to be carried when the aircraft was not employed in the aerial tanker rôle. To fulfil its multi-rôle capability, a standard BAe type Large Freight Door would have been fitted although the prototype was not so converted. A standard lash-down cargo layout or roller conveyor system with ball mats and the BAe Air Transportable Hoist were available as options. The Macavia BAe 748 could also have been configured for 24 stretchers with attendants or in mixed passenger/cargo layouts.

The prototype was first flown from Cranfield without the pannier attached on 21st August 1987 and with the pannier on 4th September 1987. "Fire bombing" trials were undertaken at Cranfield, using water to test the aircraft's changed flying characteristics whilst dropping retardant. In November 1987 the aircraft was flown to the South of France for demonstrations to the Securité Civile who are responsible for aerial fire fighting throughout France. On returning to the United Kingdom, the aircraft was used for development flying which led to it being granted a Certificate of Airworthiness for Aerial Work by the Civil Aviation Authority on 11th March 1988. It was later

G-BNJK c/n 1594, the Macavia International BAe 748 Turbine Tanker, seen on a demonstration flight during 1987.   *(Macavia International)*

involved in a programme to update the aircraft's avionics and to improve the tanks and dropping mechanism before being shown at the Paris Air Show in June of the same year.

It was hoped to market the Macavia BAe 748 Turbine Tanker in the Insect Control, Aerial Spraying, Acid Rain Control, Oil Spillage, Fish Stocking, Fishery Protection, Coast Guard Service, Casualty Evacuation, Ambulance and Rescue, Supply Dropping and mixed passenger/freight rôles. It is believed that the aircraft was flown for at least one fire-fighting season in southern France before being put in storage and no further conversions were carried out.

THE EARLY 1990s

In Canada, V Kelner Airways purchased a Series 2A from Springer Aerospace in April 1990, returning its first aircraft to the same company for conversion to a pure freighter with a large rear cargo door between March 1990 and February 1991. This aircraft was unfortunately declared a structural write-off after a fire on the ground when the aircraft was being used as a fuel tanker in August of the same year. An aircraft was leased from Northland Air Manitoba until October 1991 when two Series 2Bs were obtained from Niger, one of which had a Large Freight Door. Yet another Large Freight Door equipped aircraft was obtained from British Aerospace in April 1992, before the company was renamed Wasaya Airways in January 1993. Northland Air Manitoba, soon to be marketed as Air Manitoba, obtained Springer Aerospace's third ex Dan-Air Series 2A in January 1990. In September 1993 the company bought two Series 2As from Bahamasair but one was reduced to spares and the other stored in Canada without use. Another new Canadian 748 operator was West Wind Aviation, based at Saskatoon, which took delivery of a Series 2A from Chevron Canada in June 1993 and a Series 2B from British Aerospace in October of the same year. The aircraft were used in support of the mining industry, carrying either staff or cargo. Thunderbird Tours was another new carrier based in Vancouver which leased a Series 2B from Bradley Air Services in April 1994.

In the United Kingdom, British Independent Airways commenced scheduled air services from Lydd to Le Touquet and Beauvais in April and July 1990 respectively with a leased Series 2A and a Series 1A. Dan-Air Services Ltd retired the last of its fleet in March 1992 and sold its remaining six flyable 748s to Janes Aviation 748 Ltd in July the same year. These comprised three Series 1s and three Series 2As, one of which was fitted with a Large Freight Door. Janes Aviation 748 Ltd, known as Janes Aviation Ltd prior to this, was already a 748 operator, having purchased a Series 2A in November 1991 which was used for a small parcels contract. The company was renamed Emerald Airways Ltd in September 1993 and would later become one of the 748's largest operators. The company later added another Series 1 in March and two Series 2As in June 1994. Jersey European Airways added a third Series 2A in April 1990, but they were replaced gradually in the passenger rôle by a fleet of Fokker Friendships purchased in Australia from September 1990. The 748s were returned to the lessor between September and November 1991, after spending the last few months of their time flying night-mail contract flights between Scotland and England. After leasing a ninth Series 2B from April 1990, British Airways withdrew its 748 fleet between November 1991 and 15th April 1992, when the last revenue flight was flown. Newly delivered BAe ATPs had gradually displaced them.

Air Saint-Pierre added a second Series 2A in April 1990 that it had purchased from Bahamasair. The Sri Lanka Air Force doubled its fleet to four aircraft with the addition of a Series 2A and Large Freight Door equipped Series 2B in December 1991. Airfast Services Indonesia leased a Series 2A from Transvalair from October 1991 until it was replaced by a similar aircraft from Euroair Transport Ltd in July 1992. Emirates Air Services leased

two Series 2Bs from British Aerospace in April 1992 to operate on a shuttle service between Abu Dhabi and Dubai. This was a short-lived operation and the aircraft were returned in January 1993.

There was an expansion of 748 operations in Nepal from 1992, adding to the Royal Nepal Airways and military operations. Necon Air took delivery of two Series 1s in September and November 1992 while a Series 2A was added in May 1993 and a Series 2B in October 1994. In March 1993 a Series 2B was leased from British Aerospace by Nepal Airways, another new 748 operator. Two similar types leased from the same source in February and March 1994 replaced this. Both operators used their aircraft on domestic networks, catering for the much increased tourist trade.

In Africa, Shabair sold its two Series 2s to Trans Service Airlift in June 1992, while in South Africa two new 748 operators were Intensive Air and Executive Aerospace. The first purchased a Series 2A in November 1993 which it operated initially on behalf of Care Airlines, while the second obtained its first Series 2B from British Aerospace in December 1994.

In Australasia, Mount Cook Airlines added a Series 2A on lease from Clewer Aviation in December 1993, and Impulse Airlines in Australia took delivery of two former British Airways Series 2Bs in October and November 1994.

1995 TO 2000

The second half of the 1990s saw further long-term users of the type retiring their aircraft, while newer operators expanded their fleets. In Canada, a new operator was Awood Air which obtained two Series 2Bs in May 1995 to operate on schedules and charters in British Columbia, while Air North Charter & Training Ltd of Whitehorse, Northwest Territories took delivery of two former Mount Cook Airlines Series 2As in July 1996 and a former Air Manitoba example in September 1998. Air North used its aircraft on schedules both within Northwest Canada and to Alaska. Another newcomer to the Canadian scene was Aerial Recon Surveys which flew the former AMOCO Canada Series 2A on schedules from Calgary from December 1997 to April 1998. Calm Air International added one of the former Awood Air Series 2Bs in May 1997 before taking delivery of the previously mentioned former AMOCO Canada Series 2A in April 1999. This last aircraft had been much modified with a glass cockpit when in AMOCO service and was to be converted further with a large rear freight door by Calm Air. Wasaya Airways, having sold one of its Series 2Bs in May 1998, bought two former Air Manitoba Series 2As in January 1999, having leased them previously from November 1996 and February 1997. The company obtained Air Creebec's specialised unpressurised freighter Series 2A with a Large Freight Door in May 1999. One of the company's Series 2As was converted to a specialised fuel tanker in August 1996, while in December 1996 its passenger configured Series 2B was fitted with an Auxiliary Power Unit. Finally Bradley Air Services purchased one of Air Creebec's Series 2As in June 1999 to replace an earlier written-off aircraft.

In Europe, a new 748 operator was West Air Sweden, which obtained the last four former BFS Series 2s for use in the cargo rôle in September 1995. The company later expanded its fleet considerably by adding a Series 2A from Norway in September 1996 and another from Heliglobe of France in February 1997. In August 1997 a Series 2B with a Large Freight Door and a Series 2A were obtained from the Fuerza Aérea Colombiana. This last purchase comprised the last two airworthy 748s in the Colombian fleet but the second aircraft, although flown to Sweden, was purchased for spares use only and was subsequently broken-up. In May 1998 a Series 2B with a Large Freight Door was bought from Wasaya Airways, while Transportes Aéreos de Guine-Bissau's single Series 2A was obtained in May of the same

SE-LEG c/n 1723 of West Air Sweden awaiting its next cargo load at Münich on 5th July 2001. (Keith Gaskell)

year. The final 748 purchase was the two RAAF Series 2 VIP aircraft obtained in March 1999. All aircraft were brought up to a similar pure freighter standard. In a weight-saving measure, each aircraft was stripped of all non-essential equipment which included APUs (where fitted), autopilots and all fittings that had been installed originally for the carriage of passengers. E-Class cargo compartments were installed with fire doors to the cockpits, smoke detector systems, new wall panels and a system of restraining straps and nets stressed to 9G. New avionics were installed and Dart hush-kits were also fitted to make the aircraft more acceptable throughout Europe. After modifications, the payload was increased to 13,890 lbs (6.3 tonnes) and the volumetric capacity to 1,942 ft³ (55 m³). The company additionally leased a Series 2A with a Large Freight Door from Air Inuit of Canada from March 1999 to January 2000.

In France, Air Provence International of Marseille commenced using two Series 2As in the freight rôle from July 1995.

Emerald Airways Ltd in the United Kingdom continued with the expansion of its fleet with additional Series 2As in May 1995, February 1996 and August 1996, while two Series 2Bs were added in March and November 1996. The airline commenced passenger charter work in May 1995 with a single Series 2A. Both Series 2Bs were fitted out in passenger configuration and a scheduled route was inaugurated between Liverpool and the Isle of Man in April 1996. The scheduled routes were withdrawn at the end of March 1999 and the company's single remaining Series 2B was sold in South Africa. Additions to the fleet were single Series 2As in April and November 1998.

In October 1996, the airfield calibration duties performed by the Civil Aviation Authority were handed over to private interests in the shape of Flight Precision Ltd. The two Series 2As which had performed faithfully for twenty-seven years were also sold to the new organisation, but within two years had been withdrawn and were sold to Emerald Airways who used them for spares only.

The Royal Air Force's six standard CC.Mk.2 748s came onto the market during this period. 32 (The Royal) Squadron based at Northolt withdrew its four aircraft in early 1995. Three of these found their way to Africa in 1995, carrying various registrations and operating with several carriers undertaking relief flights in East Africa and the Sudan. The fourth of these aircraft was preserved initially at Bruntingthorpe in the UK before being broken up. Of the two remaining RAF CC.Mk.2s, one failed to reach its reserve price at auction and was broken up, while the other headed for Africa in June 1997 and was last heard of flying for Gabon Express.

New Zealand's Mount Cook Airlines, after leasing a Series 2B from Clewer Aviation in May 1995, progressively withdrew its fleet from service from November of the same year. Replaced by ATR-72s, the 748s had served Mount Cook faithfully for twenty-seven and a half years by the time the last service was flown on 12th February 1996, the fleet reaching a peak of eight aircraft. Most of the aircraft were disposed of quickly, but two officially remained on strength after this. One aircraft was leased to Royal Tongan Airlines for schedules among the Pacific Islands in November 1995 but its ownership was eventually transferred to Clewer Aviation in early 1999 for continued lease to the Tongan carrier. Royal Tongan leased another Mount Cook 748 in October and November 1997 while its own aircraft underwent maintenance. This last aircraft, c/n 1689 ZK-DES, was the last to leave New Zealand in early February 1998, on sale to Emerald Airways in the UK. Interestingly it was still flying in full Mount Cook colours without titles in February 2000.

International Aviation of Sydney, Australia obtained the two Impulse Airlines Series 2Bs in October 1996. These had been converted for freighting use, but were fitted later with Large Freight Doors at Bankstown in late 1998 and early 1999 for use by Horizon Airlines on ad hoc and contract freight and mail charter work. The two Series 2Bs of Nepal Airways were also purchased, one for spares use only. The airworthy example

ZS-PLO c/n 1797 of Executive Aerospace. The fixed registration was chosen to honour the company's Flight Operations Director, Peter Leeson Ovenstone.
(Richard J Church)

arrived in Bankstown in July 2000 and was used for passenger work. This company also took delivery of an ex-RAAF Series 2 in July 1999 but the aircraft never entered service.

In South Africa, Executive Aerospace expanded its fleet with the addition of a former British Airways' Series 2B in October 1995, a Sun Air Series 2B in August 1996, a Series 2A from Mount Cook Airlines in July 1997, a Series 2A from France in August 1997 and a Series 2B from Emerald Airways in June 1999. The aircraft were operated on behalf of scheduled carriers in many countries including Botswana, Gabon, Madagascar, Malawi, the Maldives, Nigeria, South Africa, Uganda, Zambia and Zimbabwe. They were also used on executive charters and flown for government agencies and the United Nations. Intensive Air, originally based at Johannesburg-Rand, expanded its fleet to three aircraft operating ad hoc charter work from Johannesburg International Airport together with a schedule to Margate. The two additional aircraft were a Series 2A with a Large Freight Door added in September 1996 and a Series 2A in October 1997. Another new South African 748 operator was Lanseria-based AirQuarius Aviation (Pty) Ltd which purchased Air Marshall Islands' Series 2B in March 1999 and a Series 2B from Canada in October 1999.

Finally in Nepal, Necon Air purchased the last two Series 2B 748s to be completed when they were disposed of by Uni Air of Taiwan in November and December 1997 although unfortunately one of these was written-off in September 1999.

INTO THE NEW MILLENIUM

The demand for well-maintained 748s continued unabated into the new millenium as the type began to establish itself in very specialised areas where its ruggedness, reliability and unmatched performance made it the ideal choice. The Rolls-Royce Dart engine, though not the most fuel-efficient turbo-propeller engine in the modern world, is renowned for its reliability and is still used extensively worldwide.

In Canada such operators as Air Inuit, Calm Air and First Air, although operating more modern types on their southern routes have found the 748 very difficult to replace on their northern scheduled and charter work. The 748 can operate long sectors routinely with good payloads into severely restricted airfields in all conditions. In Canadian winters these conditions can be extremely severe. With very short daylight hours and temperatures down to minus 40°C, the gravel runways used become covered in compacted snow and ice. To cope with these severe conditions, individual operators have carried out numerous modifications to their aircraft and have adapted operating techniques to further improve the reliability and efficiency of the type. From December 2001 First Air began the gradual replacement of its high time 748s with new ATR42s, but surprisingly in October and December 2006 and in May 2007 Air Creebec bought three aircraft from West Air Sweden to once again expand its fleet.

Recently, the 748 has re-established itself in Southern and Central Africa where once again its performance eclipses more modern types out of hot and high airfields. The 748 can lift full passenger and/or freight loads out of strips which younger designs can find severely restricting, the latter's users frequently having to offload both passengers and freight in order to fly at all.

For similar reasons, the 748 operated successfully out of extremely high and restricted airfields in the Himalayan mountains of Nepal for many years, although it was withdrawn from regular commercial service by Necon Air and Royal Nepal Airlines during 2001 with two retired Necon Air aircraft eagerly snapped up by Executive Aerospace in South Africa.

In South Africa, Intensive Air ceased operations in April 2002 and its three 748s were due to be sold in Australia as indicated below but remained in South Africa under care and maintenance with AirQuarius Air Charter (Pty) Ltd, with whom two were converted to pure freighters. AirQuarius lost both of its own 748s in serious accidents in April and June 2002. Executive Aerospace expanded its fleet with the addition of two Series 2Bs from Necon Air in August and September 2001. The company found additional work for its aircraft operating in both Sri Lanka and Gabon. Lion Air of Sri Lanka flew the last-built 748 on schedules from Colombo to Jaffna from September 2002 until summer 2004, while Air Excellence of Gabon flew both domestically and internationally with one of Executive Aerospace's 748s from October 2002 to May 2003. Executive Aerospace later standardised on Series 2B versions and disposed of its two Series 2As in October 2002 and October 2003. The company found further work for one if its aircraft with Island Aviation Services of the Maldives in July and August 2004, with Comores Aviation from late June 2004 and with Euroguineana de Aviación from early June 2006. In more recent years Executive Aerospace gradually ran down its operational fleet of 748s and was eventually liquidated in February 2008. One of its aircraft moved to Avro Express of Kenya in August 2012 where it joined a Series 2A that came from International Air Parts in November 2010. Avro Express took delivery of four additional freighter configured HS748s one of which is fitted with a Large Freight Door in late 2014. These aircraft have all been in long term storage and all but one are expected to see service in Southern Sudan on relief flights. Three of these aircraft were used on relief flights in South Sudan.

In Australia, Horizon Airlines further expanded its 748 fleet with the purchase of two Large Freight Door equipped Series 2Bs from Madagascar in July 2001. The first two were converted into specialist freighters with similar interior work carried out to that completed on their original two aircraft, though only one entered service. In August 2002 International Air Parts (IAP) of Australia announced the purchase of the three-strong fleet of Intensive Air of South Africa, one of these being fitted with a large rear freight door. Horizon Airlines went into Administration in October 2003 and ceased operations soon after this, with the 748s returned to International Air Parts. The passenger-configured Srs.2B/426 was sold to Aero Lanka Airlines (Pvt) Ltd in September 2004 while one of the freight configured aircraft was leased to Z-Airways and Service Limited in Bangladesh in mid-December 2004. One of the Srs.2B/424s was sold to start-up carrier Stars Away Aviation of South Africa in March 2005, with the second following in March 2006. Of the three South African aircraft, one went on lease in Kenya with Trackmark Cargo in October 2004, one went to Best Air in Bangladesh in March 2005 and the third was reduced to spares. IAP's last 748, a Srs.2B/360, was sold to Trackmark Cargo in July 2006.

In Europe, 748 operations continued with two operators but in both cases in the small parcels, freight and mail rôles only. West Air Sweden built up a large fleet of aircraft, which came from a variety of sources, and brought all the aircraft up to a similar standard at its Hovby engineering base near Lidköping.

In August 2002 the company took over Air Provence International, but that company's two 748s were not part of the deal and they are now retired. West Air began the slow rundown of its fleet with the retirement of its Srs.2A/264 in April 2004, its Srs.2A/333 in September 2004 and was due to dispose of the first of its two Large Freight Door equipped aircraft to freight operator Stellair of Spain in April 2005 under a lease/purchase agreement. However, this last deal was not completed and the aircraft remained in service with West Air.

ALAIRE of Spain took delivery of the first of two all-freight-configured aircraft from West Air Sweden in early May 2006 to be operated out of a new Palma hub. On 24th May 2007 West Air flew its last revenue 748 service, having sold three of its aircraft in Canada in October and December 2006 and May 2007. The ALAIRE deal failed to reach a conclusion and the aircraft were returned to West Air, who managed to sell the last two aircraft to 748 Air Services of Kenya in late November 2007.

Emerald Airways in the United Kingdom had also built up a sizeable fleet of pure freighter 748s and operated these in the various colour schemes of the companies for which it was contracted to fly. Two further Series 2As were added in May 2001 and October 2002, raising the company's operational fleet to fourteen aircraft. However, the fleet was grounded when its AOC was suspended on 4th May 2006 and it subsequently went into administration on 11th May 2006.

On 16th October 2006 Emerald Airways was sold to IAP of Australia, who planned to bring the 748 fleet to airworthy condition and market them worldwide. The first three of these were leased to Bismillah Airlines, Best Aviation and Easy Fly Express in Bangladesh in May 2007 and April 2008, two more went to a rejuvenated Janes Aviation in April 2008 and another to Elysian Airlines of the Guinea Republic in March 2009.

G-OJEM c/n 1791 of Emerald Airways is seen here at Manchester in 1996.

(George Jenks)

The Belgian Air Force withdrew its three aircraft in 2001 and 2002 after some twenty-five years of service. Two of these were donated to Benin by the Belgian government in 2002, while the third was used for spares.

Demand for large cargo door equipped aircraft was particularly strong and several aircraft were converted to this configuration by robbing written-off aircraft of their doors.

In October 2001, the Força Aérea Brasileira retired its initial batch of six aircraft, having served the Brazilians for nearly forty accident-free years. The second batch of five large cargo door equipped aircraft was some thirteen years younger and continued in service after major upgrade work in 2001. At this time, the only other military user of the type in South America was Ecuador. The Fuerza Aérea Ecuatoriana had been flying the type for over thirty years and were still using two aircraft when in 2006 they obtained the five Large Freight Door equipped Srs.2A/281s previously operated by the Força Aérea Brasileira. One of these five aircraft was for spares use only. However, the Fuerza Aérea Ecuatoriana finally withdrew the type on 7th August 2014, so ending South America's association with the 748.

The Royal Australian Navy had retired its two aircraft earlier in June 2000, while the RAAF finally retired the last five of its Navigational Trainers at the end of June 2004. Of these one was reduced to spares, one was sold to GGG Aviation in March 2005 while the other three were all ferried to the United Kingdom by Clewer Aviation for subsequent disposal. Sadly, these three aircraft have not been found operational homes. The RAAF's two communications configured aircraft had been sold in Sweden in March 1999 (as recorded earlier), while two of its Navigational Trainers had been disposed of to International Air Parts in March 1999 and January 2001. The first of the Navigational Trainers was donated to the RAAF Museum at Point Cook, Victoria in January 2004.

Of the thirty-one Andover C.Mk.1s built, no fewer than fifteen found their way to Africa when their military use had finished. Here their capacious cabins and ease of loading through the rear doors together with the novel kneeling undercarriage have made them much in demand in war-torn or drought-stricken areas, delivering supplies and equipment and evacuating the injured from improvised strips.

In India, the military and government agencies continue to fly over fifty examples of the Indian-produced 748, though civilian use of the type has long since ceased.

At the time of writing, 78 748s of all versions remain operational with 22 in storage and capable of being returned to service. Reported hours flown by all versions of the 748 (excluding Andover C.Mk.1 and Indian military types) have exceeded 7 million, while landings have passed 7½ million. The first aircraft to pass the 60,000 flying hours figure was C-GJVN (c/n 1640) of Bradley Air Services in January 2005, while fifteen other aircraft are known by the author to have flown over 50,000 hours with several others nearing this figure. Five aircraft have passed the 70,000 landings mark.

LICENCE PRODUCTION IN INDIA

Throughout the early design stage of the Avro 748, the Indian Ministry of Defence expressed interest in the project as a suitable replacement for the Douglas C-47 Dakota in service with the Indian Air Force. The Indian Government was also keen to have an aircraft that would be licence-built in India. After negotiations with the various parties concerned, the Indian Ministry of Defence entered into an agreement with Hawker Siddeley Aviation in July 1959 for licence production of the 748 aircraft in India. Initially, Hawker Siddeley would supply kits from the A.V. Roe production line for assembly in India and at a later stage the complete aircraft would be constructed there. Included in the arrangement was the licence production of the Rolls-Royce Dart engine by Hindustan Aeronautics at their Bangalore facilities. In January 1960 four hangars were taken over at Kanpur and the new plant became known as the Indian Air Force Manufacturing Depot.

On 16th July 1960 the first aircraft was despatched from Woodford in kit form aboard a Hawker Siddeley Argosy. The Argosy delivered the kit to Kanpur as part of a sales tour to India and Pakistan. Production facilities, including jigs and tooling, were set up in Kanpur and full production was targeted for early 1964. A team of engineers was sent from Woodford to assist in setting up the new production line and to help in producing the prototype aeroplane. A decision was then taken to construct all subsequent aircraft for the Indian Air Force order at Kanpur although some components would be shipped out from the UK.

The Indian 748s were slightly different from those produced by Avro and had a larger freight door with a strengthened fuselage floor and had the maximum take-off weight increased to 37,500lbs (17,014kgs). Later another project, the HS 758 was offered to the Indian Air Force, as detailed in the section 'Projected versions of the 748', but this was not proceeded with. The Indian Government was still hopeful of finalising sales of locally-produced 748s to Indian Airlines Corporation.

First flight of the Indian-assembled aircraft, a Series 1 with c/n 500 registered BH572, took place at Kanpur on 1st November 1961 with the then Squadron Leader Kapil Bhargava in command. Also on board were Squadron Leaders Ripu Daman Sahni and Chandrakant Vishwanath Gole. All three crew had qualified as test pilots at the Empire Test Pilots School at Farnborough in the United Kingdom. The same aircraft was named "Subroto" in a ceremony that took place on 26th November 1961 in the presence of the Indian Prime Minister (Mr Nehru), the Minister of Defence (Mr Krishna Menon) and the Minister of Transport and Communications (Dr P. Subbarayan). The aircraft's name came from a former Chief of Air Staff of the Indian Air Force, Air Marshall Subroto Mukerjee. A promotional tour of south-east Asia was made in August 1962, when the aircraft visited Burma, Cambodia, Indonesia, Malaya and Thailand. The aircraft was used for development flying and registered VT-DRF for a while in 1964. It was delivered to the

Highest recorded flown aircraft

Type	c/n	Regn	Operator	Figures
Series 1	1549	9N-ACM	Necon Air	50,044 hours
	1549	9N-ACM	Necon Air	57,345 landings
Series 2/2A	1640	C-GJVN	Bradley Air Service	62,521 hours
	1584	G-11-4	BAe plc	79,014 landings
Series 2B	1790	C-GHSC	Calm Air	37,242 hours
	1790	C-GHSC	Calm Air	40,907 landings
HAL 748	518	VT-DXK	Indian Airlines	53,033 hours
	518	VT-DXK	Indian Airlines	50,556 landings
C.Mk.1	09	3C-KKB	748 Air Services	17,428 hours
	18	3C-KKC	748 Air Services	21,638 landings

The first two HAL 748s, BH572 c/n HAL/K/500 and BH573 c/n HAL/K/501, are seen here in the final assembly hall at Kanpur.

Indian Air Force on 17th April 1964. Indian production was very slow and the first wholly Indian built 748, c/n 501, made its first flight on 13th March 1963 in the hands of Squadron Leaders Bhargava and Tapsall.

The Series 1 aircraft reportedly fell short of specifications and the Tata committee undertook a review of the entire licence production concept. The committee's report suggested ending 748 production and starting licence production of the de Havilland Canada Caribou aircraft for the Indian Air Force instead. After consideration, the report was rejected. On 8th May 1963 an HS 748 Series 2 (G-ARAY) was demonstrated to Indian officials in Delhi. Following this, the Indian Government decided to suspend Series 1 production after the fourth aircraft in favour of Series 2 production to satisfy the requirements of the Indian Air Force. In 1964 Hindustan Aircraft Limited took over the Kanpur facilities in an endeavour to improve the poor production rate. On 1st October 1964 this company's name was changed to Hindustan Aeronautics Ltd (HAL). The aircraft would, from henceforth, be known as the HAL 748 and new production targets were set as follows: - 7 aircraft in 1964 and 12 aircraft in 1965. HAL's Bangalore facilities started to produce licence-built Dart RDa.7 Mk 531 engines in lieu of the earlier RDa.6 version. On 28th January 1964 the first production HAL 748 Series 2, c/n 504, was flown for the first time from Kanpur by Squadron Leader Tapsall and Flight Lieutenant Ramachandran. It has been reported that three of the first four aircraft were upgraded to Series 2 standard. Production was still very slow and by mid-1965 only four aircraft had flown. The Indian Air Force had considered licence production of the HS 780 Andover, but in view of the poor production rate of the 748 at Kanpur, the plan was dropped in favour of a direct purchase of 16 DHC-4 Caribou aircraft.

A breakthrough for Hindustan Aeronautics came in December 1965 when Indian Airlines Corporation (IAC) ordered fifteen 748s to replace their DC-3s. The order came after IAC had evaluated the first HAL 748 Series 2 aircraft early in 1965. Deliveries were planned between September 1966 and December 1968 with targets for 5 aircraft in 1966, 6 in 1967 and 4 in 1968. First flight of the HAL 748 for Indian Airlines took place on 11th February 1966 with c/n 506, registered VT-DUO. That aircraft was flown subsequently to Woodford for fitting out to commercial standards and remained there from March 1966 to May 1967. On 22nd June 1967, VT-DUO was loaned to IAC, being handed over officially at Chakeri on 28th June. Revenue services were started from Hyderabad on 8th August 1967 with the aircraft operating in a 40-seat configuration.

The production rate was still a major problem and only two aircraft were delivered in 1966. IAC could not wait any longer to replace their remaining DC-3s and purchased a further batch of Fokker F.27s. The HAL 748 order was reduced subsequently to fourteen aircraft and contract delivery dates were renegotiated. During 1968 and 1969 the production rate at last began to improve and the last of the fourteen 748s contracted for by IAC, c/n 525 VT-DXR, was delivered on 26th February 1970. Indian Airlines Corporation then ordered a further batch of ten aircraft but only three of these would be accepted. Problems arose with the remaining seven aircraft when HAL suggested modifications. IAC would not accept the proposals, as the modifications would increase the aircraft basic weight and operating costs.

In March 1973 the Indian Minister of Civil Aviation, Dr. Karan Singh, set up an investigation to examine the Indian 748 in detail. Dr. Satish Dhawan, Director of the Institute of Science and

H-1181 c/n HAL/K/537 of the Indian Air Force, seen during a visit to Chabua.   (Simon Watson)

Above: VT-EFR c/n HAL/K/547 with National Airports Authority titles, with whom it operated from September 1978 to September 2000. (WHC)

Above: VT-EAX c/n HAL/K/544 of Indian Airlines at Woodford on 26th February 1973 for performance trials.   (Ralph Harrison)

Secretary of the Space Department, was appointed to head a high-level team of engineers drawn from the Indian Air Force, Indian Airlines, Air India and government agencies. One aircraft, c/n 544 VT-EAX, was ferried to Woodford where it arrived on 11th January 1973 to undergo performance trials by Hawker Siddeley and Rolls-Royce. After examination, Rolls-Royce stated that the licence-produced Dart engines were up to standard and performance specification and suggested a modified water-methanol system to enhance performance. Indian-produced aircraft were still fitted with the original Dart RDa.7 Mk 531 engines, which had a lower power rating when compared to contemporary UK built Series 2A aircraft. Some IAC pilots had complained of poor single-engined performance. VT-EAX was returned to India, departing Woodford on 19th April 1973 for tropical trials under Hawker Siddeley supervision. The same version of the Dart RDa.7 Mk 531 engine continued to be produced and was used in all Hindustan Aeronautics built 748 production except the last batch of twenty.

The Indian Air Force ordered more HAL 748s for operation in the VIP, pilot training, and signal training rôles. Once the production rate had improved, the Indian Air Force received a total of 45 aircraft by 1975. After Hawker Siddeley had introduced the Large Rear Cargo Door (LFD) in 1971, Hindustan Aeronautics produced their own conversion, using c/n 532 from the Indian Air Force order. The aircraft made its first flight so fitted on 16th February 1972 and was designated the HAL 748 Series 2M. In June 1975 the Indian Air Force ordered a batch of ten Series 2M aircraft as freighters. Late in 1980 a second batch of ten similar aircraft was ordered and all were delivered by 1984.

All seven aircraft that Indian Airlines had rejected were completed and placed in storage at Kanpur. In October 1977 one aircraft was delivered to the National Remote Sensing Agency, and between 1978 and 1979 three aircraft were transferred to the Indian Air Force and fitted out for photographic survey work. Two aircraft were later allocated to the Indian Civil Aviation Department for use in Flight Inspection duties in January 1981. The final aircraft was allocated to the Indian Border Security Force in March 1982.

Indian Airlines Corporation used their aircraft on domestic schedules with aircraft centred on Bombay (Mumbai), Delhi, Hyderabad and Madras (Chennai) at various times during the type's service. As airfields were improved and traffic increased, Boeing 737s replaced the type and Indian Airlines progressively transferred the aircraft to Vayudoot, leading to the retirement of the 748 in April 1989. Vayudoot operated eleven aircraft, receiving them between July 1986 and April 1989, having earlier leased a few aircraft from 1982. The company ceased operations in mid-1994 and the aircraft were retired.

The Indian Air Force has operated its aircraft in a variety of rôles including VIP, general freighting, training and paradropping. HAL 748s operated as multi-engine pilot and navigation trainers from the base at Yelahanka near Bangalore. One of the last batch of Series 2Ms, c/n 587, was transferred to the Indian Border Security Force as VT-EIR. The original prototype c/n 500 was transferred from the Indian Air Force and became the personal transport of the Chairman of Hindustan Aeronautics Limited. Ten of the Indian Air Force Series 2s were converted later to Series 2M standard with Large Freight Doors. Another modification was the conversion of an aircraft to the ASP (Airborne Surveillance Platform) prototype with a large rotodome mounted above the fuselage. This aircraft, c/n 569 H-2175, initially flew from Kanpur without the rotodome fitted, before ferrying to Bangalore for the fitment of the 24ft x 5ft rotodome. It made its public debut at the Aero India Show in December 1996, but was unfortunately written-off on 11th January 1999. It is believed that the rotodome broke free from the aircraft causing loss of control.

The aircraft had been converted by the Defence Research and Development Organisation (DRDO) and sadly eight persons, including four of the DRDO's senior scientists, were killed in the ensuing crash 2.5 kilometres short of the runway at the Arakkonam naval airbase near Chennai. The aircraft had carried out over nine years of research and testing but following the crash the programme was cancelled in January 2000. Over this period this aircraft had become known locally as the 'Flying Chapatti'.

A second aircraft was being similarly converted, but following the cancellation of the programme, the aircraft was de-modified and converted for flight testing avionics systems and airborne radars destined for the indigenous Light Combat Aircraft (LCA). This aircraft, H-2176, has been modified in several ways. The most visible external changes were the new nose cone which housed the LCA's Multi-mode Radar (MMR) antenna and the air scoops for cooling purposes. Inside the cabin, racks were installed for mounting various items for in-flight testing. Known locally as Line Replaceable Units or LRUs, these included items for the MMR, Radio Altimeter and Laser Ranger. A Turbomeca APU was fitted to provide additional electrical power and to assist in equipment cooling, while a Solid State Flight Data Recorder was also utilised. More recently, the aircraft was used by the 'Centre for Airborne Systems' (CABS) for flight testing the jointly developed Indian/Israeli ELTA Systems Ltd Airborne Warning Radar due to be fitted in the Embraer 135.

H-2176 c/n HAL/K/570 was used as a radar testbed by the Indian Defence Research and Development Organisation (DRDO).   *(Simon Watson)*

(Simon Watson)

H-2182 c/n HAL/K/576 of the Indian Air Force with a Hindustan Aeronautics Large Freight Door conversion.

H-2183 c/n HAL/K/577 of the Indian Air Force; its Large Freight Door is on the port side.　　　　　　　　　　*(Simon Watson)*

Prime users of the type with the Indian Air Force are detailed below. The Air Headquarters Communications Squadron, the 'Pegasus' Squadron, has used 748s continually since they were introduced into service in 1964 from its base at Palam (Delhi), until the type was due to be withdrawn from use officially in the VIP rôle on 28th April 2006. At its peak this Squadron operated seven 748s. Three newly-delivered Embraer 135s replaced the VIP 748s at this time with a fourth due for delivery later. However, service experience found that the Embraer 135s were unable to operate into some airfields and the 748 was returned to service. The primary task of this Squadron is to convey Indian VVIPs and VIPs together with visiting Heads of State and Governments. It has also been called upon to carry out emergency relief duties when so required.

In the general transport rôle, two Squadrons are known to have used 748s. No 11 Squadron (the 'Rhino') introduced the type into service in April 1979 based at Gwalior, Madhya Pradesh where the type joined C-47 Dakotas. The last Dakota was withdrawn on 17th July 1980, from which time the 748 was the sole type in service. With effect from January 1996, Antonov 32s began to replace the 748s in a process that was completed in August 1996. In March 2000 this squadron moved to Baroda, Gujarat and replaced some of its Antonov 32s with 748s once again.

More recently No 41 Squadron 'A' Flight (the 'Otters') based at Palam (Delhi) took delivery of 748s in 1996, where they joined the Squadron's locally-produced HAL/Dornier 228s, doing VIP flying, communications and light load carrying duties. Other units that used 748s include 106 Squadron (the 'Lynxes') based at Agra in Uttar Pradesh and 59 Squadron (the 'Hornbills') based at Guwahati (formerly Gauhati) in Assam.

106 Squadron operated two (possibly three) 748s in the photo reconnaissance rôle alongside Canberra PR.Mk.57/67s though the latter were retired on 31st May 2007. The 748s photo-mapped both India and Sri Lanka using Carl Zeiss RMK Alpha cameras mounted in a special fairing beneath the fuselage aft of the wing spar and carried out similar work reportedly from 2001 until they were withdrawn in December 2013. No 59 Squadron took 748s

on strength in 1999 when they replaced Dornier 228s, carrying out similar duties to those used by 41 Squadron. Based at Hindon (Delhi), 181 Flight operates a pair of 748s in the ELINT/SIGINT (Electronic and Signals Intelligence) rôle for work on the Pakistan and China borders. The Indian Air Force Navigation and Signals Training School at Begumpet, Hyderabad has operated 748s since February 1972, while the Transport Training Wing also flew 748s from its base at Yelahanka, Bangalore from October 1968 until 1999, when they were replaced by Dornier 228s. The Indian Air Force had a Flight Inspection Unit which flew two 748s out of Palam. This unit later became part of the Air Examining Board based at the military airfield at Hindon.

Several Commands have Headquarters Flights which fly 748s. These are Maintenance Command based at Nagpur (Maharashtra), Central Air Command based at Allahabad (Uttar Pradesh), Eastern Air Command based at Guwahati (Assam), Southern Air Command based at Sulur (Tamil Nadu), South West Air Command based at either Baroda or Gandhinagar (Gujarat) and finally Western Air Command at Palam which uses the Pegasus Squadron fleet and has no aircraft of its own.

Another Air Force department which flies a single 748 is ASTE, the Aircraft & Systems Testing Establishment. ASTE can best be described as the Indian equivalent of the United Kingdom's old A & AEE at Boscombe Down and was established on 23rd August 1972, evolving from the Aircraft & Armaments Testing Unit (A&ATU). From July 1973 it has been based at Bangalore where it evaluates aircraft and systems for their suitability for use by the Indian military.

Indian production ended after the completion of 89 aircraft including the original prototype. The main problem in the early years was very slow production and later the inability of the manufacturer to update the aircraft and powerplant to Series 2A standards. The final batch of twenty Series 2Ms was delivered to the Indian Air Force with Rolls-Royce Dart RDa.7 Mk 536-2T engines to improve the overall performance. No HAL built aircraft were sold abroad and information regarding Indian-produced aircraft has been generally difficult to obtain.

ANDOVER

Delivery of the Andover C.Mk.1 aircraft to the Royal Air Force started in mid-1966 and was completed in February 1968 (the facing page features a three-view drawing of the aircraft). Most of the aircraft were allocated to No.46 Squadron, the Andover Operational Conversion Unit (OCU) or the Station Flight at RAF Abingdon. The majority of the aircraft passed through No.46 Squadron prior to further allocation. Six aircraft saw service with No.52 Squadron from 1st December 1966 until its disbandment on 31st December 1969 and were based at Seletar (Singapore). A further six aircraft were allocated to No.84 Squadron based at Sharjah from August 1967. No.84 Squadron converted from Beverley aircraft to the Andover C.Mk.1 and the Squadron moved to Muharraq (Bahrain) in December 1970.

Aircraft from the Squadron were rotated to the Search and Rescue Flight, with individual Andovers based at various locations in the Gulf area throughout that period. No.84 Squadron was disbanded on 31st October 1971 and the aircraft were returned to the UK.

A single aircraft went via No.21 Squadron to the Middle East Communications Squadron in July 1967 as a VIP aircraft. That aircraft was transferred subsequently to No.84 Squadron prior to returning to the UK. Set 31, serial XS 647, was not used for true RAF service and, after a short period with the Ministry of Technology, was stored at RAF Kemble in the charge of No.5 Maintenance Unit (MU) from January 1969. Eventually Set 31 went to British Aerospace at Woodford in January 1981 to be used as a centre-section design rig for the new ATP aircraft. In 1970 a number of aircraft that had become surplus to requirements were stored with 5 MU at Kemble. Late in 1970, XS637 was delivered to Fornebu airport in Oslo for the use of the Commander Air Force North (NATO) where it remained for some time.

By the early 1970s successive government cutbacks on defence spending and progressive withdrawal from overseas commitments rendered the Andover C.Mk.1. surplus to requirements.

The aircraft had become a victim of the wind of change in Whitehall and some aircraft were used for alternative duties during that period. One aircraft went to Boscombe Down for use by the Empire Test Pilots' School in August 1975 where it was used until August 2012. In January 1973 a single aircraft went to the Royal Aircraft Establishment at Farnborough, followed by a second in April 1976. No.32 Squadron at Northolt, already operating three Andover CC.Mk.2 aircraft, received two Andover C.Mk.1s in November 1975, one of which was later transferred to No.115 Squadron in September 1976.

No.46 Squadron had moved to Thorney Island in September 1970, where it joined the Andover Training Squadron and No.242 OCU already based there. When No.46 Squadron was disbanded on 31st August 1975 a large number of aircraft went into storage with No.5 MU at Kemble.

Between November 1976 and January 1978, No.115 Squadron based at Brize Norton converted from Argosy E.Mk.1 to Andover C.Mk.1 aircraft. The Squadron was tasked with calibrating landing aids and related equipment to ICAO standards at Ministry of Defence, RAF and Royal Navy airfields worldwide. It moved to RAF Benson in January 1983. Four of the Andovers, serials XS603/605/610 and 640, were upgraded and converted to E.Mk.3 standard having being fitted earlier with Rover Gas Turbines 2S/150A APUs located in a similar position to the APUs on the production 748s. They were fitted with an Inertial Reference Flight Inspection System (IRFIS) in 1985 produced by Litton of Canada. They were crewed by two pilots, a navigator, an Air Electronics Officer (AEO), who operated the new IRFIS equipment, and one or two radar assessors who calibrated Precision Approach Radar (PAR), Area and Air Defence radars. After the navigator established the aircraft on the required approach path utilising his assortment of aids including Decca/TANS, VOR, TACAN, ADF and Litton INS equipment, the AEO brought the IRFIS equipment into use. This calibrated the ILS accurately from six stations simultaneously for a position fix, reportedly accurate to within six inches in any direction.

XS596 (Set 3) Andover C.Mk.1 (PR) of QinetiQ at Fairford on 12th July 2002 with 'United Kingdom Open Skies' titles.   *(Keith Gaskell)*

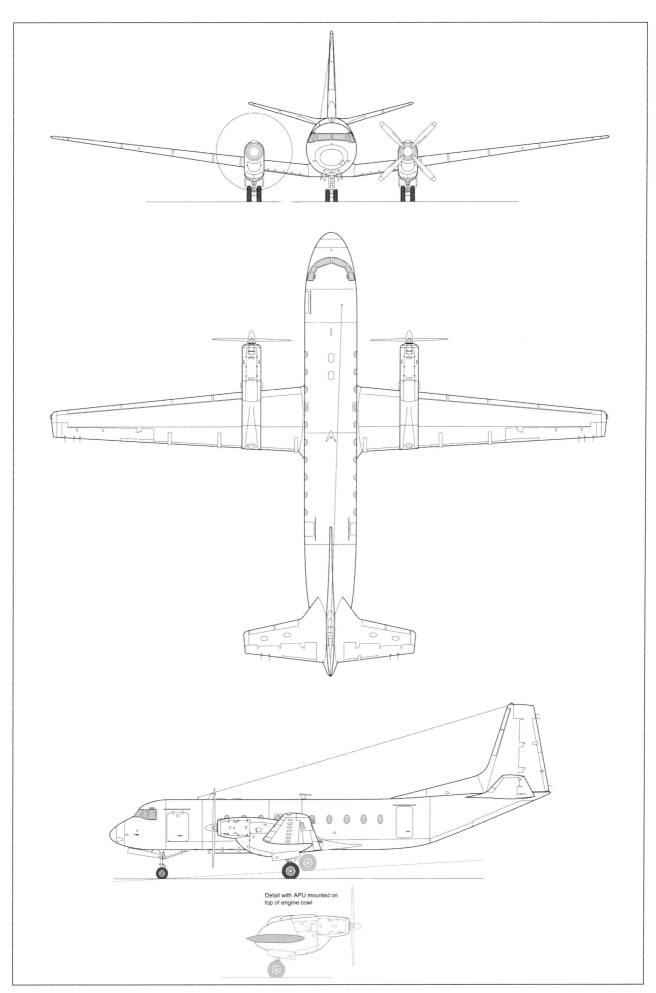

Detail with APU mounted on
top of engine cowl

Andover C.Mk.1.

This Andover, G-BEBY (Set 14), was civil registered for a demonstration tour to India, and was photographed at Manchester on 10th August 1976.
(Ralph Harrison)

Three aircraft were converted to E.Mk.3A standard, serialled XS639/643 and 644. Not IRFIS equipped, these aircraft were basically standard C.Mk.1s with an extra crew position alongside the navigator. They were used for radar calibration, transport, training, casualty evacuation and VIP flights. One of these aircraft (XS644) was loaned to the Electronic Warfare and Avionics Unit at Wyton. 115 Squadron disbanded on 19th October 1993 and its duties were taken over by Hunting Aviation Ltd who also took over the operation of the four E.Mk.3s. One of the aircraft was retired early in 1995 and ferried to Northolt for storage until it was finally broken up in November 1997. The last three aircraft soldiered on until 19th October 1996, when they were retired and disposed of for mainly humanitarian work in Africa, after removal of their specialised equipment. The three 115 Squadron E.Mk.3A aircraft were all moved on to No.32 Squadron at Northolt in early 1992. One (XS639) was donated to the Cosford Museum for preservation in July 1994, one was sold in Africa in November 1994 and the last was dismantled and taken to Manston in Kent for the use of the fire school.

Four aircraft in their later years were operated by No.60 Squadron at Wildenrath in Germany (XS596/7 and XS637/641), two of which were converted to C.Mk.1 (PR) standard for use in the photographic reconnaissance rôle. However, the Squadron disbanded on 18th July 1992 and the aircraft were put in storage. Of these four aircraft, two were sold subsequently in Africa, one of them went to QinetiQ as detailed below with the fourth becoming an instructional airframe with the School of Technical Training at Cosford in June 1993. The last operational Andovers in UK military marks were all based at Boscombe Down with QinetiQ, the former Defence Evaluation and Research Agency (DERA). XS596, a C.Mk.1 (PR), was used for exercising British rights under the "Open Skies" policy, XS606 was operated on behalf of the Empire Test Pilots' School, while the third aircraft, XS646, was used as a large flying laboratory for research and development work. However, the last of these was withdrawn at the end of August 2012 and departed to a new user in Africa in April 2013.

A single Andover C.Mk.1 received a civil registration, G-BEBY, when registered to Hawker Siddeley Aviation in July 1976 for a demonstration tour to India the following month. On return to the UK, the registration was cancelled and the aircraft, restored as XS607, went to the Royal Aircraft Establishment at West Freugh in September 1976 where it was operated by the Electronic Warfare and Avionic Unit until transferred to Boscombe Down in April 1994. It was finally sold in the Democratic Republic of Congo in August 1996.

In 1976, ten RAF Andover C.Mk.1s were sold to the Royal New Zealand Air Force to replace Bristol 170 Mk.31 Freighters and DC-3s in service at that time. No.241 O.C.U. at Brize Norton was used for the initial training of RNZAF crews. Six aircraft in camouflage went to No.1 Squadron RNZAF, based at Whenuapai, whilst the remaining four aircraft went to No.42 Squadron RNZAF, based at Ohakea as VIP and General Communications aircraft. The VIP aircraft were painted in an attractive livery with white top, blue cheat line and grey undersurfaces.

By 1981, the RNZAF had purchased two Boeing 727s, plus a third for spares, to supplement the Lockheed C.130s already in service on long and medium range tasks. Three Cessna 421C Golden Eagles were also purchased in 1981 for use in the VIP rôle. When passenger loads were small, the Cessna 421Cs were flown, these being cheaper to operate than the larger Andover. By late 1984 some Andover C.Mk.1s had became surplus to requirements and were stored at Whenuapai. No.1 Squadron was deactivated on the 7th December 1984 and all Andover tasks were taken over by No.42 Squadron from the 10th December. No.42 Squadron subsequently moved from Ohakea to Whenuapai and the Cessna 421Cs were transferred to a new RNZAF Cessna Flight based at Woodbourne. In mid-1985 the New Zealand Ministry of Defence offered three Andovers for lease to any New Zealand commercial operator provided that the aircraft were maintained to RNZAF standards and they did not leave New Zealand airspace. The offer was not taken up and five aircraft were withdrawn in 1996, four of which were put in store at

Ardmore pending their disposal, while the fifth was donated to the RNZAF Museum at Wigram. All four stored aircraft were sold to Eureka Aviation in February 1997 and after registration in the Democratic Republic of Congo departed for Belgium. A sixth aircraft was withdrawn in 1992 and broken up at Whenuapai.

The final four aircraft were withdrawn from service on 20th June 1998 and all were sold for use in Africa. After registration in Equatorial Guinea, two departed New Zealand in September 1998 and the last two in March and April 1999.

It is virtually impossible to follow the subsequent histories of Andovers on the African continent where identities are confused by multiple changes and multiple uses of similar registrations. It is however clear that the type has proved most versatile in delivering essential supplies and ferrying out injured people from isolated jungle strips in war-torn areas, where there are no navigational aids or turnaround facilities. The aircraft is self-sufficient and the novel kneeling undercarriage makes loading and unloading much less of a problem. Details of fleet changes, where known, are shown in the Andover C.Mk.1 Individual Aircraft Histories section.

PROJECTED VERSIONS OF THE 748

From the outset, the Design Department of A.V. Roe & Co Ltd inevitably considered variations on the basic 748 airframe. As many of these projects were shelved and then resurrected for various reasons, chronology is difficult to ascertain. In addition to the basic development that actually took place as detailed in this chapter, many more options were considered. A simple fuselage stretch is always a possibility when a transport aircraft is designed and the 748 was no exception. This section is therefore divided into four smaller sections, covering developments that in many cases were running concurrently:

a) Civil variants
b) Military variants
c) STOL/VTOL projects
d) Pure jet developments

Drawings of several of these projected versions are given at the end of this section.

a) Civil variants

1) The Avro 748E was a project for a Series 2 aircraft with a 6ft (1.83m) fuselage stretch, retaining the Rolls-Royce Dart 7 engine and seating 52 passengers with a reduced range of around 200nm.

2) The 748E was also proposed to have the more powerful Rolls Royce Dart 10 engines of 2,400 shp to improve payload/range and would have been known as the 748 10/E.

3) An even longer stretch of 9ft (2.74m) was proposed, known as the Avro 748 Super E, also with Dart 10 engines. If either project had been built, a type similar in capacity to the Japanese YS-11 would have evolved.

4) With later engine improvements, fuselage stretches of 13.5ft (4.11m) seating 60 passengers and 16.5ft (5.03m) seating 64 passengers were also considered, leading eventually to the ATP.

5) An executive version designated the 748X, representing a Series 2 with extra fuel tankage offering a range of 2,250 miles (3,618km), was studied but not proceeded with.

3C-JJX (Set 6) at Johannesburg-Lanseria on 18th October 2002 fresh off a repaint and ready for delivery to 748 Air Services Ltd in Kenya, where it became 5Y-SFE.

(Keith Gaskell)

6) Another 'stretch' considered was the 748L employing a larger wing with a span of 109ft 2in (33.27m) and an area of 950ft^2 (88.25m^2), Rolls-Royce Dart 10s driving 14ft (4.27m) diameter propellers and a fuselage diameter increased to 10ft 6in (3.20m). This approach had worked well in earlier days when Douglas developed the DC-3 from the DC-2.

7) Once the RAF 748MF type had been finalised and had become known as the Andover C.Mk.1, Hawker Siddeley explored the possibilities of a civil version designated the HS 748CF in 1963. The 748CF would have been powered by Rolls-Royce Dart RDa.10 engines, would have had the same rear loading facilities as the 748MF and would have carried 8 tons of freight or up to 54 passengers or a mix of both.

8) Another project based on the 748CF would have offered the capability of carrying up to three family-sized cars and was intended as a Bristol 170 replacement.

9) Alternative powerplants were also considered, as were civil freighter versions, including the 748F with Dart 6 or 7 engines. Large Freight Doors, swing noses and even swing engines were also considered.

b) Military variants

To satisfy anticipated military customers' needs, many variations of the basic 748 were proposed during the sixties and early seventies. The 748MF was of course built as the Type 780 Andover C.Mk.1 for the RAF, but was also the subject of much projected development. This included a version powered by four Dart 6s and a shortened version powered by two Dart 6s or two DH Gnomes, designated the type 782. As with the 748, alternative power plants were also considered for many of the proposals including the Pratt and Whitney T-64. Other developments known to have been proposed but which in the event were not proceeded with are listed below:

1) The 748M featured a large side-loading door and a strengthened cabin floor and was a proposal for the Indian Air Force. It was later given the Avro type number 757.

2) Another interesting proposal, also for the Indian Air Force, known initially as the 748R and later allocated the type number 758 was an aircraft with a high wing and rear ramp. Engines were mounted Fokker Friendship style and the fuselage width and depth were extended to 11ft 3in (3.43m) and 10ft 4in (3.15m) respectively while the undercarriage was housed in pods on the fuselage side.

3) In 1961 the 748MR with wing-tip and leading edge podded sensors together with a retractable ASV21 scanner was proposed. This would have been powered by Dart 8 engines and had a wing span of 95ft (28.95m) and a wing area of 795ft^2 (73.86m^2).

4) In 1962 the 748EW was proposed. This had an AWACS type dish and twin fins and rudders. An alternative version had a large ventral scanner similar to the later Coastguarder.

5) Another projected EW version was the carrier-based Type 768 to Naval Staff Target NA107T. Also fitted with twin fins, it had a shorter fuselage and a 24ft (7.32m) dish mounted on top of the fuselage. Wing span was reduced to 85ft (25.90m) but with wing folding an overall width of 30ft (9.14m) was obtained to ease stowage on crowded carrier decks and hangars.

6) The 748AEW was a projected version based on the Series 2A with nose and tail radomes similar to the later Nimrod AEW.3. Dimensions were the same as for the Series 2A 748 except for the overall length which was extended to 84ft 6in (25.75m).

7) A carrier-on-board delivery (COD) type was also proposed for the US Navy. This Large Freight Door equipped version of the 748 had a redesigned and strengthened undercarriage to cope with deck landing and was also fitted with an arrester hook and catapult attachments. It was also designed to have a flight refuelling probe above the cabin which extended forward of the cockpit glazing. As with 5), this version incorporated wing folding outboard of the engines which reduced the overall width of the aircraft to 48ft 6in (14.8m).

8) The type 818 was an AEW study to AST400 powered by four Rolls-Royce Darts.

c) STOL/VTOL Projects

The basic 748 had a good short field performance, but many schemes were put forward to improve this even more - right up to VTOL. As early as 1959, the 748R (Type 758) was projected in a STOL version using Dart 12s while a VTOL version had additional RB162 lift engines. The following year, a Deflected Slipstream development of the Type 758 was considered using four Dart 12s or DH Genies. A number of four-engined STOL schemes based on the 748 were considered using Garrett ATF3s, Darts with booster engines and T-53s. The 780 Andover got similar treatment with engine variations including four Dart 6s and six Viper 11s. A STOL type 780 was projected for a NATO requirement under the separate type number 783. VTOL versions of the Type 780 included the use of ten RB162-31s mounted in under-wing pods. Perhaps the ultimate use of the 748 fuselage was for a VTOL transport based on the use of Circulation Controlled Rotors, a system devised by the NGTE (National Gas Turbine Establishment) in the early sixties by which wing-tip mounted rotors were stopped after take-off and folded for conventional flight.

d) Pure Jet Developments

A pure jet version, the 748J, was envisaged as early as April 1960 using two rear-mounted Armstrong/Bristol Siddeley engines such as the P.216 or BS75. A new type number 778 was allocated to cover such developments. These included the use of two RB161 or BS216 engines, three General Electric CF700s (mounted Trident style) and a shorter 30-seat version with two CF700s designated type 781. The fuselage forward of the rear pressure bulkhead was virtually unchanged from that of the 748 as was the wing apart from a reduction in span to 84ft (25.60m). The main undercarriage retracted forwards into pods protruding forward of the wing. From 1961, four Armstrong Siddeley Viper 20s were also considered as powerplants, either rear-mounted or paired under the wing similar to the Avro Ashton research aircraft. Jet versions of the Type 780 were also considered using engines such as the RB180, BS75 or CF700. In mid-1967, design work centred about a rear mounted twin jet with a swept fin designated the Type 806. The 748 fuselage was extended to accommodate 72 passengers and power was to be supplied by the Rolls-Royce RB203 Trent engine of 9,970 lb thrust. The project was later renumbered Type 860, reportedly because the square typeface used on the publicity model appeared to read "BOG" instead of "806". The Trent engine was not continued with, ending work on this project. A much simpler variation to the basic 748 was known as the HS748 Series 5. This employed the mounting of two Rolls-Royce M45H engines in a similar position to the Darts on the 748s with the engines exhausting over the wing. Apart from the horizontal tailplane being changed to a dihedral position, the engine mountings being redesigned and the wing span being reduced to 95ft 6in (29.11m), the airframe was virtually identical to the basic 748. Strangely, this last engine's only other application was on the German VFW614 airliner which also had the engines mounted over the wing. An alternative engine proposed was the Avco-Lycoming ALF502 for which the type would have been known as the 748/502.

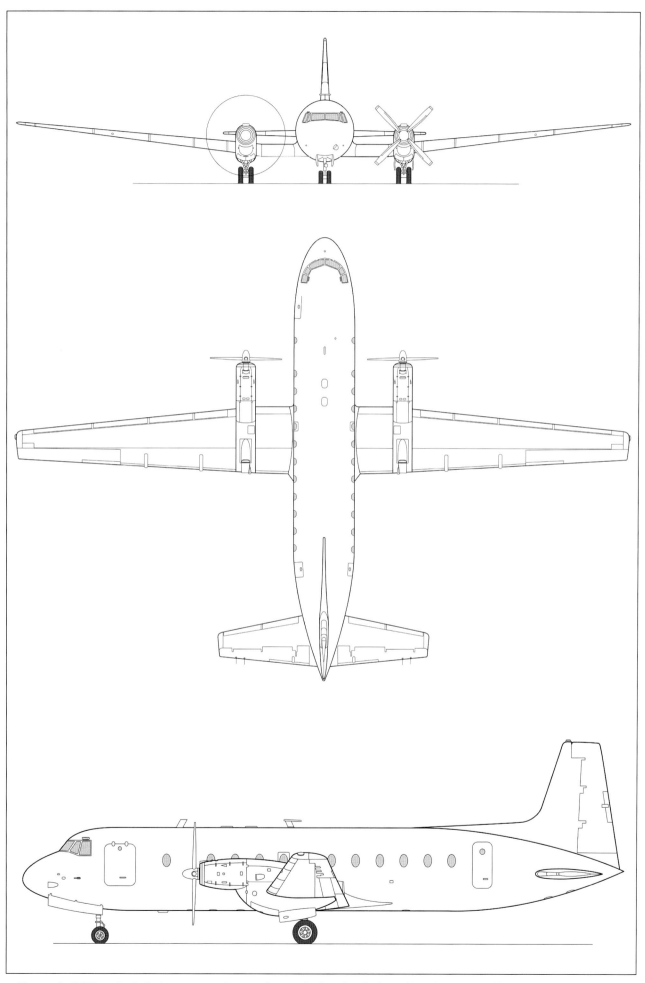

The stretched 748L version had a larger wing and greater diameter fuselage than the Series 2B, with more powerful Rolls-Royce Dart 10 engines.

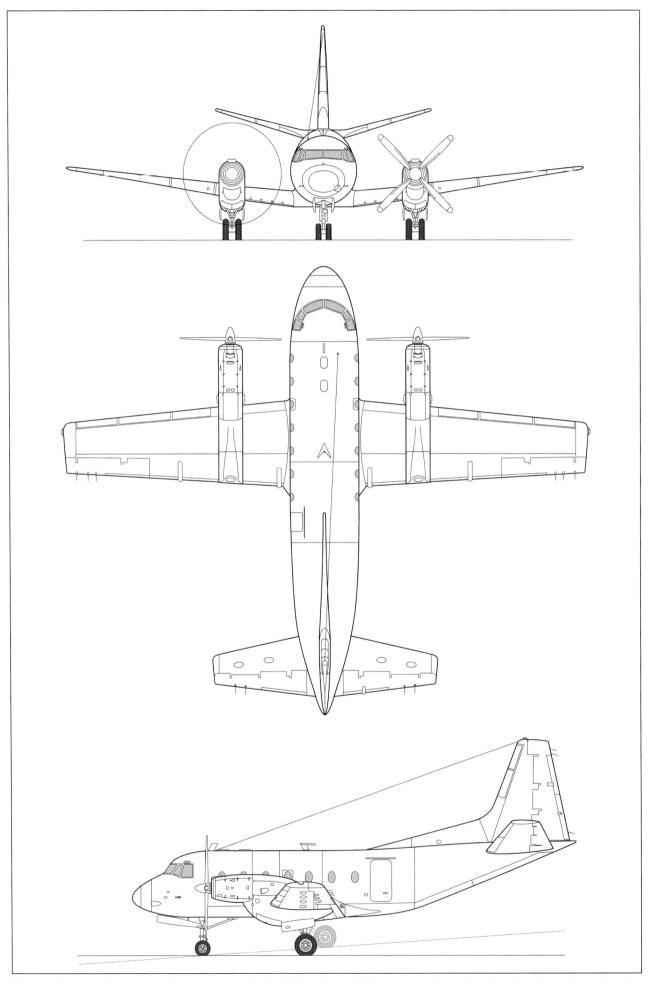

The Avro 782 was a military variant with versions powered by four RR Dart 6s, two DH Gnomes or, as shown above, by two Dart 6s in a shortened version.

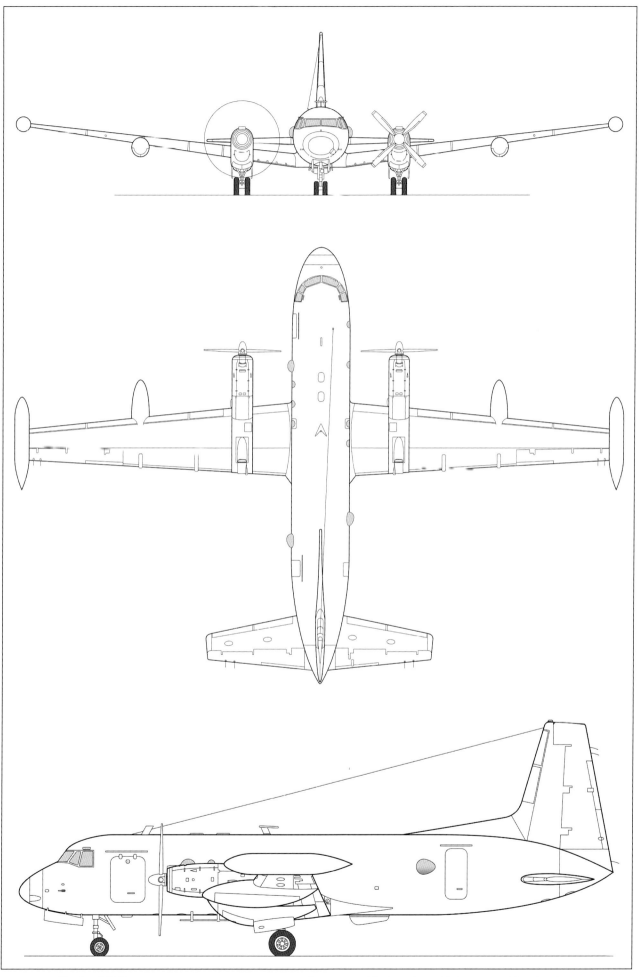

The Avro 748MR was a maritime reconnaissance project with wing tip and leading edge podded sensors and Dart 8 engines.

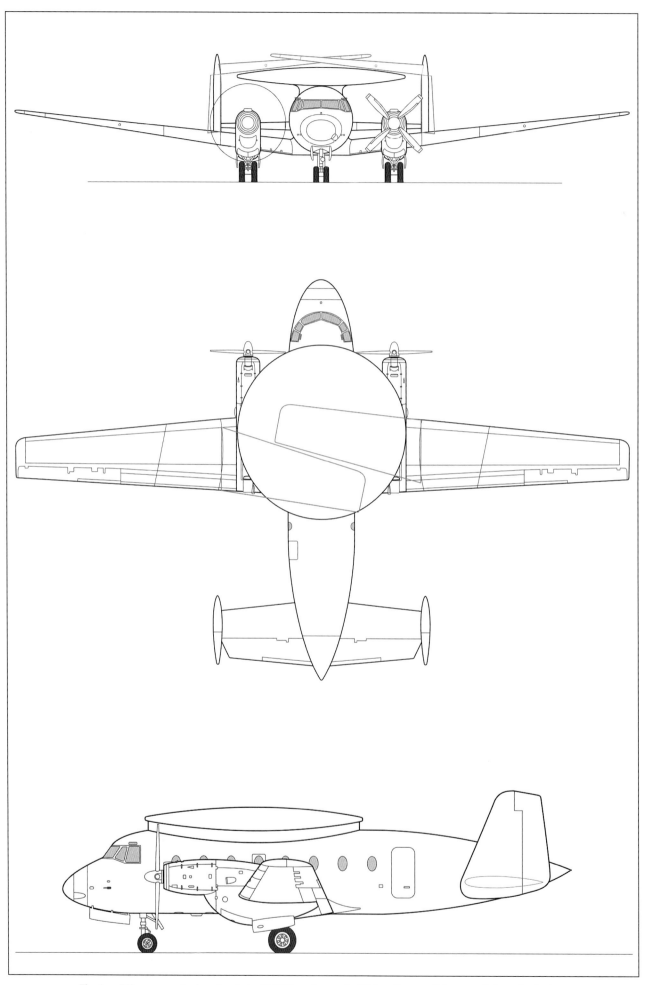

The Avro 768 was a carrier-based project with folding wings and a 24-foot diameter disk mounted above the fuselage.

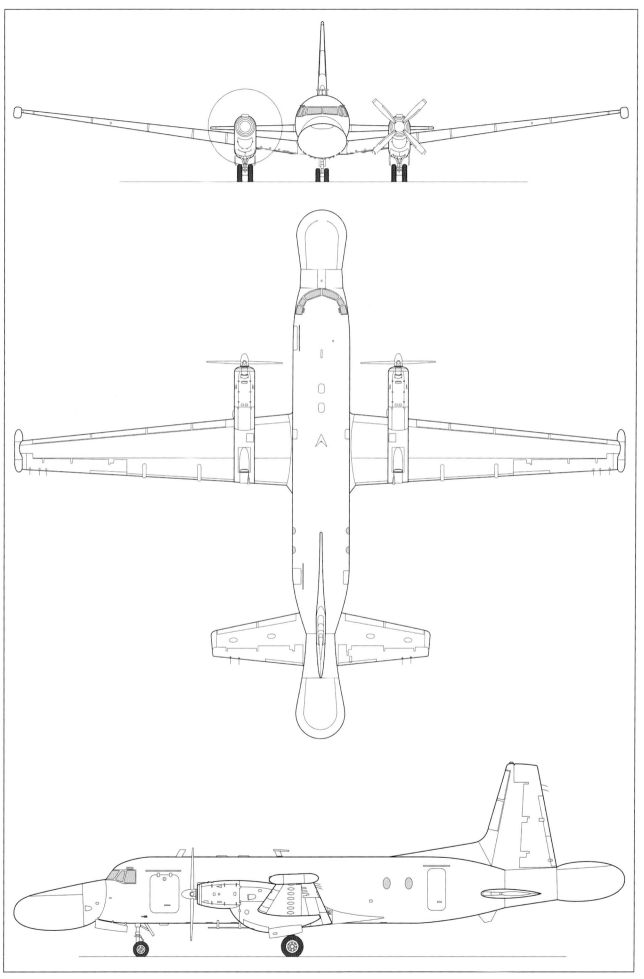

The 748 AEW version was based on the Series 2A with nose and tail radomes similar to the later Nimrod AEW.3.

The 748R was originally a proposal for the Indian Air Force, and was later allocated the type number 758, featuring a high wing and a rear ramp. The undercarriage was housed ATR42/72-style in pods on the side of the fuselage and the version illustrated shows a VTOL proposal with additional RB162 lift engines.

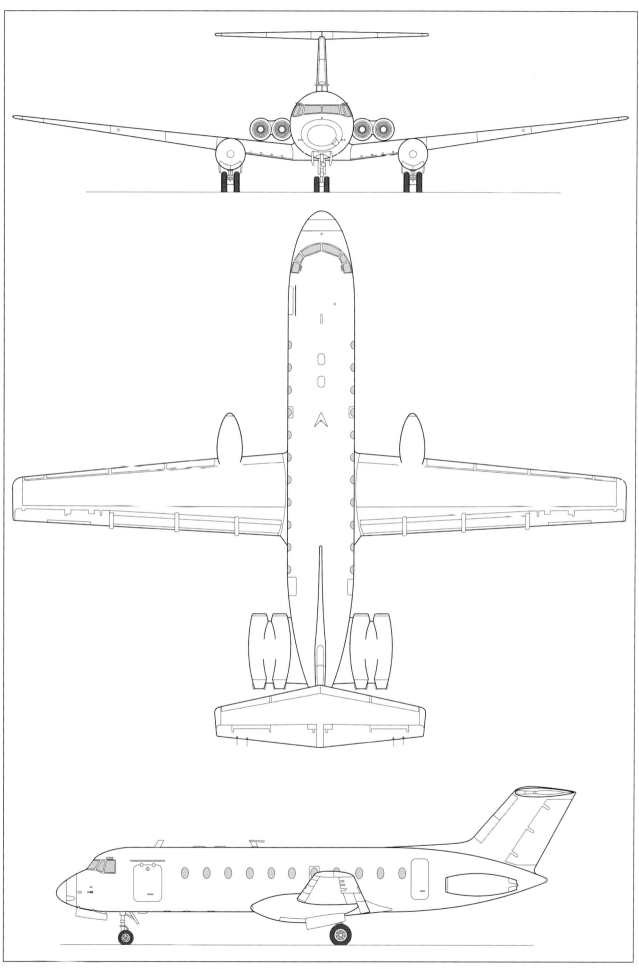

Several pure jet developments of the 748 were proposed, including one from 1961 involving four Armstrong Siddeley Viper 20s, shown rear-mounted VC-10-style in this Avro 778 version.

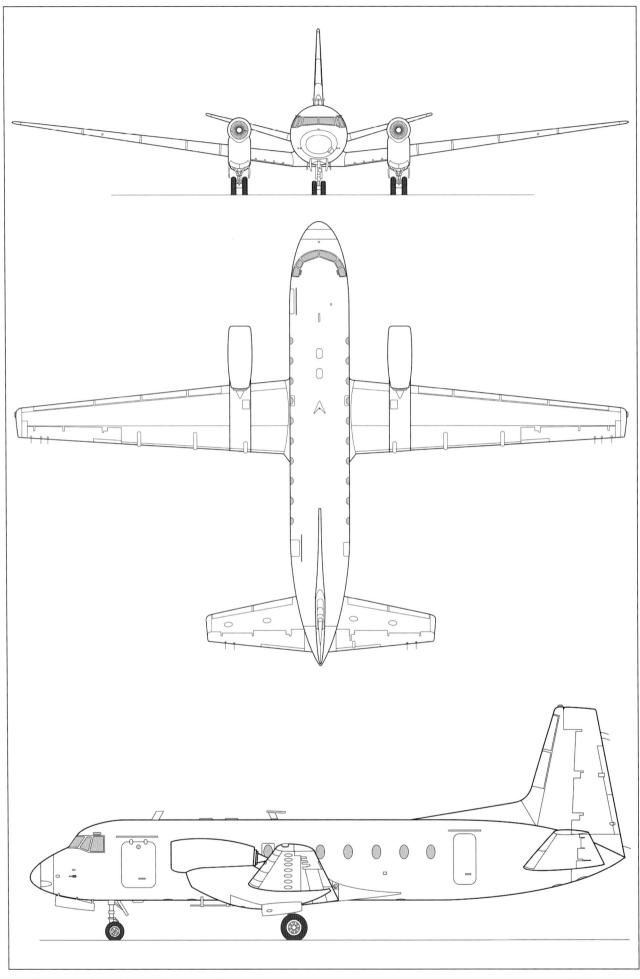

The HS 748 Series 5 featured two Rolls-Royce M45H jet engines mounted above the wings in a configuration reminiscent of the German VFW614 airliner.

Chapter 2
Technical Description

The following technical description refers to the British Aerospace 748 Series 2B aircraft except where otherwise stated. The BAe design philosophy, even at the beginning of the project in the days of A.V. Roe, was to produce a simple, rugged and easily maintained aircraft with good handling characteristics using existing 'state of the art' technology. From the outset the aircraft structure was designed and constructed to fail-safe principles with the notable exception of the engine sub-frame and landing gear which are 'safe-life' items. Design for the 748 extended the normal fail-safe concept by using alternative load paths to maintain structural integrity should a failure occur, by offering safety after failure. The aircraft is capable of operating until a regular inspection period, when any structural damage can be assessed and repaired. Fail-safe capability includes:

a) Use of alloys with slow crack propagating characteristics in all structural members, with wide use of crack-stoppers to contain the effects of a failure. All components are also protected by multiple anti-corrosion barrier treatment.

b) Secondary structural elements are incorporated where necessary to take up the load in the event of a primary element failure.

c) The entire airframe is designed for low working stress levels and there are no completely closed sections in the primary structure.

During the design stage and through subsequent development all sections of the airframe became readily accessible for structural examination and general maintenance is made easy by offering large numbers of maintenance hatches, removable panels and inspection holes of adequate size. Construction techniques requiring sophisticated back-up equipment for inspection and repair have been avoided so that repairs can be carried out 'in the field'.

WING

The low wings are of cantilever construction comprising an all-metal two spar fail-safe structure with no cut-outs in the spars for landing gear or engines. Wing section is NACA 23018 at root, NACA 4412 at tip with 7° dihedral, incidence of 3° and sweepback of 2° 54' at quarter-chord. Attached to the wings are all-metal set-back hinge, shielded horn-balance, manually operated ailerons and electrically actuated Fowler flaps. The port aileron tab is a geared tab and the starboard aileron is a geared trim tab. Along the leading edges are pneumatic de-icing boots.

FUSELAGE

The fuselage is an all-metal semi-monocoque riveted fail-safe structure and is of circular cross-section. Design of the fuselage offers an unobstructed cabin with constant headroom and level

Cockpit detail from FAE742 c/n 1733 of the Fuerza Aérea Ecuatoriana, showing partial EFIS modification at Tachina General Rivadeneira on 28th November 2008. The aircraft's former Força Aérea Brasileira serial C-91 2510 is still visible. *(Stefano Rota)*

floor. The passenger door is located at the rear of the cabin to port and opens outwards and forwards. Hydraulic airstairs, which slide away aft of the door when not in use, are built into the door. A baggage-loading door is installed on the starboard side opposite the passenger door and also opens outwards and forwards. In the forward fuselage on the port side a crew entrance/freight door is installed which opens outwards and upwards. The forward freight door is sufficiently large to accept a Dart engine complete with trestle.

A large rear cargo door could be installed as a customer option. This is located in the port rear fuselage and incorporates a passenger entrance door which opens outwards and rearwards. The forward section opens outwards and forwards parallel to the fuselage. Total door size is 8ft 9ins wide (2.67m) x 5ft 8in (1.72m) high. Cabin floor strengthening increased floor loading to 200lbs/ft² (976kg/m²) overall. An air transportable hoist was also available as a customer option with a lifting capability of 5,600lbs (2,540kgs). The door sill height is 6ft (1.83m) and permits direct loading. A roller-track system could be fitted for freighting or for military versions and the large rear door can be opened in flight for paradropping.

In the standard passenger aircraft ten oval cabin windows size 1ft 7in x 1ft 1in (48.26cm x 33.02cm) are installed on either side of the fuselage but when a large cargo door is installed only nine windows are fitted on the port side.

TAIL UNIT

The tail unit is a cantilever all-metal structure. A fixed incidence tailplane is fitted with manually-operated controls with geared trim tabs in the elevators and a trim tab plus a spring-tab in the rudder. The rudder trim tab has three sizes for Series 1, Series 2, 2A and 2B or Series 2 with Dart RDa.8 engines, which is the longest. Pneumatic de-icing boots are fitted to the leading edges of the tailplane and fin. Fin and tailplane and all ancillaries are detachable for ease of maintenance.

LANDING GEAR

The landing gear is of the retractable tricycle type with hydraulically operated nosewheel steering. All units are held in the extended and retracted positions by both hydraulic pressure and mechanical locks. All wheels retract forward hydraulically with mainwheels retracting into bulbous housings beneath the engine nacelles forward of the front wing spar and the nosewheel into the lower forward fuselage after automatic self-centreing. All units are twin-wheeled and fitted with Dowty-Rotol oleo-pneumatic shock absorbers and Dunlop tyres. Hydraulic brakes are fitted on the mainwheels with an automatic Maxaret anti-skid system. Nosewheel steering through 45° either side is controlled from the Captain's position. Runway loading at maximum take-off weight is LCN 9-18.

Tyre Pressures	Mainwheels	Nosewheels	
Series 1	59lb/in²	40lb/in²	
	4.15kg/cm²	2.80kg/cm²	
Series 2	64lb/in²	43lb/in²	
	4.50kg/cm²	3.02kg/cm²	
Series 2A	73lb/in²	55lb/in²	1
	5.13kg/cm²	3.87kg/cm²	
	65lb/in²		2
	4.57kg/cm²		
Series 2B	85lb/in²	55lb/in²	1
	5.98kg/cm²	3.87kg/cm²	
Andover C.Mk.1	63lb/in²	55lb/in²	
	4.40kg/cm²	3.87kg/cm²	
1. Standard pressures			
2. Optional low pressures for soft surfaces			

DOORS AND EMERGENCY EXITS

Five emergency exits are provided, three of which are Type 1 via the rear passenger door, rear baggage door and by the forward freight door (assuming the propeller has stopped). Two Type IV emergency window exits are provided, one on each side of the fuselage, over the wing section size 1ft 7in x 2ft 2in (48.26cm x 66.04cm). Escape chutes and ropes are fitted at the main cabin Type 1 exits. Sliding windows with escape ropes on the flight deck provide additional facilities for the pilots.

FLYING CONTROLS

The flying controls are of the direct mechanical linkage type and are designed with "fail-safe" characteristics. Teleflex tension regulators are fitted to all circuits of the flying controls and although many cables and rods are identical, it is impossible to cross-connect them due to a stagger at the connecting points.

On the flight deck dual control columns and dual rudder bars with toe brakes are standard. Trim-tabs are fitted to the rudder, geared trim-tabs on both elevators and on the right hand aileron and are controlled by hand wheels on the centre console. The trimmers can provide adequate control in the event of a failure in the primary control linkage. Control locks are fitted to the rudder, elevators and ailerons and when locked sufficient engine power is only available for taxying and not for take-off. A stall warning system is fitted operating a control column stick shaker.

Large Fowler type flaps are fitted under the trailing edges of the wing. The increased chord available with this type of flap ensures safer and more efficient control during take-off and landing. There are five selected flap settings: 0°, 7°, 15°, 22° and 27°. The positions used for take-off are 7°, 15° and 22° while 22° and 27° are used for landing. A full-span hinged tab deflects a further 27° when 27° of flap is selected. Each flap is supported on four "I" section tracks. The flaps are operated through duplicated torque tubes powered by an electric motor. The drive from the flap gearbox is transmitted through the primary shaft, which is connected directly to the gearbox. Interconnection between the primary and secondary shafts is by sprocket and chain loops. For emergency use a hand winding gear is fitted. On Large Freight Door and Special Fit aircraft a second electric motor was fitted due to difficulty in accessing the emergency handle when the aircraft was loaded. Operation of the flaps is not affected by failure of any single cable or torque shaft.

The 748 Series 2B is fitted with a Sperry SPZ-500 autopilot providing automatic stabilisation in pitch, roll and yaw axes, a split axis (pitch and roll) flight director and an attitude alerting system.

FLIGHT DECK LAYOUT

Dual flying controls and blind flying instrumentation are fitted as standard on the Series 2B flight-deck which is both spacious and ergonomically designed for a normal crew of two pilots. Crew seats are adjustable forwards, backwards and vertically and the seat rake can also be varied. The crew seat armrests hinge upwards for easy access. A folding third seat is provided for training purposes or for an occasional extra crew member. Large stowage is provided adjacent to the two main crew seats for flight documents and manuals.

The 748 flight-deck provides ample space for all equipment and instrumentation to be laid out in logical and functional groups. Controls and switches are positioned to make them readily available to both pilots and the electrical panels are situated to allow the pilots to replace fuses or reset circuit breakers.

An excellent field of view is available to the pilots through large windscreens. Both main and direct vision windscreens are electrically heated for de-misting and anti-icing and a two-speed

Dunlop wiper system is fitted to both main windscreens. White floodlights in the roof provide flight deck lighting and red lights are utilised for night flying. The instruments are illuminated by pillar lights arranged in pairs on different wiring circuits, in order that any single failure leaves the instruments well-lit.

The flight deck has been designed around the crew and is sufficiently large to enable easy access for maintenance. Throughout the long production run the flight deck was updated continually to enable the use of modern equipment and technology to maximum benefit.

ACCOMMODATION

Normal airline accommodation is provided for two pilots and two cabin staff with provision for extra crew seating when required. Passenger seating is available from 44 to 62 (maximum high density at 28in (71cm) pitch) in paired seats either side of a central gangway, the number depending on customer requirements.

The cabin interior was refined and updated continually. The final Series 2B offered a "wide-body look" interior with diffused lighting, overhead baggage lockers, amenity panels and tasteful colour shading. Passenger seating is comfortable with reclining seats, armrests and foldaway tray tables. A typical seating configuration is 48 seats at 30in (76cm) pitch offering 303ft ($8.6m^3$) of baggage space. An additional 76ft ($2.2m^3$) is available in the overhead bins and under seat stowage is available for hand luggage.

A galley is provided for cold meals and hot/cold drinks whilst an oven could be installed for hot food as a customer option. Toilet facilities include a removable toilet with the option of an externally serviced unit. Hot and cold water is supplied to the washbasin.

The cabin was designed specifically to permit quick changes in seat pitch and baggage capacity to suit customers' operational requirements. A mixed passenger/freight layout is possible and the cabin can be converted speedily to all-freight configuration. Moveable bulkheads, clip-on fibreglass side panels and foldaway seats were designed to make "quick-change" capability simple, offering great flexibility for customers with operational multi-rôle tasks. In pure freighter configuration up to 6,000kgs of cargo can be carried. It is possible for a team of six men to convert the cabin from all-passenger to all-freight configuration in under fifteen minutes.

POWERPLANT

The two Rolls-Royce Dart turbo-propeller engines installed in the 748 come in two basic versions, the Dart RDa.6 or the Dart RDa.7 depending on the mark of the aircraft. Early production aircraft, designated as Series 1s, were fitted with Dart RDa.6 engines. Later the Dart RDa.7 engine offering increased power was introduced and became standard for all Series 2 production aircraft with the exception of a few specialised aircraft that used Dart RDa.8 engines for high altitude performance. The basic difference between the two variants is that the Dart RDa.6 is a two-stage turbine while the Dart RDa.7 is a three-stage turbine. A Dart RDa.6 cannot be modified to RDa.7 standard and vice versa. Each basic version of the Dart engine was developed and improved continually through various power ratings with mark numbers allocated to distinguish each variant. The Dart RDa.6 Mk 514 (with a maximum take-off rating of 1,740 eshp) was used for production Series 1 aircraft and the RDa.7 Mks 531/532/534/535 and 536 were used for production Series 2, 2A and 2B aircraft. The maximum take-off rating of the RDa.7 engines was increased progressively from 1,910 to 2,280 eshp during the production run of Series 2, 2A and 2B 748 aircraft. The late production HAL Series 2Ms and those aircraft converted to this standard were fitted with Mk.536-2T engines of 2280 eshp.

Always a comforting sight and sound, the Rolls-Royce Dart in action on G-EDIN c/n 1757 between Frankfurt and Edinburgh on 7th May 1987.
(Fred Barnes)

The few aircraft using Dart RDa.8 engines used Mk 550 variants with a maximum take-off rating of 2,250 eshp.

A further development, the Dart RDa.7 Mk 552 was due to be introduced in late production aircraft after 1985. By offering a higher dry power rating than previous variants, the new Mk 552 engine would have virtually eliminated the need for the use of water-methanol to restore performance in hot and high conditions, improving engine life and saving costs. Fuel consumption was expected to be up to 12% better than previous variants. The Mk 551 would also have been offered to customers making the same fuel savings but with a lower dry power rating for those not requiring the extra performance. A standby water-methanol system was due to be fitted as standard in both variants for use in the event of an engine failure. The later-developed hush kit was also due to be a standard fit. Although flight-tested in c/n 1790 registered G-11-6 in May and June 1985, no new 748s were fitted with these updated engines.

The final BAe 748 Series 2B aircraft were fitted with Rolls-Royce Dart RDa.7 Mk 536-2 engines developing 2,280 eshp at take-off power. Aircraft built for the USA market had Dart RDa.7 Mk 535-2 engines installed.

Each engine drives a Dowty-Rotol 12ft (3.66m) diameter four bladed, constant speed, fully feathering propeller through a gearbox. The gearbox produces a reduction ratio of 0.086:1 for the RDa.6 engine and 0.093:1 for the RDa.7 engine. Engine speeds are 14,500 rpm for the RDa.6 engine and 15,000 rpm for the RDa.7 engine. The propellers have ground-fine pitch stop to produce drag during the landing roll but are not reversible. In the event of an engine failure, pitch coarsening and feathering are automatic.

Through an accessory gearbox, each Dart engine drives a 9kW, 28 volt DC generator, a 22kVA three-phase alternator, a hydraulic pump and a supercharger for cabin pressurisation. The left hand gearbox incorporates propeller braking.

Each engine nacelle has a Graviner fire detection and extinguisher system fitted. The extinguisher system comprises a pressurised BCF bottle in each nacelle, which is dischargeable through spray rings, and the bottles are crossed in order that both bottles are capable of being discharged into either nacelle. The detection system incorporates a continuous resetting facility.

Engine instrumentation includes oil pressure, oil inlet temperature, engine torque, turbine gas temperature, engine rpm and fuel datum. Automatic engine synchronisation is fitted.

The engine controls comprise a throttle control interconnected with propeller and water-methanol control units, a fuel trimmer control and a high-pressure fuel cock interconnected with the feathering selector.

AUXILIARY POWER UNIT

A Rover Gas Turbines 2S/150A APU could be fitted as an optional extra. The APU is mounted behind the starboard engine in a re-contoured housing above the jet pipes and drives the normal engine auxiliaries through the accessory gearbox. APU controls are mounted in the cockpit roof panel.

This APU consists of a gas-generator and a power turbine section. The single stage centrifugal compressor feeds an annular reverse flow combustion chamber. The gas flow from the combustion chamber is directed by a radial inward-flow compressor turbine and then, via a short duct, to a single stage axial-flow power turbine. The power turbine drives the output shaft through a 6.818 to 1 ratio reduction gear. Engine accessories include fuel and oil pumps and an electric starter motor together with a fully automatic engine control system. The unit weighs approximately 160lbs (72.5kgs), has an overall length of 3ft 1in (0.94m) and has an output of 103shp. Specific fuel consumption is 1.2lb (0.54kg)/shp/hr.

The APU option was employed mainly by military users but at least one airline customer is known to have taken it up. Those customers who purchased aircraft with the APU fitted are shown in the 'Model Numbers and Engine Marks' listing towards the end of this chapter. The four RAF Andovers that were converted later to E.Mk.3s also had the Rover 2S/150A APU fitted at the time they were converted.

SYSTEMS

FUEL

Fuel types normally used are Jet A, A-1, JP4 and JP5. Integral tanks in the outer wings have a usable capacity of 1,440Imp Gals (1,730US Gals, 6,546litres) and supply fuel to the powerplants.

Refuelling or defuelling of each tank is provided through underwing pressure connections accessible from ground level. Maximum refuelling rate is 90Imp Gals/min (108US Gals/min, 408litres/min) while the maximum defuelling rate is 60Imp Gals/min (72US Gals/min, 273litres/min). The aircraft can also be fuelled by overwing gravity refuelling enabling operation from primitive airstrips with no facilities.

Fuel is gravity fed from each tank into its own collector tank. The main cell of each tank is emptied first then the float valves are activated and the contents of the tip cells are used. Two electrically driven LP fuel pumps are mounted in each collector box and deliver fuel into a common feed line. The fuel then passes through the LP cock and filter to the engine HP fuel pumps. Each LP pump is capable of supplying full engine requirements and a cross-feed system allows fuel from both tanks to feed either engine. A fuel heater is installed for each engine.

A capacitance type fuel contents indicating system is installed and dipsticks fitted to the underside of each tank allow direct measurement on the ground.

WATER-METHANOL

A water-methanol system is provided to maintain engine power in hot and high altitude conditions to offset performance denigration thus maintaining payload/range capability. Flexible bag tanks with a capacity of 30Imp Gals (36US Gals, 136litres) complete with electric feed pump are fitted in each wing root fillet. These tanks are gravity fuelled via a wing root filler cap directly accessible from ground level.

Water-methanol is fed to an engine mounted control unit via a non-return valve, shut-off cock, filter and LP switch. The control unit automatically regulates the flow rate to the engine according to ambient pressure, engine rpm and engine torque. Water-methanol from both tanks can be fed to either engine via a cross-feed connection. When using water-methanol to boost take-off power, the take-off is termed as 'wet' while a normal take-off would be termed 'dry'.

Water-methanol had become expensive and Rolls-Royce in conjunction with British Aerospace developed a standby water-methanol system allowing take-offs from airfields of suitable length using "dry" power but at operating weights close to the "wet" power limits. In the event of an engine failure on take-off this standby system automatically increases the live engine to "wet" take-off power. On sensing an engine failure from a signal generated by the low torque switch on the failed engine, water-methanol is fed to the live engine. The flow is at a controlled rate to prevent power overswing and "wet" power builds up to full normal level after a few seconds. The use of the standby system also improves engine life as the number of "wet" take-offs required is reduced in normal operations.

HYDRAULICS

Hydraulic power is supplied by two engine driven pumps and in the event of a pump failure non-return valves ensure that pressure is maintained in the system by means of the remaining pump. The system operates landing gear, brakes, nose-wheel steering, propeller brakes and airstairs. Pressure in the system ranges from 2,000 to 2,500lb/in² (140 to 175kg/cm²).

An independent emergency reservoir provides fluid capacity to an auxiliary hand pump in the crew compartment to lower the undercarriage in an emergency. The same system can be used via the hand pump to provide power for brake/nosewheel steering, for towing and pressure for system ground testing.

Total system fluid capacity is 6.5Imp Gals (7.8US Gals, 29litres) and the main system components are located in the right-hand engine nacelle and nose-wheel bay.

The aircraft windscreen wipers are operated hydraulically by a separate self-contained system.

ELECTRICS

The primary electrical system comprises a 28Volt DC supply from two 9kW engine driven generators, one in each accessory drive gearbox. A secondary system is supplied by two 1,500VA static inverters. Variable frequency AC power supply comes from 22kVA engine driven alternators. Four 24Volt 23AH nickel-cadmium batteries are also fitted for internal engine starting and emergency use.

The 748 is equipped with a comprehensive range of contemporary electronics, depending on customer specification, including communication, navigation and weather radar as standard on all late-produced aircraft.

AIR CONDITIONING AND PRESSURISATION

Two engine-driven superchargers, one on each accessory gearbox, provide air conditioning and pressurisation either of which is capable of supplying sufficient air for all requirements. Cabin pressure is controlled automatically offering an 8,000ft (2,438m) cabin altitude at 25,000ft (7,620m) with a maximum cabin differential pressure of 5.5lb/in² (0.387kg/cm²). Air heating is provided by blower compression and choke valve. A bootstrap cold air unit and air-to-air heat exchangers provide air cooling. A standard 5in (12.7cm) connection for an external air conditioning unit is fitted.

ICE PROTECTION

Wing, tailplane and fin leading edges are fitted as standard with a pneumatic rubber boot de-icing system actuated by engine compressor air. Either engine is capable of operating the complete airframe de-icing system in the event of an engine failure. When the system is not in use, vacuum is applied to all boots holding them flat against the leading edge. The crew can select light or heavy ice removal.

Anti-icing of the propellers, spinners, engine air intakes and windshields is provided from the aircraft's electrical system.

A pressure sensing device detects any ice forming in the fuel filter and de-icing is carried out by a flow of hot air from the engine compressor.

AVIONICS

On any aircraft type the avionics fit is usually a customer option and depends upon the level of equipment required by the operator and the amount the operator is prepared to spend. A typical Series 2B 748 package would include:

1)	Twin VHF Communications	(Collins 618M-3)
2)	Twin VHF Navigation with glide slope	(Collins 51RV-4B)
3)	Twin ADF	(Collins DF206)
4)	Weather Radar	(Bendix RDR-1300 with colour)
5)	Marker Receiver	(Collins 51Z-4)
6)	DME Transceiver	(Collins 860E-5)
7)	ATC Transponder	(Collins 621A-6A)
8)	Interphone	(Ultra UA60)
9)	Passenger Address/ IFE System	(Field Tech Helicon FT-100-1)
10)	Radio Navigation System with dual C14 Gyro Compass	(Sperry RN-200)
11)	Autopilot	(Sperry SPZ-500)

A flight data recorder could be provided as a customer option (in many countries this is mandatory).

One of the main features of the final cockpit layout was the Bendix Colour Weather Radar. This unit provides three colours (green, yellow and red) to highlight different intensities of rainfall with storm centres being highlighted further by cycling on and off in the red area. The terrain mapping display is depicted in the same manner with the three colours depending upon the amount of reflected energy; ie high ground in red.

An azimuth track line can be selected by the pilot and superimposed over the weather or terrain display to depict the heading to a selected waypoint. A range scale is provided for both weather and terrain displays. Another feature of the Series 2B, again a customer option, is a checklist display facility containing

32 pages of data. The data stored can include take-off and landing checklists, standard instrument departures, standard arrival routes and en route navigation aids, all of which can be selected by the pilots as required on the same screen as used for the weather radar.

All radio equipment is fitted in one enclosed module, including a built-in cooling system, behind the first pilot's seat and is easily accessible. The DME and Transponder equipment is located beneath the aircraft floor and is reached easily through one of the belly inspection hatches. Access to the radar scanner and battery bay is by opening the hinged nose cone.

EMERGENCY EQUIPMENT

Two water/glycol fire extinguishers are located one at each end of the cabin and a carbon dioxide extinguisher is situated on the flight deck.

A manually operated emergency high-pressure oxygen system with a single bottle of 750 litres capacity is installed for use by both pilots. Smoke protection masks and goggles are available for the flight-deck crew. The first pilot's mask, incorporating a low carbon microphone, is fitted with a toggle switch to select 100% oxygen/air mixture as required. A portable oxygen set is provided for a third crew member. In the cabin, five portable oxygen sets are provided for emergency use by passengers and a first-aid box is situated at the rear.

Life jacket stowage is provided under all passenger seats and provision is made for the installation of dinghies as a customer option. In the event of ditching, all valves through which water could enter are closed by a cable operated ditching security system. Emergency lights situated at intervals along the main cabin roof illuminate the passenger cabin. These are activated by frangible crash switches that also disconnect the batteries from the centre busbar and activate the power plant BCF extinguishers. On late production Series 2As and on Series 2Bs these crash switches were of the inertia type. Emergency exits are identified by Phoenix lamps, each incorporating an inertia switch and battery. On Series 2Bs updated emergency lighting replaced the Phoenix lamps.

The emergency flap handle and an axe are located adjacent to the crew entrance door.

UPGRADING AIRCRAFT

The Series 2B and Super 748 represent the final production models of this aircraft and many of the design improvements could be retrofitted to the earlier Series 2 and 2A aircraft. Similarly, most Series 2 aircraft were updated to Series 2A standard mainly by updating the early Rolls-Royce Dart RDa.7 engines to a later marque offering improved operating weights and performance. In the Dan-Air fleet, a small number of Series 1 aircraft were upgraded by installing Rolls-Royce Dart RDa.7 engines and making some structural changes such as "beefing up" the undercarriage and other modifications. These aircraft were operated at lower weights than true Series 2 aircraft and were known as Series 1As, an internal Dan-Air type specification only. In one case, c/n 1560 G-ASPL, the aircraft was upgraded completely from Series 1 to Series 2 standard and ultimately to Series 2A standard.

LICENCE-BUILT AIRCRAFT

A total of eighty-nine aircraft were built under licence in India by Hindustan Aeronautics at Kanpur. These aircraft are technically similar to the British-built examples but to the Series 2 standard.

The initial four aircraft were completed to Series 1 standard using Rolls-Royce Dart RDa.6 Mk 514 engines. The majority were constructed to the basic standard using Rolls-Royce Dart RDa.7 Mk 531 engines with the exception of the final batch of twenty aircraft. These were built for the Indian Air Force as freighters with large rear freight doors and were fitted with Dart RDa.7 Mk 536-2T engines. Some of the aircraft were modified subsequently for specialist tasks with the Indian Air Force and Government agencies while nine earlier-produced Indian Air Force aircraft were fitted later with large rear freight doors.

ANDOVER C.Mk.1

The thirty-one Andover C.Mk.1 aircraft originally built for the Royal Air Force were of similar basic construction to the Series 2 748 aircraft with some major differences:

a) Rear fuselage upswept, incorporating an integral rear loading ramp and two rear doors measuring 5ft 6in x 3ft 0in (1.68m x 0.91m). Total fuselage length extended from the 67ft (20.42m) of the Series 2 to 78ft (23.77m). Overall height increased from 24ft 10in (7.57m) of the Series 2 to 30ft 1in (9.15m)

b) Tailplane moved upwards from the rear fuselage to the base of the fin, given dihedral and increased chord on inboard leading edges

c) Wing centre section redesigned with engines located further from the fuselage walls to facilitate the use of larger diameter propellers. Overall wingspan slightly less than the production Series 2A aircraft with 3ft (0.91m) added to the centre section but 3ft 6in (1.06m) removed from the tips of the 748 wing

d) Two Rolls-Royce Dart RDa.12 engines of 3,245 eshp driving 14ft 6in (4.42m) diameter four bladed Dowty-

Rotol propellers through a reduction gearbox with a ratio of 0.079:1

e) Larger mainwheel tyres (size 34 x 11.75-14), revised nose oleo and longer mainwheel oleo legs to accommodate increased diameter propellers

f) Kneeling undercarriage designed to lower the rear fuselage for easier loading/unloading in the field

g) Spring-tabs (inner) and trim-tabs (outer) on both ailerons

h) Increased operating weights

j) Hydraulically operated rear loading ramp capable of opening in flight for paradropping

k) Removable HS Skydel lightweight roller track and side guidance rails

l) Flight Deck for two pilots and optional navigator/radio operator position

m) Toilets forward and aft to starboard (rear toilet removable when used in the freighter rôle)

n) Accommodation for a variety of military rôles:
    1. 56/58 troops or 40 paratroops and despatchers
    2. 24 stretcher patients and attendants
    3. 3 Land Rovers
    4. 15,350lbs (6,936kgs) of freight

Some of the Royal Air Force aircraft were modified later for other duties as the need arose. In some cases new designations were created. These were E.Mk.3, E.Mk.3A and C.Mk.1 (PR) and are described in the "General History" chapter under Andover C.Mk.1.

G-ARAY c/n 1535 was fitted briefly with rear extensions to its engine nacelles in a drag reduction programme, illustrated here at Woodford on 30th January 1967.
(Tom Singfield collection)

SPECIFICATION DATA

OVERALL DIMENSIONS

	Imperial	Metric	Type
Wing span	102ft 6in	31.24m	Srs.2B
	98ft 6in	30.02m	Srs.1/2/2A
	98ft 3in	29.95m	C.Mk.1
Wing chord at root	11ft 5¼in	3.49m	All versions
Wing chord at tip	4ft 5in	1.34m	All versions
Wing aspect ratio	12.668		Srs.2B
	11.967		Srs.1/2/2A
	11.61		C.Mk.1
Wing incidence	3°		All versions
Sweepback at quarter chord	2° 54'		All versions
Overall length	67ft 0in	20.42m	Srs.1/2/2A/2B
	78ft 0in	23.77m	C.Mk.1
Maximum fuselage diameter	8ft 9in	2.67m	All versions
Overall height	24ft 10in	7.57m	Srs.1/2/2A/2B
	30ft 1in	9.15m	C.Mk.1
Tailplane span	36ft 0in	10.97m	Srs.1/2/2A/2B
	30ft 0in	9.14m	C.Mk.1
Fuselage ground clearance	4ft 0in	1.22m	Srs.1/2/2A/2B
	-	-	C.Mk.1
Wheelbase	20ft 8in	6.30m	Srs.1/2/2A/2B
Wheel track	24ft 9in	7.54m	Srs.1/2/2A/2B
	27ft 9in	8.45m	C.Mk.1
Mainwheel turning circle radius	39ft 0in	11.82m	Srs.1/2/2A/2B
	-	-	C.Mk.1
Propeller diameter	12ft 0in	3.66m	Srs.1/2/2A/2B
	14ft 6in	4.42m	C.Mk.1
Propeller ground clearance	2ft 0in	0.61m	Srs.1/2/2A/2B
	1ft 9in	0.53m	C.Mk.1
Passenger door (port rear)			
Height	5ft 2in	1.57m	Srs.1/2/2A/2B
	5ft 9in	1.75m	C.Mk.1
Width	2ft 6in	0.76m	Srs.1/2/2A/2B
	3ft 0in	0.91m	C.Mk.1
Height to sill	6ft 0½in	1.84m	Srs.1/2/2A/2B
	Variable	-	C.Mk.1
Freight/Baggage door (forward)			
Height	4ft 6in	1.37m	All versions
Width	4ft 0in	1.22m	All versions
Height to sill	6ft 0½in	1.84m	Srs.1/2/2A/2B
	Variable	-	C.Mk.1
Baggage door (rear starboard)			
Height	4ft 1in	1.24m	All versions
Width	2ft 1in	0.64m	Srs.1/2/2A/2B
	2ft 6in	0.76m	C.Mk.1
Height to sill	6ft 0½in	1.84m	Srs.1/2/2A/2B
Optional freight door (rear port)			
Height	5ft 7¾in	1.72m	Srs.2A/2B
Width	8ft 9in	2.67m	Srs.2A/2B
Height to Sill	6ft 0½in	1.84m	Srs.2A/2B
Rear Loading Ramp			
Height	6ft 3in	1.91m	C.Mk.1
Width	6ft 11in	2.11m	C.Mk.1
Height to Sill variable over the range	7ft 3in	2.21m	C.Mk.1
	3ft 6in	1.07m	

INTERNAL DIMENSIONS

	Imperial	Metric	Type
Maximum cabin length *	46ft 6in	14.17m	Srs.1/2/2A/2B
	53ft 9½in	16.40m	C.Mk.1
Constant section cabin length	34ft 7in	10.54m	Srs.1/2/2A/2B
Maximum cabin height	6ft 4in	1.92m	All versions
Maximum cabin width	8ft 1in	2.46m	All versions
Maximum floor width	6ft 7in	2.01m	All versions
Usable floor area *	296ft²	27.50m²	Srs.1/2/2A/2B
	375ft²	34.83m²	C.Mk.1
Usable cabin volume *	1,990ft³	56.35m³	Srs.1/2/2A/2B
	2,200ft³	62.30m³	C.Mk.1
Total freight holds (maximum)	337ft³	9.54m³	Srs.1/2/2A/2B
* Excludes flight deck			

EXTERNAL AREAS

	Imperial	Metric	Type
Gross wing area	828.87ft²	77.00m²	Srs.2B
	810.75ft²	75.35m²	Srs.1/2/2A
	831.40ft²	77.20m²	C.Mk.1
Ailerons (total)	42.90ft²	3.98m²	Srs.1/2/2A/2B
	42.40ft²	3.94m²	C.Mk.1
Trailing edge flaps (total)	159.80ft²	14.83m²	All versions
Fin	105.64ft²	9.81m²	Srs.1/2/2A/2B
	135.10ft²	12.65m²	C.Mk.1
Rudder including tabs	39.36ft²	3.66m²	Srs.1/2/2A/2B
	46.00ft²	4.27m²	C.Mk.1
Tailplane	188.90ft²	17.55m²	Srs.1/2/2A/2B
	192.00ft²	17.84m²	C.Mk.1
Elevators including tabs	54.10ft²	5.03m²	Srs.1/2/2A/2B
	41.10ft²	3.82m²	C.Mk.1

G-ARAY c/n 1535 visited Ifrane in the middle Atlas region of Morocco during its May 1963 demonstration tour in Africa.   *(Tom Singfield collection)*

WEIGHTS AND LOADINGS

	Imperial	Metric	Type
Basic operating weight	22,614lb	10,257kg	Srs.1
(including crew)	24,580lb	11,149kg	Srs.2
	26,806lb	12,159kg	Srs.2A
	25,453lb	11,545kg	Srs.2A(Military)
	27,176lb	12,327kg	Srs.2B
	25,697lb	11,656kg	Srs.2B(Military)
	28,650lb	12,996kg	C.Mk.1
Maximum payload	10,586lb	4,802kg	Srs.1
	12,420lb	5,634kg	Srs.2
	11,694lb	5,304kg	Srs.2A
	13,047lb	5,918kg	Srs.2A(Military)
	17,476lb	7,927kg	(1)
	11,323lb	5,136kg	Srs.2B
	12,802lb	5,807kg	Srs.2B(Military)
	17,302lb	7,848kg	(2)
	15,350lb	6,963kg	C.Mk.1
Maximum take-off weight	36,800lb*	16,690kg*	Srs.1
	43,500lb	19,750kg	Srs.2
	46,500lb	21,092kg	Srs.2A/2B
	46,500lb	21,092kg	Srs.2A/2B(Military)
	51,000lb	23,133kg	(3)
	50,000lb	22,680kg	C.Mk.1
Maximum zero fuel weight	33,200lb	15,060kg	Srs.1
	37,000lb	16,783kg	Srs.2
	38,500lb	17,463kg	Srs.2A/2B
	43,000lb	19,504kg	(4)
	44,000lb	19,958kg	C.Mk.1
Maximum landing weight	36,300lb	16,465kg	Srs.1
	41,500lb	18,824kg	Srs.2
	43,000lb	19,504kg	Srs.2A/2B
	47,500lb	21,546kg	(5)
Maximum wing loading	41.5lb/ft²	202.6kg/m²	Srs.1
	53.7lb/ft²	262.2kg/m²	Srs.2
	57.3lb/ft²	279.8kg/m²	Srs.2A
	56.1lb/ft²	273.9kg/m²	Srs.2B
	60.1lb/ft²	293.8kg/m²	C.Mk.1

(1) Series 2A optional overload military payload
(2) Series 2B optional overload military payload
(3) Series 2A/2B and HAL 748M optional overload military MTOW
(4) Series 2A/2B optional overload military MZFW
(5) Series 2A/2B optional overload military MLW

* Operating weights for early Series 1 and early Series 2 aircraft were increased progressively during early 748 development
  Series 1 aircraft had MTOW increased to 38,000lb (17,235kg)

PERFORMANCE

		Type
Cruising speed (1)	257mph (223kt, 413km/h)	Srs.1
	266mph (232kt, 430km/h)	Srs.2
	281mph (244kt, 452km/h)	Srs.2A/2B
	265mph (230kt, 426km/h)	C.Mk.1
Airspeed Limitations		
Never exceed speed V_{NE} *	260kt IAS	Srs.2B
Normal operation V_{NO} *	225kt IAS below 15,000ft/4,572m	Srs.2B
	215kt IAS above 15,000ft/4,572m	Srs.2B
Never exceed speed V_{FE}	180kt IAS (7½° or 15°flap)	Srs.2B
Flaps extended	140kt IAS (22½° flap)	Srs.2B
	120kt IAS (27½° flap)	Srs.2B
Never exceed speed landing gear extended V_{LO}/V_{LE}	160kt IAS	Srs.2B
Minimum control air speed V_{MCA}	87kt IAS (15° flap)	Srs.2B
	81kt IAS (22½° flap)	Srs.2B
Manoeuvring rough air speed V_A	155kt IAS	Srs.2B
Stalling Speed	81mph (70.3kt, 130km/h)	Srs.1/2/2A
(flaps and wheels down)	88.5mph (76.8kt, 143km/h)	C.Mk.1

(1) Speeds quoted at 38,000lb/17,235kg for Series 2A/2B

* For aircraft certificated to FAA requirements a V_{MO} (maximum operating speed) of 225kt IAS is quoted in lieu of V_{NE} and V_{NO}

	Imperial	Metric	Type
Maximum rate of climb (2)	1,150ft/min	(350m/min)	Srs.2
	1,420ft/min	(433m/min)	Srs.2A/B
	1,180ft/min	(360m/min)	C.Mk.1
Service ceiling at MTOW (3)	25,000ft	7,620m	Srs.1/2/2A/2B
	24,000ft	7,300m	C.Mk.1
Take-off run (BCAR) (4)	4,020ft	1,225m	Srs.2A
	2,480ft	756m	Srs.2A(Military)
	3,720ft	1,134m	Srs.2B
	3,100ft	945m	Srs.2B(Military)
	1,260ft	384m	C.Mk.1
Balanced field length (BCAR)	3,860ft	1,175m	Srs.1
	3,640ft	1,110m	Srs.2
	5,380ft	1,640m	Srs.2A
	4,570ft	1,393m	Srs.2B
Take-off to 50ft/15m	3,040ft	927m	Srs.2A(Military)
	3,800ft	1,158m	Srs.2B(Military)
	1,926ft	585m	C.Mk.1
Landing field length (BCAR)	3,400ft	1,036m	Srs.2A/2B
Landing from 50ft/15m	2,170ft	660m	Srs.1
	2,270ft	692m	Srs.2
	1,860ft	567m	Srs.2A(Military)
	2,050ft	625m	Srs.2B(Military)
	1,410ft	430m	C.Mk.1
Landing run	1,140ft	347m	Srs.2A(Military)
	1,270ft	387m	Srs.2B(Military)
	760ft	232m	C.Mk.1

(2) Rate of climb quoted at 38,000lb/17,235kg for Series 2A/2B and at maximum AUW for Andover C.Mk.1

(3) Service ceiling quoted at maximum AUW for Andover C.Mk.1

(4) Take-off run quoted at maximum AUW for Andover C.Mk.1

PERFORMANCE (continued)

Maximum payload range	630 st ml (548nm, 1,010km)	Srs.1 (1)
	930 st ml (809nm, 1,495km)	Srs.2 (1)
	904 st ml (785nm, 1,455km)	Srs.2B (2)
	1,066 st ml (926nm, 1,715km)	Super (2)
	282 st ml (245nm, 454km)	C.Mk.1 (3)
Maximum fuel range	1,750 st ml (1,522nm, 2,815km)	Srs.1 (1)
	1,910 st ml (1,660nm, 3,070km)	Srs.2 (1)
	1,946 st ml (1,690nm, 3,132km)	Srs 2A (2)
	1,635 st ml (1,420nm, 2,630km)	Srs.2B (2)
	1,158 st ml (1,008nm, 1,865km)	C.Mk.1 (3)

(1) Data based on figures produced in 1961/2 assuming no allowances for diversion or holding

(2) Data based on figures produced from late 1960s using different criteria. Allowances made for reserve fuel for 230 statute miles (200nm, 370km) plus 45 minutes holding

(3) Data based on figures produced from 1967 using different criteria. Allowances made for reserve fuel for 230 statute miles (200nm, 370km) plus 30 minutes holding plus 5% block fuel

OPERATIONAL NOISE LEVELS
FAR PART 36

Flight phase	Series 2A/B*	Series 2B Super	FAR part 36 Limit
Take-off	92.5 EPNdB	88.7 EPNdB	93.0 EPNdB
Approach	103.8 EPNdB	92.8 EPNdB	102.0 EPNdB
Sideline	96.3 EPNdB	93.3 EPNdB	102.0 EPNdB
* Series 2B not hush-kitted			

MAINTENANCE

The 748 was designed from the outset to be a type that would be "on line" for the operator as much as possible by keeping maintenance simple and at low cost. To achieve these objectives the design team incorporated reliable systems with logically grouped components and made access easy to all parts of the aircraft.

Many components are maintained "on condition" and the few which are "lifed", often have a long Time Between Overhaul (TBO). This further improves maintenance schedules. The Dowty Rotol undercarriage for example was lifed for 10,000 landings but has since been increased to 12,000 landings between overhaul. The propeller life is 3,000 hours. Many components are interchangeable between left and right-hand sides of the aircraft thus simplifying replacement and reducing costly spares holdings. "On condition" items are kept under constant review by the manufacturer to ensure safety standards. The low wing design enables systems to be located below floor level for easy ground level servicing.

The basic structure of the 748 is simple, robust and designed with fail-safe principles with safety-after-failure capability. Repairs, when necessary, can be undertaken without the need for specialised equipment and can often be deferred to the next scheduled inspection. All structural components were protected by multiple anti-corrosion treatments during manufacture. Access for inspection and repair is easy and there are no completely closed sections in the primary structure. In certain cases accidental structural damage has proven easy to repair even at remote sites or sufficient to "patch-up" the aircraft for ferry home to base.

With some sixty years operating experience throughout the world, the Rolls-Royce Dart engine has proven one of the most reliable powerplants ever built with an average of one in-flight shutdown for every 100,000 hours of operation. A long TBO is another feature of the Dart engine which now has a starting point of 5,400

hours for new operators. With experience some operators are now achieving a figure of 8,000 hours. In the 748 the engines are positioned for easy access with the large nacelle panels opening like petals in a few seconds to allow inspection. Theoretically, four maintenance staff can accomplish a complete engine change in three hours. Throughout its long service life the Dart engine has been updated and improved continually for fuel consumption, power, noise reduction and maintenance requirements.

MAINTENANCE PROGRAMME

The manufacturers devised a progressive maintenance schedule for the 748 aircraft in order to maximise aircraft utilisation and keep maintenance costs down. The schedule was flexible and could be adapted to suit the operational requirements and standard of equipment of individual operators.

The 748 basic maintenance schedule comprised the following checks:
1) **Pre-flight Check**.
   Before the first flight of the day, with selected items only prior to subsequent flights
2) **Check "A"**.
   At 55 elapsed hours
3) **Period Inspection**.
   At 150 flying hours with a never exceed period of 31 days

By January 1964 enough flying hours had been accumulated to allow a review leading to a revised schedule with the Period Inspections increasing to 200 flying hours or 42 days. Over the years the Period Inspections increased through 250, 500 and 700 to 750 flying hours, not exceeding 120 days. The Check "A" was increased to 7 days and a Check "B" was introduced at 300 flying hours or 65 days.

An alternative system of equalised checks was also developed for the basic schedule to spread the maintenance workload over the life of the aircraft. A number of different programmes were included to give operators the opportunity to find the most suitable one for their particular operation.

With the introduction of the Super 748, a new maintenance schedule was introduced affecting all 748 operators. That new schedule comprised:

1) **Check "A"** - Every 14 days
2) **Check "B"** - Every 250 flight hours
3) **Check "C"** - Every 500 flight hours
4) **Period Inspection** - Every 1,000 flight hours

Once again the new schedule was flexible and could be adjusted to suit the requirements of individual operators.

A further change in the programme was introduced in the early 1990s and continues to this day as follows:

1)   **Check "A"** - Every 16 days
2)   **Check "B"** - Every 375 flight hours or 120 days
3)   **Check "C"** - Every 750 flight hours or 240 days
4)   **Period Inspection** - Every 1,500 flight hours or 2 years

A small number of special schedules were developed for non-typical VIP and military operators etc, where elapsed time was the driver.

In line with CAA requirements, a structural audit was carried out resulting in the issue of the Supplementary Structural Inspection Document and later a Corrosion Prevention and Control Programme. These documents covered all the mandatory structural inspections for the life of the ageing aircraft.

CUSTOMER SUPPORT

Over the years Avro, Hawker Siddeley and British Aerospace developed a comprehensive and experienced organisation to provide operators with the necessary back-up in the customer support rôle. Customer Support Service has continued throughout the life of the aeroplane to enable operators to make the most efficient use of their 748s and more recently ATPs.

Aspects of Customer Support are as follows:

1)   Technical and Flying Training

Operators, engineers, pilots and own instruction staff attended courses at the modern Customer Training Centre at Woodford Aerodrome near Manchester. Theoretical classroom training was given to engineers with practical lessons on the Woodford production line. Pilots received classroom training covering all aspects of the aircraft together with operating techniques and flying conversion training at the Woodford base. Assistance with ferry flights and subsequent flying training was also available. Specialist flight crew training was also available for cabin crew and paradropping dispatchers.

2)   Customer Liaison

From the initial sales presentation, through the pre-delivery phase and up to actual handover a Senior Customer Liaison Engineer was available to assist the new operator and offer advice. Once

the type had been introduced satisfactorily into service, subsequent visits were made periodically to update the operator on any new modifications or developments that had been introduced. At the same time, any problems encountered by the operator would be investigated.

3)   Field Support Engineers

Two manufacturer's engineers covering airframe and electrics were provided for the initial introductory period at no cost. At Woodford the Field Support Section investigated any in-service queries or problems to determine the required corrective action. A data exchange was also maintained in a bi-monthly newsletter containing items of technical interest, operational statistics and unscheduled component removal rates.

Field Support could also provide specialist personnel in the event of a major accident to advise if a repair was practicable, the components required and the best means of undertaking the work.

4)   Technical Publications

This department covers all of the operational and maintenance manuals provided with the aircraft. Service Bulletins, amendments and updates to all manuals are sent regularly to operators.

5)   Spares Support

British Aerospace provides a 24-hour, every day of the year AOG (Aircraft on Ground) service. A computer-controlled spares store with a comprehensive stock for both routine and non-routine items is maintained. Spares are inspected to UK/CAA standards prior to despatch from the stores and shipment was from nearby Manchester International Airport. Operators could use pre-delivery planning to order and budget for spares requirements. The 748 Spare Parts Price Catalogue was available to customers and 90 days' notice was given of any price changes. The product support organisation for BAe's turbo-propeller products was moved from Woodford to Prestwick in 1993 at which time the spare parts store was moved to Weybridge in Surrey. This last site is particularly convenient for early despatch of AOG spares world-wide, being close to London's Heathrow and Gatwick Airports.

The commercial aircraft division of British Aerospace was split into two divisions in mid-1994 with the Prestwick location concentrating on turbo-propeller airliners, being renamed Jetstream Aircraft Ltd, while the Woodford site, renamed Avro International Aerospace, concentrated on the RJ Series of four-engined turbofan airliners. In June 1996 the product support

Various maintenance activities and products are illustrated in this West Air Sweden brochure selection.

AIRCRAFT DELIVERIES BY YEAR

Year	Total	Srs							HAL		
		1	2	2A	2A LFD	2B	2B LFD	C Mk.1	Srs 1	Srs 2	Srs 2M
1962	12 a	11	1								
1963	11 b	6	5								
1964	10 c	1	7						2		
1965	16		12					1	1	2	
1966	31		14					15	1	1	
1967	37		18					14		5	
1968	33		24	3				1		5	
1969	27		15	5						7	
1970	20		1	16						3	
1971	19		0	10						9	
1972	18		2	9						7	
1973	13		3	10						0	
1974	13		0	4						9	
1975	20		4	2	8					6	
1976	12		1	2	5					4	
1977	8			1	6					1	
1978	16			2	6					4	4
1979	14			7	2					1	4
1980	6			1	0	1	2			0	2
1981	11				1	8	1			0	1
1982	6					2	1			1	2
1983	10					6	1				3
1984	10					6	0				4
1985	5					4	1				
1986	0					0					
1987	0					0					
1988	1					1					
1989	1					1					
Total	**380**	**18**	**107**	**72**	**28**	**29**	**6**	**31**	**4**	**65**	**20**

a - including 2 leased to Skyways Coach Air

b - including 1 leased to Skyways Coach Air and 1 leased to BKS Air Transport

c - including 1 leased to BKS Air Transport

organisation was moved to Toulouse in France when the Aero International Regional - 'AIR' organisation was set up to jointly market and support the operation of all BAe, Avro International, Jetstream Aircraft Ltd and Avions de Transport Regional - ATR produced airliners. Although the AIR grouping was short lived, the product support organisation for BAe and later BAE Systems' airliners remained based at Toulouse while the spares and AOG stores organisation remained based at Weybridge.

RF Saywell Ltd of Woods Way, Goring by Sea, West Sussex, UK became the sole distributor for HS748 spares and AOG supply with effect from 1st September 2001. The complete BAE Systems inventory of 748 items both in the United Kingdom and the USA (amounting to a value of over £18 million sterling) was added to the already comprehensive spares holding held by RF Saywell. BAE Systems is still responsible for ATP spares provisioning as described above. Technical Support and Customer Liaison was still provided by BAE Systems from their bases at Toulouse, Washington and from September 1998 Sydney for both the 748 and ATP, although the European base had moved to Prestwick by the end of 2002. Product support for the 748 had been guaranteed until at least the year 2015 by BAE Systems.

To further disseminate technical information a "748 Operators Conference" was held periodically where operators could discuss and compare experiences and put forward ideas and suggestions for improving the aircraft. Experts were at hand at these conferences to discuss matters and advise where necessary.

MODEL NUMBERS AND ENGINE MARKS

Listed in this section are the numbers of aircraft built by model number. It also shows the original Series type, the customer and the original mark of Rolls-Royce Dart engine with which the aircraft were either built or delivered. Also listed here are details of firm contracts signed but subsequently cancelled.

A model number was allocated when a prospective customer had been identified and thereafter indicated the individual build standard relative to his requirements. In certain circumstances that customer might have specified differing requirements for individual aircraft. These could have included aircraft fitted with or without Large Freight Doors, quick-change VIP kits etc... In this case more than one model number would be allocated. Missing numbers from the enclosed list were either allocated to prospective customers who failed to purchase or were relative to customer build standards not taken up. Some unlisted numbers were allocated to batches of unordered aircraft laid down and indicated their basic build standard. Examples of these were: - 250, 251, 252, 280, 293, 300, 317, 380 and 410. Eventually these aircraft were allocated new model numbers when customers were found for them and the build standard was modified according to their individual requirements. Aircraft built for sale in the United States of America were not issued with model numbers. In all cases these aircraft were referred to as Model FAA, thus indicating that they were built to comply with Federal Aviation Authority requirements. The second listing is that of assigned model numbers, where known, which did not result in sales.

MODEL NUMBERS AND ENGINE MARKS ASSIGNED TO CUSTOMERS
AND MANUFACTURERS

Model	Srs	Customer	Engine Type	No. Built	Remarks
100	1	A.V. Roe & Co Ltd	RDa.6 Mk 514	1	First Prototype Later C.Mk.1 development prototype
101	1	Skyways Coach Air Ltd	RDa.6 Mk 514	3	
102	1	B.K.S. Air Transport Ltd	RDa.6 Mk 514	-	Order for 5 cancelled
103	1	Indian Air Force	RDa.6 Mk 514	1	
104	1	Indian Air Force	RDa.6 Mk 514	3	VIP
105	1	Aerolíneas Argentinas	RDa.6 Mk 514	12	
106	1	B.K.S. Air Transport Ltd	RDa.6 Mk 514	1	
107	1	S. Smith & Sons Ltd	RDa.6 Mk 514	1	
108	1	B.K.S. Air Transport Ltd	RDa.6 Mk 514	1	
200	1/2	A.V. Roe & Co Ltd	RDa.6 Mk 514 RDa.7 Mk 531	1 -	Second Prototype Later Srs.2 development and demo aircraft. Later to Falcks Flyvetjeneste
201	2	Aden Airways	RDa.7 Mk 531	-	Order for 3 cancelled
203	2	Indian Air Force	RDa.7 Mk 531	6	VIP
204	2	Força Aérea Brasileira	RDa.7 Mk 531	1	
205	2	Força Aérea Brasileira	RDa.7 Mk 531	5	
206	2	Royal Air Force	RDa.7 Mk 531	6	VIP
207	2	Thai Airways Co Ltd	RDa.7 Mk 531	3	
208	2	Royal Thai Air Force	RDa.7 Mk 531	2	VIP
209	2	Philippine Airlines Inc	RDa.7 Mk 531	12	
210	2A	British Aerospace plc	RDa.7 Mk 535-2	-	Ex COPA Model 227 Demo Coastguarder prototype. Later to Calm Air
212	2	Air Ceylon Ltd	RDa.7 Mk 531	1	
214	2	B.K.S. Air Transport Ltd	RDa.7 Mk 531	1	
215	2	Lineas Aereas Venezolana	RDa.7 Mk 531	6	*
216	2A	Bouraq Indonesia Airlines	RDa.7 Mk 535-2	3	
217	2	LIAT	RDa.7 Mk 531	3	
218	2	Indian Air Force	RDa.7 Mk 531	6	VIP
219	2	Indian Air Force	RDa.7 Mk 531	7	Navigation Trainer
220	2	Indian Air Force	RDa.7 Mk 531	4	Signals Trainer
221	2	Fuerza Aérea Argentina	RDa.7 Mk 531	1	VIP
222	2	Channel Airways Ltd	RDa.7 Mk 531	4	
223	2	Fuerza Aérea Venezolana	RDa.7 Mk 531	1	* VIP
224	2	Indian Airlines Corp	RDa.7 Mk 531	17	Order for 8 cancelled
	2	Indian Air Force	RDa.7 Mk 531	3	
	2	Indian Directorate General of Civil Aviation	RDa.7 Mk 531	2	
	2	Indian Border Security Force	RDa.7 Mk 531	1	
	2	Indian National Remote Sensing Agency	RDa.7 Mk 531	1	
225	2	Autair International Ltd	RDa.7 Mk 531	2	
226	2	Austrian Airlines	RDa.7 Mk 531	2	
227	2	COPA	RDa.7 Mk 531	1	
	2A	COPA	RDa.7 Mk 534-2	1	
228	2	RAAF	RDa.8 Mk 550-2	8	* Navigation Trainer
229	2	RAAF	RDa.7 Mk 531	2	* VIP
230	2	Aerotaxi del Sureste SA	RDa.7 Mk 531	2	
231	2	Zambia Air Force	RDa.7 Mk 531	1	* VIP
232	2	Bahamas Airways Ltd	RDa.7 Mk 531	4	
233	2	Fiji Airways Ltd	RDa.7 Mk 531	1	
	2A	Fiji Airways Ltd	RDa.7 Mk 535-2	2	
234	2	LAN – Chile	RDa.7 Mk 531	9	
235	2	VARIG	RDa.7 Mk 531	10	

238	2	Board of Trade	RDa.7 Mk 531	2	Calibration
239	2A	Hawker Siddeley Avn Ltd	RDa.7 Mk 534-2	1	Srs 2A Prototype Later Transgabon
240	2	Fuerza Aérea Argentina	RDa.7 Mk 531	-	Order for 8 cancelled
242	2	Mount Cook Airline Ltd	RDa.7 Mk 531	1	
	2A	Mount Cook Airline Ltd	RDa.7 Mk 534-2	2	
243	2	Thai Airways Co Ltd	RDa.7 Mk 531	6	
244	2	BFS	RDa.8 Mk 550-2	7	* Calibration
245	2A	AVIANCA	RDa.7 Mk 534-2	2	
246	2A	Fuerza Aérea Ecuatoriana	RDa.7 Mk 534-2	2	
247	2	Indian Air Force	RDa.7 Mk 531	18	Pilot Trainer
248	2A	Republic of Korea Air Force	RDa.7 Mk 534-2	2	VIP
253	2A	Royal Nepal Airlines	RDa.7 Mk 534-2	2	
254	2A	Ghana Airways Corp	RDa.7 Mk 534-2	2	
256	2A	Air Malawi	RDa.7 Mk 534-2	2	
257	2A	Midwest Aviation Ltd	RDa.7 Mk 534-2	1	
258	2A	AMOCO (Canada) Petroleum	RDa.7 Mk 534-2	1	
259	2A	SAESA	RDa.7 Mk 534-2	3	
260	2A	Fuerza Aérea Colombiana	RDa.7 Mk 534-2	4	
263	2A	Zambia Airways Corp	RDa.7 Mk 534-2	4	
264	2A	Rousseau Aviation	RDa.7 Mk 534-2	3	
265	2A	Zambia Air Force	RDa.7 Mk 534-2	1	* VIP
266	2A	Polynesian Airlines Ltd	RDa.7 Mk 534-2	2	
267	2A	Fuerza Aérea Ecuatoriana	RDa.7 Mk 534-2	1	VIP
268	2	Royal Australian Navy	RDa.8 Mk 550-2	2	*
269	2A	Hawker Siddeley Avn Ltd	RDa.7 Mk 534-2	1	Demonstrator. Later Chevron Standard Oil
270	2A	SATA	RDa.7 Mk 534-2	2	
271	2A	Hawker Siddeley Avn Ltd	RDa.7 Mk 534-2	1	LFD Prototype. Later to Royal Nepal Air Force
272	2A	South African Airways	RDa.7 Mk 534-2	3	
273	2A	Royal Brunei Malay Regiment	RDa.7 Mk 534-2	1	VIP
274	2A	Merpati Nusantara	RDa.7 Mk 534-2	2	
275	2A	Hawker Siddeley Avn Ltd	RDa.7 Mk 534-2	1	Demonstrator. Later to Dakota & South Bend Securities
276	2A	Air Gaspé Inc	RDa.7 Mk 534-2	1	
278	2A	TACV	RDa.7 Mk 534-2	2	
281	2A	Força Aérea Brasileira	RDa.7 Mk 534-2	6	LFD
282	2A	Tanzanian Government	RDa.7 Mk 534-2	1	VIP
283	2A	Lineas Aereas Venezolana	RDa.7 Mk 534-2	2	
284	2A	Fuerza Aérea Ecuatoriana	RDa.7 Mk 534-2	2	LFD
286	2A	Williamson Diamonds Ltd	RDa.7 Mk 535-2	1	LFD
287	2A	British Airways plc	RDa.7 Mk 535-2	2	
288	2A	Force Aérienne Belge	RDa.7 Mk 535-2	3	LFD
301	2A	Hawker Siddeley Avn Ltd	RDa.7 Mk 535-2	1	LFD Demonstrator. Later to Sri Lanka Air Force
309	2A	Guyana Airways Corp	RDa.7 Mk 535-2	2	LFD
310	2A	Cameroon Air Force	RDa.7 Mk 535-2	2	LFD
314	2A	Tanzania Air Force	RDa.7 Mk 535-2	3	LFD
320	2A	Upper Volta Air Force	RDa.7 Mk 535-2	1	LFD
329	2A	Air Liberia	RDa.7 Mk 535-2	1	LFD
333	2A	Linhas Aéreas da Guiné-Bissau	RDa.7 Mk 535-2	1	
334	2A	Trinidad & Tobago A/S	RDa.7 Mk 535-2	2	
335	2A	Trinidad & Tobago A/S	RDa.7 Mk 535-2	2	LFD
343	2A	LIAT (1974) Ltd	RDa.7 Mk 535-2	1	LFD
344	2A	Bahamasair Ltd	RDa.7 Mk 535-2	3	
347	2A	Trinidad & Tobago A/S	RDa.7 Mk 535-2	2	
348	2A	Bahamasair Ltd	RDa.7 Mk 535-2	1	LFD

351	2A	Transkei Airways Corp	RDa.7 Mk 536-2	1	
352	2A	Royal Nepal Airlines	RDa.7 Mk 534-2	1	LFD
353	2A	Air Sénégal	RDa.7 Mk 534-2	1	
357	2B	British Aerospace plc	RDa.7 Mk 536-2	1	LFD – Series 2B prototype and demonstrator. Later to British Airways
360	2B	Air Madagascar	RDa.7 Mk 536-2	2	LFD
362	2B	Air Madagascar	RDa.7 Mk 536-2	1	VIP
369	2B	Upper Volta Air Force	RDa.7 Mk 535-2	1	LFD
371	2B	Fuerza Aérea Colombiana	RDa.7 Mk 536-2	1	LFD
372	2A	SATA	RDa.7 Mk 535-2	1	
376	2B	British Aerospace plc	RDa.7 Mk 535-2	1	Trials A/C for Sperry SPZ-500 autopilot. Later to Cascade Airways as a Srs.2B/FAA
378	2B	DLT	RDa.7 Mk 536-2	6	
398	2B	Air Niger Ste Nle	RDa.7 Mk 536-2	1	
399	2B	Air Niger Ste Nle	RDa.7 Mk 536-2	1	LFD
400	2B	Airline of the Marshall Islands	RDa.7 Mk 536-2	1	
401	2B	Bouraq Indonesia Airlines	RDa.7 Mk 536-2	1	LFD
402	2B	Bouraq Indonesia Airlines	RDa.7 Mk 536-2	5	
424	2B	LIAT (1974) Ltd	RDa.7 Mk 536-2	4	Super
426	2B	British Airways plc	RDa.7 Mk 536-2	2	
435	2B	Cameroon Airlines	RDa.7 Mk 536-2	2	Super
501	2B	Makung Airlines Co Ltd	RDa.7 Mk 536-2	2	Super
FAA	2A	Air Illinois Inc	RDa.7 Mk 535-2	1	
FAA	2B	Air Illinois Inc	RDa.7 Mk 535-2	1	
FAA	2B	Air Virginia Inc	RDa.7 Mk 535-2	2	
FAA	2B	Cascade Airways Inc	RDa.7 Mk 535-2	2	
—-	2M	Indian Air Force	RDa.7 Mk 536-2T	19	LFD - Freighter
—-	2M	Indian Border Security Force	RDa.7 Mk 536-2T	1	LFD
C.Mk1	—	Royal Air Force	RDa.12 Mk 301	31	
* Fitted with Rover APU on delivery					
Rolls-Royce Dart Mk 534-2 engines were known earlier as Mk 532-2L Rolls-Royce Dart Mk 535-2 engines were known earlier as Mk 532-2S					
Models 103, 104, 203, 218, 219, 220, 224, 247 and Series 2M aircraft were all produced in India					

C/n 1587 was preserved at the Sri Lankan Air Force Museum at Colombo-Ratmalana from 5th November 2009, marked with its operational serial CR-831 in this January 2015 photograph.
(Tom Singfield)

OTHER ASSIGNED MODEL NUMBERS

Model	Potential Customer	Model	Potential Customer
109	Unknown	346	Trinidad & Tobago Air Services
110	Unknown	349	Unallocated civil
202	Build standard CAA Series 200	350	Unallocated civil - LFD
211	Standard aircraft	354	Unknown
213	Standard aircraft	355	Production Batch 17
236	Fuerza Aérea Chile	356	Set 261 SEP 2E Autopilot
237	Unallocated	358	Unallocated Srs.2B – Sets 262/8
241	Fuerza Aérea Argentina	359	Unallocated Srs.2B – Set 269
245	Colombia	361	Air Madagascar – Civil no LFD
249	Thai Government – VIP	363	Unallocated Batch 17 – Srs.2A
250	Production Batch 12	364	Unallocated Batch 17 – Srs.2B
251	Production Batch 13	365	Coastguarder
252	Production Batch 14	366	Air Mali
255	Transair Canada	367	Coastguarder - Standard
261	Romania	368	Coastguarder - Algeria
262	President of Colombia – VIP	370	Unknown military
277	Transgabon	373	Unallocated Srs.2A - LFD
279	Bundesministerium der Verteidgung	374	Unallocated Srs.2B - LFD
280	Production Batch 15	375	Unallocated Srs.2A
285	Fuerza Aérea Ecuatoriana	377	Batch 17 – Basic Military
289	BECASA	379	Coastguarder – Hellenic Navy
290	Air Niger	380	Batch 18 – basic build
291	ENN Niger - Military	381	SATA
292	Basic military	382	Wing Tours (Pty) Ltd
293	Unallocated Batch 15	383	Unknown
294	Basic Coastguarder	384	Unallocated - Sets 269/270
295	ENN Niger – VIP	385	AVIANCA
296	Unknown	386	Maersk Air
297	Unknown	387	Tunisavia
298	Unknown	388	Gulf Air - LFD
299	Unknown	389	Improved Model 364
300	Production Batch 16	390	Egyptian A/F
302	Yemen Airways	391	Egyptian A/F
303	Egyptian A/F (Nav Trainer)	392	Egyptian A/F
304	Egyptian A/F (Pax)	393	Egyptian A/F
305	Egyptian A/F (Military)	394	Set 253 - Libya
306	Egyptian A/F (General Purpose)	395	Set 255 - Libya
307	Spanish Coastguarder	396	Batch 17 – Civil LFD
308	Spanish Coastguarder	397	SATENA – Set 260
311	Cameroon A/F (Civil version)	403	SATENA
312	Basic military from Batch 16	404	SATENA
313	Not used	405	Bouraq Indonesia Airlines
315	Bouraq Indonesia Airlines	406	Wing Tours (Pty) Ltd
316	Unallocated Batch 16	407	Batch 18 - Coastguarder
317	Production Batch 17	408	Unknown
318	Mauritania A/F - Civil	409	Unknown
319	Mauritania A/F - Military	410	Batch 19 – Basic build
321	Libyan A/F	411	Eastern Provincial
322	Tanzania A/F – Coastguarder	412	Unknown
323	Unallocated Batch 17	413	Unused
324	Basic Military – Batch 17	414	East West Airlines
325	Basic Coastguarder – Batch 17	415	Set 273
326	Standard Coastguarder – Batch 16	416	Palau – Small door
327	Armada del Ecuador	417	Palau - LFD
328	Basic Coastguarder - Batch 16	418	Intercor/Carbocol of Colombia
330	Burundi – Civil LFD	419	Egyptair
331	Burundi – Military LFD	420	New Batch 18 - Coastguarder
332	Philippine A/F	421	Congo A/F
336	French - Coastguarder	422	Fuerza Aérea Colombiana
337	French Navy - Trainer	423	SATENA
338	Libyan A/F	425	Coastguarder
339	Trinidad & Tobago Air Services	430	Coastguarder - ASW
340	Merpati Nusantara - Standard	433	British Airways leased aircraft
341	Merpati Nusantara – LFD	434	Coastguarder - ASW
342	Royal Thai Army - LFD	500	Fuerza Aérea Venezolana
345	Basic civil - LFD		

Seen on this page are three examples showing the world-wide distribution of 748 operators. Above: Air Lanka 4R-SER c/n 1799, seen at Colombo-Ratmalana on 14th October 2004, soon after entering service. (Roger Thiedema)

Seen above at Woodford on 26th July 1966, prior to its delivery as 0111, c/n 1591 was destined for operation as a VIP transport by the Ministerio de la Defensa of the Venezuelan Government. (Tom Singfield)

Above: After 26 years' use by the Force Aerienne Belge, TY-21A c/n 1741 has been operated by the Force Aerienne du Populaire Benin since 2002, and was in excellent condition when seen at Cotonou on 3rd October 2013. (Keith Parkinson)

Possibly the final occasion on which Rolls-Royce Dart engines were heard in the UK, as former ETPS Hawker Siddeley Andover C.Mk.1 TL-AEW starts to run up her engines in the maintenance area at Hurn Airport on 16th April 2013 in preparation for her ferry flight to Africa. (Keith Gaskell)

Ferry Flight

What could well be the last flight of an aircraft from the Avro 748/Andover line of aircraft within the United Kingdom and also Europe took place on 16th April 2013 when the former Empire Test Pilots School (ETPS) Hawker Siddeley Andover C.Mk.1 **XS606** (Set 13) departed from Bournemouth Airport (Hurn) on the first stage of its ferry flight to Algiers en-route to Kenya carrying the marks TL-AEW in its familiar red, white and blue colour scheme of the ETPS. It was a really nostalgic time for those who had gathered to witness this departure and to hear those wonderful, distinctive sounds of the Rolls-Royce Dart engines powering the aircraft on its way. This was almost certainly also the last flight from the UK by an aircraft powered by this most famous of all turboprops.

The aircraft had earlier been ferried from Boscombe Down to Hurn on 19th December 2012 in full ETPS colours with a QinetiQ crew. Within two days all the identity markings had been removed, and the aircraft awaited the attention of an engineer from Kenya to prepare the Andover for its forthcoming ferry flight to the Dark Continent.

First flown from the old Avro airfield at Woodford on 5th October 1966, after a short spell with the Andover OCU at Abingdon from 2nd November to 22nd December 1966, the Andover was assigned to 52 Squadron, Royal Air force, based initially at Seletar and later at Changi in the Far East. XS606 remained with the unit until it was disbanded on 31st December 1969. Having returned to the UK, after a period of inactivity, it was loaned to the Ministry of Defence (Procurement Executive) on 3rd August 1972 for use by the Royal Aircraft Establishment. Between 9th May and 13th September 1973 it was based at RAE Thurleigh with the Bedford Aero Flight for use on STOL and steep approach trials before carrying out parachute drop trials at RAE Farnborough. On 24th September 1975 it was transferred to the Empire Test Pilots School as a flying classroom for STOL, autopilot and asymmetric flight exercises. The aircraft continued to fly for the ETPS, which came under the control of QinetiQ from 2nd July 2001, until it carried out its last sortie for them from Boscombe Down on 31st August 2012, by which time it had flown 10,289 hours completed during 11,525 cycles.

On 7th March 2013 New Zealander Allan Fantham arrived at Hurn to prepare the aircraft for the ferry flight to its new owners,

Westwind Aviation Ltd, part of the Wilken group of companies. Allan is an engineer who has been working on Hawker Siddeley 748s and, more recently, Andovers since September 1973 when Mount Cook Airlines took delivery of their third 748, ZK-MCA. He stayed with Mount Cook until they retired their last 748 in 1996, and since then he has worked on 748s for Horizon Airlines in Australia, Emerald Airways at Blackpool, Executive Aerospace in South Africa and 748 Air Services in Kenya, while he has also worked on the aircraft of the Royal Thai Air Force and Aero Lanka. A man of enormous experience, he has also been involved with the ferry flights of 748s from Madagascar to Australia, and from Australia to Sri Lanka and South Africa.

While the Andover was at Hurn, Allan and local engineer Mark Jones fitted the aircraft with two 1,000 litre ferry tanks in the cabin, together with all the associated plumbing. They also fitted four large water methanol tanks in the cabin. This is used to improve take-off performance at hot and high airfields. Most of the cabin seats were removed from the seat rails and stowed in the cabin. The flight had been delayed awaiting arrival of a spare Rolls-Royce Dart R.Da.12 engine to be roaded from Boscombe Down. This, too, was loaded into the cabin, together with a spares pack containing wheels and oils. Allan also removed the nose boom which had been used by the ETPS for free air measurement of pitot, sideslip, etc, for test pilot instrumentation. A further complication arose when a revolution took place in Bangui in the Central African Republic, necessitating a revised flight routing avoiding a stop in this country.

Andover TL-AEW engages water methanol as she speeds along the runway at Hurn on 16th April 2013, leaving her homeland for adventures anew in East Africa. (Keith Gaskell)

*Left: Everything but the kitchen sink! Interior shot of Andover TL-AEW showing the extra cabin fuel tanks, spare Dart engine, spares and other paraphernalia, all well stowed for the ferry flight.
(Keith Gaskell)*

On board the ferry flight to Africa were two pilots supported by Allan Fantham and the head of Westwind Aviation, Ruben Isaac. The two pilots were Jeremy Robinson (who had, interestingly, ferried the Conroy CL-44-0 'Guppy' into Hurn many years ago) and Guy Terken. Both pilots had flown Andovers in the past and have experience flying many types of aircraft.

The first sector to Algiers took 4 hours 30 minutes, and employed the use of just one of the ferry tanks in the cabin. The spirited acceleration along the runway at Hurn could be attributed to the crew using water methanol in order to check out the system before it would be used in earnest later in the ferry flight. The aircraft was refuelled in Algiers, before the crew retired to a local hotel for a night stop.

The second sector of the ferry flight took place on 17th April, taking the aircraft across the Sahara to Tamanrasset, also in Algeria, with the flight being made in 4 hours 36 minutes. Here the aircraft was refuelled using both cabin mounted ferry tanks, before departing to N'Djamena in Chad, where the Andover touched down late in the evening after a flight of 4 hours 57 minutes. Having been directed to an area on the airfield for refuelling, after a long wait nothing had happened so, eventually, the crew retired to their hotel.

The original plan was to set off early the following morning for Juba in southern Sudan and onwards to Nairobi-Wilson, but due to their late arrival and lack of rest, it was decided to depart mid-morning for Juba and night stop there. However, on arrival at

N'Djamena Airport at nine o'clock in the morning local time, the crew were denied access to the Andover due to the imminent arrival of the President of Ghana for an African Leaders' Conference in a Boeing 777. The airfield remained closed for yet another VIP arrival, so by the time the Andover crew were given permission to depart, they had insufficient time to make Juba before that airfield closed for the night.

All the crew could do was refuel the aircraft and return to their hotel for a relaxing afternoon and night in temperatures of 43°C! An early morning departure ensued on 19th April for the longest sector of the trip, from N'Djamena to Juba – taking 6 hours 13 minutes. Here the aircraft was refuelled for the relatively short 2 hour 59 minute-long sector to Nairobi-Wilson Airport, where it arrived safely in the early evening ahead of a rainstorm.

Over the course of the next few days, the Central African Republic CAA inspected the aircraft and gave it full certification and approvals. After removing various military equipment and fittings in order to reduce the aircraft weight, the Andover set out for Juba on 7th June to begin revenue earning flying throughout East and Central Africa, where its capabilities and the kneeling undercarriage would be much appreciated at rough strips in the area. – RICHARD CHURCH

The author thanks Allan Fantham for ferry flight and other details.

———————————

This article is reproduced with kind permission of Tony Merton-Jones from Propliner, *No. 134, Spring 2013.*

*Hawker Siddeley Andover C.Mk.1 XS606 painted as TL-AEW and awaiting delivery to Westwind Aviation in the sunshine at Hurn on 7th April 2013.
(Mark Empson)*

Chapter 3
748 Operators

This section lists all companies known to have operated or owned 748 aircraft in alphabetical order with two-letter flight code where known, ICAO three letter code where known, base and country. Included is a brief history of each operator's use of the type where known. For each operator a fleet list is shown by registration with constructor's number. Bracketed registrations were anticipated but not in fact used by the operator. Dealers and finance companies are generally not included. In a few cases commercial operators of Andover C.Mk.1s are included where the carrier has also operated 748s. For several African commercial operators of Andover C.Mk.1s so little detail is available that, for most, it was not considered worthy of inclusion. Following this section is a separate section detailing military users of Andover C.Mk.1s and CC.Mk.2s under the heading 'Andover Operators'.

Aberdeen Airways Ltd (SM/AAW)
Aberdeen, Scotland

This company leased one Srs.1A/105 from British Independent Airways Ltd in early Dec89 and a Srs.2A/266 from Euroair Transport Ltd in late Nov89. A Srs.2A/232 and a Srs.2A/245 leased from Dan-Air Services Ltd replaced these two aircraft in Feb and Mar90, the first of these being purchased outright in Mar90. A Srs.1A/101 was then obtained from the same source in Sep90 but was returned to the previous owner in late Dec90

following a decline in the company's business. The type was introduced into scheduled service on the company's Aberdeen to East Midlands via Edinburgh route on 04Dec89. The aircraft were used additionally to operate a twice-weekly charter from Aberdeen to Lerwick on behalf of British Petroleum and for ad hoc charter work within the United Kingdom and Europe. Schedules were flown on behalf of British Airways plc between Aberdeen and Wick from summer 1991 until Feb92. The scheduled licence was suspended on 01Aug92 and the company was put into the hands of receivers on 18Aug92.

G-ARMW 1537	G-BEKG 1557	G-BMFT 1714
G-AZSU 1612	G-BFLL 1658	

Aden Airways Ltd (AD)
Khormaksar, Aden

Aden Airways ordered three Srs.2/201s on 26Apr60, the contract being signed by BOAC Associated Companies Ltd who wholly owned Aden Airways Ltd at the time. A fuselage mock-up of the aircraft was displayed at the Farnborough Air Show 1960 in full company colours. The order was cancelled in Jun62 before delivery had been made.

(VR-AAU) 1550	(VR-AAV) 1551	(VR-AAW) 1552

Dan-Air's Series 2A G-BEBA c/n 1613 shown in the later Dan-Air livery with additional black cheatline and full fin colour-scheme.

Aerolíneas Argentinas' Series 1 LV-PUM c/n 1544 in ferry marks. This aircraft would later become LV-HHE on arrival in Argentina.

Aerial Recon Surveys Ltd ( )

Whitecourt, Alberta, Canada

This organisation purchased a Srs.2A/258 in Jun97. The aircraft was leased to West Wind Aviation Inc for two weeks in Aug97. A thrice-weekly scheduled service was operated from Calgary to Whitecourt, Grand Prairie and Rainbow Lake from Dec97 to Apr98 after which the aircraft was withdrawn.

C-FAMO 1669

Aero Lanka Airlines (Pvt) Ltd (QL/RNL)

Colombo, Sri Lanka

Aero Lanka obtained a Srs.2B/426 on long term lease from International Air Parts Pty Ltd in mid Sep04 in a 48-seat passenger configuration for operations on domestic services and to nearby Indian destinations. The company, which formerly flew as Serendib Express, inaugurated 748 services on 05Oct04 initially linking Colombo-Ratmalana with Jaffna-Palaly four days per week and via Trincomalee to Jaffna two days per week. By Sep07 this company was only operating twice daily schedules between Ratmalana and Jaffna direct seven days per week, and by summer 2010 had ceased operations.

4R-SER   1799

Aerolíneas Argentinas (AR/ARG)

Buenos Aires, Argentina

This company ordered twelve Srs.1/105s in two batches of nine and three with delivery from Jan to Aug62 and Aug to Nov63

respectively. The world's first 748 revenue service was flown when LV-HGW departed Buenos Aires Aeroparque for Bahía Blanca on 02Apr62, the aircraft being appropriately named "Ciudad de Bahía Blanca". An extensive domestic network was built up rapidly, while internationally the 748s replaced Short Sandringham flying boats from 03May62 on the Asunción via Rosario and Corrientes, Posadas via Mercedes and the Montevideo routes and also operated to Punta del Este and Colonia in Uruguay all from Buenos Aires.

Domestic points served included Bahía Blanca, Catamarca, Comodoro Rivadavia, Concordia, Córdoba, Curuzú Cuatiá, Esquel, Formosa, General Pico, Gobernador Gregores, Gualeguaychú, Iguazú, Jujuy, La Cumbre, Lago Argentino, La Rioja, Mar del Plata, Mendoza, Monte Caseros, Neuquén, Orán, Paraná, Paso de los Libres, Perito Moreno, Presidencia Roque Sáenz Peña, Puerto Deseado, Resistencia, Río Cuarto, Río Gallegos, Río Grande, Río Hondo, Río Turbio, Rosario, Salta, San Carlos de Bariloche, San Juan, San Julián, San Luis, San Rafael, Santa Cruz, Santa Fe, Santa Rosa, Santiago del Estero, Sarmiento, Tartagal, Trelew, Tucumán, Ushuaia, Viedma and Villa Dolores. As airfields were paved and upgraded and as passenger loads increased, the 748s were replaced by Boeing 737 and later Fokker F-28 equipment. The disposal of surplus 748s began in Mar73 until the last aircraft was sold in Jul77.

LV-HGW	1539	LV-HHI	1547	LV-PUF	1543
LV-HHB	1540	LV-IDV	1556	LV-PUM	1544
LV-HHC	1541	LV-IEE	1557	LV-PUP	1545
LV-HHD	1542	LV-IEV	1558	LV-PVF	1547
LV-HHE	1543	LV-PIZ	1539	LV-PVH	1546
LV-HHF	1544	LV-PJA	1540	LV-PXD	1556
LV-HHG	1545	LV-PRJ	1541	LV-PXH	1557
LV-HHH	1546	LV-PUC	1542	LV-PXP	1558

Aerolíneas de Guatemala – Aviateca (GU/GUG)
Guatemala City, Guatemala

Aviateca leased one Srs.2/222 from Transair Ltd from Aug74 to 22Feb75 in full Aviateca colour scheme. No other details are known.

TG-MAL 1587

Aeromaya SA (YA)
Mérida, México

Aeromaya was formed on 01Nov66 from the merger of three Mexican operators including Aerotaxi del Sureste S.A. which company's order for two Srs.2/230s it took over. The aircraft were delivered in Nov66 and Jan67. The lease of a Srs.2/214 from BKS Air Transport Ltd was continued until receipt of the second new aircraft. The airline operated domestic services linking the following Mexican destinations:- Acapulco, Chichén Itza, Cozumel, Isla Mujeres, Manzanillo, Mérida, Mexico City, Puerto Vallarta and Tuxpan. On 10May69 the company ceased operations and entered receivership. In Sep69 many of the routes of Aeromaya and its HS 748 aircraft were absorbed into Servicios Aéreos Especiales SA – SAESA (qv).

XA-SEI 1576   XA-SEV 1598   XA-SEY 1599

Aeronaves de México, SA - Aeroméxico
See Servicios Aéreos Especiales, SA

Aeropostal
See Línea Aeropostal Venezolana – LAV

Aero Service (5R/RSR)
Brazzaville, Congo Brazzaville

By Feb98 this company was using an unidentified 748 to operate scheduled domestic services between Brazzaville, Pointe Noire and Loubomo and internationally from the first two points to Kinshasa in the Democratic Republic of Congo.

Aero Spacelines Inc
Van Nuys, California, USA

The company was employed by British Aerospace plc to complete 'green' aircraft for the United States market. It was later taken over by Tracor Aviation Inc in Sep81 (qv).

Aerotaxi del Sureste SA – ASSA ( )
Mérida, México

Aerotaxi leased one Srs.2/214 from BKS Air Transport Ltd from Jul66. Two Srs.2/230s were ordered but the company ceased operations on 30Oct66 before delivery could be made following the purchase of the airline by Aeromaya SA. The company was marketed as Aerotaxis Aerosafari.

XA-SEI 1576   (XA-SEV) 1598   (XA-SEY) 1599

Aerotaxis Aerosafari
See Aerotaxi del Sureste, SA – ASSA

Aerovías Caribe SA (FO)
Mérida, México

Aerovias Caribe purchased one Srs.2A/230 from Servicios Aéreos Especiales SA (SAESA) in Jan77. The aircraft was disposed of in Aug79 and it is not known which destinations were served with the aircraft.

XA-SEY 1599

Aerovías Nacionales de Colombia SA - AVIANCA (AV/AVA)
Bogotá, Colombia

AVIANCA ordered two Srs.2A/245s which were delivered in Sep and Oct68, while a Srs.2A/234 was leased from Línea Aérea Nacional de Chile from Sep74 to Sep75. The aircraft were used

Aerovías Caribe SA's sole aircraft, a Series 2A, XA-SEY c/n 1599, seen at an unidentified location circa 1977.   *(John Roach collection)*

AVIANCA's Series 2A, HK-1408 c/n 1657, in the early AVIANCA livery, which was used until the early 1970s, when the dark blue and purple colours were replaced by the bright red scheme.

on domestic routes including those to Barrancabermeja, Barranquila, Bogotá, Bucaramanga, Cartagena, Cúcuta, Medellin and Santa Marta until the last was sold in Mar78.

HK-1408 1657   HK-1409 1658   HK-1698X 1620

Africana Air (3F)
Banjul, The Gambia

A division of Africana Enterprises Ltd, this carrier commenced scheduled operations with HS748s on 02Sep86 from Banjul to Dakar and Ziguinchor in Sénégal. Air Sénégal aircraft were leased for these services and flew in that company's colours.

6V-AEO 1769   6V-AET 1676

African Commuter Services Ltd ( )
Lokichoggio, Kenya

This company took delivery of a Srs.2/206 in early Mar97 which was disposed of before Feb99. It later purchased another Srs.2/206 in Mar03 to operate relief flights from its home base to destinations in southern Sudan. It was written-off in Feb05 and the company ceased operations soon after this.

9L-LBG 1566   9XR-AB 1564

Air Açores
See Sociedade Açoreana de Transportes Aéreos - SATA

Air ADS Inc ( )
Manila, Philippines

This organisation obtained a Srs.2/209 freighter from LBC Express Airways In Oct95. The Certificate of Airworthiness expired in Oct97.

RP-C1023 1659

Air Afrique
(Société Aeriénne Africaine Multinationale) (RK/RKA)
Abidjan, Ivory Coast

Air Afrique leased one Srs.2A/239 from Hawker Siddeley Aviation Ltd for evaluation during Nov and Dec69. A Transgabon 748 was operating a twice-monthly Port Gentil to Lomé schedule by 1974. Air Sénégal 748s were also operated between Dakar and Banjul on Air Afrique schedules from 01May86 to 23Oct86.

G-AVRR 1635

Air Atlantique (ES/AAG)
Coventry, Warwickshire, England

Air Atlantique leased a Srs.1A/105 from Euroair Transport Ltd to commence scheduled services between Southampton and Jersey. Initially flown three times daily with effect from 20May88, service continued until 31Oct88 after which the aircraft was used for ad hoc charter work. The aircraft was finally returned to the lessor on 24Mar89.

G-BEKG 1557

Air Bissau
See Transportes Aéreos da Guiné-Bissau – TAGB

Air Botswana (Pty) Ltd (BP/BOT)
Gaborone, Botswana

Air Botswana used three aircraft at different times wet-leased from Air Services Botswana (Pty) Ltd. The first two aircraft, both Srs.2A/232s, were in turn leased from Inexco Oil and Dan-Air Services Ltd and were used from the beginning of Apr to the end of Sep74 and from early Oct74 to the end of Dec75 respectively. From this time a Srs.2A/264 owned by Air Services Botswana (Pty) Ltd was used. The first aircraft entered service on 01Apr74 between Johannesburg and Gaborone and the aircraft were used both on this route and on that between Gaborone and Lusaka until

Air Botswana's leased Series 2A A2-ABA c/n 1611. This aircraft was operated on lease from Inexco Oil in 1974.

31Aug81. From this date Air Services Botswana lost the contract to operate Air Botswana schedules to Commercial Airways (Pty) Ltd. Management of the 748 operation during Air Botswana service was provided by Protea Airways (Pty) Ltd. From mid-August to late Oct88 a Srs.2A/263 was leased from Lesotho Airways Corporation for services between Johannesburg and Gaborone. Following the loss of all but one of its ATR fleet on 11Oct99, 748s of Executive Aerospace and Intensive Air operated the company's schedules until replacement ATRs were obtained in Jan00.

A2-ABA 1611   A2-ABC 1681   9J-ABK 1677
A2-ABB 1612

Air BVI Ltd (BL/BLB)
Tortola, British Virgin Islands

This company first leased a Srs.2A/225 from Dec81 to Apr82. In Nov83 the first of two Srs.1A/101s was delivered followed by the second late in Oct85. Both of these aircraft remained in service until Apr90, all three machines having been leased from Dan-Air Services Ltd. In Jan88 a Srs.2A/256 was obtained from Air

Malawi under a lease/purchase agreement. The company additionally leased five of the six Trinidad & Tobago (BWIA International) Airways Corporation fleet of 748s at various times from Nov84 to May86 for short periods. The aircraft were used on a network of scheduled services linking Beef Island in the British Virgin Islands with San Juan, St. Kitts, St. Maarten, St. Thomas, Anguilla and Antigua together with charter work. By 1988 the network had been expanded to Dominica and La Romana (Dominican Republic) and to North Sound and Virgin Gorda in the Virgin Islands. Dan-Air Services Ltd repossessed the two Srs.1A/101s in Apr90 while the third aircraft had been abandoned earlier in Canada in Aug89 bringing all HS748 operations to an end.

G-ATMI 1592   VP-LVQ 1666   9Y-TGD 1759
VP-LVN 1538   9Y-TFS 1756   9Y-TGH 1766
VP-LVO 1537   9Y-TFT 1757   9Y-TGI 1767

Air Canada (AC/ACA)
Montréal, Québec, Canada

The scheduled operations of Austin Airways Ltd and Air Ontario Inc came together on 26Apr87 under Air Canada's 'Connector' programme. This followed Air Canada taking a 75% holding in both carriers and merging the two as Air Ontario Inc. See under both operators for full details. Following the takeover of CP Air (which owned 45% of Calm Air International Ltd at the time) by Air Canada in 2000, the Calm Air International 748 schedules started operating with the AC (Air Canada) flight prefix. This ended on 07Apr02 when Calm Air shareholders bought back the 45% shareholding that had been held by Air Canada.

Air Cape (Pty) Ltd (SA,KP/ACP)
Cape Town, South Africa

Air Cape bought one Srs.2A/264 from Rousseau Aviation in Nov74. Earlier in Dec69 the company had utilised an HSA demonstrator for evaluation on the coastal schedules, substituting

Air Cape's Series 2A ZS-JAY c/n 1717, seen here in one of the many liveries it carried.

The same Air Cape aircraft, ZS-JAY c/n 1717, shown on the previous page, in another of its many liveries.

for a DC-3. The aircraft was used to fly South African Airways' multi-sector service from Cape Town to Port Elizabeth via Oudtshoorn, George and Plettenberg Bay under an eight-year contract from 01Dec74 to 30Nov82. This was later extended to 31Mar83 when the route was later taken over by Air Cape in its own right. The aircraft was used to operate both the above route and the route from Cape Town to Walvis Bay in Namibia via Alexander Bay and Lüderitz together with charter work. The company was taken over by Safair Freighters (Pty) Ltd in May88 which was renamed Safair Lines (Pty) Ltd later in the same year. The 748 was finally disposed of late in Oct88 after it had been replaced by two Convair 580s at the time of the takeover.

ZS-IGI   1635   ZS-JAY   1717

Air Cargo Express Pty Ltd ( )
Perth, Western Australia

This company commenced a Monday to Thursday scheduled cargo service over the Perth-Port Hedland-Karratha-Perth route on 30Sep02 using a Srs.2B/287 of Horizon Airlines Pty Ltd. The lease was terminated on 08Apr03.

VH-IMI   1736

Air Ceylon Ltd (AE)
Colombo, Sri Lanka

Air Ceylon ordered one Srs.2/212 with delivery in Oct64 and purchased a Srs.2/222 from Canada in May75. The first aircraft was used initially on routes from Colombo-Ratmalana to Bombay, Madras and Tiruchirapalli in India. By late 1965 Jaffna was linked to both Ratmalana and Tiruchirapalli. In 1969 further domestic destinations served by the 748 included Anuradhapura, Gal Oya, Batticaloa and Trincomalee, the last point also linked to Jaffna. In 1970 the only international destination still served by the 748, Tiruchirapalli, was connected with Colombo-Katunayake. In 1973 all 748 scheduled operations were transferred to Katunayake, and Male in the Maldive Islands was added to the network. With the addition of the second aircraft in May 1975, the 748s took over all the domestic schedules that then linked Ratmalana with Jaffna and Trincomalee while Male and Tiruchirapalli were still served from Katunayake and the latter from Jaffna. The 748 network then remained unchanged until the last aircraft was disposed of in Sep79, shortly before the airline ceased operations.

4R-ACJ   1571   4R-ACR   1587

Air Commuter Ltd
See Venture Airways Ltd

Air Comores (Société Nationale des Transport Aériens) (OR/AOR)
Moroni, Grande Comore, Comoros Islands

Air Comores leased a Srs.2A/264 from United Air Services (Pty) Ltd from Sep81 until Apr82 for use on the airline's scheduled domestic services from Moroni to Dzaoudzi, Anjouan and Mohéli.

A2-ABC   1681

Air Ceylon's attractive bright red and yellow colour-scheme is shown on Series 2 4R-ACJ c/n 1571.   (WHC)

Air Creebec Cargo Series 2A C-FPJR c/n 1725 . The aircraft was photographed at Timmins, Ontario, on 13th June 2008 fresh off its repaint.
(Marty Boisvert)

Air Condal SA – Compañia de Aéro Taxis (JID)
Palma de Mallorca, Spain

Air Condal leased a Srs.1/105 from Dan-Air Services Ltd with effect from Jul83. The aircraft was purchased outright in early Oct85 and was used to operate charter and government contract flights until the carrier ceased operations in Jan86.

EC-DTP   1544

Aircraft & Systems Training Establishment - (ASTE)
Bangalore, India

This Indian Air Force organisation is the equivalent of the United Kingdom's A & AEE organisation and has operated a HAL 748 throughout its existence.

H-1517   555

Air Creebec Inc (YN/CRQ)
Val d'Or, Québec and Timmins, Ontario, Canada

This company purchased a Srs.2A/234 from Austin Airways Ltd in Dec83. A Srs.2A/215 was leased from Nov85 to mid Aug86, this being replaced immediately by a Srs.2A/234 both from Austin Airways Ltd. This last aircraft was purchased outright in Jan88. On 06Dec88 details were completed for the purchase of Air Ontario's HS748 fleet. This comprised one Srs.2A/215, two Srs.2A/272s, one Srs.2A/221, one Srs.2A/259 and a Srs.2A/234. Early in 1989 a specialised pure freighter conversion of a Srs.2A/214 was obtained from the same source. A Srs.2A/257 was leased additionally from Calm Air from Oct89 to Mar90. The company, which was a joint venture between the Deluce family (who formerly owned Austin Airways Ltd) and the Cree Indians of the James Bay area, inaugurated service with the type on 31Jan84. Initial schedules were flown from Val d'Or to Matagami and Moosonee and on charters in a mixed passenger/cargo

configuration delivering food, fuel, building materials and essential supplies to Northern Cree settlements. Most of the runways used are 3,500 ft gravel strips. By Oct86 the following additional points had been added to the scheduled network: Rupert House, Eastmain, Wemindji, Fort George and Kuujjuarapik.

The company became 100% Cree-owned during 1988 and with the purchase of the Air Ontario 748s in Dec88 the company took over the Air Ontario routes northwards from Timmins, formerly part of the Austin Airways network. The fleet was withdrawn progressively starting in Jan91 until by Jun99 only two aircraft remained in service, one of which was converted to an unpressurised pure freighter during 1998. The other aircraft operated in either mixed passenger/cargo or 47-seat all-passenger configuration on ad hoc charter work and during summer 2001 on up to twice daily schedules linking Timmins with Attawapiskat via Moosonee, Peawanuk, Fort Albany and Kaschechewan. The passenger aircraft was withdrawn at the end of Oct01 leaving the freighter aircraft primarily supplying fuel to remote communities in the James Bay area.

However, the company took delivery of a freight-configured Srs.2A/229 in late Oct06, which entered service in Feb07, and two low-time similarly-configured Srs.2A/244s in early Dec06 and late May07 to primarily support De Beers Canada Inc diamond mining operations at the Victor Project in Northern Ontario, Canada. The first Srs.2A/244 aircraft was fitted with a Large Freight Door and entered service at the end of Jan08 when it replaced the Srs.2A/229. The third aircraft was put in storage initially but after maintenance replaced the Srs.2A/221 in mid-Jul08. When used in the bulk fuel delivery rôle, the aircraft are fitted with 8 x 250 gallon lightweight aluminium tanks. The aircraft can be converted from bulk fuel to the standard cargo rôle or vice versa in 45 minutes. The two Srs.2A/244s remain in service.

C-FLIY	1723	C-GGNZ	1690	C-GQSV	1618
C-FLJC	1596	C-GGOO	1692	C-GQTG	1619
C-FMAK	1668	C-GMAA	1576	C-GQWO	1597
C-FPJR	1725	C-GOUT	1621	C-GSXS	1674
C-GFFU	1579				

Air Écosse Ltd (SM/ECS)
Aberdeen, Scotland

Euroair Transport Ltd commenced operation of its Srs.1/105 on the Air Écosse route from Dundee to London-Heathrow via Carlisle on 18Nov85 before taking over the operation in its own name later.

G-VAJK   1557

Air Éspace ( )
Pointe Noire, Congo Brazzaville

Operated a Srs.2A/232 between at least Apr99 and Jul99.

TN-AGA   1611

Air Excellence ( )
Libreville, Gabon

This carrier leased a Srs.2B/378 from Executive Aerospace (Pty) Ltd from early Oct02 until late May03 to operate on domestic passenger services within Gabon. The aircraft also operated on behalf of Cameroon Airlines.

ZS-NWW   1786

Air Facilities GmbH

This company purchased one Srs.2/244 from Bundesanstalt für Flugsicherung (BFS) in Jul84. The aircraft was registered to PK Finance International in Iceland one month after purchase and was stored at Brussels until sold in Canada in Nov85.

D-AFSE   1711   TF-GMB   1711

Airfast Services Indonesia PT (FS/AFE)
Jakarta, Indonesia

Airfast Services bought its first aircraft, a Srs.2/209, from Philippine Airlines Inc in May80. This was followed by a Srs.2/222 in Feb81 and a Srs.2/207 in May81. A Srs.2/217 was obtained for spares use only in Mar87. Following the loss of one of these aircraft a Srs.2A/264 was leased from France until a Srs.2A/347 was purchased in Jul92. By Oct93 a Srs.2A/266 had been leased from Euroair Transport Ltd, being returned in early Nov97. The aircraft were employed mainly in support rôles for mining and oil industry work both domestically and as far afield as Australia, Cambodia, Myanmar, Singapore and Vietnam and were also used for general charter work. The company's last 748 was sold in Jan07.

F-GFYM	1717	PK-OBV	1585	VP-BFT	1714
G-BMFT	1714	PK-OBW	1567	VR-BFT	1714
(N43AZ)	1583	PK-OCH	1766	V2-LIK	1583
PK-OBQ	1638				

Air France (AF/AFR)
Paris-Orly and Charles de Gaulle, France

The Réunion Air Service (later known as Air Réunion) Srs.2A/254 was employed on joint Air France/Air Madagascar schedules from Dec86 between Réunion Island and Antananarivo and on joint Air France/Air Mauritius schedules between Réunion Island and Mauritius for some considerable time until mid 88. Rousseau Aviation 748s were also employed on jointly operated AF/RU services from Dinard, Nantes and Quimper to London in summer 1973.

F-BSRA   1678

Air Gabon
See Société Nationale Transgabon

Air Gaspé Inc (GP)
Havre de Gaspé, Québec, Canada

Air Gaspé ordered one Srs.2A/276 which was delivered in Apr71 and used on a scheduled network radiating from its home base until the aircraft was sold in May75. The airline became a subsidiary of Québecair Inc in 1973. The aircraft was also used for charter work, sometimes in a mixed passenger/freight layout, both domestically and internationally operating as far south as the Bahamas.

CF-AGI   1699

Air Illinois Inc (UX/AIL)
Carbondale, Illinois, USA

This company ordered a Srs.2A/FAA and a Srs.2B/FAA with delivery in Oct73 and Dec80 respectively. The aircraft were used on a scheduled network linking Chicago (Meigs Field and O'Hare) with Springfield, Carbondale, Decatur and St Louis until 11Oct83 when the initial aircraft was written-off, the second aircraft having been earlier returned to BAe in Oct82.

N748LL   1716   N749LL   1783

Air Inter
(Lignes Aériennes Intérieures) (IT/ITF)
Paris-Orly, France

Kel Air's two Srs.2A/263s and single Srs.2A/264 were employed on Air Inter scheduled services over several French domestic routes from late Dec88 to early 1990.

F-GFYM   1717   F-GHKA   1680   F-GHKL   1677

Air Inuit (1985) Ltd/Ltée (3H,7F/AIE)
Montréal-Dorval, Québec, Canada

Air Inuit leased a Srs.2A/234 from Austin Airways Ltd from Apr84 to May85. This was replaced by a used Srs.2A/343 fitted with a Large Freight Door bought from British Aerospace in Jan85 following service with LIAT (1974) Ltd. In Jan89 a used Srs.2A/310 fitted with a Large Freight Door was added to the fleet. Two Srs.2A/244s were added in Sep89 and 1990 while a third aircraft of the same type was leased from Jan to Apr89. The company adopted its current title in 1985 after it had been purchased by the Makivik Corporation. It had previously been known as Air Inuit Ltd. The aircraft were used on scheduled services from Québec City to Kuujjuaraapik via La Grande and to Kuujjuaq from Kuujjuaraapik via Ivujivik returning via Salluit operating in the First Air name.

More recently the type has been used on schedules in the extreme north of mainland Québec Province serving Aupaluk, Kangiqsujuaq, Kangirsuk, Kuujjuaq, Quaqtaq and Tasiujaq from Salluit and Kuujjuarapik, Sanikiluaq and Umiujaq from La Grande together with ad hoc passenger and freight charter work. One of the aircraft was leased to Western EXpress Airlines for one month late in 1998, to West Air Sweden from late Mar99 to early Jan00 and to Emerald Airways Ltd from Jul00 to late Dec00. By 2006 two of the aircraft were operated as pure freighters and two in the passenger/cargo combi rôle. The last four aircraft were advertised for sale in Summer 2009, but two were still operational in Jan11 on ad hoc services after one of the Srs.2A/244s was withdrawn in Jul10 and the Srs.2A/343 was

Air Gaspé's sole aircraft, Series 2A CF-AGI c/n 1699, is shown as originally delivered, in the early 1970s, prior to undergoing the Canadian registration change to C-FAGI.

Above: Air Illinois' second aircraft, a Series 2B, N749LL c/n 1783, was delivered over seven years after the airline's original Series 2A and saw three years' service before the airline ceased operations.

withdrawn in Sep10. With the withdrawal from service of the last Srs.2A/244 in Apr12, just the Srs.2A/310LFD remained operational at the end of 2014.

C-FDOX	1749	C-GCUK	1762	C-GLTC	1656
C-FGET	1724	C-GEGJ	1711	C-GOUT	1621

Air Katanga

See International Trans Air Business – ITAB

AirLanka Ltd (UL/ALK)

Colombo, Sri Lanka

After the company's Boeing 737-2Y5 4R-ULH was damaged in a heavy landing at Madras on 10Jan92, two HS748s were pressed into service by AirLanka Ltd to cover the shortfall on their short-haul routes. These two aircraft were a Srs.2A/344 and a Srs.2B/357 with a Large Freight Door which had only just been delivered to the Sri Lanka Air Force. They were painted with AirLanka titles while retaining their original basic British Airways or Scottish European Airways colour schemes and were flown by Helitours, the Air Force's tourist operations section, for an unknown period while the Boeing 737 was being repaired.

4R-HVA 1768   4R-HVB 1757

Air Liberia's only 748, a Series 2A, EL-AIH c/n 1755, is seen at a wintery Woodford in early 1978 prior to delivery to the airline. (George Jenks)

Air Liberia (NL/ALI)
Monrovia, Liberia

Air Liberia ordered a Srs.2A/329 fitted with a large rear freight door which was delivered in Feb78. The aircraft was used on a scheduled domestic network radiating from Monrovia, Spriggs-Payne to Cape Palmas, Sinoe and Tchien together with some charter work until it was written off in Apr83.

EL-AIH   1755

Airline of the Marshall Islands
See Air Marshall Islands Inc

Air Madagascar (Société Nationale Malgache de Transports Aériens) (MD/MDG)
Antananarivo, Madagascar

Air Madagascar ordered two Srs.2B/360s and a Srs.2B/362. The first two, fitted with large rear freight doors, were delivered in Jan and Nov80. The third aircraft was delivered in a VIP configuration for government use in Apr81 but was used on Air Madagascar schedules as and when required. Pending delivery of the first aircraft a Srs.2A/301 was leased from BAe from Dec79 to Feb80. The aircraft were used on an extensive domestic network to points including Antalaha, Antananarivo, Diego Suarez, Farafangana, Fianarantsoa, Fort Dauphin, Maintirano, Majunga, Manakara, Mananara, Mananjary, Maroantsetra, Morombe, Morondava, Nossi-bé, Sainte Marie, Sambava, Tuléar, Tamatave and Vohemar.

Aircraft were leased to SATA Air Açores from mid-Jun to mid-Sep86 and again over the same period in 1988, to Réunion Air Service/Air Réunion for two weeks in Apr83 and for five weeks in Jan/Feb88 and to Ecuato Guineana de Aviación from Aug86 to Aug87. From late 1986 until Mar88 the Réunion Air Service/Air Réunion Srs.2A/264 operated a once weekly joint Air France/Air Madagascar schedule from Antananarivo to Réunion Island. The two airline-configured aircraft were withdrawn from service in May99 and sold in Jul01 while the Srs.2B/362 had been withdrawn from use by Oct96.

F-BSRA	1678	5R-MJB	1773	5R-MTI	1780
5R-MJA	1772	5R-MJS	1746		

Air Malawi Ltd (QM/AML)
Blantyre, Malawi

Air Malawi ordered two Srs.2A/256s which were delivered in Dec69 and Jan70. The aircraft were used domestically between Lilongwe, Blantyre, Karonga, Mzuzu and Salima while internationally they served Harare/Salisbury, Beira, Lusaka and Ndola. The first aircraft was disposed of in Jan88 and the second was withdrawn in Nov91. In January 2000 a Series 2A/344 of Intensive Air was noted flying with 'Air Malawi' titles at Johannesburg.

ZS-XGY	1764	7Q-YKA	1666	7Q-YKB	1667

Air Malta plc (KM/AMC)
Luqa, Malta

Air Malta leased a Srs.2A/353 from Tunisavia during the summer of 1981. The aircraft was used to operate scheduled services from Malta to Catania, Italy and Tunis.

6V-AEO   1769

Air Manitoba Ltd (7N/NAM)
Winnipeg, Manitoba, Canada

Originally known as Ilford Riverton Airways Ltd, this company took the name Northland Air Manitoba Ltd with effect from 13Feb86. In 1991 Air Manitoba was adopted. The company took delivery of its first 748 in Jan84 after the Deluce family had taken a 50% interest in the carrier. The first aircraft, a Srs.2A/234, came from Austin Airways. An ex South African Srs.2A/264 was added in Jan86 and a Srs.2A/276 came from Québecair in late Apr88. A Srs.2A/209 and a Srs.2A/226 were bought from Springer Aerospace in Oct89 and Jan90 respectively, the former being operated by subsidiary company Nunasi-Northland Airways Ltd until its demise in Feb90. A Srs.2A/344 was bought in Sep93 and a Srs.2A/310 with a large rear freight door was obtained in Apr94. The type entered service in Feb84 on Class 3 schedules from Winnipeg to Theresa Point, Gardenhill and God's Narrows. The aircraft were used additionally to operate from both Winnipeg and Minneapolis to remote gravel strips in the Canadian sub-arctic carrying both passengers and cargo. Charterers included fishing parties, remotely situated industrial concerns and the Department of Indian Affairs, who used the airline to provide essential services to isolated native settlements and to carry schoolchildren

Air Madagascar received its first Series 2B, 5R-MJA c/n 1772, in January 1980. It is seen here prior to delivery from the UK. (WHC)

Air Malawi Series 2A 7Q-YKA c/n 1666 is seen in the airline's first livery in 1970.

Air Malawi's Series 2A 7Q-YKB c/n 1667, illustrated the airline's modernised later colour-scheme with red cheat-line outlined in black and an all red fin with the airline emblem.

south to high schools and teachers north to public schools. With fleet expansion, schedules had been added by late Apr86 to Gillam, God's River and Oxford House from Winnipeg. During 1988 Island Lake, Jenpeg, Sandy Lake and Thompson were added to the network. The company had ceased trading by November 1996.

C-FAGI	1699	C-FQPE	1761	C-GQTH	1617
C-FFFS	1663	C-FTTW	1681	C-GTAD	1750
C-FGGE	1589				

Air Maritime

See Eastern Provincial Airways (1963) Ltd

Air Marshall Islands Inc (CW/MRS)

Majuro, Marshall Islands, UN Trust Territory of the Pacific

This company ordered a Srs.2B/400 and leased a Srs.2B/357 fitted with a large rear freight door from British Aerospace from Jul82 until its own aircraft was delivered in Dec82. A Srs.2A/242 was leased from Mount Cook Airlines in late Aug and early Sep89 while their own aircraft underwent maintenance. A Srs.2A/226 was leased from Northland Air Manitoba Ltd from late Aug to late Nov91 for similar reasons. The type was used to operate inter-island passenger and freight services after entering service on 10Jul82. Points served included Bikini Atoll, Kosrae, Kwajalein, Majuro and the islands of Eniwetok and Kili. From Nov84 the aircraft was used to operate services on behalf of the Air Tungaru Corporation between Tarawa and Majuro (Marshall Islands), Funafuti (Tuvalu) and Nadi (Fiji). However, the weekly Fiji service was operated in the airline's own name from 1986 while the Air Tungaru Corporation reduced its lease of the aircraft to a weekly Tarawa to Majuro schedule until 1988 when this too was discontinued. In the same year the Fiji service was increased to twice weekly, with one service operating to Nadi and the other to Suva. The airline was known formerly as Airline of the Marshall Islands. With the arrival of a SAAB 2000 in Jun95, the 748 was leased to Royal Tongan Airlines Ltd from Wednesday to Saturday each week from 05Jul95 to 28Oct95. The aircraft was finally disposed of in Mar99.

C-FGGE	1589	MI-8203	1796	ZK-MCA	1712
MI-GJV	1768	V7-8203	1796		

Air Martinique (Compagnie Antillaise d'Affrètements Aériens) (PN/NN)

Fort de France, Martinique

This company operated a twice-weekly combined service with LIAT (1974) Ltd between Fort de France and Port of Spain, Trinidad from Feb86 for approximately two months with 748s drawn from the LIAT (1974) fleet.

Air Mauritius Ltd (MK/MAU)

Port Louis, Mauritius

Réunion Air Service operated their Srs.2A/264 on behalf of this operator from Mauritius to Réunion Island and to Rodrigues Island on Fridays by Sep84. This arrangement was terminated in Nov86.

F-BSRA   1678

Air Max-Gabon S.A. (   )

Libreville, Gabon

Air Max-Gabon employed a Srs.2B/FAA of Executive Aerospace (Pty) Ltd from 01Apr02 to Sep02 to operate on domestic schedules and charters within Gabon.

ZS-LSO   1783

Series 2A C-FTTW c/n 1681 is seen in its Air Manitoba colour scheme post-1991. Previously the airline had been known as Ilford Riverton Airways and had been renamed as Northland Air Manitoba in 1986.

Airline of the Marshall Islands leased Series 2B G-BGJV c/n 1768. It is seen here at Woodford on 17th January 1983 after its return from the Marshall Islands lease in BAe house colours. *(Ralph Harrison)*

Airline of the Marshall Islands Series 2B MI-8203 c/n 1796 was photographed awaiting delivery at Woodford on 3rd November 1982. *(Ralph Harrison)*

Air New Zealand Ltd (TE,NZ/ANZ)
Auckland, New Zealand

From Oct68 Mount Cook Airlines' 748s operated a twice-daily schedule between Christchurch and Oamaru via Timaru for a short time. While the runway at Rarotonga (Cook Islands) was being made suitable for jet operations, HS748 aircraft of Fiji Airways Ltd/Air Pacific Ltd were used to operate Air New Zealand services from Rarotonga to Nadi via Pago Pago and Aitutaki. These were used from Sep70 to Dec72 whereafter similar aircraft of Polynesian Airlines Ltd took over until Nov73. Air New Zealand Ltd also owns Mount Cook Airlines (qv), a long time HS748 operator in New Zealand.

Air Niger - Société Nationale (AW/AWN)
Niamey, Niger

Air Niger ordered a Srs.2B/398 and a Srs.2B/399, the latter fitted with a large rear freight door, with delivery in Dec81 and Jan82.

The aircraft operated scheduled services from Niamey to Agadès, Arlit, Maradi, Tahoua, Zinder and to Lomé (Togo) until early 1985. The aircraft were stored from this time until sold in Canada in Oct91.

5U-BAR 1779   5U-BAS 1778

Air North Charter & Training Ltd (4N/ANT)
Whitehorse, Yukon, Canada

Air North obtained two aircraft, a Srs.2A/233 and a Srs.2A/273 in Jul96 with a Srs.2A/276 added in Sep98, a Srs.2A/269 in Apr06 and a Srs.2A/335 with a large rear freight door in May12. This last aircraft was then converted to a pure freighter and was expected to enter service late in 2016. The type was introduced into service in early spring 1997 on schedules which are operated from the company's home base to Dawson City, Fairbanks (summer only with effect from 22Jun98), Inuvik and Old Crow with a seasonal route to Fort McPherson and ad hoc charter work

Air Niger's Series 2B G-11-20 c/n 1778 would become 5U-BAS prior to delivery in January 1982.   *(WHC)*

An unusual shot of one of Air North's 748s taxying at Whitehorse, Yukon Territory, in November 2008 with the fin missing!   *(Kyle Cameron)*

throughout Canada and to the USA. All aircraft are operated in the combi rôle with either 4, 20, 28, 32, 40 or 44 passenger seats with the forward section as cargo or baggage. By the end of 2007 all aircraft were fitted with movable bulkheads while two of the aircraft have a vent system enabling them to bulk-haul fuel oil in eight rigid 250 gallon tanks. In more recent years two aircraft have been based in Vancouver in the summer months for charter work, mainly serving fishing lodges, leaving a third aircraft to cover the scheduled passenger services out of Whitehorse, serving points such as the Minto gold and copper mine. Points served from Vancouver include Bella Bella, Denny Island and Sandspit. The Srs.2A/223 has been stored for the winters of 2011/12, 2012/13 and 2013/14 to conserve hours/cycles on this high-time aircraft. By September 2016, only two 748s were operating, C-FAGI and C-FCSE. Plans to return C-FYDU to service were cancelled, while C-GANA was intended to return to service in late 2016.

C-FAGI	1699	C-FYDU	1694	C-GANA	1758
C-FCSE	1679	C-FYDY	1661		

Air Ontario Inc (AC, GX/ONT)
London, Ontario, Canada

Austin Airways Ltd and Air Ontario Ltd were merged after Air Canada had taken a 75% holding in both carriers in Jun87. The surviving name became Air Ontario Inc and all flights were promoted with the AC (Air Canada) flight prefix from 26Apr87 under the Air Canada 'Connector' scheme. At the time of the merger eight HS748s were on strength including one on lease to Air Creebec Inc. This last aircraft was sold to that operator in

Jan88 while a Srs.2/244 was leased from the Royal Bank of Canada in early Nov87 until the end of Dec88. From the autumn of 1987 the type was introduced onto routes linking Thunder Bay with Kenora, Winnipeg and Minneapolis and was retained on some services out of Toronto until a deal was struck with Air Creebec Inc on 06Dec88 for the sale of all but one of the 748 fleet and the airline's northern assets.

Prior to the decision being made to dispose of the 748 fleet and the northern network, it had been planned to convert three of the fleet to pure freighters. In the event, only one such aircraft was converted. Work started in the spring of 1988 to convert a Srs.2A/214 and continued until it was completed in Jan89. Work involved removal of all the pressurisation systems, avionics, doors and windows and then fitting a large rear freight door and forward crew door on the port side. Unlike the Hawker Siddeley LFD, these were designed by ACS of Winnipeg and are hinged, opening outwards. The aperture is however the same size. Windows were blanked over and new King Gold Crown avionics were installed together with a pair of auxiliary heaters for the cockpit and cabin. Finally the aircraft was stripped of paint in a further effort to reduce weight. The net result was a specialised unpressurised freighter version of the HS748 which had the basic weight reduced by more than 2,500 lbs, increasing the payload by a similar figure. This aircraft was also sold to Air Creebec Inc as a pure freighter early in 1989. Other aircraft in the fleet were also used for passenger and cargo charter flights.

C-GFFU	1579	C-GLTC	1656	C-GQTG	1619
C-GGNZ	1690	C-GMAA	1576	C-GQWO	1597
C-GGOO	1692	C-GOUT	1621	C-GSXS	1674

Air Pacific Ltd (FJ/FJI)
Suva, Fiji

Known as Fiji Airways Ltd until 23Sep70 and then for a brief period as Pacific Island Airways Ltd until 31Jul71, this company ordered a Srs.2/233 and two Srs.2A/233s in three separate contracts with delivery in Sep67, Dec68 and Oct69. The aircraft were employed on an inter-island network beginning on 01Oct67 and over the years flew from Suva to Labasa and Nadi domestically and to Apia (Samoa), Funafuti (Tuvalu), Honiara (Solomon Islands), Nauru, Port Moresby (Papua New Guinea), Espiritu Santo and Port Vila (Vanuatu), Tarawa (Gilbert and

Ellice Islands) and Tongatapu (Kingdom of Tonga). From 30Sep70 to 08Dec72 the aircraft were used additionally to operate services on behalf of Air New Zealand Ltd between Nadi and Rarotonga (Cook Islands) via Pago Pago (American Samoa) and Aitutaki (Cook Islands). The aircraft were replaced eventually on international services by BAC One-Eleven 479s and the last 748 was disposed of in Nov80. In early Dec85 a Srs.2A/273 was leased from Mount Cook Airlines Ltd to increase capacity over the peak Christmas period. It was returned at the end of Jan86.

DQ-FAL	1613	VQ-FAL	1613	VQ-FBK	1665
DQ-FBH	1661	VQ-FBH	1661	ZK-MCP	1694
DQ-FBK	1665				

Air Portugal
See Ligações Aéreas Regionais, SA

Air Provence International (DG/APR)
Marseille, France

This organisation leased a Srs.2A/232 in May95 and a Srs.2A/245 in Jul95. With effect from 01Jul00 the company was renamed Société Nouvelle Air Provence International. The aircraft were used on cargo flights within France. In Jul02 it was announced that this company was being taken over by West Air Sweden AB and the HS748s were withdrawn by Mar03.

F-GODD	1658	F-GPDC	1612

AirQuarius Air Charter (Pty) Ltd (SSN)
Lanseria, Johannesburg, South Africa

AirQuarius obtained a Srs.2B/400 in late Mar99 and a Srs.2B/FAA in Oct99 for use in the charter market in Southern and Central Africa. Both aircraft were fitted initially with 44 passenger seats and were registered in the name of Hering Aviation (Pty) Ltd. The company's operating name was formerly AirQuarius Aviation (Pty) Ltd. Regular cargo charters were flown when the passenger seats were removed, these including night flights for the South African postal service.

Aircraft were operated on behalf of Trackmark Ltd of Kenya from Apr to Aug99 and GAMEC of Angola from Apr00 to Feb01. One 748 was severely damaged in Apr02 which led to its write-off and the other crashed in early Jun02. The company's engineering arm was also involved in converting two former Intensive Air 748s to pure cargo configuration on behalf of International Air Parts Pty Ltd.

ZS-OJU	1782	ZS-XGE	1770	ZS-XGZ	1740
ZS-OLE	1796				

Air Réunion
See Réunion Air Service

Air Saint-Pierre SA (PJ,CP/SPM)
Îles Saint-Pierre et Miquelon

With effect from 1976 scheduled services were flown on behalf of this carrier from Saint-Pierre to Halifax and Sydney, Nova Scotia under contract by HS748s drawn from the Eastern Provincial Airways (1963) Ltd/Air Maritime fleet, when the aircraft carried additional 'Air St Pierre' titles, until a Srs.2A/232 was purchased from that carrier in Oct86. Air Saint-Pierre then operated the schedules in its own right.

In 1987 the company joined the Canadian 'Partner' programme and operated schedules from Saint-Pierre to Halifax and to Montréal via Sydney. A Srs.2A/283 was leased additionally from Canadian Pacific Air Lines Ltd from early Apr87 for approximately six weeks and a Srs.1A/105 from Euroair Transport Ltd from early Apr to late May89. May90 saw the fleet

Fiji Airways Series VQ-FAL c/n 1613 overflying impressive cloud formations. The aircraft is pictured in the original livery.

*Above: Eastern Provincial Airways'
Series 2A C-FINE c/n 1611 on lease to
Air St Pierre in circa 1982.*
(Fred Barnes/Mike Ody)

*Left: Air Sénégal's Series 2 6V-AFX
c/n 1588 photographed at Southend
after return from lease in July 1989.*
(WHC)

Air Sénégal Series 2A 6V-AEO c/n 1769 on an air test from Woodford on 3rd July 1979, seen here in the full colour-scheme of the airline.   *(WHC)*

Air Virginia's first Series 2B, N748AV c/n 1782, in the airline's attractive livery. (J Roach collection)

doubled when a Srs.2A/344 was obtained from Bahamasair. Following the delivery of an ATR42 in Jan84, one of the aircraft was leased to First Air for the summer of that year. The fleet was withdrawn subsequently and disposed of in Oct95.

F-ODQQ 1745 F-OSPM 1611 G-BEKG 1557
F-ODTX 1764

Air Sénégal (Sonatra, Société Nationale de Transport Aériens) (DS/DSB)
Dakar, Sénégal

Air Sénégal ordered a Srs.2A/353 which was delivered in Jul79. A Srs.2A/263 was purchased from Zambia Airways Corporation Ltd in Mar80 while a Srs.2/222 was leased from late Dec88 to mid-Jul89 and a Srs.2A/264 by Mar90. The aircraft were used for charter work and on a scheduled basis to Banjul (Gambia), Guinea-Bissau, Nouakchott (Mauritania), Praia (Cape Verde Islands) and to Cap Skirring, Tambacounda and Ziguinchor domestically. The aircraft were also used for a short while from 02Sep86 to operate services between Banjul, Dakar and Ziguinchor on behalf of Africana Air and at various times on behalf of Air Afrique between Banjul and Dakar to connect with their international services.

The company's Srs.2A/353 was leased to Tunisavia for at least eighteen months from May80. One of the two owned aircraft was written off in Feb97 and it is believed the second was withdrawn from service soon afterwards.

F-BSRA 1678 6V-AET 1676 6V-AFX 1588
6V-AEO 1769

Air Services Botswana (Pty) Ltd
See Air Botswana (Pty) Ltd

Air Sinai (4D)
Cairo, Egypt

In Apr83 a Srs.2A/210 and a Srs.2B/357 were painted at Woodford with Air Sinai titles for a leasing deal which it is believed was not completed.

G-BCDZ 1662 G-BGJV 1768

Air Tungaru Corporation (RT,VK/TUN)
Tarawa, Republic of Kiribati

Airline of the Marshall Islands operated their Srs.2B/400 on behalf of Air Tungaru from Nov84 on scheduled flights between Tarawa and Majuro (Marshall Islands), Funafuti (Tuvalu) and Nadi (Fiji). However, during 1986 this lease was reduced to a once-weekly schedule from Tarawa to Majuro, until this was discontinued during 1988.

MI-8203 1796

Air Virginia Inc (CE/FVA)
Lynchburg, Virginia, U.S.A.

Air Virginia ordered two Srs.2B/FAAs with delivery in Oct81 and May82. A second-hand example of a similar type was leased from British Aerospace Inc with effect from Aug83. The aircraft linked Lynchburg, Richmond, Charlottesville and Roanoke in Virginia with Newark, Baltimore, Philadelphia and Washington-National on a scheduled basis until the type was withdrawn at the end of Jun84.

N748AV 1782 N749AV 1790 N749LL 1783

Airworks India Engineering Pvt Ltd
See Indian National Remote Sensing Agency

Airworld (Pty) Ltd (SPZ)
Pretoria-Wonderboom and Cape Town, South Africa

Airworld chartered a Srs.2A/242 from Executive Aerospace (Pty) Ltd with effect from May98 for operation in the freight rôle over the Johannesburg to George route via Bloemfontein. A second aircraft, a Srs.2B/378, was chartered from the same source to operate as a freighter on the Johannesburg to East London route with effect from late May01.

ZS-NWW 1786 ZS-OCF 1647

ALAIRE – Líneas Aéreas Alaire SL (ALR)
Madrid, Spain

This company took delivery of a Srs.2B/371 in early May06 with a Srs.2A/244 and a Srs.2B/399 following later on lease from West Air Sweden AB. Two of these aircraft were fitted with Large

Freight Doors and all three were fitted out as pure freighters. The first aircraft were initially flown and maintained by West Air Sweden while ALAIRE's 748 approvals were being obtained and only two aircraft were operated at any one time. The 748s initially operated from Palma and Ibiza to the Spanish mainland. The Srs.2A/244 was returned to West Air for onward sale in late May07 and the Srs.2B/399 in early Aug07 after operating its last service on 03Aug07. The Srs.2B/371 flew its last service between Madrid and Santiago de Compostela on 26Oct07 and the aircraft was returned to West Air.

SE-LEK   1725   SE-LIB   1776   SE-LIC   1778

Albarka Air Services Ltd (F4/NBK)
Abuja, Nigeria

This airline leased a Srs.2B/378 from Executive Aerospace (Pty) Ltd from Aug to Oct01 to operate on schedules between Abuja and Yola.

ZS-PLO   1797

Alliance Air (Y2/AFJ)
Entebbe, Uganda

From Aug98 to 31Aug99 Executive Aerospace (Pty) Ltd 748s were operated on scheduled services on behalf of Alliance Air from Kigali (Rwanda) to Bujumbura (Burundi), Mwanza (Tanzania), Nairobi and Entebbe.

AMOCO (Canada) Petroleum Co Ltd ( )
Calgary, Alberta, Canada

AMOCO ordered one Srs.2A/258 which was delivered in Aug69 and was used as a company transport carrying personnel and equipment to northern oil and gas sites. The aircraft was sold in Jun97 after nearly twenty-eight years service and a lease to Chevron Canada Resources Ltd from Jan to Mar97.

CF-AMO   1669   C-FAMO   1669

Arch Aviation Ltd ( )
Nairobi, Kenya

Arch Aviation purchased a used Srs.2/206 in May95 but it was reported to have been sold soon after delivery.

5Y-IAK   1564

Askar Melayu Diraja Brunei
See Royal Brunei Malay Regiment

ASSA
See Aerotaxi del Sureste, SA

ASTE
See Aircraft & Systems Testing Establishment

Astral Aviation Ltd (8V/ACP)
Nairobi, Kenya

By Oct06 Astral Aviation was operating a Srs.2A/245 in freighter configuration leased from Best Aviation Ltd, but it was written off very quickly at Alek in Southern Sudan. It was leased to operate humanitarian relief flights on behalf of the United Nations.

S2-ABE   1658

Atlantic Airlines de Honduras, S de RL (ZF/HHA)
La Ceiba, Honduras

This airline leased a Srs.2B/424 from mid-Aug02 but the aircraft had not entered service by Mar03. The aircraft was impounded in Grand Cayman in Apr03 but later released. A second similar aircraft had been due for delivery later but was not accepted. The company ceased operations in Oct08.

C-GBCS   1801   HR-ATC   1801

Atlantic Aviation Inc

Atlantic Aviation is the United States Company through which the first Air Illinois aircraft was delivered.

Austin Airways Ltd (UH/AAW)
Timmins, Ontario, Canada

This company obtained its first Srs.2A/214 from Air Gabon in Jun76 followed by two Srs.2A/259s from Servicios Aéreos Especiales SA (SAESA) at the end of 1976. Earlier, the airline had evaluated the same Srs.2A/214 in Sep71. The Fuerza Aérea Argentina was the source of a Srs.2/221 in Sep78 while the four remaining Srs.2A/234s were purchased from Línea Aérea Nacional de Chile (LAN) on 30Mar79. Late in 1980 the entire fleet of Línea Aeropostal Venezolana was obtained in a deal that included the two aircraft that had been passed to the Venezuelan Military. The majority of this last purchase failed to see service with Austin Airways and passed directly to other Canadian operators. These last types were a Srs.2A/283 and Srs.2/215s. The final acquisitions were the three Srs.2A/272s of South African Airways in Nov83. Two additional aircraft were leased from Aug to Nov86. These were a Srs.2A/254 and a Srs.2A/227 which came from Canadian Pacific Air Lines Ltd.

The aircraft were used on scheduled services throughout Ontario from hubs at Timmins and Pickle Lake to Big Trout Lake, Attawapiskat, Deer Lake, Forts Albany, Hope and Severn, Kaschechewan, Moosonee, Pikangikum, Sioux Lookout, Winisk and Red, Round and Sandy Lakes. A twice-daily service was operated from Thunder Bay to Minneapolis St. Paul until early 1985. From this time a twice-daily schedule was begun between Timmins and Toronto, one of these originating in Kapuskasing and competing with Air Canada DC-9s over the first sector. From late 1985 the following additional destinations were added to the network from Toronto: Attawapiskat, Elliot Lake, Fort Albany, Geraldton, Kaschechewan, Manitouwadge, Marathon and Moosonee.

The aircraft were also used extensively for charter work and, apart from operating flights for sports teams and hunting parties, they were used additionally for freighting fuel, food and other essential supplies to distant communities in the extreme north of Canada.

The company also leased aircraft to overseas operators in Denmark and Réunion Island and to several Canadian airlines. Surplus aircraft were sold in both Canada and Sri Lanka. Following Air Canada's purchase of a 75% holding of both this airline and Air Ontario Ltd in Jun87, the two carriers were merged in the name of Air Ontario Inc and the Austin Airways name was dropped. For further information see Air Ontario Inc.

C-GDOP	1745	C-GFFU	1579	C-GPAA	1675
C-GDOV	1582	C-GGNZ	1690	C-GQSV	1618
C-GDUI	1577	C-GGOB	1691	C-GQTG	1619
C-GDUL	1578	C-GGOO	1692	C-GQTH	1617
C-GDUN	1581	C-GMAA	1576	C-GQWO	1597
C-GEPB	1686	C-GOUT	1621	C-GSXS	1674
C-GEPI	1594				

Australian air Express Pty Ltd (XM/XME)

Melbourne, Victoria, Australia

This carrier wet-leased a Srs.2B/287 from Horizon Airlines Pty Ltd from 29Mar to 21Jun99. From 17Sep01 both Horizon Airlines Srs.2B/287s were contracted to fly regular freight schedules from Sydney to Adelaide and Brisbane. A third aircraft, a Srs.2B/360, was wet-leased from the same source from late Apr02. The 748s were last flown on 24Oct03 after the collapse of Horizon Airlines.

VH-IMI 1736   VH-IMK 1737   VH-IPB 1773

Austrian Airlines (Oesterreichischer Inlandflugdienst Luftverkehrs AG) (OS/AUA)

Vienna, Austria

Austrian Airlines ordered two Srs.2/226s which were delivered in Apr and May66. The aircraft were employed on domestic schedules linking Vienna with Graz, Innsbruck, Klagenfurt, Linz and Salzburg and internationally served Belgrade, Budapest, Frankfurt, Prague and Warsaw during the day and on all cargo services to London at night. The aircraft were disposed of in Nov69 and Sep70.

OE-LHS 1589   OE-LHT 1590

Austrian Airlines' first Series 2 OE-LHS c/n 1589, seen taxying at an unknown location in the late 1960s.

(WHC)

Autair International Airways Ltd (OU)

Luton, Bedfordshire, England

Autair ordered two Srs.2/225s which were delivered in Mar and Apr66. The aircraft were used initially from 31May66 on the summer Luton to Blackpool and Glasgow schedule together with charter work which included flights to Alghero, Barcelona, Basel, Bastia, Beauvais, Calvi, Copenhagen, Corfu, Dublin, Düsseldorf, Ljubljana, Milan, Palma, Perpignan, Rennes, Rimini, Rotterdam and Tarbes. During the winter 1966/7 period the type was employed on schedules from Luton to Hull (Brough) and to Carlisle via Blackpool. From the end of 1967 they were leased permanently to other operators in the Caribbean and Europe. The company became known as Court Line Aviation Ltd from Jan70 following its take-over by the Court Line Group. The aircraft were sold finally in Dec71 and Oct72 after seeing service with many operators, of which full details can be found in the 'Individual Aircraft Histories' chapter.

G-ATMI 1592   G-ATMJ 1593

AVIANCA

See Aerovías Nacionales de Colombia, SA

Aviateca

See Aerolíneas de Guatemala

Aviation Division of S Smith & Sons (England) Ltd

Staverton, Gloucester, England

This company ordered one Srs.1/107 with delivery in Oct63. It was used by the Flying Unit of this company for flight development of its Series 6 Flight Control System, gyroscopes and air data computers until the unit was closed down at the end of Oct69. The company's name had been changed earlier to Smith's Industries Ltd with effect from Feb66.

G-ASJT 1559

Avro Express, Ltd ( )

Nairobi-Wilson, Kenya

This more recent operator took delivery of a Srs.2A/266 freighter with a large rear freight door in Oct09 on lease and flown under the Planes for Africa AOC and took delivery of a Srs.2B/378 in Sep12. The first aircraft entered service on 15Nov10 and has since flown charters out of Goma (DRC), Juba (Southern Sudan) and Lokichoggio in Kenya. In Sep14 the company purchased a Srs.2B/287, a Srs.2A/242, a Srs/2A/270 and a Srs/2A/275. The Srs.2B/387 has since entered service and was based in Mogadishu, Somalia, in August 2015.

One of the other three aircraft is due to be reduced to spares, though by June 2016 no movement of these aircraft had been noted. Avro Express and Planes for Africa parted company by early 2016 and the Srs.2B/287 was transferred to Planes for Africa, Ltd.

5Y-BXT 1701   5Y-PFA 1736   5Y-??? 1689
5Y-CBI 1784   5Y-??? 1687   5Y-??? 1697

Awood Air Ltd (8D/AWO)

Sidney, British Columbia, Canada

Awood Air leased two used Srs.2B/FAAs from BAe Asset Management with delivery in Mar95. Schedules were flown between Vancouver and Masset while extensive charter work was also undertaken. The company ceased operations in Jan97.

C-GHSC 1790   C-GHSF 1782

BAC Express Airlines Ltd (RPX)

London Gatwick, England

BAC Express wet-leased a Srs.2A/245 from 02Jan to 15Feb03 to operate night postal flights based on Edinburgh.

F-GODD 1658

Bahamasair (UP/BHS)

Nassau, Bahamas

Bahamasair ordered three Srs.2A/344s and one Srs.2A/348, the latter fitted with a large rear freight door. All aircraft were delivered in 1979 while a Srs.2A/301 was leased from the manufacturer from Jan to Aug79. The aircraft were employed on a comprehensive network of services throughout the Bahamas Islands and to Miami, Fort Lauderdale and West Palm Beach in Florida and to South Caicos.

Bahamian points served from Nassau included Andros Town, Arthur's Town, Crooked Island, Deadman's Cay, Freeport, George Town, Governor's Harbour, Inagua, Mangrove Cay,

Bahamas Airways' Series 2 VP-BCL c/n 1611 sporting the airline's livery which was based on the contemporary BOAC scheme.

Marsh Harbour, Mayaguana, North Eleuthera, Rock Sound, San Andros, San Salvador, South Andros, Stella Maris and Treasure Cay. The aircraft were withdrawn from service by 1991.

C6-BEA	1746	(C6-BEC)	1763	C6-BEE	1764
(C6-BEA)	1761	C6-BED	1763	(C6-BEE)	1765
C6-BEB	1761	(C6-BED)	1764	C6-BEF	1765

Bahamas Airways Ltd (BH)
Nassau, Bahamas

Bahamas Airways ordered four Srs.2/232s with delivery from Dec66 to Apr67. The company operated the aircraft throughout the Bahamas Islands with schedules to Andros Town, Bimini, Cat Island, Crooked Island, Deadman's Cay, Freeport, George Town, Governor's Harbour, Inagua, Marsh Harbour, Mayaguana, North Eleuthera, San Andros, San Salvador, Stella Maris, Treasure Cay and West End.

Internationally, 748s were flown from Nassau to Grand Turk and to Fort Lauderdale via Bimini until the airline ceased operations on 16Oct70. One of its aircraft was disposed of prior to the company's closure in June of the same year.

VP-BCJ	1609	VP-BCL	1611	VP-BCM	1612
VP-BCK	1610				

Bali Air (Bali International Air Services PT)
(BO/BLN)
Jakarta, Indonesia

Bouraq Indonesia Airlines P.T., the parent company of Bali Air, ordered one Srs.2A/216 on behalf of this subsidiary. Initially it was operated as one of the Bouraq fleet but in later years was painted with Bali Air titles. Bali Air operated charter flights to both domestic and international destinations with both its own aircraft and others from the Bouraq fleet. By Sep00 a Srs.2B/402 was noted in Bali Air colours with a further Srs.2A/235 appearing by Apr01. Later a further Srs.2A/235 and a further Srs.2B/402 were transferred from the parent company. Bali Air ceased operations in Mar05.

PK-IHH	1629	PK-IHT	1793	PK-KHL	1735
PK-IHJ	1630	PK-IHV	1795		

Bangkok Airways Co Ltd (PG/BKP)
Bangkok, Thailand

From 13Oct86 Bangkok Airways operated a Srs.2/234 on lease from Thai Airways Co Ltd on a scheduled service from Bangkok to Nakhon Ratchasima on Fridays, Saturdays and Sundays. The aircraft carried Bangkok Airways titles when so used. This arrangement ceased in July 1987.

HS-THH 1707

Belgische Luchtmacht
See Force Aeriénne Belge

Bengal Air Services, Pvt. Ltd ( )
Calcutta, India

This company took delivery of the first of four Srs.2B/424s in late Nov98. However, due to certification problems with the Indian authorities, this aircraft never entered service and the remaining aircraft were stored in Canada.

VT-BAA	1800	(VT-BAC)	1802	(VT-DOA)	1800
VT-BAB	1801	(VT-BAD)	1803		

Benin Air Force
See Force Aeriénne du Benin

Best Aviation Ltd (5Q/BEA)
Dhaka, Bangladesh

Trading as Best Air this company, which was part of the IPSSL Group, obtained a freighter-configured Srs.2A/245 in Feb04, a Srs.2A/351 freighter in Mar05 and a Srs.2A/242 freighter in late May07. The aircraft were employed primarily ferrying shrimp fry from Cox's Bazar to Jessore. The first aircraft was leased to Astral Aviation for UN humanitarian aid based in Kenya in early Oct06 but was written-off soon after this. The Srs.2A/242 was repossessed by the lessor by Jun09 and the company ceased operations in the same year.

S2-AAT	1770	S2-ABE	1658	S2-AEE	1647

Bismillah Airlines Ltd (5Z/BML)
Dhaka, Bangladesh

A member of the Mollah Group of Industries, this carrier leased a freight-configured Srs.2A/347 from International Air Parts Pty Ltd in May07 and a freight-configured Srs.2A/242 by Jun09. Points served include Chittagong, Cox's Bazar, Dhaka and Jessore. A third Srs.2A/347 was acquired from Easy Fly Express Ltd by Apr15.

S2-AAX	1767	S2-ADW	1766	S2-AEE	1647

BKS Air Transport Ltd (BK)
London-Heathrow and Leeds/Bradford, England

BKS ordered two Srs.1/102s in Sep59 and a further three in Sep60. The orders were later cancelled when the airline was hit by financial problems. When conditions improved the airline ordered a Srs.2/214 which was delivered in Feb65, while a Srs.1/106 and a Srs.1/108 were leased from the manufacturer from Apr63 and Apr64 respectively. The type entered service with the carrier on 01Oct62 when G-ARMW, a Srs.1/101 leased from Skyways Coach Air Ltd, flew from Leeds/Bradford to Heathrow. This was the first of many leases between these two airlines. The aircraft were used on scheduled services from Leeds to London, Dublin, Belfast, Amsterdam and Düsseldorf, from Dublin to Newcastle and from London to Bilbao (with effect from 30Apr64) and San Sebastian in northern Spain. The Srs.2 aircraft was sold back to Hawker Siddeley Aviation Ltd in Jul67 while the two Srs.1 aircraft went to Skyways Coach Air Ltd in March of the same year. The type was last used by BKS in Mar68 with aircraft leased from Skyways Coach Air Ltd.

G-ARMV 1536	G-ARMX 1538	G-ASPL 1560
G-ARMW 1537	G-ARRW 1549	G-ATAM 1576

BOAC Associated Companies Ltd

This company became the owner of three Bahamas Airways Ltd Srs.2/232s when that company ceased trading on 16Oct70 pending their disposal. It had also ordered the three Srs.2/201s on behalf of Aden Airways Ltd, being the parent company at that time.

G-AZSU 1612	VP-BCL 1611	VP-BCM 1612
VP-BCK 1610		

Board of Trade, The (United Kingdom)
Stansted, Essex & Teesside, Durham, UK

Two Srs.2/238s were ordered by this organisation with delivery in Jul and Sep69 for airfield calibration duties by the Civil Aviation Flying Unit (CAFU) from its Stansted, Essex base. Nominal changes of ownership were made to the Department of Trade and

Industry in Jan71 and to the Civil Aviation Authority in Apr72. A third aircraft, a Srs.2/225, was bought from Court Line Aviation Ltd in Oct72 but was later sold to Dan-Air Services Ltd in Jul78. This last aircraft had been used for some VIP flying duties while with the CAFU and had flown Dan-Air schedules at weekends during the summer of 1975. It was also used for educational flights for local schoolchildren on occasion. The operating base was moved to Teesside Airport in 1993. In Oct96 the calibration duties and the two 748s were taken over by Flight Precision Ltd.

G-ATMJ 1593	G-AVXI 1623	G-AVXJ 1624

Bop-Air (Pty) Ltd (BV/MAW)
Mmabatho, Republic of Bophuthatswana

Previously known as Mmabatho Air Services (Pty) Ltd, Bop-Air took delivery of a used Srs.2B/FAA in Feb86. The aircraft was put into service on 28Mar86 on routes linking Mmabatho and Sun City with Johannesburg. From 1994 the company traded as Sun Air. The aircraft was sold in May96.

ZS-LSO 1783

Botswana Airways Corporation Ltd (BP)
Gaborone, Botswana

Botswana Airways leased new aircraft, firstly a Srs.2A/272 from South African Airways from early Feb to mid-May71 and then a Srs.2A/263 from Zambia Airways Corporation Ltd from Feb to Jun72 for flights from Gaborone to Johannesburg and Lusaka.

A2-ZFT 1691   A2-ZGF 1706

Bouraq Indonesia Airlines, PT (BO/BOU)
Jakarta, Indonesia

Bouraq ordered three Srs.2A/216s in three separate orders with delivery in 1973 and 1974. The company then became a major buyer of second-hand fleets, taking six Srs.2A/235s from Viação Aérea Rio-Grandense (VARIG) in Dec76 and Jan77 and five Srs.2A/234s from Línea Aérea Nacional de Chile (LAN) during 1978. Later, the company ordered six new aircraft, one

Botswana Airways' Series 2A A2-ZFT c/n 1691, photographed in 1971.

Srs.2B/401 fitted with a large rear freight door and five Srs.2B/402s all of which were delivered in 1983. The aircraft were used on a comprehensive domestic scheduled network eastwards from Jakarta throughout the Java chain of islands as far as Timor, northwards to Banjarmasin, Bandung and Tarakan in Borneo and north eastwards to North, Central and South Sulawesi and to Ternate in the North Moluccas. Other points served included Balikpapan, Bima, Denpasar, Gorontalo, Kupang, Mataram, Maumere, Menado, Palu, Semarang, Surabaya, Ujung Pandang, Waingapu and Yogyakarta. Charter flights were undertaken by a subsidiary company named Bali Air using aircraft drawn from the Bouraq fleet. Many of the aircraft were withdrawn from service and put in storage prior to the company ceasing operations in Jul05.

PK-IHA	1614	PK-IHI	1626	PK-IHP	1787
PK-IHB	1615	PK-IHJ	1630	PK-IHR	1722
PK-IHC	1616	PK-IHK	1633	PK-IHS	1615
PK-IHD	1700	(PK-IHL)	1735	PK-IHT	1793
PK-IHE	1620	PK-IHM	1634	PK-IHV	1795
PK-IHF	1622	PK-IIN	1794	PK-IHW	1788
PK-IHG	1627	PK-IHO	1774	PK-KHL	1735
PK-IHH	1629				

Bradley Air Services Ltd (7F/BAR/FAB)

Carp & later Kanata and Ottawa, Ontario, Canada

Bradley Air Services obtained a Srs.2A/216 from Bouraq Indonesia Airlines PT in Feb79, a Srs.2 /209 from Philippine Airlines Inc in Oct of the same year and a Srs.2A/233 from Air Pacific Ltd in Dec80. In Sep and Oct84 two Srs.2A/215s were obtained from Québecair Inc while a further two ex Québecair Srs.2A/215s were obtained in Sep87. In Sep87 two Srs.2A/335s were bought from Trinidad & Tobago (BWIA International) Airways Corporation, these being fitted with large rear cargo doors. The last aircraft purchased were the two ex Cascade Airways Srs.2B/FAAs which were obtained in Apr88 while a Srs.2A/272 was added in May99 to replace one of the Srs.2A/335s lost in an accident. Leased aircraft that have been used have included a Srs.2B/FAA from British Aerospace from Jul to Nov85 and a Srs.2/244 from the Royal Bank of Canada from Jul to the end of Sep87. A Srs.2A/243 with a large rear

freight door was leased from Air Inuit (1985) Ltd from Jun93 to Jan95 and a Srs.2A/344 was leased from Air Saint-Pierre for summer 1994.

The first 748 was introduced into service on 10Sep79 out of Frobisher Bay (Iqaluit) while the type replaced DC-3s between Ottawa and Montréal-Mirabel with effect from 13Mar81. An Ottawa to Boston schedule was inaugurated on 17Nov84 and was operated twice daily for six years. Ottawa was also linked with Rouyn and Val d'Or for a while at the start of 748 operations. All scheduled 748 operations from Ottawa ceased in 1990. The second base of Iqaluit on Baffin Island has been linked with Cape Dorset, Clyde River, Coral Harbour, Hall Beach, Igloolik, Nanisivik, Pangnirtung, Pond Inlet, Qikiqtarjuak (Broughton Island), Rankin Inlet and Resolute Bay, while internationally it was linked with Nuuk in Greenland. Kangerlussuak (Søndre Strømfjord) was an added destination on a once-weekly schedule from summer 1996. Another hub set up at Yellowknife was linked to Cambridge Bay, Gjoa Haven, Holman Island, Kugluktuk (Coppermine), Pelly Bay and Taloyoak (Spence Bay). The company's 748s were also flown on the former Ptarmigan Airways Ltd schedules to Fort Simpson, Hay River and Whitehorse after Bradley purchased Ptarmigan Airways late in 1995. All scheduled routes are marketed in the name of 'First Air' although in later years all operations were marketed in this name.

From late 1987 the two freight door equipped aircraft were based on Hall Beach re-supplying stations on the DEWline from the Alaskan border in the west to Greenland in the east and were joined by a third 748 at peak times. This last contract ended in late 1994 with the wind-up of the DEWline. The aircraft were also used extensively for passenger and cargo charter flights. From 2001 748s were used to carry scientists and equipment from Resolute Bay via Alert to the Russian Environmental Observatory at Borneo only 60 miles from the North Pole. A 3,100 ft strip was used at this floating ice station.

The company has been owned by the Inuit-led Makivik Corporation (which also owns Air Inuit (1985) Ltd/Ltée) since 28Sep90. With effect from Dec01, ATR42s started to displace the 748s initially from the Yellowknife hub and with effect from Nov04 the Iqaluit hub. From May07 only two 748s remained operational but the type was introduced onto the Iqaluit,

Bouraq Indonesia Airlines Series 2A PK-IHD c/n 1700 photographed prior to delivery in November 1972. Bouraq's aircraft were instantly recognisable at an airport in their bright emerald green colour-scheme.
(WHC/BAe)

British Airways Series 2A G-AZSU c/n 1612 carrying the short-lived 'British' titles at Jersey on 13th October 1984. *(Keith Gaskell)*

Nanisivik, Resolute Bay schedule in Dec05 replacing Boeing 727s. The type was still serving Resolute Bay, the most northerly station on First Air's scheduled network, from the Iqaluit hub in Jul07. By Oct07 only one aircraft, a Srs.2A/335 with a large rear freight door, remained in service, which is still based in Iqaluit doing ad hoc work. By early 2007 the company's head office had moved to Kanata and the main engineering base from Carp to Ottawa Macdonald-Cartier International Airport with secondary bases at Iqaluit and Yellowknife. This company's last 748 was withdrawn in mid Feb11, so ending 32 years of service with the type.

C-FBNW	1759	C-GDUN	1581	C-GRXE	1783
C-GBFA	1781	C-GFFA	1789	C-GTLD	1722
C-GCUK	1762	C-GFNW	1758	C-GYMX	1665
C-GDOV	1582	C-GGNZ	1690	CG-TLD	1722
C-GDUI	1577	C-GJVN	1640	F-ODTX	1764
C-GDUL	1578	C-GLTC	1656		

British Air Ferries Ltd (VF/BAF)
Southend, England

This company leased two Srs.2/225s from Court Line Aviation Ltd, the first from Nov70 to Oct71 and the second from Apr to Nov71. The aircraft were used to operate schedules from Southend to Ostend and Le Touquet together with charter flights.

G-ATMI	1592	G-ATMJ	1593

British Airways plc (BA/BAW)
London-Heathrow, England

British Airways ordered two Srs.2A/287s, two Srs.2B/426s and one Srs.2B/357. The last, fitted with a large rear freight door, had previously been a BAe demonstrator and was obtained under a lease/purchase agreement. The two Srs.2A/287s were delivered in Jul and Sep75 and the type entered service on 04Aug75 on routes linking Aberdeen with Kirkwall, Sumburgh and Glasgow. Three aircraft were leased from Dan-Air Services Ltd, a Srs.2A/232 from Mar82 to Feb85, a Srs.2A/245 from Apr82 to Jan85 and again in Sep85 and a Srs.2A/225 from Mar82 to the end of Mar89

while a second Srs.2A/225 was leased from the same source on several occasions during 1983 and 1984. In addition a Srs.2A/210 was leased from BAe from May to Nov82. The two Srs.2B/426s were delivered in Dec84 and the Srs.2B/357 in Jan85. Between Jan and Jun85 the two Srs.2A/287s were modified to Series 2B standard at the airline's Glasgow base. These were the only such conversions carried out by any operator and were done with kits of parts supplied by British Aerospace plc.

On receipt of the leased aircraft in 1982, all Viscounts were withdrawn from service and the Highlands Division of British Airways became a self-contained operation within the parent company. Two Srs.2A/227s were leased from Euroair Transport Ltd in May and Jun86 until Apr89 while a Srs.2A/284 was leased from the same source from mid-May to early Jul86 while the first two were being prepared for service. At the beginning of Nov86 a Srs.2A/245 was leased from Dan-Air Services Ltd, this being replaced by a Srs.2A/266 on lease from Euroair Transport Ltd from early Apr87 to Apr89. Further expansion of the Highland Division took place when three Srs.2B/378s were leased from Deutsche Luftverkehrsgesellschaft mbH with delivery in Mar and Jun88. A fourth Srs.2B/378 was leased from BAe early in Mar90. The division operated all services totally within Scotland and flew from Aberdeen to Edinburgh, Glasgow, Kirkwall and Sumburgh and from Glasgow to Benbecula, Stornoway, Inverness and Kirkwall and additionally to Belfast in Northern Ireland. From the summer of 1984 weekend services were started from Aberdeen and Edinburgh to Jersey, while from 07Jun85 the division started its first international service from Lerwick to Bergen in Norway. One month earlier the 748s commenced services to Manchester and Birmingham from Aberdeen and Glasgow, while Birmingham to Cork and Jersey to Düsseldorf services were started on behalf of the parent company.

With the return to service of the second converted Series 2B and the fleet strength up to six, daily weekday services were commenced between Aberdeen and Birmingham via Edinburgh or Manchester with an extension to Southampton added from 18Nov85. The last destination was dropped early in 1988. German internal services were commenced with the type on 17May86 with schedules from Berlin-Tegel to Münster and Bremen with Hannover and Westerland/Sylt being added later. For summer 1986 a Manchester to Cork schedule was started, while twice weekly services were inaugurated from Manchester to Berlin via Münster or Düsseldorf. Wick was added to the network from 21Jan87 and from 19Jan87 daily night-time newspaper flights were started between Glasgow and Dublin. The Dublin newspaper charter was terminated in Apr91 at which time a Monday to Friday night-time postal contract was started between Edinburgh and Luton. At the start of the summer schedules on 28Mar88 four daily flights between Glasgow and Manchester and a third daily frequency between Birmingham and Scotland were introduced, while weekend flights from Manchester to Jersey were started.

Aircraft remained based in Berlin until 08Apr89 when the last such aircraft was replaced by British Aerospace ATPs. This allowed the last Series 2A aircraft to be withdrawn after operating the last Berlin-based service on 22Apr89. All such aircraft were then returned to their owners. From this time the 748 fleet was employed mainly on Scottish internal scheduled services together with some schedules from Scotland to Birmingham and Manchester, while Bergen was served internationally during summer weekends only. Charter flights were also flown, mainly in support of the oil industry both domestically and to Northern Europe. The BAe ATP fleet was gradually built up leading to the last HS748 flight operating on 15Apr92 when G-HDBD flew from Belfast to Glasgow as flight BA5845.

G-ATMI	1592	G-BFLL	1658	G-BOHZ	1785
G-ATMJ	1593	G-BGJV	1768	G-HDBA	1798
G-AZSU	1612	G-BGMN	1766	G-HDBB	1799
G-BCDZ	1662	G-BGMO	1767	G-HDBC	1786
G-BCOE	1736	G-BMFT	1714	G-HDBD	1797
G-BCOF	1737	G-BOHY	1784		

British Eagle International Airlines Ltd (EG)
London-Heathrow, England

British Eagle wet-leased a Srs.1/101 from Skyways Coach Air Ltd from 24May to 04Jun65 to operate twice daily Liverpool-Glasgow and once daily Liverpool-Heathrow schedules.

G-ARMX   1538

British Independent Airways Ltd (RX/BXH)
Lydd, Kent, England

This company leased a Srs.2A/266 from Euroair Transport Ltd for crew training for a week in Aug89 before leasing a Srs.1A/105

from the same source immediately afterwards. A Srs.1A/106 was added in late Mar90 leased from London European Airways Ltd. The type entered revenue service on 04Dec89 operating on behalf of Aberdeen Airways between Aberdeen and East Midlands. This lease continued until 03Feb90. Ryanair Ltd leased an aircraft throughout the summer of 1990 to operate schedules from Dublin to Cardiff and Liverpool and from Luton to Carrickfin and Sligo at weekends while the same aircraft was leased again over the Christmas period in 1990. The aircraft were also used to operate numerous ad hoc charters. Scheduled services commenced between Lydd and Le Touquet with effect from 12Apr90 and to Beauvais with effect from 11Jul90 both on a twice-daily frequency. Operations ceased on 05Jul91 after the Srs.1A/105 had been earlier returned to the lessor in Feb91.

| G-ARRW | 1549 | G-BMFT | 1714 | G-FBMV | 1537 |
| G-BEKG | 1557 | | | | |

British West Indian Airways Ltd (BW/BWA)
Port of Spain, Trinidad

BWIA ordered a Srs.2/217 on behalf of Leeward Islands Air Transport Services Ltd. See also Trinidad & Tobago Air Services Ltd.

(9Y-TDH)   1670

Brunei Government
See Royal Brunei Malay Regiment

Brymon Airways Ltd (BC/BRY)
Plymouth, Devon, England

This operator leased a Srs.1/105 from Euroair Transport Ltd from late Oct87 until late Jan88 for use on its charter programme primarily in Scotland.

G-BEKG   1557

Bundesanstalt für Flugsicherung (BFS) ( )
Frankfurt & Lechfeld, Germany

BFS ordered seven Srs.2/244s fitted with Rolls-Royce Dart RDa.8 engines in three contracts for one, one, and five aircraft. The first was delivered in Dec69, the second in Nov73 and the

The Bundesanstalt für Flugsicherung operated seven Series 2 aircraft, including D-AFSF c/n 1723. These were used for calibration duties throughout West Germany.
(WHC)

last five between Oct75 and Apr76. All aircraft were used for calibration of navigational aids including Instrument Landing Systems, Air Surveillance Radars and Precision Approach Radars at German civilian and military airfields and were modified extensively with specialised equipment for that task including a Ferranti inertial platform updated by an Omnitrac triple DME and a Decca navigation system. The aircraft were also fitted with a third crew position behind the cockpit to starboard opposite the forward door. The base was moved from Frankfurt to the military airfield at Lechfeld in May77. The first two aircraft were disposed of in 1984 following a period of storage while a third was sold in Canada in Jul89. The organisation's title was changed to DFS Deutsche Flugsicherung GmbH in Dec92 and the last of the fleet was disposed of in Sep95.

D-AFSD	1656	D-AFSG	1724	D-AFSI	1726
D-AFSE	1711	D-AFSH	1725	D-AFSJ	1727
D-AFSF	1723				

Business Air, Ltd (II/GNT)
Aberdeen, Scotland

Business Air leased a Srs.2A/225 from Janes Aviation 748 Ltd in a 44-seat passenger configuration from Oct92 until May93 for ad hoc charter work.

G-ATMI	1592

Caicos International Airlines ( )

This organisation reportedly obtained Guyana Airways' two Srs.2A/309s fitted with large rear freight doors in Jun96. One was reportedly beyond economic restoration prior to this and nothing further has been reported on this carrier. Calm Air International Ltd subsequently obtained both airframes for spares use only.

8R-GEU	1747	8R-GEV	1748

Calm Air International Ltd (AC,CP,MO & PW/CAV)
Thompson, Manitoba, Canada

This company, which was based at Lynn Lake, Manitoba until 1986, purchased one Srs.2A/257 from Northward Airlines Ltd in Dec79. Following an accident with this aircraft the airline leased a Srs.2A/276 from Regionair (1981) Inc from Apr to Jun82, a Srs.2A/275 from Mount Cook Airlines Ltd from Jun82 to Sep84 and a Srs.2B/FAA from British Aerospace Inc from late Aug84 to early Oct84. In the meantime, the initial aircraft had been rebuilt and returned to service in Jul83. In early Oct84 a Srs.2A/210 was leased from BAe plc, the aircraft being purchased outright at the end of Aug85. The fleet was doubled to four aircraft with the addition of a Srs.2A/254 in Jun87 and a Srs.2A/283 in Jan88, both being obtained from Canadian Pacific Airlines Ltd.

Two later additions to the fleet have been a Srs.2B/FAA in Apr97 and a Srs.2A/258 in Mar99. The latter was fitted with a large rear freight door at the company's Thompson base by Aerometal Fabrications of Calgary prior to entering service as a pure freighter in Oct99. The Srs.2B/FAA was converted similarly and returned to service in Jun04. The Srs.2A/254 was also converted to a pure freighter but without the fitment of a large cargo door and entered service in this form in Feb01. The source of the doors was two Srs.2A/309s from Guyana that were obtained for spares use only.

The type entered service with Calm Air on 04Apr80 on a network of scheduled services linking Churchill with Thompson, Eskimo Point, Rankin Inlet, Baker Lake, Coral Harbour and Repulse Bay on the Arctic Circle where temperatures regularly fall to between -35 and -40 degrees Centigrade. By the summer of 1986 Leaf

Rapids, Lynn Lake, Brochet, Lac Brochet, Gillam and Shamattawa had been added to the scheduled network. With effect from 14Sep86 the airline came under the Pacific Western "Spirit" banner in a joint marketing programme with Pacific Western Airlines Ltd and Time Air Ltd. At this time the network was expanded to link Winnipeg with The Pas, Flin Flon and Thompson.

Further changes came when the airline joined the Canadian Airlines International Ltd commuter network as a "Canadian Partner" with effect from 26Apr87. In July of the same year Canadian Airlines International Ltd purchased a 45% holding in this carrier. In the summer of 1988 a twice-daily schedule was reportedly flown between Winnipeg and Brandon, while in the same year a daily service was started between Thompson and Winnipeg via Oxford House, God's Narrows and Island Lake. This last service was terminated early in 1990 at which time scheduled services were severely curtailed.

From early 1995 SAAB 340Bs replaced 748s on the more southerly routes, leaving the 748s to operate the more demanding northerly routes from Churchill and Thompson to Arviat (Eskimo Point), Baker Lake, Brochet, Chesterfield Inlet, Coral Harbour, Lac Brochet, Lynn Lake, Rankin Inlet, Repulse Bay, Shamattawa, Tadoule Lake and Whale Cove. Some schedules were also flown from Winnipeg to Churchill and Thompson.

In 2000 CP Air was taken over by Air Canada and Calm Air schedules began operating with the 'AC' flight prefix, but on 07Apr02 all flights reverted to the independent 'MO' flight prefix after the Morberg family bought back the 45% shareholding from Air Canada. However, on 08Apr09 the company was sold to what is now the Exchange Industrial Corporation, which also owns Perimeter Airlines Ltd and Keewatin Air Ltd.

The aircraft have been used additionally for charter work, mainly freighting to northern settlements but have been seen as far away as Seattle, when on one occasion three live Beluga whales were flown from Churchill. The three pure freighters were used regularly for bulk fuel deliveries and cargo charters, although the Srs.2A/254 was withdrawn from use in late Jun09. The last passenger-configured aircraft, a Srs.28/283, operated as a combi with either 12, 20, 32 or 40 passenger seats to the rear with cargo in the forward section on either charters or as a back-up for the scheduled flights until it was retired in mid-Dec08. The earlier used passenger-configured aircraft were withdrawn in Nov02 and Sep06 as the SAAB 340Bs took over the northern schedules while an ATR42-300 was introduced into service on some of the southern schedules in summer 2007.

By Jul09 the two remaining Large Freight Door-equipped pure freighters were operating regular ad hoc services from Churchill and Thompson to Brochet, God's Lake Narrows, God's River, Lac Brochet, Island, Red Sucker and Tadoule Lakes, Oxford House, St Teresa Point and Shamattawa in Manitoba and to Arviat, Baker Lake, Chesterfield Inlet, Coral Harbour, Hall Beach, Igloolik, Kugaaruk (Pelly Bay), Meadowbank, Pond Inlet, Rankin Inlet, Repulse Bay and Whale Cove in Nunavut Territory. The Srs.2A/258 was withdrawn from service in Aug11 leaving just the Srs.2B/FAA flying for Calm Air until 05Jun15 when it flew its last service, from Island Lake to Thompson, Manitoba, where it was placed in storage. Both engines had preservation runs carried out on 15Jun15, and the aircraft was permanently withdrawn from service on 24Jun15.

C-FAGI	1699	C-GEPB	1686	N748BA	1783
C-FAMO	1669	C-GHSC	1790	(8R-GEU)	1747
C-FMAK	1668	C-GRCU	1697	(8R-GEV)	1748
C-GDOP	1745	C-GSBF	1662		

Cameroon Air Force
See L'Armée de l'Air du Cameroun

Cameroon Airlines Series 2B TJ-CCF c/n 1804, seen prior to delivery in the airline's orange and green scheme, in November 1985.   *(BAe)*

One of two aircraft operated by Cascade Airways Inc, Series 2B N117CA c/n 1781 was photographed in the early 1980s.

Cameroon Air Lines (UY/UYC)

Douala, Cameroun

Cameroon Air Lines purchased two Srs.2A/310s fitted with large rear freight doors from L'Armée de l'Air du Cameroun in Feb82. These were replaced by two Srs.2B/435 Super 748s in Oct/Nov85. The aircraft flew from Douala and Yaoundé to Bali, Bafoussam, Bertoua, Batouri, Koutaba, Kribi, Mamfé and Ngaoundéré domestically and internationally served Cotonou (Benin) and Malabo (Equatorial Guinea) from Douala. One of these aircraft was written off in Jun89 and the other was later withdrawn from service.

TJ-CCD   1749   TJ-CCF   1804   TJ-CCG   1805
TJ-CCE   1750

Canadian Airlines International Ltd (CP/CDN)

Vancouver, British Columbia, Canada

Under this company's 'Canadian Partner' scheme various operators provided feeder services to this airline's schedules or provided services where jet operations were inappropriate. Aircraft so used were painted in Canadian Partner colours. HS748s were used by two such operators, these being Air Saint-Pierre and Calm Air International Ltd. This last operator became 45% owned by Canadian Airlines International with effect from Jul87. Full details are shown under the individual operators' listings.

Canadian Pacific Air Lines Ltd

See Eastern Provincial Airways (1983) Ltd

Cape Aero Services (Pty) Ltd

See Stars Away Aviation (Pty) Ltd

Care Airlines (Pty) Ltd (CE)

Johannesburg, South Africa

This operator purchased a used Srs.2A/351 in Jul93. Scheduled services were flown between Johannesburg and Margate. The aircraft and the route were operated by Intensive Air Ltd from Nov93 initially in Care Airlines' name.

ZS-XGE   1770

Cascade Airways Inc (CZ/CCD)

Spokane, Washington, U.S.A.

Cascade Airways ordered two Srs.2B/FAAs, both delivered in Dec81. A third aircraft was optioned but not taken up. The aircraft were introduced into service on 01Feb82 and served most of the airline's network at various times. Points served included Boise, Idaho Falls, Kalispell, Lewiston, Medford, Pasco, Pocatello, Pullman, Seattle, Spokane, Twin Falls, Walla Walla and Yakima. The type was used exclusively on scheduled work. The carrier filed for Chapter 11 bankruptcy protection on 21Aug85 and withdrew its 748 fleet.

N117CA 1781   N118CA 1789   (N119CA) 1791

Cayman Airways Ltd (KX/CAY)
Georgetown, Grand Cayman

Cayman Airways bought one Srs.1A/105 from Dan-Air Services Ltd that was operated from Feb82 until Sep83 on routes linking Grand Cayman with Cayman Brac, Miami International and Kingston (Jamaica).

VR-CBH 1557

Centre for Airborne Systems – (CABS)
See Defence Research & Development Organisation (DRDO)

Channel Airways Ltd (CW)
Southend, Essex, England

Channel Airways ordered four Srs.2/222s which were delivered between Sep65 and Mar66, the first two being leased immediately in Panamá and the Leeward Islands before seeing service with the company. The type entered service on 24Feb66 on a network linking Southend and Portsmouth with Jersey, Guernsey and Paris while on 22Jan69 the type was introduced onto a new 'bus-stop' multi-sector service from Portsmouth to Aberdeen marketed as the "Scottish Flyer". Intermediate points served were Southend, Luton, East Midlands, Leeds, Teesside, Newcastle and Edinburgh. The aircraft were also used on an extensive charter programme together with several overseas leases until the last aircraft was disposed of in Aug70.

G-ATEH 1585   G-ATEJ 1587   G-ATEK 1588
G-ATEI 1586

Chevron Standard Oil ( )
Calgary, Alberta, Canada

This organisation ordered one Srs.2A/269 with delivery in Oct70 while the aircraft, a manufacturer's demonstrator, was being shown in Canada. The company was later known as Chevron Canada Resources Ltd. The aircraft was used to carry personnel

Channel Airways Series 2 G-ATEH c/n 1585. The airline operated their 748s in the same gold, black and white scheme as their Viscounts.
(WHC)

and equipment to northern oil and gas sites until the aircraft was disposed of in Jun93. The company later leased a Srs.2A/258 from AMOCO (Canada) Petroleum Ltd from Jan to Mar97.

C-FAMO 1669   CF-CSE 1679   C-FCSE 1679

Chieftain Airways plc (PQ)
Glasgow, Scotland

Chieftain Airways purchased two Srs.2A/334s from Trinidad & Tobago (BWIA International) Airways Corp in Dec86. Scheduled services were started on 30Mar87 on two routes from Glasgow to Brussels and Frankfurt, both via Edinburgh. It also carried out charter flights and flew some schedules for Loganair Ltd between Belfast Harbour and Manchester. A twice-daily service from Hamburg to Gatwick on behalf of British Caledonian Airways Ltd, although advertised, was never operated. The company was put into receivership on 13May87 with the last flight taking place on the same day.

G-EDIN 1757   G-GLAS 1756

Civil Aviation Authority (UK)
See Board of Trade

Civil Aviation Flying Unit (CAFU)
See Board of Trade

Clewer Aviation Ltd ( )
London, England

This company has been involved in trading used 748s for several years and has owned several aircraft, which have been leased to operators in Madagascar, Nepal, New Zealand, South Africa, Tonga and the United Kingdom. The most recent acquisitions have been three Srs.2/228s from the RAAF in Feb and Mar05 and a Srs.1/107 from QinetiQ in Nov06, but efforts to place these aircraft have so far proved fruitless.

Comores Aviation (KR/05/KMZ)
Moroni, Grande Comore, Comoros Islands

Comores Aviation leased a Srs.2B/378 from Executive Aerospace (Pty) Ltd in a 48-seat single class configuration from late Jun04. This aircraft was replaced by other Srs.2B/378s and a Srs.2B/501 at various times (for more comprehensive details see 'Individual Aircraft Histories') until mid-2007. The aircraft were used from 07Jul04 to operate scheduled services to points within the Comoros Islands including Anjouan, Mohéli and Moroni and to Dzaoudzi on Mayotte and to Nossi-bé in Madagascar. Charters were also flown to Madagascar, Tanzania and Zanzibar.

ZS-AGB 1807   ZS-PLO 1797   ZS-TPW 1784
ZS-NWW 1786

Compañía Aérea de Navegación Alaire SL
See ALAIRE – Líneas Aéreas Alaire, SL

Compañía Panameña de Aviación SA (COPA) (CM/CMP)
Panamá City, Panamá

COPA ordered a Srs.2/227 and a Srs.2A/227 with delivery in Aug66 and May69, while a Srs.2/222 was leased from Channel Airways Ltd from Oct65 to May66. One aircraft was sold back to

Hawker Siddeley Aviation Ltd in May74 and was converted later into the Coastguarder prototype while the second aircraft was disposed of in Apr78. The aircraft replaced Martin 404s and were used from Panamá City to David, Bocas del Toro, Changuinola and Puerto Armuelles domestically and to Kingston (Jamaica), Managua (Nicaragua) and San José (Costa Rica).

HP-416   1585   HP-432   1594   HP-484   1662

Court Line Aviation Ltd
See Autair International Airways Ltd

CP Air (Canadian Pacific Air Lines Ltd) (CP/CPC)
Vancouver, British Columbia, Canada

In Aug84 this operator finalised the purchase of Eastern Provincial Airways (1963) Ltd and its subsidiary Air Maritime. Both companies continued to operate in their own names until 12Jan86, when their aircraft and operations became fully integrated into those of the parent company. At the same time, CP Air reverted to its former name of Canadian Pacific Air Lines Ltd. For details see entry under Eastern Provincial Airways (1963) Ltd.

Dakota and South Bend Securities

This organisation ordered one Srs.2A/275 that was not delivered but stored at Woodford at the customer's request from Nov73. Following the death of Howard Hughes (who had ordered the aircraft through the above company), the aircraft was sold to Mount Cook Airlines Ltd in Sep76.

G-AYYG   1697

Dan-Air Services Ltd (DA/DAN)
London-Gatwick, England

This company obtained its first 748 when it purchased the second prototype from Maersk Air I/S in May71 while in Oct of the same year one Srs.2/226 was bought from International Skyways Ltd. Apr72 saw the company absorb International Skyways Ltd together with its fleet of four Series 1 aircraft. In the same month a Srs.2/232 was obtained from BOAC Associated Companies Ltd. In May75 a Srs.2/225 was bought which was joined by its sister ship on lease from the Civil Aviation Flying Unit at weekends during the summer of the same year. A Srs.2/233 was added in late Jun76 before a deal was concluded with Argentina to buy the remaining seven Srs.1/105s that had seen service with Aerolíneas Argentinas and in some cases more recently with Yacimientos Petrolíferos Fiscales. These aircraft were delivered between Dec76 and Sep77. In Mar78 a used Srs.2A/245 was bought followed by the earlier leased Srs.2/225 in July of the same year. A Srs.2/209 was obtained from Philippine Airlines Inc in Nov79 before the airline's final purchase of the type in late May81. This last aircraft, a Srs.2A/266 that came from Polynesian Airlines Ltd, was fitted by Dan-Air with a large rear cargo door supplied in kit form by British Aerospace. This was the first aircraft so modified by anybody other than British Aerospace and was used on cargo services when required following the completion of the work in Mar82. Of note was c/n 1697 which was ferried from Mount Cook Airlines Ltd of New Zealand on three separate occasions between 1978 and 1981 on lease to cope with the summer peak operations.

The airline commenced 748 operations with the second prototype on the Newcastle to Kristiansand (Norway) route on 18May71. After the takeover of International Skyways Ltd a new division was set up at Ashford to operate 748s on the Ashford to Beauvais, Clermont Ferrand and Montpellier schedules, though the last two routes were transferred to Gatwick by 1973. Aircraft so used were painted for a while with 'Dan-Air Skyways' titling. From 11Apr72 748s started flying the company's 'Link City' domestic services between Bournemouth and Newcastle via varying intermediate points over the next few years, these being Bristol, Cardiff, Birmingham, Liverpool, Manchester and Teesside. In the same year the type was also introduced onto Jersey routes from many places in the United Kingdom including Ashford, Carlisle, Bournemouth, Gatwick, Newcastle and Swansea and from Guernsey to Bournemouth and Jersey. The type was used internationally from Gatwick to Berne (with effect from 05Jun72), Ostend, Clermont Ferrand and Montpellier and from Newcastle to Bergen, Kristiansand and Stavanger while Dublin and Cork were served from Bristol and Cardiff. Amsterdam was

Compañia Panameña de Aviación SA - COPA Series 2 HP-432 c/n 1594. Note the additional 'vuele' (fly) before the airline titles and the rather indistinct advertising that the aircraft was 'jet-prop' on the tail-fin!   *(WHC/HAS)*

Dan-Air Series 2 G-AYYG c/n 1697 at Teesside on 26th April 1980 during its third lease to Dan-Air in Mount Cook Airline/Airlines Ltd light blue colours, but with Dan-Air London titles. *(Keith Gaskell)*

linked with Liverpool, Teesside, Bristol and Cardiff and the last two for a short while with Paris. Domestically, schedules were flown from Leeds to Glasgow, Bristol, Cardiff and Luton, from Belfast to Bristol, Cardiff and Newcastle, from Carlisle to Newcastle and from the Isle of Man to Bristol, Cardiff, Carlisle, Newcastle and Prestwick.

On 31Oct74 the Ashford base was moved from Lympne to Lydd. Later an aircraft was based in Berlin-Tegel for schedules to Saarbrücken and weekend flights to Amsterdam. From 27Oct86 a second aircraft was deployed to Tegel to cover a twice-daily Amsterdam schedule previously operated by One-Elevens. This route reverted to jet operations during 1990 when a BAe146 replaced the 748. On 04Jan87 the last scheduled service was operated from Bournemouth to Jersey, so ending fifteen years of continual 748 operations from Hurn. Service was later reinstated during 1988 summer weekends only. From 1974 aircraft were based in Aberdeen in support of the North Sea oil programme, mainly flying rig crews up to Lerwick for onward travel by helicopter to the rigs out of range of Aberdeen-based helicopters. At the peak of this operation fourteen of the company's 748 fleet were employed on this work and flying associated charters to Europe and other destinations in the United Kingdom. The short runway at Scatsta, near the pipeline terminal on Sullom Voe to the north of Zetland, was an added secondary base from Jul78. From here tankers ferried the crude oil to refineries.

Aircraft were also employed on night-time flights under contract to the Post Office from 1979 until Mar92. Two of the Srs.1/105s were converted to pure freighters for this work but without the costly fitment of large rear cargo doors. As the North Sea oil support work diminished, surplus aircraft capacity was made good by leasing aircraft to various operators both in the United Kingdom and the Azores, British Virgin Islands, Canada, the Philippines and Spain. The last of the fleet were withdrawn from service on 28Mar92 and the remaining six aircraft were all sold to Janes Aviation 748 Ltd together with the entire remaining spares stocks on 15Jul92. However one 748, G-BEKE, was leased back by Dan-Air to operate an outstanding British Petroleum contract over the Aberdeen to Scatsta route before being retired finally on 30Sep92.

G-ARAY	1535	G-AYYG	1697	G-BEKE	1545
G-ARMW	1537	G-AZSU	1612	G-BEKF	1542
G-ARMX	1538	G-BEBA	1613	G-BEKG	1557
G-ARRW	1549	G-BEJD	1543	G-BFLL	1658
G-ASPL	1560	G-BEJE	1556	(G-BFUA)	1599
G-ATMI	1592	G-BEKC	1541	G-BHCJ	1663
G-ATMJ	1593	G-BEKD	1544	G-BIUV	1701
G-AXVG	1589				

Defence Evaluation and Research Agency
See Defence Research Agency

Defence Research Agency

The UK Ministry of Technology purchased one Srs.1/107 from Smith's Industries Ltd in Jan70 for the use of the Royal Aircraft Establishment at Farnborough. It was transferred to the RAE at Bedford in 1971 initially with the Blind Landing Unit and later with the Flight Systems Division. The RAE was renamed the Royal Aerospace Establishment with effect from 01Apr88. The RAE was merged into a new body entitled the Defence Research Agency (DRA) with effect from 01Apr91.

A Srs.2A/206 Andover CC.Mk.2 was transferred to the DRA after retirement from the RAF Queen's Flight in Mar91. After extensive modifications as a flying laboratory the aircraft first flew on 13Feb92. It was withdrawn from service in late Jul97 and subsequently broken up. The organisation was renamed the Defence Evaluation and Research Agency – DERA with effect from 01Apr95 and QinetiQ from 02Jul01. The Srs.1/107 was put in storage with effect from late Jan05 and sold in Nov05.

XS790   1562   XW750   1559

Defence Research & Development Organisation (DRDO)
Bangalore, India

This Indian organisation leased two HAL Srs.2Ms from the Indian Air Force and after extensive modifications, both aircraft were flown on research projects. More specific details can be found in the 'Individual Aircraft Histories' and 'Licence Production in India' sections of this book. A sub-division of this organisation is called the Centre for Airborne Systems – (CABS).

H-2175   569   H-2176   570

Department of Trade and Industry
See Board of Trade

DERA
See Defence Research Agency

Series 2A G-BCDZ c/n 1662 was operated in full bright red DLT colours for eight months in 1981 on lease from British Aerospace.

Eastern Provincial Airways Series 2A C-GEPI c/n 1594 in the airline's red livery with black titles.

Elysian Airlines' Series 2A 3X-GEW c/n 1701 was photographed at Nairobi-Wilson on arrival in July 2009. The Large Freight Door opening is seen to good effect in this hangar view.
(Allan Fantham)

Deutsche Lufthansa AG
See Deutsche Luftverkehrsgesellschaft mbH (DLT)

Deutsche Luftverkehrsgesellschaft mbH (DLT) (DW,LH/DLT)
Frankfurt, West Germany

DLT ordered three Srs.2B/378s that were delivered between Mar and Jul81 while a Srs.2A/210 was leased from Jan to Sep81 and a Srs.2B/357 from Feb to May and again for a short period in Jun81. This last aircraft was leased again in Feb and Mar82. All leases were from British Aerospace. Three repeat orders, each for a single Srs.2B/378, were placed later with delivery in Nov83 and May and Sep84. The aircraft were flown between Cologne, Düsseldorf, Frankfurt, Hamburg, Hannover, Munich, Münster, Nuremberg, Saarbrücken, Stuttgart and Westerland/Sylt, while internationally they served Amsterdam, Bastia, Brussels, Copenhagen, Geneva, Göteborg, Guernsey, Jersey, Milan, Paris, Venice, Vienna, Zagreb and Zurich. All scheduled routes flown by the 748 fleet were done so on behalf of Deutsche Lufthansa AG of which DLT was a subsidiary. However, when the 748s first entered service, the domestic services were flown with the DLT 'DW' flight designator. DLT specialised in opening new routes on behalf of Lufthansa until traffic levels built up sufficiently to warrant the use of jet equipment. From Mar88 the company leased two of its 748s to British Airways plc with a third following in June of the same year. The remaining aircraft were sold back to British Aerospace in Nov88 and Jan and May89 from which time the type was no longer operated.

D-AHSA	1784	D-AHSD	1791	G-BCDZ	1662
D-AHSB	1785	D-AHSE	1792	G-BGJV	1768
D-AHSC	1786	D-AHSF	1797		

DFS Deutsche Flugsicherung GmbH
See Bundesanstalt für Flugsicherung (BFS)

DRDO
See Defence Research & Development Organisation

Eastern Provincial Airways (1963) Ltd
(PV,CP/EPA)
Gander, Newfoundland, Canada

Eastern Provincial purchased its first aircraft, a Srs.2A/232, from Inexco Oil in Mar75 and introduced the type into service on 08Mar75. One Srs.2A/239 was added in Mar76 from Air Gabon, while a Srs.2A/227 was bought from Compañia Panameña de Aviación SA in Apr78. Ghana Airways Corp was the source of a Srs.2A/254 in May81. Two aircraft were leased from Dan-Air Services Ltd, a Srs.2A/226 in Jun and Jul81 and a Srs.2A/233 from Aug to Oct of the same year. In Apr82 a Srs.2A/283 was obtained from Austin Airways Ltd while a Srs.2A/234 was leased from the same operator from May84 for a nine-month period. The final lease was a Srs.2B/FAA from BAe Inc from Oct84 to Apr85. With effect from Jan82 a separate division within the company known as 'Air Maritime' operated the 748 aircraft. In Aug84 the purchase of Eastern Provincial Airways and Air Maritime by CP Air was finalised. However, both companies continued to operate with their individual identities until 12Jan86. From this date all aircraft and schedules were integrated fully into those of CP Air, which reverted to its former name of Canadian Pacific Air Lines Ltd on the same date. The aircraft were employed on a network of services based on Halifax, Nova Scotia to Saint John, Moncton, Fredericton, Charlottetown, Îles de la Madeleine, Saint-Pierre, Sydney, Stephenville, St. Johns, Deer Lake and Gander. The aircraft also operated services on behalf of Air Saint-Pierre between Saint-Pierre and Halifax or Sydney, Nova Scotia. The type was withdrawn progressively from service from early 1986.

C-FINE	1611	C-GEPI	1594	G-AXVG	1589
C-GDOP	1745	C-GQTG	1619	G-BEBA	1613
C-GEPB	1686	C-GRXE	1783	N748BA	1783
C-GEPH	1635				

East Horizon Airlines (EA/EHN)
Kabul, Afghanistan

A passenger configured Srs.2B/426 was leased via Ivoirienne de Transports Aériens (ITA) from the owners of Aero Lanka in late Dec11. The aircraft was due to operate domestic schedules from Kabul to Bamiyan, Chaghcharān, Feyzābād, Herāt, Kunduz and Trinkot from early 2012, but it is not known if this ever took place.

TU-PAD   1799

Easy Fly Express Ltd (8E/EFX)
Dhaka, Bangladesh

This more recent Bangladeshi carrier took delivery of an ex Emerald Airways Ltd Srs.2A/347 freighter in late Apr08. Domestic cargo services have been flown from Cox's Bazar to Jessore and from Chittagong to Dhaka after the company's AOC was issued on 01Jul08. International charter flights are also carried out. The GETCO Group obtained 60% of the company's shares on 01Oct10, and the aircraft was sold to Bismillah Airlines Ltd by Apr15.

S2-AAX   1767

Ecuato Guineana de Aviación (ZH)
Malabo, Equatorial Guinea

This company leased a Srs.2B/360 fitted with a large rear freight door from Air Madagascar from late Aug86 until it was damaged in a ground incident in Aug87. The aircraft was employed on a scheduled network comprising a twice-weekly service from Malabo to Douala (Cameroon) and a five times weekly service from Malabo to Bata of which two continued to Libreville (Gabon).

5R-MJB   1773

Elysian Airlines SA (E7)
Conakry, République de Guinée

This organisation leased a Srs.2A/266 freighter fitted with a Large Freight Door from International Air Parts Pty Ltd in Mar09. Although delivered to Conakry, this aircraft never entered service with this company and was returned to the lessor in late Jul09.

3X-GEW   1701

Emerald Airways Ltd (G3/JEM)
Liverpool, Merseyside and Blackpool, Lancashire, UK

When this company obtained its first 748, a Srs.2A/334 in Nov91, it was known as Janes Aviation Ltd. On 15Jul92 the company purchased Dan-Air Services' fleet of six remaining 748s together with a large spares holding. These aircraft comprised three Srs.1/105s, two Srs.2A/225s and one Srs.2A/266 fitted with a large rear freight door. At the same time the company was renamed Janes Aviation 748 Ltd. All aircraft were used as freighters on contract newspaper flights, on Post Office contract flights and on ad hoc charters. On 15Sep93 the company adopted the Emerald Airways' title. In Mar94 a Srs.1A/105 was bought from Alexandra Aviation, while in Jun94 two Srs.2A/270s and a Srs.2A/372 were purchased from British Aerospace after long periods of storage. The second of these aircraft was the first in the fleet to be fitted out for ad hoc passenger charter work and entered service in May95. A Srs.2A/263 was leased for a period of two and a half weeks in Dec95. A Srs.2A/347 was purchased in Feb96 followed by two Srs.2B/378s in Mar96. Later additions to the fleet were a Srs.2A/275 in Nov96, a Srs.2A/266 in Dec97, a Srs.2A/242 in Feb98, two Srs.2A/238s in Sep98 (which were destined to never enter service), a Srs.2A/347 in Nov98, a second Srs.2A/242 that entered service in May01 and a third Srs.2A/242 in Oct02. A Srs.2A/310 with a large rear freight door was leased from Air Inuit of Canada with effect from Jul to late Dec00 and a Srs.2A/263 was bought for spares use in Oct04.

A twice-daily scheduled passenger service between Liverpool and the Isle of Man was started on 29Apr96 and although later increased to thrice daily, all scheduled passenger flights ceased on 28Mar99. The one remaining passenger-configured aircraft was sold and the company then concentrated on flying mail and express parcel services on behalf of several organisations including the Royal Mail, Reed Aviation, Parcel Force and the Lynx group together with ad hoc freight charter work. Several of

the Royal Mail contracts were terminated on 10Jan04 but by August 2004 five aircraft had been relocated to Europe flying contract freight flights. Points served on a regular basis included Belfast, Bournemouth, Bristol, Coventry, Dublin, East Midlands, Edinburgh, Isle of Man, Liverpool and Newcastle. In 2000 a regular daytime flight was flown to the Channel Islands from Bournemouth on behalf of Channel Express Ltd. The company's engineering base was set up at Blackpool. The fleet was grounded when their AOC was suspended on 04May06. Administrators were appointed on 11May06 and the organisation was sold to International Air Parts Pty Ltd in Oct06. It was not planned for Emerald Airways to fly again but to market the Emerald fleet of aircraft worldwide.

C-FDOX	1749	G-BEKE	1545	G-DAAL	1557
F-GHKA	1680	G-BGMN	1766	G-EMRD	1797
G-ATMI	1592	G-BGMO	1767	G-OJEM	1791
G-ATMJ	1593	G-BIUV	1701	G-OPFW	1714
G-AVXI	1623	G-BMFT	1714	G-ORAL	1756
G-AVXJ	1624	G-BPDA	1756	G-ORCP	1647
G-AYIM	1687	G-BPNJ	1680	G-OSOE	1697
G-AYYG	1697	G-BVOU	1721	G-OTBA	1712
G-BEJD	1543	G-BVOV	1777	G-SOEI	1689
G-BEJE	1556				

Emerald Airways Series 2A G-OPFW c/n 1714 in the bright red Parcel Force colours. The aircraft was photographed on 8th July 1998.   *(WHC)*

Emerald Airways Series 2A G-BVOV c/n 1777 is seen here landing at Hurn, UK on 26th June 2001, in the airline's full colour-scheme. (Keith Gaskell)

Emirates Air Services Ltd (RF/EAS)
Abu Dhabi, United Arab Emirates

Emirates Air Services leased two Srs.2B/426s from British Aerospace from Apr92 to Jan93. They were used to operate a five times daily shuttle between Abu Dhabi-Bateen and Dubai.

A6-ABM	1799	A6-GRM	1798

Euroair Transport Ltd (EZ)
Gatwick, West Sussex, UK

Euroair purchased a Srs.1A/105 in Jun85, which had been operated previously by Venture Airways Ltd and in Oct of the same year bought a Srs.2A/266 from Polynesian Airways Ltd. In Apr86 two Srs.2A/347s were bought from Trinidad & Tobago (BWIA International) Airways Corporation for onward leasing to British Airways plc. In Sep92 a Srs.2A/232 and a Srs.2A/245 were purchased. The company commenced scheduled operations with the type when it began flying the Air Écosse route between Dundee and Heathrow via Carlisle on 18Nov85. Later it operated this route in its own name.

From 07Apr86 the Carlisle stop ceased and the Dundee-Heathrow route was flown twice daily. The company ceased flying this route on 03Apr87 and apart from a Dundee-Carlisle-Isle of Man route which was flown on Saturdays from 23May87, from this time the company specialised in leasing out its aircraft to operators both in the UK and abroad mainly through associate companies BAC Leasing Ltd and Alexandra Aviation Ltd.

G-AZSU	1612	G-BGMN	1766	G-VAJK	1557
G-BEKG	1557	G-BGMO	1767	VP-BFT	1714
G-BFLL	1658	G-BMFT	1714	VR-BFT	1714

Euroguineana de Aviación SL (8Y/ECV)
Malabo, Equatorial Guinea

This airline leased a Srs.2B/378 from Executive Aerospace (Pty) Ltd in early Jun06 for one year though the aircraft had returned to its owners by mid Nov06.

ZS-TPW	1784

Executive Aerospace (Pty) Ltd (EA/EAS)
Johannesburg, South Africa

This company, which was based in Durban until Mar99, purchased two used Srs.2B/378s with delivery in late Nov94 and Oct95 followed by a Srs.2B/FAA in May96, a Srs.2A/242 in Aug97, a Srs.2A/263 in late Sep97 and a Srs.2B/378 in Jun99. Later acquisitions were a Srs.2B/378 and a Srs.2B/501 from Necon Air in Aug & Sep01, the latter being the last 748 built. Aircraft were operated in a single class 44-seat configuration. In the contract airline support market, aircraft were operated on behalf of Albarka Air Services, Alliance Air, Air Botswana, Air Excellence of Gabon, Air Malawi, Air Max-Gabon, Air Namibia, Air Zimbabwe, Comores Aviation, Euroguineana de Aviación, Kalanga Air Services, Island Aviation Services Ltd of the Maldives, Lion Air of Sri Lanka, Ocean Air, Pelican Air Services, SAA Express, SA Airlink, Sonavam of Madagascar, Zambian Express and Zimbabwe Express.

One of the aircraft was stripped out as a pure freighter and chartered to Airworld (Pty) Ltd from May98 with a second similarly converted aircraft joining it in late May01. Ad hoc charter work to the tourist, sports and conference markets was also carried out while relief work was performed on behalf of the United Nations and the Red Cross. The Srs.2A/242 and Srs.2A/263 were returned to Clewer Aviation in mid-Oct02 and late-Oct03 respectively. It is believed that 748 operations came to an end in early 2007 and the company was liquidated by the Durban High Court on 27Feb08.

ZS-AGB	1807	ZS-NNW	1785	ZS-ODJ	1680
(ZS-KLC)	1784	ZS-NWW	1786	ZS-PLO	1797
ZS-LSO	1783	ZS-OCF	1647	ZS-TPW	1784

Falcks Flyvetjeneste A/S – Falckair (FV/FLK)
Odense, Denmark

Falckair purchased the second prototype from Hawker Siddeley Aviation Ltd in Aug67. The aircraft was used on a network of scheduled services linking Copenhagen with Odense, Skrydstrup, Stauning and Thisted until the company was taken over by Maersk Air I/S in Nov69.

OY-DFV	1535

Fiji Airways Ltd
See Air Pacific Ltd

First Air
See Air Inuit (1985) Ltd/Ltée and Bradley Air Services Ltd

Flight Precision Ltd ( )
Teesside Airport, Durham, UK

This company took over the UK airfield calibration duties from the Civil Aviation Authority in Oct96 together with the two Srs.2A/238s. The aircraft were withdrawn from service in late Aug98 and sold the following month.

G-AVXI	1623	G-AVXJ	1624

Força Aérea Brasileira – FAB

The Força Aérea Brasileira ordered a Srs.2/204 and five Srs.2/205s with delivery from Nov62 to Sep63. Six Srs.2A/281s, all fitted with large rear freight doors, were ordered later and delivered between Jan and Dec75. The first six aircraft were operated initially by the Grupo de Transporte Especial – GTE. They were used primarily for transporting government officials and VIPs between Rio de Janeiro - Galeão and Brasilia. The aircraft were transferred to 2 Grupo de Transporte, 1 Esquadrão (the Condor Squadron) on 01Apr69, also based at Galeão Air Base where they replaced Douglas C-54s. The fleet was used on the main routes of the 'Correio Aéreo Nacional' - CAN (National Air Mail service) both domestically and to nearby South American countries together with flights for the GTE.

The second order went direct to 2 Grupo de Transporte, 2 Esquadrão (the Privateer Squadron) also based at Galeão where they replaced Douglas C-118s. The new aircraft, known as C-91As but not painted as such, carried out similar work to those of 1 Esquadrão but were tasked additionally with work for the Army Parachute Brigade and for supplying Força Aérea Brasileira bases with material from their maintenance depots. From 04Apr78 all 748 aircraft were operated by 1 Esquadrão.

The first six aircraft were withdrawn from service and struck off charge on 01Oct01 while the five remaining large cargo door

The second of the Series 2 aircraft of the Força Aérea Brasileira, C-91 2501 c/n 1551, is seen in an impressive view in the early 1960s.   *(WHC)*

The third aircraft for the Força Aérea Brasileira, Set 207 c/n 1731, is seen here being fitted with its Large Freight Door at Woodford. This aircraft would become C-91 2508.
(WHC)

equipped aircraft commenced a major upgrade programme in Sep01. The last of the Srs.2A/281 fleet was withdrawn from use on 30Sep05 and the five aircraft were donated to the Fuerza Aérea Ecuatoriana with the first delivery in late Mar06.

C-91 2500	1550	C-91 2506	1729
C-91 2501	1551	C-91 2507	1730
C-91 2502	1552	C-91 2508	1731
C-91 2503	1553	C-91 2509	1732
C-91 2504	1554	C-91 2510	1733
C-91 2505	1555	C-91 2511	1734

Force Aeriénne Belge/Belgische Luchtmacht

The Belgian Air Force ordered three Srs.2A/288s fitted with large rear freight doors with delivery between Jun and Sep76. The aircraft were operated by 21 Squadron, Melsbroek until finally withdrawn from use on 20Feb02. Initially used as tactical transport aircraft supporting the armed services in Europe and the Mediterranean area, they were used later for the carriage of the Belgian Royal Family, Government ministers and NATO diplomats. Two were donated to the Force Aériénne du Benin in 2002.

CS-01	1741	CS-02	1742	CS-03	1743

Force Aeriénne de Burkina Faso

Prior to 04Aug84 this country was known as Upper Volta and the air force was known as Force Aeriénne de Haute-Volta. It ordered a Srs.2A/230 and a Srs.2A/369, both fitted with large rear freight doors, with delivery in Sep77 and Aug81. By early 2009 only one aircraft was reported to be operational.

XT-MAL	1754	XT-MAN	1775

Force Aeriénne Populaire du Bénin

The Benin government obtained two Large Freight Door equipped Srs.2A/288s which were donated by the Belgian government in 2002 for the use of the country's Air Force.

TY-21A	1741	TY-22A	1742

Force Aeriénne de Haute-Volta

See Force Aeriénne de Burkina Faso

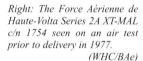

Above: The Force Aeriénne Belge / Belgische Luchtmacht Series 2A CS-02 c/n 1742 in the Force's tactical camouflage livery.

Right: The Force Aérienne de Haute-Volta Series 2A XT-MAL c/n 1754 seen on an air test prior to delivery in 1977.
(WHC/BAe)

Fred Olsens Flyselskap A/S (FO/FOF)

Oslo, Norway

In Sep75 this airline purchased a Srs.2A/235 from Viaçao Aérea Rio-Grandense (VARIG). Following its introduction to service in Oct75, it was used exclusively for the calibration of navigational aids at Norwegian airfields under contract to the government. It was flown initially with 'Luftfartsdirektoratet' titles but by 1978 these had been changed to 'Luftfartsverket'. A DHC-8-103 was ordered to replace it in this rôle early in 1995 although the 748 was still in service in late Sep95. The aircraft was disposed of in Aug96.

LN-FOM 1631

Fuerza Aérea Argentina

Buenos Aires, Argentina

The Fuerza Aérea Argentina ordered one Srs.2/221 as a VIP transport with delivery in Dec66. Later eight Srs.2/240s were ordered for the use of Líneas Aéreas del Estado - LADE but the order was cancelled. The initial VIP aircraft was sold in Sep78.

(LV-PGG)	1597	(TC-71)	1648	(TC-75)	1652
T-01	1597	(TC-72)	1649	(TC-76)	1653
T-02	1597	(TC-73)	1650	(TC-77)	1654
T-03	1597	(TC-74)	1651	(TC-78)	1655

Fuerza Aérea Colombiana (ZT/NSE)

Bogotá, Colombia

After the demonstration of a Srs.2A/227 by Hawker Siddeley in May69, the Fuerza Aérea Colombiana ordered four Srs.2A/260s all of which were delivered in Mar72. A Srs.2B/371 fitted with a large rear freight door was ordered later and delivered in Aug81. All aircraft were operated by Servicio de Aeronavegación a Territorios Nacionales - SATENA. This division of the Air Force operates essential services throughout Colombia with a varied fleet of aircraft. The 748s were employed on the more demanding routes over the Andes range from Bogotá to numerous

Fuerza Aérea Colombiana Series 2A FAC-1102 c/n 1703 in the livery of the Colombian military airline SATENA.   (J Roach collection)

points including Apiay, Arauca, Bahía Solano, Baranquilla, Bucaramanga, Buenaventura, Cali, Corozal, Cúcuta, El Yopal, Florencia, Ibagué, La Macarena, Maicao, Medellín, Neiva, Puerto Asis, Puerto Carreño, Quibdó, Riohacha, San José del Guaviare, San Vicente del Caguán, Tame, Tumaco, Turbo, Valledupar and Villavicencio on the eastern plains or within the Amazon basin. The last two operational aircraft were disposed of in Aug and Sep97.

FAC-1101	1702	FAC-1103	1704	FAC-1108	1776
FAC-1102	1703	FAC-1104	1705		

Fuerza Aérea Ecuatoriana (EQ/TAE)

Quito, Ecuador

The Fuerza Aérea Ecuatoriana (FAE) ordered two Srs.2A/246s and two Srs.2A/285s, the latter two fitted with large rear freight doors. A fifth aircraft, a Srs.2A/267, was ordered as a convertible VIP version for Presidential use when required. The first two aircraft were delivered in Oct70, the VIP version in Nov70 and the remaining two in Nov75 and Apr76. The first of four Srs.2A/281s fitted with Large Freight Doors was donated to the FAE by the Força Aérea Brasileira and was noted ready for

Fuerza Aérea Argentina 748 Series 2, T-01 c/n 1597, is seen here at Woodford in late 1966.   (WHC/BAe)

Above: The Fuerza Aérea Ecuatoriana Series 2A FAE 001/HC-AUK c/n 1684, which was ordered for VIP use and also carried the registration HC-AUK, which was usual for military transport aircraft in Ecuador which were used by the military airline TAME. (J Roach collection)

delivery in late Mar06. A fifth aircraft was obtained from the same source for spares use only. The fleet was operated by Escuadrón de Transporte 1112 of the Ala de Transporte No.11. The aircraft were operated earlier by the Transportes Aéreos Militares Ecuatorianos - TAME which was later named Transportes Aéreos Nacionales Ecuatorianos, then TA Mercantiles Ecuatorianos before finally becoming TAME - Línea Aérea del Ecuador. This military airline operates scheduled and charter flights. TAME used its 748s to operate to numerous destinations including Bahía de Caraquez, Coca, Cuenca, Esmeraldas, Guayaquil, Lago Agrio, Loja, Machala, Manta, Portoviejo, Quito, Tarapoa and Tulcan until the last aircraft was withdrawn from use on 07Aug14, when it was replaced by an Airbus Military CASA C295. The HS 748 had, by then, served the FAE for just short of forty-four years.

FAE 001	1684	FAE 740	1734	HC-AUE	1683
FAE 682	1682	FAE 741	1731	HC-AUK	1684
FAE 683	1683	FAE 742	1733	HC-BAZ	1738
FAE 684	1684	FAE 743	1729	HC-BEY	1739
FAE 738	1738	FAE 744	1730		
FAE 739	1739	HC-AUD	1682		

Fuerza Aérea Venezolana

The Fuerza Aérea Venezolana ordered one Srs.2/223 for the use of the Ministerio de la Defensa which was delivered in Aug66. In Oct77 a Srs.2/215 was obtained from Línea Aeropostal Venezolana but it was operated only for seven months.

0111	1591	6201	1578

Gabon Express (GEX/GBE)
Libreville, Gabon

Gabon Express commenced scheduled operations on 26Oct98 with an Andover C.Mk.1 in a 44-seat passenger configuration between Libreville and Port Gentil. This route was extended later to Gamba and new destinations of Oyem, Bitam and Franceville were added to the network later. A Srs.2A/206 was added in Oct99 and a Srs.2A/232 in Nov00. The Andover C.Mk.1 was disposed of in Oct02 and one of its 748s was written-off in Jun04

after which the company was grounded by the Gabonese Government on 15Jun04.

TR-LFW	1611	3C-KKP	1565	3D-BAE	1611
3C-CPX	Set 19				

GAMEC ( )
Luanda, Angola

GAMEC used an AirQuarius Air Charter (Pty) Ltd Srs.2B/FAA to operate ad hoc charter work from Apr00 to Feb01.

ZS-OJU   1782

Gateway Aviation Ltd (WG)
Edmonton, Alberta, Canada

This operator purchased one Srs.2A/257 from Transair Ltd in Apr72. It was used for charter flights to the Northwest Territories in support of the mining industries until the company was taken over by Northward Airlines Ltd in 1979.

CF-MAK   1668

GGG Aviation ( )
Arusha, Tanzania

This organisation took delivery of an ex-RAAF Srs.2/228 in Mar06. The aircraft was employed in running relief flights to Akot in Southern Sudan but had been sold by early Jun07 to Guinée Air Cargo.

3D-POZ   1602

Ghana Airways Corporation (GH/GHA)
Accra, Ghana

Ghana Airways ordered two Srs.2A/254s which were delivered in Dec70 and Jan71. The lease of a company demonstrator had been arranged earlier with Hawker Siddeley Aviation Ltd but was not proceeded with. The aircraft were used on a domestic network from Accra to Takoradi, Kumasi and Tamale until the last aircraft was disposed of in Mar81.

(9G-ABV)	1576	9G-ABW	1685	9G-ABX	1686

Ghana Airways Series 2A 9G-ABX c/n 1686, photographed pre-delivery on a test flight.   *(WHC)*

Guyana Airways Series 2A 8R-GEU c/n 1747, seen on a pre-delivery test flight. The airline used an attractive yellow and green livery at the time.   *(WHC)*

Goa Way Ltd ( )
Bombay, India

Two Srs.2B/378s were painted in this company's colour scheme in Aug93 for lease from Independent Airways (Leasing) Ltd. The deal was not completed and the aircraft were not delivered.

(VT-GOA) 1786   (VT-WAY) 1785

GPA Jet Prop Ltd

This leasing company purchased six Srs.2/209s from Philippine Airlines Inc in mid-1987 and leased them back to the same carrier until Fokker 50s replaced them during 1989.

RP-C1015 1637   RP-C1021 1642   RP-C1024 1660
RP-C1017 1639   RP-C1023 1659   RP-C1026 1664

Guinée Air Cargo SA (GJH)
Conakry, République de Guinée

By early Jun07 this company was operating a Srs.2/228 freighter, acquired from GGG Aviation.

3X-GEE   1602

Guyana Airways Corporation (GY/GYA)
Georgetown, Guyana

Guyana Airways ordered two Srs.2A/309s fitted with large rear freight doors. These were delivered in Mar and Jun77 and were used on a domestic network between Georgetown and Aishalton, Annai, Bemichi, Kamarang, Kato, Lethem, Lumid Pau and Matthews Ridge. Internationally they served Barbados, Port of Spain (Trinidad) and Boa Vista (Brazil). Charter work was also undertaken. The type was withdrawn from use in 1988.

8R-GEU 1747   8R-GEV 1748

Heliglobe Finet France Cargo (HGF)
Lyon, France

This company purchased two Srs.2A/263s in Aug91 for use in the cargo rôle. After operating ad hoc charter work, the last aircraft was withdrawn in Feb97.

F-GHKA 1680   F-GHKL 1677

Helitours
See Sri Lanka Air Force

Hering Aviation (Pty) Ltd
See AirQuarius (Pty) Ltd

Horizon Airlines Pty Ltd (YK,KH,BN/HZA)
Sydney-Bankstown, NSW, Australia

This company, initially a subsidiary of International Air Parts Pty Ltd, was known as International Aviation Pty Ltd until 10Dec98 and obtained two freight configured Srs.2B/287s in Oct96. The aircraft were fitted with large rear freight doors in Nov98 and Jul99 together with strengthened floors incorporating roller systems and a new 9G forward bulkhead. This enabled the carriage of standard LD3 containers for quick turnarounds. A weight and drag-reducing programme was also embodied. Two Srs.2B/426s were obtained early in 1999, one for spares use only, while the second was ferried to Bankstown in Jul00 and was operated in a 44-seat passenger configuration on ad hoc charter work.

Two Srs.2B/360s fitted with large rear freight doors were purchased from Air Madagascar in Jul01. These last two aircraft were converted to pure freighters after similar cabin work had been carried out as completed on the two Srs.2B/287s but only one had entered service by the time the company ceased operations.

The pure freighter aircraft were used for ad hoc charter work together with regular operations for both Australian air Express and Ansett Air Freight (until this company's demise on 14Sep01) while from 30Sep02 to 08Apr03 one 748 was based in Perth to operate regular four times weekly freight schedules to Karratha and Port Hedland on behalf of Air Cargo Express. Horizon Airlines was sold to new owners in April 2003 but was placed in Administration on 14Oct03 and the last of the 748s ceased flying on 24Oct03. All the 748s were leased from International Air Parts Pty Ltd and were returned subsequently to their owner.

VH-IMI   1736   VH-IMK   1737   VH-IPB   1773
VH-IMJ   1799   VH-IPA   1772

Ilford Riverton Airways Ltd
See Air Manitoba Ltd

Imperial Air Cargo (Pty) Ltd (FA/SFR)
Johannesburg, South Africa

Imperial Air Cargo commenced service on 01Aug06 operating cargo services within South Africa. The company is 70% owned by Safair (Pty) Ltd and 30% owned by Comair Ltd. A Stars Away Aviation (Pty) Ltd 748 freighter operated a five times weekly rotation between Johannesburg and Durban from 01Aug06.

ZS-DBM 1736

Impulse Airlines Pty Ltd (VQ/IPY & OAA)
Sydney, NSW, Australia

Impulse Airlines leased two Srs.2B/287s from BAe Asset Management with delivery in Oct and Nov94. The aircraft were operated in cargo configuration from Mar to Jul95 on newspaper contract flights from Sydney to Brisbane and Melbourne replacing Beech 1900Ds. They were handed over to Jetstream Aircraft Ltd in Jul95.

VH-IMI   1736   VH-IMK   1737

Horizon Airlines Series 2B VH-IMK c/n 1737 'The Beast' is seen at an unknown location in 1995. Note the additional 'Big Door' on the freight door fitted after cargo conversion.
(WHC)

Independent Airways Ltd ( )
Stansted, Essex, U.K.

Clewer Aviation Ltd reformed the failed British Independent Airways Ltd in this name with a Srs.1A/101 and a Srs.1A/106 with first operations taking place in Apr92. General charter work was undertaken until the last revenue flight took place on 30Aug92 after which the aircraft were sold.

G-ERMV 1537   G-MRRV 1549

Indian Air Force

The Indian Air Force ordered one Srs.1/103, three Srs.1/104s, six Srs.2/203s, six Srs.2/218s, seven Srs.2/219s, four Srs.2/220s, eighteen Srs.2/247s and finally three Srs.2/224s which had been ordered originally by Indian Airlines Corporation but not accepted. A further two batches of ten Srs.2Ms were ordered, these being fitted with large rear freight doors. All aircraft were produced locally on the Indian production line. The first aircraft was delivered in Apr64 and since then the type has been used in a variety of rôles. These have included VIP transport, navigation training, signals training, multi-engine pilot training, photographic survey and general transport for which the aircraft are fitted with either 48 or 49 seats. The last of the twenty Srs.2Ms was delivered in 1985 (the last of the Indian produced 748s to be taken on strength), after one of this order was diverted to the Indian Border Security Force prior to its handover. Eleven of the early production aircraft have been converted to Srs.2M standard with large rear freight doors, these being ten Srs.2/247s and one Srs.2/219. Approximately fifty 748s were reportedly still in service with the military in mid-2008 and the type is expected to remain in service until the year 2020 with updates by Hindustan Aeronautics Ltd. Two aircraft have been loaned to the DRDO and another is operated by the Aircraft & Systems Testing Establishment (ASTE). In 2012, India's Defence Ministry proposed to procure 56 tactical transport aircraft to replace their 748s, eventually deciding on the CASA295 in a contract valued at $1.87 billion. For details of individual Squadron use see the 'Licence Production in India' section in Chapter 1 (page 43).

BH572	500	BH-1011	507	H-914	516
BH573	501	BH-1012	508	H-915	517
BH574	502	BH-1013	509	H-1030	526
BH575	503	BH-1047	503	H-1031	527
BH576	504	BH-1048	504	H-1032	528
BH-1010	505	H-913	510	H-1033	529

H-1034	530	H-1520	558	H-2178	572
H-1175	531	H-1521	559	H-2179	573
H-1176	532	H-1522	560	H-2180	574
H-1177	533	H-1523	561	H-2181	575
H-1178	534	H-1524	562	H-2182	576
H-1179	535	H-1525	563	H-2183	577
H-1180	536	H-1526	564	H-2184	578
H-1181	537	H-1527	565	H-2372	579
H-1182	538	H-1528	566	H-2373	580
H-1386	539	H-1529	567	H-2374	581
H-1512	550	H-1530	568	H-2375	582
H-1513	551	H-2064	543	H-2376	583
H-1514	552	H-2065	544	H-2377	584
H-1515	553	H-2066	545	H-2378	585
H-1516	554	H-2175	569	H-2379	586
H-1517	555	H-2176	570	(H-2380)	587
H-1518	556	H-2177	571	H-2381	588
H-1519	557				

Indian Airlines Corporation (IC/IAC)
New Delhi, India

This airline leased an Indian Air Force Srs.2/203 from Jan to Nov65 for evaluation. It then ordered fifteen Hindustan Aeronautics Ltd built 44-seat Srs.2/224s, later reduced to fourteen. A further ten Srs.2/224s were ordered later of which only three were accepted. Delivery was made between Jun67 and Feb70 for the first order, the remaining three being delivered between Apr and Jun72. The company later leased a Srs.2/224 from the Civil Aviation Department from Feb78 to Sep80.

The first aircraft entered service on 08Aug67 operating out of Hyderabad. As aircraft were delivered they replaced DC-3s on routes radiating from the three other hubs of Bombay (Mumbai), Delhi and Madras (Chennai) to points including Agra, Ahmadabad, Allahabad, Aurangabad, Bangalore, Belgaum, Bhavnagar, Bhopal, Bhubaneshwar, Bhuj, Chandigarh, Cochin, Coimbatore, Dabolim, Goa, Gorakhpur, Gwalior, Indore, Jabalpur, Jaipur, Jamnagar, Jodhpur, Kandla, Keshod, Lucknow, Madurai, Mangalore, Nagpur, Porbandar, Pune, Raipur, Rajkot, Srinigar, Tiruchchirappalli, Tirupati, Trivandrum, Udaipur, Vadodara (Baroda), Varanasi, Vijayawada and Vishakhapatam. Internationally the type flew from Tiruchchirappalli and Trivandrum to Colombo in Sri Lanka. As airfields were improved

Below: An early Indian Air Force licence-built 748 Series 2 H-913 c/n HAL/K/510 in the VIP-passenger scheme coded 'A'.   (Simon Watson)

An Indian Airlines licence-built 748 Series 2, VT-DUO c/n HAL/K/506. The aircraft were originally flown with titles in English on the port side (as seen here) and Hindi on the starboard side. *(WHC/BAe)*

and traffic figures increased, the aircraft were replaced by Boeing 737 equipment and the type was transferred progressively to Vayudoot. In Apr89 the last of the type was transferred to Vayudoot together with a network of routes that could not support jet service. Vayudoot was merged into Indian Airlines Corporation with effect from 25May93, the transaction being completed in Mar94. The 748s were not returned to service after the merger was completed.

BH-1048	504	VT-DXM	520	(VT-EAW)	543
VT-DUO	506	VT-DXN	521	(VT-EAX)	544
VT-DXF	511	VT-DXO	522	(VT-EAY)	545
VT-DXG	512	VT-DXP	523	(VT-EAZ)	546
VT-DXH	513	VT-DXQ	524	(VT-EBA)	547
VT-DXI	514	VT-DXR	525	(VT-EBB)	548
VT-DXJ	515	VT-EAT	540	(VT-EBC)	549
VT-DXK	518	VT-EAU	541	VT-EFQ	546
VT-DXL	519	VT-EAV	542		

Indian Border Security Force
New Delhi, India

This organisation, a part of the Ministry of Home Affairs, ordered one Srs.2/224 from the cancelled Indian Airlines Corporation order with delivery in Mar82 while in Sep84 a Srs.2M was diverted from the Indian Air Force order. During 1991 two Srs.2/224s were obtained from Vayudoot with a fourth aircraft of the same type being delivered in 1994.

VT-DXH	513	VT-EAV	542	VT-EIR	587
VT-EAT	540	VT-EHL	549		

Indian National Airports Authority
New Delhi, India

Two Srs.2/224s from the cancelled Indian Airlines Corporation order were ordered by the Director General of Civil Aviation for use in the airfield calibration rôle. The aircraft were delivered in Feb and Sep78, the first aircraft immediately going on lease to Indian Airlines Corporation until Sep80. The two aircraft were operated by the Flight Inspection Unit of the renamed body shown above, but are believed to have been withdrawn at Delhi for some years.

VT-EFQ	546	VT-EFR	547

Indian National Remote Sensing Agency
Hyderabad, India

This organisation ordered one Srs.2/224 from the cancelled Indian Airlines Corporation order with delivery in Oct77. The aircraft, which was operated on this organisation's behalf by Airworks India Engineering Pvt Ltd, was used in the survey rôle, but is now believed to be withdrawn from use.

VT-EFN	548

Inexco Oil
Canada

Inexco Oil purchased a Srs.2/232 from BOAC Associated Companies Ltd in Feb73. This was converted into a Srs.2A/232 and entered service the following month carrying both personnel and equipment to northern points in Canada. The aircraft was leased in Botswana from Mar to Oct74 prior to its sale in Feb75.

CF-INE	1611

Intensive Air (Pty) Ltd (IM/XRA)
Johannesburg, South Africa

Intensive Air purchased a Srs.2A/351 in Nov93, a Srs.2A/236 with a large rear freight door in Sep96 and a Srs.2A/344 in Oct97 for ad hoc charter work. By Apr98 the company was operating a scheduled service between Johannesburg and Margate. Services were flown on behalf of several African operators including Air Botswana and Air Malawi. The company ceased operations on 08Apr02 and the aircraft were sold to International Air Parts Pty Ltd of Australia.

ZS-XGE	1770	ZS-XGY	1764	ZS-XGZ	1740

Inter City Airways Series 2 C-GLTC c/n 1656 photographed at Oshawa, Ontario, on 16th March 1986.   *(Fred Barnes collection)*

Inter City Airways Inc (5C)
Oshawa, Ontario, Canada

Inter City Airways bought two Srs.2/244s which had seen service previously with Bundesanstalt für Flugsicherung (BFS) with delivery in Mar and Jun86. After extensive modifications from its earlier calibration rôle, the first 748 entered service on 07Apr86. The aircraft still retained their original Rolls-Royce Dart RDa.8 engines and as such were the first 748s to be operated commercially with this mark of engine installed. By 08Jul86 schedules were flown from Oshawa to Montréal-Dorval (3 times daily, Monday to Friday), Ottawa (twice daily, Monday to Friday) and Windsor (4 times daily, Monday to Friday) while the aircraft were used additionally on a much reduced scheduled programme at weekends together with charter work. An Oshawa to Buffalo schedule was due to be operated at a later date but the airline ceased trading on 04Oct86 following the withdrawal of reservations facilities two days earlier by Canadian Pacific Air Lines Ltd after a rift between the two carriers. This reduced loads to an unacceptable level. The carrier, which had been identified previously as the possible user of a British Aerospace Inc-owned Srs.2B/FAA in a deal which was not concluded, was declared bankrupt and went into receivership on 11Oct86.

C-GEGJ   1711   C-GLTC   1656   (C-GRXE)   1783

International Aviation Pty Ltd
See Horizon Airlines Pty Ltd

International Air Parts Pty Ltd
Sydney, Australia

This company specialises in providing spares for worldwide distribution for various aircraft types including the 748. The company has purchased several aircraft for reduction to spares including eight of the former Vayudoot fleet of HAL-built Srs.2/224s in Oct96, a former TACV Srs.2A/278 in Sep97, a damaged Srs.2B/426 from Nepal in 1999, a Srs.2/228 from the RAAF in Jan01 and a Philippines Government Srs.2/209 in Mar02. Two former Australian military 748s were also obtained for possible use, though the Srs.2/228 was loaned to a museum at

Sydney-Bankstown where it remained in store until it replaced the Srs.2/228 at the Bankstown Museum in May04. The Srs.2/228 was broken-up subsequently. The company also purchased the three-strong fleet of Intensive Air (Pty) Ltd in 2002 of which the Srs.2A/286 with a Large Freight Door and the Srs.2A/351 were converted to pure freighters for remarketing. These were leased to Trackmark Cargo of Kenya in Oct04 and Best Aviation of Bangladesh in Mar05 respectively. The remaining Srs.2A/344 is expected to be reduced to spares. The company has also specialised in purchasing written-off aircraft for recovery of their large cargo doors for future fitting in active 748s. These have been obtained in the Bahamas, Canada, Nepal and Tanzania.

The company also set up its own airline subsidiary in the shape of International Aviation Pty Ltd/Horizon Airlines Pty Ltd in 1996 to operate company-owned 748s, though it and the engineering base at Bankstown were sold to new owners in Apr03. The airline was short-lived with its new owners and collapsed in Oct03 being later sold on to Macair Airlines Pty Ltd. Macair were not interested in the 748 operations and the aircraft were returned to International Air Parts at Bankstown. The engineering base and hangar were bought back by International Air Parts in mid-Mar04. The active aircraft comprised two freighter-configured Srs.2B/287s which were fitted with Large Freight Doors at the company's base in Nov98 and Jul99, two Srs.2B/360s fitted with Large Freight Doors and a passenger-configured Srs.2B/426. Details can be found under Horizon Airlines Pty Ltd.

The list below excludes aircraft that were only purchased for reduction to spares. The Srs.2B/426 was lease/purchased by Aero Lanka Airlines (Pvt) Ltd in Sep04, the Srs.2B/361 was leased to Z-Airways and Service Limited of Bangladesh from Dec04 until Oct08 and the Srs.2B/287s were sold to Stars Away Aviation of South Africa in Mar05 and Mar06. The company's last 748, a Srs.2B/360, was sold to Trackmark Cargo Ltd of Kenya in Jul06. In Sep06 International Air Parts merged with Pacific Turbine Brisbane Pty Ltd but the two companies continue to operate independently of each other. On 16Oct06 International Air Parts purchased Emerald Airways Ltd in the UK which included their fleet of fifteen freight configured 748s with the intention of marketing these worldwide through subsidiary company, PTB (Emerald) Pty Ltd. These aircraft comprised a Srs.1/105, a Srs.2A/225, 3 Srs.2A/242s, a Srs.2A/263, 2 Srs.2A/266s (one with an LFD), 2 Srs.2A/270s, a Srs.2A/275, a Srs.2A/344, 2 Srs.2A/347s and a

Srs.2A/372. Of these one Srs.2A/270 and the Srs.2A/275 were sold to Janes Aviation, the two Srs.2A/347s were sold to Bismillah Airlines and Easy Fly Express, one Srs.2A/242 was sold to Best Aviation and a Srs.2A/266 was sold to Elysian Airlines of Guinea. The company later purchased a Srs.2A/209 from Airfast Services Indonesia PT and a damaged Srs.2A/245 for spares only in Jan07. The remainder of the ex-Emerald 748 fleet was broken up for spares.

G-ATMJ	1593	G-ORAL	1756	(VH-IMJ)	1720
G-AYIM	1687	G-ORCP	1647	VH-IMJ	1799
G-BEJD	1543	G-OSOE	1697	VH-IMK	1737
G-BGMN	1766	G-OTBA	1712	VH-IPA	1772
G-BGMO	1767	G-SOEI	1689	VH-IPB	1773
G-BIUV	1701	N339C	1720	ZS-XGE	1770
G-BPNJ	1680	PK-OBQ	1638	ZS-XGY	1764
G-BVOU	1721	S2-ADL	1773	ZS-XGZ	1740
G-BVOV	1777	VH-IMG	1604	3C-QQP	1709
G-OPFW	1714	VH-IMI	1736	4R-SER	1799

International Red Cross Organisation

The IRC leased one Srs.2A/242 from Mount Cook Airlines Ltd for use in Thailand and Kampuchea from Jun81 to Aug82.

ZK-MCA 1712

International Skyways Ltd

See Skyways Coach Air Ltd

International Trans Air Business – ITAB (WQ9)

Lubumbashi, Democratic Republic of Congo

This company had obtained its first Srs.2A/206 by Jun98. It had earlier taken delivery of three Andovers (two C.Mk.1s and an Mk.3A) in Apr95, Nov96 and Apr97 respectively. An E.Mk.3 was taken on strength in Feb99 and two C.Mk.1s in May and June. Later marketed as Air Katanga, the company operated passenger

and cargo flights throughout southern and central Africa. It would appear that the company reverted to the ITAB name in late 2004 and still had the Srs.2 /206 and three active Andover C.Mk.1s in mid-Jun05 though one of these was sold later in the same year.

9Q-CJJ	Set 21	9Q-COE	Set 20	9Q-CVC	Set 29
9Q-CLL	Set 21	9Q-COE	Set 28	9Q-CYB	Set 22
9Q-CLL	1561	9Q-CVC	Set 24		

Island Aviation Services Ltd (Q2/DQA)

Male, Maldives

This company leased a Srs.2B/501 from Executive Aerospace (Pty) Ltd to carry out inter-island schedules from mid-July to early September 2004 linking Male with Gan Island, Hanimaadhoo, Kaadedhdoo and Kadhdhoo.

4R-LPV 1807

Ivoirienne de Transports Aériens – ITA (ITA)

Abidjan, Côte d'Ivoire

Leased a Srs.2B/246 from late Dec11 for sub-lease to East Horizon Airlines of Afghanistan.

TU-PAD 1799

Jamaica Air Services (1967) Ltd (JT)

Kingston, Jamaica

Jamaica Air Services leased one Srs.2/225 from Autair International Airways Ltd from Jan68 to Apr69. The aircraft was used on routes between Kingston, Montego Bay, Ocho Rios and Port Antonio.

6Y-JFJ 1593

ITAB Andover 9Q-CVC Set 29 photographed at Manono, Democratic Republic of Congo, on 18th June 2005. (Jérôme Cassart)

Jambo Air Lines Ltd ( )
Bauchi, Nigeria

Jambo Airlines purchased one used Srs.2A/310 fitted with a large rear freight door from the manufacturer at the end of Dec86. It was flown to Exeter for storage at the beginning of Oct87 before being leased to British Aerospace for sub-lease to Ligações Aéreas Regionais SA from Apr88 to Apr90. The aircraft was not flown by Jambo Airlines again.

CS-TAU   1750   5N-ARJ   1750

Janes Aviation Ltd (JAN)
Southend, Essex, UK

For the original Janes Aviation Ltd see Emerald Airways Ltd. The new company had its AOC issued on 25Apr08 and commenced operations in Jul08 with a Srs.2A/270 and a Srs.2A/275, both freighters, formerly operated by Emerald Airways Ltd after their type 'A' Operating Licence was issued on 28Apr08. Very little flying took place and the aircraft were stored at Southend from February and Mar09.

G-AYIM   1687   G-OSOE   1697

Jersey European Airways Ltd (JY/JEA)
Exeter, Devon, UK

Jersey European Airways leased two Srs.2A/347s and a Srs.2A/266 from Euroair Transport Ltd with delivery in late Oct89, early Dec89 and early Apr90. The type was introduced onto scheduled services from Blackpool to the Isle of Man and Belfast Harbour on 14Nov89 and later from Jersey to Bournemouth, Dinard, Exeter, Paris, Southampton and Stansted. With effect from 17Nov89 services were also flown on behalf of Manx Airlines Ltd from the Isle of Man to Belfast Harbour, Dublin and Blackpool, the Dublin route being dropped at the start of the summer schedules 1990. Fokker Friendship 500s replaced the HS748s with effect from 08Sep90 on this Manx contract. With effect from 24Sep90 and 02Jan91 aircraft were based in Glasgow and Edinburgh respectively to cover mail flights to East Midlands and Manchester. These contracts continued until 05Oct91 at Edinburgh and 02Nov91 at Glasgow when the last of the aircraft was returned to the lessor.

G-BGMN   1766   G-BGMO   1767   G-BMFT   1714

Jeshi la Wananchi la Tanzani – JWTZ ( )
See Tanzanian Peoples' Defence Force.

Kalanga Air Services ( )
Congo Brazzaville

This company leased a Srs.2B/378 from Executive Aerospace (Pty) Ltd from mid-May to early Jul05.

ZS-PLO   1797

Kalt, NA
San Antonio, Texas, USA

NA Kalt purchased one Srs.2/244 from Bundesanstalt für Flugsicherung (BFS) in 1984. It was disposed of in Mar86 reportedly without being used.

N57910   1656

Kamaria Air, SARL ( )
Moroni, Grande Comore, Comoros Islands

The Srs.2A/232 was noted fully-painted at Johannesburg-Rand in Feb99, but by Apr99 was operating with Air Éspace titles at Pointe Noire, Congo Brazzaville.

9L-LBH   1611

Kel Air (CEETA - Compagnie Européenne d'Exploitation et de Transports Aériens Kel Air) (CET)
Nice-Côte d'Azur, France

Kel Air leased a Srs.2A/264 from Transvalair in late Oct88 and two Srs.2A/263s from Guide Leasing Ltd at the end of Mar and the end of Jun89. These last two aircraft were purchased outright in Jun89.

The company commenced operations on 22Dec88 with regional passenger schedules on behalf of both Air Inter and Touraine Air Transport. A nightly newspaper freight contract was flown on behalf of *Nice-Matin* between Nice and Corsica. The initial TAT contract was for a Lyons to Mulhouse service while a twice-daily service was operated between Metz and Paris-Orly by Oct89. The company ceased operations on 14Jun90.

F-GFYM   1717   F-GHKA   1680   F-GHKL   1677

Below: Kel Air Series 2A F-GHKL c/n 1677 in a photograph taken in 1989/90.   (WHC)

LIAT Series 2 VP-LIK c/n 1583 photographed in the original livery carried by the airline's 748s in the 1960s.　　　*(WHC/BAe)*

V Kelner Airways Ltd
See Wasaya Airways Ltd

LADE
See Fuerza Aérea Argentina

LAN - Chile
See Línea Aérea Nacional de Chile

L'Armée de l'Air du Cameroun

The Cameroon Government ordered 2 Srs.2A/310s fitted with large rear freight doors with delivery in Sep77 for the use of the L'Armée de l'Air du Cameroun. They were sold to Cameroon Airlines in Feb82.

TJ-AAN	1749	TJ-XAF	1749	TJ-XAH	1750
TJ-AAO	1750				

LAR - Transregional
See Linhas Aéreas Regionais SA

LAV
See Línea Aeropostal Venezolana

LBC Express Airways Inc ( )
Manila, Philippines

LBC Airways purchased three ex-Philippine Airlines Inc Srs.2/209s, two in May and one in Sep89 to operate cargo services. One was written-off in Jun91, one was sold in Oct95, and the other aircraft had its Certificate of Airworthiness expire in Oct97.

RP-C1017	1639	RP-C1023	1659	RP-C1024	1660

Leeward Islands Air Transport Services Ltd
(LI/LIA)
St. Johns, Antigua

LIAT ordered three Srs.2/217s after leasing a Srs.1/101 from Skyways Coach Air Ltd from Jan to May65 when the first new aircraft was delivered. A Srs.2/222 was leased from Channel Airways Ltd from Dec65 to May66. This aircraft was replaced by a Srs.1/200 leased from Hawker Siddeley Aviation Ltd from Apr to Aug66 when the second new aircraft was delivered. A Srs.2/225 was leased from Autair International Airways Ltd to cope with the peak traffic period from Nov67 to May68. The first of two Srs.2/222s bought from Channel Airways Ltd was delivered in May68, the second following a month later. The third new Srs.2/217 was delivered in Oct69. A Srs.2/225 was leased from Court Line Aviation Ltd from Dec69 to Apr70 and again from Dec70 to Mar71 before it was purchased outright in Dec71. A second aircraft of the same mark was leased from Court Line Aviation Ltd from Nov71 to Apr72.

Following the collapse of the Court Line Group, which had taken over the 75% British West Indian Airways Ltd holding in the company during 1971, Leeward Islands Air Transport Services Ltd ceased operations on 15Aug74. The airline and aircraft were taken over by the governments of the islands served and a new company was formed on 20Sep74 named LIAT (1974) Ltd. The new company ordered a Srs.2A/343 fitted with a large rear freight door which was delivered in Dec78, this following a short lease of a Srs.2/215 from Línea Aeropostal Venezolana from Aug to Nov77. A Srs.2A/334 was leased from Trinidad & Tobago (BWIA International) Airways Corporation from Nov80 to Jun82. Late in 1984 the airline ordered four Srs.2B/424s, the first Super 748s ordered, under a lease/purchase agreement with delivery of the first two in Dec84, the third in May and the fourth in Jun85. These new aircraft replaced older Series 2 aircraft, one of which was the lead 748 aircraft for landings recorded of almost 75,000 at that time. Some older 748s were traded to British Aerospace as part of the new aircraft deal and were leased back immediately for varying periods of time. A Srs.2B/FAA was leased from British Aerospace Inc for two weeks in late Nov and early Dec85 while one of the Super 748s was demonstrated in Ecuador. Yet further leases were a Srs.2A/347 from Trinidad & Tobago (BWIA

LAN-Chile Series 2 CC-CEC c/n 1614 at Woodford prior to delivery in 1967.   *(WHC)*

International) Airways Corporation from mid-Dec85 to mid-Jan86, a Srs.2B/378 from British Aerospace plc from late Dec88 to Feb91 and a Srs.2A/221 from Air Creebec Inc from Jan to Jun91.

The original company performed its inaugural 748 revenue service out of Antigua on 01Feb65. From this time the 748 was the largest aircraft and the mainstay of the airline, apart from the expansionist policy pursued for a short while during Court Line control when BAC One-Eleven 500s were employed on an expanded route structure. The 748s were used throughout the Leeward and Windward chain of islands northwards to St Thomas and St Croix in the US Virgin Islands, Beef Island in the British Virgin Islands and San Juan in Puerto Rico (with effect from 01Dec67).

During the summer of 1967 services were flown on behalf of BWIA twice daily over the route Antigua to St Thomas via St Kitts and return, while in the summer of 1968 the aircraft flew fourteen services a week between Port of Spain and Tobago on behalf of Trinidad & Tobago (BWIA International) Airways Corporation. Most southerly point served was Port of Spain, Trinidad until the summer of 1985 when service was started to Caracas from Bridgetown. Georgetown, Guyana was an added destination twice weekly from Bridgetown from 1988. Tobago was added to the network again with effect from 01Nov90 with daily flights operating from Bridgetown via this point to Port of Spain. The two main hubs of the operation were Antigua and Bridgetown, with additional points served by the 748s over the years including Dominica, Grenada, Montserrat, St Kitts, St Lucia, St Vincent, Tobago, Fort de France (Martinique), Pointe-á-Pitre (Guadeloupe) and St Maarten (Netherlands Antilles). The last of the fleet was retired early in 1995.

C-GQWO	1597	VP-LIP	1584	V2-LCS	1802
VP-LAA	1670	VP-LIU	1592	V2-LCT	1803
VP-LAJ	1593	VP-LIV	1588	V2-LDA	1783
VP-LAX	1581	VP-LIW	1585	V2-LDB	1767
VP-LAZ	1762	V2-LAA	1670	V2-LDK	1791
VP-LCG	1757	V2-LAZ	1762	V2-LIK	1583
VP-LII	1537	V2-LCG	1757	V2-LIP	1584
VP-LIK	1583	V2-LCQ	1800	V2-LIV	1588
VP-LIN	1586	V2-LCR	1801	(9Y-TDH)	1670
VP-LIO	1535				

Les Ailes du Nord Ltée/Northern Wings Ltd (WS)
Sept Îles, Québec, Canada

This company's first 748, a Srs.2A/276, was purchased from another Québecair subsidiary named Air Gaspé Inc in May75. In Aug79 a Srs.2A/230 was bought from Aerovías Caribe SA, while in Jan81 Austin Airways Ltd sold them a Srs.2A/215. In mid-1981 the company's aircraft and operations were merged into a new Québecair subsidiary named Regionair (1981) Inc. The airline operated scheduled routes to many points within Québec from its home base.

CF-AGI	1699	C-GAPC	1599	C-GDOV	1582
C-FAGI	1699				

Lesotho Airways Corporation (QL/LAI)
Maseru, Lesotho

Lesotho leased a Srs.2A/266 from Zambia Airways Corporation Ltd from mid-Aug to early Nov88 while their Fokker Friendship underwent maintenance. The aircraft flew schedules to Johannesburg, Gaborone and Harare from Maseru and was sub-leased to Air Botswana (Pty) Ltd for services between Johannesburg and Gaborone.

9J-ABK   1677

LIAT (1974) Ltd
See Leeward Islands Air Transport Services Ltd

Ligações Aéreas Regionais SA
See Linhas Aéreas Regionais SA

Línea Aérea Nacional de Chile SA - LAN Chile (LA/LAN)
Santiago, Chile

LAN Chile ordered nine Srs.2/234s, one of which was delivered as a convertible VIP version for Presidential use when required.

Delivery took place between Jul67 and Jun69 and the type entered commercial service on 01Sep67. The aircraft were used on an extensive domestic network from Arica in the extreme north to Puerto Williams in the extreme south of the country. Internationally the aircraft served Río Gallegos and San Carlos de Bariloche in Argentina from Punta Arenas and Puerto Montt respectively. Additional domestic points served included Antofagasta, Balmaceda, Calama, Chañaral, Concepción, Copiapó, Iquique, La Serena, Los Angeles, Osorno, San Carlos, Santiago, Taltal, Temuco, Tocopilla, Valdivia and Vallenar. The last service took place on 02Jun79 with the aircraft being disposed of between Feb78 and Jun79. One aircraft was leased to AVIANCA in 1974/5.

CC-CEC	1614	CC-CEF	1617	CC-CEI	1620
CC-CED	1615	CC-CEG	1618	CC-CEJ	1621
CC-CEE	1616	CC-CEH	1619	CC-CEK	1622

Línea Aeropostal Venezolana - LAV (LV/LAV)
Caracas, Venezuela

LAV ordered six Srs.2A/215s with delivery taking place between May65 and May66 following the lease of the second prototype from the manufacturer between Feb and Jul65. Two Srs.2A/283s were ordered later with delivery in Nov76. The aircraft were employed on a domestic network which included Acarigua, Barcelona, Barinas, Barquisimeto, Caracas, Carúpano, Coro, Cumaná, Guanare, Las Piedras, Maracaibo, Maturin, Mérida, Porlamar, Puerto Ayacucho, San Fernando, Santa Barbara Zulia and Valera. Regional services were also flown to Curacao, Georgetown in Guyana and Port of Spain in Trinidad. The last of the fleet was disposed of in Apr81. The airline was generally marketed as 'Aeropostal'.

YV-C-AMC	1535	YV-C-AMY	1580	YV-08C	1582
YV-C-AMC	1582	YV-04C	1577	(YV-09C)	1744
YV-C-AME	1577	YV-05C	1578	(YV-10C)	1745
YV-C-AMF	1581	YV-06C	1579	YV-45C	1744
YV-C-AMI	1578	YV-07C	1581	YV-46C	1745
YV-C-AMO	1579				

Líneas Aéreas Alaire SL
See ALAIRE - Líneas Aéreas Alaire SL

Líneas Aéreas del Estado - LADE
See Fuerza Aérea Argentina

Linhas Aéreas da Guiné-Bissau
See Transportes Aéreos da Guiné-Bissau

Linhas Aéreas Regionais SA (TH,TP/PDF)
Lisbon, Portugal

This company, which was known as Ligações Aéreas Regionais, SA until 30Dec88, leased five aircraft from British Aerospace plc, two Srs.2A/270s from Apr88 to Jun90, a Srs.2A/310 fitted with a large rear freight door from Apr88 to Apr90, a Srs.2 /222 from mid Sep to mid-Dec88 and a Srs.2A/372 from Oct89 to mid-Jun90. The type entered service on 16Apr88 operating schedules on behalf of Air Portugal from Lisbon to Faro and Oporto while an aircraft was based in Funchal to operate a four times daily schedule to Porto Santo from 01Jul88 to Jun90. From 01Jan90 all flights operated from the mainland of Portugal were operated in the company's own name and marketed as LAR Transregional. The last of the type was withdrawn in Jun90 after replacement by British Aerospace ATPs.

CS-TAG	1687	CS-TAO	1777	CS-TAV	1588
CS-TAH	1721	CS-TAU	1750		

Lion Air (Pvt) Ltd (LEO)
Ratmalana Airport, Colombo, Sri Lanka

Lion Air leased a Srs.2B/501 from Executive Aerospace (Pty) Ltd from early Sep02. It commenced a daily schedule between Ratmalana and Jaffna-Palaly on 26Sep02 which was increased later to twice-daily. From 02Jan03 frequency was increased to

Línea Aeropostal Venezolana Series 2 YV-C-AMF c/n 1581 'Aeropostal', at Mérida, Venezuela, showing the early-style of Venezuelan registration used by the airline.
(WHC/BAe)

three times per day. Additional weekend schedules were due to commence from Colombo to Trincomalee in May04 and to Trivandrum and Tiruchirapalli in India from Jun04 but the aircraft had been returned to its owners by Jul04.

4R-AGB 1807   4R-LPV 1807

London European Airways Ltd (UQ)
Luton, Bedfordshire, UK

A Srs.1A/106 was transferred to this airline by its parent company, Ryanair Ltd, in Jan90. In Mar90 the aircraft was leased to British Independent Airways Ltd, never having been used by London European.

G-ARRW 1549

Macavia International Inc
Santa Rosa, California, USA

This company marketed an updated 748 aircraft that it called the 'Macavia BAe 748 Turbine Tanker'. It could be used in a variety of rôles including water bombing, casualty evacuation, cargo, mixed passenger/cargo or in all-passenger configuration. The aircraft was fitted with a quickly removable tank system when used in the fire-fighting rôle that was bolted to the underbelly through twelve permanent hard points. This unit comprised eight compartments of 250 US gallons capacity each together with a 108 US gallon foam concentrate tank. The mix of foam and water, door sequencing and rate of flow were all computer-controlled. In the cargo rôle, the aircraft was fitted with a roller conveyor system and could be fitted with a hoist and winch for ease and speed of loading. In the casualty evacuation rôle the aircraft could carry 24 stretcher cases with their attendants. Any further conversions would have been fitted with a large rear freight door, although the prototype was not so fitted.

The first conversion, a Srs.2A/227 previously operated by Canadian Pacific Air Lines Ltd, first flew with the tank attached on 04Sep87 from Cranfield in Bedfordshire, UK. Cranfield Aeronautical Services, the engineering arm of the Cranfield Institute of Technology, had converted this aircraft. The aircraft is known to have flown in southern France in its fire-fighting rôle for at least one season but is believed to have been in storage since then.

G-BNJK 1594

Maersk Air I/S (DM/DAN)
Copenhagen, Denmark

Maersk Air inherited the second prototype 748 when the airline took over Falcks Flyvetjeneste A/S in Nov69. In Jan and Feb70 the company leased a Srs.2A/214 from the manufacturer while three Srs.2A/234s were leased from Austin Airways Ltd over a period from Jun80 to Jul81. The aircraft operated scheduled routes linking Copenhagen with Billund, Esbjerg, Odense, Skrydstrup, Stauning and Thisted.

OY-APT 1621   OY-DFV 1535   OY-MBY 1618
OY-DFS 1576   OY-MBH 1617

Magnum Airlines Ltd (LE)
Johannesburg, South Africa

For one week from 01-07Feb82 this operator leased Srs.2A/272s from South African Airways to operate services between Margate and Johannesburg. All three aircraft were used at some time during this period.

ZS-SBU 1690   ZS-SBV 1692   ZS-SBW 1691

Makung International Airways Co Ltd (B7/UIA)
Kaoshiung, Taiwan

Makung International Airways ordered two Srs.2B/501s with delivery in Dec88 and Feb89. The aircraft were used on schedules between Makung, Taipei, Tainan, Kaoshiung and Chiayi. The company's name was changed to Uni Air on 31Mar96. The type was withdrawn in Dec97 and the aircraft were sold in Nepal.

B-1771 1806   B-1773 1807

Mandala Airlines PT (YM/MDL)
Jakarta, Indonesia

Mandala Airlines purchased a Srs.2/232 from BOAC Associated Companies Ltd in Jun71. For a while following the merger with Seulawah Air Services PT, the company was known as Seulawah-Mandala Airlines PT but later reverted to the former name. The aircraft was employed on a scheduled domestic network linking Ambon, Gorontalo, Kendari, Manado, Palu, Surabaya and Ujung Pandang until it was written off in Oct77.

PK-RHQ 1610   PK-RHS 1610

Manx Airlines Ltd (JE/MNX)
Isle of Man, UK

Jersey European Airways Ltd HS748s were used to operate Monday to Friday schedules on a once-daily basis in each direction between the Isle of Man and Blackpool and Belfast Harbour from 17Nov89 to 07Sep90 and also on the Isle of Man to Dublin route over the following initial winter period.

G-BGMN 1766   G-BGMO 1767   G-BMFT 1714

Merpati Nusantara Airlines PT (MZ/MNA)
Jakarta, Indonesia

This airline ordered two Srs.2A/274s previously having leased a Srs.2A/239 from the manufacturer from Jan to Jun71. In Jun71 the first of the new aircraft was delivered on lease until it was purchased in Dec of the same year. At the same time the second aircraft was handed over. The aircraft were used on domestic schedules mainly in the Java chain of islands. From Surabaya and Jakarta schedules were flown to points including Balikpapan, Banjarmasin, Denpasar, Kupang, Maumere, Palambang, Palangkaraya, Palu, Pangkalpinang, Pontianak, Semarang, Tarakan, Telukbetung, Ujung Pandang and Waingapu. The aircraft were advertised for sale in Nov92 and broken-up at Surabaya in 1999.

G-AVRR 1635   PK-MHD 1695   PK-MHR 1696
G-AZAE 1695   PK-MHM 1695

Midwest Aviation Ltd (UW)
Winnipeg, Manitoba, Canada

Midwest Aviation ordered one Srs.2A/257 with delivery in Jul69 previously having bought a Srs.2/222 from Channel Airways Ltd in Dec67. The airline and aircraft were taken over by Transair Ltd in 1969.

CF-MAK 1668   CF-MAL 1587

Ministry of Technology
See Defence Research Agency

Maersk Air Series 2A OY-MBY c/n 1618 photographed in the airline's full livery with light blue cabin roof and fin plus white star.

Series 2B G-BPEP c/n 1806 awaiting delivery to Makung Airlines in late 1988. This aircraft was the penultimate 748 to be completed and would become B-1771 on arrival in Taiwan.
(WHC/BAe)

Merpati Nusantara Airlines Series 2A PK-MHD c/n 1695 photographed in April 1971. It would later be leased to them as G-AZAE before becoming PK-MHM in December 1971.
(WHC/BAe)

MK Airlines Ltd (7G/MKA)
Accra, Ghana

MK Airlines obtained a Srs.2B/287 pure freighter with a Large Freight Door in May09 believed for use in providing feeder services to the company's long-haul cargo services. It was returned to the owner by early Sep09.

9G-MKV 1736

Mmabatho Air Services (Pty) Ltd
See Bop-Air (Pty) Ltd

Mount Cook Airline/Airlines (NM,ZK/NZM)
Christchurch, New Zealand

Mount Cook Airline/Airlines ordered one Srs.2/242 and two Srs.2A/242s with delivery in Sep68, Jul71 and Sep73. In Sep76 the airline took delivery of a Srs.2A/275 that had remained in store with the manufacturer for nearly three years at the request of the original buyer, Dakota and South Bend Securities. An Air Pacific Srs.2A/233 was bought in Oct79 while a Srs.2A/266 was leased from Polynesian Airlines Ltd from Jun to Oct82. A Srs.2A/273 was obtained from Royal Brunei Airlines in May84 while a Srs.2A/347 was leased from Euroair Transport Ltd from Dec93 until Feb96. The last 748 to be taken on strength was a

Mount Cook Airlines Series 2A ZK-CWJ c/n 1647 and ZK-DES c/n 1689 in the original livery, probably at the Mount Cook airfield, South Island, New Zealand.   *(Fred Barnes/Mount Cook Airlines)*

A later Mount Cook Airlines livery is seen on Series 2A ZK-MCA c/n 1712 and ZK-CWJ c/n 1647 with the airline marketed as 'Mount Cook Line'. The scene was photographed at Christchurch, probably in the 1980s.

Srs.2B/378, the company's first and only Series 2B to have been operated, leased from Clewer Aviation that entered service on 01Jul95. This last lease ended in Dec95.

The type was introduced into scheduled service on the Christchurch to Queenstown via Mount Cook route in Oct68. It was also flown on behalf of Air New Zealand in the early days over the Christchurch-Timaru-Oamaru route twice daily. Christchurch-Rotorua was added to the network in Oct70 with an extension to Auckland the year after. An Auckland-Kerikeri route was added in Oct76. By Oct84 direct flights were flown between Rotorua and Mount Cook while frequencies on the existing routes had been increased. In Oct87 the network was expanded to include a twice-daily service to Nelson from Christchurch and an additional service to Rotorua via Wellington and Taupo.

In 1988 a four times daily schedule was introduced between Nelson and Wellington together with a third daily frequency between Nelson and Christchurch. On 01Nov90 service was started to Chatham Island from Wellington and Christchurch on temporary authority following the demise of SAFE Air. This authority was later made permanent. From Apr92 a Christchurch-Palmerston North schedule was started up to three times daily and the Queenstown route was extended to Te Anau on a daily basis.

The type was withdrawn progressively from Nov95 as a newly ordered fleet of ATR-72s was delivered. The company's final commercial 748 flight took place on 12Feb96 when ZK-MCF flew from Wellington to Christchurch was flown by Captains Peter Banks and Alister McLeod, the latter having been in command on the inaugural Mount Cook 748 service in Oct68. The airline specialised in leasing out its aircraft worldwide with their 748s seeing service in the Azores, Canada, Fiji, Kampuchea, the Marshall Islands, Tonga, Western Samoa and the United Kingdom. The airline became a wholly-owned subsidiary of Air New Zealand on 01Apr91. Mount Cook's last owned 748, which was leased to Royal Tongan Airlines Ltd, was finally sold to Clewer Aviation Ltd in early 1999 for continued operation in Tonga.

ZK-CWJ	1647	ZK-MCB	1767	ZK-MCJ	1661
ZK-DES	1689	ZK-MCF	1697	ZK-MCP	1694
ZK-MCA	1712	ZK-MCH	1791	5W-FAO	1714

National Airways Corporation (Pty) Ltd ( )
Johannesburg, South Africa

A company demonstrator was evaluated during Dec69.

ZS-IGI   1635

Necon Air Ltd (3Z/NEC)
Kathmandu, Nepal

This airline obtained its first used aircraft, a Srs.1A/101 and a Srs.1A/106, with delivery in Sep and Nov92. These were followed by a Srs.2A/256 in May93 and the first of two Srs.2B/378s in Oct94. The second of the last-named was not accepted but leased to Mount Cook Airline by Clewer Aviation from Jun95. Two Srs.2B/501s were obtained in Nov and Dec97. The type was used to operate scheduled services throughout Nepal from its introduction to service on 14Sep92 and flew from Kathmandu to Bhadrapur, Bhairawa, Biratnagar, Janakpur, Nepalganj, Pokhara, Simra and Tumlingtar. The type was withdrawn from regular operations in Apr01.

9N-ACH	1537	9N-ADE	1784	9N-AEG	1806
9N-ACM	1549	(9N-ADF)	1791	9N-AEH	1807
9N-ACP	1667				

Nepal Airways Pvt Ltd (7E)
Kathmandu, Nepal

The company's first aircraft was a used Srs.2B/287 which was leased from British Aerospace from Mar93. This aircraft was replaced by two Srs.2B/426s, also leased from British Aerospace, with delivery in Feb and Mar94. These were used on a network of scheduled services linking Kathmandu with Bhairawa, Biratnagar, Nepalganj and Pokhara. Operations were suspended on 31Jul97 and one of their aircraft was written off later in a ground incident in Nov97.

9N-ACN	1736	9N-ACW	1798	9N-ACX	1799

Nepal Army Air Wing
See Royal Nepal Army Air Wing

Norcanair
See North Canada Air Ltd

Nordair Metro Ltd (ND/NDM)
Québec City, Québec, Canada

This carrier took over Québecair Inc with effect from 31Jul86 but operations were continued in the Québecair name. Following this take-over, the 748s were withdrawn gradually from service.

North Canada Air Ltd (NK/NKA)
Saskatoon, Saskatchewan, Canada

Trading as Norcanair, this company leased a Srs.2A/234 from Air Creebec Inc between early Jun and late Aug91. The aircraft was operated over the Saskatoon to Uranium City schedule via Prince Albert, La Ronge, Stony Rapids and Fond-du-Lac.

C-GQTG   1619

Northern Wings Ltd
See Les Ailes du Nord Ltée

Northland Air Manitoba Ltd
See Air Manitoba Ltd

Northward Airlines Ltd (NN)
Edmonton, Alberta, Canada

This operator inherited a Srs.2A/257 when the company took over Gateway Aviation Ltd during 1979. The aircraft was disposed of in December of the same year.

C-FMAK   1668

The Northwest Company Inc ( )
Churchill, Manitoba, Canada

The Northwest Company leased a Srs.2A/266 in Apr/May90 and a Srs.2A/209 from Apr90 to Mar91, both from Air Manitoba Ltd. This company was a division of the Hudson Bay Company until 1987 when it became independent. It used its 748s to supply its stores in the region.

C-FFFS	1663	C-FGGE	1589

Philippine Air Lines Series 2 PI-C1018 c/n 1640 is seen with its original registration marks (possibly prior to delivery).   *(WHC)*

Nunasi-Northland Airways Ltd (6N/NUN)
Churchill, Manitoba, Canada

Nunasi-Northland Airways purchased a Srs.2A/209 from Springer Aerospace early in Nov89, having operated a Srs.2A/234 leased from Northland Air Manitoba Ltd earlier in the same year. The company ceased operations in Feb90.

C-FFFS   1663   C-GQTH   1617

Ocean Air Pvt Ltd (OCR)
Gan, Addu Atoll, Maldives

From 01Nov00 to 31Oct01 a Srs.2A/263 of Executive Aerospace (Pty) Ltd operated services on behalf of this operator. A daily rotation was flown between Gan and Male of which two services per week operated via Kaadedhdhoo. Both Sri Lankan textile workers employed in Gan and tourists were carried on these flights.

ZS-ODJ   1680

Olympic Airways SA (OA/OAL)
Athens, Greece

A Srs.2A/239 company demonstrator was evaluated from Jun to Oct69.

G-AVRR   1635

Pacific Island Airways Ltd
See Air Pacific Ltd

Pacific Western Airlines Ltd (PW/PWA)
Calgary, Alberta, Canada

This airline formed a joint marketing programme with Calm Air International Ltd effective from 14Sep86 known as the Pacific Western 'Spirit'. All Calm Air schedules came under this programme from this date and flew with Pacific Western flight numbers. See 'Calm Air International Ltd' for full details.

Pelican Air Services CC (7V/PDF)
Johannesburg, South Africa

Pelican Air Services leased a Srs.2B/FAA from Executive Aerospace (Pty) Ltd from late May03 to operate a daily scheduled route between Johannesburg International and Vilanculos (Mozambique) primarily serving the Bazaruto Islands' tourist centres. From Jul04 the aircraft was replaced by Grumman Gulfstream 1s with occasional substitutions to Executive Aerospace 748s when capacity demanded.

ZS-LSO   1783

Philippine Airlines Inc (PR/PAL)
Manila, Philippines

Philippine Airlines ordered twelve Srs.2/209s, the first order for eight being delivered between Sep67 and Aug68. The second prototype was leased from the manufacturer prior to receipt of these from Feb to Jun67 for service evaluation on DC-3 routes. From Oct67 to Mar69 a Srs.2/214 was leased from the same source. The penultimate pair of new aircraft was delivered in Mar69 while the last two were delivered in Oct and Nov69 after a short-term lease from new to Transair Ltd in Canada. In Jun70 a Srs.2/232 was bought from Bahamas Airways Ltd and in Sep of the same year two further 748s were purchased, a Srs.2/266 from Austrian Airlines and a Srs.2/222 from Channel Airways Ltd. The fleet was reduced gradually to six with BAC One-Eleven 500s replacing them. However, with effect from 23Oct84 a Srs.2A/209, a Srs.2A/226 and a Srs.2A/233 were leased from Dan-Air Services Ltd enabling the company's NAMC YS-11s to be phased out. This lease continued until Feb89 when Fokker 50s replaced them. Three further aircraft were leased from British Aerospace plc. These comprised two Srs.2/217s and a Srs.2/222 with the leases running from Sep85 until Jun87.

Following the type's entry into service on 15Nov67, it was used throughout the many islands in the Philippines on a comprehensive network of schedules from hubs at Manila, Cebu and Zamboanga to numerous points from Tawitawi in the extreme south west to Bislig in the east and to Basco in the extreme north of the island group. Other points served included Alah, Aparri, Bacolod, Bagabag/Baguio, Butuan, Cagayan de Oro, Calbayog, Catarman, Cauayan, Cotabato, Daet, Dipolog, Dumaguete, General Santos, Iligan, Iloilo, Jolo, Kalibo, Laoag, Legaspi,

Malabang, Mamburao, Marinduque, Masbate, Naga, Ozamiz, Pagadian, Puerto Princesa, Roxas, San Jose, Surigao, Tablas, Tacloban, Tagbilaran, Tandag, Tuguegarao and Virac.

The last Philippine Airlines revenue service was flown by an HS748 when RP-C1023 flew from General Santos City to Manila as the PR454 on 31May89 whereupon the aircraft were withdrawn from service.

PI-C784	1535	PI-C1025	1663	RP-C1023	1659
PI-C1014	1636	PI-C1026	1664	RP-C1024	1660
PI-C1015	1637	PI-C1027	1609	RP-C1025	1663
PI-C1016	1638	PI-C1028	1590	RP-C1026	1664
PI-C1017	1639	PI-C1029	1586	RP-C1028	1590
PI-C1018	1640	RP-C1014	1636	RP-C1029	1586
PI-C1019	1641	RP-C1015	1637	RP-C1030	1663
PI-C1020	1576	RP-C1016	1638	RP-C1031	1589
PI-C1021	1642	RP-C1017	1639	RP-C1032	1613
PI-C1022	1643	RP-C1018	1640	RP-C1041	1588
PI-C1023	1659	RP-C1019	1641	RP-C1042	1584
PI-C1024	1660	RP-C1021	1642	RP-C1043	1670

Planes for Africa, Ltd ( )
Nairobi, Kenya

Originally the AOC provider for Avro Express Ltd, this company had set up its own HS 748 operation with a Series 2B/287 with a Large Freight Door by Jun16. The aircraft is used on a United Nations 'World Food Programme' contract based in Mogadishu, Somalia, flying to destinations including Garbaharey in South West Somalia.

5Y-PFA   1736

Polynesian Airlines Ltd (PH/PAO)
Apia, Western Samoa

Polynesian Airlines ordered two Srs.2A/266s with delivery in Jan and Nov72, while a Srs.2A/242 was leased from Mount Cook Airlines Ltd from May to Jul81. The last aircraft was withdrawn in Jun82 when it was replaced by a Boeing 737. Scheduled services were operated from Apia to Nadi, Niue Island, Pago Pago, Rarotonga, Tongatapu and Wallis Island together with charter work.

From 15Dec72 to Nov73 the aircraft were used additionally to operate on behalf of Air New Zealand Ltd between Nadi and Rarotonga (Cook Islands) via Pago Pago and Aitutaki.

ZK-CWJ	1647	5W-FAN	1701	5W-FAO	1714

Protea Airways (Pty) Ltd
Johannesburg, South Africa

This company provided management services to Air Botswana (Pty) Ltd when that company operated HS748 aircraft from Apr74 to Dec81.

Ptarmigan Airways Ltd (5P/PTA)
Yellowknife, North West Territories, Canada

HS748s drawn from the First Air fleet were used to operate schedules on behalf of this operator from late 1995 over the routes Yellowknife to Fort Simpson and Hay River. Later, the company was absorbed completely into the First Air/Bradley Air Services organisation.

PTB (Emerald) Pty Ltd
See International Air Parts Pty Ltd

Québecair Inc (QB/QBA)
Montréal, Québec, Canada

This operator, whose subsidiary companies had been operating HS748 aircraft from Apr71, formed a new company in mid-1981 named Regionair (1981) Inc. This concern took over the operations and aircraft of its subsidiary, Les Ailes du Nord Ltée and at the same time purchased three Srs.2A/215s from Austin Airways Ltd.

A network of services based on Sept Îles was operated to Baie Comeau, Blanc-Sablon, Bonaventure, Gagnon, Gaspé, Harrington, Havre-Saint-Pierre, Îles de la Madeleine, Mingan, Mont-Joli, Natashquan, Port-Menier, Rouyn-Noranda, Saint Augustin, Val d'Or and Québec City. All these services were operated with Québecair flight numbers. Early in 1984 Regionair ceased to exist and all operations came under the Québecair name together with the HS748 operations. The airline was taken over by Nordair Metro Ltd on 31Jul86 and the 748s were withdrawn from service.

C-FAGI	1699	C-GDOV	1582	C-GDUL	1578
C-GAPC	1599	C-GDUI	1577	C-GDUN	1581

QinetiQ
See Defence Research Agency

Polynesian Airlines' first Series 2A, 5W-FAN c/n 1701, is seen prior to delivery in 1972.

Regionair (1981) Ltd
See Québecair Inc

Republic of Korea Air Force

This Air Force ordered two Srs.2A/248s with delivery in Apr and Jul74. Both aircraft are operated in the VIP rôle by 296 (Black Bat) Squadron from the Seongnam Air Base near Seoul.

1713   1713   1718   1718

Republic of the Philippines Bureau of Air Transportation

This organisation purchased one Srs.2/209 from Philippine Airlines Inc in Mar79. The aircraft was still maintained by its former owner and was used for airfield calibration duties. The aircraft had been withdrawn from use by Mar02.

RP-122 1641   RP-1019 1641   RP-2001 1641
RP-211 1641

Réunion Air Service (UU/REU)
Réunion Island

Réunion Air Service operated one Srs.2A/264 obtained from Touraine Air Transport in Aug77. The company additionally leased other aircraft to cover maintenance downtime on their own aircraft. These comprised a Srs.2A/221 from Austin Airways Ltd from Apr to Jun80, a Srs.2B/360 from Air Madagascar for two weeks in Apr83 and a similar aircraft from the same source for five weeks in Jan/Feb88. The company was renamed Air Réunion with effect from 06Mar87. The aircraft was used to fly from Réunion Island to Dzaoudzi (Comoro Islands) and on behalf of Air Mauritius from Mauritius to Réunion and Rodrigues Island. This last destination was dropped in Nov86 at which time a once-weekly flight was started from Réunion to Antananarivo. A once-weekly flight from Réunion to Tamatave and Saint Marie (Madagascar) was started early in 1988 while later in the same year Saint Pierre in Réunion was added to the network. A Fokker 28 replaced the 748 on all other routes with effect from Mar88. The aircraft was withdrawn soon after this and leased to Air Sénégal by Mar90.

C-GQWO 1597   5R-MJA   1772   5R-MJB   1773
F-BSRA 1678

Rousseau Aviation (RU)
Dinard, France

Rousseau Aviation ordered three Srs.2A/264s, the first two being delivered in May and Oct70 and the third in Jun73. Prior to delivery of the second aircraft a Srs.2/222 was leased from Channel Airways from May to Aug70 and a Srs.2/225 from Court Line Aviation Ltd from Aug to Oct of the same year. This last aircraft was leased again from Apr to Oct72. The aircraft were operated domestically to many destinations including Clermont Ferrand, Dinard, Lannion, Lille, Metz, Morlaix, Mulhouse, Nantes, Paris, Quimper, St. Brieuc and Toulouse, and internationally to the Channel Islands and to London from Dinard, Nantes and Quimper in conjunction with Air France, together with charter work. In 1976 the airline and remaining aircraft were absorbed fully into the operations of Touraine Air Transport, the aircraft having appeared in that company's colours from early 1974.

F-BSRA 1678   F-BUTR 1717   VP-LAJ 1593
F-BSRU 1681   G-ATEI 1586

Royal Aerospace Establishment
See Defence Research Agency

Royal Aircraft Establishment
See Defence Research Agency

Royal Air Force

The Royal Air Force ordered six 748 Srs.2/206s under contract KU/11/015/CB.31(a) with serials allotted 14Jan63. They were known as Andover CC.Mk.2s in RAF service, and were all delivered in a VIP configuration between Jul64 and Sep65. Their use by various Communications Squadrons and The Queen's Flight is described in the *Andover Operators* section at the end of this Chapter. The RAF also ordered Andover C.Mk.1s under contract KU/11/02/CB.31(a), serials for this contract being allotted between 9Aug63 and 3Oct63. Details of the service histories of the C.Mk.1s are also given in the *Andover Operators* section of this Chapter. The type was finally retired from RAF service on 31Mar95.

Below: The first Series 2A for the Republic of Korea Air force is seen in its pre-delivery markings as G-BBGY c/n 1713 on take-off for a test flight in 1974. The aircraft was serialled 1713 on arrival in Korea.   (WHC)

G-ATEI c/n 1586 of Channel Airways on lease to Rousseau Aviation at Dinard in the summer of 1970. *(Kurt Lang)*

Royal Air Lao (RY)
Vientiane, Laos

One of the two Royal Thai Air Force Srs.2/243s fitted with Large Rear Freight Doors was painted in full Royal Air Lao colour scheme for use in the 1990 film 'Air America'. The actual aircraft involved has not yet been determined. It was never operated by the airline, however.

XW-PNA 1645 or 1646

Royal Australian Air Force

For a unit cost of A$2,000,430, the RAAF ordered two Srs.2/229 C.2s, described as type A10-A, and eight Srs.2/228 T.2s, described as type A10-B, the former being delivered in Mar and May67 to 34 Squadron at Fairbairn, ACT as 18-seat VIP aircraft. The remainder were delivered between Sep68 and Jul69 to the School of Air Navigation at East Sale, Victoria. All aircraft were fitted with a navigator's station immediately behind the cockpit to starboard opposite the cargo door and with a sextant in the roof panel for Astral navigation. They also had a periscope/driftmeter through the floor at the same station. The T.2s were used as flying classrooms for the training of navigation and air electronics officers (AEOs) for the RAAF and observers for the Royal Australian Navy and visited points throughout Australia and also RNZAF Wigram in New Zealand during their service life.

The Srs.2/228 aircraft were powered by the higher rated Rolls-Royce Dart RDa.8 engines. They had three navigator stations forward (one instructor and two students) while to the rear behind the observation section with bubble windows were three AEO stations (one instructor and two students). The AEO area was replaced with a crew rest area in the mid-1990s with two double seat units and a table. These eight aircraft also had a free drop hatch in the floor. With effect from 01Jul89 32 Squadron was reformed at East Sale to fly all ten RAAF HS748s. The T.2s were

operated on behalf of the School of Air Navigation. The C.2s were operated in the communications rôle from the end of 1989 after their replacement at Fairbairn by Falcon 900s but by Jun96 had been withdrawn from service. These two aircraft operated extensively throughout Australia in the VIP rôle and also travelled abroad visiting such places as Honiara (Solomon Islands), Lord Howe Island, Port Vila (Vanuatu), Daru Island, Girua, Goroka, Gurney, Kieta, Lae, Madang, Mendi, Mount Hagen, Port Moresby, Rabaul, Tari, Telefomin and Wewak (all in Papua New Guinea) and also flew to destinations throughout New Zealand. An Airborne Navigation Training System upgrade was under way for the Srs.2/228s in late 1998 and two of the aircraft were undergoing conversion and trials when it was decided to retire the 748s. In consequence the upgrade programme was cancelled and of the remaining six aircraft, one was donated to the RAAF Museum at Point Cook, Victoria in Jan04. The last five aircraft were retired after performing a three-hour final farewell flight over the Gippsland region on 30Jun04.

During over thirty-seven years of service the aircraft had been called upon to do a variety of additional tasks. These included search and rescue, maritime surface surveillance patrols, relief supplies delivery to flood and bushfire areas and ferrying emergency supplies to Darwin and evacuating refugees after Cyclone Tracy hit the city on Christmas Day 1974. Three of the aircraft were fitted out with 26 passenger seats and flew emergency schedules linking Canberra, Launceston, Hobart, Melbourne and Sydney for several months in 1989 during the long Australian pilots' dispute. Affectionately known as "Draggies" in RAAF service, the 748s also flew a formation team at several air shows, known as the "Howlettes". By the time the type was retired, the fleet had flown 192,404 accident-free hours and carried out 180,764 landings.

A10-595	1595	A10-603	1603	A10-606	1606
A10-596	1596	A10-604	1604	A10-607	1607
A10-601	1601	A10-605	1605	A10-608	1608
A10-602	1602				

Royal Australian Air Force Series 2 A10-607 c/n 1607, the penultimate T.2 aircraft for the School of Air Navigation.

The "Howlettes", the unique formation team of 32 Squadron of the Royal Australian Air Force.   (WHC/BAe)

N15-709 c/n 1709 of the Royal Australian Navy.   *(WHC)*

Royal Australian Navy

The Royal Australian Navy ordered two Srs.2/268s with delivery in May and Aug73. Like the RAAF model 228 aircraft, these two machines were powered by Rolls-Royce Dart RDa.8 engines and also had a similar navigator's position. They were used initially in the transport rôle replacing Dakotas with 851 Squadron based at HMAS Albatross at Nowra, New South Wales. Between 1978 and 1981 the two aircraft were modified extensively into Electronic Warfare (EW) trainers. Fitted with electronic countermeasures (ECM) jamming equipment and chaff dispensers, the aircraft were tasked as airborne trainers to simulate a hostile EW environment.

The Squadron was disbanded on 31Aug84 and the aircraft transferred to 723 Squadron, also based at Nowra, where they continued performing similar tasks. The aircraft were decommissioned at Nowra on 23Jun00.

N15-709 1709   N15-710 1710

Royal Brunei Airlines Ltd (BI/RBA)
Bandar Seri Begawan, Brunei

This airline purchased one Srs.2A/273 from the Royal Brunei Malay Regiment in Aug81. The aircraft was sold in Apr84 following a prolonged period of inactivity after conversion for civilian use by Singapore General Aviation Services Pte Ltd during late 1981 and early 1982.

VR-UEH 1694   VS-UEH 1694   V8-UEH 1694

Royal Brunei Malay Regiment

The Royal Brunei Malay Regiment ordered one Srs.2A/273 with delivery in Jan71. The aircraft was flown by the Air Wing of the Regiment as a VIP transport on behalf of the Brunei Government. It was used additionally for the carriage of passengers and freight and in the Search and Rescue rôle for which it was modified to drop dinghies through a chute in the rear fuselage. The aircraft was sold to Royal Brunei Airlines Ltd in Aug81.

AMDB-110 1694

Royal Nepal Airlines Corporation (RA/RNA)
Kathmandu, Nepal

Royal Nepal Airlines ordered two Srs.2A/253s and a Srs.2A/352, the latter fitted with a large rear freight door. The aircraft were delivered in Jan and Mar70 and Nov79. They were used on routes from Kathmandu to Calcutta, Delhi and Patna in India and to many Nepalese domestic points including Bhairawa, Biratnagar, Meghauli, Pokhara and Simra following the type's introduction to service on 26Jan70. The first two aircraft were withdrawn from service late in 1989 though one was overhauled subsequently and returned to service. The type was withdrawn from use in Mar00.

9N-AAU 1671   9N-AAV 1672   9N-ABR 1771

Royal Nepal Army Air Wing
Kathmandu-Tribhuvan, Nepal

The Royal Nepal Army Air Wing ordered one Srs.2A/271 fitted with a large rear freight door, the aircraft being the first so fitted and previously the manufacturer's demonstrator. Delivered in Jan75, it was operated on behalf of the Royal Flight until transferred to the Army Air Wing for full time use by the 11th Brigade in Apr80. With effect from 17Apr06 the organisation was renamed the Nepal Army Air Wing.

RAN-20 1698   9N-RAC 1698

Royal New Zealand Air Force
See Andover Operators section

The sole 748 Series 2A, AMDB-110 c/n 1694, operated by the Royal Brunei Malay Regiment is seen prior to delivery in 1971.   *(WHC)*

Royal Thai Air Force Series 2 HS-TAF c/n 1570, seen prior to delivery to the King's Flight in 1965.

Royal Thai Air Force

See also Royal Air Lao

The Royal Thai Air Force ordered two Srs.2/208s with delivery in Jan65 and Jan73, both aircraft being delivered initially to the King's Flight. One Srs.2/207 and three Srs.2/243s were purchased from Thai Airways Co Ltd with delivery between Sep83 and Jan84. Two aircraft in the fleet have been fitted with large rear freight doors from kits supplied by British Aerospace plc. All aircraft are operated by 603 Squadron of the 6th Wing 1st Air Division, Don Mueang, although one aircraft was struck off charge after a landing accident in Nov04. An unidentified RTAF 748 was used in the 1990 film 'Air America', painted in full Royal Air Lao colour scheme as XW-PNA. The type was formally withdrawn from service at a special ceremony at Bangkok Don Mueang Air Base on 30Mar16 after over 51 years' service.

HS-TAF	1570	60205	1646	60304	1644
HS-TAF	1715	60206	1645	60305	1646
11-111	1570	60301	1570	60306	1645
60203	1569	60302	1715	99-999	1715
60204	1644	60303	1569		

Royal Tongan Airlines Ltd (WR/HRH)

Tongatapu, Tonga

This airline leased a Srs.2B/400 from Air Marshall Islands Inc in Jul95. The aircraft was used to operate schedules from Tongatapu to Apia, Nadi, Ha'apai, Niue and Vava'u after inaugurating service on 05Jul95. The aircraft operated from Wednesday to Saturday each week until the last service was flown on 28Oct95. A Srs.2A/242 was leased from Mount Cook Airline in mid-Nov95 to fly similar schedules. Another Srs.2A/242 was leased from Mount Cook Airline to cover a maintenance input on the other aircraft from mid-Oct to late Nov97. Early in 1999 the ownership of the aircraft was transferred to Clewer Aviation Ltd but its operation continued with Royal Tongan until it flew its last service on 18Aug00.

A3-MCA	1712	ZK-DES	1689	V7-8203	1796

Ryanair Ltd (IW/FR/RYR)

Dublin, Eire

Ryanair purchased a Srs.1A/106 from Dan-Air Services Ltd in Apr86 and a Srs.1/105 that had seen service previously with Air Condal S.A. in May86. The type entered service on 23May86 on routes linking Luton with Dublin (four times daily) and Waterford (once daily). On 01Dec86 the 748s were replaced by ROMBAC One-Eleven 561s on the Dublin route while on 16Dec86 a three times weekly service was started with 748s between Luton and Connaught/Knock. The aircraft were used additionally for charter work. One of the aircraft was withdrawn in Jan87 while the second was retired in early Nov88.

This last aircraft was returned to service in the summer of 1989 as a back-up for the company's ATR42 fleet. This aircraft was leased to British Independent Airways Ltd through Ryanair's subsidiary, London European Airways Ltd, in Mar90. It was then leased back to operate weekday schedules from Dublin to Cardiff and Liverpool and from Luton to Carrickfin, Dublin and Sligo at weekends during the summer of 1990 and again over the Christmas period in the same year for services out of Luton.

EI-BSE	1549	EI-BSF	1544	G-ARRW	1549

SAESA

See Servicios Aéreos Especiales SA

Safair Freighters (Pty) Ltd

See Air Cape (Pty) Ltd

Safair Lines (Pty) Ltd

See Air Cape (Pty) Ltd

Safe Air Company Kenya, Ltd (SAC) ( )

Nairobi, Kenya

This organisation took delivery of a Srs.2B/360 pure freighter fitted with a large rear freight door in late Nov09 for operations from a forward base at Juba in Southern Sudan.

5Y-TCO	1772

SATA

See Sociedade Açoriana de Transportes Aéreos

SATENA

See Fuerza Aérea Colombiana

The photographs on this page and the next show three of the five HS 748s which celebrated the 50th Anniversary
of the 748 in Royal Thai Air Force service at Don Mueang Air Base on 30th July 2014
(all photographs by AVM Sakpinit Promthep, RThaiAF, via Steve Darke)

Above and below: 60301, serial L5-1/08, c/n 1570, was the first RThaiAF HS748 delivered in January 1965. Initially a Royal Flight aircraft, coded 11-111, it moved to 603 Squadron in 2005 and was recoded 60301.

Above: HS748 60304, serial L5-4/26, c/n 1644, was transferred from Thai Airways with whom it had operated as HS-THD between October 1968 and August 1983. It was initially operated by 602 Squadron, coded 60204, then transferred to 603 Squadron and recoded 60304.

Above and below: HS748 60303, serial L5-3/26, c/n 1569, was transferred from Thai Airways with whom it had operated as HS-THC between November 1964 and August 1983. It was initially operated by 602 Squadron, coded 60203, then transferred to 603 Squadron and recoded 60303. It has been repainted in a special scheme to celebrate the 50th Anniversary in service of the 'Avro', as they are known by RThaiAF. Of the six HS748s operated by the RThaiAF, five remain in service. Only one (L5-2/16) is out of use following an accident in 2004. It is preserved at one of the palaces of the Thai Crown Prince.

Above: The 'winged star' is the Wing 6 emblem. The wings represent Wing and the five small stars plus the big one represent number 6, i.e. Wing 6. The Thai script at the top says 'Valour without arms', and at the bottom 'Wing 6'.

Above: The 'leaping horse' emblem has been used by Wing 6 (of which 603 Squadron, which operates the HS748s, is part) as tail marking for many years, going back to the C-47 and C-123. There is no real significance to the 50th Anniversary of the HS748 (Wing 6 has not itself been in existence for 50 years yet), but that's how they decided to paint it!

Scottish European Airways Ltd (WW/SEU)
Glasgow, Scotland

This airline purchased two ex Chieftain Airways Ltd Srs.2A/334s in Oct88 and dry leased a Srs.2A/266 from Jul to Nov89. The company commenced ad hoc charter operations on 05Oct88 including operating some schedules on behalf of British Airways and British Midland Airways. With effect from 14Nov88 scheduled services were started from Glasgow to Brussels and Frankfurt with the aircraft reconfigured with 32 passenger seats. The network was expanded further to include Edinburgh to Brussels services with effect from May89, Edinburgh to Frankfurt services with effect from Jul89 and Newcastle to Frankfurt services with effect from Sep89. After the two aircraft were impounded in Manchester and Frankfurt, the company ceased trading on 27Apr90.

G-BMFT 1714   G-BPDA 1756   G-BPFU 1757

Serendib Express (Pvt) Ltd
See Aero Lanka Airlines (Pvt) Ltd

Servicio de Aeronavegación a Territorios Nacionales (SATENA)
See Fuerza Aérea Colombiana

Servicio de Aviación Naval Venezolana

This organisation purchased a Srs.2/215 from Línea Aeropostal Venezolana in Oct77. It was disposed of in Aug81.

TR-0203 1579

Servicios Aéreos Especiales SA - SAESA
(AM/AMX)
México City, México

SAESA ordered three Srs.2A/259s with delivery in Feb and Mar70 having taken over two Srs.2/230s from Aeromaya S.A. in Sep69. At this time Mexican carriers were subjected to major reorganisation and this carrier came under the Aeronaves de México directed integrated air transport system. Among domestic points served were Campeche, Chetumal, Ciudad del Carmen, Ciudad Lázaro Cárdenas, Cozumel, Guadalajara, La Paz, Leon, Mazatlán, Mérida, Mexico City, Poza Rica, Reynosa, Tapachula, Torreón, Tuxtla Gutiérrez and Villahermosa. The last aircraft was disposed of in Nov77.

XA-SAB 1673   XA-SAF 1675   XA-SEY 1599
XA-SAC 1674   XA-SEV 1598

Servico Acoriano de Transportes Aéreos EP
See Sociedade Acoriana de Transportes Aéreos - SATA

Seulawah-Mandala Airlines PT
See Mandala Airlines PT

748 Air Services Ltd (SVT)
Nairobi-Wilson, Kenya

This company, which specialises in operating emergency relief cargo and passenger services to numerous airstrips in southern Sudan, Eritrea and Somalia from a forward base at Lokichoggio in northern Kenya, has operated two 748s and four Andover C.Mk.1s. Relief flights have also been flown from Nairobi to the Democratic Republic of Congo, Rwanda and Tanzania.

The first 748, a Srs.2/206, was written off in Feb99. The first two Andovers were delivered in Oct98 and a Srs.2B/399 was obtained in Feb04. The second pair of Andover C.Mk.1s was obtained in Oct02 and late 2005. A Srs.2B/371 and a Srs.2B/399 both fitted with Large Freight Doors and in cargo configuration were bought from West Air Sweden together with a large spares package with the first aircraft delivered in late Nov07 and the second in late Feb08. Maintenance is provided by Aviation International Support Ltd (AIS). The company's only passenger-configured 748 was written-off in Dec09, while the Srs.2B/371 LFD was written-off in Feb14, and their last operational HS 748/Andover, the Srs.2B/399 LFD, was written-off in Nov14. With effect from Sep13, the 748s had been operated on behalf of Global Airlift Ltd.

3C-KKB Set 9   5Y-HAJ 1776   (5Y-YKN) 1776
3C-KKC Set 18   5Y-SFE Set 6   (5Y-YKO) 1778
5Y-BSX Set 20   5Y-YKM 1779   9L-LBG 1566
5Y-BVQ 1778

Shabair Sprl (SS)
Lubumbashi, Zaire

Shabair purchased two Srs.2/209s from Philippine Airlines Inc which were delivered in late Oct and early Dec89. Scheduled services were operated from Lubumbashi to Kolwezi together with charter work. The aircraft were sold to Trans Service Airlift in Jun92.

9Q-CSR 1664   9Q-CST 1642

Simba Air Cargo Ltd (QG)
Nairobi, Kenya

This company obtained a Srs.2A/344 in Nov95 from Air Saint-Pierre which was prepared for service in Malta. Nothing is known of this company's operations with the aircraft.

5Y-SAL 1764

Singapore General Aviation Services Pte Ltd (SINGAS)
Singapore

This company specialised in the care and maintenance of HS748 aircraft in the Far East and has, in the course of its business, become the owner of certain aircraft. The first of these was a Srs.2/209 obtained from Philippine Airlines in Dec79. The aircraft was subsequently sold to Airfast Services Indonesia PT in May80. One of the Bouraq Indonesia Airlines fleet of Srs.2A/235s was transferred temporarily to this company when major maintenance was carried out from Jan to Jun81.

One Srs.2A/266 was on care and maintenance with this company from its withdrawal from service by Polynesian Airlines Ltd in Feb83 until it was sold in Oct85. The company also modified a Srs.2A/273 from military to civilian status on behalf of Royal Brunei Airlines Ltd late in 1981 and early 1982. The entire fleet of Srs.2B/401 and 402 aircraft purchased by Bouraq Indonesia Airlines PT was delivered through SINGAS and received their Indonesian marks while in the company's care.

PK-IHM 1634   RP-C1016 1638   5W-FAO 1714

Skyservices Ltd
See Springer Aerospace Ltd

Former Royal New Zealand Air Force Andover 3C-KKB c/n 9, seen at Auckland prior to its delivery to 748 Air Services (PTY) Ltd of Nairobi, Kenya.
(WHC)

The original Skyways Coach Air livery is seen on Series 1 G-ASPL c/n 1560, a former BKS aircraft, at Liverpool (Speke) in the mid-1960s.

Skyways International Series 1 G-ARMW c/n 1537 seen in the later colour-scheme flying over Southern England in October 1971.   *(WHC/BAe)*

Skyways Coach Air Ltd (SX)
Lympne, near Hythe, Kent, UK

Skyways Coach Air leased three Srs.1/101s from the manufacturer with delivery in Apr and Jun62 and Apr63. Two of these aircraft were purchased outright in Jan71, the third having been written-off earlier. One Srs.1/106 and one Srs.1/108 had been purchased previously in Mar67, these having been operated on lease from the manufacturer by BKS Air Transport Ltd prior to this. Many leases took place between Skyways Coach Air Ltd and BKS Air Transport Ltd in both directions. Other leased aircraft used were the second prototype from Hawker Siddeley Aviation Ltd in Aug and Sep65 and a Srs.2/225 from Autair International Airways Ltd from May to Oct68. The first company owned Series 2, a 226, was obtained from Austrian Airlines in Dec69 following the short lease of a Srs.2A/235 from the manufacturer in early Apr of the same year.

The company ceased operations on 20Jan71 and was reformed as International Skyways Ltd with the first service taking place on 08Feb71 after refinancing. The new company was marketed as Skyways International. This concern was taken over by Dan-Air Services Ltd in Apr72 and for a while after this, the aircraft were painted with Dan-Air Skyways titling. The company had become the second operator to introduce the Avro 748 when G-ARMV entered service on 17Apr62. The aircraft were used between Lympne and Beauvais, Montpellier, Clermont Ferrand, Lyon and Vichy. Charter work was also undertaken including a twice daily 'schedule' on behalf of the Ford Motor Company between Stansted and Cologne.

G-ARAY	1535	G-ARMX	1538	G-ATMI	1592
G-ARMV	1536	G-ARRW	1549	G-AVRR	1635
G-ARMW	1537	G-ASPL	1560	G-AXVG	1589

Smith's Industries Ltd
See Aviation Division of S Smith & Sons (England) Ltd

Sociedade Acoriana de Transportes Aéreos - SATA (SP/SAT)
Ponta Delgada, Azores, Portugal

The first 748 aircraft operated by SATA was a Srs.2A/239 leased from Hawker Siddeley Aviation Ltd in Jan and Feb69. Two Srs.2/225s were leased from Autair International Airways Ltd/Court Line Aviation Ltd., one from Apr69 to May70 and the other from May to Aug70. Prior to the delivery of the first of two Srs.2A/270s ordered, a Srs.2A/264 was leased for one week in Oct70 in Rousseau Aviation colours. The first new aircraft was delivered on lease from Aug70 until Apr72 when it was purchased. The second Srs.2A/270 was delivered in Jun73 while a Srs.2A/372 was ordered with delivery in May80. Two Srs.2B/FAAs were purchased from the manufacturer with delivery in May and Jun87 for which the two Srs.2A/270s were traded in part exchange. From 1980 when the company became state-owned, it was marketed as 'SATA Air Açores' with the official company name as Servico Acoriano de Transportes Aéreos EP.

To cover the peak summer schedules, one extra aircraft was leased each year from 1980 from a variety of sources. Mount Cook Airlines Ltd Srs.2A/242s were used in 1980 and 1982, Dan-Air Services Ltd Srs.2A/209 and Srs.2A/232s were used in 1981 and 1985 respectively while a Srs.2A/210 was leased from the manufacturer in 1983 and 1984. A Srs.2B/360 was leased from Air Madagascar during the summers of 1986 and 1988 while a Srs.2A/270 was leased from the manufacturer in 1987. In 1989 a Srs.2B/378 was leased followed by a Srs.2A/372 in 1990, both

SATA CS-TAO c/n 1777, photographed on a pre-delivery sortie in the airline's early livery in 1980. (WHC)

from British Aerospace. Schedules linked Ponta Delgada, Horta, Santa Maria and Terciera with the islands of Graciosa, Flores, Pico and São Jorge. The type was replaced by BAe ATPs and the last of the HS748s were traded in to British Aerospace in mid Jan91.

CS-TAF	1681	CS-TAR	1797	G-BCDZ	1662
CS-TAG	1687	G-ATMI	1592	G-BHCJ	1663
CS-TAH	1721	G-ATMJ	1593	ZK-DES	1689
CS-TAO	1777	G-AVRR	1635	ZK-MCA	1712
CS-TAP	1782	G-AZSU	1612	5R-MJA	1772
CS-TAQ	1790				

Société de Navigation Aérienne Malgache – SONAVAM ( )

Antananarivo, Madagascar.

SONOVAM utilised a Srs.2B/378 and a Srs.2A/263 of Executive Aerospace (Pty) Ltd over the periods Aug01 to May02 and from Mar to Jul02 respectively to operate on both schedules and charters within Madagascar.

ZS-NWW	1786	ZS-ODJ	1680

Société Nationale Transgabon (GN/AGN)

Libreville, Gabon

Transgabon ordered one Srs.2A/239 and one Srs.2A/214, the former being leased from Hawker Siddeley Aviation Ltd from

Oct71 until purchased in Dec72 while the second aircraft was delivered in Oct72. Both aircraft had been former manufacturer's demonstrators. The company was renamed Air Gabon with effect from mid-1974. The aircraft were disposed of in Mar and May76 after operating domestic services to Bitam, Franceville, Lambaréné, Lastoursville, Libreville, Makokou, Mayoumba, Mitzic, Moanda, Mouila, Okandja, Oyem, Port Gentil and Tchibanga. A twice-monthly schedule was also flown on behalf of Air Afrique between Port Gentil and Lomé by Apr74.

TR-LQJ	1635	TR-LQY	1576

Société Nouvelle Air Provence International
See Air Provence International

SONAVAM
See Société de Navigation Aérienne Malgache

South African Airways (SA/SAA)

Johannesburg, South Africa

This airline ordered three Srs.2A/272s, one of which was leased from new to Botswana Airways Corporation Ltd from early Feb to mid-May71. The remaining two aircraft were delivered in Feb71. Prior to delivery of their own aircraft, two machines were leased from the manufacturer. The first, a Srs.2A/239, was used initially for route proving in late Dec69 and early Jan70 before returning in May of the same year and then leased until Sep70.

Transgabon Series 2A TR-LQY c/n 1576 in the airline's striking livery of orange and white. (WHC)

ZS-SBU c/n 1690 of South African Airways, seen in the airline's older livery of dark blue cheatline and bright orange fin with white and blue stylised arrow. The airline's name appeared in Afrikaans on one side and English on the other. (WHC)

The second aircraft, a Srs.2A/214, immediately replaced the former and was used until late Feb71.

The type entered revenue service on 04May70 when ZS-HSI (on lease from Hawker Siddeley Aviation Ltd) flew from Johannesburg to Durban via Manzini in Swaziland. Services were progressively introduced to Gaborone and Francistown (Botswana) from 05May70, to Maseru (Lesotho) from 08May70, to Windhoek and Keetmanshoop (Namibia) via Bloemfontein and/or Kimberley from 01Feb72, while Cape Town was served from Windhoek via Alexander Bay the following day.

On 11Feb75 the type was introduced onto services to Victoria Falls (Zimbabwe), while on 01Apr76 direct services were started to Selebi Pikwe (Botswana), the destination having been served previously via Gaborone from 06Apr74. Other points added to the network were Lourenço Marques/Maputo (Mozambique) from 01Apr76, Umtata from 02Feb80 and Richards Bay from 01Nov82.

The last revenue HS748 flight took place on 31May83 when ZS-SBW landed at Johannesburg from Gaborone. Additionally Air Cape (Pty) Ltd were contracted to fly their Srs.2A/264 on the South African Airways route from Cape Town to Port Elizabeth via Oudtshoorn, George and Plettenberg Bay. This it did from 01Dec74 to 31Mar83.

Following the withdrawal of the 748 fleet, all routes unable to support jet operations were handed over to other smaller operators. From 1999 Executive Aerospace (Pty) Ltd 748s operated several domestic routes on behalf of SAA Express and SA Airlink from Johannesburg on an ad hoc basis.

ZS-HSA	1576	ZS-JAY	1717	ZS-SBV	1692
ZS-HSI	1635	ZS-SBU	1690	ZS-SBW	1691
ZS-IGI	1635				

Springer Aerospace Ltd
Bar River, Sault Ste. Marie, Ontario, Canada

This maintenance organisation obtained one Srs.2A/209, one Srs.2A/226 and a Srs.2A/233 from Dan-Air Services Ltd in Jun and Jul89. A Srs.2/244 was obtained from the Royal Bank of Canada later in the same year and converted to a Srs.2A/244 for onward sale to V Kelner Airways Ltd in Mar90.

Two of the former Dan-Air aircraft were sold to Northland Air Manitoba Ltd in Nov89 and Jan90 after conversion to pure freighters, the first being operated initially by Nunasi-Northland Airways Ltd. The third ex Dan-Air aircraft after initial lease to V Kelner Airways Ltd was converted later to a specialist unpressurised pure freighter with oversize double rear freight doors and a modernised avionics package. It was sold subsequently to V. Kelner Airways Ltd. Two other Srs.2/244s which had been imported from Germany were also converted to Srs.2A/244s on behalf of Air Inuit (1985) Ltd/Ltée.

The company merged with Skyservices Ltd in the late 1990s but continued to market itself in the original name. Springer Aerospace completed an LFD modification on a Srs.2A/244 on behalf of Air Creebec Inc in Jan08.

C-FFFS	1663	C-FKTL	1613	C-GLTC	1656
C-FGGE	1589				

Sri Lanka Air Force
Ratmalana, Sri Lanka

The Sri Lanka Air Force bought one Srs.2/222 from Air Ceylon Ltd for use by No.2 (Transport) Squadron in Sep79. This was followed by a Srs.2A/272 obtained from Austin Airways Ltd in May75 and a Srs.2A/301 fitted with a large rear freight door obtained from the manufacturer in Mar86. A Srs.2B/357 fitted with a large rear freight door and a Srs.2A/334 were added in Dec91. Initially based at Katunayake, the Squadron moved to Ratmalana in Apr85, from where the aircraft were used for general military transport and for tourist flying.

Tourist charter flights were undertaken in the name of Helitours by Nov86 and continued until Oct96. Destinations served from both Katunayake and Ratmalana included Bangalore, Bombay, Delhi, Calcutta, Gaya, Hyderabad, Kuala Lumpur, Madras, Madurai, Male, Tirupati and Varanasi. On 28 and 29Apr95 two of the aircraft were destroyed in the air after being hit apparently by SAM missiles. Two of the three remaining aircraft were initially pressed into service in early 1992 to operate on behalf of AirLanka Ltd by Helitours to cover for a damaged Boeing 737. They were then stored at Ratmalana and there were plans to return them to service after the last one was withdrawn from service on 23Aug02. However, they were eventually roaded to military-run restaurants near Koggala Lake and Weerewila for external display. The third aircraft is displayed at the Sri Lanka Air Force Museum.

CR-830	1691	CR-834	1768	SCM-3102	1746
CR-831	1587	CR-835	1757	4R-HVA	1768
CR-833	1746	SCM-3101	1691	4R-HVB	1757

Stars Away Aviation (Pty) Ltd (STX)
Cape Town, South Africa

This company took delivery of two Srs.2B/287 freighters fitted with large freight doors in Mar05 and Mar06 for use initially on a night freight operation between George and Johannesburg via Bloemfontein from Jul06 until Mar09. A Johannesburg to Durban route was operated five times weekly on behalf of Imperial Air Cargo (Pty) Ltd from 01Aug06. The company name was originally referred to as Cape Aero Services (Pty) Ltd. One aircraft was leased to MK Airlines of Ghana from early Apr to Aug09 and from May to Sep12 to Tropicana Airlines in Ghana. The second aircraft was leased to Timbis Air Services of Kenya from 10Nov10 until 22Jan11 and again from Oct11 until 22Apr12 when it was written-off in Southern Sudan. Stars Away Aviation went into liquidation in Nov12.

ZS-DBL	1737	(ZS-OEO)	1737	5Y-HVS	1736
ZS-DBM	1736	5Y-BZR	1737		

Stellair – Compañia de Actividades y Servicios de Aviación SL (8X/LCT)
Madrid, Spain

Stellair was due to lease a Srs.2B/371 with a large rear freight door from West Air Sweden AB in Apr05. A Srs.2B/399 also with a large rear freight door was also due to be leased later in 2005. The company, which specialises in operating cargo flights throughout Europe, the Canary Islands and North Africa, failed to complete the contract and the work that was destined initially for the first aircraft was taken over by West Air Sweden itself.

(SE-LIB)	1776	(SE-LIC)	1778

Suidwes Lugdiens (Eiendoms) Beperk (SW)
Windhoek, Namibia

A company demonstrator was evaluated by this company in Dec69.

ZS-IGI	1635

The Tanzanian Government's sole 748, Series 2A 5H-MPG c/n 1728, photographed with 'United Republic of Tanzania' titles. The registration marks were changed to 5H-STZ prior to delivery. (WHC)

Thai Airways Series 2 HS-THD c/n 1644 seen in the final, very attractive, livery carried by the airline's 748s.

Sun Air
See Bop-Air (Pty) Ltd

TACV
See Transportes Aéreos de Cabo Verde

TAME
See Fuerza Aérea Ecuatoriana

Tanzanian Government

The Tanzanian Government ordered one Srs.2A/282 for VIP use with delivery in Apr74. It has not flown for several years and remains in storage at Dar-es-Salaam.

5H-MPG 1728   5H-STZ 1728   (5H-RJN) 1728

Tanzanian Peoples' Defence Force

The Tanzanian Peoples' Defence Force (also known as Jeshi la Wananchi la Tanzani - JWTZ) ordered three Srs.2A/314s all fitted with large rear freight doors. They were delivered in Nov77 and Jan78. None is believed still to be flying.

JW-9008 1751   JW-9009 1752   JW-9010 1753

TAP Air Portugal
See Sociedade Açoreana de Transportes Aéreos - SATA

TAT
See Touraine Air Transport

Thai Airways Co Ltd (TH/TAC)
Bangkok, Thailand

Thai Airways ordered three Srs.2/207s which were delivered between Aug and Nov64. A further six Srs.2/243s were ordered in batches of three, one and two with delivery of three in Oct and Nov68, one in Dec70 and the last two in Jan and Feb72. As traffic built up, the aircraft were replaced by Boeing 737s and from Jun82, the shorter, less densely travelled routes, by Shorts 330 aircraft.

The aircraft was introduced into service on 01Nov64 replacing DC-3s and gradually served numerous points within Thailand from the hubs of Bangkok, Ubon Ratchath, Chiang Mai and Hat Yai (Songkhla) together with international routes to Hanoi (from 17May78), Penang, Siem Reap and Vientiane. Other points served within Thailand included Chiang Rai, Khon Kaen, Mae Hongson, Lampang, Nakhon Phanom, Nan, Narathiwat, Pattani, Phitsanulok, Phrae, Phuket, Trang, Udon and Utapao. One aircraft was sold to Airfast Services Indonesia in Feb81 and four to the Royal Thai Air Force between Sep83 and Jan84. By May87 only one aircraft remained in service and this shared its time flying schedules on behalf of both Thai Airways and Bangkok Airways until it was involved in a landing accident in Dec of the same year.

HS-THA	1567	HS-THD	1644	HS-THG	1693
HS-THB	1568	HS-THE	1645	HS-THH	1707
HS-THC	1569	HS-THF	1646	HS-THI	1708

Thunderbird Tours Inc (4A/TBD)
Vancouver, British Columbia, Canada

This company leased First Air's surviving Srs.2B/FAA from Apr94 to operate schedules from Vancouver via Bella Bella to Masset and Sandspit in the Queen Charlotte Islands. The aircraft was introduced into service on 26Apr94 in a mixed passenger/cargo configuration with a moveable bulkhead. These schedules mainly serviced holiday lodges in the islands and appealed especially to United States salmon fishing parties. Extensive charter flights were also undertaken both for passenger and freight work. Jasper and Calgary in Alberta were due to be added destinations to the scheduled network with effect from 21Dec95. The company's operating licence was suspended by the Canadian Transport Agency on 11Jan96 and cancelled with effect from 08Mar96. The aircraft was returned to the lessor.

C-GBFA 1781

Timbis Air Services ( )
Nairobi - Jomo Kenyatta, Kenya

Timbis Air Services leased a Srs.2B/287 freighter from Nov10 until 22Jan11, when the aircraft was parked at Nairobi. After registration in Kenya in Oct11, the lease restarted until the aircraft was written-off in early Apr12. Points served included Juba, Malakal and Wau in South Sudan, Mwanza (Tanzania), Mogadishu (Somalia) and Khartoum (Sudan).

ZS-DBL	1737	5Y-BZR	1737

Touraine Air Transport - TAT (IJ/TAT)
Tours, France

At the time of the complete integration of Rousseau Aviation services into the network of Touraine Air Transport in 1976, one Srs.2A/264 still remained on strength and was painted in full TAT

Thunderbird Tours Inc Series 2B C-GBFA c/n 1781 at Vancouver, British Colombia, on 11th June 1995. *(Fred Barnes)*

Sporting joint TAT-Rousseau Aviation titling, Series 2A F-BSRA c/n 1678 was photographed at Jersey, Channel Islands, on 8th May 1970. *(Ray Turner)*

colours. It was operated on routes mainly out of Dinard until sold for use by Réunion Air Service in Aug77. Other HS748s from the Rousseau fleet had appeared in TAT colours with Rousseau titling by Mar74. From late Dec88 to at least Oct89 Kel Air's two Srs.2A/263s and single Srs.2A/264 were used to operate domestic schedules on behalf of TAT, which by then had been renamed Transport Aérien Transrégional, that included the routes from Metz to Paris-Orly and from Lyon to Mulhouse.

F-BSRA	1678	F-GHKA	1680	F-GHKL	1677
F-GFYM	1717				

Trackmark Cargo Ltd ( )
Nairobi-Wilson, Kenya

Trackmark Cargo utilised a Srs.2B/400 of AirQuarius Air Charter (Pty) Ltd for ad hoc charter work. The aircraft was in service by early Apr99 but was returned to the lessor in late Aug99. In mid-Oct04 a Srs.2A/286 with a large rear freight door and configured as a pure freighter was leased from International Air Parts Pty Ltd on a two-year contract for use primarily on relief flights to the Sudan.

This last aircraft was written-off in late Mar06 and was replaced by a Srs.2B/360 freighter with a large rear freight door in early Aug06. The new aircraft was flown on behalf of the United Nations World Food Programme between Nairobi and Somalia and additionally flew ad hoc freight charters from Kenya to Sudan until it was withdrawn from use in late Sep08.

ZS-OLE	1796	5Y-TCA	1740	5Y-TCO	1772
ZS-XGZ	1740				

Tracor Aviation Inc
Goleta, California, USA

This company took over Aero Spacelines Inc soon after that company had contracted to complete 'green' aircraft for the United States market. It continued with this work and between them, the two companies completed a total of five aircraft for Air Virginia, Cascade Airways and British Aerospace plc.

Transair Ltd (TZ/TTZ)
Winnipeg, Manitoba, Canada

Transair leased one Srs.2A/239 in Apr and May69 and then two Srs.2/209s, one from May to Sep and the other from Jun to Sep69. A fourth, a Srs.2/222, was leased from May to Nov of the same year. The airline inherited two further aircraft, a Srs.2A/257 and a Srs.2/222 when it took over Midwest Aviation Ltd late in 1969. These last two aircraft were disposed of in Apr72, the second after a lease in Guatemala in May75. The aircraft flew scheduled services to numerous points in Canada including Churchill, Coral Harbour, Dauphin, Flin Flon, Gillam, Lynn Lake, Rankin Inlet, Red Lake, Regina, Saskatoon, The Pas, Thompson, Yorkton and Yellowknife.

CF-MAK	1668	CF-TAX	1586	CF-YQD	1635
CF-MAL	1587	CF-TAZ	1663	C-GCZY	1587
CF-TAG	1664				

Transair Cambodia Co Ltd (6H)
Phnom Penh, Cambodia

Two used Srs.2B/FAAs were painted in Transair Cambodia's colour scheme in Jun92 at Manchester but lack of Cambodian Government approval for a licence to operate stopped the import of the aircraft.

(XU-???)	1782	(XU-???)	1790

Trans Air Cargo Services ( )
Kinshasa-Ndjili, DRC

In Aug07 an Andover C.Mk.1 was noted being prepared for this carrier at its home base, but nothing further has been reported.

9Q-CPW Set 14

Transgabon
See Société Nationale Transgabon

Transkei Airways Corporation (KV/TAK)
Umtata, South Africa

Transkei Airways ordered one Srs.2A/351 which was delivered in Aug79. The aircraft entered service on 01Nov79 on the route between Johannesburg and Umtata. Charter work was also undertaken until the aircraft was disposed of in Jul93.

ZS-XGE 1770

Transport Aérien Transrégional – TAT
See Touraine Air Transport – TAT

Transportes Aéreos de Cabo Verde – TACV (VR/TCV)
Praia, Cape Verde Islands

TACV ordered two Srs.2A/278s that were delivered in Oct and Nov73. The aircraft were used on a domestic network linking Praia, Ilha do Sal, São Nicolau and São Vicente and to Dakar (Sénégal). The aircraft were replaced by ATR42s late in 1994 and subsequently disposed of.

CR-CAV	1719	D4-CAV	1719	D4-CAW	1720
CR-CAW	1720				

Transportes Aéreos da Guiné-Bissau - TAGB (YZ/GBU)
Bissau, Guiné-Bissau

LAGB ordered a Srs.2A/233 which was delivered in Nov78. The aircraft was used by the renamed Transportes Aéreos da Guiné-Bissau on domestic services and on routes between Bissau and Banjul (Gambia), Dakar (Sénégal), Conakry (Guinea), Praia (Cape Verde Islands) and with effect from 1989 to Las Palmas (Canary Islands). In later years the company traded as Air Bissau. The aircraft was disposed of in May98.

J5-GAT 1760

Transportes Aéreos Mercantiles Ecuatorianos
See Fuerza Aérea Ecuatoriana

Transportes Aéreos Militares Ecuatorianos
See Fuerza Aérea Ecuatoriana

Transportes Aéreos Nacionales Ecuatorianos
See Fuerza Aérea Ecuatoriana

Trackmark Cargo Ltd's Series 2A 5Y-TCA c/n 1740, seen after its landing accident at Old Fangak, Sudan, on 17th March 2006.   *(Allan Fantham)*

Transkei Airways' sole 748, a Series 2A, ZS-XGE c/n 1770, was photographed in southern Africa in the 1980s.

One of Transportes Aéreos de Cabo Verde's two 748 Series 2As, G-BBPT c/n 1720, photographed prior to delivery in 1973.

Transportes Aéreos da Guiné-Bissau was formerly known as Linhas Aéreas da Guiné-Bissau. Their Series 2A G-BFVR c/n 1760 was seen taxying as such at Woodford prior to delivery. (WHC/BAe)

Trinidad & Tobago Air Services flew six Series 2As between December 1977 and June 1986. 9Y-TFX c/n 1758 is seen here prior to its delivery on 23rd December 1977. (WHC/BAe)

Trans Service Airlift (TSR)
Kinshasa, Zaire

This company obtained 2 Srs.2/209s from Shabair in Jun92 but no further details are known of this carrier or its aircraft since that time.

9Q-CSR   1664   9Q-CST   1642

Transvalair (VY/CHX)
Paris, France

Transvalair purchased a Srs.2A/264 from Safair Lines (Pty) Ltd in late Oct88. The aircraft was leased immediately to Kel Air of Nice until Jun90 and to Airfast Services Indonesia P.T. from Oct91 until Aug92. The aircraft was sold in Feb97.

F-GFYM 1717

Trinidad & Tobago Air Services Ltd - TTAS
(HU,BW/BWA)
Port of Spain, Trinidad

Trinidad & Tobago Air Services ordered two Srs.2A/334s, two Srs.2A/347s and two Srs.2A/335s, the last fitted with large rear freight doors. Delivery took place between Dec77 and Nov79. The company was merged with BWIA International on 01Jan80 and renamed Trinidad & Tobago (BWIA International) Airways Corporation. The type entered service with the company on 28Dec77 between Piarco Airport, Port of Spain and Crown Point, Tobago replacing DC-6B equipment. A high frequency service was operated between these two points under the name 'Airbridge'.

From Oct84 the aircraft were also used on a twice-daily schedule between Port of Spain and Grenada and in Jul85 commenced services to St. Lucia and Fort de France, Martinique. Charter flights were also undertaken. One of the aircraft was leased to LIAT (1974) Ltd from Nov80 to Jun82 while several short-term leases were made to Air BVI Ltd. Disposal of the aircraft took place between Apr86 and Sep87 with regular use of the type ending by Jun86.

| 9Y-TFS | 1756 | 9Y-TFX | 1758 | 9Y-TGH | 1766 |
| 9Y-TFT | 1757 | 9Y-TGD | 1759 | 9Y-TGI | 1767 |

Tropicana Airlines Ltd ( )
Accra, Ghana

Tropicana Airlines took delivery of a freight configured Srs.2B/287 in late May12 on lease. The aircraft was flown to points which included Abidjan (Ivory Coast), Douala (Cameroon), Malabo (Equatorial Guinea) and Pointe-Noire (Republic of the Congo) but had been withdrawn by Sep12.

ZS-DBM 1736

Tunisavia (Société de Transports, Services et Travaux Aériens) (TT/TAJ)
Tunis, Tunisia

Tunisavia leased one Srs.2A/353 from Air Sénégal from May80 which was used on Air Malta services during the summer of 1981 between Malta and nearby North African points before its return to Air Sénégal in 1983. In Jul85 one Srs.1A/105 was leased from Euroair Transport Ltd. This was replaced in Nov85 by a Srs.2A/266 leased from the same source until it was returned the following year. The aircraft were used to operate scheduled services from Tunis to Constantine, Malta and Sfax and from Sfax to Malta.

| G-BMFT | 1714 | G-VAJK | 1557 | 6V-AEO | 1769 |

Uni Airways Corporation - Uni Air
See Makung International Airways Co Ltd

United Air Services (Pty) Ltd (UE/UTD)
Johannesburg, South Africa

This company purchased one Srs.2A/264 from Air Services Botswana (Pty) Ltd in Sep81. The aircraft was leased immediately to Air Comores for six months and from Jul83 to Apr84 to Zambia Airways Corporation Ltd. The aircraft was sold to Ilford Riverton Airways Ltd in Canada in Jan86.

| A2-ABC | 1681 | ZS-LHN | 1681 | 7P-LAI | 1681 |

VARIG
See Viaçao Aérea Rio-Grandense

Vayudoot Ltd (PF/VDT)
New Delhi, India

This company was formed to operate services to previously unserved areas of India and inaugurated service on 26Jan81. Hindustan Aeronautics Ltd built HS748s were leased firstly and later transferred from Indian Airlines Corporation to operate services from Bombay and Delhi to points including Chandigarh, Dehra Dun, Kandla, Kulu, Ludhiana and Pantnagar. The Indian Airlines 748 fleet was transferred progressively to Vayudoot with the last of the type being received in Apr89. At this time this operator started serving many of the destinations previously served by Indian Airlines for which jet service was not warranted. From this time 748s were based at Bombay, Delhi, Hyderabad and Madras with service added to Agatti Island, Agra, Allahabad, Belgaum, Bhatinda, Calicut, Cochin, Coimbatore, Goa, Jabalpur, Jaipur, Jaisalmer, Jodhpur, Kanpur, Keshod, Khajuraho, Kolhapur, Lucknow, Nasik, Porbandar, Pune, Rajahmundry, Rajkot, Tirupati, Trivandrum, Varanasi and Vijaywada. The company was merged officially into Indian Airlines Corporation with effect from 25May93, the transaction being completed in Mar94.

VT-DXH	513	VT-DXN	521	VT-DXR	525
VT-DXK	518	VT-DXO	522	VT-EAT	540
VT-DXL	519	VT-DXP	523	VT-EAV	542
VT-DXM	520	VT-DXQ	524		

Vayudoot Ltd Hindustan 748 VT-DXM c/n HAL/K/520 seen at an unknown location in India. (WHC)

Venezuelan Government

See Fuerza Aérea Venezolana

Venture Airways Ltd (HC)

Coventry, West Midlands, UK

Venture Airways obtained one Srs.1A/105 from Cayman Airways Ltd in Feb84 at which time this company was known as Air Commuter Ltd. The name Venture Airways was adopted on the eve of delivery of the company's HS748. The type was introduced into service on the Coventry to Paris route on 22May84 in a 33 seat executive configuration. The schedule was flown twice on weekdays and once on Sundays. The aircraft was also available for charter in either a 44- or 33-seat layout. The company ceased trading in Aug84.

G-VAJK   1557

Viação Aérea Rio-Grandense (VARIG)

(RG/VRG)

Rio de Janeiro, Brazil

After leasing the second prototype for demonstrations from Dec65 to Jan66, this company ordered ten Srs.2/235s on 04Apr66 with delivery from Nov67 to Sep68. The aircraft were flown over an extensive domestic network throughout Brazil, at one time serving no less than fifty-nine different points from hubs at Brasília, Rio de Janeiro and São Paulo. Among points served were Alegrete, Almenara, Alto Parnaiba, Araxá, Bagé, Balsas, Barra, Barra do Corda, Barreiros, Belém, Belo Horizonte, Bom Jesus, Campina Grande, Carolina, Crateus, Cruz Alta, Curitiba, Floriano, Fortaleza, Foz do Iguaçu, Gilbués, Goiânia, Governado Valadares, Grajau, Iguatu, Ilhéus, Imperatriz, Itabuna, Itajai, João Pessoa, Joinville, Juazeiro, Livramento, Marabá, Miracema, Montes Claros, Nanuque, Paulo Alfonso, Parnaiba, Pedro Afonso, Pelotas, Petrolina, Põrto Alegre, Põrto Nacional, Recife,

Final production at Woodford in early 1968, with VARIG Series 2 PP-VDS c/n 1630 in the foreground, plus VARIG PP-VDR and VDT and a LAN Chile aircraft identifiable in the background on the line.   *(WHC/BAe)*

VARIG's Series 2 PP-VDU c/n 1632 photographed at Woodford in June 1968.   *(WHC/BAe)*

Wasaya Airways Ltd Series 2B C-GDTD c/n 1779. Note the fleet number '803' on the nosewheel door. (Colin Carswell)

Remanso, Salvador, Santa Maria, Santo Angelo, São Luíz, Teresina, Uberaba, Uberlândia, Uruguaiana, Vitória and Xique-Xique. Many flights were of ten sectors with turnarounds as short as ten minutes at jungle strips. Disposal of the fleet commenced in Sep75 and had been completed by Jan77.

PP-VDN	1625	PP-VDR	1629	PP-VDV	1633
PP-VDO	1626	PP-VDS	1630	PP-VDX	1634
PP-VDP	1627	PP-VDT	1631	PP-VJQ	1535
PP-VDQ	1628	PP-VDU	1632		

Wasaya Airways Ltd/LP (WG/WT/WSG)
Thunder Bay, Red Lake, Sioux Lookout and Pickle Lake, Ontario, Canada

Previously known as V Kelner Airways Ltd., this company bought a Srs.2A/233 from Springer Aerospace in Aug89 followed by a Srs.2A/244 from the same source in Apr90. The first aircraft was converted to a specialised unpressurised pure freighter with large double cargo doors between Mar90 and Feb91. After this aircraft was written off in Aug91, a Srs.2A/209 was leased from Air Manitoba Ltd until late Nov of the same year. In Oct91 a Srs.2B/398 and a Srs.2B/399, the latter fitted with a large rear freight door, were leased from Holter Leasing Inc, who had in turn purchased the aircraft from Air Niger.

In Apr92, a Srs.2A/310 fitted with a large rear freight door was purchased. Two further aircraft were leased, firstly a Srs.2A/264 in Nov96 and then a Srs.2A/209 in Feb97. Both these aircraft were purchased in Jan99. The Srs.2B/399 was sold in Feb98 while the Srs.2A/310 was written off in Aug98. The Srs.2B/398 was returned to Holter Leasing Inc in Oct 2000. A Srs.2A/214 specialised pure freighter with a large rear freight door was leased in Sep98 prior to its purchase in Jan99. The most recent purchase has been two Srs.2B/424s which were bought for spares recovery only in Sep05.

The company specialises in passenger and cargo charter operations throughout central and northern Canada, supplying fuel, food and equipment to far-flung settlements. Fire fighting teams are also flown to remote areas. To cater for the specialised nature of the company's work, two aircraft have undergone major engineering work. In Aug96 the Srs.2A/244 was fitted out as a specialised tanker and is used exclusively in this rôle, while in Dec96 the Srs.2B/398 was fitted with an APU to maintain acceptable cabin temperatures on turnarounds when used in the passenger rôle. This

last aircraft was withdrawn from service in Oct00 and sold in Feb04 and the four remaining aircraft are now only used in the freight/fuel delivery rôle to numerous destinations in Northwestern Ontario including Bearskin Lake, Big Trout Lake, Fort Severn, Kasabonika, Kingfisher Lake, Webequie and Wunnummin Lake and also to destinations in Manitoba mainly from Red and Pickle Lakes. Heavy HS 748 maintenance is carried out at Thunder Bay while secondary maintenance bases are located at Pickle Lake and Red Lake. The Srs.2A/264 was destroyed by fire on the ground in Jun12 leaving just three aircraft on strength. C-FFFS was placed into storage at Pickle Lake on 07Apr16.

C-FFFS	1663	C-GBCY	1803	C-GMAA	1576
C-FTTW	1681	C-GDTD	1779	C-GTAD	1750
C-FKTL	1613	C-GLTC	1656	(V2-LCS)	1802
C-FKTL	1778				

West Air Sweden AB (PT/SWN)
Göteborg & Lidköping, Sweden

West Air Sweden obtained the four remaining Srs.2/244s of DFS Deutsche Flugsicherung in Sep95 which were converted subsequently into Srs.2A/244s. A Srs.2A/235 was obtained in Aug96, a Srs.2A/264 in Feb97, a Srs.2B/371 with a Large Freight Door in Aug97 and for spares use only a Srs.2A/260 in Sep97. A Srs.2B/399 with a large rear freight door was purchased in Mar98 while a Srs.2A/333 was bought in May98. The last aircraft to be obtained were two Srs.2/229s, purchased from the Royal Australian Air Force in Mar99 which were converted into Srs.2A/229s. The second of these entered service in Jun00 and raised the company's operational fleet of 748s to eleven. All aircraft were brought up to a similar standard and conformed with the latest JAR rulings, while several aircraft were fitted with Dart hush kits. In a programme to reduce airframe weight and to increase payload, all non-essential equipment was removed which included the APUs from the ex-RAAF, DFS and Fred Olsen aircraft. A Srs.2A/310 with a large rear freight door was leased from Air Inuit of Canada from Mar99 to early Jan00.

The aircraft, which were all converted to pure freighters, were used primarily on contract night mail services on behalf of the Swedish Postal Service to many domestic points from Luleå and Umeå in the north to Malmö in the south hubbing on Stockholm-Arlanda. Other points served on the postal contract included Göteborg, Jönköping, Karlstad, Norrköping, Sundsvall, Växjo and Visby. Contract night freight flights were also flown for

The view from West Air Sweden's SE-LEG c/n 1723 on finals to Lidköping, Sweden, after a special photographic sortie.   *(Christian Lindberg)*

A composite image of West Air Sweden's 748s showing two of the company's basic colour schemes..   *(Christian Lindberg)*

DHL linking Copenhagen with Århus, Billund and Stavanger. Later other destinations served on behalf of both DHL and Federal Express included Berlin-Tempelhof, Cologne, Frankfurt, Munich and Paris-Charles de Gaulle. Daytime ad hoc freight flights were also flown to numerous points within Europe. These included Bratislava, Bucharest, Budapest, Ljubljana, Prague, Vienna and Warsaw. From early Aug00 an aircraft was based in Dublin to cover a nightly flight to Stansted on behalf of Federal Express.

The Srs.2A/235 was withdrawn in late Nov00 as British Aerospace ATPs came on line to augment the fleet while a Srs.2A/244 was written-off in a ground incident in Dec01. In Jul02 it was announced that the company was taking over Air Provence International of France which would have added a Srs.2A/232 and a Srs.2A/245 to the company fleet. However, neither of these aircraft was involved in the deal and initial plans to transfer a 748 to France and operate as West Air France had been abandoned by Dec03. In Aug03 the first 748 appeared with West Air Europe titles in a new marketing scheme.

The company continued the slow rundown of its fleet with the retirement of its Srs.2A/264 in Apr04 and its Srs.2A/333 in Sep04 as more ATPs came on line. A deal to sell its two Large Freight Door equipped aircraft to Stellair of Spain was not completed, but a further deal to lease two aircraft to ALAIRE of Spain was finalised with the first delivery in May06, though initially West Air continued to fly and maintain these aircraft on the new company's behalf. The last 748 still flying on West Air's own flights flew its last revenue service on 24May07 and was transferred to ALAIRE while a Srs.2A/229 and two Srs.2A/244s were sold in Canada in Oct, early Dec06 and late May07 respectively. In early Aug and late Nov07 the two aircraft on lease to ALAIRE were returned to West Air and were sold in Kenya in late Nov07.

C-FDOX	1749	SE-LEY	1631	(SE-LIC)	1703
SE-LEG	1723	(SE-LIA)	1736	SE-LIC	1778
SE-LEK	1725	SE-LIA	1717	SE-LID	1760
SE-LEO	1726	(SE-LIB)	1737	SE-LIE	1595
SE-LEX	1727	SE-LIB	1776	SE-LIF	1596

Western EXpress Air Lines Inc (WG/WES)
Vancouver, B.C., Canada

Western EXpress Air Lines leased a Srs.2A/310 fitted with a large rear freight door from Air Inuit Ltd for a one month period from late Oct98. The aircraft was used to operate a DHL contract for parcel flights between Vancouver and Seattle while a company Friendship was on a D check.

C-FDOX 1749

Westwind Aviation Ltd ( )
Nairobi-Wilson, Kenya

Westwind Aviation, part of the Wilken Group, took delivery of an Andover C.Mk.1 in mid-Apr13. Since this time the aircraft has been mainly employed on the United Nations World Food Programme (WFP) relief flights in Southern Sudan from the forward base at Juba. Points served have included Lankien, Maban, Malakal, Pochalla, Rubkona, Rumbek and Yida. The aircraft was written off in Nov15.

TL-AEW   Set 13

West Wind Aviation Inc (WE/WEW)
Saskatoon, Saskatchewan, Canada

This airline purchased a Srs.2A/269 from Chevron Canada Resources Ltd in Jun93 and a Srs.2B/378 from British Aerospace in Oct93. The aircraft were used in the support of the uranium mining industry in northern Saskatchewan either carrying equipment in the cargo rôle or for mine crew changes when the aircraft were fitted with 46 or 47 seats respectively mainly on behalf of Cameco. Points served included Cigar Lake Mine, Cluff Lake Mine, Collins Bay Mine, Key Lake Mine, La Ronge, McArthur River Mine, Points North Landing for McLean Lake Mine and Prince Albert.

Additional points were also served including Stony Rapids for fishing charters. A Srs.2A/258 was leased from Aerial Recon Surveys Ltd for two weeks in Aug97. The Srs.2B/378 was withdrawn in late Jan04 and the Srs.2A/269 was sold in Apr06 after operating its last service on 25Feb06.

C-FAMO 1669   C-FCSE 1679   C-FQVE 1792

Williamson Diamonds Ltd ( )
Dar-es-Salaam, Tanzania

This organisation ordered one Srs.2A/286 fitted with a large rear freight door, which was delivered in Apr76. It was used in a rapid change all passenger, all freight or mixed passenger/freight configuration in support of the company's mining operations in Tanzania, carrying both equipment and personnel. The aircraft was sold in Jun95.

5H-WDL 1740

Yacimientos Petrolíferos Fiscales - YPF ( )
Buenos Aires, Argentina

YPF purchased six Srs.1/105s from Aerolíneas Argentinas between 1973 and 1975. This Argentine oil company was state-owned at the time and used its aircraft for flying personnel and equipment throughout Argentina until they were disposed of between Dec76 and Mar77. Main bases of operations were Cutral-Có, Malargue and Tartagal.

LV-HHB	1540	LV-HHD	1542	LV-HHG	1545
LV-HHC	1541	LV-HHE	1543	LV-IDV	1556

Z-Airways and Services Ltd (3Z/ZAW)
Dhaka, Bangladesh

Z-Airways leased a Srs.2B/360 fitted with an LFD in early Dec04 under an initial three year contract from International Air Parts Pty Ltd. The aircraft was employed in a pure freight configuration ferrying shrimp fry from its operational base at Cox's Bazar to Chittagong. From 1995 the company also traded in the name of Zoom Airways, Ltd. The aircraft was repossessed by International Air Parts in Oct08.

S2-ADL 1773

Zambia Air Force

The Zambian Air Force ordered one Srs.2/231 which was delivered in Jun67. This was replaced by a Srs.2A/265 in Feb71 after the former aircraft had been written off. It operated in a VIP

The sole 748 Series 2A of Williamson Diamonds Ltd, 5H-WDL c/n 1740, seen on a pre-delivery flight in 1976.   *(WHC/BAe)*

The ill-fated first 748, a Series 2, AF601 c/n 1600, of the Zambia Air Force, probably seen prior delivery in 1967. (WHC)

Zambia Airways' leased Series 2A A2-ABB c/n 1612. The aircraft, owned by Dan-Air Services Ltd, was leased to Zambia Airways from January to March 1976 after a lease to Air Botswana (Pty) – hence the Botswanan registration.

configuration for Government use but was believed to have been in store for several years. In 2001 it was overhauled and returned to service and was still active in Apr14.

AF601   1600   AF602   1688

Zambia Airways Corporation Ltd (QZ/ZAC)

Lusaka, Zambia

Zambia Airways ordered four Srs.2A/263s with delivery in Apr, Jul and Sep70 while the fourth aircraft was delivered in Jun72, after a four-month lease to Botswana Airways Corporation Ltd.

Additional aircraft were leased from Hawker Siddeley Aviation Ltd, a Srs.2A/239 in Jan and again in Mar and Apr70 and a Srs.2A/214 from early Apr to early Sep of the same year. A Srs.2A/232 was leased from the same source from Jan to Mar76.

One aircraft was sold to Air Sénégal in Mar80 while another was damaged severely in Jul83 eventually leading to its write-off. From Jul83 to Apr84 this last aircraft was replaced by a Srs.2A/264 leased from United Air Services (Pty) Ltd.

The aircraft were used on an extensive domestic network from Lusaka and Ndola to Balovale, Chipata, Kalabo, Kasama, Kasaba Bay, Kitwe, Livingstone, Lukulu, Mansa, Mbala, Mfuwe, Mongu, Ngoma, Senanga and Sesheke. They also served Blantyre and Lilongwe (Malawi), Lubumbashi (Zaire) and Harare/Salisbury

(Zimbabwe). The last two aircraft were disposed of in Dec88 and Mar89.

A2-ABB	1612	9J-ABJ	1676	9J-ABM	1635
G-AVRR	1635	9J-ABK	1677	9J-ABW	1680
ZS-LHN	1681	9J-ABL	1576	9J-ADM	1706
7P-LAI	1681				

Zambia Express Airways (1995) Ltd (OQ/SZX)

Lusaka, Zambia

From 26Dec95 to 08Aug96 scheduled services were operated by Zambia Express Airways with Executive Aerospace (Pty) Ltd 748s over the routes Lusaka-Livingstone-Johannesburg and Lusaka-Ndola-Lilongwe.

Zimbabwe Express Airlines Ltd (Z7)

Harare, Zimbabwe

From late Jan96 Zimbabwe Express commenced scheduled operations linking Harare with Hwange National Park, Kariba and Victoria Falls, with Beira in Mozambique an added destination later in the same year. Aircraft used were operated by Executive Aerospace (Pty) Ltd of South Africa. The contract was concluded in late Apr97.

ZS-LSO 1783   ZS-NNW 1785   ZS-NWW 1786

Zoom Airways Ltd

See Z-Airways & Services Ltd

Andover Operators

Note: Military Andover operators and contractors operating on behalf of the military are described below. Civilian-registered Andover operators can be found in the preceding section of this Chapter.

A & AEE

Boscombe Down, Wiltshire, UK

The Aircraft and Armament Evaluation Establishment was known as the Aeroplane and Armament Experimental Establishment until May92. Several aircraft were used at different times for CA [Controller (Air)] clearance release trials from Dec65 including parachuting tests

XS594	Set 1	XS598	Set 5	XS644	Set 28
XS595	Set 2	XS607	Set 14	XS647	Set 31
XS596	Set 3	XS611	Set 18		
XS597	Set 4	XS640	Set 24		

Defence Evaluation and Research Agency – DERA

See Defence Research Agency

Defence Research Agency

Boscombe Down, Wiltshire, UK

One aircraft was assigned to the Royal Aircraft Establishment at Farnborough in Dec72. Its base was changed to Bedford in 1973 where it flew with Aero Flight. This same aircraft was also used for parachuting trials at Farnborough before transfer to the ETPS at Farnborough in Aug75. A second aircraft was used for a time in 1974, while in the same year Farnborough took one aircraft on permanent strength. From Sep76 a further aircraft was used, initially based at West Freugh. The Royal Aircraft Establishment was renamed the Royal Aerospace Establishment but was absorbed into the Defence Research Agency (DRA) in Apr91. All operations were moved to Boscombe Down in Apr94. The DRA was renamed the Defence Evaluation and Research Agency (DERA) with effect from 01Apr97 and as QinetiQ from 02Jul01.

The last operational Andover was withdrawn from service on 31Aug12.

XS596	Set 3	XS607	Set 14	XS646	Set 30
XS606	Set 13	XS611	Set 18		

Empire Test Pilots' School – ETPS

Boscombe Down, Wiltshire, UK

One aircraft was on permanent strength for use by the ETPS as a flying classroom from Aug75, coming under the control of QinetiQ from 02Jul01 until making its last flight at Boscombe Down on 31Aug12.

XS606   Set 13

Hunting Aviation Ltd

East Midlands, UK

With effect from 19Oct93 this company was contracted to carry out airfield calibration duties formerly performed by 115 Squadron of the Royal Air Force. Four Andover E.Mk.3s were used initially for this task. One aircraft was withdrawn in 1995 and the remaining aircraft were withdrawn from service after the contract was terminated on 19Oct96.

XS603	Set 10	XS610	Set 17	XS640	Set 24
XS605	Set 12				

North Atlantic Treaty Organisation

One aircraft was based at Fornebu, Oslo with the Commander Air Forces Northern Europe from 1970 and carried Viking Ship markings from at least 1975 until it was transferred to 32 Squadron in Dec85.

XS637   Set 21

QinetiQ

See Defence Research Agency

Royal Aircraft/Aerospace Establishment

See Defence Research Agency

Royal Air Force Andover C.Mk.1 XS644 Set 28 seen at Brize Norton, Oxfordshire, on 5th June 1993 in its final RAF colour scheme.   (WHC)

Royal Aircraft Establishment Andover C.Mk.1 XS646 Set 30 at Greenham Common, Berkshire, on 27th June 1981, in the colourful 'raspberry ripple' scheme of red, white, black and blue.   *(Keith Gaskell)*

Royal Air Force

Details of Andover use by RAF Squadrons and Units are given below. Full service histories can be found under the Individual Aircraft Histories in Chapter 4.

21 Squadron

Based at Khormaksar, Aden and later Sharjah (Trucial States), the squadron had one CC.Mk.2 aircraft on strength from 01Mar66 until 28Oct67, while a C.Mk.1 was also used from 15Feb-17Jul67.

XS793	1565	XS611	Set 18

32 Squadron

Based at Northolt, Middlesex. When the type was first introduced, this squadron was known as the Metropolitan Communications Squadron, and operated a single CC.Mk.1 from early 1969. It used several C.Mk.1s and CC.Mk.2s from its formation on 01Feb69 until the type was withdrawn from use on 31Mar95.

XS597	Set 4	XS644	Set 28	XS792	1564
XS637	Set 21	XS789	1561	XS793	1565
XS639	Set 23	XS791	1563	XS794	1566
XS643	Set 27				

46 Squadron

Formed on 01Dec66 at Abingdon, Oxfordshire. 46 Squadron moved to Thorney Island on 11Sep70 and was disbanded on 31Aug75. Most aircraft passed through this squadron at some time. Listed below are those aircraft known to have been used operationally.

XS594	Set 1	XS604	Set 11	XS613	Set 20
XS595	Set 2	XS605	Set 12	XS637	Set 21
XS596	Set 3	XS606	Set 13	XS638	Set 22
XS597	Set 4	XS607	Set 14	XS639	Set 23
XS599	Set 6	XS608	Set 15	XS640	Set 24
XS600	Set 7	XS609	Set 16	XS641	Set 25
XS601	Set 8	XS610	Set 17	XS644	Set 28
XS602	Set 9	XS611	Set 18	XS645	Set 29
XS603	Set 10	XS612	Set 19	XS646	Set 30

48 Squadron

Based at Changi, Singapore.

XS791	1563	XS792	1564

52 Squadron

Formed on 01Dec66 at Seletar, Singapore, moving to Changi on 17Feb69. The squadron was disbanded on 31Dec69.

XS606	Set 13	XS608	Set 15	XS613	Set 20
XS607	Set 14	XS612	Set 19	XS637	Set 21

60 Squadron

A Communications squadron based at Wildenrath, Germany, 60 Squadron used several C.Mk.1s, C.Mk.1(PR)s and CC.Mk.2s from Nov71 until it disbanded on 31Mar92.

XS596	Set 3	XS637	Set 21	XS791	1563
XS597	Set 04	XS641	Set 25	XS793	1565

84 Squadron

Based at Sharjah, Trucial States, this squadron converted to Andover C.Mk.1s from Blackburn Beverley aircraft in Aug67. It moved to Muharraq (Bahrain) in Dec70 and disbanded on 31Oct71. Aircraft were rotated to the Search and Rescue Flight which had aircraft based at various locations in the Gulf area at different times.

XS595 A	Set 2	XS642 C	Set 26	XS646 F	Set 30
XS611	Set 18	XS643 D	Set 27	XS647	Set 31
XS641 B	Set 25	XS645 E	Set 21		

115 Squadron

Based at Brize Norton, Oxfordshire, this squadron converted to the Andover from Argosy aircraft between Nov76 and Jan78. 115 Squadron was employed in the calibration of navigational aids at all Ministry of Defence airfields worldwide. The C.Mk.1s were used for crew training while the E.Mk.3 and E.Mk.3As were used in the calibration rôle.

The squadron moved to Benson on 04Jan83 and disbanded on 19Oct93. Three of these aircraft (Sets 10, 23 and 28) were used on detachment to the Electronic Warfare and Avionics Unit at Wyton.

XS596	Set 3	XS610	Set 17	XS641	Set 25
XS597	Set 4	XS637	Set 21	XS643	Set 27
XS603	Set 10	XS639	Set 23	XS644	Set 28
XS605	Set 12	XS640	Set 24		

152 Squadron

Based at Muharraq, Bahrain. The squadron used a CC.Mk.2 for 10$\frac{1}{2}$ weeks from late Oct67.

XS793   1565

Andover OCU

Based at Abingdon, Oxfordshire, this Operational Conversion Unit received aircraft from early Jul66 and remained operational until Aug70.

XS598 E	Set 5	XS600 B	Set 7	XS602 D	Set 9
XS599 A	Set 6	XS601 C	Set 8	XS603 F	Set 10

Queen's Flight

The RAF ordered six Srs.2/206s, known as Andover CC.Mk.2s in RAF service, all in a VIP configuration with delivery between Jul64 and Sep65. Two of the aircraft went straight to The Queen's Flight at Benson (XS789 and XS790), one to the Middle East Communications Squadron (XS793), eventually becoming the third aircraft for the Queen's Flight in Jan68, with XS794, used at Abingdon in the VIP rôle, spending time on loan to The Queen's Flight in 1967 and 1971.

The Queen's Flight aircraft were used extensively all over the world on official duties for several members of the United Kingdom Royal Family. Countries visited included Fiji, Tonga and Papua New Guinea in the Pacific, India and the Gulf States, Canada and the West Indies and numerous countries in North, West and East Africa. Most countries in Europe were also visited during the type's twenty-six years' service with The Queen's Flight.

In Aug and Oct86 two of The Queen's Flight aircraft were transferred to 32 and 60 Squadrons after replacement by BAe 146

Series 100s. The last Queen's Flight aeroplane (XS790) was transferred to the Defence Research Agency early in 1991.

XS789	1561	XS793	1565	XS794	1566
XS790	1562				

241 OCU

Based at Brize Norton, Oxfordshire. This Operational Conversion Unit was used to provide crews for 115 Squadron and initial conversions for the Royal New Zealand Air Force. NZ7624 of the RNZAF was used together with C.Mk.1s of 115 Squadron for a short while between its handover and departure for New Zealand.

242 OCU

Based at Thorney Island, West Sussex. Previously named Air Training Squadron, but also known as Andover Training Squadron, the Air Training Squadron was formed at Abingdon on 01Apr68 and moved to Thorney Island on 01Aug70. 242 OCU was formed in Nov of the same year.

XS599	Set 6	XS605	Set 12	XS638	Set 22
XS600	Set 7	XS610	Set 17	XS644	Set 28
XS603	Set 10	XS613	Set 20		

EWAU

The Electronic Warfare and Avionics Unit was based at Wyton, Cambridgeshire and used one C.Mk.1 from Aug-Oct75. This was replaced by another C.Mk.1 from Oct75. This last aircraft was converted to an E.Mk.3A in Apr83. An additional E.Mk.3A was employed from Jul-Nov83.

XS603	Set 10	XS639	Set 23	XS644	Set 28

FEAF

The Far East Air Force VIP Flight operated a single CC.Mk.2 from Sep-Nov71.

XS792   1564

FECS

The Far East Air Force Communications Squadron operated two CC.Mk.2s from Jul65 and Feb67 until 31Dec69.

XS791	1563	XS792	1564

MCS

The Metropolitan Communications Squadron based at Northolt, Middlesex, operated one CC.Mk.2 from Jan69 until it was reformed as 32 Squadron on 01Feb69.

XS794   1566

MECS

The Middle East Communications Squadron was based at Muharraq, Bahrain, and used two CC.Mk.2s from March and Jul65 until Mar66 and Feb67. A single C.Mk.1 in the VIP rôle was operated from Jul67 to Dec70.

XS611	Set 18	XS791	1563	XS793	1565

5 MU

MU's are fundamentally Aircraft Storage Units, and No. 5 Maintenance Unit was based at Kemble, Gloucestershire.

15 MU

This Aircraft Storage Unit was based at Wroughton, Wiltshire.

60 MU

No. 60 Maintenance Unit was based at Leconfield, Yorkshire.

71 MU

No. 71 Maintenance Unit was based at Bicester, Oxfordshire and was used as a mobile unit for Andover repairs.

Royal New Zealand Air Force

1 Squadron

Based at Whenuapai. Andover C.Mk.1 aircraft replaced Bristol 170 Mk.31s over the period from Dec76 to Oct77. They were used in the Short/Medium range tactical transport rôle of troop lift, casualty evacuation, paratrooping and paradropping of supplies. The Squadron was deactivated on 07Dec84.

NZ7620	Set 6	NZ7624	Sct 15	NZ7626	Set 19
NZ7621	Set 7	NZ7625	Set 18	NZ7629	Set 29
NZ7623	Set 11				

42 Squadron

Based at Ohakea as a VIP and General Communications Squadron. The aircraft were configured in either rôle and were delivered between Feb and May77. With effect from 10Dec84 the Squadron moved to Whenuapai and took over the tasks performed by the deactivated 1 Squadron in addition to its own work.

One aircraft was based in Teheran, Iran with UNIMOG from Sep88 until Dec90 in support of the United Nations. On 01Jan93 three aircraft were despatched to Mogadishu in Somalia on similar relief work for the United Nations returning to New Zealand in May93. The last aircraft were retired from service on 20Jun98.

NZ7620	Set 6	NZ7624	Set 15	NZ7627	Set 20
NZ7621	Set 7	NZ7625	Set 18	NZ7628	Set 22
NZ7622	Set 9	NZ7626	Set 19	NZ7629	Set 29
NZ7623	Set 11				

Democratic Republic of Congo Air Force

This organisation was reportedly operating two Andover C.Mk.1s obtained in 2009, the origins of which are still to be confirmed and whose status is uknown.

9T-TCO	Set ??	9T-TCP	Set ??

A line-up of four Royal New Zealand Air Force Andovers including the two VIP aircraft NZ7622 (Set 9) and NZ7628 (Set 22). (WHC)

One of the two Royal New Zealand Air Force VIP-configured Andovers seen in a stunning inflight photograph. (Fred Barnes/RNZAF)

Chapter 4
Individual Aircraft Histories

The history of each 748 built is described in the following pages in constructor's number order. This is followed by a similar listing for Andover C.Mk.1s and then Kanpur production. Constructor's numbers run from 1534 onwards, the only omissions being 1648-1655 inclusive which were not built while 1534 was rebuilt as 1548 as the aerodynamic prototype for the Andover C.Mk.1. The first four production C.Mk.1s were allocated constructor's numbers but the remainder of production was only identified by set numbers. UK Set 6 was purely a fatigue test airframe and was never allocated a constructor's number. Kanpur production ran from constructor's number 500 to 588 inclusive, the first twenty-eight aircraft also being identified by United Kingdom set numbers from kits or part kits supplied from the British production line. All first flights of British built aircraft were from Woodford unless otherwise stated, while delivery dates of new aircraft were all ex Woodford (excepting c/ns 1723, 1806 and 1807) and are official BAc handover dates. Where aircraft have been leased to other operators, dates quoted are from/to the owners' home base unless otherwise stated. For completeness, known leases are recorded, although it is to be expected that several transactions may well have gone unrecorded while dates can on occasions be difficult to ascertain. Leases of under one week are not shown.

Since delivery, most Series 2 aircraft are believed to have had their engines uprated from Mk.531 to Mk.533-2, while many aircraft have been further upgraded to Series 2A standard by substituting Mk.534 engines for Mk.531 or 533-2. Only those definitely known to have been uprated are recorded. Models 228, 244 and 268 although classified as Series 2 aircraft, were delivered from new with the higher rated Dart Mk.550-2 engines for either prolonged high altitude performance or in the case of the RAAF aircraft for improved dry rated performance. Kanpur produced Series 2s are believed to have retained their originally delivered modification standard engines. However the last twenty Indian produced aircraft, which were fitted with large freight doors, are powered by Rolls-Royce Dart RDa.7 Mk.536-2T engines. This mark of engine had earlier been flight tested in the Andes when fitted in c/n 1662.

Details of Indian production are regrettably somewhat abbreviated due to the lack of reliable information, while it can be expected that Vayudoot Limited may well have temporarily leased 748s from the Indian Airlines fleet for short periods from earlier dates than those indicated.

At the end of the histories can be found an alphabetical registration/constructor's number cross reference for civilian, military and finally Class 'B' registrations. Bracketed registrations in this section are those which were anticipated but never in fact used on the aircraft.

The UK Civil Aviation Authority has registered all British built 748 aircraft from c/n 1534 to 1559 inclusive as Avro 748s when they have used United Kingdom marks. All other United Kingdom registered 748s have been registered as HS.748s.

G-APZV c/n 1534, the first prototype, seen in an early photograph probably taken while on a test flight from Woodford. (WHC/AV Roe & Co Ltd))

The information given in each aircraft entry is in the following order (where applicable):

C/n   Set No   Series

1534   Srs.1/100

Regd as **G-APZV** to A.V. Roe & Co Ltd 24Mar60 (CofR R.6576/1) as first prototype. R/o 26May60. F/f 24Jun60 from company's Woodford Airfield with Avro's chief test pilot, Jimmy Harrison in command, Colin Allen in the right hand seat and flight test observers Bob Dixon-Stubbs and Mike Turner also on board. CofA issued 06Sep60. Displayed at Farnborough Air Show in Sep60. C/o grass landing trials at Coventry 20Jul61. Regn cld 09May63 after last flight on 11Jul62 and converted into HS780/748MF prototype at Woodford as c/n 1548 regd as G-ARRV.

TT 841 hrs, 857 ldgs

1535   Srs.1/100

Regd as **G-ARAY** to A.V. Roe & Co Ltd 21Apr60 (CofR R.6861/1) as second prototype. Construction delayed by fire at Avro's Chadderton works. F/f 10Apr61, CofA issued 29May61. C/o Series 1 tropical trials in Cyprus and Spain in July and August61. Converted to Srs.1/200 with Rolls-Royce Dart Mk.531 engines as a Srs.2 development prototype and f/f as such 06Nov61. Regd as a Series.2 09Nov61. C/o competitive rough field trials against the Handley Page Herald at Martlesham Heath in Feb62 which led to the Andover C.Mk.1 order. Named "Pride of Perth" 07Mar62 at Woodford, carrying this name until the first overseas lease. C/o Srs.2 tropical trials in Kenya and Nigeria 08Mar-19Apr62. Demonstrated at the Hannover Air Show 04-09May62. C/o SEP2 Autopilot trials 13-24Aug62. C/o a demonstration tour of the Middle East and India 18Oct-05Nov62 and a similar tour of Europe between 24-29Mar63 when it visited Amsterdam, Brussels, Copenhagen, Milan, Paris, Vienna and Zurich. This was followed by further demonstrations in Africa and the Far East between 04Apr63 and 25May63 (all dates from/to Woodford). Shown Paris Air Show 05-17Jun63. Demonstrated to Austrian Airlines at Innsbruck and Salzburg on 20-21Jun63. Regd to Hawker Siddeley Aviation Ltd, Avro Whitworth Division 11Jul63 (CofR R.6861/2). A demonstration tour of the Americas and the Caribbean was c/o between 31Dec63 and 10Mar64, before the aircraft ferried Ringway-Woodford the following day. Loaned to the Royal Air Force Queen's Flight for crew training at various times between 31Mar64 and 02Jul64 but also demonstrated to Channel Airways at Portsmouth, Ipswich and Southend on 19-20Apr64. Regn cld 18Jan65 as transferred Venezuela. Lsd Línea Aeropostal Venezolana 09Feb65 to 07Jul65

regd as **YV-C-AMC**. Restored to Hawker Siddeley Aviation Ltd as **G-ARAY** 07Jul65 (CofR R.6861/3) for demonstrations in South and Central America before returning Woodford 24Jul65. Lsd Skyways Coach Air Ltd 13Aug to Sep65. Departed Woodford for lse to Viaçao Aérea Rio Grandense (VARIG) 13Dec65 via Stornoway, Keflavik, Søndre Strømfjord, Frobisher Bay, Sept Îles, Albany, Wilmington, Nassau, Antigua, Georgetown, Belem and Brasilia to São Paulo. Regd as **PP-VJQ** 17Dec65 and UK regn cld 18Dec65 as transferred Brazil. C/o inaugural proving flight from São Paulo to Iguaçu Falls 23Dec65. Restored as **G-ARAY** to Hawker Siddeley Aviation Ltd 24Jan66 (CofR R.6861/4) returning to Woodford 14Feb66. Used for Autair crew training 02-08Mar66. Regn cld 27Apr66 as transferred Windward & Leeward Islands and lsd to Leeward Islands Air Transport Services Ltd as **VP-LIO** from 27Apr66 to 23Aug66. Departed Antigua same day via San Juan, Bermuda, Sept Îles, Frobisher Bay, Søndre Strømfjord and Keflavik arriving Woodford 25Aug66. Shown at Farnborough Air Show Sep66 in full LIAT c/s as VP-LIO. Used for crew training and trials until restored as **G-ARAY** to Hawker Siddeley Aviation Ltd 18Nov66 (CofR R.6861/5). Fitted with rear extensions to the engine nacelles in a drag reduction programme and noted as such at Woodford 20Jan67. Reverted to standard fit. Lsd Philippine Airlines Inc for service evaluation on DC-3 routes with del ex Woodford as G-ARAY 20Feb67 arriving Manila 25Feb67. Regn cld 27Feb67 as transferred Philippines and regd **PI-C784**. Restored as **G-ARAY** to Hawker Siddeley Aviation Ltd 01Jun67 (CofR R.6861/6) and ferried ex Manila 02Jun67 arriving Woodford 08Jun67. Regn cld 10Jul67 as transferred Denmark. Flight tested as **G-11** 23Jul67 in Falckair c/s prior to sale and del to Falcks Flyvetjeneste A/S as **OY-DFV** as a Srs.2/200 04Aug67. Airline and aircraft absorbed into Maersk Air I/S Nov69. Sold Dan-Air Services Ltd with del Gatwick 01May71. Restored to Dan-Air Services Ltd as **G-ARAY** 03May71 (CofR R.6861/7). CofA issued 17May71. In service 18May71. Converted back to a Srs.1/200 with Rolls-Royce Dart 514 engines 15Mar72. Converted to Srs.1A/200 25Jul77. WFU 17Oct89 and stored Gatwick, U.K. Ferried Lasham 31Oct89 where wings, engines and tail unit were removed. Regn cld 02Nov92 as PWFU. The complete fuselage was taken away by lorry to an unknown destination in Feb93.

TT 40,029 hrs, 52,285 ldgs

1536   (1)   Srs.1/101

Regd as **G-ARMV** to A.V. Roe & Co Ltd 28Apr61 (CofR R.7271/1). First production aircraft. F/f 31Aug61, CofA issued 02Sep61. Shown at Farnborough Air Show Sep61. Ferried Lympne 02Nov61. Used for route proving with Skyways Coach

G-ARMV c/n 1536 at Ma'an, Jordan, during Avro demonstrations in December 1961.   *(WHC/AV Roe & Co Ltd)*

Air Ltd 06-26Nov61. Returned Woodford 30Nov61. C/o sales tour to Italy, Jordan and Syria 06-13Dec61. Lsd Skyways Coach Air Ltd with del 03Apr62. Entered service 17Apr62 between Lympne and Beauvais. Regd to Hawker Siddeley Aviation Ltd, Avro Whitworth Division 02Dec64 (CofR R.7272/2). Sub-lsd B.K.S. Air Transport Ltd from 29Mar65 when del Lympne–Leeds/Bradford until Apr65. W/o landing Lympne, Kent, U.K. 11Jul65 while operating flight SX716 from Beauvais. No fatalities among 4 crew and 48 pax on board. Regn cld 18Nov65 as PWFU.

TT 3,432 hrs, 4,791 ldgs

1537 (15) Srs.1/101

Regd as **G-ARMW** to A.V. Roe & Co Ltd 28Apr61 (CofR R.7273/1). F/f 08May62, CofA issued 28May62. Lsd Skyways Coach Air Ltd with del 05Jun62. Sub-lsd B.K.S. Air Transport Ltd with del from Lympne to Leeds 30Sep62 entering service 01Oct62 on the Leeds-Heathrow route as BK401. Returned Skyways Coach Air Ltd 25May63. Regd to Hawker Siddeley Aviation Ltd, Avro Whitworth Division 02Dec64 (CofR R/7273/2). Regn cld 06Jan65 as transferred Leeward Islands and regd **VP-LII**. Lsd Leeward Islands Air Transport Services Ltd with del 27Jan65 arriving Antigua 31Jan65. In service 01Feb65. Returned U.K. 26May65 as VP-LII. Restored as **G-ARMW** to Hawker Siddeley Aviation Ltd 28May65 (CofR R.7273/3) and lease to Skyways Coach Air Ltd continued. Lsd B.K.S. Air Transport Ltd from Oct66 to Apr67 and from 03Oct67 to 09Dec67. Regd to Skyways Coach Air Ltd 28Jan71 (CofR R.7273/4) after sale to them. Regd to Spakey Ltd 25Feb71 (CofR R.7273/5). Name changed to International Skyways Ltd 05Mar71. Regd to Dan-Air Services Ltd 26Apr72 (CofR R.7273/6) following purchase of airline and aircraft by them on 12Apr72. Converted Srs.1A/101 03Mar79. Lsd Air BVI Ltd after roll out Manchester as **VP-LVO**. Del ex Manchester as G-ARMW 28Oct85 via Stornoway, Keflavik, Søndre Strømfjord, Frobisher Bay, Schefferville, Halifax, Bangor, Wilmington and Nassau arriving Tortola 31Oct85. Regn cld 01Nov85 as transferred Virgin Islands (UK) and regd **VP-LVO**. Named "BVI Hope". Del Manchester for Major Check 12Sep86. Departed Manchester 22Oct86 for continued lse to Air BVI Ltd. Returned Manchester at end of lse 21Apr90. Restored as **G-ARMW** to Dan-Air Services Ltd 18May90 (CofR G-ARMW/R7). CofA issued 11Jun90. Entered service 12Jun90. Flew last service 07Sep90 and sold Hawk Aviation 13Sep90 for operation by Aberdeen Airways Ltd. Del from Manchester to Aberdeen the following day. Repossessed by Dan-Air Services Ltd 28Dec90 and ferried from East Midlands to Lasham. Sold Clewer Aviation Ltd to whom regd as **G-FBMV** 19Mar91 (CofR G-FBMV/R1). Del from Lasham to Lydd 21Mar91 and operated by British Independent Airways Ltd. Company ceased operations 05Jul91. Restored as **G-ARMW** to Clewer Aviation Ltd 13Jan92 (CofR G-ARMW/R8). Re-regd **G-ERMV** 16Mar92 (CofR G-ERMV/R1) for use by Independent Airways Ltd. Regn cld 04Sep92 as transferred Nepal. Lsd Necon Air Ltd and del from Southend via Forli as **9N-ACH** 05Sep92 arriving Kathmandu 09Sep92. Entered service 14Sep92. Flew last revenue flight 06Nov94 and put in store Kathmandu, Nepal. Noted derelict 14Mar08.

TT 42,290 hrs, 54,542 ldgs

1538 (18) Srs.1/101

Regd as **G-ARMX** to A.V. Roe & Co Ltd 28Apr61 (CofR R.7274/1). F/f 19Oct62, CofA issued 15Mar63. Lsd Skyways Coach Air Ltd with del 02Apr63. Sub-lsd B.K.S. Air Transport Ltd 18-21Jun63 and from 20-24Aug63. Regd to Hawker Siddeley Aviation Ltd, Avro Whitworth Division 02Dec64 (CofR R.7274/2). Wet lsd British Eagle International Airlines Ltd and ferried Lympne-Heathrow-Liverpool 24May65. Entered service 25May65 between Liverpool and Glasgow. Returned lessor 04Jun65. Lsd B.K.S. Air Transport Ltd from 03Nov66 to Apr67 and again from 10Oct67 to 29Mar68. Regd to Skyways Coach

Air Ltd 28Jan71 (CofR R.7274/3) after sale to them. Regd to Spakey Ltd 25Feb71 (CofR R.7274/4). Name changed to International Skyways Ltd 05Mar71. Regd to Dan-Air Services Ltd 26Apr72 (CofR R.7274/5) following purchase of airline and aircraft by them on 12Apr72. Converted to Srs.1A/101 27Sep77. Lsd Air BVI Ltd 13Nov83 with del ex Manchester as G-ARMX 21Nov83. Regn cld 03Dec83 and regd **VP-LVN**. Named "BVI Perseverance". Del Manchester 20Oct87 for maintenance with Dan-Air Engineering Ltd. Departed Manchester 21Nov87 for continued lease to Air BVI Ltd. Sold Air BVI Ltd 30Nov89. Flew last service for Air BVI Ltd 22Apr90. Returned Manchester, U.K. 30Apr90 after repossession by Dan-Air Services Ltd and put into storage. Restored as **G-ARMX** to Dan-Air Services Ltd 18May90 (CofR G-ARMX/R6) but never returned to service and reduced to produce by Sep90. To Manchester Airport Fire Service, fuselage in fire dump, removed Aug 00. Regn cld 21Oct92 as transferred British Virgin Islands.

TT 38,249 hrs, 48,861 ldgs

1539 (3) Srs.1/105

F/f 10Dec61 as **LV-PIZ**. H/O 11Jan62. Del Aerolíneas Argentinas 18Jan62 via Stornoway, Keflavik, Goose Bay, Detroit and Belize arriving Buenos Aires 26Jan62. Re-regd **LV-HGW** and named "Ciudad de Bahía Blanca". C/o a proving flight to Punta del Este, Uruguay on 15Feb62. Became the first Avro 748 to enter regular commercial service on 02Apr62. W/o 6 minutes after take-off from Corrientes for Rosario and Buenos Aires-Aeroparque as AR707 on 04Feb70 after entering severe turbulence. 4 crew and 33 pax killed.

TT 19,049 hrs, 15,739 ldgs

1540 (4) Srs.1/105

F/f 20Feb62 as **LV-PJA**. Del Aerolíneas Argentinas 24Mar62 arriving Buenos Aires 31Mar62. Re-regd **LV-HHB** and named "Ciudad de Corrientes". Pax door blew off when operating AR737 from Resistencia to Buenos Aires 30Aug62 and stewardess lost. Repaired. Sold Yacimientos Petrolíferos Fiscales 28Mar73. W/o during cruise in Cerro de la Esperanza hills near Neuquén, Argentina 14Apr76 while en route Rincón de los Sauces and Cutral-Có after separation of the starboard outer wing and tailplane. 3 crew and 31 pax killed.

TT 25,759 hrs, 24,130 ldgs

1541 (5) Srs.1/105

F/f 02Apr62 as **LV-PJR**. Repainted as **LV-PRJ** and del Aerolíneas Argentinas 24Apr62 arriving Buenos Aires 01May62. Re-regd **LV-HHC** and named "Ciudad de Concordia". Sold Yacimientos Petrolíferos Fiscales 1973. Sold Dan-Air Services Ltd and regd to them as **G-BEKC** 28Feb77 (CofR G-BEKC/R1), the same date it departed Ezeiza on del. Arrived Manchester 08Mar77. CofA issued 04Aug77. Entered service 05Aug77 from Manchester to Newcastle. Withdrawn from service 21Nov87 after operating its last flight from Belfast to Manchester, U.K. on the same date. Noted robbed of numerous parts 26Apr89. Dismantled May89 with nose section going to Reflectone Inc for ATP simulator use and other parts to Woodford. Regn cld 21Oct92 as transferred USA.

TT 37,199 hrs, 35,272 ldgs

1542 (7) Srs.1/105

F/f 21Apr62 as **LV-PUC**. Del Aerolíneas Argentinas 07May62 arriving Buenos Aires 15May62. Re-regd **LV-HHD** and named "Ciudad de Salta". Sold Yacimientos Petrolíferos Fiscales 19Mar73. Sold Dan-Air Services Ltd being regd to them as **G-BEKF** 24Mar77 (CofR G-BEKF/R1). Painted as G-BEKF 26Mar77 and ferried from Comodoro Rivadavia to Buenos Aires for pre-ferry maintenance. Departed Buenos Aires 05Apr77 arriving Manchester 14Apr77. Ferried Lasham 22Apr77. CofA issued

09Jul77. Ferried Aberdeen 21Jul77. W/o Sumburgh Airport, Scotland 31Jul79. Aborted take-off but overran into sea. 2 crew and 15 pax killed, 30 survived. Regn cld 14Dec79 as aircraft destroyed.

TT 29,007 hrs, 26,578 ldgs

1543   (10)   Srs.1/105

F/f 19May62 as **LV-PUF**. Del Aerolíneas Argentinas 05Jun62 arriving Buenos Aires 13Jun62. Re-regd **LV-HHE** and named "Ciudad de Resistencia". In service 14Jul62. Sold Yacimientos Petrolíferos Fiscales 18Apr75. Sold Dan-Air Services Ltd being regd to them as **G-BEJD** 17Dec76 (CofR G-BEJD/R1) and painted as such on the same date. Del Manchester 24Dec76 in full Yacimientos Petrolíferos Fiscales c/s. CofA issued 07Mar77. In service 08Mar77. Interior stripped for use as a pure freighter without fitment of large freight door 14Feb87. In service 31Mar87. Stored Manchester with effect from 28Mar92. Sold Janes Aviation Ltd 15Jul92 with del Manchester-Blackpool 16Jul92. Ferried Glasgow 02Aug92 and entered service between Glasgow and Coventry the following day. Regd to Janes Aviation 748 Ltd 03Aug92 (CofR G-BEJD/R2). Named "John Case" after JEA Engineering's Quality Assurance Manager late 1992 and noted as such 15Sep93 painted overall white. Company renamed Emerald Airways Ltd 15Sep93. Painted in Reed Aviation c/s Nov94 named "Sisyphus". Reed titles and fin marks removed. Ferried Liverpool-Blackpool as JEM65E 13Mar05 and WFU. CofA expired 29Mar06. Company's AOC suspended 04May06. Sold International Air Parts Pty Ltd 16Oct06. Regd PTB (Emerald) Pty Ltd 12Dec06 (CofR G-BEJD/R3). Regn cld as PWFU 08Apr10. Dismantled and fuselage transferred to the Speke Aerodrome Heritage Group for preservation on 20Oct11 with the wings following a day later. The engines/propellers had been moved earlier.

TT 49,914 hrs, 50,882 ldgs

1544   (12)   Srs.1/105

F/f 09Jun62 as **LV-PUM**. Del Aerolíneas Argentinas 30Jun62 arriving Buenos Aires 09Jul62. Re-regd **LV-HHF** and named "Ciudad de San Juan". In service 01Aug62. Nosewheel collapsed during take-off from General Pico 06Aug63. Repaired. Sold Dan-Air Services Ltd being regd to them as **G-BEKD** 10Jun77 (CofR G-BEKD/R1). Del Manchester 18Jun77. CofA issued 26Oct77 and ferried Aberdeen the same day. Lsd Air Condal S.A. with del ex Lasham 04Jul83 as G-BEKD. Regn cld 29Jul83 as transferred Spain and regd **EC-DTP** named "Francisca" and later "St Raphael". Purchased outright Oct85. Air Condal ceased operations and aircraft del Shannon for storage 21Jan86 pending sale. R/o out 03Apr86 as **EI-BSF** at Shannon in full Ryanair colours named "The Spirit of Tipperary". Regd to Ryanair Ltd as EI-BSF 21May86 following CofA issue the previous day. In service as IW200 from Dublin to Luton 23May86. Withdrawn from service 07Jan87. Engines removed by 09Jan87 and regn cld 01Jul87 as WFU. Fuselage used as a cabin crew trainer by Ryanair Ltd at Dublin by 1994. Sold Aer Rianta Sep99 for use as a rescue trainer by the fire department. Trucked out 03Mar05 to the Irish Air Corps base at Baldonnel-Casement for use by the fire service. Moved to Fairyhouse Racecourse, County Meath, in an emergency response exercise 02Oct14. Moved to Weston Airport, Dublin, for fire service use by 07Oct14.

TT 37,234 hrs, 34,039 ldgs

1545   (13)   Srs.1/105

F/f 29Jun62 as **LV-PUP**. Del Aerolíneas Argentinas 20Jul62 arriving Buenos Aires 28Jul62. Re-regd **LV-HHG** and named "Ciudad de Mar del Plata". In service 16Aug62. Later renamed "Ciudad de La Rioja". Damaged in ground collision with DC-3 at Comodoro Rivadavia 28Jan67. Repaired. Sold Yacimientos Petrolíferos Fiscales 12Apr73. Sold Dan-Air Services Ltd being regd to them as **G-BEKE** 24Mar77 (CofR G-BEKE/R1). Ferried from Cutral Có to Buenos Aires for pre-ferry maintenance 29Mar77. Del Manchester 22Apr77. CofA issued 17Sep77. Ferried from Lasham to Aberdeen 18Sep77 and entered service

the same day. Sold Janes Aviation Ltd and ferried Aberdeen to Hurn 07Jul92. Positioned Exeter 16Jul92. Lsd back to Dan-Air Services Ltd and ferried Aberdeen 15Aug92. Regd to Janes Aviation 748 Ltd 21Aug92 (CofR G-BEKE/R2). Flew last revenue Dan-Air 748 service as DA7276 from Scatsta to Aberdeen 30Sep92 and returned Janes Aviation at Blackpool 14Oct92. Damaged Coventry 23Jul93. Ferried Liverpool 24Jul93 and withdrawn 26Jul93. B/U Oct93. Regn cld as PWFU 10Sep96.

TT 41,181 hrs, 39,393 ldgs

1546   (16)   Srs.1/105

F/f 14Jul62 as **LV-PVH** from Hawarden where final assembly took place. Del Aerolíneas Argentinas 10Aug62 arriving Buenos Aires 18Aug62. Re-regd **LV-HHH** and named "Ciudad de Neuquén". Hard landing Colonia Catriel when opting AR682 from Esquel 19Dec70 tearing off nose leg, damaging both propellers and fuselage. No fatalities among 4 crew and 24 pax. Temporary repairs c/o and ferried Buenos Aires, Argentina where declared as w/o 20Jan71.

TT 21,542 hrs, 17,282 ldgs

1547   (17)   Srs.1/105

F/f 20Jul62 as **LV-PVF** from Hawarden where final assembly took place. Del Aerolíneas Argentinas via Stornoway and Keflavik 20Aug62 arriving Buenos Aires 27Aug62. Re-regd **LV-HHI** and named "Ciudad de Río Gallegos". W/o on approach Santa Rosa, La Pampa, Argentina 27Nov69. No fatalities among 4 crew and 24 pax on board.

TT 20,149 hrs, 16,099 ldgs

1548   HS780/748MF

Prototype rebuild of c/n 1534 G-APZV. Regd as **G-ARRV** to A.V. Roe & Co Ltd 29Jun61 as an Avro 748 Srs 1 (CofR R.7347/1). Amended to an Avro 748 MF 14Feb63. R/o 12Dec63. F/f 21Dec63, CofA issued 04Sep64. Built to Andover C.Mk.1 standards without Royal Air Force equipment. Regd Hawker Siddeley Aviation Ltd 02Dec64 as an HS 748 MF (CofR R.7347/2). To Boscombe Down for trials 20Feb/05Mar65. C/o an Indian demonstration tour departing Woodford 08Apr65 returning 07May65. WFU 16Jun65 prior to CofA expiry 03Sep65. Handed over to the Apprentice School Woodford 12Jan68. Regn cld 03Apr69 as PWFU. Painted in Soviet Air Force marks as '57' in mid-80 for use in a television film named "Invasion" on the 1956 Russian invasion of Hungary. To Royal Air Force Benson, U.K. Mar81 in exchange for Andover C.Mk.1 XS647. Used as an instructional airframe with serial **8669M** allotted at RAF Benson on 28Jan81. Reportedly B/U May90 but large sections were still present on 13Jul91.

TT 491 hrs, 823 ldgs

1549   (25)   Srs.1/106

Regd as **G-ARRW** to A.V. Roe & Co Ltd 29Jun61 (CofR R.7348/1). F/f 09Apr63, CofA issued 18Apr63. Lsd B.K.S. Air Transport Ltd with del Woodford-Southend 23Apr63 for crew training. Ferried Southend-Heathrow 26Apr63 and entered service 27Apr63 on the Heathrow-Leeds route. Received a nominal change of ownership to Hawker Siddeley Aviation Ltd, Avro Whitworth Division on 02Dec64 (CofR R.7348/2). Sold Skyways Coach Air Ltd with del from Leeds/Bradford to Lympne 13Mar67. Skyways Coach Air Ltd became regd owners from 30Mar67 (CofR R.7348/3), the aircraft having Lsd back to B.K.S. Air Transport Ltd from 03-13Apr67 and again from 09Dec67 to 27Mar68. Regd to Spakey Ltd 25Feb71 (CofR R.7348/4). Name changed to International Skyways Ltd 05Mar71. Regd to Dan-Air Services Ltd 26Apr72 (CofR R.7348/5) following purchase of airline and aircraft by them on 12Apr72. Regd Dan-Air Skyways Ltd 30May74 (CofR R.7348/6). Regd to Dan-Air Services Ltd 14Apr77 (CofR G-ARRW/R7). Converted to Srs.1A/106

24Apr77. WFU 20Mar86. UK regn cld 26Mar86, the same date as regd to Ryanair Ltd as **EI-BSE**. Sold Ryanair Ltd with del from Manchester to Shannon 01Apr86 as EI-BSE in Dan-Air colours. Painting in Ryanair colours commenced 03Apr86. Named "The Spirit of Ireland". CofA issued 20May86. In service as IW212 from Dublin to Luton 23May86. Renamed briefly "The Spirit of Mgr Horan" Mar87 and thereafter "The Spirit of Waterford" 1987. Withdrawn from service early Nov88. Put back into service summer 1989 as a back up for the ATR42 fleet. Restored as **G-ARRW** to London European Airways plc 09Jan90 (CofR G-ARRW/R8). Lsd British Independent Airways Ltd in their c/s 28Mar90. CofA issued 29Mar90, the date training commenced. In service 07Apr90 operating between Stansted and Jersey on behalf of Air UK. Company ceased operations 05Jul91. Ferried from Lydd to Hurn 10Aug91 for storage. Regn cld by the CAA 11Oct91. Restored to Clewer Aviation Ltd 13Jan92 (CofR G-ARRW/R9). Re-regd **G-MRRV** 28Feb92 (CofR G MRRV/R1). Ferried Southend 03Mar92 and flown by Independent Airways Ltd. Last revenue flight Liège to Stansted 30Aug92. UK regn cld 10Nov92 as transferred Nepal. Regd **9N-ACM** and del ex Southend via Forli 12Nov92 arriving Kathmandu 15Nov92 on lse to Necon Air Ltd. Entered service 18Nov92. Overran runway on landing Pokhara, Nepal 06Nov97 and collided with Nepal Airways 748 9N-ACW (c/n 1798). No fatalities among 4 crew and 44 pax on board. Subsequently w/o.

TT 50,044 hrs, 57,345 ldgs

1550　(19)　Srs.2/201

Originally allocated to Aden Airways Ltd as **VR-AAU**. Order cld. **Srs.2/204** F/f 27Aug62 as **C-91 2500**. Shown Farnborough Air Show with ferry from and to Woodford on 02 & 10Sep62. Del Força Aérea Brasileira 17Nov62 and initially operated by the Grupo de Transporte Especial - GTE. Transferred to 2 Grupo de Transporte, 1 Esquadrão 01Apr69. Stored Rio de Janeiro, Gallegos, Brazil by Sep01. Struck off charge 01Oct01.

TT 16,615 hrs, in excess of 11,141 ldgs

1551　(22)　Srs.2/201

Originally allocated to Aden Airways Ltd as **VR-AAV**. Order cld. **Srs.2/205** F/f 16Jan63 as 1 **C-91 2501**. Del Força Aérea Brasileira 26Feb63 and initially operated by the Grupo de Transporte Especial - GTE. Transferred to 2 Grupo de Transporte, 1 Esquadrão 01Apr69. Struck off charge 01Oct01 and stored Rio de Janeiro, Gallegos, Brazil.

TT in excess of 21,346 hrs, 14,838 ldgs (figures at 30Nov98)

1552　(21)　Srs.2/201

Originally allocated to Aden Airways Ltd as **VR-AAW**. Order cld. **Srs.2/205** F/f 22Feb63 as **C-91 2502**. Del Força Aérea Brasileira 20Mar63 and initially operated by the Grupo de

Transporte Especial - GTE. Transferred to 2 Grupo de Transporte, 1 Esquadrão 01Apr69. Stored Rio de Janeiro, Gallegos, Brazil by Sep01. Struck off charge 01Oct01. By Jun04 displayed outside Força Aérea Brasileira Galeão main base entrance. Still present 18Feb12.

TT in excess of 20,120 hrs, 14,715 ldgs (figures at 30Nov98)

1553　(23)　Srs.2/205

F/f 19Mar63 as **C-91 2503**. Del Força Aérea Brasileira 19Apr63 via Stornoway and initially operated by the Grupo de Transporte Especial - GTE. Transferred to 2 Grupo de Transporte, 1 Esquadrão 01Apr69. Reportedly stored Rio de Janeiro, Gallegos, Brazil by Jun01. Struck off charge 01Oct01.

TT in excess of 20,216 hrs, 14,035 ldgs (figures at 30Nov98)

1554　(24)　Srs.2/205

F/f 10Jun63 as **C-91 2504**. Del Força Aérea Brasileira 04Jul63 and initially operated by the Grupo de Transporte Especial - GTE. Transferred to 2 Grupo de Transporte, 1 Esquadrão 01Apr69. Reportedly stored Rio de Janeiro, Gallegos, Brazil by Jun01. Struck off charge 01Oct01. Del Museu Aeroespacial - MUSAL at Campo dos Afonsos, Rio de Janeiro 25Oct01 for preservation and display. Still present 17Jan10.

TT in excess of 19,157 hrs, 12,362 ldgs (figures at 30Nov98)

1555　(30)　Srs.2/205

F/f 30Aug63 as **C-91 2505**. Del Força Aérea Brasileira 28Sep63 and initially operated by the Grupo de Transporte Especial - GTE. Transferred to 2 Grupo de Transporte, 1 Esquadrão 01Apr69. Reportedly stored Rio de Janeiro, Gallegos, Brazil by Jun01. Struck off charge 01Oct01.

TT in excess of 19,378 hrs, 12,541 ldgs (figures at 30Nov98)

1556　(26)　Srs.1/105

F/f 19Jul63 as **LV-PXD**. Del Aerolíneas Argentinas 31Aug63 via Stornoway and Keflavik arriving Buenos Aires 08Sep63. Re-regd **LV-IDV** and named "Ciudad de Montevideo". In service 12Oct63. Sold Yacimientos Petrolíferos Fiscales and named "Mendoza". Sold Dan-Air Services Ltd and regd to them as **G-BEJE** 07Feb77 (CofR G-BEJE/R1). Del ex Buenos Aires 10Feb77 via São Paulo, Brasília, Belém, Paramaribo, Port of Spain, San Juan, Miami, Wilmington, Boston, Goose Bay, Sudbury, Søndre Strømfjord, Kulusuk and Stornoway arriving Manchester 17Feb77. CofA issued 01May77. Entered service from Manchester to Aberdeen 02May77. Withdrawn from service and ferried from Gatwick to Teesside 29Jan86 for storage. Ferried to Manchester 10Oct86 for Major Check and interior strip for use as a pure freighter without large freight door. In service 27Nov86.

G-BEJE c/n 1556 of Emerald Airways in Royal Mail Skynet colours at Liverpool on 2nd July 1995, while operating postal services for the Royal Mail.
(Keith Gaskell)

G-VAJK c/n 1557 of Venture Airways Ltd, named 'Lady Godiva', in a photograph taken in 1984.

G-ASPL c/n 1560 of BKS Air Transport showing off the company's later livery.   *(Fred Barnes/HSA)*

G-ASPL c/n 1560 of Dan-Air London at Newcastle on 6th April 1980 in the later colour-scheme with a black outline to the red cheatline.

(Keith Gaskell)

Stored Manchester with effect from 28Mar92. Sold Janes Aviation Ltd 15Jul92 and del 16Jul92 (18Jul also quoted). Regd to Janes Aviation 748 Ltd 03Aug92 (CofR G-BEJE/R2). Painted in Royal Mail Skynet overall red c/s with yellow trim. Ferried from Exeter to Edinburgh 28Sep92 and entered service the same date from Edinburgh to Liverpool. Company renamed Emerald Airways Ltd 15Sep93. Ferried Blackpool, U.K. for reduction to spares 17Jan97. B/u May97. Regn cld 16May97 as PWFU.

TT 41,140 hrs, 41,323 ldgs

1557   (27)   Srs.1/105

F/f 06Sep63 as **LV-PXH**. Del Aerolíneas Argentinas 30Sep63 via Stornoway and Keflavik arriving Buenos Aires 07Oct63. Re-regd **LV-IEE**. In service 13Nov63. Named "Ciudad de Santa Fe" at a ceremony on 03May64 at Santa Fe, when a new runway was opened. Sold Dan-Air Services Ltd being regd to them as **G-BEKG** 08Jul77 (CofR G-BEKG/R1). Del Manchester 19Jul77. CofA issued 29Dec77 having been converted to a Srs.1A/105 prior to this on 22Dec77. In service from Manchester to Hurn 29Dec77. Sold Cayman Airways Ltd with del ex Manchester as G-BEKG 24Feb82. Regn cld 03Mar82 as transferred Cayman Islands and regd **VR-CBH** named "Cayman Brac Pride". Del Manchester 08Sep83 as VR-CBH for care and maintenance pending sale. Sold Air Commuter Ltd 17Feb84 and regd to them as **G-VAJK** 29Feb84 (CofR G-VAJK/R1). CofA issued 11May84 after being fitted with an executive 33 seat interior. Company name changed to Venture Airways Ltd 11May84. Del Coventry 12May84 and used on a proving flight to Paris the same day. In service 22May84 from Coventry to Paris, Charles de Gaulle as HC101 and named "Lady Godiva" in a ceremony prior to departure. Company ceased operations Aug84. Del Lasham 19Sep84 for storage. Sold Euroair Transport Ltd Jun85 and regd to Alexandra Aviation Ltd 13Jun85 (CofR G-VAJK/R2). Ferried Stansted 13Jun85. Ferried to Exeter for maintenance 24Jun85. Lsd Tunisavia as G-VAJK and del ex Gatwick 12Jul85, Returned UK 28Sep85 and repainted in full Euroair colours at Exeter. Del 15Nov85 and entered service 18Nov85 on the Air Écosse route between Dundee, Carlisle and Heathrow as SM/EZ724. Re-regd/restored as **G-BEKG** to Euroair Transport Ltd 03Jul86 (CofR G-BEKG/R2). Flew last scheduled service on behalf of this operator as EZ724 from Dundee to Heathrow 03Apr87. Lsd Brymon Airways and painted in their colours 26Oct87. Ferried Exeter 25Jan88 for storage. Lsd Air Atlantique and del Coventry 07Apr88 in full Air Atlantique c/s. Used for crew training 08-21Apr88. Operated first commercial service 30Apr88. Operated first scheduled service as ES21 from Southampton to Jersey 20May88. Flew last scheduled service for Air Atlantique 31Oct88. Ferried from Coventry to Exeter at end of lse 24Mar89 Lsd Air Saint-Pierre with del ex Exeter 06Apr89. Returned Euroair Transport Ltd 01Jun89. Lsd British Independent Airways Ltd and used for crew training briefly with effect from 30Aug89 before return lessor. Lsd British Independent Airways Ltd again with del 10Nov89 and used for crew training with effect from 11Nov89. Sub-lsd Aberdeen Airways Ltd with del to Aberdeen 03Dec89. In service 04Dec89 from Aberdeen to East Midlands via Edinburgh. Lse continued until 03Feb90 with a short break over the Christmas period. Painted in British Independent Airways c/s. Returned Euroair Transport Ltd 05Feb91. Painted overall white and stored Hurn from 06Apr91. Ferried from Hurn to Exeter 22May92 for further storage. Regd as **G-DAAL** to Alexandra Aviation Ltd 11Aug92 (CofR G-DAAL/R1) for operation by Euroair. Lsd Emerald Airways Ltd Sep93 and ferried Belfast-Liverpool 04Oct93. Sold Emerald Airways Ltd and regd to them 29Mar94 (CofR G-DAAL/R2). Flew last revenue service from Liverpool to Stansted 04Oct96. Ferried Blackpool, U.K. 05Oct96 and WFU. B/u Jan97. Regn cld as WFU 18Mar97.

TT 41,101 hrs, 40,023 ldgs

1558   (28)   Srs.1/105

F/f 24Oct63 as **LV-PXP**. Del Aerolíneas Argentinas 15Nov63 via Stornoway and Keflavik arriving Buenos Aires 22Nov63.

Re-regd **LV-IEV** and named "Ciudad de Gualeguaychú". W/o landing Bahía Blanca, Argentina 15Jul69. No fatalities among 4 crew and 35 pax on board.

TT 16,137 hrs, 12,930 ldgs

1559   (29)   Srs.1/107

Regd as **G-ASJT** to A.V. Roe & Co Ltd 04Jul63 (CofR R.7956/1). F/f 11Oct63, CofA issued 18Oct63. Del 28Oct63 to The Aviation Division of S. Smith & Sons (England) Ltd to whom regd 04Dec63 (CofR R.7956/2). Regd to Smith's Industries Ltd 23Feb66. Departed Staverton 06Jun67 on a four week tour of Canada and the USA demonstrating Smith's Series 6 Cat 2 flight control system. Flying unit closed down 31Oct69. Sold Ministry of Technology for operation by the Royal Aircraft Establishment at Farnborough and del ex Staverton as G-ASJT 13Jan70. Regn cld 20Jan70 as transferred to military marks and regd **XW750**. Initially used by Radio Flight. To RAE Bedford 06Dec71 initially with the Blind Landing Experimental Unit and later with the Flight Systems Division. Fitted with a Microturbo Gevauden 8 (045-1) APU located in the tail cone in 1985. RAE absorbed into Defence Research Agency 01Apr91. Ferried Farnborough 24Mar94 as RAE Bedford run down. To Boscombe Down as a Large Flying Laboratory 01Jun94. Operator renamed Defence Evaluation and Research Agency 01Apr97 and QinetiQ from 02Jul01. Last flew 31Jan05 and put into storage Boscombe Down. Advertised for sale by tender by the Disposal Services Agency of the Ministry of Defence with a closing date of 03Oct06. Sold Clewer Aviation Ltd Nov06. Military marks removed Dec06 and restored to Clewer Aviation Ltd as **G-ASJT** 09Jan07 (CofR G-ASJT/R1). UK marks cld the same date as transferred to the USA and regd as **N748D** to Aerospace Trust Management LLC 18Jan07. US regn taped on 23Jan07 and ferried Finningley 25Jan07. Used as a ground based training airframe for Doncaster College's New Aviation Academy. Noted hangared Finningley airfield, U.K. newly painted white with blue/green engines with large 'directions' on fuselage 08Feb08. Sold Aerowings 3A of Switzerland 21May08. US regn cancelled but still painted on aircraft 29May08. Restored as N748D to Aerospace Trust Management LLC 02Dec08 and ferried to Southend 20Dec08 after 'directions' titles removed. Regn cld 26Mar09. Noted being dismantled at Southend 20Jul09. After removal of fin and wings, roaded out of Southend on 03Nov09 on two low loaders.

TT 5,866 hrs, 11,696 ldgs

1560   (37)   Srs.1/108

Regd as **G-ASPL** to Hawker Siddeley Aviation Ltd, Avro Whitworth Division 28Feb64 (CofR R.8120/1). F/f 31Mar64, CofA issued 13Apr64, Lsd B.K.S. Air Transport Ltd with del Leeds/Bradford 14Apr64. In service 16Apr64. Sold Skyways Coach Air Ltd 18Mar67, the company becoming regd owners 30Mar67 (CofR R.8120/2) after a previous nominal change of ownership to Hawker Siddeley Aviation Ltd 24Nov65. Lsd B.K.S. Air Transport Ltd Dec67 to Mar68. Made emergency landing Manston 09May68 when nose leg failed to extend. Repaired. Regd Spakey Ltd 25Feb71 (CofR R.8120/3). Name changed to International Skyways Ltd 05Mar71. Amended to a Srs.2/108 21Mar72. Regd to Dan-Air Services Ltd 26Apr72 (CofR R.8120/4) following the purchase of the airline and aircraft by them on 12Apr72. Inaugurated the 'Link City' service from Hurn the day before this. Regd Dan-Air Skyways Ltd 30May72 (CofR R.8120/5). Converted to a Srs.2A/108 15Apr75. Named "City of Berne" 1975. Regd Dan-Air Services Ltd 14Apr77 (CofR G-ASPL/R6). W/o Nailstone, Leicestershire, U.K. on approach East Midlands Airport 26Jun81. 3 crew killed. Regn cld as aircraft destroyed 19May83.

TT 34,587 hrs, 35,281 ldgs

1561   (34)   Srs.2/206

Andover CC.Mk.2. F/f 15May64 as **XS789**. To A & AEE Boscombe Down 04Jun64 and used for hot weather trials at Bahrain. Returned Woodford 26Jun64. Del to the RAF at Benson for use by the Queen's Flight 07Aug64. Converted to Srs.2A/206 and re-delivered to RAF Queen's Flight 03Sep64. To 5 MU Kemble 06Nov79 and re-del to RAF Queen's Flight 18Dec79. To 5 MU Kemble for repaint 23Nov81 and re-del to RAF Queen's Flight 05Jan82. To RAF St Athan for repaint 24Feb86 and re-del to RAF Queen's Flight 07Mar86. To RAF 32 Sqn (Northolt) 23Jun86. To ASF Benson 14Jul86. To Luton 25Aug86 for repaint by McAlpine Aviation Ltd in standard white/grey colours. To 32Sqn (Northolt) 12Nov86 and to ASF Benson 17Mar88. SOC 31Mar95. Ferried Southend 21Apr95. Painted as **D2-MAG** and del via Nice 26Apr95. Regd Ibis Air Transport Ltd as **9L-LBF** Jun95 and noted stored Malta as such 16Jun96. Noted Lanseria, South Africa painted overall white 29Aug97. Re-regd **9Q-CLL** and noted as such Lanseria with ITAB titles 15Jun98 (although not officially regd as such until 28Jan99). Noted Lanseria 23Sep01 named 'Kikondja' with fish motif on fin. Noted Lanseria 06Dec06 on maintenance input, repaint and interior refurbishment still with ITAB titles and fish motif. Seen Lanseria 02Feb08 and again 17Feb08 painted overall white with red, silver and gold trim and no titles named "Fatima". Noted still looking immaculate in same c/s at Rand 05Mar09 and Goma, DRC 18Feb11. Noted operational at Shabunda, DRC, reportedly flown by Steffavia sprl 04Sep12.

1562 (35) Srs.2/206

Andover CC.Mk.2. F/f 26Jun64 as **XS790**. Del RAF Benson for use by the Queen's Flight 10Jul64. Returned Woodford 21Aug64 for conversion to Srs.2A/206 before re-del Benson 03Sep64 for RAF Queen's Flight. To 5 MU Kemble 02Feb81 for repaint. Re-del to RAF Queen's Flight 03Mar81. To 5 MU Kemble 10Jan83 for repaint. Re-del to RAF Queen's Flight 21Feb83. To St Athan 30Sep85 for repaint and re-del to RAF Queen's Flight 08Nov85. To St Athan 06Apr88 for repaint and re-del to RAF Queen's Flight 20May88. Fitted with a Matador IRCM as an extension of the tail cone at Benson and f/f as such 16Nov89. Ferried from Benson to RAE Bedford 31Jan91 for use as a flying laboratory after wfu by the Queen's Flight. Painted in 'Raspberry Ripple' c/s at East Midlands Mar91. Transferred to the RAE with del Farnborough 26Mar91. Operator renamed the Defence Research Agency 01Apr91. F/f after a Major Check 13Feb92 before completion of the modifications. Modified with a recontoured and bulbous nose while the weather radar was relocated to a pod above and behind the cockpit. F/f after modifications 01Sep93. The new nose housed infra-red sensors and a steerable turret for SIRSA (Study Into Infra-red Sensor Algorithms) trials. Used on SAR (Synthetic Aperture Radar) trials for which the antenna was housed in a panel on the starboard side of the rear fuselage. The cabin was modified with six operational observer positions. SAR and TV trials early 95. The aircraft was also used by the DRA Malvern. Operator renamed Defence Evaluation and Research Agency 01Apr97. Last flew 28Jul97 and put in store Boscombe Down. Was due for sale by auction 24Sep98 but after parts recovery during early Nov the aircraft was finally b/u on 23/24Nov98 at Boscombe Down having failed to reach its reserve price. Nose section retained Boscombe Down, U.K. for long term rebuild by the Boscombe Down Aviation Collection (BDAC). Nose section relocated by road to the new location of the BDAC at Old Sarum airfield 28Jun12. Museum officially opened to the public 01Jul12.

TT 14,210 hrs, 15,969 ldgs

1563 (46) Srs.2/206

Andover CC.Mk.2. F/f 18Nov64 as **XS791**. Del RAF Station Flight Abingdon as a VIP aircraft 22Dec64. To Middle East Communications Squadron (Khormaksar) which later moved to Sharjah. Issued to Far East Air Force 24Feb67, and to Far East Communications Squadron (Changi) 02Mar67, then to 48 Squadron (Changi) 31Dec69. To Far East Air Force VIP Flight 01Sep71. To 60 Squadron (Wildenrath) 05Nov71. Noted Berlin-Gatow 30Jun74 in use as a personal aircraft by the CinC RAF Germany and marked with three star emblem below cockpit

window. To 32 Squadron (Northolt) 28Nov75. To Station Flight (Brize Norton) 24Jul79, returning to 32 Sqn Station Flight 20Aug87. To Hurn 12Jul88 for repaint by Lovaux Ltd, returning to 32 Sqn (Northolt) 13Sep88. SOC 28Nov94 and dismantled Northolt 22Mar95. Transported Bruntingthorpe by road and reassembled for static display by Phoenix Aviation. Fuselage noted at scrapyard at Stock, Essex, U.K. 27Apr05.

TT in excess of 10,629 hrs, 11,932 ldgs (figures at 29Jan93)

1564 (49) Srs.2/206

Andover CC.Mk.2. F/f 14Jan65 as **XS792**. Del RAF Station Flight Abingdon as a VIP aircraft 09Feb65 (08Feb65 also quoted). Issued to Far East Air Force 31Mar65 and to Far East Air Force Andover Flight 06Apr65. To Far East Communications Squadron (Changi) 20Jul65. To 48 Squadron (Changi) 31Dec69. To Far East Air Force VIP Flight 01Sep71. To 32 Sqn (Northolt) 23Nov71, to Station Flight 10Nov77 and to 32 Sqn (Northolt) 19Jan78. Noted at Frankfurt 11Oct78. To Station Flight (Brize Norton) 21Mar80, then to 32 Sqn (Northolt) 18Apr80. To St Athan 25Jun81 for repaint and returned to 32 Sqn (Northolt) 27Jun81. To Benson for modifications 16Sep85 and back to 32 Sqn (Northolt) 10Oct85. To Luton 23Mar87 for repaint by McAlpine Aviation Ltd and then to 32 Sqn (Northolt) 20May87. Refurbished by Wesco Aircraft at Hurn from 05Dec88 and returned to 32 Sqn (Northolt) 06Feb89. To Jecco Aviation 27Nov89 for modifications. Sold at auction 26Nov94 for £75,000. Regd as **G-BVZS** to Arch Aviation Ltd of Kenya 08Mar95 (CofR G-BVZS/R1). Regn cld 10Apr95 as sold in Kenya and regd **5Y-IAK**. Reportedly sold in Rwanda on an unknown date and suffered wing damage in the D.R.C with unknown marks (possibly 9L-LBE). Repaired and ferried Kigali for storage. Sold African Commuter Services Ltd as **9XR-AB** approx Mar03. Overshot on landing Old Fangak in Southern Sudan from Lokichoggio approx Feb05 and subsequently w/o.

TT in excess of 11,656 hrs, 15,536 ldgs (figures at 28Jan93)

1565 (50) Srs.2/206

Andover CC.Mk.2. F/f 11Mar65 as **XS793**. Del RAF Station Flight Abingdon as a VIP aircraft 14Apr65. Returned Woodford for modifications 24Jun65 and re-del Abingdon 04Jul65. To Air Force Middle East 15Jul65 and to Middle East Communications Squadron (Khormaksar) 17Jul65, which later moved to Sharjah. Cat.3R flying accident 26Jul65, to Middle East Communications Sqn 29Oct65. Cat.3R flying accident 22Jan66, then to 21 Sqn (Sharjah) 01Mar66 with 'Royal Air Force Middle East' titles. To 152 Sqn (Muharraq) 21Oct67. To RAF Benson for use by the Queen's Flight 09Jan68. Converted to Srs.2A/206. In service 26May68. Cat.3R Disposal Account 17Mar70, repaired on site. To RAF Queen's Flight (Benson) 13Apr70. To 5 MU (Kemble) 08Feb82 for repaint and returned to RAF Queen's Flight (Benson) 12Mar82. To RAF St Athan 01Aug84 for repaint and returned to Queen's Flight (Benson) 10Sep84. To Luton 03Nov86 for repaint by McAlpine Aviation Ltd in standard white/grey colour scheme. To 60 Sqn (Wildenrath) 02Mar87. Shown at RIAT show at Fairford 18Jul87. To Hurn 25May89 for repaint, returned to Wildenrath 14Jul89. Loaned to Queen's Flight mid-Aug89 and returned to 60 Sqn (Wildenrath) 21Nov89. Squadron disbanded 31Mar92. To Bruggen as the personal aircraft of the CinC RAF Germany, Air Marshall Andrew Wilson. Damaged in heavy landing RAF Northolt Sep92. Noted stored Northolt Feb93 with 30 Sqn. Ferried No.2 School of Technical Training (Cosford) 23Apr93 as RR726. Allotted **9178M** 08Mar93 and painted as such. Unit later renumbered No.1 School of Technical Training. Sold at auction to Andila Aviation 08May97 and regd to Eureka Aviation as **EL-AIF**. Ferried Cosford-Wevelgem 04Jun97. R/o Ostend 03Nov97 in full Liberia World Airlines Inc c/s. Seen Abidjan 04/05Feb98. Departed Ostend without titles after maintenance 01May98. Sold Gabon Express as **3C-KKP** Oct99. Company grounded 2004. Status unknown.

TT in excess of 12,949 hrs, 13,618 ldgs (figures at 22Jul92)

1566　　(54)　　Srs.2/206

Andover CC.Mk.2. F/f 06May65 as **XS794**. Handed over to Ministry of Aviation 31May65 at Woodford. Arrived at the A&AEE 09Jul65 for radio, navigation and tropical trials. Returned to Woodford 19Aug65 and del to RAF Station Flight Abingdon as a VIP aircraft 09Sep65. Cat.3R flying accident 02Oct66, repaired on site 03Oct66 and returned to Station Flight (Abingdon) 19Nov66. Loaned to the RAF Queen's Flight 26Jun67-24Jul67. To 60 MU (Leconfield) 06Aug68 for modifications, and returned to Station Flight (Abingdon) 27Aug68. To Metropolitan Communications Squadron (Northolt) 01Jan69 which reformed as 32 Sqn (Northolt) 01Feb69. Loaned to the RAF Queen's Flight 28Jan71-04Feb71. Flying accident 30Dec71, repaired on site by 71 MU 04Jan72 and returned to 32 Sqn (Northolt) 31Jan72. Displayed at RAF Finningley Jubilee Air Show 30Jul77. To Station Flight (Abingdon) 21Apr80 and to 32 Sqn (Northolt) 14May80. To Kemble 03May83 for repaint and returned to 32 Sq (Northolt) 29Jun83. To Hurn 13Sep88 for repaint by Lovaux Aviation Ltd and returned to 32 Sqn (Northolt) 11Nov88. Arrived Jecco Aviation for repaint 18Aug89. SOC 31Mar95. Ferried Southend 21Apr95. Painted as **D2-MAF** and del via Nice 26Apr95. Regd to Ibis Air Transport Ltd as **9L-LBG** and arrived Malta as such 17Apr96. Painted with 'African Commuter Services Ltd' titles Feb97 and departed Malta 06Mar97. Noted Goma 23Aug and 09Sep97 without titles but named "Hanna Nell". When operated by 748 Air Services Ltd veered off Foxtrot Airstrip in the Sudan when landing after a flight from Lokichoggio in Kenya 14Feb99. 2 crew survived. Damaged beyond repair.

TT in excess of 12,772 hrs & approx 15,500 ldgs (hours figures at 26Apr95)

1567　　(44)　　Srs.2/207

F/f 14Aug64 as **HS-THA**. Del Thai Airways Co Ltd 27Aug64, arriving Bangkok 31Aug64 and regd to same 03Nov64. Sold Airfast Services Indonesia P.T. as **PK-OBW** through Kenneth Green Pte Ltd 28Feb81 with del ex Bangkok 30May81. Converted to Srs.2A/207. W/o Lombok Island, Indonesia 25Jan90. Flew into Mount Rijani while en route Djayapura to Denpasar. 3 crew and 16 pax killed.

TT in excess of 38,220 hrs, 32,493 ldgs (figures at 01Nov89)

1568　　(38)　　Srs.2/207

F/f 27Sep64 as **HS-THB**. Del Thai Airways Co Ltd 08Oct64 and regd to same 29Oct64. W/o on approach Bangkok, Thailand from Khon Kaen 27Apr80 while operating flight TH231. 4 crew and 40 of 49 pax on board killed.

TT in excess of 29,282 hrs, 25,833 ldgs (figures at 24Mar79)

1569　　(39)　　Srs.2/207

F/f 12Nov64 as **HS-THC**. Regd Thai Airways Co Ltd 06Nov64 and del 19Nov64. Made emergency landing at Lampang airport after cargo door broke off in flight 09Jan69. Repaired. Withdrawn from service 08Aug83. Sold Royal Thai Air Force 03Sep83 and del 09Sep83 coded **60203**. Allotted serial L5-3/26 but not carried by aircraft. Operated by 603 Squadron Don Muang. Re-coded **60303** Feb95 and noted still active as such Phuket, Thailand 19Mar10 looking immaculate and again Don Muang 18Nov11. Noted still active at Phuket Feb13. Noted at Chiang Mai painted with '50th Anniversary of 603 Squadron' titles and with a leaping horse on its fin 11Sep14. Noted flying at Chiang Mai 04Jan16. Withdrawn from use 30Mar16 at a special ceremony at Bangkok-Don Mueang Air Force Base and ferried to Royal Thai Air Force Base at Takhli the same day for storage.

TT in excess of 33,407 hrs, 31,665 ldgs (figures at 28Feb93)

1570　　(48)　　Srs.2/208

F/f 23Dec64 incorrectly painted as **HS-RTAF**. Del Royal Thai Air Force as a King's Flight aircraft 15Jan65 as **HS-TAF**. Coded as **11-111** Sep70 and operated by 61st Squadron of the 6th Wing, Royal Thai Air Force. Allotted serial L5-1/08 but not carried by aircraft. Transferred 603 Squadron, Don Muang 1984. Re-painted with new code **60301** Nov05 and first noted as such at Bangkok 15Nov05. Damaged 25May07. Repaired and noted still active Bangkok, Thailand 04Nov08. Damaged by flood water Don Muang, Bangkok late Oct11. Seen flying at Phuket, Thailand 07Jan13, and again at Don Mueang, Bangkok 09Feb14. Withdrawn from use 30Mar16 at a special ceremony at Bangkok Don Mueang Air Force Base and put into storage.

TT in excess of 9,428 hrs, 14,176 ldgs (figures at 28Feb93)

1571　　(20)　　Srs.2/212

F/f 09Oct64 as **4R-ACJ**. Del Air Ceylon Ltd 27Oct64 arriving Colombo-Ratmalana 30Oct64. In service 07Nov64. Became the first airliner to land at the newly opened Male airport in the Maldive Islands on 12Apr66. W/o Ratmalana Airport following destruction by saboteurs 07Sep78.

TT 28,851 hrs, 24,562 ldgs

1572 - 1575

See Andover C.Mk.1 listing.

1576　　(14)　　Srs.2/214

Regd as **G-ATAM** to B.K.S. Air Transport Ltd 28Jan65 (CofR R.8457/1). F/f 09Feb65, CofA issued 16Feb65. Del Leeds/Bradford 17Feb65. Structural damage to nose wheel bay and fwd fuselage landing Leeds/Bradford in deep snow 21Mar65. Repaired and declared serviceable 07Apr65. WFU Leeds 05Jun66 and ferried Southend the same day. Del ex Southend to Woodford 13Jun66. Lsd Aerotaxi del Sureste S.A. and del ex Woodford as G-ATAM 01Jul66 via Stornoway and Keflavik in basic B.K.S. c/s with 'Aerotaxis Aerosafari' titles. Regn cld 06Jul66 as transferred Mexico and regd **XA-SEI**. Company merged into Aeromaya S.A. 01Nov66. Returned Woodford as XA-SEI with Aeromaya titles 10Jan67 at end of lse. Del Leeds/Bradford the following day. Restored as **G-ATAM** to B.K.S. Air Transport Ltd 16Jan67 (CofR R.8457/2) with CofA renewed 16Feb67. Sold to Hawker Siddeley Aviation Ltd and regd to them 04Aug67 (CofR R.8457/3) after del Woodford 12Jul67. Regn cld 05Oct67 as transferred Philippines and lsd Philippine Airlines Inc as **PI-C1020** with del ex Woodford 12Oct67. Overshot runway landing San Fernando, Philippines 30Aug68 causing severe damage to undercarriage, forward fuselage and port nacelle. Repaired and declared serviceable 22Feb69. Restored as **G-ATAM** to Hawker Siddeley Aviation Ltd as a Srs.2A/214 25Feb69 (CofR R.8457/4) with CofA renewed 28Feb69 and del ex Manila 07Mar69 via Labuan, Singapore and Bangkok arriving Woodford at end of lse 12Mar69 from Teheran, Ankara, Corfu and Nice. Ferried to Coventry for maintenance 14Mar69 returning Woodford 28Mar69. Regn cld 08Apr69 as

9J-ABL c/n 1576 of Zambia Airways Corp Ltd, who leased the aircraft for five months in 1970.

C-GMAA c/n 1576 of Wasaya Airways at Red Lake, Ontario, on 18th September 2009. This aircraft is one of the oldest active 748s in the world.
(Fred Barnes)

transferred Ghana and aircraft painted for lse to Ghana Airways Corporation as **9G-ABV**. Reverted to **G-ATAM** for air test 11Jun69. Reverted to **9G-ABV** 13Jun69 for crew training and demonstrations. Restored as **G-ATAM** to Hawker Siddeley Aviation Ltd 16Jul69 (CofR R.8457/5). C/o African demonstration tour 22Jul to 15Aug69. Regn cld 08Jan70 as transferred Denmark and lsd Maersk Air I/S as **OY-DFS** from 07Jan70 to 17Feb70. Ferried Coventry for maintenance 18Feb70. Restored as **G-ATAM** to Hawker Siddeley Aviation Ltd 06Mar70 (CofR R.8457/6). CofA renewed 16Mar70 and returned Woodford the same day. Regn cld 29Mar70 as transferred Zambia and lsd Zambia Airways Corporation Ltd as **9J-ABL** the same day. Aircraft briefly restored as **G-ATAM** to Hawker Siddeley Aviation Ltd from 07Sep70 (CofR R.8457/7) to 10Sep70 when transferred South Africa for ferry flight to Johannesburg 09Sep70. Repainted in South African Airways c/s as **ZS-HSA** 11Sep70 for lse to them. In service 15Sep70 as SA100 from Johannesburg to Gaborone and Francistown. Operated last service as SA132 from Maseru to Johannesburg 24Feb71. Restored as **G-ATAM** to Hawker Siddeley Aviation Ltd 26Feb71 (CofR R.8457/8) and painted as such 03Mar71 with del ex Johannesburg 05Mar71. Flown at Hatfield Open Day 03Jul71. Demonstrated to Air Anglia Ltd 12Jul71. Demonstrated with Merpati Nusantara titles Jul71. Repainted with Hawker Siddeley titles Aug71. Evaluated by Austin Airways Ltd 01Sep71 to 02Oct71 in HSA c/s with Austin Airways titles. Ferried Hawarden 30Mar72 for maintenance returning 26Jun72. Regn cld 26Sep72 as transferred Gabon. F/f as **TR-LQY** 03Oct72. Sold Société National Transgabon as TR-LQY named "Libreville" and del 10Oct72. Company renamed Air Gabon with effect from mid 1974. Sold Austin Airways Ltd with CofR issued 27May76. Del as **C-GMAA** via Manchester 29/31May76 arriving Canada 01Jun76. CofA issued 19Jul76. Company merged with Air Ontario Inc Apr87 using Air Ontario as the operating name. From spring 1988 a start was made on converting the aircraft to a specialised unpressurised pure freighter with large rear freight door and windows blanked out. This was completed in Jan89. (see Air Ontario Inc for full details). Sold Air Creebec Inc Sep90. Regd Air Creebec (1994) Inc 23Mar95. Lsd Wasaya Airways Ltd 22Sep98. Sold Wasaya Airways Ltd 03Jan99 and regd to them 06May99 with f/n 807. Regd Wasaya Airways Limited Partnership 22Jun00. WFU Thunder Bay, Ontario, Canada 09Mar05 and put in storage. Overhauled, repainted in new c/s and returned to service 29Dec06. Repainted in Wasaya's latest fin c/s Nov10.

TT 50,691 hrs, 73,582 ldgs (figures at 28Apr16)

1577   (36)   Srs.2/215

F/f 26Apr65 as **YV-C-AME**. Del Línea Aeropostal Venezolana 15May65 named "Paramagay". Re-regd **YV-04C** 1975. Made wheels-up landing Caracas 18Apr80. Repaired. Sold Austin Airways Ltd Apr81 as **C-GDUI**. Converted to Srs.2A/215. Sold Regionair (1981) Inc 1981 never having been operated by Austin Airways. Airline and aircraft absorbed into Québecair Inc early 1984. Company taken over by Nordair Metro 31Jul86. Withdrawn from service and stored Montréal-Dorval. Advertised for sale by tender by Québec Government in Flight International of 25Jul87. Sold Bradley Air Services Ltd/First Air with del Carp, Ontario, Canada 25Sep87. Remained unconverted and in long-term storage devoid of many parts, not having flown since del. Reportedly B/U Mar/Apr91. Regn cld 24Jun01.

TT 32,343 hrs, 49,317 ldgs

1578   (40)   Srs.2/215

F/f 07May65 as **YV-C-AMI** (04Jun65 has also been quoted but considered less likely). Del Línea Aeropostal Venezolana 02Jul65. Struck by taxiing C-46 (YV-C-AMN) 04Apr73 at Puerto Ayacucho, Venezuela. Repaired. Re-regd **YV-05C** 1975. Lsd Fuerza Aérea Venezolana Oct77 as **6201**. Returned Línea Aeropostal Venezolana May80 as **YV-05C**. Sold Austin Airways Ltd Dec80 as **C-GDUL** and converted to Srs.2A/215. Sold Regionair (1981) Inc 1981 never having been operated by Austin Airways. Airline and aircraft absorbed into Québecair Inc early 1984. Company taken over by Nordair Metro 31Jul86. Withdrawn from service and stored Montréal-Dorval. Advertised for sale by tender by the Québec Government in Flight International of 25Jul87. Sold Bradley Air Services Ltd/First Air with del 19Sep87. CofR issued 29Sep87, CofA issued 07May88. In service 07May88 painted in First Air c/s with f/n 403. Regd Bradley Air Services Ltd 24Jun98. WFU 05May04 and ferried from Iqaluit to Carp, Ontario, Canada the same day for storage. Still intact early Jul07. Regn cld 09Oct07. Fuselage noted at Ed's Autoparts at Arnprior, Ontario 09Oct09 and still present 06Sep10.

TT 48,048 hrs, 59,568 ldgs

1579   (47)   Srs.2/215

F/f 06Jul65 as **YV-C-AMO**. Del Línea Aeropostal Venezolana 30Jul65. Veered off runway when landing Santa Bárbara del Zulia, Venezuela and tore off starboard undercarriage 23May73. Repaired. Re-regd **YV-06C** 1975. Sold Servicio de Aviación Naval Venezolana as **TR-0203** 23Jul77. Sold Austin Airways Ltd as **C-GFFU** 10Aug81 and converted to Srs.2A/215. CofR and CofA issued 03Jul82. Lsd Air Creebec Inc Nov85 to 12Aug86. Company merged with Air Ontario Inc Apr87 using Air Ontario as the operating name. Sold Air Creebec Inc 06Dec88 never having been painted in Air Ontario c/s. Last flown 28Jan92 after an engine failure caused a wing fire and stored Timmins, Ontario, Canada. Regn cld 29Mar94. B/U Jul95.

TT 33,507 hrs, 47,488 ldgs

1580   (57)   Srs.2/215

F/f 22Oct65 as **YV-C-AMY**. Del Línea Aeropostal Venezolana
12Nov65. W/o 10 minutes after take-off from Maturín, Venezuela
20Aug68. 2 crew and 2 pax killed, 1 crew and 2 pax survived.

TT 5,614 hrs, 7,668 ldgs

1581   (59)   Srs.2/215

F/f 23Dec65 as **YV-C-AMF**. Del Línea Aeropostal Venezolana
04Feb66 named "Paramaconi". Re-regd YV-07C 1975. Lsd LIAT
(1974) Ltd as **VP-LAX** from 10Aug77 to 06Nov77 in full
Aeropostal c/s with additional LIAT titles. Restored as **YV-07C**.
Sold Austin Airways Ltd Dec80 as **C-GDUN** and converted to
Srs.2A/215. Sold Regionair (1981) Inc Dec81 never having been
operated by Austin Airways. Airline and aircraft absorbed into
Québecair Inc early 1984. Sold Bradley Air Services Ltd/First Air
with del 25Oct84. Entered service 02Nov85. Painted in First Air
colours with f/n 404. Regd Bradley Air Services Ltd 24Jun98.
WFU and ferried Yellowknife to Carp, Ontario, Canada 12Dec01
for parts recovery. Regn cld 23Dec02.

TT 55,216 hrs, 63,790 ldgs

1582   (61)   Srs.2/215

F/f 08May66 as **YV-C-AMC**. Del Línea Aeropostal Venezolana
24May66. Damaged Maiquetía Airport, Caracas, Venezuela
15Mar73. Returned to service by May73. Re-regd YV-08C 1975.
Sold Austin Airways Ltd as **C-GDOV** 05Dec80 and converted to
Srs.2A/215. Sold Les Ailes du Nord Ltée/Northern Wings Ltd
26Jan81. Company known as Regionair (1981) Inc with effect
from mid 1981. Airline and aircraft absorbed into Québecair Inc
early 1984. Sold Bradley Air Services Ltd with del 01Oct84.
Entered service 19Nov84. Painted in First Air c/s. W/o soon after
take-off Dayton, Ohio, U.S.A. 12Jan89. 2 crew killed. Regn cld
06Sep89.

TT 35,772 hrs, 49,357 ldgs

1583   (45)   Srs.2/217

F/f 09May65 as **VP-LIK**. Del Leeward Islands Air Transport
Services Ltd 21May65 with CofA issued the same day routing via
Stornoway, Reykjavik, Søndre Strømfjord, Frobisher Bay, Sept
Îles, Washington and Nassau arriving Antigua 23May65. In
service the same day. Named "Halcyon Cove" and repainted in
Court Line turquoise c/s in 1971. Made heavy landing St Croix,
US Virgins 01May73. Repaired. Company ceased operations
15Aug74, being reformed as LIAT (1974) Ltd 20Sep74. Engines
uprated to Mk.533-2. Overran runway on landing St Lucia
26Aug75. Repaired. Re-regd **V2-LIK** Mar82 after Antiguan
Independence on 01Nov81. Sold Airfast Services Indonesia P.T.
27Mar83 and immediately lsd back to LIAT (1974) Ltd. WFU
25Dec84 being at that time the lead 748 aircraft for total recorded
landings of 74,945. Del ex Antigua 22Jan85 to El Paso, Texas for
storage by Aviation Consultants. Regd as **N43AZ** to Charles
Weitz of Singapore Mar87. Ferried through Toronto 16/17Mar87
to Glasgow and Gatwick 20Mar87. Departed Southend for
Ajaccio, Corsica 22Mar87 en route Singapore to its owners,
Airfast Services Indonesia P.T. Stored Seletar, Singapore and
subsequently reduced to spares. Regn cld 17Jul89.

TT 35,636 hrs, 74,971 ldgs

1584   (71)   Srs.2/217

F/f 04Aug66 as **VP-LIP**. Del Leeward Islands Air Transport
Services Ltd 16Aug66 routing via Stornoway, Reykjavik, Søndre
Strømfjord, Frobisher Bay, Sept Îles, Washington, Miami and San
Juan arriving Antigua 20Aug06. In service the same day. Named
"Halcyon Sun" and painted in Court Line orange c/s in 1971.
Company ceased operations 15Aug74, being reformed as LIAT
(1974) Ltd 20Sep74. Engines uprated to Mk.533-2. Re-regd
V2-LIP Mar82 after Antiguan Independence on 01Nov81. Sold
British Aerospace plc in part exchange for Super 748s 20Dec84

and immediately lsd back to LIAT (1974) Ltd. Flew last service
30Dec85. Lsd Philippine Airlines Inc with del ex Antigua
05Jan86 via Manchester 15-20Jan86 arriving Manila 26Jan86.
Regd **RP-C1042** and entered service 04Mar86. Del ex Manila
08Jun87 at end of lse arriving Exeter 16Jun87 for open storage.
Regd **G-11-4** for an Active Noise trials programme by British
Aerospace plc in conjunction with Southampton University and
their ANC System after earlier trials with a 'Topexpress' system.
F/f as G-11-4 from Exeter 11Feb88 in basic PAL c/s without
titles. A series of 21 flights was flown between 25Feb and
16Jun88 as Stage 2 of the 'Open Rotor Technology' programme
which began with c/n 1790 in late 1985. Regd as **G-BPNW** to
British Aerospace (Commercial Aircraft) Ltd 07Feb89 (CofR
G-BPNW/R1) for proposed use as a company shuttle aircraft after
refurbishment and white painting by JEA Engineering Ltd.
Programme cld and regn not used. Regd to British Aerospace plc
Airlines Division 20Sep90 (CofR G-BPNW/R2). Regn cld as
PWFU 05Nov90. WFU and dismantled Aug/Sep91. Moved to
Woodford airport, U.K. by road for use as a systems rig for ATP
Rudder Boost system trials Sep91. Fuselage to Maxi Haulage
Scrapyard, Irvine, by Sep94.

TT 39,281 hrs, 79,014 ldgs

1585   (55)   Srs.2/222

Regd as **G-ATEH** to Channel Airways Ltd 26May65 (CofR
R.8548/1). F/f 24Aug65, CofA issued 24Sep65. Del 29Sep65
Woodford-Southend-Woodford. Lsd Compañia Panameña de
Aviación S.A. being del via Prestwick 08Oct65 as G-ATEH.
Ferried Prestwick-Keflavik 10Oct65 after aborted attempts on 08
and 09Oct65. Regn cld 14Oct65 as transferred Panama and regd
HP-416. Del Woodford at end of lse as HP-416 21May66.
Restored as **G-ATEH** to Channel Airways Ltd 26May66 (CofR
R.8548/2) and del Langar-Southend 30May66. Entered service
01Jun66 from Southend to Belfast. Severely damaged
Portsmouth, U.K. 15Aug67 in landing accident after a scheduled
flight from Jersey via Guernsey with no injuries to 4 crew and 66
pax on board. Del Southend 16May68 after repairs. Air tested
20Jun68. Regn cld 21Jun68 as transferred Windward/Leeward
Islands. Sold Leeward Islands Air Transport Services Ltd as
VP-LIW and del ex Southend via Keflavik 21Jun68. Painted in
Court Line orange c/s 1971. Company ceased operations
15Aug74, being reformed as LIAT (1974) Ltd 20Sep74. Engines
uprated to Mk.533-2. Undershot landing St Vincent, E.T. Joshua
Airport 31May77 with collapse of starboard main landing gear.
Repaired. Sold Airfast Services Indonesia P.T. 28Feb81, having
been del ex Antigua to Hayes International of Alabama, U.S.A.
for refurbishing 27Jan81. Del via Dublin as VP-LIW in Airfast c/s
14Feb81. Regd **PK-OBV**. Converted to Srs.2A/222. W/o
07Sep93. Undershot runway landing Tanahmerah, Indonesia. No
fatalities among 2 crew and 4 pax on board.

TT 40,197 hrs, 62,684 ldgs

1586   (56)   Srs.2/222

Regd as **G-ATEI** to Channel Airways Ltd 26May65 (CofR
R.8549/1). F/f 01Nov65, CofA issued 18Nov65. H/o 24Nov65
but did not leave Woodford. Regn cld 01Dec65 as transferred
Windward/Leeward Islands and f/f as **VP-LIN** 02Dec65. Lsd
Leeward Islands Air Transport Services Ltd as VP-LIN 04Dec65.
Del Woodford at end of lse as VP-LIN 02May66. Ferried Langar
for maintenance. Restored as **G-ATEI** to Channel Airways Ltd
17May66 (CofR R.8549/2) the same day returned from Langar
and del 20May66. Entered service from Southend to Paris-Le
Bourget 21May66. Shown at Paris Air Show 29May to 03Jun67.
Flew final Scottish Flyer schedule from Aberdeen to Southend
14May69. Regn cld 23May69 as transferred Canada. Lsd Transair
Ltd as **CF-TAX** from 24May69 to 21Nov69. Restored as
G-ATEI to Channel Airways Ltd 05Jan70 (CofR R.8549/3) and
stored until lsd Rousseau Aviation as G-ATEI from 19May70
when del from Southend to Dinard until returned Southend
19Aug70. Regn cld 28Aug70 as transferred Philippines. Test
flown 14Sep70. Sold Philippine Airlines Inc as **PI-C1029** with

del ex Southend via Rome-Ciampino 16Sep70. Re-regd **RP-C1029** 01Mar74. W/o soon after take-off from Manila, Philippines 10May75. Force landed in paddy field after tyre burst after undercarriage retraction caused port engine to fail. No fatalities among 4 crew and 39 pax on board.

TT 17,072 hrs, 21,391 ldgs

1587   (60)   Srs.2/222

Regd as **G-ATEJ** to Channel Airways Ltd 26May65. (CofR R8582/1). F/f 20Jan66, CofA issued 02Feb66. Del 21Feb66 entering service from Southend to Guernsey and Jersey with Captain Walsh in command 25Feb66. Damaged after collision with ground power unit Jersey 08Aug66. Ferried Southend for repairs 10Aug66. Re-entered service from Southend to Paris-Le Bourget 22Aug66. Flew last service from Ostend to Southend 29Nov67. Test flown 12Dec67. Regn cld 13Dec67 as transferred Canada and aircraft ferried to Woodford the same day. Sold Midwest Aviation Ltd and del as **CF-MAL** 14Dec67. Airline and aircraft absorbed into Transair Ltd 1969. Lsd Aerolíneas de Guatemala - Aviateca from Aug74 to 22Feb75 as **TG-MAL** in full Aviateca c/s. Re-regd **C-GCZY** on return from lse. Sold Air Ceylon Ltd 04May75 as **4R-ACR** and del via Gatwick 29Apr75. Sold Sri Lanka Air Force 01Sep79 as **CR-831** and operated by No2 (Transport) Squadron/Helitours. Reportedly stored Ratmalana, Sri Lanka by Mar94. Displayed at the new Sri Lanka Air Force Museum at Ratmalana from 05Nov09 after conversion to a flying simulator as an educational item for school parties.

TT 24,848 hrs, 26,778 ldgs

1588   (58)   Srs.2/222

Regd as **G-ATEK** to Channel Airways Ltd 26May65. (CofR R8583/1). F/f 10Feb66, CofA issued 03Mar66. Del from Woodford to Southend 28Mar66 entering service from Southend to Guernsey and Jersey 30Mar66. Severely damaged Portsmouth, U.K. 15Aug67 in landing incident after a flight from Southend which was due to continue to Paris with no injuries to 4 crew and 19 pax on board. Partially repaired and ferried undercarriage down to Southend 21Feb68. Test flown 09Apr68 and returned to service from Southend to Castle Donnington 11Apr68. Flew last service from Ostend to Southend 21Apr68. Regn cld 16May68 as transferred Leeward Isles. Sold Leeward Islands Air Transport Services Ltd and del as **VP-LIV** 16May68 via Luton, Keflavik, Goose Bay and Washington-National and onwards via Miami to Antigua 17May68. In service 19May68. Painted in Court Line orange c/s 1971. Company ceased operations 15Aug74, being reformed as LIAT (1974) Ltd 20Sep74. Engines uprated to Mk.533-2. Re-regd **V2-LIV** Mar82 after Antiguan Independence 01Nov81. Sold to British Aerospace plc in part exchange for Super 748s 10Jun85 and immediately lsd back to LIAT (1974) Ltd. Flew last service 25Aug85. Lsd Philippine Airlines Inc with del ex Antigua 26Aug85 via Manchester 29-31Aug85 arriving Manila 07Sep85. Re-regd **RP-C1041** 23Sep85 and entered service 09Oct85. Del ex Manila 28May87 at end of lse arriving Exeter, U.K. 03Jun87 for storage. Sold S. Hully 08Mar88. Restored as **G-ATEK** to Sean T. Hully (Sales) Ltd 01Aug88 (CofR G-ATEK/R2). Regn cld 16Sep88 as transferred Portugal. Lsd British Aerospace plc for sub-lse to Ligações Aéreas Regionais S.A. as **CS-TAV** with del 16Sep88. In service

G-ATEK c/n 1588 of Channel Airways Ltd at Jersey, UK.   (WHC)

G-AXVG c/n 1589 of Dan-Air London, seen here landing in full Dan-Air red scheme with tail fin logo.   (Fred Barnes Collection)

OE-LHT c/n 1590, seen on the ramp at Innsbrück on 25th April 1969 during its 4½ years' service with Austrian Airlines.   (Fred Barnes)

VP-LIU c/n 1592 of LIAT – a brilliant 1972 image taken soon after take-off with undercarriage tucking away. This aircraft was leased by LIAT three times.
(Kurt Lang)

19Sep88. Withdrawn from service after last flight on 07Dec88. Del Southend at end of lse 12Dec88. Painted as **6V-AFX** and lsd Air Sénégal painted overall white with AIR SENEGAL titles from Dec88 to 18Jul89 when returned Southend for storage. Restored as **G-ATEK** to STH (Sales) Ltd 29Nov89 (CofR G-ATEK/R3) but never painted as such. Broken up Southend, U.K. 11Jul91. Regn cld by the CAA 17Jun92.

TT in excess of 37,612 hrs, 72,374 ldgs (figures at 31Dec88)

1589 (64) Srs.2/226

F/f 22Apr66 as OE-LHS. Del Austrian Airlines 29Apr66 named "Franz Lehar" of the Belvedere class. Sold Skyways Coach Air Ltd 15Nov69 and regd to them as **G-AXVG** 31Dec69 (CofR R.8983/1). CofA issued 17Jan70. Name changed to International Skyways Ltd 05Mar71. Sold and regd to Dan-Air Services Ltd 01Nov71 (CofR R.8983/2) being del to Lasham 04Oct71. Converted to Srs.2A/226 30Aug75. On push back at Paris, Charles de Gaulle 23Feb77 nose leg collapsed causing damage to nose. Repaired. Lsd Eastern Provincial Airways (1963) Ltd as G-AXVG from 15Jun81 to 14Jul81. Regn cld 16Oct84 as transferred Philippines and lsd Philippine Airlines Inc as **RP-C1031** with del ex Manchester 17Oct84 arriving Manila 20Oct84. In service 30Oct84. Converted back to Srs.2/226 27Dec84 when engines demodified to Mk.533-2. Returned to Dan-Air Services Ltd at Manchester 03Feb89 at end of lse. Ferried Lasham 06Feb89 for storage. Converted back to Srs.2A/226 and restored as **G-AXVG** to Dan-Air Services Ltd 05Jun89 (CofR G-AXVG/R3). Sold Springer Aerospace of Canada for conversion to a freighter and del ex Lasham via Gatwick, Glasgow and Keflavik 06Jul89. Regn cld 17Jul89 as transferred Canada. Sold Northland Air Manitoba as **C-FGGE** being regd to them 24Jan90. Lsd The Northwest Company Inc in Apr/May90. Converted back to passenger configuration and lsd Air Marshall Islands Inc 22Aug91 to 27Nov91. Later named "Spirit of Winnipeg". WFU Winnipeg, Manitoba, Canada and dismantled Oct95. Regn cld 17Feb97.

TT 42,528 hrs, 47,463 ldgs

1590 (66) Srs.2/226

F/f 23May66 as **OE-LHT**. Del Austrian Airlines 31May66 named "Anton Bruckner" of the Belvedere class. Sold Philippine Airlines Inc as **PI-C1028** 03Sep70. Re-regd **RP-C1028** 01Mar74. W/o shortly after take-off from Manila, Philippines 03Feb75 following No.2 engine failure. 4 crew and 29 pax killed, 2 pax survived.

TT 6,449 hrs, 8,320 ldgs

1591 (68) Srs.2/223

F/f 01Jul66 as **0111**. Del Venezuelan Government for the use of the Ministerio de la Defensa as a VIP transport 05Aug66 and operated by the Fuerza Aérea Venezolana. Regn **G-BIOV** rsvd 1981 but not taken up. Seen Caracas, Venezuela Mar87 in full Aeropostal c/s with no external regn visible. By 13Jun87 was reportedly painted as **YV-39C** and used as an instructional airframe. Status unknown.

TT 4,506 hrs, 5,783 ldgs

1592 (62) Srs.2/225

Regd as **G-ATMI** to Autair International Airways Ltd 04Jan66 (CofR R.8834/1). F/f 15Mar66, CofA issued 29Mar66. Del 30Mar66. Regn cld 13Nov67 as transferred Windward and Leeward Islands and aircraft painted as **VP-LIU** the same date, being airtested in these marks the following day. Lsd Leeward Islands Air Transport Services Ltd with del ex Luton as VP-LIU 15Nov67 arriving Antigua 19Nov67. In service 20Nov67. Ferried ex Antigua via Bermuda and Halifax to Gander 13May68 and onwards to Søndre Strømfjord and Keflavik the following day before del Luton via Southend 15May68 at end lse. Restored as **G-ATMI** to Autair International Airways Ltd 27May68 (CofR R.8834/2). Immediately lsd to Skyways Coach Air Ltd until 01Oct68 and again from 15Mar69 to 11Nov69, Lsd Leeward Islands Air Transport Services Ltd as **VP-LIU** with del ex Luton 01Dec69 arriving Antigua 04Dec69. In service 06Dec69, the UK regn not being cld until 09Dec69 as transferred Windward and Leeward Islands. Flew last service 26Apr70 and del ex Antigua 27Apr70 arriving Luton 29Apr70 at end of lse. Restored as **G-ATMI** to Court Line Aviation Ltd 07May70 (CofR R.8834/3) and painted as such 11May70. Lsd Sociedade Açoreana de Transportes Aéreos (SATA) with del from and to Luton 13May70 to 15Oct70. Lsd Leeward Islands Air Transport Services Ltd as **VP-LIU** named "Halcyon Breeze" in Court Line's lilac c/s with del ex Luton 24Nov70 arriving Antigua 28Nov70. In service 01Dec70. UK regn cld 04Dec70 as transferred Windward and Leeward Islands. Flew last service 17Mar71. Del Luton at end of lse 24Mar71 and restored as **G-ATMI** to Court Line Aviation Ltd 30Mar71 (CofR R.8834/4). Lsd British Air Ferries Ltd from 06Apr to 28Nov71. Sold Leeward Islands Air Transport Services Ltd with del ex Luton as **VP-LIU** 18Dec71 arriving Antigua 21Dec71. In service 22Dec71, the same day the UK regn cld as transferred Windward and Leeward Islands. Flew last service 15Mar75. Sold Dan-Air Services Ltd and del ex Antigua 08May75 arriving Lasham via Gatwick 13May75. Restored as **G-ATMI** to Dan-Air Services Ltd 09Jun75 (CofR G-ATMI/R5). In service 29Jun75. Converted to Srs.2A/225 01May77. Lsd Air

BVI Ltd as **G-ATMI** with del from and to Manchester 11Dec81 and 17Apr82. Lsd British Airways for use by the Highlands Division from 02-30Mar83, 01-15Oct83, 06-19Apr84 and 13May to 12Jun84. Flew last flight 09May91 and put into storage Manchester. Sold Janes Aviation 15Jul92 and del from Manchester to Exeter 22Jul92. Regd Janes Aviation 748 Ltd 03Aug92 (CofR G-ATMI/R6). Lsd Business Air 11Oct92 to 31May93. Painted in Reed Aviation c/s named "Old Ben" and r/o Exeter 17Jun93. Del Liverpool 22Jun93. Janes Aviation renamed Emerald Airways Ltd 15Sep93. Severely damaged after take-off accident Liverpool 16Aug96. Repaired by BAe working party. F/f after repair 19May97 and returned to service in freighter config. WFU 15May99 and ferried Blackpool the same day. Placed in storage. Noted being reduced to spares Mar01. Regn cld 30Jul01 as PWFU. Nose section to RAF Millom Aviation & Military Museum Oct07 for conversion as a flight simulator. Museum entered into voluntary liquidation 11Aug10 and nose section later advertised for sale on Ebay.

TT 53,552 hrs, 59,705 ldgs

1593   (63)   Srs.2/225

Regd as **G-ATMJ** to Autair International Airways Ltd 04Jan66 (CofR R.8835/1). F/f 06Apr66, CofA issued 19Apr66. Del 20Apr66, being displayed at the Farnborough Air Show 05-09Sep66. Regn cld 15Jan68 as transferred Jamaica. Lsd Jamaica Air Service (1967) Ltd as **6Y-JFJ** with del ex Luton 15Jan68 in Autair c/s with Jamaica Air Service titles and fin flash. Entered service 20Jan68. Flew last flight 27Mar69 and departed Kingston at end of lse 29Mar69 arriving Luton 02Apr69. Restored as **G-ATMJ** to Autair International Airways Ltd 17Apr69 (CofR R.8835/2). Lsd Sociedade Açoreana de Transportes Aéreos (SATA) from 29Apr69 to 15May70, Rousseau Aviation from 17Aug70 to 10Oct70 and British Air Ferries Ltd from 02Nov70 to 30Oct71 all as G-ATMJ and all dates quoted to and from Luton. Lsd Leeward Islands Air Transport Services Ltd with del ex Luton as G-ATMJ named "Halcyon Beach" in Court Line pink c/s 21Nov71 via Prestwick & Keflavik arriving Antigua 24Nov71. Regn cld 25Nov71 as transferred Antigua and regd **VP-LAJ** entering service the same day. Flew last service 09Apr72 and del Luton at end of lse as VP-LAJ 12Apr72. Lsd Rousseau Aviation as VP-LAJ in full LIAT c/s with Rousseau titling from 17Apr72. Entered service 20Apr72. Returned Luton at end lse 02Oct72.

Sold to the Civil Aviation Authority 02Oct72 being restored to them as **G-ATMJ** 28Dec72 (CofR R.8835/3) after del Stansted as VP-LAJ 20Oct72. Antiguan regn cld 10Nov72. F/f after conversion to the Civil Aviation Flying Unit standards as G-ATMJ 29Jan73. Lsd Dan-Air Services Ltd at weekends from May to Oct75 flown by C.A.A. crews. Sold Dan-Air Services Ltd with ferry to Manchester for repaint in Dan-Air c/s and conversion to Srs.2A/225 21Jul78 and regd to them 26Jul78 (CofR G-ATMJ/R4). Ferried ex Manchester to Aberdeen as DA99MJ 31Jul78. Lsd British Airways for use by the Highlands Division and del ex Manchester 01Mar82. In service 02Mar82 and regd to British Airways Board 07Jun82 (CofR G-ATMJ/R5). Named "Glen Nevis" on starboard and "Gleann Nibheis" on port side Mar83. Regd to British Airways plc 01Apr84. Repainted in British Airways' new colour scheme 19Jun85. Ferried from Glasgow to Heathrow as BA8917E 03Mar89. Repainted in full Dan-Air c/s and r/o 10Mar89. Ferried back to Glasgow as BA8929E the same date and returned to service with British Airways. Flew last revenue service as BA8935H 27Mar89 from Glasgow to Dublin before positioning back to Glasgow as BA8936P 27Mar89. Handed back to Dan-Air Services Ltd 31Mar89. Regd to Dan-Air Services Ltd 14Jan91 (CofR G-ATMJ/R6). Stored Manchester by 10Dec91. Sold Janes Aviation 15Jul92 and del from Manchester to Exeter 21Jul92. Regd to Janes Aviation 748 Ltd 03Aug92 (CofR G-ATMJ/R7). Company renamed Emerald Airways Ltd 15Sep93. Stored Exeter from 07Aug96. Ferried Woodford for repaint 22Sep97. Ferried Woodford-Liverpool as JEM748P 04Oct97 and returned to

service in freighter config. Starboard engine fire during ground runs Isle of Man 11Apr02 causing extensive damage. Repaired and ferried Blackpool 16Nov02. Air tested 18Nov02. Ferried Liverpool as JEM03T 21Nov02 and returned to service. Company's AOC suspended 04May06 and aircraft stored Blackpool, U.K. Sold International Air Parts Pty Ltd 16Oct06. Regd PTB (Emerald) Pty Ltd 12Dec06 (CofR G-ATMJ/R8). Wings removed by early Apr09 at start of b/u process. Regn cld as PWFU 15Jun09.

TT 44,551 hrs, 58,641 ldgs

The end of the line. G-ATMJ c/n 1593 being broken up at Blackpool in April 1970.   *(Mike Davey)*

1594   (70)   Srs.2/227

F/f 15Jul66 as **HP-432**. Del Compañia Panameña de Aviación S.A. (COPA) 05Aug66 named "Chiriqui". Sold Eastern Provincial Airways (1963) Ltd as **C-GEPI** with del Gander 24Apr78, fleet number 302. Converted to Srs.2A/227. CofR and CofA issued 05Jul78. Operated by Air Maritime with effect from Jan82. Del Manchester for attention by Dan-Air Engineering Ltd 01Nov85. Departed 14Dec85 on return to Air Maritime. Company fully integrated into Canadian Pacific Air Lines Ltd with effect from 12Jan86. WFU and ferried Toronto for storage 16May86. Lsd Austin Airways Ltd Aug86 to Nov86 in full Air Maritime c/s. Sold Macavia International 01Mar87 and ferried to Cranfield via Reykjavik and Prestwick 04Apr87. Regd as **G-BNJK** to Macair International Ltd 05May87 (CofR G-BNJK/R1) for conversion to the prototype Macavia BAe748 Turbine Tanker by Cranfield Aeronautical Services, the engineering section of the Cranfield Institute of Technology. F/f as G-BNJK 21Aug87 without the bolt on belly tank. F/f with belly tank attached 04Sep87. CofA issued 30Jan88. Full details of the conversion shown in the 'General History' section. Displayed at the Paris Air Show Jun88 and Woodford Air Show 25Jun89. Stored Châteauroux, France by Jun95. Regn cld by the CAA 29Feb96.

TT in excess of 29,103 hrs, 34,214 ldgs (figures at 27May90)

1595   (76)   Srs.2/229

F/f 13Jan67 as **A10-595**. H/o 17Mar67. Taken on charge by RAAF Staff London 23Mar67 and del Royal Australian Air Force 29Mar67 and used as a VIP aircraft by 34 Squadron, Fairbairn A.C.T. To 32 Squadron, East Sale 16Jan90 for use in the communications rôle. Withdrawn East Sale by Jun96. Advertised for sale by tender Nov98. Regn SE-LIE rsvd 23Feb99. Sold West Air Sweden AB as **SE-LIE** and del ex Essendon 01Mar99. Converted Srs.2A/229, stripped out and converted to a pure freighter. Painted in full West Air c/s with the RAAF grey as the base. Regd as SE-LIE to West Air Sweden AB 15Jun00. Regd European Turboprop Management AB 27Sep01. Regd SG Finans AS Norge 17Jun05. Noted Lidköping late Jul06 being used for training Alaire crews. Ferried Lidköping, Sweden 22Aug06 and WFU. Regn cld as scrapped 06Dec06.

TT 21,279 hrs, 23,964 ldgs

1596   (77)   Srs.2/229

F/f 10Mar67 as **A10-596**. Del Royal Australian Air Force 04May67 and used as a VIP aircraft by 34 Squadron, Fairbairn A.C.T. On 10Apr70 used to transport HM Queen Elizabeth, Prince Philip and Princess Anne on an official visit to RAAF Williamstown, NSW. To 32 Squadron, East Sale 13Nov89 for use in the communications rôle. Withdrawn East Sale by Jun96. Advertised for sale by tender Nov98. Regn SE-LIF rsvd 23Feb99. Sold West Air Sweden as **SE-LIF** and del ex Essendon 01Mar99. Converted Srs.2A/229, stripped out and converted to a pure freighter. Painted in full West Air c/s using the RAAF grey as the base. Regd as SE-LIF to West Air Sweden AB 08Sep99. Named "Number 10". Regd European Turboprop Management AB 27Sep01. Regd SG Finans AS Norge 17Jun05. Flew last revenue flight 02Oct06 and then used for crew training at Lidköping. Painted overall grey and sold Air Creebec Inc and ferried ex Lidköping via Bergen and Keflavik 29Oct06. Ferry continued via Søndre Strømfjord and Iqaluit to Timmins 30Oct06. Regn cld 01Nov06 as exported Canada. Regd as **C-FLJC** to Air Creebec Inc 06Dec06. Fitted with a roller floor, smoke detectors and 8 X 250 gallon internal removable fuel cells. CofA issued 20Jan07 and entered service 15Feb07 still painted overall grey. PWFU Timmins, Ontario, Canada 29Jan08 and put in store. Regn cld 15Jul08. B/U Nov11.

TT 24,312 hrs, 26,677 ldgs

1597   (75)   Srs.2/221

F/f 18Nov66 as **T-01** although regn **LV-PGG** had been reserved for ferry flight but not used. Del Fuerza Aérea Argentina 20Dec66 for Presidential use. Re-regd **T-02** Jan71 and named "Libertad". Re-regd **T-03** 1975. Sold Austin Airways Ltd as **C-GQWO** and del 29Sep78. Converted to Srs.2A/221. CofR and CofA issued 28Feb79. Lsd Réunion Air Service and del via Manchester as C-GQWO 07Apr80. In service 15Apr80. Flew last service 21Jun80 and del ex Réunion 01Jul80 via Copenhagen 05-07Jul80. Austin Airways Ltd merged with Air Ontario Inc Apr87 using Air Ontario as the operating name. Sold Air Creebec Inc 06Dec88 never having been painted in Air Ontario c/s. Reportedly lsd LIAT (1974) Ltd Jan to Jun91. Regd Air Creebec (1994) Inc 13Mar91. Converted to an unpressurised pure freighter in 1998 and fitted with a removable fuel tankering unit comprising 8 X 250 gallon tanks interconnected via a manifold system. Cabin windows and rear baggage door removed and cockpit heaters installed at the same time. PWFU at Timmins, Ontario, Canada 10Jul08 and put in store. Donated to the Canadian military and was due to be used in an emergency response exercise in Feb12. Regn cld 20Feb12.

TT 37,981 hrs, 50,950 ldgs

1598   (72)   Srs.2/230

F/f 31Aug66 as **G11**. F/f as **XA-SEV** 26Oct66. Del Aeromaya S.A. 10Nov66 in the c/s of the original customer, Aerotaxi del Sureste S.A. with 'Aerotaxis Aerosafari' titles. Transferred to Servicios Aéreos Especiales S.A. (SAESA) Sep69 and named "Chichenitsa". Later named "Puerto Vallarta". Converted to Srs.2A/230. W/o 25 miles north-west of Chetumal attempting a forced landing in a jungle clearing following a reported fire on board. 5 crew and 20 passengers killed (other reports state 18 passengers killed). The aircraft was flying from Chetumal to México City via Mérida.

TT 10,081 hrs, 8,800 ldgs

1599   (73)   Srs.2/230

F/f 23Sep66 as **G-11**. Painted as **XA-SEY** 09Nov66. Del Aeromaya S.A. 02Jan67 in the c/s of the original customer, Aerotaxi del Sureste S.A. Transferred to Servicios Aéreos Especiales S.A. (SAESA) Sep69 and named "Palenque". Converted to Srs.2A/230. Sold Aerovías Caribe S.A. Jan77 named "Cozumel". Regd **G-BFUA** to Dan-Air Services Ltd 18May78 (CofR G-BFUA/R1) but regn cld 06Jun78 as not

imported. Sold Les Ailes du Nord Ltée/Northern Wings Ltd and del Toronto 19Aug79 as **C-GAPC**. Company renamed Regionair (1981) Inc with effect from mid 1981. Airline and aircraft absorbed into Québecair Inc early 1984. WFU Montréal-Dorval 86. Company taken over by Nordair Metro 31Jul86. Sold Aerocontracts Ltd and broken up Dorval, Québec, Canada for spares 15/30Apr87. Regn cld 26Feb88.

TT 34,060 hrs, 35,177 ldgs

1600   (90)   Srs.2/231

F/f 09May67 as **AF601**. Del Zambia Air Force as a Presidential/VIP aircraft 21Jun67. W/o on take-off Lusaka, Zambia 26Aug69. 3 crew killed, one survived.

TT 957 hrs, 1,209 ldgs

1601   (108)   Srs.2/228

Regd as **G-AVZD** to Hawker Siddeley Aviation Ltd 06Dec67 (CofR R.9243/1). F/f 21Feb68, CofA issued 05Apr68. Used as a certification aircraft for Rolls-Royce Dart 8 engines with tropical trials at Asmara, Eritrea leaving Woodford 06Apr68 via Ciampino and Nicosia. Returned Woodford 20Apr68 via Cairo, Malta and Nice. Development trials ended 29Jun68 and aircraft modified to standard RAAF fit. Regn cld 09Aug68 as transferred RAAF. H/o RAAF at Woodford 30Aug68. Arrived RAAF School of Air Navigation, East Sale as **A10-601** 20Sep68 after departing Woodford 07Sep68 via Athens, New Delhi, Bangkok, Singapore, Denpasar, Darwin and Alice Springs. Operated by 32 Squadron with effect from 01Jul89 on behalf of former operator. WFU and ferried to the RAAF Museum at Point Cook, Victoria, Australia for preservation 20Jan04 in the overall grey c/s. Later completely covered in protective coating.

TT 20,485 hrs, 18,040 ldgs

1602   (121)   Srs.2/228

F/F 01Aug68 as **A10-602**. Del RAAF School of Air Navigation, East Sale 03Oct68. Operated by 32 Squadron with effect from 01Jul89 on behalf of former operator. WFU after last flight on 30Jun04. Sold TAG Aviation Jul04. Ferried West Sale as 'Turbo 602' 10Aug04 for storage. Regd as **VH-POZ** to Edge Aviation Pty Ltd 15Sep04. Ferried West Sale-Broome 06Mar05 en route Tanzania on sale to GGG Aviation. Regn cld as sold in Tanzania 07Apr05 and subsequently regd **3D-POZ**. Regd as **3X-GEE** to S Höcherl 07Aug06. Noted Nairobi-Wilson 22May06. Seen Conakry painted as **3X-GEE** with Guinée Air Cargo titles 07Jun07 after preparation at Wilson. Regn cld 26Feb08. Reportedly used for ground training when seen Conakry 29Jan11.

TT in excess of 19,864 hrs, 18,865 ldgs (figures at 30Jun04)

1603   (124)   Srs.2/228

F/f 13Sep68 as **A10-603**. Del RAAF School of Air Navigation, East Sale 30Oct68 having previously been displayed at the Farnborough Air Show. Operated by 32 Squadron with effect from 01Jul89 on behalf of former operator. WFU after last flight on 30Jun04. Sold Thameside Aviation Jul04. Ferried West Sale as 'Turbo 603' 06Aug04 for storage. Regd as **VH-AMQ** to Ross Michael Hornblower 02Feb05. Ferried ex West Sale 16Feb05 via Broome (same date) and onwards via Kuala Lumpur, Colombo, Muscat, Alexandria & Bari arriving Southend 20Feb05 in white top/blue cheat line c/s. Put in store. Regn cld 25Sep08 as exported USA but remained in store Southend, U.K. still painted as VH-AMQ. Sold Skylark Hotel, Southend Airport for preservation and lifted onto hotel site 19Jul10.

TT in excess of 19,998 hrs, 18,260 ldgs (figures at 30Jun04)

1604   (127)   Srs.2/228

F/f 07Nov68 as **A10-604**. Del RAAF School of Air Navigation, East Sale 15Dec68. Operated by 32 Squadron with effect from 01Jul89 on behalf of former operator. Sold International Air Parts

Pty Ltd and regd to Horizon Airlines Pty Ltd as **VH-IMG** 22Mar99. Ferried from Kingsford-Smith to Bankstown as VH-IMG 15Jul99 and stored. Loaned to Australian Aviation Museum at Bankstown 16Apr03 for static display. Horizon Airlines placed in Adminstration 14Oct03 and later ceased operations. Replaced at museum by c/n 1709 19May04. Reduced to spares by Jul04. Regn cld 12May05.

TT 18,048 hrs, 16,405 ldgs

1605   (130)   Srs.2/228

F/f 19Dec68 as **A10-605**. Del RAAF School of Air Navigation, East Sale 28Feb69. Operated by 32 Squadron with effect from 01Jul89 on behalf of former operator. WFU after last flight on 30Jun04. Sold TAG Aviation Jul04. Ferried West Sale as 'Turbo 605' 10Aug04 for storage. Ferried to Bankstown as 'Turbo 5' 18Sep04 in overall grey c/s. Regd as **VH-AMQ** to IAP Group Australia Pty Ltd 23Sep04. Reduced to spares by 28Oct04. Regn cld 15Dec04. *TT 21,106 hrs, 19,290 ldgs*

1606   (133)   Srs.2/228

F/f 24Feb69 as **A10-606**. Del RAAF School of Air Navigation, East Sale 15May69. Operated by 32 Squadron with effect from 01Jul89 on behalf of former operator. WFU after last flight on 30Jun04. Sold Thameside Aviation Jul04. Ferried West Sale as 'Turbo 606' 06Aug04 for storage. Regd as **VH-AHL** to Ross Michael Hornblower 04Feb05. Ferried ex West Sale 27Feb05 via Broome, Kuala Lumpur, Colombo, Muscat and Heraklion arriving Southend 03Mar05 in white top/blue cheat line c/s. Put in store. Regn cld 25Sep08 as exported USA but remained in store Southend, U.K. still painted as VH-AHL. Sold Skylark Hotel, Southend Airport for preservation and lifted onto hotel site 19Jul10.

TT in excess of 19,322 hrs, in excess of 16,400 ldgs
(figures at 30Jun04)

1607   (136)   Srs.2/228

F/f 28Mar69 as **A10-607**. Del RAAF School of Air Navigation, East Sale 27Jun69. Operated by 32 Squadron with effect from 01Jul89 on behalf of former operator. WFU and put in store East Sale 31May98. Dismantled. Fuselage to DTSO Salisbury 01Jun98 for trial installation work but contract cld. Components sold International Air Parts Pty Ltd and transported Bankstown by road 08Jan01. Fin & rudder displayed on a plinth outside 32 Squadron building at East Sale, Victoria, Australia.

TT 17,474 hrs, 15,314 ldgs

1608   (139)   Srs.2/228

F/f 02Jun69 as **A10-608**. Del RAAF School of Air Navigation, East Sale 29Jul69. Operated by 32 Squadron with effect from 01Jul89 on behalf of former operator. WFU after last flight on 30Jun04. Sold Thameside Aviation Jul04. Ferried West Sale as 'Turbo 608' 06Aug04 for storage. Ferried to Bankstown as 'Turbo 8' 19Sep04 in overall grey c/s. Regd as **VH-AYS** to IAP Group Australia Pty Ltd 23Sep04. Ferried ex Bankstown 11Mar05 via Broome and Kuala Lumpur arriving Southend 14Mar05 from Heraklion and Dubai in the overall grey c/s and put in store. Moved into Inflite hangar 21Apr08. Regn cld 30May08 as exported USA but remained in store Southend, UK still painted as VH-AYS. B/U 05/20May09.

TT in excess of 19,609 hrs, 17,294 ldgs (figures at 30Jun04)

1609   (74)   Srs.2/232

F/f 09Dec66 as **VP-BCJ**. Del Bahamas Airways Ltd 22Dec66. Sold Philippine Airlines Inc and del via Gatwick as VP-BCJ 22Jun70. Regd as **PI-C1027**. W/o following heavy landing Bislig, Philippines 28Nov72. No fatalities among 4 crew and 24 pax.

TT 13,230 hrs, 17,303 ldgs

1610   (81)   Srs.2/232

F/f 20Feb67 as **VP-BCK**. Del Bahamas Airways Ltd 07Mar67. Company ceased operations 16Oct70. Del Manchester 06Nov70 prior to storage at East Midlands from del 09Nov70. Sold Mandala Airlines P.T. and del as **PK-RHQ** 24Jun71 after f/f as such 24May71. Re-regd **PK-RHS** and named "Djajawidjaja" on arrival Indonesia. W/o landing Manila, Philippines 18Oct77 on a test flight with No2 engine shut down. 2 crew and 3 killed on ground, 3 on board survived.

TT 14,993 hrs, 16,498 ldgs

1611   (82)   Srs.2/232

F/f 16Mar67 as **VP-BCL**. Del Bahamas Airways Ltd 13Apr67. Company ceased operations 16Oct70. Stored East Midlands from 13Nov70 until sold Inexco Oil as **CF-INE** 23Feb73 after f/f as such 20Feb73 (initially r/o 19Feb73 incorrectly painted as **LF-INE**). Del ex East Midlands two days later. Converted to Srs.2A/232. In service 03Mar73. Lsd Air Services Botswana (Pty) Ltd with del via Manchester 22Mar74 arriving Johannesburg 26Mar74. Painted as **A2-ABA** 27Mar74 and wet lsd to Air Botswana (Pty) Ltd. In service 01Apr74. Flew last service 30Sep74 and del ex Johannesburg 05Oct74 arriving East Midlands 08Oct74. Underwent maintenance before ferry to Canada 19Oct74. Restored to Inexco Oil as **C-FINE** 01Nov74. Last flight for Inexco Oil 21Jan75 before sale to Eastern Provincial Airways (1963) Ltd 01Feb75. Repainted in full colours at Dorval before del to Gander 07Mar75. In service 08Mar75. Operated by Air Maritime with effect from Jan82. Company fully integrated into Canadian Pacific Air Lines with effect from 12Jan86. Regn cld 25Sep86 and regd to SAEMI 15Oct86 on sale to them as **F-OSPM** for operation by Air Saint-Pierre. Named "Ville de Saint-Pierre". Ferried East Midlands 15Oct95 via Narsarsuaq and Keflavik and onwards to Nice 18Oct95 on sale to Ibis Air Transport Ltd/Executive Outcomes. Regn cld 31Oct95, regd **9L-LBH** and stored Malta. Noted Lanseria, South Africa 30Aug97 still in basic Air Saint-Pierre c/s without titles. By Oct97 had "Kamaria Air" titles added. Seen Rand 10Feb98 in a new green and white Kamaria Air c/s. Noted Pointe Noire, Congo Brazzaville with 'Air Éspace' titles 14Apr99. Regd **TN-AGA**. Rear freight door separated 16 minutes into flight out of Brazzaville on 28Jul99 when operated by Air Éspace. Landed safely with no injuries to 39 pax and 5 crew. Repaired and later regd **3D-BAE**, being noted in the latter marks at Rand 08Mar00 with no titles. Noted in store Rand Sep00. Sold Gabon Express Nov00 and noted Rand 09Dec00 in full Gabon Express c/s. Re-regd as **TR-LFW** to Liberavia 04May01 and noted as such Lanseria 19Sep01 all white with Gabon Express titles. Noted Rand in same c/s 27Mar03. Returned Liberavia and departed Rand 29Jul03 for further lease Gabon Express. W/o soon after take-off from Libreville, Gabon when operating flight GBE221 to Franceville 08Jun04. Crashed into sea just offshore when returning on full emergency. 1 crew and 18 pax killed, 3 crew and 8 pax survived.

TT in excess of 31,909 hrs, 43,329 ldgs (figures at 20Mar96)

1612   (83)   Srs.2/232

F/f 04Apr67 as **VP-BCM**. Del Bahamas Airways Ltd 23Apr67. In service 27Apr67. Company ceased operations 16Oct70. Stored East Midlands from 31Oct70 after ferry via Montréal, Goose Bay, Narsarsuaq, Rekjavik and Manchester. Lsd Dan-Air Services Ltd with del Ashford as VP-BCM 07Apr72. Regd as **G-AZSU** to BOAC Associated Companies Ltd 20Apr72 (CofR R.9247/1). CofA issued 20May72. In service with Dan-Air Services Ltd 21May72. Inaugurated Gatwick to Berne service 05Jun72. Converted to Srs.2A/232 27Sep74. Lsd Hawker Siddeley Aviation Ltd 26Sep74 and sub-lsd Air Services Botswana (Pty) Ltd with del ex Ashford 27Sep74 arriving Johannesburg 01Oct74. Regn cld 01Oct74 as transferred Botswana. Regd as **A2-ABB** and wet lsd to Air Botswana (Pty) Ltd. In service 05Oct74. Last flight 30Dec75 before lse to Zambia Airways Corporation Ltd regd as

The much-travelled 3D-BAE c/n 1611 at Johannesburg-Rand, untitled, on 6th September, 2000. (Keith Gaskell)

A2-ABB with del Lusaka 05Jan76. In service 08Jan76. Last flight 24Mar76 and del ex Lusaka 26Mar76 arriving Manchester from Dinard 29Mar76. Restored as **G-AZSU** to Dan-Air Services Ltd 09Apr76 (CofR G-AZSU/R2) and departed for Teesside 16Apr76. Left runway Sumburgh 10Jan77 causing nose leg to collapse. After temporary repair, flown unpressurised to Manchester landing gear down for permanent repair 29Jan77. Departed Manchester 29Mar77. Lsd British Airways for the use of the Highlands Division and del Glasgow 15Mar82. Regd to British Airways Board 30Mar82 (CofR G-AZSU/R3). Named "Glen Clova" on starboard and "Gleann Clovaigh" on port side Mar83. Regd British Airways plc 01Apr84. Flew last service as BA5543 from Belfast to Glasgow 08Feb85 and del Manchester as BA9864P at the end of lse 13Feb85. Regd to Dan-Air Services Ltd 20Feb85 (CofR G-AZSU/R4) and operated with a white top and red upper half to fin with 'Dan-Air London' titles. Lsd Sociedade Açoreana de Transportes Aéreos (SATA) as G-AZSU from 26Jun85 to 07Sep85. Ferried from Manchester to Aberdeen 04Feb90 for lse to Aberdeen Airways Ltd. Sold Aberdeen Airways Ltd 02Mar90. Regd Hawk Aviation Ltd 20Mar90 (CofR G-AZSU/R5). Regd to Wisdom Investments Ltd 25Mar91 (CofR G-AZSU/R6) and continued to be operated by Aberdeen Airways Ltd. Company ceased operations 01Aug92. Ferried Glasgow 25Sep92 on sale to Euroair Ltd. Entered service 30Sep92. Ferried Glasgow 30Dec93 for storage. Ferried Prestwick Apr94 for further storage. Departed Prestwick 16Aug94. Regn cld 25Apr95 as sold in France. Regd as **F-GPDC** to Wisdom Investments Ltd 02May95 for lse to Air Provence International. Noted Le Bourget with 'Air Provence Cargo' titles 02Mar97. Stored Marseille, France engineless by 17Aug03. B/u Feb04.

TT in excess of 42,778 hrs, 47,453 ldgs (figures at 31Aug01)

1613 (100) Srs.2/233

F/f 16Aug67 as **VQ-FAL**. Del Fiji Airways Ltd 11Sep67 arriving Suva 21Sep67. In service 01Oct67. Company name change to Pacific Island Airways Ltd 23Sep70. Regd to Air Pacific Ltd 31Jul71 following company name change. Re-regd **DQ-FAL**

01Oct71. Last flight 17Jun76 and sold Dan-Air Services Ltd with del ex Suva the same day arriving Lasham 29Jun76. Regd as **G-BEBA** to Dan-Air Services Ltd 01Jul76 (CofR G-BEBA/R1). Converted to Srs.2A/233 31Jul76, CofA issued 01Aug76. In service 02Aug76. Lsd Eastern Provincial Airways (1963) Ltd as G-BEBA from 01Aug81 to 08Oct81. Regn cld 29Oct84 as transferred Philippines. Lsd Philippine Airlines Inc as **RP-C1032** with del ex Manchester 03Nov84 arriving Manila 06Nov84. Converted back to Srs.2/233 12Nov84 after engines de-modified to Mk.533-2. In service 16Nov84. Del Lasham for storage 06Mar89 at end of lse. Converted back to Srs.2A/233 and restored as **G-BEBA** to Dan-Air Services Ltd 24May89 (CofR G-BEBA/R2). Sold Springer Aerospace of Canada for conversion to a freighter. Ferried from Lasham to Manchester 30May89. Del ex Manchester via Stornoway 03Jun89. Regn cld 07Jun89 as transferred Canada. CofR issued 10Aug89 as **C-FKTL**. CofA issued 11Aug89, the same day del to V. Kelner Airways Ltd on sale to them with fleet number 801. Regd to V. Kelner Airways Ltd 05Sep89. Returned Springer Aerospace 06Mar90 for modifications. Converted to an unpressurised pure freighter with double rear freight doors and fitted with a modernised avionics package. Re-del V. Kelner Airways Ltd 26Feb91. Used as a freighter/tanker with new fleet number 802. Rear of aircraft damaged by fire at Big Trout Lake, Ontario while defuelling aircraft when being used in its tanker rôle 14Aug91. Ferried Bar River Airport, Sault Ste. Marie, Ontario, Canada 16Aug91 and subsequently declared a write-off. Regn cld 19Nov91.

TT 40,982 hrs, 43,001 ldgs

1614 (87) Srs.2/234

F/f 12Jun67 as **CC-CEC**. Del Línea Aérea Nacional de Chile 13Jul67 with fleet number 741 and ferried via Stornoway, Keflavik, Søndre Strømfjord, Frobisher Bay, Sept Îles, Philadelphia, Jacksonville, Montego Bay, Panama City, Guayaquil, Lima and Antofagasta arriving Santiago 19Jul67. Entered service 01Sep67. Converted to Srs.2A/234. Sold Bouraq Indonesia Airlines P.T. and del via Shannon as **PK-IHA** 19Feb78.

In service 03Mar78. Severely damaged Banjarmasin, South Kalimantan, Indonesia 04Jan89 when aircraft belly-landed after main undercarriage failed to extend. No fatalities among 5 crew and 47 pax on board. Repair reportedly abandoned and stripped for spares 1992.

TT 33,415 hrs, 24,844 ldgs

1615   (92)   Srs.2/234

F/f 21Jul67 as **CC-CED**. Del Linea Aérea Nacional de Chile 18Aug67 with fleet number 742. Converted to Srs.2A/234. Sold Bouraq Indonesia Airlines P.T. and del via Shannon as **PK-IHB** 24Aug78 arriving Jakarta 29Aug78. Re-regd **PK-IHS** 20Sep78. Damaged Gorontalo, North Sulawesi, Indonesia 10Feb88 when nose leg collapsed during landing roll. Repaired and returned to service 05Mar89. Nose gear collapsed on landing Tarakan, Indonesia 10Oct90. Repaired. Stored Jakarta from Apr93. PWFU 07Apr94. Still there May00.

TT in excess of 37,050 hrs, 27,303 ldgs (figures at 31Oct92)

1616   (102)   Srs.2/234

F/f 19Sep67 as **CC-CEE**. Del Línea Aérea Nacional de Chile 05Oct67 with fleet number 743. Converted to Srs.2A/234. Sold Bouraq Indonesia Airlines P.T. Mar78 and del via Larnaca as **PK-IHC** 18Mar78 arriving Jakarta 24Mar78. In service 08Apr78. Stored Jakarta from Feb91. PWFU 07Apr94. Still there May00.

TT 33,625 hrs, 24,973 ldgs

1617   (106)   Srs.2/234

F/f 27Nov67 as **CC-CEF**. Del Línea Aérea Nacional de Chile 15Dec67 with fleet number 744. Converted to Srs.2A/234. Sold Austin Airways Ltd May79 as **C-GQTH** arriving Canada 16Jul79. Lsd Maersk Air I/S with del to Copenhagen as C-GQTH 07Dec80. Regd as **OY-MBH** 11Dec80 and entered service 16Dec80 in basic LAN - Chile c/s. Departed Copenhagen 27Mar81 for Stansted where painted as **C-GQTH**. Danish regn cld 31Mar81. Del Canada via Reykjavik 04Apr81. CofR and CofA issued 09Apr81. Sold Ilford Riverton Airways Ltd as C-GQTH 01Jan84. Operator renamed Northland Air Manitoba Ltd with effect from 13Feb86. W/o on take-off from Sandy Lake, Ontario, Canada when operating as 7N206 10Nov93. 3 crew and 4 pax killed. Regn cld 12Dec94.

TT 29,242 hrs, 35,785 ldgs

1618   (114)   Srs.2/234

F/f 27Mar68 as **CC-CEG**. Del Línea Aérea Nacional de Chile 02May68 with fleet number 745. Converted Srs.2A/234. Operated last scheduled service by HS748 for this operator as LA1990 from Punta Arenas to Santiago 02Jun79. Sold Austin Airways Ltd as **C-GQSV** arriving Canada Jul79. Lsd Maersk Air I/S with del to Copenhagen as C-GQSV 21Aug80. Painted in full Maersk Air c/s. Regd as **OY-MBY** 25Aug80 and entered service 31Aug80. Departed Copenhagen 14Jul81 for Manchester where painted as **C-GQSV**. Danish regn cld 17Jul81. Del via Reykjavik 21Jul81 arriving Canada 23Jul81. CofR and CofA issued 31Jul81. Sold Air Creebec Inc 01Dec83. In service 31Jan84 from Val d'Or to Rupert House, La Grande, Sanikiluak and back to Val d'Or. W/o on fifth attempt at landing Waskaganish (Rupert House), Québec, Canada 03Dec88. No fatalities among 3 crew on board. Regn cld 30Jan89.

TT 23,559 hrs, 28,022 ldgs

1619   (132)   Srs.2/234

F/f 18Oct68 as **CC-CEH**. Del Línea Aérea Nacional de Chile 20Nov68 with fleet number 746. Converted to Srs.2A/234. Sold Austin Airways Ltd May79 as **C-GQTG** arriving Canada 29May79. CofR issued 06Nov79, CofA issued 26Nov79. Lsd

Eastern Provincial Airways (1963) Ltd from 01May84 and operated by Air Maritime until 02Mar85. Fitted with wide body look interior and lsd Air Creebec Inc Aug86. Austin Airways Ltd merged with Air Ontario Inc Apr87 using Air Ontario as the operating name. Sold Air Creebec Inc 01Jan88. Lsd Norcanair early Jun91 to end Aug91 in Austin Airways c/s with 'Norcanair' titles. Regd Air Creebec (1994) Inc 08Mar95. WFU 29Oct01 and reduced to spares. Regn cld 09May02. Fuselage noted stored with Skywagon City Inc at Peter Muehlegg, Ontario, Canada 01Oct05.

TT 35,726 hrs, 47,872 ldgs

1620   (125)   Srs.2/234

F/f 12Dec68 as **CC-CEI**. Del Línea Aérea Nacional de Chile 22Jan69 with fleet number 747. Converted to Srs.2A/234. Lsd Aerovías Nacionales de Colombia S.A. (AVIANCA) in full AVIANCA c/s with dual regn **HK-1698X/CC-CEI** from Sep74 to Sep75. Sold Bouraq Indonesia Airlines P.T. Mar78 and del via Larnaca as **PK-IHE** 18Mar78 arriving Jakarta 24Mar78. In service 29Apr78. W/o 09Jan93 at Surabaya, Indonesia. Starboard engine failure soon after take-off. Crashed into swamp. 4 crew and 13 pax killed, 1 crew and 26 pax survived.

TT 37,143 hrs, 27,922 ldgs

1621   (149)   Srs.2/234

F/f 14May69 as **CC-CEJ**. Del Línea Aérea Nacional de Chile 18Jun69 with fleet number 748. Converted to Srs.2A/234. Sold Austin Airways Ltd May79 as **C-GOUT** arriving Canada Aug79. CofR and CofA issued 17Aug79. Lsd Maersk Air I/S with del via Manchester as C-GOUT 04/07Jun80 and to Copenhagen 07Jun80. Regd as **OY-APT** 12Jun80 and painted in full Maersk Air c/s. In service 16Jun80. Departed Copenhagen 22Jun81 for Manchester where painted as **C-GOUT**. Danish regn cld 26Jun81. Ferried to Canada 27Jun81. Lsd Air Inuit Ltd from 07Apr84 to 10May85. Company merged with Air Ontario Inc Apr87 using Air Ontario as the operating name. Became the first and believed only HS748 to be painted in Air Canada's 'Connector' c/s. Sold Air Creebec Inc 06Dec88. Last flown 09Jan91 and stored Timmins, Ontario, Canada. Regn cld 29Mar94. B/U Aug95.

TT 23,749 hrs, 27,005 ldgs

1622   (120)   Srs.2/234

F/f 08Jul68 as **CC-CEK**. Del Línea Aérea Nacional de Chile 07Aug68 with fleet number 749. Aircraft fitted with a quick change VIP interior for Presidential use when required. Converted to Srs.2A/234. Sold Bouraq Indonesia Airlines P.T. Mar78 and del via Larnaca as **PK-IHF** 18Mar78 arriving Jakarta 24Mar78. In service 17Apr78. Stored Jakarta from Feb91. Returned to service. Left runway on landing Menado, Indonesia 08Jan97. Company ceased ops Jul05.

TT 35,987 hrs, 26,909 ldgs

1623   (122)   Srs.2/238

Regd as **G-AVXI** to The Board of Trade 02Nov67 (CofR R.9584/1). F/f 13Feb69, CofA issued 04Jul69. Del 15Jul69 to the Civil Aviation Flying Unit for airfield calibration duties. Regd to the Secretary of State, Department of Trade and Industry 20Jan71. Regd to the Civil Aviation Authority 04Apr72 (CofR R.9584/2). Converted to Srs.2A/238. Named "Eddie Stockton". Regd to Flight Precision Ltd 28Oct96 (CofR G-AVXI/R3) after airfield calibration duties transferred to them. Last flew 25Aug98 and sold Emerald Airways Ltd Sep98. Noted Exeter 19Sep98. Ferried Southend 22Sep98 in Flight Precision c/s still named "Eddie Stockton". Regd Emerald Airways Ltd 05Oct98 (CofR G-AVXI/R4). Stored Southend, U.K. without use. Regn cld by the CAA 24Oct01. B/U 05-08Nov01.

TT 16,590 hrs, 8,619 ldgs

LAN-Chile operated Series 2A CC-CEI (1620) from January 1969 until it was leased for operation in AVIANCA colours in September 1974.

(J Roach collection)

G-AVXI c/n 1623 of the CAA Flying Unit at Gatwick in 1985.

(Kurt Lang)

1624 (137) Srs.2/238

Regd as **G-AVXJ** to The Board of Trade 02Nov67 (CofR R.9720/1). F/f 04Jun69, CofA issued 27Aug69. Del 04Sep69 to the Civil Aviation Flying Unit for airfield calibration duties. Regd to the Secretary of State, Department of Trade and Industry 20Jan71. Regd to the Civil Aviation Authority 04Apr72 (CofR R.9720/2). Converted to Srs.2A/238. Lsd to Hawker Siddeley Aviation Ltd for display at Farnborough Air Show Sep74. Regd to Flight Precision Ltd 28Oct96 (CofR G-AVXJ/R3) after airfield calibration duties transferred to them. Ferried Exeter 01Aug98 for storage. Sold Emerald Airways Ltd Sep98. Regd Emerald Airways Ltd 05Oct98 (CofR G-AVXI/R4). Remained in store Exeter without use. Components used to repair G-ATMJ c/n 1593

in 2002. Regn cld 17Jan03 as PWFU. B/U 14May04. Fuselage donated to Vobster Quay Ltd and sunk in three sections into a lake near Mells in Somerset, U.K. as an interesting item at an inland diving centre.

TT 17,301 hrs, 9,877 ldgs

1625 (101) Srs.2/235

F/f 12Oct67 as **PP-VDN**. Del Viaçao Aérea Rio Grandense (VARIG) 14Nov67. Converted to Srs.2A/235. W/o landing Pedro Afonso, Brazil 17Jun75. Overran and crashed into house. 1 crew + 3 on ground killed, 3 crew and 11 pax survived.

TT 19,382 hrs, 19,465 ldgs

1626   (105)   Srs.2/235

F/f 12Dec67 as **PP-VDO**. Del Viação Aérea Rio Grandense
(VARIG) 03Jan68. Converted to Srs.2A/235. Sold Bouraq
Indonesia Airlines P.T. 13Dec76. F/f as **PK-IHI** 31Dec76 and del
via Manchester 04/06Jan77. W/o landing Manado, North
Sulawesi, Indonesia 10Dec82. No fatalities among 3 crew and
42 pax.

TT 32,675 hrs, 27,670 ldgs

1627   (109)   Srs.2/235

F/f 09Jan68 as **PP-VDP**. Del Viação Aérea Rio Grandense
(VARIG) 25Jan68. Converted to Srs.2A/235. Sold Bouraq
Indonesia Airlines P.T. 05Dec76 and del via Manchester as
PK-IHG 16/22Dec76. In service 29Dec76. Damaged
Yogyakarta, Java 29Oct86. Repaired. Aft service door detached
soon after take-off from Tarakan/Juwata 24Feb97. Company
ceased operations Jul05.

TT in excess of 47,937 hrs, 38,156 ldgs (figures at 31Oct92)

1628   (110)   Srs.2/235

F/f 26Jan68 as **PP-VDQ**. Del Viação Aérea Rio Grandense
(VARIG) 17Feb68 being demonstrated to Aerovías Nacionales de
Colombia S.A. on the way. W/o landing Uberlandia, Brazil
14Dec69. No fatalities among 5 crew and 4 pax.

TT 3,408 hrs, 3,341 ldgs

1629   (111)   Srs.2/235

F/f 07Mar68 as **PP-VDR**. Del Viação Aérea Rio Grandense
(VARIG) 11Apr68. Converted to Srs.2A/235. Sold Bouraq
Indonesia Airlines P.T. 05Jan77. F/f as **PK-IHH** 05Jan77 leaving
Porto Alegre the same day via Brasilia, Belem, Barbados,
Antigua, Bermuda, Goose Bay, Søndre Strømfjord and Reyjavik
to Manchester 09/13Jan77 before eventually arriving Jakarta
18Jan77. In service 07Feb77. Reportedly transferred Bali Air in
2001. Company ceased operations Mar05. Noted stored Jakarta-
Soekarno, Indonesia 06Oct05 & again 06Nov08 in full purple
Bali Air c/s.

TT in excess of 51,461 hrs, 40,702 ldgs (figures at 31Oct92)

1630   (112)   Srs.2/235

F/f 18Apr68 as **PP-VDS**. Del Viação Aérea Rio Grandense
(VARIG) 16May68. Converted to Srs.2A/235. Sold Bouraq
Indonesia Airlines P.T. 08Jan77. F/f as **PK-IHJ** 07Jan77 and del
via Manchester 12/14Jan77 arriving Jakarta 20Jan77. In service
27Jan77. Withdrawn from service 20Mar87 for major inspection.
Returned to service 23Jan89. Noted operational with all white
fuselage, purple fin and 'Bali Air' titles at Batham Apr01.
Company ceased operations Mar05. Noted stored Surabaya,
Indonesia 11Oct08. Noted late 2010 with fictitious regn
'**EX-DLT**' and B737-900ER titles after use in a training exercise.

TT in excess of 47,618 hrs, 37,882 ldgs (figures at 31Oct92)

1631   (113)   Srs.2/235

F/f 02May68 as **PP-VDT**. Del Viação Aérea Rio Grandense
(VARIG) 26Jun68. Converted to Srs.2A/235. Sold Fred Olsens
Flyselskap A/S and del ex Porto Alegre regd as **LN-FOM**
23Sep75 via Brasília, Belém, Port of Spain, an unknown airport,
West Palm Beach, New Philadelphia, Goose Bay, St Johns and
Keflavik arriving Oslo 29Sep75, a ferry of 41 hrs 13 mins and 10
sectors. In service 13Oct75 from Oslo to Sola being used
exclusively as a calibration aircraft for airfield navigational aids.
Fitted with an APU in rear fuselage aft of pressure bulkhead.
Regn cld 30Aug96 on sale to West Air Sweden AB. Regn
SE-LEY rsvd to Vikingarna AB/West Air Sweden AB 15Aug96.
Regd as SE-LEY to West Air Sweden AB 25Sep96. Ferried from
Oslo to Karlstad 26Sep96. Regd GE Capital Equipment Finance
AB Jul99 for continued operation by West Air Sweden in basic
Fred. Olsen's c/s after removal of APU. Regd Commuter Aircraft
Support Ltd 09Nov99. Flew last revenue service and ferried
Lidköping, Sweden 24Nov00. Used for spares. Regn cld
03Sep01. Hulk to Lidköping Airport fire service and noted
dumped in trees 18May07.

TT 34,016 hrs, 32,205 ldgs

1632   (115)   Srs.2/235

F/f 13Jun68 as **PP-VDU**. Del Viação Aérea Rio Grandense
(VARIG) 18Jul68. Converted to Srs.2A/235. W/o on take-off
Porto Alegre 04 or 09Feb72 on a training detail. No fatalities.

TT 8,705 hrs, 8,218 ldgs

G-AVXJ c/n 1624 in Civil Aviation Authority titles on final approach to Farnborough in the 1970s.

PP-VDR c/n 1629 of VARIG photographed on a test flight prior to delivery from Woodford in 1968. (WHC/BAe)

1633 (116) Srs.2/235

F/F 19Jul68 as **PP-VDV**. Del Viaçao Aérea Rio Grandense (VARIG) 21Aug68. Converted to Srs.2A/235. Sold Bouraq Indonesia Airlines P.T. 05Dec76. F/f as **PK-IHK** 03Dec76 and del via Manchester 09/11Dec76. W/o landing Ujung Pandang, Indonesia 09Feb77. No fatalities among 5 crew and 46 pax on board.

TT 19,212 hrs, 18,771 ldgs

1634 (117) Srs.2/235

F/f 14Aug68 as **PP-VDX**. Del Viaçao Aérea Rio Grandense (VARIG) 15Sep68. Converted to Srs.2A/235. Sold Bouraq Indonesia Airlines P.T. 05Dec76. F/f as **PK-IHM** 05Dec76 and del via Manchester 09-11Dec76 arriving Jakarta 17Dec76. In service 23Dec76. Nominal change of ownership to Singapore General Aviation Services Pte Ltd from 31Dec80 to 11Jun81 as PK-IHM while major maintenance carried out before returning to service with Bouraq Indonesia Airlines P.T. Stored Jakarta, Indonesia from Dec93. PWFU 07Apr94. Still there May00.

TT in excess of 45,829 hrs, 36,101 ldgs (figures at 31Oct92)

1635 (88) Srs.2A/239

Regd as **G-AVRR** to Hawker Siddeley Aviation Ltd 14Jul67 (CofR R.9587/1). F/f 05Sep67, CofA issued 15Sep67. Series 2A development aircraft and used for tropical trials leaving Woodford for Asmara, Eritrea on 22Jan68 returning via Cairo, Malta and Nice on 02Feb68. Left Woodford for Jeddah via Rome and Nicosia 12May68. Used for desert demo before returning via Cairo, Malta and Nice arriving Woodford 16May68. Displayed Farnborough Air Show 15/23Sep68. C/o U.S.A demo tour leaving Woodford 10Oct68. Points visited included La Guadia (for demo to Eastern Airlines and American Airlines), Washington (demo to National Airlines), Atlanta, Huntsville, St Louis, Denver, San Francisco (demo to United Airlines), Cheyenne and Chicago before returning Woodford 24Oct68. C/o African tour early

Nov68 visiting Nairobi, Johannesburg and many points in South Africa, Kinshasa, Accra and Dakar before continuing via Las Palmas and Palma to Athens for demo to Olympic Airways 26Nov68. Finally returned Woodford via Nice 29Nov68. Lsd Sociedade Açoreana de Transportes Aéreos (SATA) Jan69 to 25Feb69. Demonstrated Bucharest 02/06Mar69. Lsd Skyways Coach Air Ltd from 31Mar to 07Apr69. C/o Canadian demonstration tour 11-25Apr69. Lsd Transair Ltd as **CF-YQD** 26Apr69. UK regn cld 27Apr69 as transferred Canada. Returned Manchester 28May69 as CF-YQD with del to Woodford 30May69. Restored as **G-AVRR** to Hawker Siddeley Aviation Ltd 30May69 (CofR R.9587/2). Shown Paris Air Show 31May to 09Jun69. Lsd Olympic Airways from 16Jun69 to 04Oct69 and to Air Afrique from 10Nov69 to 08Dec69 both as G-AVRR. Regn cld 10Dec69 as transferred South Africa after del to Johannesburg 08Dec69. Painted as **ZS-IGI** 15Dec69 and demonstrated to Air Cape (Pty) Ltd, South African Airways, National Airways Corporation and Suidwes-Lugdiens. Restored as **G-AVRR** to Hawker Siddeley Aviation Ltd 24Dec69 (CofR R.9587/3) and departed Johannesburg 05Jan70 for Lusaka for lse to Zambia Airways Corporation Ltd. Returned Woodford 04Feb70 with Zambia Airways titling. Refurbished Coventry 05/16Feb70. Regn cld 22Mar70 as transferred Zambia with lse to Zambia Airways Corporation Ltd again as **9J-ABM** from 12Mar70 to 26Apr70. Restored as **G-AVRR** to Hawker Siddeley Aviation Ltd 30Apr70 (CofR R.9587/4) for ferry to Johannesburg 01May70, the date regn cld as transferred South Africa. Lsd South African Airways as **ZS-HSI** and painted in their full c/s. In service 04May70 when aircraft inaugurated South African Airways first HS748 service, operating SA125 from Johannesburg to Durban via Manzini. Flew last service as SA126 14Sep70 and restored as **G-AVRR** to Hawker Siddeley Aviation Ltd 15Sep70 (CofR R.9587/5). Painted as such the following day. Returned Woodford 19Sep70. Refurbished Bitteswell 21-29Sep70. C/o African demonstration tour 25Nov to 22Dec70. Lsd Merpati Nusantara Airlines P.T. as G-AVRR with del from Luton 11Jan71 until return UK 26Jun71. Regn cld 22Oct71 as transferred Gabon and lsd Société Nationale Transgabon as **TR-LQJ** with del the same day until returned

ZS-IGI c/n 1635 in Hawker Siddeley colours on one of its many demonstration tours in December 1969.

9J-ABM c/n 1635 of Zambia Airways at a typical bush strip at Kasaba Bay, Zambia, on 2nd April 1970, on its second short lease to them. (Kurt Lang)

Woodford 10Oct72. Subsequently sold to the same company with re-del 28Dec72. Company renamed Air Gabon with effect from mid74. Sold Eastern Provincial Airways (1963) Ltd as **C-GEPH** 07Mar76 and del via Prestwick 09Mar76 arriving Gander 11Mar76. CofR and CofA issued 26Mar76 and entered service the same day. W/o Sydney, Nova Scotia, Canada 29Dec81. Taxied into terminal building following hydraulic failure. No fatalities among 3 crew and 15 pax on board. Regn cld 10Nov87.
TT 15,186 hrs, 21,750 ldgs

1636   (89)   Srs.2/209
F/f 12Sep67 as **PI-C1014**. Del Philippine Airlines Inc 30Sep67 arriving Manila 03Oct67. Re-regd **RP-C1014** 01Mar74. Engines uprated to Mk.533-2. W/o on aborted take-off Jolo, Philippines 11Jul82. 1 crew killed of 5 crew and 25 pax on board.
TT 27,822 hrs, 30,644 ldgs

1637   (91)   Srs.2/209
F/f 17Oct67 as **PI-C1015**. Del Philippine Airlines Inc 02Nov67 arriving Manila 05Nov67. Re-regd **RP-C1015** 01Mar74. Engines uprated to Mk.533-2 23Jul69. Sold GPA Jet Prop Ltd 1987 and lsd back by Philippine Airlines Inc. W/o Mount Ugos near Baguio, Philippines 26Jun87. 4 crew and 46 pax killed.
TT 33,273 hrs, 37,342 ldgs

1638   (93)   Srs.2/209
F/f 25Oct67 as **PI-C1016**. Del Philippine Airlines Inc 21Nov67 arriving Manila 24Nov67. Re-regd **RP-C1016** 01Mar74. Sold Singapore General Aviation Services Pte Ltd 28Dec79. Sold Airfast Services Indonesia P.T. May80 and regd **PK-OBQ**. Converted to Srs.2A/209. Stored Jakarta, Halim by Jun02. Sold International Air Parts Pty Ltd Jan07. B/U for spares Apr08.
TT 48,906 hrs, 48,950 ldgs

1639 (103) Srs.2/209

F/f 15Nov67 as **PI-C1017**. Del Philippine Airlines Inc 13Dec67 arriving Manila 16Dec67. Re-regd **RP-C1017** 01Mar74. Engines uprated to Mk.533-2 27Dec77. Sold GPA Jet Prop Ltd 1987 and lsd back by Philippine Airlines Inc. Sold LBC Express Airways Inc 07May89. CofA expired 09Oct97. Noted stored Manila, Philippines without engines, windows or undercarriage 01May99.

TT in excess of 41,871 hrs, 48,191 ldgs (figures at 28Feb93)

1640 (104) Srs.2/209

F/f 21Dec67 as **PI-C1018**. Del Philippine Airlines Inc 16Jan68 arriving Manila 19Jan68. Re-regd **RP-C1018** 01Mar74. Engines uprated to Mk.533-2. Sold Bradley Air Services Ltd 01Oct79 and del via Shannon as **C-GJVN** 18Feb80. CofA issued 26Feb80, CofR issued 17Mar80. In service 22Mar80 in Bradley Air Services Ltd c/s. Converted Srs.2A/209. F/n 406. Regd Bradley Air Services Ltd 24Jun98. Became the first 748 to fly 60,000 hrs Jan05. WFU and ferried Trois-Rivières, Québec, Canada for storage 30Apr07 and still present engineless 09Sep10. Regn cld 28Aug12. Still present in Bradley c/s without titles 11Apr15. Currently the highest time HS748 of all time.

TT 62,521 hrs, 56,413 ldgs

1641 (107) Srs.2/209

F/f 13Feb68 as **PI-C1019**. Del Philippine Airlines Inc 13Mar68 arriving Manila 17Mar68. Re-regd **RP-C1019** 01Mar74. Engines uprated to Mk.533-2 15Mar78. Sold Republic of the Philippines Bureau of Air Transportation as RP-C1019 21Mar79 and used as a calibration aircraft. Re-regd **RP-122** Aug86 but noted still active Manila as RP-C1019 with 'Philippines' titles and a yellow cheat line 07Feb88. Re-regd **RP-211** 1991. Regn **RP-2000** rsvd but not used. Re-regd **RP-2001** Nov93 and noted painted as RP2001 (no dash) overall white with Philippine flag on fin at Manila 24Mar94. CofA expired 30Jul94. WFU and sold International Air Parts Pty Ltd for reduction to spares Jan02. B/u Manila, Philippines Feb02.

TT 22,287 hrs, 23,374 ldgs (lndgs figure at 26Feb93)

1642 (118) Srs.2/209

F/f 24May68 as **PI-C1021**. Del Philippine Airlines Inc 18Jul68 arriving Manila 22Jul68. Re-regd **RP-C1021** 01Mar74. Engines uprated to Mk.533-2 11Aug78. On landing at Alah 23Apr85 aircraft left runway causing collapse of starboard undercarriage. Repaired. Sold GPA Jet Prop Ltd 1987 and lsd back by Philippine Airlines Inc. WFU 27May89 and returned to GPA Jet Prop Ltd. Sold Shabair Sprl of Zaire and ferried to Brussels 14Oct89. Regd **9Q-CS1** and departed via Basel 24Oct89. Sold Trans Service Airlift Jun92. Status unknown.

TT in excess of 36,480 hrs, 42,415 ldgs (figures at 14Oct89)

1643 (119) Srs.2/209

F/f 24Jun68 as **PI-C1022**. Del Philippine Airlines Inc 03Aug68 or 04Aug68. W/o eighty miles north of Manila, Philippines 21Apr70. Explosive devise in rear toilet blew off tail while en route Cuayan to Manila. 4 crew and 32 pax killed.

TT 4,892 hrs, 5,127 ldgs

1644 (123) Srs.2/243

F/f 18Sep68 as **HS-THD**. Regd Thai Airways Co Ltd 15Aug68 and del to same 05Oct68. In service 21Oct68. Made heavy landing Bangkok 07Aug76 (14 & 18Aug76 also quoted). Repaired. WFU 30Aug83. Sold Royal Thai Air Force coded **60204** and del 03Oct83. Operated by 603 Squadron, Don Mueang. Allotted serial L5-4/26 but not carried by aircraft. Re coded **60304** Oct95. Noted still active Phuket, Thailand 27Jun12. Withdrawn from use 30Mar16 at Bangkok - Don Mueang Air Force Base and put into storage.

TT in excess of 26,304 hrs, 23,777 ldgs
(figures as at 28Feb93)

1645 (135) Srs.2/243

F/f 29Oct68 as **HS-THE**. Regd Thai Airways Co Ltd 15Aug68 and del to same 07Nov68. In service 19Nov68. WFU 06Dec83. Sold Royal Thai Air Force coded **60206** and del 07Jan84. Operated by 603 Squadron, Don Mueang. Allotted serial L5-6/26 but not carried by aircraft. Fitted with a large rear freight door in Bangkok from a kit supplied by British Aerospace plc. Re-coded **60306** Oct95. Noted still active Bangkok, Thailand 09Jan10. Damaged by flood water Don Mueang, Bangkok late Oct11. Noted active at Don Mueang, Bangkok with Royal Thai Air Force 100th anniversary emblem on fin 05Jul12 and again 05Nov13. Withdrawn from use 30Mar16 at Bangkok - Don Mueang Air Force Base and put into storage.

TT in excess of 27,842 hrs, 25,555 ldgs
(figures as at 28Feb93)

1646 (138) Srs.2/243

F/f 13Nov68 as **HS-THF**. Regd Thai Airways Co Ltd 15Aug68 and del to same 29Nov68. In service 10Dec68. WFU 03Oct83. Sold Royal Thai Air Force coded **60205** and del 28Oct83. Operated by 603 Squadron, Don Mueang. Allotted serial L5-5/26 but not carried by aircraft. Fitted with a large rear freight door in Bangkok from a kit supplied by British Aerospace plc. Re-coded **60305** Jul94. Noted active Chiang Mai, Thailand 22Jan10 and again at Donn Mueang, Bangkok 27Jun12 and 12Jan13. Withdrawn from use 30Mar16 at Bangkok - Don Mueang Air Force Base and put into storage.

TT in excess of 27,404 hrs, 25,597 ldgs
(figures as at 28Feb93)

60206 c/n 1645 of Royal Thai Air Force immediately after fitting the Large Freight Door at Don Mueang, Thailand. (George Jenks/WHC)

1647   (131)   Srs.2/242

F/f 05Sep68 as **ZK-CWJ**. Demonstrated at Farnborough Air Show Sep68. Del Mount Cook Airlines Ltd 26Sep68. Converted Srs.2A/242. Named "Aorangi". Regd to The Mount Cook Group Ltd 07Feb78. Lsd Polynesian Airlines Ltd as ZK-CWJ from 31May81 to 26Jul81. Flew last service as NZ5091 from Chatham Island to Christchurch 20Jan96 and stored. Sold Clewer Aviation Ltd and after air test 28May97 departed Christchurch via Norfolk Island and Brisbane 29May97 then across Pacific and via Churchill 06Jun97, Søndre Strømfjord, Reykjavik and Belfast International arriving Southend 07Jun97 for storage. Regn cld 30Jul97 and lsd Executive Aerospace (Pty) Ltd. Regd Aerospace Express (Pty) Ltd 30Jul97. R/o as **ZS-OCF** 31Jul97 and f/f as such the same date. Departed via Corfu on del 02Aug97. Stripped out for use as a pure freighter from Mar98. Chartered Airworld (Pty) Ltd Apr98. WFU and painted with white top, grey undersides and natural metal engines and wings. Returned Clewer Aviation Ltd and ferried ex Johannesburg 18Oct02 for Blackpool where it arrived 22Oct02 after transitting Cairo, Malta, Nice and Southend. Regn cld 13Dec02. Regd as **G-ORCP** to Emerald Airways Ltd 02Jan03 (CofR G-ORCP/R1) after sale to them. Stripped out as a pure freighter. Air tested as JEM65E both 18Feb and 19Feb03. CofA issued 19Feb03. Ferried Liverpool as JEM70E 21Feb03 and entered service. Company's AOC suspended 04May06 and aircraft stored Coventry. Sold International Air Parts Pty Ltd 16Oct06. Ferried Blackpool 23Nov06. Regd PTB (Emerald) Pty Ltd 11Dec06 (CofR G-ORCP/R2). Regn cld 04May07 as transferred Bangladesh. Painted as **S2-AEE** 09May07 for lse Best Aviation Ltd and after a short air-test 28May07 departed the same day on del via Marseille. Repossessed by International Air Parts Pty Ltd and lsd Bismillah Airlines Ltd by 24Jun09 when noted Cox's Bazaar as such.

TT 58,893 hrs, 66,208 ldgs (figures at 28May07)

1648 to 1655   Srs.2/240

Ordered by Fuerza Aérea Argentina for operations by Líneas Aéreas del Estado (LADE) with serials **TC-71** to **TC-78** reserved. Order subsequently cld and aircraft not built.

60305 c/n 1646 of the Royal Thai Air Force at Chiang Mai on 22nd January 2000.   *(Stephen Darke)*

N57910 c/n 1656 awaiting painting in Inter City colours at Toronto in March 1986, still in the colour-scheme carried during its service with the Bundesanstalt für Flugsicherung and with the last letter of previous registration D-AFSD on the nosewheel door and fin.   *(Michael L. Baker)*

S2-ABE c/n 1658 of Astral Aviation Ltd at Alek, Sudan, on 19th November 2006 after its earlier accident. *(Steve Ferris/Allan Fantham)*

1656 (146) Srs.2/244

F/f 12Sep69 as **D-AFSD**. Del Bundesanstalt Für Flugsicherung (B.F.S.) 19Dec69 for airfield calibration duties. Regn cld 02Nov84. Sold N.A. Kalt of San Antonio, Texas, U.S.A. to whom regd as **N57910** Dec84 after storage at Lechfeld. Del from Frankfurt to Stansted 07Mar85 and to Keflavik 10Mar85. Noted in storage at San Antonio, Texas 23Oct85. Del Toronto 01Mar86. Regn cld Apr86 and regd to Inter City Airways Inc as **C-GLTC** Jun86. CofA issued 02Jun86. In service 16Jun86 in full Inter City c/s. Company ceased operations 04Oct86 and went into receivership 11Oct86. Repossessed by the Royal Bank of Canada. Lsd Bradley Air Services Ltd from Jul87 to 30Sep87. Lsd Air Ontario Inc from 06Nov87 to 31Dec88 flying in Inter City blue and white c/s on the Kapuskasing to Toronto via Timmins schedules. Lsd Air Inuit Ltd 25Jan89 to 24Apr89. Ferried Toronto for storage 01May89. Sold Springer Aerospace Ltd 07Dec89 when ferried Bar River airport near Sault Ste. Marie. Converted Srs.2A/244 Mar90 with Dart RDa.7 Mk 534-2 engines replacing the RDa.8 Mk 550-2s and test flown as such 05Apr90. Sold V. Kelner Airways Ltd and entered service 09Apr90 with fleet number 801. Company renamed Wasaya Airways Ltd and regd to them 05Jan93. Converted to a specialised Tanker by Springer Aerospace Inc Aug94 with all doors except forward freight door removed. Painted in Wasaya c/s with additional 'Super Tanker' titles. Regd Wasaya Airways Ltd Partnership 22Jun00. Active Pickle Lake, Ontario, 2001.

TT 42,707 hrs, 72,622 ldgs (figures at 28Apr16)

1657 (129) Srs.2A/245

F/f 16Aug68 as **HK-1408**. First production Series 2A. Del Aerovías Nacionales de Colombia S.A. (AVIANCA) 07Sep68 named "Jose Antonio Galan". W/o landing Bucaramanga, Gómez Niño airport, Colombia 05Jul73. Overshot landing hitting houses and stopping short of a precipice. No fatalities among 4 crew and 40 pax on board, 3 children on ground killed.

TT 10,158 hrs, 11,239 ldgs

1658 (134) Srs.2A/245

F/f 04Oct68 as **HK-1409**. Del Aerovías Nacionales de Colombia S.A. (AVIANCA) 25Oct68 named "Garcia Rovira". Sold Dan-Air Services Ltd being regd to them as **G-BFLL** 03Mar78 (CofR G-BFLL/R1). Del ex Bogotá 04Mar78 arriving Manchester 21Mar78. CofA issued 22Apr78 and ferried Aberdeen the same day. Lsd British Airways for the use of the Highlands Division with del Glasgow 17Apr82. Regd to British Airways Board 07Jun82 (CofR G-BFLL/R2). Named "Glen Esk" on starboard and "Gleann Uisgue" on port side Mar83. Regd British Airways plc 01Apr84. Flew last service 23Jan85 and del Manchester as BA9853P 30Jan85 at end of lse. Regd to Dan-Air Services Ltd 08Feb85 (CofR G-BFLL/R3). Lsd British Airways again from 05Sep85 to 03Oct85, from 06Jan86 to 25Jan86, from

01Nov86 to 01Apr87 (last service as BA9835H Glasgow-Dublin & ferried Dublin-Manchester as BA9803P), from 21Oct87 (first service as BA5542 from Glasgow to Belfast) to 29Oct87 (last service as BA5549 from Belfast to Glasgow & ferried to Newcastle the same date) and from 15Oct88 to 11Nov88. Lsd Aberdeen Airways Ltd with del to Aberdeen 04Mar90. Returned Dan-Air Services Ltd from 01May90 to 31May90. Re-entered service with Aberdeen Airways Ltd 03Jun90. Regd Hawk Aviation Ltd 07Sep90 (CofR G-BFLL/R4). Regd to Wisdom Investments Ltd 25Mar91 and continued to be operated by Aberdeen Airways Ltd in basic Dan-Air c/s with 'Aberdeen Airways' titles. Company ceased operations 01Aug92. Sold Euroair Transport Ltd and ferried from Aberdeen to Glasgow 28Sep92. Entered service 29Sep92. Ferried Glasgow 31Dec93 for storage. Ferried Prestwick for further storage Apr94. Ferried Le Bourget via Glasgow 18Aug94. Regn cld 01Jun95 on export France. Regd as **F-GODD** to Wisdom Investments Ltd 03Jul95 for lse to Air Provence International. Damaged on ground Marseille 24Jul00. Repaired. Regd Citicapital Locavia 13Nov01. Wet lsd BAC Express Airlines Ltd from 02Jan03 with del Edinburgh 03Jan03. Ferried Edinburgh to Le Bourget at end lse 15Feb03 and subsequently stored Marseille. Regn cld 16Feb04. Noted Marseille with 'Best Air' titles and regn **S2-ABE** Mar04. Ferried ex Dhaka 07Oct06 for Nairobi where noted 22Oct06 lsd to Astral Aviation Ltd with Astral titles and fin logo. Reportedly struck trees landing at Wunrok in southern Sudan on its first flight, was repaired and then w/o landing on its next flight at Alek in southern Sudan in the first week of Nov06. Nose undercarriage ripped off and port main undercarriage went through wing causing damage to both propellers and lower forward fuselage. Sold International Air Parts Pty Ltd for spares recovery and b/u on site Feb07.

TT in excess of 39,159 hrs, 44,080 ldgs (figures at 31Aug01)

1659 (126) Srs.2/209

F/f 29Jan69 as **PI-C1023**. Del Philippine Airlines Inc 08Mar69 arriving Manila 17Mar69. Re-regd **RP-C1023** 01Mar74. Engines uprated to Mk.533-2 25Oct75. Sold GPA Jet Prop Ltd 1987 and lsd back by Philippine Airlines Inc. Flew last revenue HS748 service for Philippine Airlines as PR454 from General Santos City to Cebu 31May89. Sold LBC Express Airways Inc 01Sep89. Sold Air ADS Inc Oct95 and painted in their c/s. Seen Subic Bay 22Nov96 in full Air ADS c/s with 'Island Hopper' titles. CofA expired 09Oct97. Noted stored Manila, Philippines without engines, windows or undercarriage 01May99.

TT in excess of 36,921 hrs, 41,736 ldgs (figures at 31Oct95)

1660 (128) Srs.2/209

F/f 19Feb69 as **PI-C1024**. Del Philippine Airlines Inc 26Mar69 arriving Manila 30Mar69. Re-regd **RP-C1024** 01Mar74. Engines uprated to Mk.533-2 10Apr78. Sold GPA Jet Prop 1987 and lsd

VQ-FBH c/n 1661 in its original Fiji Airways livery.   *(WHC/HSA)*

ZK-MCJ c/n 1661 of Mount Cook Line.

G-BCDZ c/n 1662 at the Farnborough Air Show in September 1978 as the "Coastguarder" prototype. Note the forward fuselage radome.   (Kurt Lang)

back by Philippine Airlines Inc. WFU 03May89. Sold LBC Express Airways Inc 04May89. W/o circumstances unknown 30Jun91 and noted still stored Manila, Philippines without engines, windows or undercarriage 01May99.

TT in excess of 31,681 hrs, 35,532 ldgs (figures at 04May89)

1661 (140) Srs.2A/233

F/f 27Nov68 as **VQ-FBH**. Del Fiji Airways Ltd 08Dec68. Company name change to Pacific Island Airways Ltd 23Sep70. Regd to Air Pacific Ltd 31Jul71 following company name change. Re-regd **DQ-FBH** 01Oct71. Sold Mount Cook Airlines Ltd 06Oct79 and regd to The Mount Cook Group Ltd as **ZK-MCJ** the same day. Del Christchurch 07Oct79 named "Rotorua". Flew last service as NZ5718 from Mount Cook to Christchurch 31Dec95 and stored. Sold Air North Charter and Training Ltd and ferried ex Christchurch via Norfolk Island to Brisbane 26Jun96 and through Chitose, Japan 30Jun96. Noted Whitehorse 25Jul96 still regd ZK-MCJ. Regd as **C-FYDY** to Air North Charter and Training Ltd 29Aug96. CofA issued 27Sep96. Stored Whitehorse after a freight flight from Minto Mine 23Dec11. Air tested 13May12 and returned to service 14May12 operating a pax flight from Whitehorse to Minto Mine. Stored Whitehorse after last flight on 09Oct12. Re-entered service on 18May13 from Whitehorse to Minto Mine. Into winter storage at Whitehorse by 01Nov13. Air-tested 13Jun14 and returned to service. Flew from Whitehorse to Minto Mine and return 02Jan15 and put into store, used as spares source.

TT 56,885 hrs, 60,665 ldgs

1662 (143) Srs.2A/227

F/f 22Apr69 as **HP-484**. Del Compañia Panameña de Aviación S.A. (COPA) 10May69 via Reykjavik, Søndre Strømfjord, Sept Îles, Washington and Nassau arriving Panamá City, Tocumen 13May69. Lsd Hawker Siddeley for demo to Fuerza Aérea Colombiana from 27-29May69 being flown to Bogotá, Florencia, Loquisimo, Neiva, Puerto Asis, Tres Esquinas, San Vicente and Villavicencio. Departed Panamá City 10May74 via Freeport, Washington and Montréal arriving Manchester 18May74 and Woodford 20May74 following sale to Hawker Siddeley Aviation Ltd to whom regd as **G-BCDZ** 10Jun74 (CofR R.14291/1). F/f with these marks 18Jan75, CofA issued 04Feb75. Departed Woodford 05Feb75 for high altitude trials at La Paz, Bolivia fitted with Rolls-Royce Dart Mk.536-2T engines. The trials were completed 06Mar75. Stored at Cochabamba awaiting frustrated sale. Returned Woodford 27Oct75. Used as a trials/demonstration and crew training aircraft in 1976, being based Hawarden from 13Feb76. Conversion to the Coastguarder prototype commenced 14May76. F/f as such 18Feb77. Demonstrated in Spain 08-11Mar77, at the Paris Air Show 31May to 13Jun77, in Denmark, Norway and Sweden between 16 & 22Jun77, and at Kerkyra, Corfu 02Dec77 en route to Philippines demonstration tour, returning 21Dec77. Regd to British Aerospace plc Aircraft Group 18Jan78 (CofR G-BCDZ/R2). C/o African demonstration tour 14-30Apr78 and Far East tour 07May to 28Jun78. Shown Farnborough Air Show 06-11Sep78. C/o second Far East tour 02-17Mar79 and shown at the Paris Air Show 07-18Jun79 with Show No. '234'. Last flight as a Coastguarder 13Nov79 and converted to a Srs.2A/210. Fitted with Rolls-Royce Dart hush kits and f/f with these installed 04Mar80. Hush-kit trials took place from 14-25Mar80 and again from 07-26May80. Engines reverted to standard fit. Refurbished, painted overall red and reflown 27Aug80. Lsd Deutsche Luftverkehrsgesellschaft mbH (D.L.T.) in full overall red c/s from 15Jan81 to 16Jun81 and again from 24Jun81 to 01Sep81, having previously been del to Dan-Air Engineering Ltd at Manchester 23Dec80 for preparation. Lsd British Airways for use by the Highlands Division from 09May82 to 01Nov82. Noted Woodford in British Airways c/s with Air Sinai titles 14Apr83. Lsd Sociedade Açoreana de Transportes Aéreos (SATA) from 29Jun83 to 08Sep83 and again from 28Jun84 to 07Sep84. Regn cld 21Sep84 as transferred Canada. Lsd Calm Air International Ltd as **C-GSBF** and del via Prestwick

01Oct84 in full colours having previously been test flown as **G-11-3** on 29Sep84. Arrived Canada 02Oct84. CofR and CofA issued 05Oct84. In service 08Oct84. Purchased outright from British Aerospace plc 31Aug85. R/o Kelowna B.C. 13Sep86 in full Pacific Western Spirit/Calm Air c/s for use on new routes from Winnipeg to Thompson, The Pas and Flin Flon. Painted in Canadian Partner colours 1987. WFU Thompson, Manitoba, Canada after last flight 26Sep06 and put in store. Allocated f/n 742 2007 but not used. Later B/U.

TT 46,683 hrs, 45,774 ldgs

1663 (141) Srs.2/209

Originally painted for Philippine Airlines Inc but repainted in Transair c/s for f/f 14May69 as **CF-TAZ**. Lsd Transair Ltd 28May69 to 22Sep69. Repainted in Philippine Airlines c/s as **PI-C1025** and del ex Woodford 07Nov69 arriving Manila 10Nov69. Stored from 21Dec70 to 07Mar71. Overshot at Basco, Philippines 14Jun72 and after temporary repair was ferried Manila 03Aug72. Returned to service 19Oct72. Re-regd **RP-C1025** 01Mar74. WFU 11Jul79. Sold Dan-Air Services Ltd and regd to them as **G-BHCJ** 29Oct79 (CofR G-BHCJ/R1). Del ex Manila 30Oct79 arriving Lasham via Gatwick 10Nov79. Amended to a Srs.2A 07Dec79 after conversion to Srs.2A/209. CofA issued 10Dec79 and entered service 13Dec79. Lsd Sociedade Açoreana de Transportes Aéreos (SATA) from 31May81 to 16Sep81 as G-BHCJ. Regn cld 22Oct84 as transferred Philippines. Lsd Philippine Airlines Inc as **RP-C1030** with del ex Manchester 25Oct84 arriving Manila 28Oct84. Converted back to Srs.2/209 30Oct84 when engines de-modified to Mk.533-2. Repainted in full Philippine Airlines c/s. In service 12Nov84. Nose leg collapsed during landing roll Bacolod 08Nov85. Repaired. Del Lasham for storage at end of lse 16Feb89. Converted back to Srs.2A/209 and restored as **G-BHCJ** to Dan-Air Services Ltd 05Jun89 (CofR G-BHCJ/R2). Sold Springer Aerospace of Canada. Del ex Lasham via Gatwick, Stornoway and Keflavik 15Jun89. Regn cld 19Jun89 as transferred Canada. Fitted with a large rear freight door. Regd to Northland Air Manitoba Ltd as **C-FFFS** 03Oct89. CofA issued 01Nov89. Sold Nunasi-Northland Airlines Ltd 04Nov89, being regd to them 08Nov89. Company ceased operations Mar90 and aircraft returned Northland Air Manitoba Ltd. Lsd to The Northwest Company Inc Apr90 to Mar91. Lsd V. Kelner Airways Ltd from 21Aug91 to 25Nov91. Last flew for Air Manitoba Ltd 20Feb97 and lsd Wasaya Airways Ltd the same day and regd to them 28Apr97. Sold Wasaya Airways Ltd 15Jan99 with f/n 806. Regd Wasaya Airways Limited Partnership 22Jun00. Nose leg collapsed while taxiing at Kenora, Ontario 16Oct13 also causing damage to both propellers. Nose leg and propellers replaced and ferried to Thunder Bay 29Oct13 for structural repairs. Returned to service 19Nov13 and last flew 07Apr16 Red Lake-Pikangikum-Pickle Lake where it was placed into storage at TT 57,993 hrs, 73,996 ldgs.

1664 (148) Srs.2/209

Originally painted for Philippine Airlines Inc but repainted in Transair c/s for f/f 09Jun69 as **CF-TAG**. Lsd Transair Ltd 25Jun69 to 17Sep69. Repainted in Philippine Airlines c/s as **PI-C1026**. F/f as such 22Oct69 and del ex Woodford 29Oct69 arriving Manila 01Nov69. Re-regd **RP-C1026** 01Mar74. Engines uprated to Mk.533-2 06Aug79. Sold GPA Jet Prop Ltd and lsd back by Philippine Airlines Inc. WFU 31May89 and returned to GPA Jet Prop. Sold Shabair Sprl of Zaire 1989 and ferried to Brussels 08Nov89. Painted as **9Q-CSR** with 'SHABAIR' titles and departed for Zaire Dec89. Sold Trans Service Airlift Jun92. Status unknown.

TT in excess of 35,415 hrs, 40,051 ldgs (figures at 08Nov89)

1665 (150) Srs.2A/233

F/f 22Aug69 as **VQ-FBK**. Del Fiji Airways Ltd 06Oct69. Company name change to Pacific Island Airways Ltd 23Sep70. Regd to Air Pacific Ltd 31Jul71 following company name

Air Malawi's Series 2A 7Q-YKB c/n 1667.

change. Re-regd **DQ-FBK** 01Oct71. Sold Bradley Air Services Ltd 26Nov80 and del via Manchester as **C-GYMX** 18Dec80 in full Air Pacific c/s arriving Canada 19Dec80. CofR and CofA issued 30Dec80. In service 13Mar81 inaugurating appropriately the Ottawa to Montréal, Mirabel (YMX) schedule. Operated in First Air c/s with f/n 408. Nose leg collapsed while taxiing at Pangnirtung 30Jul91 after a flight from Iqaluit. Repaired. Regd Bradley Air Services Ltd 24Jun98. WFU Iqaluit and ferried Carp, Ontario, Canada for storage 21Mar03. Sold Royal Canadian Mounted Police Dec03 for anti-terrorist training. Wings and tail removed. Regn cld 20Apr04.

TT 50,964 hrs, 55,821 ldgs

1666   (158)   Srs.2A/256

F/f 13Nov69 as **7Q-YKA**. Del Air Malawi Ltd 06Dec69. Sold Air BVI Ltd and del ex Lilongwe 06Jan88 arriving Manchester 10Jan88 for maintenance by Dan-Air Engineering Ltd. Painted in Air BVI c/s as **VP-LVQ** with f/f as such 27Apr88. Del ex Manchester 29Apr88. B/U Timmins, Ontario, Canada Aug89 after overhaul abandoned by Air Creebec Inc.

TT 27,628 hrs, 26,692 ldgs

1667   (159)   Srs.2A/256

F/f 09Dec69 as **7Q-YKB**. Del Air Malawi Ltd 10Jan70. WFU Nov91. Restored incorrectly as **G-BPNK** to Clewer Aviation Ltd 20Nov92 (CofR G-BPNK/R2) and del Southend as such 27Nov92. Regn cld by the CAA 14Dec92. Regd as **G-BURJ** to Clewer Aviation Ltd 14Dec92 (CofR G-BURJ/R1). Painted as such 04May93 in Necon Air c/s. Regn cld 12May93 as transferred Nepal on lse to Necon Air Ltd and del ex Southend as **9N-ACP** via Brindisi the same date arriving Kathmandu 15May93. Entered service 22May93. Ferried via Muscat 13May02 arriving Johannesburg 17May02 for storage on behalf of Clewer Aviation Ltd. Noted Johannesburg, South Africa painted overall white with no marks or regn and reportedly awaiting ferry to UK Oct05. Restored as **G-BURJ** to Clewer Aviation Ltd 26Nov07 (CofR G-BURJ/R2). Last noted Johannesburg Apr09 and B/U Jun12. Regn cld 24Feb15.

TT 39,045 hrs, 43,555 ldgs

1668   (142)   Srs.2A/257

F/f 17Jun69 as **CF-MAK** having previously been marked as **G-11**. Del Midwest Aviation Ltd 17Jul69. CofR and CofA issued

18Jul69. Airline and aircraft absorbed into Transair Ltd the same year. Sold Gateway Aviation Ltd as CF-MAK 14Apr72. Made wheels-up landing Port McMurray, Alberta 05Dec74. Repaired. Aircraft and company taken over by Northward Airlines Ltd 1979. Sold Calm Air International Ltd as **C-FMAK** 17Dec79. Del Churchill 03Apr80 and entered service the following day. Crash landed after take-off from Churchill 19Mar82. Ferried to Calgary with undercarriage locked down and unpressurised named "Phoenix". Rebuilt at Calgary. R/o 17Jul83 and returned to service. Painted in Canadian Partner c/s 1987. Lsd Air Creebec Inc Oct89 to Mar90. Regd Calm Air International Ltd 29Nov90. Last flew 17Nov02 and stored Thompson, Manitoba, Canada. Fin removed late Oct05 at start of B/U process. Allocated f/n 741 2007 but not used. Regn cld 21Dec07.

TT 50,571 hrs, 49,786 ldgs

1669   (144)   Srs.2A/258

F/f 30Jul69 as **CF-AMO**. Del AMOCO (Canada) Petroleum Ltd 21Aug69. Re-regd **C-FAMO**. Fitted with a 'glass' cockpit. On 12Dec91 passed the 20,000 hour mark of accident/incident free flying with AMOCO. Lsd Chevron Canada Resources Ltd 02Jan to 14Mar97. Sold Aerial Recon Surveys Ltd Jun97 and regd to them 04Jun97. Lsd West Wind Aviation Inc 13/27Aug97. WFU Apr98 and stored Calgary. Sold Calm Air Air International Ltd 27Mar99 and regd to them 04May99. Converted to a pure freighter and fitted with a large rear freight door robbed from c/n 1748 8R-GEV between Apr and Oct99. Fitted with a roller floor system, cabin windows removed and plugged and painted with 'Calm Air Cargo' titles. Carried f/n 746F from 2007. Last flew 08Aug11 and now used as an engine test bed at Thompson, Manitoba, Canada.

TT 46,453 hrs, 43,784 ldgs

1670   (145)   Srs.2/217

F/f 12Sep69 as **9Y-TDH**. Ordered by British West Indian Airways Ltd on behalf of Leeward Islands Air Transport Services Ltd. Re-regd **VP-LAA** and f/f as such 07Oct69. Del 08Oct69. Entered service 14Oct69. Engines uprated to Mk.533-2. Company ceased operations 15Aug74, being reformed as LIAT (1974) Ltd 20Sep74. Re-regd **V2-LAA** Mar82 after Antiguan Independence on 01Nov81. Sold British Aerospace plc in part exchange for Super 748s 28Jun85 and immediately lsd back to LIAT (1974) Ltd. Flew last service 22Mar86. Lsd Philippine Airlines Inc with del ex Antigua 26Mar86 via Manchester 28/30Mar86 arriving

Manila 07Apr86. Regd **RP-C1043** and entered service 07Jun86. Del ex Manila at end of lse 21Jun87 arriving Exeter 28Jun87 for open storage. Sold S. Hully 08Mar88. Regd as **G-BORM** to Sean T. Hully (Sales) Ltd 29Jul88 (CofR G-BORM/R1) but not flown from arrival Exeter. Used by Exeter Airport Fire Service, U.K. as a training aircraft by Nov91. Regn cld by the CAA 18Jun92 but still present in natural metal finish unmarked Jun03. B/U at Exeter 08Dec05.

TT 33,172 hrs, 65,407 ldgs

1671 (161) Srs.2A/253

F/f 16Dec69 as **9N-AAU**. Regd as **G-AXVZ** to Hawker Siddeley Aviation Ltd 12Jan70 (CofR R,11352/1) with f/f in these marks 15Jan70. CofA issued 31Dec69. Del Royal Nepal Airlines Corporation as G-AXVZ 21Jan70. Regn cld 26Jan70 as transferred Nepal and entered service the same day regd as **9N-AAU**. WFU by 31Mar91 and noted present Kathmandu, Nepal Oct06 in a derelict state.

TT 21,491 hrs, 26,410 ldgs

1672 (162) Srs.2A/253

F/f 07Jan70 as **9N-AAV**. Painted as **G-11** 19Jan70 and f/f as such 21Jan70. Del Royal Nepal Air-lines Corporation as **9N-AAV** 03Mar70. Aircraft left runway on landing Kathmandu 29Jul83 and came to rest beyond perimeter fence on a crew training flight. Repaired. WFU 1991/2. Returned to service Mar94. WFU Mar00 & stored Kathmandu, Nepal. Still present 04Feb09. Sold Aero Partners Ltd and reduced to spares 16/17Nov09.

TT 27,547 hrs, 36,545 ldgs

1673 (151) Srs.2A/259

F/f 02Feb70 as **XA-SAB**. Del Servicios Aéreos Especiales S.A, (SAESA) 27Feb70. W/o on take-off Acapulco, México 27Jul73 (28Jul73 also reported) while on a night crew training flight. No fatalities among 3 crew on board.

TT 10,248 hrs, 8,310 ldgs

1674 (152) Srs.2A/259

F/f 11Feb70 as **XA-SAC**. Del Servicios Aéreos Especiales S.A. (SAESA) 16Mar70 via Reykjavik, Søndre Strømfjord, Sept Îles, Washington, New Orleans to México City named "Mulege" or possibly "Mulega". Sold Austin Airways Ltd 11Nov77 and del

Toronto 14Nov77 as XA-SAC. Re-regd **C-GSXS**. CofR and CofA issued 02Jun78. Company merged with Air Ontario Inc Apr87 using Air Ontario as the operating name. Sold Air Creebec Inc 06Dec88. Regd Air Creebec (1994) Inc 08Mar95. Last flown 28Sep94 and stored Timmins, Ontario, Canada. Reduced to spares. Regn cld 18Jun99 as WFU.

TT 38,464 hrs, 45,054 ldgs

1675 (153) Srs.2A/259

F/F 02Mar70 as **XA-SAF**. Del Servicios Aéreos Especiales S.A. (SAESA) 25Mar70 named "Zihuatanejo". Sold Austin Airways Ltd 03Dec76 being del via Miami as **C-GPAA** 11Dec76. W/o Moosonee, Ontario, Canada 15Jul79. Fumes from AVGAS bladder tanks exploded on engine start and aircraft burnt out. No fatalities among 2 crew on board.

TT 24,395 hrs, 23,044 ldgs

1676 (163) Srs.2A/263

F/f 24Mar70 as **9J-ABJ**. Del Zambia Airways Corporation Ltd 17Apr70 and later named "Sumbu". Regn **G-BHRG** reserved 1980 but not used. Sold Air Sénégal as **6V-AET** 25Mar80. Hydraulic failure after take-off Dakar 01Jul88. Returned Dakar and collided with pylons while taxiing. Repaired and returned to service. Stored by Jun96. Partially dismantled Dakar, Sénégal 1998.

TT in excess of 25,794 hrs, 28,211 ldgs (figures at 31Jul94)

1677 (166) Srs.2A/263

F/f 03Jul70 as **9J-ABK** and shown at Hatfield Open Day the following day in full Zambia Airways c/s. Del Zambia Airways Corporation Ltd 20Jul70 and later named "Nkamba Bay". Struck airport building after landing at Ndola 19Sep81 and later repaired. Returned to service 15Dec81. Lsd Lesotho Airways Corporation 15Aug88 to 02Nov88 and sub-lsd Air Botswana (Pty) Ltd for part of the time. Sold Guide Leasing Ltd to whom regd as **G-BPNK** 31Mar89 (CofR G-BPNK/R1). Del Exeter 05Apr89. Sold Kel Air and del Nice 25Jun89. Regn cld 26Jun89. Regd as **F-GHKL** to BNP Bail/Leasair Equipement (Kel Air) 04Jul89. Company ceased operations 14Jun90. Regd to Finet France/Heliglobe Inds 06Aug91. Withdrawn from service Jun95 St Rambert d'Albon, France. Regn cld 27Feb97. Noted in car scrapyard 'Auto Pièces 2001' at Le Creux de la Thine, France 28Aug97.

TT in excess of 30,400 hrs, 33,047 ldgs (figures at 05Apr89)

VP-LAA c/n 1670 of LIAT in a one-off colour-scheme at St Kitts in 1972.

(Kurt Lang)

1678   (147)   Srs.2A/264

F/f 07May70 as **G-11-2**. Regd as **G-AYDH** to Hawker Siddeley Aviation Ltd 13May70 (CofR R.11599/1) with f/f as such 15May70. CofA issued 13May70. Del Rousseau Aviation as G-AYDH 15May70. UK regn cld 03Jun70 as transferred France and regd **F-BSRA**. Airline and aircraft absorbed into Touraine Air Transport 1976 and painted in TAT's red/orange c/s. Noted Jersey 08May76 as such with both TAT & Rousseau Aviation titles. Sold Réunion Air Service 01Aug77 with del from France the same day arriving Réunion 06Aug77. In service 08Aug77. Company renamed Air Réunion 06Mar87. Company renamed Air Austral. Noted Dakar Mar90 with Air Sénégal titles. Regn cld 03Aug92. Sold Aerocontracts Ltd to whom restored as **G-AYDH** 05Aug92 (CofR G-AYDH/R2) for spares use only. Regn cld as destroyed 25Nov92. Reportedly seen Antananarivo, Madagascar 12Oct93 though thought unlikely.   *TT 27,957 hrs, 20,929 ldgs*

1679   (164)   Srs.2A/269

F/f 24Apr70 as **G-11**. Re-regd **G-11-1** and f/f as such 11May70. Regd as **G-AYFL** to Hawker Siddeley Aviation Ltd 22Jun70 (CofR R.11666/1). To Bitteswell for mods 25Jun70 to 14Jul70, not flying as G-AYFL until 14Jul70. CofA issued 14Jul70. Departed Woodford on demonstration tour of Canada 17Jul70 in Hawker Siddeley house colours. CofR and CofA issued as **CF-CSE** 01Oct70. UK regn cld 02Oct70 as transferred Canada. Sold Chevron Standard Oil 02Dec70. Re-regd **C-FCSE** and company renamed Chevron Canada Resources Ltd. Fitted with a Sunstrand APU in the tail cone. Sold West Wind Aviation Inc and del Saskatoon 04Jun93. Regd to West Wind Aviation 30Sep93. In service 01Oct93 between Saskatoon and Cluff Lake. Nosewheel collapsed after landing Saskatoon 05Nov02. Repaired and returned to service 14Jan03. WFU 25Feb06. Sold Air North Charter & Training Ltd and regd to them 27Apr06 after del 11Apr06. Entered service Dec06. Seen in service Vancouver in new c/s with orange fin with Yukon titles 04May07. Remains active.

TT in excess of 36,228 hrs, 27,860 ldgs (figures at 25May16)

1680   (165)   Srs.2A/263

F/f 12Jun70 as **G-11-4**. Repainted as **9J-ABW** and f/f as such 26Jun70. To Bitteswell for mods 01Jul70 to 25Aug70. Del Zambia Airways Corporation Ltd as 9J-ABW 02Sep70 and later named "Mfuwe". Ferried from Nice to Exeter 24Dec88. Sold Guide Leasing Ltd to whom regd as **G-BPNJ** 03Feb89 (CofR G-BPNJ/R1). Noted Exeter in full Kel Air c/s as G-BPNJ

25Mar89. Regn cld 29Mar89 as transferred France, painted as **F-GHKA** and f/f as such 29Mar89. Lsd Kel Air as F-GHKA and del from Exeter to Nice 30Mar89. Sold Kel Air Jun89. Company ceased operations 14Jun90. Regd Finct France/Heliglobe Inds 06Aug91. Lsd Emerald Airways Ltd 03Dec to 22Dec95. Sold Trygon Ltd 31Dec96. Stored Southend without titles with effect from 02Feb97. Sold Executive Aerospace (Pty) Ltd Aug97. Regd to Aerospace Express (Pty) Ltd as **ZS-ODJ** 19Sep97 and r/o Southend as such the same day. Del ex Southend via Corfu 23Sep97 still with Heliglobe Finct France titles. Noted East London in operation all white without titles. Noted Johannesburg in full Executive Aerospace c/s 14May99. Ferried Gan mid Oct00 in Executive Aerospace c/s with 'Ocean Air' titles and small 'Ocean Air, Addu Atoll, Maldives' titles. Entered service 01Nov00 on lease to Ocean Air Pvt Ltd. Contract ended 31Oct01. Aircraft noted Johannesburg 20Nov01 without titles. Sold earlier to Clewer Aviation Ltd in Aug01 and lsd back by Executive Aerospace (Pty) Ltd. Lsd SONAVAM Mar to Jul02. Noted Johannesburg 16Oct02 in Executive Aerospace c/s but without titles. Painted overall white and returned Clewer Aviation. Ferried ex Johannesburg 23Oct03 via Lilongwe, Nairobi, Djibouti, Luxor, Heraklion, Lamezia and Nice arriving Blackpool 27Oct03 at end lse. Regn cld & restored as **G-BPNJ** to Clewer Aviation Ltd 20Jan04 (CofR G-BPNJ/R2). Stored Blackpool, U.K. Sold Emerald Airways Ltd Oct04 for parts recovery. Company's AOC suspended 04May06. Regd PTB (Emerald) Pty Ltd 04Jan07 (CofR G-BPNJ/R3). Wings removed by early Apr09 at start of b/u process. Regn cld as PWFU 15Jun09.

TT 35,787 hrs, 38,352 ldgs

1681   (154)   Srs.2A/264

F/f 21May70 as **G-11-3**. Regd as **G-AYIR** to Hawker Siddeley Aviation Ltd 17Aug70 (CofR R.11775/1). F/f as G-AYIR 03Sep70. CofA issued 27Aug70 and displayed as G-AYIR in Rousseau Aviation c/s at Farnborough Air Show 06-14Sep70. Regn cld 06Oct70 as transferred France. Lsd Sociedade Açoreana de Transportes Aéreos (SATA) as **CS-TAF** in Rousseau c/s 14Oct70 to 22Oct70. Del Rousseau Aviation as **F-BSRU** 27Oct70. Sold Air Services Botswana (Pty) Ltd 23Dec75 being del Johannesburg 29Dec75 as **A2-ABC**. Wet lsd Air Botswana (Pty) Ltd from 31Dec75 to 31Aug81. Sold United Air Services (Pty) Ltd Sep81 and lsd Air Comores as A2-ABC from Sep81 to Apr82. Regd United Air Services (Pty) Ltd as **ZS-LHN** 05Apr82. Lsd Zambia Airways Corporation Ltd Jul83. Regd as **7P-LAI** to Lesotho Airways Ltd 10Sep83 and lse to Zambia continued.

FAE682/HC-AUD c/n 1682 of the Fuerza Aérea Ecuatoriana on a stormy day on 2nd October 1987, at an unknown location.   (George Jenks/BAe)

C-GEPB c/n 1686 of Air Maritime after being withdrawn from use at Toronto, Ontario, in March 1986. (Michael L. Baker)

South African regn cld 12Sep83. Restored as **ZS-LHN** to United Air Services (Pty) Ltd 04Apr84. Regn cld 17Jan86 following sale to Ilford Riverton Airways Ltd. Restored as **G-AYIR** to J. Morrison 17Jan86 (CofR G-AYIR/R2), the same day the aircraft departed Johannesburg for Stansted where it arrived 20Jan86. Regn cld 23Jan86 as transferred Canada and painted as **C-FTTW** with Ilford Riverton titles. Del ex Stansted 24Jan86 via Prestwick, Reykjavik and Frobisher Bay arriving Winnipeg 25Jan86. CofR and CofA issued 06Feb86. Regd to Northland Air Manitoba Ltd as C-FTTW Mar86 after carrier renamed as such with effect from 13Feb86. Last flew 15Nov96. Lsd Wasaya Airways Ltd 24Nov96 entering service 29Nov96 with f/n 805. After aborted take-off, nose gear collapsed Sandy Lake 06Apr98. Ferried Winnipeg via Red Lake for repair 19Apr98 undercarriage down. Positioned Pickle Lake 05Jun98 and returned to service. Sold Wasaya Airways Ltd 15Jan99 with f/n 805 having been regd to them 28Jan97. Titles and logo applied Winnipeg 20Feb99. Regd Wasaya Airways Ltd Partnership 22Jun00. Ferried Pickle Lake to Thunder Bay, Ontario 22Dec02 and put in storage. Returned to service after air test 25Mar05. Caught fire at Sandy Lake, Ontario, Canada while offloading fuel from bladder tanks soon after arrival from Pickle Lake and burned out 12Jun12. No injuries. Regn cld 22Aug13.

TT 38,784 hrs, 49,560 ldgs

1682   (168)   Srs.2A/246

F/f 02Sep70 as **FAE682**. Del Fuerza Aérea Ecuatoriana 03Oct70. By Feb77 carried both FAE682 and **HC-AUD** when used by TAME - Transportes Aéreos Militares/Nacionales Ecuatorianos. Noted at Quito in new colour scheme (white top, dark and light blue cheatline split by gold stripe) 08Jul94. Noted at Quito 11Sep97. Withdrawn from use 2008 and b/u early 2013.

TT 20,463 hrs, in excess of 26,735 ldgs (figures at 31Jan97)

1683   (169)   Srs.2A/246

F/f 18Sep70 as **FAE683**. Del Fuerza Aérea Ecuatoriana 23Oct70. Later carried both FAE683 and **HC-AUE** when used by TAME - Transportes Aéreos Militares/Nacionales Ecuatorianos. W/o between Loja and Guayaquil, Ecuador 20Jan76. 6 crew and 26 pax killed, 8 pax survived.

TT 4,518 hrs, 5,512 ldgs

1684   (155)   Srs.2A/267

F/f 09Oct70 as **FAE684**. Del Fuerza Aérea Ecuatoriana 21Nov70. Convertible VIP version for use as a Presidential aircraft when required. Veered off runway on landing Cuenca 27Apr74 and struck concrete culvert. Repaired. Re-serialled **FAE001** 1976. Carried both FAE001 and **HC-AUK** when used by TAME -

Transportes Aéreos Militares/Nacionales Ecuatorianos. Had reverted to **HC-AUK/FAE684** and with '001' in large numbers on nose by 12Dec92. Noted still flying at Quito 11Feb10. Preserved at the Museo Aeronáutico de la Fuerza Ecuatoriana at the old Mariscal Sucre Airport, Quito, Ecuador, from Feb13.

TT 9,830 hrs, in excess of 7,922 ldgs (figures at 31Oct98)

1685   (157)   Srs.2A/254

F/f 20Nov70 as **9G-ABW**. Del Ghana Airways Corporation 10Dec70. W/o Accra, Ghana 22Jan71 on crew training detail. No fatalities among 3 crew on board. *TT 256 hrs, 351 ldgs*

1686   (156)   Srs.2A/254

F/f 07Dec70 as **9G-ABX**. Del Ghana Airways Corporation 01Jan71. Sold Eastern Provincial Airways (1963) Ltd 30Mar81 and del via Shannon as **C-GEPB** 03May81 arriving Gander 05May81. CofR and CofA issued 03Jun81. Operated by Air Maritime with effect from Jan82 with f/n 303. Company fully integrated into Canadian Pacific Air Lines with effect from 12Jan86. WFU and ferried from Halifax to Toronto 13Mar86 for storage. Lsd Austin Airways Ltd Aug86 to Nov86. Sold Calm Air International Ltd with del 20Jun87. In service 22Jun87. Painted in Canadian Partner c/s 1987 with f/n 304. Hit terminal building Brochet 30Apr91 following hydraulic failure. Repaired and returned to service 24May91. Converted to pure freighter without fitment of Large Freight Door and r/o Winnipeg 05Feb01. Ferried ex Winnipeg the same day. Cabin windows removed and plugged and painted with 'Calm Air Cargo' titles. Carried f/n 743F from 2007. WFU Thompson, Manitoba, Canada after operating its last flight on 30Jun09. By mid Oct09 outer wings and tailplane removed at start of B/U process.

TT 42,928 hrs, 54,410 ldgs

1687   (167)   Srs.2A/270

F/f 17Jul70 as **G-11-5**. Regd as **G-AYIM** to Hawker Siddeley Aviation Ltd 11Aug70 (CofR R.11772/1). F/f as G-AYIM 03Sep70. Regn cld 08Oct70 as transferred Portugal. F/f as **CS-TAG** 20Oct70 and lsd Sociedade Açoreana de Transportes Aéreos (SATA) from 21Oct70, being purchased by them 30Apr72. Sold British Aerospace plc 28May87 and immediately lsd back to SATA until 31Jul87. Stored Ponta Delgada until 11Mar88. Lsd Ligações Aéreas Regionais S.A. with del 20Apr88 entering service the same day. Ferried East Midlands at end of lse 29Jun90. Test flown as **G-11-687** 12Sep90. Later stored unmarked. Restored as **G-AYIM** to Emerald Airways Ltd 21Jun94 (CofR G-AYIM/R2). Ferried to Exeter as JAN116 28Jun94. CofA issued 22Dec94. Painted in Emerald c/s and del

Liverpool 28Dec94. Operated in freighter config. Company's AOC suspended 04May06 and aircraft stored Coventry from that date. Sold International Air Parts Pty Ltd 16Oct06. Ferried Blackpool 24Nov06. Regd PTB (Emerald) Pty Ltd 11Dec06 (CofR G-AYIM/R3). Ferried from Blackpool to Norwich for repaint overall white 27Jun07. Ferried Blackpool-Southend 20Mar08 for operation by Janes Aviation Ltd. Regd Janes Aviation Ltd 03May08 (CofR G-AYIM/R4). R/o in full c/s at Southend 14May08. Ferried to Liverpool as JAN97P 08Jul08 and entered revenue service as JAN600 to the Isle of Man on 27Jul08. Ferried Blackpool for storage 10Oct08. Ferried Southend 02Mar09 as Janes01T for storage. Regn cld as transferred USA 17May11. Regd as **N687AP** to Bank of Utah Trustee, Salt Lake City, Utah, USA 18May11. Still in store painted as G-AYIM 01Jan13. Regn cld as sold in Kenya 29Oct14. Still present at Southend Jul15. Restored as N687AP 24May16. Sold to Planes for Africa Ltd for operations by Avro Express Ltd.

TT in excess of 31,854 hrs, 52,105 ldgs (figures at 04May06)

1688   (160)   Srs.2A/265

F/f 23Dec70 as **AF602**. Del Zambia Air Force as a VIP aircraft 17Feb71. Erroneously reported as crashing Ngwerere, Zambia 17Feb90 with the loss of 28 lives (believed to be another type). Underwent structural survey and heavy maintenance at Rand 2001. Noted Rand again 13Aug02. After maintenance it was returned to service with the Zambia Air Force early Sep02. Noted Rand on maintenance 22Aug03. Seen operational at Lanseria, South Africa in a new colour scheme 01Apr06, 13Jul09 and again on 07Mar11. Noted Rand in yet another new paint scheme 19Nov11. Noted active at Rand 26Apr14 and at the same location 18Sep14. Reportedly back in service by Jan16.

TT in excess of 4,887 hrs, 7,500 ldgs (figures at Sep02)

1689   (186)   Srs.2A/242

F/f 04Jun71 as **ZK-DES**. Del Mount Cook Airlines Ltd 02Jul71. Named "Tongariro". Regd to The Mount Cook Group Ltd 07Feb78. Lsd Sociedade Açoreana de Transportes Aéreos (SATA) as ZK-DES from 26Jun82 to 26Sep82. Propeller struck GPU on start-up at Queenstown 29Mar90. Repaired. Flew last service as NZ5028 from Queenstown to Christchurch 05Feb96 and stored until 15Aug97. Ferried to Tongatapu 15Oct97 for lse to Royal Tongan Airlines Ltd while A3-MCA (c/n 1712) was on maintenance. Lse ended 28Nov97 and ferried Tongatapu-Auckland-Christchurch 29Nov97. Sold Emerald Airways Ltd and arrived Southend via Luxor and Kerkira 08Feb98. Regd to Emerald Airways Ltd as **G-SOEI** 25Feb98 (CofR G-SOEI/R1). Ferried Exeter 13Apr98 still in Mount Cook c/s and air tested the following day. CofA issued 18Apr98. Entered service 21Apr98 in freighter config. Noted Hurn 22Nov05 still in Mount Cook c/s without titles. Ferried from Newcastle to Blackpool as JEM04P 04May06 and the company's AOC suspended the same date. Sold International Air Parts Pty Ltd 16Oct06. Regd PTB (Emerald) Pty Ltd 12Dec06 (CofR G-SOEI/R2). Regn cld 29Jun09 as transferred USA. Noted Blackpool on engine runs painted as **N748D** 30Jun09. Regd to Aerospace Trust Management LLC Trustee 21Jul09 although not officially sold to them until 30Jul09 after sale to IAP Group, Australia the day before. Ferried Southend 17Aug09 for further storage. Sold to Planes for Africa Ltd for operations by Avro Express Ltd. Sold 26May16 as **N743LA** to Zone 4 International LLC of Rex, Georgia, USA. Still present intact at Southend 30Jun16 still marked as N748D.

TT in excess of 54,070 hrs, 61,012 ldgs (figures at 04May06)

1690   (172)   Srs.2A/272

F/f 19Jan71 as **ZS-SBU**. Del South African Airways 17Feb71 arriving Johannesburg 22Feb71 named "Skukuza". In service 25Feb71 operating SA104 from Johannesburg to Gaborone and Francistown. Painted in new c/s 23Mar73. Used for conspicuous propeller experiment at Johannesburg 12Oct82. Retired after operating its last service as SA101 from Gaborone to Johannesburg 30May83. Sold Austin Airways Ltd 13Aug83.

Repainted as **C-GGNZ** in full Austin Airways c/s 04Nov83 reverting to **ZS-SBU** for air testing 09Nov83. Del ex Johannesburg as **C-GGNZ** 11Nov83. CofR issued 15Dec83. CofA issued 19Dec83. In service 12Dec83 on temporary authority. Company merged with Air Ontario Inc Apr87 using Air Ontario as the operating name. Painted in Air Ontario c/s. Sold Air Creebec Inc 06Dec88. Regd Air Creebec (1994) Inc 23Mar95. Sold Bradley Air Services Ltd 07May99 and regd to them 18Jun99. Flown with 'Celebration 99' titles Aug99. WFU and ferried Carp, Ontario, Canada for storage 21Jan05. Still intact early Jul07. Regn cld 09Oct07.   *TT 38,738 Hrs, 49,903 ldgs*

1691   (173)   Srs.2A/272

F/f 12Jan71 as **A2-ZFT**. Lsd by South African Airways from new to Botswana Airways Corporation Ltd in the latter company's c/s with del 29Jan71 arriving Johannesburg 01Feb71 named "Okavango". Lse terminated 13May71. Painted in South African Airways c/s as ZS-SBW named "Umfolozi". In service 19May71. Painted in new c/s 29Jan73. Collided with ground vehicle while taxiing at Johannesburg 19Aug76 severely damaging port engine. Repaired. Damaged by severe hailstorm at Johannesburg 15Jan80. Retired after operating the last South African Airways HS748 service as SA101 from Gaborone to Johannesburg 31May83. Sold Austin Airways Ltd 13Aug83. Painted as **C-GGOB** in full Austin Airways c/s 25Nov83 reverting to **ZS-SBW** for air testing 30Nov83. Del ex Johannesburg as **C-GGOB** 02Dec83. CofR and CofA issued 17Feb84. In service 15Mar84. Sold Sri Lanka Air Force and del as C-GGOB via Shannon 02May85 arriving Katunayake 11May85 for use by No2 Squadron/Helitours. Later regd **CR-830**. Canadian regn cld 16Feb88. Struck deer on take-off at unknown location 06Jun89. Returned with extensive damage to No1 engine nacelle and mounting structure. Repaired and returned to service. Noted in camouflage c/s Apr02. Flew last flight 15Oct98 and stored Ratmalana, Sri Lanka. Noted 31Mar11 carrying new serial **SCM-3101** at the same location in a grey c/s. By Oct12 had been moved to the lawn in front of the Catalina Grill at Koggala Lake and airstrip precinct in southern Sri Lanka east of Galle. Painted with a white top and dark blue undersides separated by red and yellow cheatlines sweeping up the fin. Retains its final Sri Lankan serial and Sri Lanka Air Force titles and has dummy engine cowls and spinners. It is expected to be used for on board dining.

TT 19,322 hrs, 21,800 ldgs

1692   (174)   Srs.2A/272

F/f 29Jan71 as **ZS-SBV**. Del South African Airways 17Feb71 arriving Johannesburg 22Feb71 named "Etosha". In service 01Mar71 as SA125 from Johannesburg to Manzini via Durban. Painted in new c/s 04May73. Heavy landing Maseru 29Dec80 with subsequent nose leg collapse. Repaired and del Johannesburg 19Feb81. Back in service 23Feb81. Retired after operating last service as SA101 from Gaborone to Johannesburg 29May83. Sold Austin Airways Ltd 13Aug83. Painted as **C-GGOO** in full Austin Airways c/s 09Nov83 reverting to **ZS-SBV** for air testing 15Nov83. Del ex Johannesburg as **C-GGOO** 17Nov83. CofR and CofA issued 16Dec83. In service the same day. Company merged with Air Ontario Inc Apr87 using Air Ontario as the operating name. Sold Air Creebec Inc 06Dec88 never having been painted in Air Ontario c/s. Destroyed by fire on Anticosti Island, Québec, Canada 27Nov91 as the result of an accident due to contaminated watermeth and the failure of No2 engine on aborted take-off from Rivière au Saumon. No fatalities among 3 crew and 32 pax on board. Regn cld 10Sep92.

TT 22,943 hrs, 28,007 ldgs

1693   (170)   Srs.2/243

F/f 11Nov70 as **HS-THG**. Regd Thai Airways Co Ltd 30Nov70 and del to same 09Dec70. In service 19Dec70. W/o on take-off Chiang Rai, Thailand 21Jun80. No fatalities among 3 crew and 18 pax on board.

TT 19,264 hrs, 14,642 ldgs

ZS-SBV c/n 1692 of South African Airways, seen on a test flight pre-delivery from Woodford. *(WHC/BAe)*

1694 (171) Srs.2A/273

F/f 04Nov70 as **AMB-110** direct to Hawarden for mods. Amended to **AMDB-110** for second flight back to Woodford 17Dec70. Del Brunei Government 20Jan71 and used by the Air Wing of the Royal Brunei Malay Regiment (Askar Melayu Diraja Brunei) mainly as a VIP aircraft. Sold Royal Brunei Airlines as **VR-UEH** 26Aug81. Converted to civilian status by Singapore General Aviation Services Pte Ltd. Stored from 11Aug82 to 25Apr84. Re-regd **VS-UEH** when CofA renewed 10Nov83. Re-regd **V8-UEH** 20Feb84. Sold Mount Cook Airlines Ltd being regd to The Mount Cook Group Ltd as **ZK-MCP** 26Apr84. Del Christchurch 01May84 and named "Tutoko". Lsd Air Pacific Ltd with del from Christchurch to Suva in full Mount Cook c/s with small Air Pacific titles on rear fuselage 04Dec85 returning 29Jan86. Flew last flight as NZ5036 from Queenstown to Christchurch 12Feb96 and stored. Sold Air North Charter and Training Ltd and ferried ex Christchurch via Norfolk Island to Brisbane 06Jun96 and through Chitose, Japan 12Jun96. Noted Whitehorse still regd ZK-MCP 25Jul96. Regn cld 29Aug96. Regd as **C-FYDU** to Air North Charter and Training Ltd 29Aug96. CofA issued 03Sep96. Flew Whitehorse, Dawson City, Old Crow, Inuvik, Dawson City, Whitehorse rotation on 21Jan15, put into long term storage and used for ground training. Being restored to airworthy condition Apr16 but work terminated and PWFU by Sep16.

TT 45,665 hrs, 43,080 ldgs

1695 (176) Srs.2A/274

F/f 05Apr71 as **PK-MHD**. Flown as **G-11-10** 25May71. Regd as **G-AZAE** to Hawker Siddeley Aviation Ltd 14Jun71 (CofR R11965/1). CofA issued 16Jun71. Lsd Merpati Nusantara Airlines P.T. 16Jun71 as G-AZAE until sold to them as **PK-MHM** 13Dec71 named "Mandau". UK regn cld 13Dec71 as transferred Indonesia. Later named "Mentawai". Nosewheel collapsed 15Feb86. Repaired. Advertised for sale located at Surabaya by 08Nov92. B/U Surabaya, Indonesia 1999.

Last reported TT 38,268 hrs, 28,044 ldgs in 1999

1696 (180) Srs.2A/274

F/f 24Jun71 as **PK-MHR**. Del Merpati Nusantara Airlines P.T. 15Dec71 named "Rentjong". Later named "Simeuleu". Advertised for sale located at Surabaya by 08Nov92. B/U Surabaya, Indonesia 1999. *Last reported TT 36,123 hrs, 28,818 ldgs in 1999*

1697 (179) Srs.2A/275

F/f 07May71 as **G-11-9**. Regd as **G-AYYG** to Hawker Siddeley Aviation Ltd 10May71 (CofR R.12188/1). F/f as G-AYYG 26May71. CofA issued 24May71. Company demonstrator being displayed at the Paris Air Show 27May to 07Jun71 before South American demonstration tour later the same month. Countries visited included Aruba, El Salvador, Honduras and Nicaragua before it flew to New Orleans. From here Cleveland-Lakefront, Detroit, Hopkins and White Plains were visited before the aircraft continued to Montréal, and Ottawa (with demo to the Royal Canadian Mounted Police), Timmins, Moosonee and Gaspé. Ferried Woodford via Goose Bay and Reykjavik arriving 05Aug71. Used as a support aircraft for the HS125-600 tropical trials at Madrid 08-10Sep71. C/o sales tours to Africa 08Nov to 03Dec71 and to Switzerland and Germany 10-19Jan72. C/o another U.S.A tour leaving Woodford on 03Jun72, this time visiting Buffalo, Wilmington, Baltimore, Reading, Memphis, Killeen, Dallas, Houston, Philadelphia, Atlanta, Hilton Head, Carbondale, Springfield, Chicago-Meigs Field and St Louis among others. Used as a support aircraft for Harrier demonstrations in the Middle East and India 11-25Aug72. Commenced a Canada/USA tour 01Sep72 which continued into October. Demonstrated to Widerøes Flyveselskap 24Nov72. C/o another African demonstration tour 15Feb to 13Mar73. Used in a grass landing trial at Coventry 17Oct73. Regd to Dakota and South Bend Securities Co Ltd 21Nov73 (CofR R.12188/2) but not del and stored Woodford. Flew at the Woodford Air Show 26Jun76. Regd to Hawker Siddeley Aviation Ltd 21Sep76 (CofR G-AYYG/R3). Regn cld 07Oct76 as transferred New Zealand. Sold Mount Cook Airlines Ltd as **ZK-MCF** and del 28Sep76 arriving Christchurch 07Oct76. Named "Te Wai Pounamu". Regd to The Mount Cook Group Ltd 07Feb78. Lsd Dan-Air Services Ltd with del ex New Zealand 10Jun78 arriving Manchester from Milan-Malpensa 18Jun78. Regn cld 19Jun78 and restored as **G-AYYG** to Dan-Air Services Ltd 20Jun78 (CofR G-AYYG/R4). Ferried to Aberdeen 22Jun78 and entered service. Ferried to Manchester from Aberdeen for removal of Dan-Air titles 08Oct78. Regn cld 10Oct78 as transferred New Zealand and restored as **ZK-MCF** to The Mount Cook Group Ltd the same date. Del ex Manchester via Belgrade 13Oct78 arriving Christchurch 21Oct78. Returned to service 23Oct78. Lsd Dan-Air Services Ltd and del ex Christchurch 21Apr79 arriving Manchester from Marseille 29Apr79. Regn cld 01May79 and restored as **G-AYYG** to Dan-Air Services Ltd the same day

(CofR G-AYYG/R5). Flown to Aberdeen 03May and entered service. Ferried from Aberdeen to Manchester as DA99YG 20Sep79 the same day as regn cld as transferred New Zealand and restored as **ZK-MCF** to The Mount Cook Group Ltd 22Sep79. Del ex Manchester via Marseille 24Sep79 arriving Christchurch 02Oct79 at end of lse. Lsd Dan-Air Services Ltd as **G-AYYG** being restored to them 27Mar80 (CofR G-AYYG/R6) with New Zealand regn cld 31Mar80. Del ex Christchurch 01Apr80 arriving Manchester from Nice 09Apr80. Ferried to Teesside 12Apr80 and entered service. Flown to Manchester from Cardiff as DA058 22Oct81. Del ex Manchester via Nice as DA89YG 27Oct81 at end of lse as G-AYYG arriving Christchurch 04Nov81. Regn cld 05Nov81 as transferred New Zealand and restored as **ZK-MCF** to The Mount Cook Group Ltd 07Nov81. Lsd Calm Air International Ltd and del ex Christchurch 23Jun82 via Apia, Honolulu and Los Angeles to Winnipeg, the longest sector from Apia to Honolulu taking 11 hrs 40 minutes for the 2,643 statute miles flown. Regn cld 27Jun82. Regd as **C-GRCU**. CofR and CofA issued 26Jun82. Del to Churchill 29Jun82 and entered service the same day. Departed Canada at end of lse 04Sep84 arriving Christchurch 13Sep84. Regn cld 18Sep84. Restored as **ZK-MCF** to The Mount Cook Group Ltd 21Sep84. Flew Mount Cook's last commercial flight by a 748 as NZ5043 from Wellington to Christchurch 12Feb96 and stored. Sold Clewer Aviation Ltd and ferried ex Christchurch 28May96 via Norfolk Island and Brisbane and onwards via Mount Isa and Darwin the following day. Arrived Southend for storage in full Mount Cook c/s without titles 06Jun96. Restored as **G-AYYG** to Clewer Aviation Ltd 09Aug96 (CofR G-AYYG/R7), the same date New Zealand regn cld. Ferried Exeter 14Aug96. Regd Emerald Airways Ltd 08Nov96 (CofR G-AYYG/R8) on sale to them. Conv to freighter config. Test flown 09Nov96. CofA issued 11Nov96 and ferried Liverpool the same day entering service in basic Mount Cook c/s. Ferried Liverpool-Woodford 25Oct97 where painted in Securicor Omega Express c/s. Regd as **G-OSOE** to Emerald Airways Ltd 17Nov97 (CofR G-OSOE/R1) and r/o Woodford as such 18Nov97. Returned Liverpool as G-OSOE 20Nov97 and returned to service 21Nov97 between Liverpool and Belfast. Company's AOC suspended 04May06 and aircraft stored Blackpool with effect from 05May06 after ferry from Hurn. Sold International Air Parts Pty Ltd 16Oct06. Regd PTB (Emerald) Pty Ltd 12Dec06 (CofR G-OSOE/R2). R/o overall white for engine runs 05Oct07. Operated by Janes Aviation Ltd & noted Liverpool 20Jul08 all white without titles in service. Returned Blackpool for storage 14Oct08. Ferried Stansted as JAN02P 10Nov08 to operate Royal Mail Skynet flights mainly to Belfast. Ferried Blackpool-Southend as Janes01T 24Feb09 for storage. Regn cld as transferred to Kenya 16Oct14. Sold to Planes for Africa Ltd for operations by Avro Express Ltd 2014. Registered as **N743MZ** to Zone 4 International LLC of Rex, Georgia, USA on 24May16. Still present at Southend 15Jun16.

TT in excess of 44,593 hrs, 49,062 ldgs (figures at 24May16)

1698   (190)   Srs.2A/271 LFD

First aircraft fitted with large freight door and used as a development aircraft. Regd as **G-AZJH** to Hawker Siddeley Aviation Ltd 01Dec71 (CofR R.12385/1). F/f 31Dec71, CofA issued 25Aug72. Company demonstrator and displayed at Farnborough Air Show 03-10Sep72 with 'Hawker Siddeley 748' titles. C/o a BIG DOOR demonstration tour 20Sep to 12Oct72 followed by a South American tour 21Feb to 01Apr73. Shown at the Paris Air Show 23May to 04Jun73 as the 'Hawker Siddeley Aviation HS748 Military Transport'. C/o sales tours to the Middle East 16-25Aug73, to South America 28Aug to 21Oct73 and to Africa 26Oct to 06Nov73. Acted as a support aircraft for Harrier demonstrations in Algeria 20-24Jan74. Toured Alaska 12Mar to 02Apr74 before trials at Boscombe Down 06-08May74. Regn cld 20Jan75 as transferred Nepal. Del Royal Flight Nepal as **9N-RAC** 23Jan75. Transferred to Royal Nepal Army Air Wing as **RAN-20** 13Apr80. Renamed Nepal Army Air Wing 17Apr06. Still active 27Feb08. Noted Kathmandu reserialled **NA-020** 26Nov10. Noted stored Kathmandu 18Oct13 with port engine missing.

TT in excess of 8,893 hrs, 11,181 ldgs (figures at 17May05)

1699   (175)   Srs.2A/276

F/f 04Mar71 as **G-11-6**. Del Air Gaspé Inc as **CF-AGI** 01Apr71 via Reykjavik and Frobisher Bay arriving Montréal 02Apr71. Sold Les Ailes du Nord Lteé/Northern Wings Ltd as **C-FAGI** 01May75. Company renamed Regionair (1981) Inc with effect from mid 1981. Lsd Calm Air International Ltd from 03Apr82 to 29Jun82. Airline and aircraft absorbed into Québecair Inc early 1984. Company taken over by Nordair Metro 31Jul86. WFU and stored Montréal-Dorval. Sold Northland Air Manitoba Ltd and del Winnipeg 29Apr88. Regd Air Manitoba Ltd 05May88. Painted in new owner's c/s by 06May88. CofA reissued 11May88. W/d 03Feb97. Sold Air North Charter & Training Ltd and regd to them 04Sep98. Remains active.

TT in excess of 45,596 hrs, 57,779 ldgs (figures at 25May16)

1700   (177)   Srs.2A/216

F/f 17Mar71 as **G-11-7**. Regd as **G-AYVR** to Hawker Siddeley Aviation Ltd 08Apr71 (CofR R.12169/1). CofA issued 21Apr71, the same date f/f as G-AYVR. C/o demonstration tour to Mexico 23Apr71 and to U.S.A. from 22May71 visiting New Orleans, El Paso, Van Nuys, Fresno, Orange County (for demo to Golden West Airlines) before ferrying via Great Falls, Churchill, Frobisher Bay, Reykjavik to Woodford 29May71. Regn cld 16Oct72 as transferred Indonesia as sold as **PK-IHD**, first flying as such 02Nov72. Not del and restored as **G-AYVR** to Hawker Siddeley Aviation Ltd 27Dec72 (CofR R.12169/2) having previously also flown as **G11-5** on 10Nov72. Del Bouraq Indonesia Airlines P.T. as G-AYVR 03Jan73. Regn cld 09Jan73 as transferred Indonesia and aircraft regd **PK-IHD**. W/o landing on closed runway Palu Airport, Central Sulawesi 23Jan76. No fatalities among 5 crew and 27 pax on board.

TT 6,426 hrs, 4,238 ldgs

1701   (178)   Srs.2A/266

F/f 15Apr71 as **G-11-8**. Regd as **G-AYYH** to Hawker Siddeley Aviation Ltd 10May71 (CofR R.12189/1). CofA issued 28May71. Regn cld 22Nov71 as transferred Western Samoa. Del Polynesian Airlines Ltd as **5W-FAN** 11Jan72 named "Losi" arriving Apia 25Jan72. Withdrawn after last flight 31Mar81. Sold Dan-Air Services Ltd being regd to them as **G-BIUV** 11May81 (CofR G-BIUV/R1). Painted as G-BIUV 16May81 and air tested the same day. Del ex Apia 17May81 arriving Manchester 30May81. CofA issued 17Jun81 and entered service the same day in basic Polynesian c/s with Dan-Air titles and fin logo. Withdrawn 01Oct81 for fitment of British Aerospace plc supplied large freight door kit. F/f 07Mar82 from Manchester after fitment of cargo door. Painted with 'Liberal Democrats' and 'My Vote' titles for an election charter from 18Mar92 to 08Apr92 visiting numerous points in the UK based on Heathrow. Points visited included Birmingham, Bristol, Cardiff, Chivenor, Culdrose, East Midlands, Edinburgh, Gatwick, Gloucester, Inverness, Leeds/Bradford, Liverpool, Manchester, Newcastle, Plymouth, RAF Valley and Yeovilton. Sold Janes Aviation Ltd 15Jul92 but continued flying on lse to Dan-Air Services Ltd until ferried Aberdeen-Exeter 15Aug92. Regd Janes Aviation 748 Ltd 21Aug92 (CofR G-BIUV/R2). Entered service from Glasgow to Coventry 18Sep92. Company renamed Emerald Airways Ltd 15Sep93. Named "City of Liverpool" 1997 and operated in Emerald Airlines c/s. WFU Blackpool, U.K. 09Oct05. Company's AOC suspended 04May06. Sold International Air Parts Pty Ltd 16Oct06. Regd PTB (Emerald) Pty Ltd 12Dec06 (CofR G-BIUV/R3). Lsd Elysian Airlines SA of Guinea with del Blackpool to Madrid-Torrejón 12Mar09 as G-BIUV, to Lanzarote-Arrecife 13Mar09 and onwards to Dakar 14Mar09. Regn cld 22Apr09 as transferred Guinea. Regd as **3X-GEW** to Elysian Airlines SA 11May09. Aircraft never put into service and returned International Air Parts Pty Ltd. Ferried from Conakry to Nairobi-Wilson via Accra and Bangui 26Jul09 for storage/sale. Regn cld 06Oct09. Regd as **5Y-BXT** to PTB (Emerald) Pty Ltd 18May10. Kenyan CofA issued 16Sep10. Lsd to Avro Express Ltd flying under the Planes for Africa AOC and entered service 15Nov10. Noted active at Wilson 08Apr13, all white, and in Aug13 with 'Cargo2Fly.com' titles named 'Aswin Andy Senji'. Noted still active without titles 11Nov15.

TT in excess of 37,117 hrs, 37,403 ldgs (figures at 15Nov10)

1702   (181)   Srs.2A/260

F/f 08Jul71 as **G-11-1**. Del Fuerza Aérea Colombiana as **FAC-1101** 02Mar72 for operation by Servicio de Aeronavegación a Territorios Nacionales (SATENA). On unknown date in 1974 ran off runway at San Vicente del Caguán with minor damage. Repaired. Ran off runway into ditch Arauca 09Aug76. Repaired. Damaged landing Palmaseca Airport, Cali 19Apr77 after nose leg failed to extend. Repaired. In Jun79 an emergency exit opened in flight sucking out a pax bound for Arauca. W/o Bogotá, Colombia 22Aug79. Stolen by retired mechanic, taken-off and crashed into nearby houses. Thief and 3 people on ground killed.
TT in excess of 7,885 hrs, 8,287 ldgs (figures at 28Sep78)

1703   (182)   Srs.2A/260

F/f 25Aug71 as **G-11-2**. Del Fuerza Aérea Colombiana as **FAC-1102** 03Mar72 for operation by Servicio de Aeronavegación a Territorios Nacionales (SATENA). Undercarriage collapsed on landing Bogotá, Colombia 25Feb85. Repaired. Nose leg collapsed on landing roll at Arauca 01Sep87 after flight from Bogotá. Repaired. Named "Bahia Solano". Later named "Casanare". Sold West Air Sweden AB with regn **SE-LIC(1)** rsvd 06Aug97. Ferried Narssarssuaq-Keflavik 01Sep97. Never adopted Swedish marks and stored Lidköping, Sweden for spares use only. 'Pot Rocket 11' titles painted on lower forward fuselage. Finally b/u Oct00. SE-LIC re-used on c/n 1778 (qv).
TT in excess of 32,200 hrs, 37,450 ldgs (Pre-ferry figures)

1704   (183)   Srs.2A/260

F/f 14Sep71 as **G-11-3**. Del Fuerza Aérea Colombiana as **FAC-1103** 16Mar72 for operation by Servicio de Aeronavegación a Territorios Nacionales (SATENA). W/o on Rosablanca Mountain near Florencia when flying from Capitolio Airport, Florencia to Bogotá, Colombia 09Jan74. 3 crew and 26 pax killed.
TT 1,782 hrs, 1,862 ldgs

1705   (184)   Srs.2A/260

F/f 08Oct71 as **G-11-4**. Del Fuerza Aérea Colombiana as **FAC-1104** 20Mar72 for operation by Servicio de Aeronavegación a Territorios Nacionales (SATENA). W/o landing Pasto, Colombia 07Aug83. No fatalities among 5 crew and 16 pax on board.
TT 18,846 hrs, 20,531 ldgs

1706   (185)   Srs.2A/263

F/f 20Oct71 as **G-11-5**. Lsd by Zambia Airways Corporation Ltd from new to Botswana Airways Corporation Ltd as **A2-ZGF** named "Okavango" with del 09Feb72. Returned Zambia Airways Corporation Ltd Jun72 when regd **9J-ADM** and named "Nkudu". Severely damaged Kasaba Bay, Zambia 04Jul83 after an aborted take-off. No fatalities among 4 crew and 42 pax on board. Offered for sale in 'as is where is' condition but later broken up for spares.
TT 19,849 hrs, 21,177 ldgs

1707   (187)   Srs.2/243

F/f 09Nov71 as **G-11-6**. Regd Thai Airways Co Ltd 14Jan72 as **HS-THH** and del 21Jan72. In service 29Jan72. Lsd Bangkok Airways 13Oct86 to Jul87 and flown with their titles added for scheduled services between Bangkok and Nakhon Ratchasima from Friday to Sunday, while operated by Thai Airways Co Ltd for the rest of the week. Undercarriage collapsed on landing Udon Thani 07Dec87. Dismantled and fuselage noted stored in hotel car park in Nong Khai 28Nov94. Fuselage moved to Jomtien, south of Pattaya, Thailand during 2002. Painted with Lion Air titles and regn ZS-AGB as a '748-2B'. Later painted mainly grey with fake "US. Air Force" titles markings as '208' and noted still present at Jomtien 31Dec09. By 19Dec10 painted in an overall brown/green camouflage c/s without titles. Moved to Cha Am, 45km N of Hva Hin, late 2011. Noted 06Jan16 repainted in lurid c/s with 'The Paradise Resort' titles and its interior converted to a double bedroom amidst a flower garden. See c/n 1807 for the real ZS-AGB.
TT in excess of 21,811 hrs, 18,727 ldgs (figures at 25Sep87)

1708   (189)   Srs.2/243

F/f 23Dec71 as **HS-THI**. Regd Thai Airways Co Ltd 14Jan72 and del to same 07Feb72. In service 16Feb72. Wheels-up landing Chiang Rai 28Apr87 and subsequently w/o. No fatalities among 4 crew and 39 pax on board. By 2005 had been moved to the entrance of the Siam Country Club at Pattaya, Thailand. It is displayed on a dummy undercarriage with odd two bladed propellers and showing evidence of underbelly damage. Painted white with red/pink cheatlines and no titles. Noted still present at same location 04Jan16, repainted with multi-colour bird image.
TT 21,709 hrs, 17,022 ldgs

1709   (201)   Srs.2/268

F/f 11Jan73 as **N15-709**. Del Royal Australian Navy 29May73 arriving Nowra, New South Wales 07Jun73. Later coded '800'. Fitted with specialised electronic equipment between 1978 and 1980 and subsequently used for electronic countermeasures training. Initially operated by 851 Squadron and transferred 723 Squadron 31Aug84. Decommissioned 23Jun00 and ferried East Sale for storage/sale 26Jun00. Transitted Darwin 08May01 regd as **3C-QQP** arriving Norwich 10May01 with small 'TAG' titles following sale to TAG Aviation. Departed Norwich 01Jul01 via Rome/Ciampino, Cairo, Jeddah, Djibouti, Mombasa, Mahé, Male, Colombo, Medan, Denpasar, Darwin and Mount Isa arriving Bankstown 11Jul01 following sale to International Air Parts Pty Ltd. Was due for fitment of large rear freight door from c/n 1751, JW-9008 of the Tanzanian Peoples Defence Force on behalf of Horizon Airlines Pty Ltd but airline placed in Administration 14Oct03 and later ceased operations. Stored Bankstown as 3C-QQP. Loaned to the Australian Aviation Museum at Bankstown 19May04 where it replaced c/n 1604 (A10-604, VH-IMG). Fitted with RDa.6 engines and propellers and renovated externally for display purposes.
TT 11,239 hrs, 10,690 ldgs

1710   (202)   Srs.2/268

F/f 16Mar73 as **N15-710**. Del Royal Australian Navy 03Aug73 arriving Nowra, New South Wales 17Aug73. Later coded '801'. Fitted with specialised electronic equipment in 1980/1 and subsequently used for electronic countermeasures training. Initially operated by 851 Squadron and transferred 723 Squadron 31Aug84. Decommissioned 23Jun00 and ferried East Sale for storage/sale 26Jun00. Sold TAG Aviation and reduced to spares at East Sale, Victoria, Australia late Mar01.
TT 12,788 hrs, 12,388 ldgs

1711   (209)   Srs.2/244

F/f 16Jul73 as **D-AFSE**. Del Bundesanstalt Für Flugsicherung (B.F.S.) 02Nov73 for airfield calibration duties. Sold Air Facilities GmbH 05Jul84 at auction and regd to P.K. Finance Int as **TF-GMB** 20Aug84. Ferried ex Brussels after storage 04Nov85 via Shannon to Toronto. Regn cld 06Dec85. Regd as **C-GEGJ** to Inter City Airways Inc 07Mar86 after CofA issued 31Jan86 on sale to Inter City. Painted in full c/s by 21Mar86. In service 07Apr86. Company ceased operations 04Oct86 and went into receivership 11Oct86. CofR cld 26Jun87. Repossessed by the Royal Bank of Canada. Sold Greyvest Leasing Inc and lsd Air Inuit Ltd. Converted to Srs.2A/244 by Springer Aerospace Ltd 1990. Regd Air Inuit (1985) Ltd 14Aug92. Belly landed Donaldson Lake, Québec 16Dec99. Repaired & returned to service. Advertised for sale summer 2009 but still operational mid Jan11. Flew final service 27Apr12 and ferried to Winnipeg, Manitoba, for scrapping.
TT 37,246 hrs, 37,929 ldgs

1712   (188)   Srs.2A/242

F/f 19Jan72 as **G11-7**. Stored Woodford. F/f as **ZK-MCA** 20Aug73. Regd as ZK-MCA to Mount Cook Airlines Ltd 10Sep73. Del 14Sep73 arriving Auckland 24Sep73. Named

G-BBGY c/n 1713 and G-11-7 c/n 1735 on the flight line at Woodford on 3rd April 1974. The former would later become '1713' with the Republic of Korea Air Force, and the latter would become PK-KHL with Bouraq after delivery as G-BCDM. (WHC/BAe)

"Rangitoto". Regd to The Mount Cook Group Ltd 07Feb78. Lsd Sociedade Açoreana de Transportes Aéreos (SATA) as ZK-MCA from 02Apr80 to 09Oct80. Lsd International Red Cross for use in Kampuchea and Thailand as ZK-MCA from 29Jun81 to 31Aug82. Lsd Airline of the Marshall Islands as ZK-MCA from 21Aug89 to 09Sep89. Inaugurated service to Chatham Island 01Nov90. Flew last service as NZ2691 from Chatham Island to Christchurch 04Nov95. Painted in full Royal Tongan c/s. Lsd Royal Tongan Airlines Ltd with del ex Auckland 16Nov95. Regn cld same date and regd A3-MCA. Ferried Tongatapu-Auckland-Blenheim 17Oct97 for maintenance and returned the same route 27Nov97. Sold Clewer Aviation Ltd early 1999 and lse continued to Royal Tongan Airlines Ltd. Retired after flying last service 18Aug00 and ferried Christchurch for storage 26Aug00. Del ex Christchurch 14Dec00 arriving Southend 22Dec00 for storage. Sold Emerald Airways Ltd and ferried Southend-Blackpool 27Jan01. Regd as **G-OTBA** to Emerald Airways Ltd 14Mar01 (CofR G-OTBA/R1). Converted to pure freighter and air-tested 03May01. CofA issued 04May01. Ferried Liverpool 04May01 and entered service between Liverpool and Dublin 05May01 still in Royal Tongan c/s without titles. WFU Blackpool, U.K. 03Feb06. Company's AOC suspended 04May06. Sold International Air Parts Pty Ltd 16Oct06. Regd PTB (Emerald) Pty Ltd 12Dec06 (CofR G-OTBA/R2). Wings removed by early Apr09 at start of b/u process. Regn cld as PWFU 15Jun09. Nose section to West Yorkshire Fire Service headquarters at Birkenshaw by Nov09. ***TT 51,554 hrs, 54,897 ldgs***

1713 (191) Srs.2A/248

F/f 02Mar72 as **G11-8** as a Srs.2A/280. Stored Woodford. Regd as **G-BBGY** to Hawker Siddeley Aviation Ltd 30Aug73 (CofR R.13759/1). F/f as a Srs.2A/248 still as **G11-8** 22Feb74. CofA issued 22Mar74. Del Republic of Korea Air Force as **G-BBGY** 12Apr74 as a VIP Transport. Re-regd **1713**. UK regn cld 14Jul75 as transferred Republic of Korea. Noted active at the 2011 Seoul International Aerospace and Defence Exhibition at the Seongnam Air Base on 17Oct11. Noted flying at Seoul Sinchonri Air Base 04Jan13. Present 20Oct15 on static display at the Seoul International Aerospace & Defense Exhibition at Seongnam Air Base. ***TT in excess of 5,389 hrs, 12,353 ldgs (figures at 31Dec92)***

1714 (193) Srs.2A/266

F/f 26Jun72 as **G11-10**. Del Polynesian Airlines Ltd as **5W-FAO** 17Nov72 named "Pili". Lsd Mount Cook Airlines Ltd as

5W-FAO from 22Jun82 to 08Oct82in full Polynesian Airlines c/s. Stored Christchurch until 27Feb83 when ferried to Singapore for disposal by Singapore General Aviation Services Pte Ltd. Sold Euroair Transport Ltd and regd as **G-BMFT** to Alexandra Aviation Ltd 18Oct85 (CofR G-BMFT/R1). F/f as G-BMFT 25Oct85. Del via Bombay 29Oct85 arriving Exeter 31Oct85. CofA issued 14Nov85. Seen crew training at Woodford 18/19Nov85 in basic white/grey c/s with Tunisavia titles. Lsd Tunisavia 21Nov85 to Apr86. Returned UK and operated Euroair schedules in an all white colour scheme initially without titles. Later painted with Euroair titles and fin logo. Lsd British Airways plc entering service as BA5704 from Glasgow to Aberdeen 12May86. Operated last service as BA5723 from Inverness to Glasgow 04Jul86 and returned Euroair Transport Ltd. Lsd British Airways plc for a second time in an all white c/s with black British Airways titling. In service as BA5546 from Glasgow to Belfast 04Apr87. Ferried Glasgow to Heathrow as BA9834P 15Mar88 for painting in full British Airways c/s. On completion del from Heathrow to Glasgow as BA9846E 21Mar88 named "Glen Isla" on port and "Gleann Ile" on starboard side. Flew last revenue service as BA8935H 14Apr89 from Glasgow to Dublin. Positioned back to Glasgow as BA8936P and then ferried to Heathrow as BA8958P 14Apr89 for painting all white at end of lse. Ferried back to Glasgow as BA8969E 20Apr89. Returned Euroair Transport Ltd 05May89 and ferried to Coventry the same day. Ferried Exeter 20May89. Lsd Scottish European Airways Ltd and ferried to Glasgow 25Jul89. Lse terminated 18Aug89.

Cutting up of the unsold Emerald Airways fleet took place at Blackpool in April 2009. Here G-OPFW c/n 1714 meets its end.

(Mike Davey)

Lsd British Independent Airways for crew training 24-29Aug89. Lsd Aberdeen Airways Ltd from 21Nov89 to 01Mar90 when ferried from Aberdeen to Exeter. Painted in full Jersey European c/s and f/f as such 31Mar90 prior to lse to them. Commenced crew training 03Apr90. Entered service 11Apr90 between Southampton and Jersey. Flew last service as JY833 from East Midlands to Glasgow 02Nov91 (a mail flight) and ferried to Exeter the same date as JY031 on return to Euroair Transport Ltd/Alexandra Aviation for storage at the end of lse. Painted overall white. Lsd Business Air 19Aug92 to 01Oct92. Lsd Airfast Services Indonesia P.T. 06Oct93 as G-BMFT. Regn cld 10Apr96 as transferred Bermuda and regd **VR-BFT** to Euroair (Bermuda) Ltd for continued lse to Airfast Services Indonesia P.T. Regd **VP-BFT** early 1997. Departed Selatar painted overall white 07Nov97 after a period of storage. Arrived Guernsey 14Nov97 before ferry to Exeter 28Nov97. Restored as **G-BMFT** to Emerald Airways Ltd 28Nov97 (CofR G-BMFT/R2) but remained in store Exeter painted as VP-BFT. Ferried Southend as G-BMFT 17Jan98 for maintenance and conversion freighter config. Air-tested 13 & 16Feb98. CofA issued 17Feb98 and ferried Liverpool the same date. Entered service from Liverpool to Belfast 18Feb98. Ferried Isle of Man to Woodford as JEM364 27Jun98. Regd as **G-OPFW** to Emerald Airways Ltd 01Jul98 (CofR G-OPFW/R1). Painted in overall red/white Parcel Force Worldwide c/s and ferried Liverpool 08Jul98. Returned to service 10Jul98. C/o an emergency descent while en route Pisa to Paris after severe wing icing 14Nov02. Company's AOC suspended 04May06 and aircraft ferried from Hurn to Blackpool, U.K. as JEM541Q 05May06. Sold International Air Parts Pty Ltd 16Oct06. Regd PTB (Emerald) Pty Ltd 12Dec06 (CofR G-OPFW/R2). Wings removed by early Apr09 at start of b/u process. Regn cld as PWFU 15Jun09 with nose section sold to Niall Patterson and transferred to RAF Millom Aviation & Military Museum for possible conversion into a flight simulator. Museum entered into voluntary liquidation 11Aug10. Transferred to South Yorkshire Aircraft Museum (Aeroventure) at Doncaster 04Sep10.
TT 31,736 hrs, 32,727 ldgs

1715   (198)   Srs.2/208

F/f 20Dec72 incorrectly painted as **HS-RTAF**. Corrected to **HS-TAF** 27Dec72 and f/f as such 05Jan73. Del Royal Thai Air Force as a King's Flight aircraft 26Jan73. Later coded **99-999**. Transferred 603 Squadron, Don Muang 1984. Allotted serial L5-2/16 but not carried by aircraft. Nose wheel collapsed on landing Bangkok 22Nov04. Re-painted with new code 60302 Nov05 and first noted as such at Bangkok, Thailand 15Nov05. Repair abandoned and struck off charge 10Apr06. Refurbished and moved to HRH Crown Prince Maha Vajiralongkorn's private collection at the Taweewattana Palace, Bangkok on 24Apr09 repainted in the original King's Flight c/s.
TT in excess of 6,269 hrs, 11,660 ldgs (figures at 28Feb93)

1716   (199)   Srs.2A/FAA

F/f 23Oct72 as **G11-3**. Regd as **G-BAFY** to Hawker Siddeley Aviation Ltd 23Oct72 (CofR R.13087/1). CofA issued 09Nov72. F/f as G-BAFY 10Nov72. Del Atlantic Aviation 09Jan73 and ferried via Prestwick the following day as G-BAFY. Regn cld 10Oct73 as transferred USA. Regn **N666** reserved but not used. Del Air Illinois Inc as **N748LL** 10Oct73. W/o near Pickneyville, Illinois, U.S.A. 11Oct83 when flying as UX710 from Springfield to Carbondale following failure of electrical generator system. 3 crew and 7 pax killed.   *TT 21,819 hrs, 32,350 ldgs*

1717   (192)   Srs.2A/264

F/f 16Mar73 as **G11-9**. Regd as **G-BASZ** to Hawker Siddeley Aviation Ltd 19Mar73 (CofR R.13399/1). Briefly painted in these marks but never flown as such and believed repainted as **G-11-9**. Regn cld 29May73 as transferred France. Del Rousseau Aviation as **F-BUTR** 28Jun73 after f/f as such 22Jun73. Sold Air Cape (Pty) Ltd 17Nov74 with del Cape Town as F-BUTR 29Nov74, the

final routing being via Tamanrasset, Kano, Brazzaville and Windhoek. Regd as **ZS-JAY** and used to operate South African Airways multi-sector service between Cape Town and Port Elizabeth after entering service as SA650 on 01Dec74. Painted in a revised c/s at Johannesburg 14Feb75. Flew last service for South African Airways 31Mar83. Company taken over by Safair Freighters (Pty) Ltd May88 which became known as Safair Lines (Pty) Ltd later in the year. Sold Transvalair and del ex Cape Town as **F-GFYM** 27Oct88 and immediately lsd Kel Air. Kel Air ceased operations 14Jun90 and stored Dinard. Lsd Airfast Services Indonesia P.T. by 11Oct91 until Aug92 in full company c/s. Noted stored Beauvais 10Sep93. Lsd Air Provence '96. Noted with 'Virgin' logo Oct96. Regn cld 18Feb97. Sold West Air Sweden AB and noted Lidköping 21Feb97. Regd as **SE-LIA** to ABN Amro Leasing 24Mar97. Regd GE Capital Equipment Finance AB Jul99 for continued operation by West Air Sweden as a pure freighter. Named "Mademoiselle". Regd European Turboprop Management AB 27Sep01. Was due for transfer to West Air France as **F-GMHT** but these plans were later abandoned. PWFU Lidköping, Sweden after last flight 20Apr04. Moved by road to Stockholm/Skavsta airport for use as a rescue trainer summer 2004. Regn cld 08May06.
TT 26,450 hrs, 35,083 ldgs

1718   (194)   Srs.2A/248

F/f 10Jul72 as **G11-1** as a Srs.2A/280 and put in store. Regd as **G-BABJ** to Hawker Siddeley Aviation Ltd 18Aug72 (CofR R.12996/1). F/f as G-BABJ 20Mar74 as a Srs.2A/248. CofA issued 24May74. Del Republic of Korea Air Force as G-BABJ 09Jul74 as a VIP aircraft. Regn cld 14Jul75 as transferred Republic of Korea. Received serial **1718**. Noted active at the 2011 Seoul International Aerospace and Defense Exhibition at the Seongnam Air Base on 17Oct11, and hangared 20Oct15 at the same event and location.
TT in excess of 5,235 hrs, 12,568 ldgs (figures at 31Dec92)

1719   (195)   Srs.2A/278

F/f 29Sep72 as **G11-2** and put in store. F/f as **CR-CAV** 04Oct73. Regd as **G-BBLN** to Hawker Siddeley Aviation Ltd 11Oct73 (CofR R.13880/1). CofA issued 12Oct73. F/f as G-BBLN 18Oct73. Del Transportes Aéreos de Cabo Verde (TACV) as G-BBLN 19Oct73. Regn cld 12Nov73 as transferred Portugal and regd **CR-CAV**. Returned Woodford 05Dec73 and re-del 21Jan74. Re-regd **D4-CAV** by Nov84. Last flown 05Nov94 and stored Praia, Azores. Sold Emerald Airways Ltd for spares use only 23Jan98 and b/u Praia.   *TT 25,922 hrs, 28,678 ldgs*

1720   (196)   Srs.2A/278

F/f 24Nov72 as **G11-4**. Wrongly painted as **CR-CAX** then corrected to **CR-CAW**. Regd as **G-BBPT** to Hawker Siddeley Aviation Ltd 02Nov73 (CofR R.13988/1). F/f in these marks 12Nov73. CofA issued 21Nov73. Del Transportes Aéreos de Cabo Verde (TACV) as G-BBPT 29Nov73. Regn cld 04Dec73 as transferred Portugal and regd **CR-CAW**. Re-regd **D4-CAW** by Nov84. Nose leg collapsed on start-up Praia 23Dec84. Repaired. Regn **N339C** reserved to S & H Aircraft Sales Inc 27Aug97. Sold International Aviation Pty Ltd and ferried as N339C arriving Bankstown in TACV c/s without titles 21Sep97. Regd as **VH-IMJ** to International Aviation Pty Ltd 17Oct97. Remained in storage Bankstown engineless and still painted as N339C. Dismantled and transferred by road to RAAF Amberley, Queensland, Australia 04Jul99. Reassembled for use in the fire fighting practice rôle. Regn cld 05Jun00. Last reported Nov01.
TT in excess of 24,327 hrs, 27,124 ldgs (figures at 31Dec95)

1721   (197)   Srs.2A/270

Originally painted as **G11-6** but not flown as such. F/f 19Apr73 as **CS-TAH**. Del Sociedade Açoreana de Transportes Aéreos (SATA) 05Jun73. Sold British Aerospace plc 16Jun87 and stored Ponta Delgada until 03Mar88. Lsd Ligações Aéreas Regionais S.A. with del 15Apr88. In service 16Apr88. Withdrawn 24May90 and ferried East Midlands at end of lse 05Jun90. Stored unmarked. Regd as **G-BVOU** to Emerald Airways Ltd 21Jun94 (CofR G-BVOU/R1). Ferried Blackpool as JAN125P 30Jun94 for further storage. Ferried Exeter 30Aug97 for further storage. Ferried Exeter to Southend wheels down for maintenance and conversion freighter config 27Apr98. CofA issued 31Jul98. Painted in Lynx Parcels red/white/black and gold c/s at Southend and ferried Liverpool as JEM01P 07Aug98. Air tested Liverpool as JEM03T 11Aug98. Ferried Exeter as JEM748P 15Aug98 returning Liverpool as JEM748P 17Aug98 and re-entered service the following day. Company's AOC suspended 04May06 and aircraft ferried from Belfast to Blackpool, U.K. as JEM916A the same day. Sold International Air Parts Pty Ltd 16Oct06. Regd PTB (Emerald) Pty Ltd 12Dec06 (CofR G-BVOU/R2). Wings removed by early Apr09 at start of b/u process. Regn cld as PWFU 08Apr10.

TT 25,580 hrs, 41,389 ldgs

1722   (200)   Srs.2A/216

Originally painted as **G11-6** in Hawker Siddeley Aviation c/s. Painted in Bouraq Indonesia Airlines c/s as **PK-IHR**. Regd as **G-BBTA** to Hawker Siddeley Aviation Ltd 23Nov73 (CofR R.14036/1). F/f in these marks 06Dec73, CofA issued 12Dec73. Del Bouraq Indonesia Airlines P.T. as G-BBTA 14Dec73. Regn cld 18Dec73 as transferred Singapore. Regd **PK-IHR** and named "Meranti". WFU 05Jan79. Sold Bradley Air Services Ltd and del incorrectly painted as **CG-TLD** ex Jakarta 23Jan79 and del Manchester via Nice 11Feb79. Departed Manchester for Canada via Keflavik as **C-GTLD** 27Feb79. CofR and CofA issued 07Sep79. In service 10Sep79. Painted in Bradley Air Services c/s with f/n 407. Regd Bradley Air Services Ltd 24Jun98. WFU after last flight 09Oct07 at Trois-Rivières, Québec, Canada and put in storage. Regn cld 23Dec08. Still present engineless 09Sep10 and all white with 'Commission scolaire du Chemin-du-Roy' titles 22Jul15.

TT 53,458 hrs, 40,336 ldgs

1723   (215)   Srs.2/244

F/f 12Sep75 as **D-AFSF** direct from Woodford to Hawarden where fitted out. F/f after completion at Hawarden 21Oct75. Del from Hawarden to Bundesanstalt für Flugsicherung (B.F.S.) 20Nov75 for airfield calibration duties. Regd to DFS Deutsche Flugsicherung Dec92. Sold West Air Sweden AB Sep95. Regn cld 15Sep95. Del West Air 23Nov95. Regd as **SE-LEG** to ABN Amro Leasing/ABN Amro Bank AB 12Feb96. Ferried to East Midlands 15Feb96. Ferried East Midlands to Karlstad 11Mar96 after maintenance. Converted Srs.2A/244. Regd GE Capital Equipment Finace AB Jul99 for continued operation by West Air Sweden as a pure freighter. Named "L-G P". Regd European Turboprop Management AB 27Sep01. Regd SG Finans AS Norge 17Jun05. WFU Lidköping 26May06. Sold Air Creebec Inc, painted overall grey and ferried via Bergen 30Nov06 and onwards to Keflavik, Iqaluit and Timmins 01Dec06. Ferried Bar River Airport Sault Ste. Marie the following day for major work by Skyservices Ltd including the fitting of an LFD, roller floor and mods to carry internal removable fuel cells together with a paint strip and repaint. Regn cld 06Dec06. Regd as **C-FLIY** to Air Creebec Inc 19Dec06. Painted overall white with orange & red fuselage flashes with 'airCreebec Cargo' titles. Ferried back to Timmins 23Jan08. CofA issued 31Jan08 and entered service the same day to Moosonee and the Victor Project airfield. Remains active.

TT in excess of 21,524 hrs, 19,625 ldgs (figures at 26Apr16)

1724   (218)   Srs.2/244

F/f 05Sep75 as **D-AFSG** at Hawarden where final assembly carried out. Del Bundesanstalt Für Flugsicherung (B.F.S.) 31Oct75 for airfield calibration duties. WFU 31Mar89 and stored Lechfeld. Sold at auction 26Jul89 to Air Inuit (1985) Ltd/Ltée. Del Air Inuit 07Sep89. CofR issued 29Sep89 as **C-FGET**. Converted to Srs.2A/244 by Springer Aerospace Ltd 1990. Advertised for sale summer 2009. WFU 22Jul10. Still present at Bar River Airport without engines or propellers Jan15.

TT 35,161 hrs, 36,965 ldgs

1725   (219)   Srs.2/244

F/f 29Nov75 as **D-AFSH** at Hawarden where final assembly carried out. Del Bundesanstalt Für Flugsicherung (B.F.S.) 15Dec75 for airfield calibration duties. Regd to DFS Deutsche Flugsicherung Dec92. Sold West Air Sweden AB Sep95. Regn cld 20Sep95. Reportedly arrived East Midlands from Stockholm as D-AFSH 12Dec95. Repainted as **SE-LEK** by 17Dec95. Ferried East Midlands to Billund 19Jan96 after maintenance. Regd as SE-LEK to Vikingarna HB 26Feb96. Converted Srs.2A/244. Regd GE Capital Equipment Finance AB Jul99 for continued operation by West Air Sweden as a pure freighter. Noted Lidköping 27Jul00 named "Betty Boop". Regd European Turboprop Management AB 27Sep01. Regd SG Finans AS Norge 17Jun05. Operated on behalf of ALAIRE – Líneas Aéreas Alaire, S.L. by Aug06 until May07. Sold Air Creebec Inc and ferried ex Lidköping via Bergen and Keflavik 24May07. Regn cld 31May07. Stored Timmins. Regd as **C-FPJR** to Air Creebec Inc 23Aug07. CofA issued 27Jun08. Entered revenue service 14Jul08 painted in same c/s as C-FLIY (1723). Remains active.

TT in excess of 22,518 hrs, 22,109 ldgs (figures at 23Mar16)

1726   (216)   Srs.2/244

F/f 06Dec75 as **D-AFSI**. Del Bundesanstalt Für Flugsicherung (B.F.S.) 22Dec75 for airfield calibration duties. Regd to DFS Deutsche Flugsicherung Dec92. Sold West Air Sweden AB Sep95. Regn cld 06Oct95. Regd as **SE-LEO** to ABN Amro Leasing/ABN Amro Bank AB 23Nov95. Ferried East Midlands for maintenance 29Dec95. Repainted as SE-LEO at East Midlands by 31Dec95. Regd GE Capital Equipment Finance AB Jul99 for continued operation by West Air Sweden. Converted Srs.2A/244 and operated as a pure freighter. Named "Der Loewe". Regd European Turboprop Management AB 27Sep01. No.2 engine fire on start-up and uncontrolled acceleration 13Dec01 at Lidköping, Sweden. Subsequent fire damage to wing beyond economic repair. Regn cld 12Sep02. B/U for spares.

TT 12,323 hrs, 9,872 ldgs

1727   (217)   Srs.2/244

F/f 23Jan76 as **D-AFSJ**. Del Bundesanstallt Für Flugsicherung (B.F.S.) 08Apr76 for airfield calibration duties. Regd to DFS Deutsche Flugsicherung Dec92. Sold West Air Sweden AB Sep95. Regn cld 06Oct95. Del West Air 23Nov95. Regd as **SE-LEX** to ABN Amro Leasing/ABN Amro Bank AB 23Jan96 the same day ferried East Midlands. Ferried East Midlands to Norköping after maintenance 05Mar96. Converted Srs.2A/244 and operated as a pure freighter. Regd GE Capital Equipment Finance AB Jul99 for continued operation by West Air Sweden. Regd European Turboprop Management AB 27Sep01. Regd SG Finans AS Norge 17Jun05. WFU and ferried to Lidköping, Sweden 23Dec05 and robbed of numerous parts. Regn cld 12Apr06. B/U early Oct06.

TT 13,544 hrs, 11,428 ldgs

1728   (203)   Srs.2A/282

F/f 21Mar74 as **5H-MPG**. Re-regd **5H-STZ** and f/f as such 24Apr74. Del Government of Tanzania as a VIP aircraft 29Apr74. WFU by 04Jul94. Sold Tannol Holdings Ltd Sep96 and regd to same as **5H-RJN**. Noted Dar-es-Salaam 16Oct97 semi-derelict hangared without engines or undercarriage still painted as 5H-STZ. Still present 24Sep08, derelict by 17Oct13.

TT 6,695 hrs, 5,531 ldgs

1729   (205)   Srs.2A/281 LFD

F/f 05Nov74 as **C-91 2506**. Del Força Aérea Brasileira 24Jan75 arriving Galeão 04Feb75 and operated by 2 Grupo de Transporte, 2 Esquadrão. Transferred 2 Grupo de Transporte, 1 Esquadrão 04Apr78. Seen Rio de Janeiro, Campo dos Afonsos 28Mar06 in Fuerza Aérea Ecuatoriana c/s painted as **FAE743** after donation to them by the Brazilian Government. Was present at the official

handover ceremony at Quito 23Jun06. Noted Quito engineless and being repainted 23Aug06. Seen flying Quito 19Nov07 with black cheatline and white top and noted flying again at Guayaquil 03Mar13. Decommissioned at Base Militar de Manta, Eloy Alfaro International airport, Ecuador 07Aug14.
TT 19,743 hrs, in excess of 9,649 ldgs (ldgs figures at 30Nov98)

1730 (206) Srs.2A/281 LFD

F/f 24Jan75 as **C-91 2507**. Del Força Aérea Brasileira 27Mar75 and operated by 2 Grupo de Transporte, 2 Esquadrão. Transferred 2 Grupo de Transporte, 1 Esquadrão 04Apr78. WFU 31Dec05. Donated Fuerza Aérea Ecuatoriana for spares use only. Allotted serial **FAE744** but not used. B/U Campo dos Afonsos, Rio de Janeiro, Brazil May06.
TT in excess of 14,691 hrs, 8,399 ldgs (figures at 30Nov98)

1731 (207) Srs.2A/281 LFD

F/f 13Mar75 as **C-91 2508**. Del Força Aérea Brasileira 16May75 and operated by 2 Grupo de Transporte, 2 Esquadrão. Transferred 2 Grupo de Transporte, 1 Esquadrão 04Apr78. Noted active and painted in overall grey c/s Salvador, Brazil 18Apr03. Donated Fuerza Aérea Ecuatoriana as **FAE741** and del Quito 28Jun06. Noted at Quito with Fuerza Aérea Ecuatoriana titles 10Dec06. Noted active Quito 23May08. WFU at the old Mariscal Sucre airport and reportedly b/u 2013.
TT 20,038 hrs, in excess of 9,194 ldgs (figures at 30Nov98)

1732 (208) Srs.2A/281 LFD

F/f 12May75 as **C-91 2509**. Del Força Aérea Brasileira 20Jun75 and operated by 2 Grupo de Transporte, 2 Esquadrão. Transferred 2 Grupo de Transporte, 1 Esquadrão 04Apr78. Overran runway Santa Catarina airport, Navegantes, Brazil on arrival from Rio de Janiero 09Feb98. Undercarriage collapsed and severely damaged. No fatalities. Subsequently w/o.
TT 14,160 hrs, 8,265 ldgs

1733 (211) Srs.2A/281 LFD

F/f 14Aug75 as **C-91 2510**. Del Força Aérea Brasileira 31Oct75 and operated by 2 Grupo de Transporte, 2 Esquadrão. Transferred 2 Grupo de Transporte 1 Esquadrão 04Apr78. Was present at the official handover ceremony at Quito 23Jun06 when the aircraft was donated Fuerza Aérea Ecuatoriana as **FAE742**. Noted Quito 02Aug06 in overall grey scheme with Ecuadorian national colours on rudder. Noted fully painted and operational Quito 12Jan08 and again at Tachina General Rivadeneira airport 28Nov08. WFU at the old Mariscal Sucre airport and reportedly b/u 2013.
TT 17,431 hrs, in excess of 8,206 ldgs (figures at 30Nov98)

1734 (212) Srs.2A/281 LFD

F/f 20Nov75 as **C-91 2511**. Del Força Aérea Brasileira 18Dec75 and operated by 2 Grupo de Transporte, 2 Esquadrão. Transferred 2 Grupo de Transporte, 1 Esquadrão 04Apr78. Donated Fuerza Aérea Ecuatoriana as **FAE740** and del Quito 28Jun06. Noted

D-AFSJ c/n 1727 of the BFS - Bundesanstalt für Flugsicherung (note titles on the nose).

C-91 2509 c/n 1732 of the Força Aérea Brasileira at Woodford after fitting its Large Freight Door in May 1975. (WHC)

active as such Galeão 05Oct06 in similar c/s to FAE742 above. Noted stored Quito with several parts missing 01Apr09. WFU at the old Mariscal Sucre airport and reportedly b/u 2013.

TT 19,055 hrs, in excess of 8,222 ldgs (figures at 30Nov98)

1735 (204) Srs.2A/216

F/f 02Apr74 as **G-11-7**. Regd as **G-BCDM** to Hawker Siddeley Aviation Ltd 25Apr74 (CofR R.14293/1). CofA issued 21May74. F/f as G-BCDM 30May74. Displayed at the Chester open day at Hawarden in full Bouraq c/s as G-BCDM 08Jun74. Ferried Woodford-Manchester 19Jul74 and del Bouraq Indonesia Airlines P.T. as G-BCDM 26Jul74 ex Manchester with **PK-IHL** taped over. Regn cld 01Aug74 as transferred Indonesia. Regd **PK-KHL** 08Aug74. Aircraft purchased on behalf of Bali Air P.T. but operated by Bouraq Indonesia Airlines P.T. Noted painted with Bali Air titles by 03Nov88. W/o Mount Komawa, Irian Jaya, Indonesia 09Aug95 when flying from Tual to Kaimana. 6 crew and 4 pax killed.

TT in excess of 42,169 hrs, 28,561 ldgs (figures at 02Aug95)

1736 (210) Srs.2A/287

Regd as **G-BCOE** to Hawker Siddeley Aviation Ltd 23Sep74 (CofR R.14567/1). F/f 17Jun75, CofA issued 04Jul75. Del British Airways 10Jul75 and regd to British Airways Board 17Jul75 (CofR G-BCOE/R2). In service 04Aug75. Lost rear pax door on take-off Sumburgh 16Jul77. Repaired. Named "Glen Livet" on starboard and "Gleann Liomhaid" on port side Mar83. Regd to British Airways plc 01Apr84. Flew last service 02Apr85 prior to commencement of conversion to Srs.2B/287 at Glasgow with effect from the same date. Conversion completed 03Jun85. Returned to service 07Jun85 in full new 1985 British Airways c/s. Nose undercarriage leg ripped away from aircraft by tug at Manchester 08Aug88. Repaired and ferried Glasgow as BA9844E 09Sep88. Returned to service the same date. Flew last revenue service as BA5709 from Aberdeen to Glasgow 01Apr92 and put into storage. Regd to British Aerospace Regional Aircraft 04Jun92 (CofR G-BCOE/R3). Ferried Hatfield 26Aug92. Ferried from Hatfield to East Midlands 29Jan93. Regn cld 08Mar93 as transferred Nepal. Regd **9N-ACN** and del on lse to Nepal Airways Pvt Ltd via Nice 08Mar93. Del Exeter at end of lse 20Mar94 for storage. Restored as **G-BCOE** to Jetstream Aircraft Ltd 26Apr94 (CofR G-BCOE/R4). Lsd Impulse Airlines Pty Ltd arriving Bankstown 08Oct94. Regn cld 10Oct94 as transferred Australia and regd **VH-IMI** 12Oct94. Converted to cargo configuration. In service Mar95. WFU 23Jun95 and ferried Adelaide 13Jul95 for storage on return JSX Capital Corp. Regd to Jetstream Aircraft (Sydney) Ltd 08Aug95. Ferried Bankstown by 13Aug96. Regd to International Air Parts Pty Ltd 23Oct96 on sale to them. Regn **SE-LIA** rsvd for West Air Sweden A.B. 10Jan97 but ntu. Restored to **VH-IMI**. Regd International Aviation Pty Ltd 23Jul98 and lsd to them. Fitted with a large rear freight door with completion Nov98. Item recovered from c/n 1763, C6-BED of Bahamas Airways Ltd. Company name changed to Horizon Airlines Pty Ltd 10Dec98. Lsd Australian air Express Pty Ltd 29Mar to 21Jun99 for Adelaide to Melbourne freight schedules. Lsd Ansett Air Freight Pty Ltd for four rotations per week on the Brisbane-Sydney route 22Jun99. Named "The Beast Too". Ferried from Adelaide to Perth 29Sep02 before commencing services on the Air Cargo Express schedule to Port Hedland and Karratha the following day. Lse terminated and aircraft departed Perth for Bankstown 08Apr03. Horizon Airlines placed in Administration 14Oct03 and later ceased operations. Last flew 20Oct03 when ferried Bankstown for storage. Flew shake-down flight Bankstown-Coffs Harbour-Bankstown 06Mar05. Sold Cape Aero Services (Pty) Ltd of South Africa Mar05 and del ex Bankstown via Mount Isa to Darwin 12Mar05 arriving Nelspruit, South Africa 22Mar05 as VH-IMI. Regn cld 29Mar05. Regd as **ZS-DBM** to Sonetrad (Pty) Ltd 01Apr05 and noted carrying 'Stars Away Aviation' titles. Regd Fulloutput 191 (Pty) Ltd 05Oct05. Ferried Cape Town 15Jul06 for repaint and heavy maint. Ferried from Cape Town 01Apr09 on lease to MK Airlines Ltd arriving Accra 03Apr09. Regn cld as exported Ghana

05May09 and regd as **9G-MKV.** Lse terminated Aug09 and aircraft returned to Cape Town. Regd as **5Y-HVS** to Fulloutput 191 (Pty) Ltd 02Oct09 with the lessee named as Airstream (K) Ltd of Nairobi but aircraft remained in store Cape Town. Noted hangared at Cape Town painted as 5Y-HVS 15Mar12 in similar British Airways type 'Landor' c/s as c/n 1737 below. Restored as **ZS-DBM** to Fulloutput 191 (Pty) Ltd 25Apr12 and noted flying as such at Cape Town 21May12. Ferried from Cape Town via Ondangwa, Brazzeville and Libreville on lease to Tropicana Airlines Ltd 23May12. Arrived Accra 28May12. Lse terminated Sep12 and aircraft stored in Accra. Stars Away Aviation liquidated Nov12. Regn cld as sold in Kenya 04Jun14. Sold to Planes for Africa Ltd for operations by Avro Express Ltd as **5Y-PFA**. Noted 27Mar16 with 'World Food Programme' titles operated by Planes For Africa Ltd on behalf of the United Nations.

TT in excess of 30,091 hrs, 38,420 ldgs (figures at 20Oct03)

1737 (213) Srs.2A/287

Regd as **G-BCOF** to Hawker Siddeley Aviation Ltd 23Sep74 (CofR R.14568/1). F/f 14Aug75, CofA issued 01Sep75. Del British Airways 03Sep75 and regd to British Airways Board the following day (CofR G-BCOF/R2). In service 04Sep75. Named "Glen Fiddich" on starboard and "Gleann Fithich" on port side Mar83. Regd to British Airways plc 01Apr84. Flew last service 05Jan85 prior to commencement of conversion to Srs.2B/287 at Glasgow with effect from 06Jan85. Conversion completed 01Apr85. Returned to service 02Apr85 in full new 1985 British Airways c/s. Flew last service as BA8991H from Shetland to Aberdeen 31Dec91. Ferried to Glasgow from Aberdeen as BA8994E the same date and put into storage. Sold British Aerospace plc and regd to British Aerospace (Airlines Division) plc 28Jan92 (CofR G-BCOE/R3). Ferried Glasgow-Woodford-Hatfield for storage 16Sep92. Ferried Exeter 03Feb94 for further storage. Ferried Exeter-Luton-Prestwick 29Oct94. Lsd Impulse Airlines Pty Ltd arriving Sydney 29Nov94. Regn cld 29Dec94 as transferred Australia and regd **VH-IMK** 12Jan95. Converted to cargo configuration. In service Mar95. WFU 12Jul95 and ferried Adelaide the same day for storage on return JSX Capital Corp. Regd to Jetstream Aircraft (Sydney) Ltd 08Aug95. Ferried Bankstown by 13Aug96. Regd to International Air Parts Pty Ltd 23Oct96 on sale to them. Regn **SE-LIB** rsvd to West Air Sweden A.B. 10Jan97 but ntu. By Oct97 was noted lsd to International Aviation Pty Ltd named "The Beast". I/s 21Jan98 from Brisbane to Moro, Papua New Guinea. Regd International Aviation Pty Ltd 23Jul98. Company name changed to Horizon Airlines Pty Ltd 10Dec98. Fitted with large rear freight door recovered from c/n 1771, 9N-ABR of Royal Nepal Airlines Corp early 1999. Re-entered service 01Aug99. Horizon Airlines placed in Administration 14Oct03 and later ceased operations. Flew final service for Australian air Express as XM7024 from Brisbane to Sydney 24Oct03 and ferried Bankstown the same date for storage. Noted painted in British Airways Landor c/s Dec05. Air-tested 11Mar06. Sold Stars Away Aviation and ferried ex Bankstown 20Mar06 via Alice Springs, Port Headland, Cocos Island, Colombo, Male, Seychelles, Toamasina to Kruger International 27Mar06 and onwards to Cape Town the following day. Regn cld 07Apr06 as exported South Africa. Regn as **ZS-OEO** to Fulloutput 191 (Pty) Ltd 10Apr06 but ntu and regd as **ZS-DBL** 11Apr06. Final air-test 15Jul06 and was due to ferry George 17Jul06 and enter service the same day from George to Bloemfontein and Johannesburg. Ferried from Cape Town via Johannesburg and Lilongwe to Nairobi on lease to Timbis Air Services Ltd 10Nov10. Noted active in Khartoum, Sudan Dec10. Flew last service 22Jan11 and stored Nairobi. Regn cld as exported Kenya 20Oct11 and regd as **5Y-BZR** to Fulloutput 192 (Pty) Ltd 26Oct11 for renewed lse to Timbis Air Services Ltd. W/O landing at Doro, Southern Sudan 02Apr12. No fatalities.

TT in excess of 28,232 hrs, 35,815 ldgs (figures at 24Oct03)

1738 (214) Srs.2A/285 LFD

F/f 22Oct75 as **FAE738**. Del Fuerza Aérea Ecuatoriana 21Nov75. Later carried both FAE738 and **HC-BAZ** when used by TAME -

FAE738 c/n 1738 of the Fuerza Aérea Ecuatoriana with its Large Freight Door open in flight.

Transportes Aéreos Militares/Nacionales Ecuatorianos. Overran runway after flapless landing Lago Agria, Ecuador 23Jun87. No fatalities among 38 on board. Reportedly was being air lifted by two helicopters during recovery when the HS748 became unstable. The helicopter crews released the aircraft at low level and the aircraft landed inverted sustaining much additional damage. Preserved in the Museo Aeronáutico de la Fuerza Aérea Ecuatoriana at Quito with a remarkably odd shaped nose. Replaced in the museum by FAE684 and B/U Feb13.

TT in excess of 10,115 hrs, 14,606 ldgs (figures at 31Jul88)

1739   (220)   Srs.2A/285 LFD

F/f 12Feb76 as **FAE739**. Del Fuerza Aérea Ecuatoriana 10Apr76. Later carried both FAE739 and **HC-BEY** when used by TAME - Transportes Aéreos Militares/Nacionales Ecuatorianos. Sustained severe damage to No1 engine and propeller and adjacent fuselage after taxying into a ground power unit at Guayaquil 14Jan00. Repaired. Noted still active with Fuerza Aérea Ecuatoriana titles at Quito 03Sep11 as HC-BEY/FAE739. Noted flying at Quito 24Jan13 in new c/s now as FAE739 only. WFU Latacunga/Cotopaxi airport 2014.

**TT 28,764 hrs, in excess of 23,545 ldgs
(figures at 30Oct98)**

1740   (221)   Srs.2A/286 LFD

F/f 19Mar76 as **5H-WDL**. Del Williamson Diamonds Ltd 21Apr76. Lsd BAe for a Madagascan demonstration from 31May to 08Jun79. Nose gear collapsed on landing Dar-es-Salaam 05Nov81. Repaired. WFU Madui, Tanzania from early 1987. Regn cld 22Apr96. Sold Intensive Air Sep96 and regd as **ZS-XGZ** to Dr. J.W.K. Louw 06Sep96 although still painted as 5H-WDL on 11Nov96. Noted Rand painted as ZS-XGZ 10Nov97. By Oct98 painted in new c/s incorporating South African flag fin named "Zig Zag" but without titles. Fitted with Rolls-Royce Dart Mk.536-2 engines. Company ceased operations 08Apr02 and aircraft stored Johannesburg International. Ferried Lanseria late Jul02 following sale to International Air Parts Pty Ltd of Australia. Noted Lanseria 18Oct02 with white top, dark blue undersides and no titles. Converted to a pure freighter. Regd AirQuarius Contracts (Pty) Ltd 22Jan03 and advertised for sale. Noted Lanseria 28Sep04 on engine runs with Tracmark Cargo titles. Lsd Trackmark Cargo Ltd 16Oct04 on a two year lse and noted Nairobi, Wilson on 12Nov04. Regn cld 22Nov05 and regd **5Y-TCA** for continued lse to Trackmark Cargo Ltd. Overshot landing at Old Fangak in Southern Sudan 17Mar06 and w/o. No fatalities.

TT 9,878 hrs, 6,560 ldgs

1741   (222)   Srs.2A/288 LFD

F/f 26May76 as **CS-01**. Del Force Aérienne Belge/Belgische Luchtmacht 28Jun76 in green and brown camouflage c/s. Operated by 21 Squadron, Melsbroek. Repainted in white c/s Dinard, France 09/27Nov87. WFU 20Feb02 and put in store Weelde, Belgium. Donated Benin Air Force/Force Aérienne Populaire du Bénin and ferried Cotonou mid 2002. By Feb04 regd **TY-21A**. Noted in new c/s at Johannesburg, O.R. Tambo 25Sep09 fresh off a major check, again at Rand on 28Mar10 and at Cotonou 21Sep10 and again taxying at same location on 09Feb12. Noted taking off from Ouagadougou, Burkina Faso, 18Sep12 and noted at Cotonou 23Jun13.

TT in excess of 8,926 hrs, 10,325 ldgs (figures at 31Oct99)

1742   (223)   Srs.2A/288 LFD

F/f 06Jul76 as **CS-02**. Del Force Aérienne Belge/Belgische Luchtmacht 31Jul76 in green and brown camouflage c/s. Operated by 21 Squadron, Melsbroek. Repainted in white c/s Dinard, France 24Nov/10Dec87. WFU by Feb02 and put in store Weelde, Belgium. Donated Benin Air Force/Force Aérienne Populaire du Bénin and departed Melsbroek 17Dec02 arriving Cotonou 19Dec02. Regd **TY-22A** by Feb04. Noted flying at Ouagadougou, Burkina Faso, 18Sep12 and parked at Cotonou 23Jun13, and noted again there late 2015.

TT in excess of 8,614 hrs, 9,475 ldgs (figures at 31Oct09)

1743   (224)   Srs.2A/288 LFD

F/f 11Aug76 as **CS-03**. Regd as **G-BEEM** to Hawker Siddeley Aviation Ltd 31Aug76 (CofR G-BEEM/R1). British regd for demonstration at Farnborough Air Show 03-13Sep76 but regn appeared nowhere on aircraft (call sign only). Regn cld 15Sep76 as transferred Belgian Air Force. Del Force Aérienne Belge/Belgische Luchtmacht 30Sep76 as **CS-03** in green and brown camouflage c/s. Operated by 21 Squadron, Melsbroek. Repainted in white c/s Dinard, France 06/23Dec87. WFU Aug01 and put in store Weelde, Belgium. Dismantled and transported by road to Antwerp docks 01Oct03 for shipment to Benin as spares for c/ns 1741 & 1742 above 02Oct03. Fuselage noted in two halves at Cotonou 23Jun13.

TT in excess of 8,883 hrs, 10,047 ldgs (figures at 31Oct99)

1744   (225)   Srs.2A/283

F/f 31Aug76 as **YV-45C**. Regn **YV-09C** originally rsvd but not used. Del Línea Aeropostal Venezolana 26Nov76. W/o after take-off Caracas for Cumaná, Venezuela 03Mar78. Crashed into sea. 4 crew and 43 pax killed.   **TT 2,102 hrs, 2,837 ldgs**

Above: ZS-XGZ c/n 1740 of Intensive Air at Johannesburg-Rand on 12th May 1999.   (Keith Gaskell)

Left: Interior shot of ZS-XGZ c/n 1740 at Johannesburg-Rand.
*   (Richard J. Church)*

YV-46C c/n 1745 of LAV/Aeropostal in a photograph taken in late 1976 prior to delivery.   *(WHC)*

1745   (226)   Srs.2A/283

F/f 24Sep76 as **YV-46C**. Regn **YV-10C** originally rsvd but not used. Del Línea Aeropostal Venezolana 25Nov76. Landed with nose leg retracted at unknown location 12Jun80. Repaired. Sold Austin Airways Ltd as **C-GDOP** 05Dec80. CofR issued 05Feb82. Sold Eastern Provincial Airways (1963) Ltd with del Gander 16Apr82. Operated by Air Maritime. Company fully integrated into Canadian Pacific Air Lines with effect from 12Jan86. Regn cld 31Mar87 and regd **F-ODQQ** to the same operator 09Apr87 for lease to Air Saint-Pierre. Regn cld at end of lse 20May87. Restored as **C-GDOP** 10Jun87 to Canadian Pacific Air Lines Ltd. Sold Calm Air International Ltd 02Jan88 and del 13Jan88. Entered service 17Jan88 in Canadian Partner c/s and operated in the combi rôle. Regd Calm Air International Ltd 10May88. Carried f/n 744C from 2007. WFU Thompson, Manitoba, Canada after operating its last flight on 13Dec08 and retained in storage for use as an engine run stand to carry out runs on spare Dart engines until replaced in this rôle by C-FAMO c/n 1669 in Aug11.

TT 43,735 hrs, 49,170 ldgs

1746   (228)   Srs.2A/301 LFD

Regd as **G-BDVH** to Hawker Siddeley Aviation Ltd 09Apr76 (CofR G-BDVH/R1). F/f 11Nov76, CofA issued 07Dec76. Company demonstrator in desert camouflage c/s with 'Hawker Siddeley Aviation' titles. C/o sales tours from 09-22Dec76, 05-14Jan77 and 21Feb to 10Mar77 before being shown Paris Air Show 01-13Jun77 with show number 238. C/o a Philippine tour 02-18Dec77. Regd to British Aerospace Aircraft Group 18Jan78 (CofR G-BDVH/R2). C/o Middle East tour 18Jan to 18Feb78, a North African demonstration 01-22Apr78, a Yemen/Egypt and Yugoslavia tour 22May to 01Jun78 and an African demonstration 07-12Jul78. Displayed at Farnborough Air Show 01-11Sep78. Visited Barcelona from 13-18Sep78 before conducting SEP-10 autopilot trials 08-11Nov78. Regn cld 24Nov78 as transferred Bahamas and lsd Bahamasair as C6-BEA but not del and restored to British Aerospace as **G-BDVH** 19Dec78 (CofR G-BDVH/R3). Lsd Bahamasair as **C6-BEA** 15Jan79 after f/f as such 12Dec78. UK regn cld 17Jan79 as transferred Bahamas. Del Woodford at end of lse 14Aug79 and restored as **G-BDVH** to British Aerospace plc Aircraft Group 10Sep79 (CofR G-BDVH/R4). Lsd Air Madagascar with del as G-BDVH 17Dec79. UK regn cld 27Dec79 as transferred Madagascar and regd **5R-MJS**. Del Woodford at end of lse 05Feb80 and restored as **G-BDVH** to British Aerospace plc Aircraft Group 14Feb80 (CofR G-BDVH/R5). Converted to 'Multi-Rôle 748' military type demonstrator with f/f as such 19Mar80. Shown Farnborough Air Show 30Aug to 08Sep80. Demonstrated in East Africa 19Nov to 20Dec80. Shown Paris Air Show 03-15Jun81 with Show Number 235. C/o South American tour 06-28Jul81, Indian tour 07Sep to 07Oct81, Irish Republic demonstration 19-22Oct81 and Iran tour 14-25Apr82. Shown Farnborough Air Show 03-14Sep82. Demonstrated to RSAF 06Jun83 and in Casablanca 22-30Nov83 before use as the Warton Shuttle back-up in 1984/5. Converted back to a Srs.2A/301 LFD and sold Sri Lanka Air Force with del 18Mar86. Regn cld 27Mar86 as transferred Sri Lanka and regd **CR-833** for operation by No.2 Squadron/Helitours. Noted in overall grey c/s Apr02. Last flew 23Aug02 and put in storage Ratmalana, Sri Lanka. Noted 31Mar11 carrying new serial **SCM-3102** at the same location in a camouflage scheme. Noted on display across the road from Weerawila airfield in a two tone blue and white colour scheme with 'Sri Lanka Air Force' titles and with serial **CR-833** and with Helitours titles and 'Discover Serendipity' on the fin 02Dec12. The aircraft forms an integral part of the Eagles' café, officially opened by the Speaker of the Sri Lankan parliament on 12Jun13.

TT 10,876 hrs, 17,618 ldgs

1747   (230)   Srs.2A/309 LFD

F/f 26Jan77 as **8R-GEU**. Del Guyana Airways Corporation 08Mar77. Made wheels-up landing Lethem 30Jul82. Repaired.

WFU 1987 and put into storage. Rsvd as ZS-PLO to Caicos International 24May99 but ntu. Sold Caicos International 13Jun96 but remained stored with Guyana until sold Calm Air International Ltd and dismantled for spares use only 1999. LFD removed and fitted to c/n 1790.

TT 10,009 hrs, 10,565 ldgs

1748   (232)   Srs.2A/309 LFD

F/f 11May77 as **8R-GEV**. Del Guyana Airways Corporation 22Jun77. Damage sustained to nose and propellers on take-off Georgetown 01Jul81. Struck cow on aborted take-off at Lethem 05Aug87 damaging the port engine and undercarriage. WFU 1987 and put into storage. Sold Caicos International 13Jun96 but remained stored with Guyana until sold Calm Air International Ltd and dismantled for spares use only 1999. LFD removed and fitted to c/n 1669. Fuselage to South Alberta Institute of Technology Calgary, Alberta, Canada. Seen as such 31Aug05. By 19Nov10 had moved to the Art Smith Aero Centre at Calgary.

TT 11,875 hrs, 12,064 ldgs

1749   (231)   Srs.2A/310 LFD

F/f 27Apr77 as **TJ-XAF**. Del L'Armée de l'Air du Cameroun 30Sep77. Re-regd **TJ-AAN** 19Apr79. Sold Cameroon Airlines as **TJ-CCD** 22Feb82. Del Woodford 16Dec85 after being traded in part exchange for new Srs.2B/435s. Stored Woodford. Sold Air Inuit (1985) Ltd/Ltée as **C-FDOX** 16Nov88. Ferried to Manchester 13Jan89 before del 16Jan89. CofR issued 01Aug89. Ran off runway Akulivik, Canada 16Jan92 and nose leg sheared off. Repaired. Lsd Western EXpress Air Lines Inc with del to Vancouver 22Oct98. Painted with "WEST EX" titles. Returned Air Inuit Ltd 28Nov98. Lsd West Air Sweden AB with del via Godthab and Reykjavik as AIE582 26Mar99. Returned Air Inuit (1985) Ltd/Ltée ex Lidköping 03Jan00. Lsd Emerald Airways Ltd and del Rekjavik-Liverpool as AIE800 14Jul00. Ferried Cardiff 17Jul00 and entered service the same day in full Air Inuit c/s from Cardiff to Bristol, Liverpool and Newcastle. Flew final service from Liverpool to Bristol and Cardiff 23Dec00. Returned lessor with ferry from Cardiff via Belfast and Reykjavik 27/28Dec00. Advertised for sale summer 2009 but still operational with Air Inuit 26Jun11 when noted flying Montréal-Dorval. Still operational Jan15 in old Air Inuit c/s.

TT in excess of 41,936 hrs, 39,434 ldgs (figures at 04Jan16)

1750   (235)   Srs.2A/310 LFD

F/f 01Aug77 as **TJ-XAH**. Del L'Armée de l'Air du Cameroun 30Sep77. Re-regd **TJ-AAO** 19Apr79. Sold Cameroon Airlines as **TJ-CCE** 22Feb82. Del Woodford 11Nov85 after being traded in part exchange for new Srs.2B/435s. Regd **G-11-2** and ferried Exeter 01Aug86 for maintenance and repaint by West Country Air Services Ltd in Jambo Air Lines c/s named "Yankari Express". Test flown, still as G-11-2, 03Dec86. Regd as **5N-ARJ** and del ex Exeter 29Dec86 arriving Lagos 30Dec86. Ferried Exeter 02Oct87 and stored. Del Exeter to Lisbon 12Apr88 on lse to British Aerospace plc and sub-lse to Ligações Aéreas Regionais S.A. Regd as **CS-TAU** and entered service 16Apr88. Returned Exeter at end of lse for storage 10Apr90. Regd to Merchant Enterprises Ltd as **G-JHLN** 26Jul90 (CofR G-JHLN/R1) and storage continued. Regd Twin Jet Aircraft Sales Ltd 16Apr92 (CofR G-JHLN/R2) and regn cld same date as transferred Canada. Painted as **C-GTAD** 20Apr92. Air tested 19Apr92 using call sign G-JHLN. Sold V. Kelner Airways Ltd. Del ex Exeter via Reykjavik 22Apr92. CofR and CofA issued 30Apr92. Company renamed Wasaya Airways Ltd and regd to them 05Jan93. Entered service 29May92. Regd to Air Manitoba Ltd 05Apr94 on lse to them. Returned Wasaya Airways Ltd and regd to them 19Oct95 with f/n 804. Overran runway and nose gear collapsed on landing Kasabonika, Ontario, Canada after operating cargo flight WG804 from Pickle Lake 06Aug98 and subsequently w/o. No fatalities among 4 crew on board. Regn cld as WFU 11May00.

TT 12,310 hrs, 16,308 ldgs

G-BETY c/n 1752. This aircraft was later delivered to the Tanzanian People's Defence Force where it became JW-9009.   *(WHC/BAe)*

1751   (236)   **Srs.2A/314 LFD**

Regd as **G-BETZ** to Hawker Siddeley Aviation Ltd 05May77 (CofR G-BETZ/R1). F/f 29Sep77. F/F as **JW9008** 23Nov77 but reverted to **G-BETZ** for del Tanzanian Peoples Defence Force 15Nov77. Regn cld 25Nov77 as sold Tanzania and regd **JW9008**. W/o Lake Manyara, Tanzania reportedly on 26May87. No fatalities. Sold International Air Parts Pty Ltd for spares and recovery of large cargo door by May02. Major sections moved to Sydney-Bankstown. (See also c/n 1709)

                  TT 1,698 hrs, 1,319 ldgs

1752   (237)   **Srs.2A/314 LFD**

Regd as **G-BETY** to Hawker Siddeley Aviation Ltd 05May77 (CofR G-BETY/R1). F/f 07Nov77. Del Tanzanian People's Defence Force as G-BETY 20Jan78. Regn cld 09Jan79 as sold Tanzania and regd **JW9009**. W/o soon after take-off Mbeya, Tanzania 01Jul85. Crashed 4km short of airfield attempting to return following engine failure. 4 killed.   ***TT 4,686 hrs, 3,465 ldgs***

1753   (239)   **Srs.2A/314 LFD**

Regd as **G-BETX** to Hawker Siddeley Aviation Ltd 05May77 (CofR G-BETX/R1). F/f 12Dec77. Del Tanzanian Peoples Defence Force as G-BETX 27Jan78. Regn cld 09Jan79 as sold Tanzania and regd **JW9010**. Belly landed Dar-es-Salaam, Tanzania 07Feb91. WFU and noted all white at Dar-es-Salaam 26Sep08 and again in Aug12 hangared.

    TT in excess of 2,305 hrs, 2,081 ldgs (figures at 28Feb91)

1754   (229)   **Srs.2A/320 LFD**

F/f 22Jun77 as **XT-MAL**. Del Force Aérienne de Haute-Volta 02Sep77. Following country's renaming on 04Aug84, operator renamed Force Aérienne de Burkina Faso. Noted on maintenance at Dinard, France 12Jan03 and again flying at Accra, Ghana in May07. Seen operational at Ouagadougou, Burkina Faso 25Jan09.

    TT in excess of 4,326 hrs, 4,110 ldgs (figures at 30Jun96)

1755   (240)   **Srs.2A/329 LFD**

F/f 30Jan78 as **EL-AIH**. Del Air Liberia 24Feb78. W/o soon after take-off Khartoum, Sudan 16Apr83. Following No2 engine failure and attempted return, struck house. 3 crew, 5 pax and 9 on ground killed, 1 pax survived.

    TT in excess of 6,732 hrs, 11,419 ldgs (figures at 17Oct82)

1756   (227)   **Srs.2A/334**

F/f 07Dec77 as **G-11-8**. F/f as **9Y-TFS** 21Dec77. Del Trinidad and Tobago Air Services Ltd 23Dec77. In service 28Dec77 named "James Fargo". Later named "A.P.T. James". Company renamed Trinidad & Tobago (BWIA International) Airways

Corporation with effect from 01Jan80. Lsd Air BVI Ltd as 9Y-TFS from 02May86 to 29May86. Regd to Chieftain Airways plc as **G-GLAS** 19Dec86 (CofR G-GLAS/R1) following sale to them. Del ex Port of Spain 19Dec86 stopping over at Goose Bay from 21Dec86 to 03Jan87 before arriving with McAlpine Aviation Ltd at Luton 04Jan87 for repainting. CofA issued 05Mar87. Ferried from Luton to Glasgow 05Mar87 for crew training. Returned Luton for completion of pre-service modifications 18Mar87. Re-del Glasgow 30Mar87 and named "The Lord Provost of Glasgow". In service the same day as PQ045 from Glasgow to Frankfurt via Edinburgh. Company put in the hands of receiver 13May87 and flying ceased the following day. After prolonged storage ferried Luton 02Jul88. Sold Scottish European Airways Ltd 30Sep88 and regd to them 03Oct88 (CofR G-GLAS/R2). Re-regd **G-BPDA** 07Oct88 (CofR G-BPDA/R1). Named "European Spirit of Strathclyde". Impounded Frankfurt Mar90. CAA withdrew route licences 30Mar90. Company ceased trading 27Apr90 and officially wound up 09Aug91. Ferried Exeter 04Jul90 for storage. Regd to Greyhound Financial Services Ltd 29Aug90 (CofR G-BPDA/R2). Sold Janes Aviation Ltd and painted all white with thin red cheat line below the windows and air-tested 11Nov91. CofA re-issued 13Nov91 and del Blackpool 13Nov91. Regd Janes Aviation Ltd 30Dec91 (CofR G-BPDA/R3). Regd to Janes Aviation 748 Ltd 07Jan93 (CofR G-BPDA/R4). Company renamed Emerald Airways Ltd 15Sep93. Painted in Reed Aviation c/s at Exeter 04/26Mar94 and named "John J. Goodall" and operated in freighter config. Landed Belfast 09Feb98 after a newspaper flight from Liverpool where left nose wheel found missing on arrival on stand. Had been shed on take-off from Liverpool. Ferried Woodford for repaint 09Aug99. Re-regd **G-ORAL** to Emerald Airways Ltd 13Aug99 (CofR G-ORAL/R1). R/o in new Reed Aviation c/s named "The Paper Plane" 17Aug99. Departed Woodford 19Aug99. Company's AOC suspended 04May06 and ferried from Dublin to Blackpool, U.K. as JEM910P the same date. Sold International Air Parts Pty Ltd 16Oct06. Regd PTB (Emerald) Pty Ltd 12Dec06 (CofR G-ORAL/R2). Wings removed by early Apr09 at start of b/u process. Forward fuselage section removed and roaded to Mike Davey for preservation at the Hooton Park Trust hangars on the Wirral on 29Apr09 and eventual display at cockpitfests around the country. Regn cld 15Jun09 as PWFU. Moved to the Speke Aerodrome Heritage Group 22Oct10 but still owned by Mike Davey.   ***TT 18,748 hrs, 33,217 ldgs***

1757   (233)   **Srs.2A/334**

F/f 16Jan78 as **9Y-TFT**. Del Trinidad and Tobago Air Services Ltd 04Feb78. In service 08Feb78. Company renamed Trinidad & Tobago (BWIA International) Airways Corporation with effect from 01Jan80. Lsd LIAT (1974) Ltd from 20Nov80. In service 20Dec80 regd **VP-LCG**. Re-regd **V2-LCG** from Mar82 after Antiguan Independence 01Nov81. WFU 04Jun82 and returned lessor as **9Y-TFT** the same day. Named "Uriah Butler". Lsd Air BVI Ltd as 9Y-TFT from 08Dec84 to 08Apr85 with Air BVI titles. Regd to Chieftain Airways plc as **G-EDIN** 19Dec86 (CofR G-EDIN/R1) following sale to them. Del ex Port of Spain 19Dec86 stopping at Goose Bay from 21Dec86 to 03Jan87 before arriving with McAlpine Aviation Ltd at Luton for repainting 04Jan87. CofA issued 20Mar87. Del Glasgow 20Mar87. Flew from Glasgow to Brussels via Edinburgh on a proving flight 27Mar87. Operated the company's first commercial service as PQ031 from Glasgow to Brussels via Edinburgh 30Mar87 after being named "The Lord Provost of Edinburgh". Company put in the hands of receiver 13May87 and flying ceased the following day. After prolonged storage ferried Luton 01Oct88. Sold Scottish European Airways Ltd 30Oct88 and regd to them as G-BPFU 03Nov88 (CofR G-BPFU/R1). Named "Fortune Favours the Brave". Impounded Manchester 1990. Company ceased trading 27Apr90. Regd as G-OMDS to Azedcrest Ltd 23Jan91 (CofR G-OMDS/R1). Painted as such and storage continued at Manchester. Sold Sri Lanka Air Force and del ex Manchester 28Dec91. Regn cld 07Jan92 as transferred Sri Lanka and painted as **4R-HVB** for operation by Helitours on behalf of Air Lanka with their titles added to basic Scottish European Airways c/s. Later regd as **CR-835**. W/o 28Apr95 on take-off from Jaffna-Palaly Air Force Base for Anuradhapura and Ratmalana, Sri Lanka. Hit by a SAM missile of the LTTE (Liberation Tigers of Tamil Eelam). 3 crew and 42 pax killed.

TT 10,713 hrs, 19,312 ldgs

1758   (234)   Srs.2A/335 LFD

F/f 26May78 as **9Y-TFX**. Del Trinidad and Tobago Air Services Ltd 05Jul78. Del from Woodford 05Jul78 via Keflavik, Narssarssuak, Sept Îles, Greensboro, Nassau and St. Croix to Port of Spain. Entered service 15Jul78 named "Michael Cipriani". Company renamed Trinidad & Tobago (BWIA International) Airways Corporation with effect from 01Jan80. Jumped chocks on engine runs at Port of Spain 28Jan82 and collided with GPU. Damage to No1 engine and propeller and adjacent fuselage. Repaired. WFU. Sold Bradley Air Services Ltd/First Air as **C-GFNW** with del 23Sep87. CofR issued 29Sep87, CofA issued 30Sep87 and engines modified to Mk.534-2. Painted in Bradley Air Services c/s and entered service 01Oct87 with f/n 405. Regd to Bradley Air Services Ltd 24Jun98. Ferried Trois-Rivières, Québec, Canada 29Jun09 for a Period Check. After a period of storage air tested 05Sep09, ferried Iqaluit 18Sep09 and returned to service. Flew last revenue flight 11Feb11 and ferried from Iqaluit to Trois-Rivières 15Feb11 and WFU. CofR cld 20Apr12 and re-issued as **C-GANA** to Air North Charter & Training Ltd 09May12. Arrived Whitehorse 24Jun12 after its ferry from Trois-Rivières. Under conversion to a pure freighter. Due to enter service late 2016 in new Air North c/s.

TT in excess of 39,756 hrs, 44,250 ldgs (figures at 24Jun12)

1759   (238)   Srs.2A/335 LFD

F/f 16Nov78 as **9Y-TGD**. Del Trinidad and Tobago Air Services Ltd 19Dec78. In service 23Dec78. Company renamed Trinidad & Tobago (BWIA International) Airways Corporation with effect from 01Jan80. Lsd Air BVI Ltd as 9Y-TGD from 01Nov to 07Dec84. WFU. Sold Bradley Air Services Ltd/First Air as **C-FBNW** with del 28Sep87. CofR issued 25Sep87, CofA issued 30Sep87 and engines modified to Mk.534-2. Painted in Bradley Air Services c/s and entered service 02Oct87 with f/n 401. Regd Bradley Air Services Ltd 24Jun98. Severely damaged Iqaluit, Nunavut Territory, Canada 03Dec98 after aborted take-off when operating 7F802 to Igloolik. No fatalities. Subsequently w/o. Regn cld 21Apr99.

TT 20,482 hrs, 29,248 ldgs

1760   (241)   Srs.2A/333

F/f 26Apr78 as **G11-9**. Regd as **G-BFVR** to British Aerospace 26Jun78 (CofR G-BFVR/R1) and f/f as such 29Jul78. CofA issued 08Aug78. Del Linhas Aéreas da Guiné-Bissau as G-BFVR 01Dec78 via Lisbon and Las Palmas to Bissau. Regn cld 12Dec78 as sold in Guinea Bissau and regd **J5-GAT**. Company later named Transportes Aéreos da Guiné-Bissau. Later noted newly painted with Air Bissau titles named "Madina de Boie". Sold West Air Sweden AB and ferried ex Guiné via Tenerife and Lisbon arriving Lidköping 27May98 painted as J5-GAT for conversion to a pure freighter. Regd as **SE-LID** to ABN Amro Leasing 06Aug98. Regd GE Capital Equipment Finance AB Jul99 for continued operation by West Air Sweden. Noted Lidköping 27Jul00 named "African Queen".

Regd European Turboprop Management AB 27Sep01. Ferried Lidköping, Sweden 29Sep04 for storage. Regd SG Finans AS Norge 17Jun05. Reduced to spares after cockpit section removed and relocated to the Stenbäcs Flyghistoriska Samlingar Museum 5km from Malmö-Sturup on the e65 road. Regn cld 08May06.

TT 12,859 hrs, 12,511 ldgs

1761   (244)   Srs.2A/344

F/f 22Sep78 as **G-11-10**. Painted as **C6-BEA** in Bahamasair c/s 27Nov78. Amended to **C6-BEB** the following day but not flown as such until 26Jan79. Del Bahamasair as C6-BEB 14Feb79. Regd to Air Manitoba Ltd as **C-FQPE** 30Aug93 following sale to Northland Air Manitoba Ltd. Del Winnipeg 03Sep93. Stored Winnipeg, Manitoba, Canada without use. Regn cld 04Apr05 and b/u.

TT 18,953 hrs, 36,324 ldgs

C6-BEB c/n 1761 of Bahamasair, seen prior to delivery. The fin stripes are blue, yellow and black. (WHC/BAe)

1762   (245)   **Srs.2A/343 LFD**

F/f 23Nov78 as **VP-LAZ**. Del LIAT (1974) Ltd 07Dec78. In service 10Dec78. Re-regd **V2-LAZ** Mar82 after Antiguan Independence 01Nov81. Flew last service 05Jan85 and del ex Antigua for Woodford 18Jan85 as part of Super 748 deal. Sold Air Inuit Ltd at Montréal 21Jan85 during the course of this ferry flight. Regd **C-GCUK**. Nose leg retracted on engine start at La Grande 20Mar88. Repaired. Regd Bradley Air Services Ltd 09Jun93 when lsd Bradley Air Services Ltd/First Air with First Air titles. Regd Air Inuit (1985) Ltd 01Feb95 at end of lse. By Aug04 operated as a pure freighter with cabin windows blanked out and 'Air Inuit Cargo' titles. Advertised for sale summer 2009 and WFU 07Sep10.   ***TT 49,124 hrs, 50,210 ldgs***

1763   (242)   **Srs.2A/348 LFD**

F/f 15Jun79 as **C6-BED**, C6-BEC having originally been allocated and applied to the aircraft. Del Bahamasair 06Jul79. WFU and stored Nassau, Bahamas. Cargo door removed Oct98 for fitment to c/n 1736 by International Air Parts Pty Ltd. Severely damaged by hurricane 'Mitch' 12Oct98 and dumped 10Dec98.

  TT in excess of 18,125 hrs, 35,999 ldgs (figures at 21Jan91)

1764   (248)   **Srs.2A/344**

F/f 25Jul79 as **C6-BEE**, C6-BED having originally been allocated. Del Bahamasair 24Aug79. Del from Nassau via Charlotte to Bar River Airport in Bahamasair c/s without titles 03Apr90. Painted as **F-ODTX** 10May90 and ferried as such via Sault Ste. Marie to Halifax 11May90. Regd to SAEMI Aero des Îles-St-Pierre as F-ODTX 21May90 for operation by Air Saint-Pierre. Named "Île de Miquelon". Lsd Bradley Air Services Ltd/First Air with First Air titles summer 1994. Ferried Saint-Pierre to Goose Bay 30Sep95 then onwards to Søndre Strømfjord and Keflavik 02Oct95 arriving East Midlands 03Oct95. Departed for Nice and Malta 06Oct95 on sale to Ibis Air/Executive Outcomes. Regn cld 13Oct95. Lsd Simba Air Cargo as **5Y-SAL** and ferried from Malta via Heraklion, Luxor and Djibouti to Nairobi 23/25Nov95. Noted Lanseria, South Africa 17Mar97 painted as **HR-AQV** and by May97 had been regd **TN-AFI**. Seen as such Lanseria 30Aug97. Regd as **ZS-XGY** to Dr. J.W.K. Louw 20Oct97. Del Rand 23Oct97 for operation by Intensive Air Ltd and later named "Muffin". Became wedged under rear fuselage of Iberia Airbus A340-313 EC-GJT on ground Johannesburg following hydraulic failure 20May98. Severe damage to port propeller and engine and write off of fin and rudder. Repaired and returned to service 11Sep98 using fin & rudder from c/n 1771 9N-ABR. Noted Jan Smuts with Air Malawi titles to starboard only 20Jan00. Company ceased operations 08Apr02. Sold International Air Parts Pty Ltd of Australia Aug02. Noted stored

Johannesburg International engineless, all white, with Intensive Air titles but no regn visable 17Oct02. Regd AirQuarius Contracts (Pty) Ltd 24Jan03. Due to be parted out at O.R Tambo airport, Johannesburg, South Africa.

    TT 20,114 hrs, 34,213 ldgs

1765   (254)   **Srs.2A/344**

F/f 19Oct79 as **C6-BEF**, C6-BEE having originally been allocated. Del Bahamasair 08Nov79. Sold Air Manitoba Ltd for spares use only Sep93 and b/u.   ***TT 17,123 hrs, 32,688 ldgs***

1766   (250)   **Srs.2A/347**

Regd as **G-BGMN** to British Aerospace Aircraft Group 09Mar79 (CofR G-BGMN/R1). F/f 05Jun79 as G-BGMN having been painted previously as **9Y-TGH**. CofA issued 04Jul79. Regn cld 09Jul79 as sold Trinidad & Tobago and f/f as 9Y-TGH the same day. Del Trinidad and Tobago Air Services Ltd 16Jul79. In service 26Jul79. Company renamed Trinidad & Tobago (BWIA International) Airways Corporation with effect from 01Jan80. Lsd Air BVI Ltd as 9Y-TGH from 08Mar86 to 17Mar86. Sold Euroair Transport Ltd Apr86 for lse to British Airways plc. Restored as **G-BGMN** to Euroair Transport Ltd 08Apr86 (CofR G-BGMN/R2) and del as such ex Port of Spain as BA9824P 08Apr86 arriving Exeter 14Apr86. Stripped to bare metal at Exeter. CofA issued 06Jun86. Del British Airways plc at Heathrow as BA9752E 07Jun86 for repaint in British Airways c/s. Named "Glen Finnan" on port and "Gleann Finonian" on starboard side. Ferried Glasgow for fitting out as BA9833P 14Jun86. Entered service as BA5704 from Glasgow to Aberdeen 07Jul86. Flew last revenue service as BA8935H from Glasgow to Dublin 22Apr89 before positioning back to Glasgow as BA8936P the same date. Ferried from Glasgow to Heathrow as BA8971P 25Apr89 for painting all white at end of lse. Positioned back to Glasgow as BA8975P 29Apr89. Returned Euroair Transport Ltd 05May89 and ferried to Coventry the same day. Ferried Exeter for storage 20May89. Lsd Jersey European Airways Ltd commencing crew training 02Dec89 after painting in full Jersey European c/s. Entered service 23Dec89 between Hurn and Guernsey. Left wing tip struck parked Shorts SD360 while taxiing to the north side of Exeter airport after a flight from Edinburgh 08Jun91. Repaired. Flew last service as JY828 from Manchester to Edinburgh (a mail flight) 03Sep91 and ferried to Exeter the same date as JY031 on return to Euroair Transport Ltd/Alexandra Aviation for storage at end of lse. Regn cld 16Jul92 as transferred Indonesia. Lsd Airfast Services Indonesia P.T. as **PK-OCH**. Ferried Guernsey 07Oct98 and onward to Southend 08Oct98 at end lse painted overall white with grey undersides. Sold Emerald Airways Ltd and restored to them as **G-BGMN** 03Nov98 (CofR G-BGMN/R3). Painted as such by

C6-BEC c/n 1763 at Woodford on 21st May 1979. The registration was corrected to C6-BED prior to delivery to Bahamasair.   *(Ralph Harrison)*

04Nov98. CofA issued 20Nov98 and ferried Liverpool 21Nov98 still overall white. Entered service 07Jan99. Company's AOC suspended 04May06 and aircraft stored Liverpool. Sold International Air Parts Pty Ltd 16Oct06. Ferried Blackpool 23Nov06. Regd PTB (Emerald) Pty Ltd 11Dec06 (CofR G-BGMN/R4). Regn cld 04May07 as transferred Bangladesh. Painted as **S2-ADW** 05May07 and ferried ex Blackpool via Nice 11May07 on lse to Bismillah Airlines Ltd. Noted Dhaka with Bismillah Airlines titles 12Mar08. Noted active at Dhaka 21Oct11 and at Cox's Bazar Jan16.

TT in excess of 23,679 hrs, 38,079 ldgs (figures at 11May07)

1767   (256)   Srs.2A/347

Regd as **G-BGMO** to British Aerospace Aircraft Group 09Mar79 (CofR G-BGMO/R1). F/f 29Aug79 as **9Y-TGI**. UK regn cld as sold abroad 31Aug79. Del Trinidad and Tobago Air Services Ltd 22Nov79. In service 27Nov79. Company renamed Trinidad & Tobago (BWIA International) Airways Corporation with effect from 01Jan80. Lsd Air BVI Ltd as 9Y-TGI from 26Oct85 to 27Nov85. Lsd LIAT (1974) Ltd as **V2-LDB** from 19Dec85 to 16Jan86. Restored as **9Y-TGI**. Restored as **G-BGMO** to Euroair Transport Ltd 08Apr86 (CofR G-BGMO/R2) after sale to them for lse to British Airways plc. Del ex Port of Spain as BA9825P 08Apr86 arriving Exeter 14Apr86. Stripped to bare metal at Exeter. CofA issued 12May86. Del to British Airways plc at Heathrow as BA9819P 22May86 for repaint in British Airways c/s. Named "Glen Goyne" on port and "Gleann Goinn" on starboard side. Ferried Glasgow 28May86 as BA9823P for fitting out. Entered service as BA5820 from Glasgow to Stornoway 20Jun86. Flew last service as BA5849 from Belfast to Glasgow 19Apr89. Ferried to Heathrow as BA8968E 20Apr89 for repaint all white at end of lse. Ferried back to Glasgow as BA8972P 25Apr89. Returned Euroair Transport Ltd 03May89 and ferried to Coventry and Exeter for storage the same day. Lsd Jersey European Airways Ltd commencing crew training 26Oct89 after painting in full Jersey European c/s. Entered service 14Nov89 between Blackpool and the Isle of Man. Flew last service as JY828 from Manchester to Edinburgh (a mail flight) 05Oct91 and ferried to Exeter the same date as JY031 on return to Euroair Transport Ltd/Alexandra Aviation for storage at the end of lse. Painted overall white and ferried Glasgow 07Feb92. Lsd Mount Cook Airlines and del Christchurch 02Dec93. Regn cld 07Dec93 as transferred New Zealand and regd **ZK-MCB** named "Te Anau". Painted in full Mount Cook c/s. Flew last service as NZ5721 from Taupo to Christchurch 31Dec95. Departed Christchurch 08Feb96 at end of lse on ferry to Exeter where it arrived 21Feb96. Restored as **G-BGMO** to Emerald Airways Ltd 23Feb96 (CofR G-BGMO/R3) on sale to them. CofA issued 23Apr96. Painted in full Emerald Airways c/s at Woodford between 24Apr and 06May96. Operated in pax config after del from Woodford to Liverpool 06May99. Entered service 10May96. Later converted to freighter config. Ferried Blackpool to Norwich for repaint as JEM70E 02Dec04 returning Blackpool in Emerald's new c/s as JEM70E 10Dec04. Ferried Blackpool-Liverpool as JEM75E 17Dec04 and returned to service. Company's AOC suspended 04May06 and aircraft ferried from Hurn to Blackpool as JEM983Q 05May06. Sold International Air Parts Pty Ltd 16Oct06. Regd PTB (Emerald) Pty Ltd 12Dec06 (CofR G-BGMO/R4). Regn cld 18Mar08 as transferred Bangladesh and incorrectly painted as **S2-AXX** the same date in Emerald c/s without titles. Repainted as **S2-AAX** 19Mar08. Ferried Blackpool-Nice on del to Easy Fly Express Ltd 25Apr08 and onwards to Heraklion, Sharm el Sheikh, Doha and Karachi en route Dhaka. Retains Emerald's new c/s with 'Easy Fly Express' titles. Noted 06Apr15 at Jessore, Bangladesh now with Bismillah Airlines titles and still active at Cox's Bazar 28Sep15.

TT in excess of 22,311 hrs, 37,859 ldgs (figures at 05May06)

1768   (243)   Srs.2B/357 LFD

Series 2B prototype and demonstrator although first regd as **G-BGJV** to British Aerospace 05Feb79 as a Series 2A aircraft (CofR G-BGJV/R1). F/f 22Jun79, CofA issued 29Aug80. C/o European demonstrations 24/27Jun80 and European/Middle East demonstrations 01/11Jul80. Shown Farnborough Air Show 29Aug to 08Sep80. Amended to a Srs.2B/357 08Sep80. C/o demonstrations/tours to Yugoslavia and Greece 09/13Sep80, the USA, Ecuador and Colombia 29Sep to 12Dec80, Libya 20/22Dec80, Angola 14/24Jan81 and Mexico 26Jan to 14Feb81. Shown Paris Air Show early Jun81 with show No. 236 with additional DLT titles. Lsd Deutsche Luftverkehrs-gesellschaft mbH (DLT) in BAe house c/s with DLT titles from 20Feb to 08May81 and again from 15/25Jun81 with in service dates of 25Feb81 and 16Jun81 and withdrawal from service dates of 07May81 and 24Jun81 respectively. Painted in Air Virginia c/s Jul81 and lsd Air Virginia 05Aug to 19Sep81. Returned Woodford 21Sep81. Demonstrated Cascade Airways Inc 26Oct81 to 01Dec81. Lsd Deutsche Luftverkehrsgesellschaft mbH (DLT) for a third time from 15Feb82 to 29Mar82, entering service 16Feb82 and being withdrawn from service 26Mar82. Lsd Airline of the Marshall Islands with del as G-BGJV 27Jun82 arriving Majuro 06Jul82. Regn cld 05Jul82 as transferred Marshall Islands and regd **MI-GJV** 09Jul82. In service 10Jul82. WFU 24Dec82 and Marshall Islands regn cld 25Dec82. Restored as **G-BGJV** to British Aerospace plc 26Dec82 (CofR G-BGJV/R2) and del ex Majuro 27Dec82 arriving Woodford 07Jan83. Noted at Woodford with 'Air Sinai' titles 13Apr83. Used as a support aircraft for HS125-800 demonstrations in the Middle East from 14Oct to 12Nov83. C/o Yugoslav demonstrations 22/25Nov83. F/f with Rolls-Royce Dart Mk.551s 11Jul84. C/o engine trials at Marrakech, Morocco 14Aug/18Sep84. Engines reverted to standard fit. Del British Airways plc as G-BGJV 08Jan85 under a lse/purchase agreement. In service as BA5814 from Glasgow to Benbecula 10Jan85. Inaugurated service to Southampton from Aberdeen, Manchester and Birmingham as BA5681 18Nov85. Named "Glen Avon" on port and "Gleann Athfhinn" on starboard side. Temporarily named "St Magnus of Orkney" from 01Jun87 until at least 13Nov87 when noted at Southampton still marked as such. Flew last service for British Airways as BA5704 from Birmingham to Glasgow 23Nov91. Returned BAe at end of lse 29Nov91. Positioned Manchester 05Dec91. Sold Sri Lanka Air Force and del ex Manchester 18Dec91. Regn cld 17Jan92 as transferred Sri Lanka and painted as **4R-HVA** for operation by Helitours on behalf of Air Lanka with their titles added to basic British Airways c/s. Later regd as **CR-834**. W/o 29Apr95 on approach to Jaffna-Palaly Air Force Base on a flight from Ratmalana and Anuradhapura, Sri Lanka. Hit by a SAM missile of the LTTE (Liberation Tigers of Tamil Eelam). 3 crew and 49 pax killed.

TT 13,771 hrs, 18,666 ldgs

1769   (246)   Srs.2A/353

F/f 04Apr79 as **G11-11**. Del Air Sénégal as **6V-AEO** 12Jul79. Lsd Tunisavia by 22May80 in Air Sénégal c/s with Tunisavia titling and named "Casamance". Operated Air Malta services during the summer of 1981 on a regular basis. Returned Air Sénégal 1983. W/o on take-off Tambacounda, Sénégal 01Feb97. 3 crew and 20 pax killed, 29 pax survived.

TT 17,582 hrs, 20,191 ldgs

6V-AEO c/n 1769 of Air Sénégal, seen in the airline's dark green colour-scheme with small fin logo.

ZS-XGE c/n 1770 of Intensive Air at Johannesburg-Rand.   *(Richard J. Church)*

1770   (252)   Srs.2A/351

Regd as **G-BGPR** to Hawker Siddeley Aviation Ltd 04Apr79 (CofR G-BGPR/R1). F/f 29Jun79, CofA issued 29Aug79. Del Transkei Airways Corporation as G-BGPR 30Aug79 arriving Johannesburg 02Sep79. Repainted as **ZS-XGE** named "Ulundi" 11Sep79. UK regn cld 14Sep79 as sold in South Africa. In service 01Nov79, operating as KV161 from Johannesburg to Umtata. Sold Care Airlines (Pty) Ltd Jul93. Sold Intensive Air Ltd 14Nov93 and initially operated on behalf of Care Airlines (Pty) Ltd. Noted late '97 named "Pudding". Company ceased operations 08Apr02. Sold International Air Parts Pty Ltd of Australia Aug02 and converted to a pure freighter at Lanseria. Painted in a blue/white c/s. Regd AirQuarius Contracts (Pty) Ltd 22Jan03. Regn cld 28Feb05. Sold Best Aviation Ltd as **S2-AAT** arriving Dhaka 07Mar05. Advertised for sale 14Mar11 after company ceased trading in 2009.   *TT 18,225 hrs, 11,747 ldgs*

1771   (247)   Srs.2A/352 LFD

F/f 18Oct79 as **9N-ABR**. Del Royal Nepal Airlines Corporation 12Nov79. Overran runway Meghauli, Nepal 25Apr96 and nose gear failed and subsequently w/o. No fatalities among 4 crew and 27 pax. Purchased by International Aviation Pty Ltd early '98 for spares recovery only. Large freight door fitted to c/n 1737 and fin fitted to c/n 1764.

TT in excess of 13,139 hrs, 19,453 ldgs (figures at 30Apr93)

1772   (249)   Srs.2A/360 LFD

F/f 03Dec79 as **5R-MJA**. Del Air Madagascar 04Jan80. Uprated to Srs.2B/360 after del. Named "Kandreho". Lsd Sociedade Açoreana de Transportes Aéreos (SATA) as 5R-MJA from 21Jun to 14Sep86. Lsd Air Réunion from 08Jan to 11Feb88 and to Sociedade Açoreana de Transportes Aéreos (SATA) from 23Jun to 13Sep88. WFU 28May99. Sold International Air Parts Pty Ltd for lse to Horizon Airlines Pty Ltd Jul01. Ferried Antananarivo, Mahé, Male, Padang, Broome and Alice Springs arriving Bankstown 17Oct01 in full Air Madagascar c/s with titles. Regd as **VH-IPA** to Horizon Airlines Pty Ltd 21Nov01. Converted to a pure freighter but never entered service. Horizon Airlines placed in Administration 14Oct03 and later ceased operations. Stored Bankstown. Regd IAP Group Australia Pty Ltd 06Apr05. Noted painted with all white top and fin with double red cheat lines Dec05. Air-tested 26Jun06. Sold Trackmark Cargo Ltd. Del ex Bankstown 28Jul06 via Alice Springs, Port Hedland, Cocos, Colombo, Male, Seychelles and Mombasa arriving Nairobi-

Wilson 04Aug06. Regn cld 14Aug06 as exported Kenya and regd **5Y-TCO**. Repainted in a grey, white and black c/s. WFU after several weeks of storage at Goma, DRC following an abortive sale. Ferried Nairobi-Jomo Kenyatta to Nairobi-Wilson 29Sep08 for further storage. Sold 17Sep09. Departed Wilson late Nov09 for ops by Safe Air Company Kenya Ltd (SAC) from a forward base at Juba, Sudan. In early Dec10 on a flight from Wajir (northeast Kenya) to Nairobi-Wilson, No2 engine suffered an oil loss and on shutdown in flight the engine seized. On landing Wilson all four mainwheels burst and the aircraft was put in store pending insurance assessment. Back in service by Jun12. Stored at Juba since 18Apr15 with a seized No.1 engine and propeller damage. Noted active at Nairobi-Jomo Kenyatta International 24Jun16 and late Aug16.

TT in excess of 25,401 hrs, 30,197 ldgs (figures at 29Sep08)

1773   (251)   Srs.2B/360 LFD

F/f 29Oct80 as **5R-MJB**. Del Air Madagascar 28Nov80. Lsd Réunion Air Service as 5R-MJB from 18Apr to 01May83. Lsd Ecuato Guineana de Aviacion as 5R-MJB from 20Aug86. Aircraft damaged Malabo after collision with building while taxiing 04Aug87. Repaired and re-entered service with Air Madagascar 21Jun88. WFS 28May99. Sold International Air Parts Pty Ltd for lse to Horizon Airlines Pty Ltd Jul01. Ferried Antananarivo, Mahé, Male, Medan, Denpasar, Darwin, Cairns and Brisbane arriving Bankstown 31Jul01 in Air Madagascar c/s without titles. Regd as **VH-IPB** to Horizon Airlines Pty Ltd 17Aug01. Converted to a pure freighter. Entered service late Apr02 and wet-lsd to Australian air Express Pty Ltd. Horizon Airlines placed in administration 14Oct03 and later ceased operations. Flew last service for Australian air Express as XM7022 from Melbourne to Sydney 24Oct03 before ferry to Bankstown the same date for storage. Used for crew training Oct04. Remains in storage in a derelict condition, regn cld 18Nov14.

Regn cld 05Nov04. Lsd Z-Airways & Services Ltd for three years as **S2-ADL** with del ex Bankstown as ZAW777 14Dec04 via Darwin 17Dec04 and onwards to Denpasar. Noted active Dhaka with 'Zoom Airways' titles 25Jul05. Repossessed by IAP and ferried ex Dhaka 17Oct08 via New Delhi to Karachi. On 21Oct08 it continued to Muscat-Seeb and Salalah. On 22Oct it continued via Sana'a to Addis Ababa before a final ferry to Nairobi-Jomo Kenyatta and to Nairobi-Wilson on 23Oct08 for maintenance and storage. Regd as **VH-DQY** to IAP Group Australia Pty Limited 09Jun11.

TT 22,648 hrs, 27,013 ldgs

1774 (253) Srs.2B/401 LFD

F/f 26May80 as **G-11-12** as a Srs.2A aircraft direct to Prestwick. Modified to a Srs.2B and f/f as such 25Nov81. Ferried Woodford 19Feb82. Briefly painted in British Aerospace c/s Sep82. Regd as **G-BKLD** to British Aerospace plc 17Nov82 (CofR G-BKLD/R1) and f/f as such 03Dec82. CofA issued 16Dec82. Displayed at Paris Air Show 24May to 02Jun83 in full Bouraq c/s with show No 197. Del Bouraq Indonesia Airlines P.T. 06Jun83. UK regn cld 10Jun83 as transferred Indonesia and regd **PK-IHO**, being painted in these marks in Singapore on the same date. Del Jakarta 11Jun83. In service 15Jun83. Structural damage following heavy landing Yogyakarta 13Oct97 and grounded. Company ceased operations Mar05. Still stored Yogyakarta, Indonesia in Bouraq c/s 26Nov06 minus engines, props and various components and looking beyond recovery.

TT in excess of 20,849 hrs, 13,602 ldgs (figures at 31Oct92)

1775 (255) Srs.2A/369 LFD

F/f 06Jun80 as **G-11-13** direct to Prestwick. F/f after Prestwick mods 18Mar81 as G-11-13. F/f as **XT-MAN** 28Jul81. Del Prestwick to Manchester 31Jul81 and to Woodford 02Aug81. Del Force Aérienne de Haute-Volta as XT-MAN 05Aug81. Following country's renaming on 04Aug84, operator renamed Force Aérienne de Burkina Faso. Noted parked in trees with engine cowlings off at Ouagadougou, Burkina Faso 25Jan09.

TT in excess of 2,828 hrs, 2,451 ldgs (figures at 25Aug93)

1776 (257) Srs.2B/371 LFD

F/f 20Jun80 as **G-11-14** direct to Prestwick as a Srs.2A aircraft. Modified to Srs.2B and f/f as such 12Jan81. F/f as **FAC-1108** in full Satena c/s 30Jul81 and ferried Woodford 31Jul81. Del Fuerza Aérea Colombiana as FAC-1108 01Aug81 for operation by Servicio de Aeronavegación a Territorios Nacionales (SATENA). Later named "Puerto Asis". Renamed "Arauca". Sold West Air Sweden A.B. with regn **SE-LIB** rsvd 06Aug97. Ferried via Goose Bay 09Aug97. Regd to ABN Amro Leasing as SE-LIB 10Dec97. Regd GE Capital Equipment Finance AB Jul99 for continued operation by West Air Sweden as a pure freighter. Regd European Turboprop Management AB 27Sep01. Ferried Arlanda-Southend as PT900 for repaint 06Aug03. R/o in full new West Air c/s with West Air Europe titles 15Aug03 & ferried Malmö as PT901 the same day. A lse/sale deal to Stellair of Spain due to commence in Apr05 was not finalised. Regd SG Finans AS Norge 17Jun05. Sold ALAIRE – Líneas Aéreas Alaire, S.L. and del ex Lidköping 05May06 with grey top and dark blue lower fuselage and engine cowlings with Alaire Cargo titles on fin and Alaire titles on fuselage. Initially flown and maintained by West Air Sweden. Returned West Air by Oct06. Flew last revenue West Air 748 service from Stockholm to Malmö 24May07 and re-del ALAIRE the same day. Flew last ALAIRE service as ALR7042 from Madrid to Santiago de Compostela 26Oct07. Returned West Air Sweden and remained in store Santiago until sold 748 Air Services Ltd. Ferried ex Santiago de Compostela 28Nov07 via

FAC1108 c/n 1776. The only Large Freight Door-equipped HS748 operated by SATENA, the Colombian military airline. The photo was taken at Prestwick, Scotland, prior to delivery in 1981. *(WHC/BAe)*

SE-LIB c/n 1776, the only HS748 to be painted in West Air Sweden's new colours, seen at Southend on 15th August 2003. The aircraft is seen at roll-out after painting. *(Håkan Frylén)*

Palma, Malta, Luxor and Khartoum arriving Nairobi-Wilson 30Nov07, Regn cld 05Dec07. Marks **5Y-YKN** reserved but adopted the marks **5Y-HAJ** by 01Feb08. ALAIRE titles and logo removed. Entered service 04Mar08. Sat on tail at Juba Sudan while unloading 06Aug08 sustaining some damage. Continued to Lokichoggio the same day before ferrying to Nairobi-Wilson for permanent repair 07Aug08. Returned to service 08Jul09. Painted overall white with blue engine cowlings and no titles. W/O landing Rubkona airstrip, South Sudan after a flight from Juba 17Feb14. Struck two vehicles parked near airstrip and caught fire. 1 crew killed, 3 seriously injured.

TT in excess of 34,169 hrs, 35,556 ldgs (figures at 25Jun12)

1777   (258)   Srs.2A/372

F/f 02May80 as **CS-TAO**. Del Sociedade Açoreana de Transportes Aéreos (SATA) 23May80. Sold British Aerospace plc 14Oct89 and immediately lsd Linhas Aéreas Regionais S.A. Lsd SATA - Air Açores from 10Jun90 all white with SATA titles. Ferried via Oporto to Manchester 16Oct90 at end of lse for care and maintenance by Dan-Air Engineering Ltd. Regd as **G-BVOV** to Emerald Airways Ltd 21Jun94 (CofR G-BVOV/R1). Ferried Manchester-Blackpool 12Jul94 for storage. Ferried Exeter 14Mar95. CofA issued 12May95 after air test the same day and ferried Exeter-Liverpool and entered service later the same day. Operated in Emerald Airways c/s as a pure freighter. Nose undercarriage collapsed Dublin 29May00. Repaired and returned to service 06Jul00. Overran runway on landing Guernsey 08Mar06 from Coventry and Jersey. Minor damage repaired and returned to service. Company's AOC suspended 04May06 and aircraft ferried from Isle of Man to Blackpool, U.K. as JEM40M the same date. Sold International Air Parts Pty Ltd 16Oct06. Regd PTB (Emerald) Pty Ltd 12Dec06 (CofR G-BVOV/R2). Wings removed by early Apr09 at start of dismantling process. Despatched on low loaders from Blackpool on 26May09 following sale to Capernway Diving and Leisure Ltd. Regn cld as PWFU 04Dec09. After reassembly, was sunk into the lake at Jackdaw Quarry at Carnforth, Lancs 29Mar10 as a feature at this diving school.

TT 22,180 hrs, 33,154 ldgs

1778   (259)   Srs.2B/399 LFD

F/f 12Aug81 as **G-11-20** direct to Hawarden for completion. F/f after completion Hawarden 12Dec81 still as G-11-20 and returned Woodford 22Dec81. F/f as **5U-BAS** 21Jan82. Del Air Niger Société Nationale as 5U-BAS 22Jan82. Not flown from early 1985 and stored Niamey. CofA renewed late Sep/early Oct87 and test flown before return to limited service. Sold Holter Leasing Inc and lsd V. Kelner Airways Ltd as **C-FKTL** 21Oct91.

Ferried ex Niamey 31Oct91 via Manchester 04-06Nov91 in Air Niger c/s without titles. Arrived Canada 08Nov91. CofR and CofA issued 19Nov91. Entered service 28Nov91 with f/n 802. Company renamed Wasaya Airways Ltd and regd to them 05Jan93. Sold West Air Sweden AB with regn **SE-LIC**(2) rsvd 16Feb98. Ferried via Iqaluit and Reykjavik arriving Lidköping 19Feb98. Canadian regn cld 20Feb98. Noted in full West Air Sweden c/s at Lidköping 03Mar98. Regd ABN Amro Leasing/ABN Amro Bank 20Mar98. Regd GE Capital Equipment Finance AB Jul99 for continued operation by West Air Sweden as a pure freighter. Regd European Turboprop Management AB 27Sep01. Noted Helsinki 01Jun05 painted overall white without titles. Was painted overall white for lse Stellair of Spain 2005 but the contract was not finalised. Regd SG Finans AS Norge 05Aug05. Was due for sale ALAIRE – Líneas Aéreas Alaire, S.L. Noted Palma painted overall white with West Air Europe titles 31Dec06 having been operated on behalf of ALAIRE by Jun06. Flew last service for ALAIRE as ALR119 from Menorca to Palma 03Aug07. Returned West Air at Lidköping at end of lse 04Aug07. Stored pending sale. Regn cld 25Jan08 as exported Kenya. Sold 748 Air Services Ltd and painted overall white. Marks **5Y-YKO** reserved. Reserved marks not used and painted as **5Y-BVQ**. Del ex Lidköping 23Feb08 via Sofia, Luxor and Khartoum arriving Nairobi-Wilson 25Feb08 after nightstopping Sofia and Luxor. CofA issued 24Sep08 and entered service 28Sep08 all white with blue engines and no titles. Noted Nairobi-Jomo Kenyatta with 'cargo' titles on fin 22Jan09. Temporarily parked at Nairobi-Wilson on 14Jun11. Noted active again at Juba, South Sudan 26Sep14. W/o Panyagor, Jonglei State, South Sudan, on a flight from Juba 14Nov14 while operated on behalf of Global Airlift Ltd on a relief flight for the Lutheran World Federation. Two pilots killed, one travelling engineer survived.

TT in excess of 16,095 hrs, 18,674 ldgs (figures at 14Jun11)

1779   (260)   Srs.2B/398

F/f 02Dec81 as **G-11-19**. Del Air Niger Société Nationale as **5U-BAR** 23Dec81. Not flown from early 1985 and stored Niamey. CofA renewed late Sep/early Oct87 and test flown before return to limited service. Sold Sold Holter Leasing Inc and lsd V. Kelner Airways Ltd as **C-GDTD** 21Oct91. Ferried ex Niamey 31Oct91 via Manchester 04-06Nov91 in Air Niger c/s without titles. Arrived Canada 08Nov91. CofR and CofA issued 19Nov91. Entered service 19Dec91 with f/n 803. Company renamed Wasaya Airways Ltd and regd to them 05Jan93. Garret GTCP-36-150W APU fitted by Springer Aerospace 17Dec96. Fitted in rear fuselage aft of the pressure bulkhead. Regd Wasaya Airways Limited Partnership 22Jun00. WFU 20Oct00 and returned lessor. Stored Thunder Bay, Ontario awaiting sale. APU removed. Sold 748 Air Services Ltd and del ex Thunder Bay

5Y-YKM c/n 1779 of 748 Air Services Ltd at Nairobi-Wilson.   *(Allan Fantham)*

G-BICK c/n 1782 photographed prior to being re-registered in the United States as N748AV for Air Virginia in 1981.

14Feb04 via Goose Bay & Keflavik arriving Blackpool 15Feb04. Departed via Naples 16Feb04. Regd Holter Leasing Inc 05Mar04. Seen Nairobi 08Mar04. Regn cld 10Mar04 but ferried Lockichoggio still as C-GDTD 11Mar04. Regd **5Y-YKM** and painted in company's blue & white c/s. W/o landing Tonj, Southern Sudan after a flight from Juba 20Dec09. Overran the runway and collided with a new group of houses being built. No fatalitics to 4 crew and 37 pax on board but one on ground killed and one missing. Nose severely damaged and port landing gear ripped off.

TT 15,620 hrs, 16,656 ldgs

1780 (261) Srs.2B/362

F/f 27Mar81 as **G-11-16**. Del Air Madagascar as **5R-MTI** 16Apr81 in a VIP configuration for Government use. Parked Antananarivo by 04Apr95. Re-regd as **5R-MUT** Dec96 having earlier been noted as such 17Jun96. Stored at Rand by Oct96. After lengthy legal actions, ownership still not resolved. Noted engineless in Intensive Air hangar 22Oct98 and again in same hangar Sep00 devoid of many parts. Seen outside at Rand Airport, Johannesburg, South Africa being further stripped of parts 20Nov01.

TT in excess of 5,773 hrs, 6,893 ldgs (figures at 31Dec91)

1781 (262) Srs.2B/376

F/f 21Dec80 as **G-11-15**. Used for certification flying for the Sperry SPZ-500 autopilot. Converted to Srs.2B/FAA. Regd as **G-BIRF** to British Aerospace plc 12Mar81 (CofR G-BIRF/R1). CofA issued 16Apr81, the same day aircraft del ex Woodford as G-BIRF to Aero Spacelines Inc for completion. UK regn cld 29Dec81 as transferred USA. Del Cascade Airways Inc as **N117CA** 29Dec81. In service 01Feb82. Company filed for Chapter 11 Bankruptcy Protection 21Aug85 and aircraft withdrawn from service. Advertised for sale by FAA after default on guaranteed FAA loan. Stored Phoenix with effect from 07Jan86. Regn cld Apr88. Sold Bradley Air Services Ltd/First Air as **C-GBFA** 15Apr88 and del 24May88. CofR issued 01Jun88, CofA issued 03Jun88. In service 07Jun88 in First Air c/s with f/n 402. Lsd Thunderbird Tours Inc with del Vancouver 24Apr94. Entered service on a charter from Vancouver to Muddy Lake and return 26Apr94. Regd Thunderbird Tours Inc 16Dec94. Returned Bradley Air Services Ltd/First Air Oct95. Regd Bradley Air Services Ltd 24Jun98. WFU and ferried Carp, Ontario,

Canada from Yellowknife 05Nov02 for storage. B/u 2004. Regn cld as WFU 18Nov04. Believed to be the second fuselage noted at Ed's Autoparts at Arnprior, Ontario 09Oct09 and still present 06Sep10.

TT 30,570 hrs, 32,640 ldgs

1782 (263) Srs.2B/FAA

Regd as **G-BICK** to British Aerospace Aircraft Group 27Aug80 (CofR G-BICK/R1) as a Srs.2A although aircraft built as a Srs.2B airframe. F/f 12Dec80. Del Aero Spacelines Inc as G-BICK ex Woodford 15Dec80 for completion. Finished to Srs.2B/FAA standard and f/f as G-BICK 03Sep81. UK regn cld 18Sep81 as transferred USA and f/f as **N748AV** the same date. Del Air Virginia as N748AV 01Oct81. WFU Jun84 and del to British Aerospace Inc for storage at Manassas. Flown to Oklahoma City for further storage from 10Oct95 to 02Apr86. Del Manchester 06Apr86 in full Air Virginia c/s pending sale. Painted as **G-11-3** in full Air Virginia c/s and flown as such 15Aug86. Ferried East Midlands 16Sep86. US regn cld Mar87. Painted in SATA Air Açores c/s and test flown as G-11-3 20May87 from East Midlands. Lsd SATA Air Açores and del ex East Midlands as **CS-TAP** 02Jun87. Ferried from Oporto to Manchester for storage 22Jan91 on return to British Aerospace for care and maintenance by FFV Aerotech. Painted in Transair Cambodia c/s as **G-11-782** and flown as such 19Jun92 but not del. Restored as **G-BICK** to British Aerospace plc – Regional Aircraft 22Jul92 (CofR G-BICK/R2) and flown as such 24Jul92. Storage continued at Manchester. Ferried Exeter 05Oct94. Regd Jetstream Aircraft Ltd 02Dec94 (CofR G-BICK/R3). Lsd Awood Air Ltd and painted in their c/s. Regn cld 03Mar95 as transferred Canada. Painted as **C-GHSF** and del via Newcastle 04Mar95. CofR issued 24Apr95. Ferried via Iqualuit and Reykjavik 20Sep99 arriving Blackpool 21Sep99. Ferry continued via Luton 24Sep99 and Faro 25Sep89 en route South Africa. Regn cld 04Oct99 and regd as **ZS-OJU** to Hering Aviation (Pty) Ltd 07Oct99 for operation by AirQuarius Aviation (Pty) Ltd. Lsd GAMEC (Angola) Apr00 to Feb01. Regd AirQuarius Air Charter (Pty) Ltd 09Apr01. Fitted with tailplane mounted fin spotlights and painted in a red, blue, gold and white c/s. Noted Lanseria 21Nov01 named "African Dream" stripped out as a freighter. W/o 01Jun02 in the Outeniqua mountains on go-around after intial approach George on a mail flight from Bloemfontein, South Africa. 2 crew and 1 pax (Hansie Cronje, the former South African cricket captain) killed. Regn cld 31Jan03.

TT 14,226 hrs, 19,789 ldgs

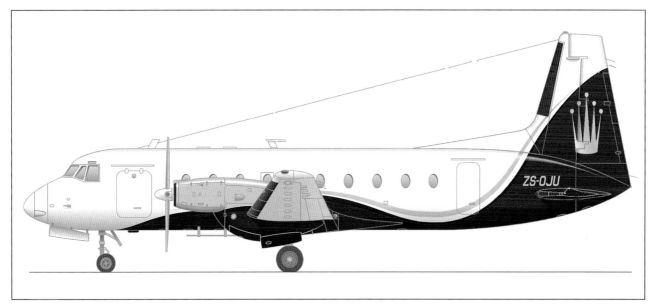

ZS-OJU c/n 1782 of AirQuarius in their smart red, blue, gold and white colour-scheme.   *(Mike Zoeller)*

C-GRXE c/n 1783 of First Air/Bradley Air Services Ltd on lease from BAe Systems in 1985.   *(Fred Barnes collection)*

1783   (264)   Srs.2B/FAA

F/f 14Dec80 as **N749LL**. Del Air Illinois Inc 20Dec80. Del British Aerospace Inc 15Oct82 at Washington-Dulles and stored. Air-tested 08Jul83 and ferried Woodford 11Jul83. Lsd Air Virginia Inc with del ex Woodford 12Aug83 in basic Air Illinois c/s without titling. Air Virginia titles applied in the USA. Withdrawn from service Jun84 and returned to British Aerospace Inc. Re-regd **N748BA** Jul84. Lsd Calm Air International Ltd from 30Aug to 04Oct84. Lsd Eastern Provincial Airways (1963) Ltd from 23Oct84 and operated by Air Maritime in full c/s. Regn cld Jan85 and regd **C-GRXE** Mar85, fleet number 306. Del Manchester at end of lse 20Apr85 regd as C-GRXE in Air Maritime c/s for care and maintenance by Dan-Air Engineering Ltd.

Painted with 'Inter City' titles for a short period for a frustrated leasing deal. Air tested as **G-11-10** from Manchester 03Jul85 before del the following day as **C-GRXE** on an initial one month lse to Bradley Air Services Ltd which was extended to 20Nov85. Operated with an all white fin and with First Air fuselage titles. Regn cld 26Nov85 and regd **V2-LDA** for lse to LIAT (1974) Ltd from 21Nov85 to 07Dec85 while c/n 1800 was loaned to British Aerospace plc for demonstrations in Ecuador. Del Woodford 11Dec85 and painted as **G-11-1**. Del as such to Dan-Air Engineering at Manchester 06Jan86 for maintenance. Regd as **G-BMJU** to British Aerospace plc Aircraft Group 10Jan86 (CofR

G-BMJU/R1). F/f as G-BMJU 03Feb86. Del ex Manchester 07Feb86 arriving Johannesburg 10Feb86 as G-BMJU with British Aerospace titles on sale to Bop-Air (Pty) Ltd. Regn cld 12Feb86 as transferred South Africa and regd as **ZS-LSO** to Mmabatho Air Services (Pty) Ltd 25Feb86. Painted in full Bop-Air orange and blue c/s at Johannesburg and h/o 26Mar86 before entering service 28Mar86. Company marketed as Sun Air from Jan94. Sold Executive Aerospace (Pty) Ltd May96 and regd to Aerospace Express (Pty) Ltd. Lsd Zimbabwe Express Airlines for a period in 1996. Seen operating for Alliance Air Sep98. Noted Johannesburg Apr02 in 'AIR MAX-GABON' c/s. Lsd Air Max-Gabon Apr to Sep02. Lsd Pelican Air Services CC May03. Noted Johannesburg International 31May03 with 'Pelican Air Services' titles and a pelican image on fin. Titles & fin scheme removed Jul04. Extended maintenance lay-up with effect from 04Jul05. Executive Aerospace liquidated on 27Feb08. Noted in external storage Johannesburg, O.R. Tambo, South Africa with several parts missing Sep08. B/u by Aug12.

TT 19,133 hrs, 21,599 ldgs

1784   (265)   Srs.2B/378

F/f 13Mar81 as **D-AHSA**. Del Deutsche Luftverkehrsgesellschaft mbH (DLT) 23Mar81. To Woodford for autopilot mods 23Jul to 12Aug81. Lsd British Airways plc with del to Glasgow from

Frankfurt as DW940 10Mar88. Regd as **G-BOHY** to British Airways plc 11Mar88 (CofR G-BOHY/R1). Ferried from Glasgow to Heathrow as BA9806E 24Mar88 for painting in full British Airways c/s. On completion del Heathrow to Glasgow as BA9819E 29Mar88 named "Glen Shee" on port and "Gleann Sidhe" on starboard side. CofA issued 02Apr88. In service as BA876 from Glasgow to Tegel via Manchester and Münster 03Apr88. Flew last service as BA5789 from Lerwick to Manchester via Aberdeen 25Oct91 before ferrying to Heathrow as BA9736E 28Oct91 for painting overall grey. Positioned from Heathrow to Glasgow 02Nov91 as BA9748E and placed in storage. Returned lessor 31Dec91. Regd to BAF Aircraft Engineering Ltd 17Jan92 (CofR G-BOHY/R2) and ferried to Southend for storage. Ferried Glasgow 29Dec93 for continued storage. Ferried Prestwick 14Apr94. Regd Clewer Aviation Ltd 29Jun94 (CofR G-BOHY/R3). Ferried Southend 18Oct94. Regn cld 26Oct94 as transferred Nepal, the same day aircraft r/o as **9N-ADE** for lse to Necon Air Ltd by Clewer Aviation Ltd. Del ex Southend 27Oct94 arriving Kathmandu 30Oct94. Entered service 06Nov94. WFU 03Jan01. Export CofA issued 02Jul01. Sold Executive Aerospace (Pty) Ltd and ferried ex Kathmandu 21Aug01 arriving Johannesburg International 27Aug01. Regn **ZS-KLC** originally assigned but not used. Regd to Aerospace Express (Pty) Ltd 18Oct01 as **ZS-TPW** (in honour of the company's former Tech Records Manager **T**om **P**ommery-**W**ard). Noted Johannesburg 20Nov01 stripped to bare metal except fin (still in Necon Air c/s). Noted hangared Johannesburg 17Oct02 still being readied for service. Seen fully painted in Executive Aerospace c/s at Johannesburg International 08Mar03. By 21Jun03 was carrying 'Sake Rapport' titles. Lsd Comores Aviation and ferried to Moroni 25Jun04 painted overall white with Comores Aviation titles named "Youmna". Entered service 07Jul04. Returned Executive Aerospace (Pty) Ltd 10Feb05. Lsd Comores Aviation for a second time 22Jul05 until Oct05 and again from ?? to 17May06. Ferried Malabo, Equatorial Guinea 06Jun06 on a 12 month lsc to Euroguineana de Aviación. Seen Douala 25Jul06 with Euroguineana de Aviación titles and Malabo 31Aug06 with orange fin, white fuselage and dark blue engines similarly titled. At Malabo 08Nov06 similarly marked but by 18Nov06 was noted Johannesburg without titles. Seen Dzaoudzi, Mayotte in full Comores Aviation c/s without name 20Jan07. Noted hangared Johannesburg, O.R. Tambo airport, South Africa 11Jul07 with 'Comores Aviation – International' titles named "Youmna" with a green map of Africa on fin. Executive Aerospace liquidated on 27Feb08. Still present in same c/s Mar10 stored outside. Noted Johannesburg, O.R. Tambo repainted overall white 30Sep10. Regd to John Wolff and Associates (Pty) Ltd 10Jan11. Advertised for lse/sale by Wolff Autohaus 14Feb12 at a cost of 200,000 $. Regd Lourens JG 22Mar12 and noted still stored 26Mar12. Regn cld as transferred to Kenya 03Aug12, for Avro Express. Arrived at Nairobi-Wilson as **5Y-CBI** 22Sep12. Noted ground running and on taxying trials 28Jun13. Port main undercarriage collapsed on landing Mayendit, Unity State, South Sudan on unknown date. Temporary repairs carried out and ferried gear down to Lokichoggio for permanent repair. Noted back at Nairobi-Wilson 24Sep14. Struck VIP Terminal Mar16 at Juba, South Sudan, after hydraulic failure. Returned to service by Jun16 after repair and replacement of No.2 engine.
TT in excess of 34,389 hrs, 37,889 ldgs (figures at 17May06)

1785   (266)   Srs.2B/378

F/f 16Apr81 as **G-11-17**. Del Deutsche Luftverkehrs-gesellschaftmbH (DLT) as **D-AHSB** 25Apr81 after first flying as such the previous day. To Woodford for autopilot mods 13Aug81 to 81. Lsd British Airways plc with del to Glasgow from Frankfurt as DW947 10Mar88. Regd as **G-BOHZ** to British Airways plc 11Mar88 (CofR G-BOHZ/R1). Ferried from Glasgow to Heathrow as BA9818E 29Mar88 for painting in full British Airways c/s. On completion del from Heathrow to Glasgow as BA9821E 04Apr88 named "Glen Turret" on port and "Gleann Turraid" on starboard side. CofA issued 04Apr88. Positioned from Glasgow to Tegel as BA9824P 05Apr88 and

entered service as BA3041 from Tegel to Bremen the same day. Flew last service as BA5732 from Manchester to Glasgow 28Oct91 before ferrying to Heathrow the same date as BA9735E for painting overall grey. Positioned from Heathrow to Glasgow 02Nov91 as BA9749E. Returned to service as BA5844 from Glasgow to Belfast 04Nov91. Flew last service as BA5843 from Belfast to Glasgow 14Dec91. Returned lessor 31Dec91 and stored Glasgow. Regd to BAF Aircraft Engineering Ltd 17Jan92 (CofR G-BOHZ/R2). Ferried Southend 24Jan92 for storage. Ferried Glasgow 12Aug93 and painted in Goa Way c/s named "Zuari" Sep93. Regn **VT-WAY** reserved but not used. Not del and ferried Prestwick 14Apr94. Regd Sharjah for storage by 08May94. Regd to Independent Airways (Leasing) Ltd 29Jun94 (CofR G-BOHZ/R3). Test flown Sharjah 29Nov94. Departed for Nairobi 30Nov94. Regn cld 15Dec94 as transferred South Africa on sale to Executive Aerospace (Pty) Ltd as **ZS-NNW**. Regd to Aerospace Express (Pty) Ltd 21Dec94. Lsd Zimbabwe Express Airlines Ltd and noted with their titles at Harare 25Jun96. Stored Durban, South Africa from last flight 27Nov97 and remained so in Dec06. Executive Aerospace liquidated on 27Feb08. B/u early 2010.
TT 25,179 hrs, 22,740 ldgs

1786   (269)   Srs.2B/378

F/f 07Jul81 as **G-11-18**. Del Deutsche Luftverkehrs-gesellschaftmbH (DLT) as **D-AHSC** 17Jul81. Lsd British Airways plc with del to Glasgow from Frankfurt as DW940 20Jun88. Regd as **G-HDBC** to British Airways plc 24Jun88 (CofR G-HDBC/R1). Ferried from Glasgow to Heathrow as BA9839E 17Jul88 for painting in full British Airways c/s. On completion del from Heathrow to Glasgow as BA9840E 22Jul88 named "Glen Drohach" on port and "Gleann Drohach" on starboard side. CofA issued 29Jul88. After crew training 30Jul88 entered service as BA876 from Glasgow to Tegel via Manchester and Münster the following day. Flew last service as BA5751 from Kirkwall to Aberdeen 26Oct91 before ferrying to Heathrow as BA9737E 29Oct91 for painting overall grey. Positioned to Glasgow as BA9747E 02Nov91. Returned to service as BA8910H from Glasgow to Belfast 09Nov91. Flew last service as BA5709 from Aberdeen to Glasgow 12Dec91. Returned lessor 31Dec91. Regd to BAF Aircraft Engineering Ltd 17Jan92 (CofR G-HDBC/R2). Ferried Southend 24Jan92 for storage. Ferried Glasgow 30Jul93 and painted in Goa Way c/s named "Mandovi" Sep93. Regn **VT-GOA** rsvd but not used. Not del and ferried Prestwick Apr94. Regd to Independent Airways (Leasing) Ltd 29Jun94 (CofR G-HDBC/R3). Ferried Southend 24Sep95. Regn cld as transferred South Africa and regd to Aerospace Express (Pty) Ltd as **ZS-NWW** 06Oct95. R/o Southend as ZS-NWW 06Oct95. Del ex Southend 07Oct95 still in Goa Way c/s on sale to Executive Aerospace (Pty) Ltd. Lsd Zimbabwe Express Airlines '96. Noted Lanseria 12Jul97 with 'British Lions Supporters' titles. Operated for Alliance Air Sep/Oct98. Chartered Airworld (Pty) Ltd late May01 as a pure freighter. Lsd SONAVAM Aug01 to May02. Lsd Air Excellence of Gabon with del ex Johannesburg 05Oct02 painted overall white with Air Excellence titles. Lse ended May03 and noted Johannesburg International 31May03. Noted on paint strip Johannesburg 25Aug03. Noted operating overall white with Executive Aerospace titles 14Nov03. Lsd Comores Aviation by Dec06 with Comores Aviation titles and fin logo. Seen in service Dzaoudzi 20Jan07. Noted stored all white 20Nov07 Johannesburg OR Tambo airport, South Africa engines fitted. Executive Aerospace liquidated on 27Feb08. Aircraft still present 09Nov16 in good condition.
TT in excess of 30,252 hrs, 26,865 ldgs (figures at 17May06)

1787   (267)   Srs.2B/402

F/f 02Aug82 as **G-11-22**. Shown at Farnborough Air Show as G-11-22 in Bouraq Indonesia Airlines colours without titling 04/13Sep82. Regd as **G-BKLE** to British Aerospace plc Aircraft Group 17Nov82 (CofR G-BKLE/R1). CofA issued 21Dec82. Del Bouraq Indonesia Airlines P.T. as G-BKLE Woodford-Ljubljana 06May83. Regn cld 10May83 as transferred Indonesia and regd **PK-IHP**, being painted in these marks in Singapore on the same date. Del Jakarta 11May83. In service 14May83. Stored Jakarta, Indonesia from Oct91. PWFU 07Apr94.

TT in excess of 16,296 hrs, 10,755 ldgs (figures at 30Jun91)

1788   (268)   Srs.2B/402

Regd as **G-BKLF** to British Aerospace plc Aircraft Group 17Nov82 (CofR G-BKLF/R1). F/f 22Dec82, CofA issued 02Feb83. Del Bouraq Indonesia Airlines P.T. as G-BKLF 28Apr83. Regn cld 02May83 as transferred Indonesia and regd **PK-IHW**, being painted in these marks in Singapore on the same date. Del Jakarta 03May83. In service 04May83. Temporarily withdrawn from service 24Jan89. PWFU 07Apr94. Stored Jakarta-Soekarno Hatto Airport May00.

TT in excess of 12,886 hrs, 8,594 ldgs (figures at 31Mar90)

1789   (270)   Srs.2B/FAA

Regd as **G-BJGI** to British Aerospace plc 24Aug81. (CofR G-BJGI/R1). F/f 20Sep81, CofA issued 25Sep81. Del Aero Spacelines Inc for completion 27Sep81. F/f after completion 20Dec81 as G-BJGI. Regn cld 29Dec81 as transferred USA. Del Cascade Airways Inc as **N118CA** 29Dec81. In service 01Feb82. Company filed for Chapter 11 bankruptcy protection 21Aug85 and aircraft withdrawn from service. Advertised for sale by FAA after default on FAA guaranteed loan. Stored Phoenix from 09Jan86. Regn cld Apr88. Sold Bradley Air Services Ltd/First Air

as **C-GFFA** 15Apr88 and del 21May88. CofR issued 31May88, CofA issued 20Jun88. In service 20Jun88 in First Air c/s. W/o between Dorval and Ottawa at Cheney, Ontario, Canada 15Sep88. 2 crew killed. Regn cld 30Nov88.

TT 10,008 hrs, 14,731 ldgs

1790   (271)   Srs.2B/FAA

Regd as **G-BJTL** to British Aerospace plc 07Dec81. (CofR G-BJTL/R1). F/f 09Dec81, CofA issued 17Dec81. Del Tracor Aviation Inc for completion 17Dec81. Regn cld 28May82 as transferred USA. Del Air Virginia Inc as **N749AV** 29May82. Withdrawn from service 01Jul84 and del to British Aerospace Inc for storage at Manassas. Test flight from Manassas to Washington-Dulles 17Jan85. Ferried ex Washington to Goose Bay 19Jan85 and onwards to Keflavik 20Jan85 arriving Woodford 21Jan85 regd as N749AV in Air Virginia c/s without titles. Regn cld Apr85. Fitted with Rolls-Royce Dart RDa.7 Mk.552 engines and regd **G-11-6**. F/f with these engines fitted 10May85 and used as a development aircraft in May/Jun85 before original MK.535-2 engines refitted. Used for Open Rotor Technology Trials from 09Oct85 to 13Dec85 (nine flights for an 'active noise control system'). Later carried out further Dart RDa.7 Mk.552 engine trials. Displayed at Hawarden Open Day 28Jun86 in Air Virginia c/s without titles. Restored as **G-BJTL** to British Aerospace plc Civil Aircraft Division 26Aug86 (CofR G-BJTL/R2) and flown as such three days later. Ferried to Field Aircraft Services Ltd at East Midlands 25Nov86. Regn cld

G-BKLF c/n 1788 of Bouraq Indonesia Airlines PT would become PK-IHW in Singapore during the delivery flight. This photo was taken pre-delivery in 1983.   *(WHC/BAe)*

N118CA c/n 1789 of Cascade Airways Inc after completion by Aero Spacelines in California in 1981.   *(WHC)*

06Apr87 as transferred Portugal. Painted in SATA Air Açores c/s and test flown as **G-11-6** 14Apr87 from East Midlands. Lsd SATA Air Açores and del ex East Midlands as **CS-TAQ** 01May87. Ferried Manchester 16Jan91 on return to British Aerospace for storage and care and maintenance by FFV Aerotech. Painted in Transair Cambodia c/s as **G-11-790** but not flown as such. Not del and restored as **G-BJTL** to British Aerospace plc - Regional Aircraft 22Jul92 (CofR G-BJTL/R3) and test flown as such 28Jul92 for CofA renewal. Storage continued at Manchester. Ferried Exeter 29Sep94. Regd to Jetstream Aircraft Ltd 02Dec94 (CofR G-BJTL/R4). Lsd Awood Air Ltd and painted in their c/s. Regn cld 14Mar95 as transferred Canada. Painted as **C-GHSC** and del from Exeter via Newcastle 14Mar95. Ferry continued ex Newcastle 15Mar95 to Saskatoon via two intermediate points. Finally arrived Victoria 16Mar95. CofR issued 11May95. WFU 15Jan97 after last flight 11Jan97. Sold Calm Air International Ltd 12Apr97 and regd to them 14May97. Entered service 18May97. Noted Winnipeg 31Jul97 with Calm Air titles and 'Canadian' fin scheme. Work commenced Dec03 in converting aircraft to a pure freighter with an LFD robbed from c/n 1747. Rear service door also removed and area sealed over. Air-tested 13Jun04 on completion of mods. Returned to revenue service 14Jun04 with 'Calm Air Cargo' titles. Carries f/n 745F from 2007. Final service flown by Captain Jacobs and First Officer Friesen on 05Jun15 between Island Lake and Thompson, Manitoba, and placed in store. Both engines had preservation runs on 15Jun15 and the aircraft was officially withdrawn from use on 24Jun15.

TT 37,242 hrs, 40,907 ldgs

1791 (272) Srs.2B/FAA

Regd as **G-BKAL** to British Aerospace plc Aircraft Group 05Apr82 (CofR G-BKAL/R1). F/f 01Apr82. Del Tracor Aviation Inc for completion from Woodford via Keflavik 08Apr82. F/f after completion 17Dec82 as G-BKAL. Originally allocated to Cascade Airways Inc as **N119CA** but order not finalised. Used as a company demonstrator in Colombia and Venezuela from 06Jan83 before del back to Woodford 28Jan83. Converted to Srs.2B/378. Regn cld 07Nov83 as transferred West Germany. Sold Deutsche Luftverkehrsgesellschaft mbH (DLT) and del as **D-AHSD** as a Srs.2B/378 08Nov83. Sold British Aerospace plc 07Nov88. Lsd LIAT (1974) Ltd as **V2-LDK** and del ex Manchester 17Dec88 in basic DLT c/s without titles arriving Antigua 20Dec88. Painted in full LIAT c/s and entered service 14Jan89. Returned British Aerospace and del Manchester 20Feb91 via Søndre Strømfjord and Reykjavik for storage with FFV Aerotech. Restored as **G-BKAL** to Clewer Aviation Ltd 28Jul94 (CofR G-BKAL/R2). Painted as G-BKAL 20Mar95. Ferried Southend 31Mar95. Painted with Necon Air titles and tail logo as **9N-ADF** with r/o 04Apr95. Reverted to **G-BKAL** for ferry to Manchester 26Apr95. Lsd Mount Cook Airlines Ltd with del ex Manchester 14May95 arriving Christchurch 21May95. Regn cld 22May95 as transferred New Zealand. Regd to Mount Cook Group Ltd as **ZK-MCH** 19Jun95. Entered service 01Jul95 in Necon Air's grey c/s with Mount Cook titles and logo. Flew last service as NZ5107 from Palmerston North to Christchurch 10Dec95. Departed Christchurch 05Mar96 on ferry to United Kingdom at end of lse arriving Exeter 14Mar96. Sold Emerald Airways Ltd and regd to them as **G-OJEM** 22Mar96 (CofR G-OJEM/R1). CofA issued 15Apr96. To Woodford for repaint 15/25Apr96. Named "Tashy's Kite". Following starboard engine failure and fire immediately after take-off from Stansted Airport, U.K. 30Mar98, aircraft put back down on runway and overshot with subsequent collapse of nose gear. No fatalities among 4 crew and 40 pax on board. Later declared a write-off with b/u starting 15Jun98. Regn cld 27Jul98 as PWFU.

TT 18,356 hrs, 19,130 ldgs

1792 (273) Srs.2B/378

Regd as **G-BJTM** to British Aerospace Aircraft Group 07Dec81 (CofR G-BJTM/1). Originally built for Air Virginia with regn

N750AV provisionally rsvd but aircraft stored unmarked and unpainted until f/f 17Jan84 as G-BJTM. Regn cld 15May84 as transferred West Germany. Sold Deutsche Luftverkehrsgesellschaft mbH (DLT) and del as **D-AHSE** 15May84 via East Midlands where aircraft painted. Del Düsseldorf 20May84. WFU Dec88. Ferried Woodford 19May89. Later ferried to Manchester for storage with FFV Aerotech Ltd. Regd as **G-SSFS** to British Aerospace plc - Regional Aircraft 06Mar92 (CofR G-SSFS/R1) and flown as such from Manchester 10Apr92. C/o a Middle East tour 01-19May92. Used as BAe company communications aircraft 26May92 until 16Apr93. Stored Hatfield from 23Apr93. Regn cld 20Oct93 as transferred Canada. Sold as **C-FQVE** and del ex Hatfield 21Oct93 to V. Kelner Airways Ltd for onward sale. Regd to West Wind Aviation Inc 20Dec93. CofA issued 07Jan94. Entered service 10Jan94 between Saskatoon and Key Lake. WFU 28Jan04 at Saskatoon for spares use. Regn cld as a/c destroyed 28Apr06. Wings removed outboard of engine nacelles (engines already removed) together with the fin 06May06, loaded on a cradle and trailer and towed to Asquith, Ontario, Canada 16May06 some 25 miles from Saskatoon. Reassembled for preservation by its new owner Cory Rousell.

TT 26,703 hrs, 27,122 ldgs

1793 (274) Srs.2B/402

Noted Woodford in primer as **G-11-23** 11Oct82. Regd as **G-BKLG** to British Aerospace plc Aircraft Group 17Nov82 (CofR G-BKLG/R1). F/f 08Apr83, CofA issued 26Apr83. Del Bouraq Indonesia Airlines P.T. as G-BKLG 27Apr83. Regn cld 01May83 as transferred Indonesia and regd as **PK-IHT**, being painted in these marks in Singapore on the same date. Del Jakarta 02May83. In service 04May83. Nose gear collapsed during heavy landing Balikpapan 28Aug96. Repaired. Transferred Bali Air in 2001. Company ceased operations Mar05. Noted stored Jakarta-Soekarno, Indonesia 06Oct05 and again 06Nov08 in full Bali Air purple c/s.

TT in excess of 20,472 hrs, 13,744 ldgs (figures at 31Oct92)

1794 (275) Srs.2B/402

Noted Woodford in primer as **G-11-24** 11Oct82. Regd as **G-BKLH** to British Aerospace plc Aircraft Group 17Nov82 (CofR G-BKLH/R1). F/f 29Mar83, CofA issued 22Apr83. Del Bouraq Indonesia Airlines P.T. as G-BKLH 26Apr83. Regn cld 30Apr83 as transferred Indonesia and regd **PK-IHN**, being painted in these marks in Singapore on the same date. Del Jakarta 01May83. In service 03May83. Cockpit damaged by fire while oxygen system being replenished at Jakarta 20Oct83. Repaired and returned to service 11Dec83. Sustained substantial damage when aircraft veered of runway during aborted take-off at Jakarta 24Jul87. Repaired. W/o after aborted take-off Ambon, Indonesia 11Jul96. No fatalities among 5 crew and 43 pax on board.

TT 22,286 hrs, 14,725 ldgs

1795 (276) Srs.2B/402

Regd as **G-BKLI** to British Aerospace plc Aircraft Group 17Nov82 (CofR G-BKLI/R1). F/f 16Apr83, CofA issued 27Apr83. Del Bouraq Indonesia Airlines P.T. as G-BKLI 29Apr83. Regn cld 04May83 as transferred Indonesia and regd as **PK-IHV**, being painted in these marks in Singapore and del Jakarta on the same date. In service 07May83. Noted Surabaya 02Oct03 in full Bali Air c/s. Company ceased operations Mar05. Noted stored Surabaya, Indonesia 08Oct05 and again 09Mar06.

TT in excess of 20,622 hrs, 13,485 ldgs (figures at 31Oct92)

1796 (277) Srs.2B/400

Regd as **G-BKIG** to British Aerospace Aircraft Group 12Oct82 (CofR G-BKIG/R1). R/o as **MI-8203** but repainted as **G-BKIG** for f/f 24Nov82, CofA issued 08Dec82. Del Airline of the Marshall Islands as G-BKIG 16Dec82. Regn cld 25Dec82 as transferred Marshall Islands and regd as **MI-8203** the same date.

D-AHSF c/n 1797 of DLT - Deutsche Luftverkehrsgesellschaft mbH; the company's colour scheme was dark blue and white.

Del Christchurch 22Nov87 for maintenance by Mount Cook Airlines Ltd. Left New Zealand 16Dec87 on return to owner. Del Christchurch for maintenance 21Aug89 before returning owner 09Sep89. Re-regd **V7-8203** by 22Mar93. Painted with Royal Tongan Airlines c/s to port and the new Air Marshall Islands c/s to starboard and lsd to Royal Tongan Airlines from Wednesday to Saturday each week. Entered service with Royal Tongan as WR821 from Tongatapu to Vava'u 05Jul95. Leasing deal terminated and last service flown with Royal Tongan as WR421 from Tongatapu via Vava'u to Nadi, Fiji 28Oct95. WFU and ferried via Nadi and Auckland to Christchurch for storage 07Feb96. Painted in full Air Marshall Islands c/s and departed for Auckland and Nadi 23Aug96 and returned to service. Sold Hering Aviation (Pty) Ltd with regn **ZS-OJU** rsvd 24Feb99. Del 30Mar99 arriving Lanseria 31Mar99 as V7-8203. ZS-OJU not taken up and regd as **ZS-OLE** to Hering Aviation (Pty) Ltd 07Apr99 for operation by AirQuarius Aviation (Pty) Ltd in an all white c/s. Noted as such Lanseria 08Apr99 with 'Trackmark' titles for a two month lse. Reportedly damaged by hailstorm at Lanseria 22Apr99 but was seen in service at Nairobi, Wilson 01Aug99 painted overall white still operating for Trackmark. Returned off lse end Aug99. Regd AirQuarius Air Charter (Pty) Ltd 25Apr01. Noted Lanseria 05Nov01 carrying name "Lojo Ka". Aircraft went off end of runway on landing Sun City, Pilanesberg Airport, South Africa 16Apr02 after reported hydraulic failure and loss of braking. Undercarriage collapsed causing extensive damage leading to the aircraft's w/o. No fatalities among 3 crew and 33 passengers. Dismantled and moved to Lanseria early Jun02. Wreckage moved to Johannesburg International by truck 21Jun02 and stored with Executive Aerospace (Pty) Ltd. Moved to Chartwell, a suburb of Johannesburg, South Africa 25Jun04 and reassembled as a cabin crew trainer for Cranfield Aviation (Pty) Ltd. Sold to nearby 'Fantasy Park Party Venue', Nicholls Road, Farmall 2013.

TT 26,975 hrs, 15,910 ldgs

1797   (278)   Srs.2B/378

F/f 16Sep84 as **G-11-2**. Del Deutsche Luftverkehrsgesellschaft mbH (DLT) as **D-AHSF** 28Sep84. Made hard landing Cologne 23Jun87 causing substantial damage. Repaired. Sold British Aerospace plc and ferried Manchester 26Jan89. After maintenance del Woodford as **G-11-1** 07Feb89. Returned Manchester 13Apr89 for CofA renewal. Lsd SATA Air Açores as **CS-TAR** with del ex Manchester 26Jun89. Positioned East Midlands at end of lse 13Jan90. Regd as **G-HDBD** to British Airways plc 26Feb90 (CofR G-HDBD/R1). Lsd British Airways

plc with del Glasgow 05Mar90 as **G-11-797** all white with SATA Air Açores titling. CofA issued 10Apr90. Reverted to **G-HBDB**. In service as BA5814 13Apr90 from Glasgow to Benbecula painted all white with British Airways titles in black. Flew last revenue HS748 flight for British Airways plc as BA5845 from Belfast to Glasgow 15Apr92. Returned British Aerospace 21May92 and ferried from Glasgow to Woodford as BA8991P the same date. Regd to British Aerospace - Regional Aircraft 11Jun92 (CofR G-HDBD/R2) for use as a company communications aircraft. WFU and ferried from Woodford to Exeter 19Aug94 for storage after CofA expiry 09Apr94. Regd to Jetstream Aircraft Ltd 02Dec94 (CofR G-HDBD/R3). Regn cld by the CAA 21Feb96. Sold Emerald Airways Ltd Mar96 and restored to them as G-HDBD 22Jul96 (CofR G-HDBD/R4). Re-regd **G-EMRD** 11Oct96 (CofR G-EMRD/R1). CofA renewed 17Oct96. Ferried from Exeter to Woodford 19Oct96 for repaint. Del Liverpool 04Nov96. Entered service 09Nov96 between Liverpool and Isle of Man in full Emerald c/s in passenger config. WFU Southend. Regn **ZS-PLO** rsvd 24May99. Sold Executive Aerospace (Pty) Ltd and del ex Southend 01Jun99. Forced down by Ethiopian Air Force Migs at Bihar Dhar during del flight but later permitted to continue. Regn cld 15Jun99 as transferred South Africa and regd as ZS-PLO (in honour of Captain **P**eter **L**eeson **O**venstone, the company's Flight Operations Director) to Aerospace Express (Pty) Ltd 22Jun99. Lsd Albarka Air Services Ltd with 'Albarka Air' titles on forward fuselage Aug to Oct01. Commenced a short term mail contract over the Johannesburg-Bloemfontein-George-Johannesburg route 03Jun02. Noted with an emblem entitled 'Proudly South African Company' on the nose 13Oct04 at Johannesburg International. Noted Johannesburg with 'Kalanga Air Services' titles and fin logo 25Jul05. Lsd Comores Aviation by Oct05 in full c/s. Noted Johannesburg 14Feb06 overall white with large '7' in black on fin and 'BMW Serie 7' titles on rear fuselage. Lsd Comores Aviation 17May06. Noted flying Zanzibar 03Dec06 all white with no titles. Noted hangared Johannesburg O.R. Tambo Airport, South Africa without engines painted overall white 11Jul07. Executive Aerospace liquidated on 27Feb08. Still present Sep08 but b/u by Aug12.

TT in excess of 19,504 hrs, 19,941 ldgs (figures at 17May05)

1798   (279)   Srs.2B/426

Regd as **G-HDBA** to British Airways plc 13Nov84 (CofR G-HDBA/R1). F/f 05Nov84, CofA issued 30Nov84. Del 13Dec84. In service from Glasgow to Lerwick via Aberdeen as BA5704 19Dec84. Inaugurated Highland Division's first international service between Lerwick and Bergen on 07Jun85.

Named "Glen Esk" on starboard and "Gleann Uisgue" on port side late 1985. Inaugurated first scheduled service from Wick as BA6707 21Jan87. Flew last revenue flight as BA8913H from Belfast to Glasgow 28Dec91. Traded to British Aerospace plc and ferried to Manchester 14Jan92. Regd to Trident Aviation Leasing Services (Jersey) Ltd 20Jan92 (CofR G-HDBA/R2). Del ex Manchester 10Apr92 via Nice arriving Abu Dhabi 12Apr92 on lse to Emirates Air Services Ltd. Regn cld 13Apr92 as transferred United Arab Emirates and regd **A6-GRM**. Returned Hatfield at end of lse 15Jan93. Restored as **G-HDBA** to Trident Aviation Leasing Services (Jersey) Ltd 23Nov93 (CofR G-HDBA/R3). Ferried Exeter 27Nov93. Regn cld 09Feb94 as transferred Nepal. Del ex Exeter via Nice to **9N-ACW** 10Feb94 on lease to Nepal Airways Pvt Ltd. WFU Pokhara 23Nov96. Damaged Pokhara, Nepal 06Nov97 after being struck by Necon Air Ltd 748 9N-ACM on ground. Impact was to starboard forward fuselage and nose causing substantial damage. Subsequently declared a write-off. Sold Inter-national Air Parts Pty Ltd for spares use only. B/u May06.

TT 14,475 hrs, 20,169 ldgs

1799 (280) Srs.2B/426

Regd as **G-HDBB** to British Airways plc 13Nov84 (CofR G-HDBB/R1). F/f 15Nov84, CofA issued 10Dec84. Del 14Dec84. Ferried Glasgow-Aberdeen as BA9832P 18Dec84 and entered service as BA5748 from Aberdeen to Kirkwall the same day. Named "Glen Clova" on starboard and "Gleann Clovaigh" on port side late 1985. Inaugurated first revenue service by British Airways 748 into Berlin-Tegel as BA924 17May86. Renamed "Glen Isla" on port and "Gleann Ile" on starboard side Mar89. Name removed later in 1989 and flown nameless until renamed "Glen Eagles" on port and "Gleann Eagais" on starboard side. Withdrawn from service after operating BA5709 from Aberdeen to Glasgow 06Nov91 and stored. Traded to British Aerospace plc 14Nov91 and storage continued at Glasgow. Regd to British Aerospace plc - Airlines Division 20Nov91 (CofR G-HDBB/R2). Regd to Trident Aviation Leasing Services (Jersey) Ltd 20Jan92 (CofR G-HDBB/R3). Ferried Manchester 30Jan92. Del ex Manchester 02Apr92 via Nice arriving Abu Dhabi 06Apr92 on lse to Emirates Air Services Ltd. Regn cld 06Apr92 as transferred United Arab Emirates and regd **A6-ABM**. Returned Hatfield at end of lse 15Jan93. Restored as **G-HDBB** to Trident Aviation Leasing Services (Jersey) Ltd 23Nov93 (CofR G-HDBB/R4). Ferried Exeter 27Nov93. Regn cld 09Mar94 as transferred Nepal. Painted as **9N-ACX** and del ex Exeter via Nice 10Mar94 on lse to Nepal Airways Pvt Ltd. Sold International Air Parts Pty Ltd for lse to Horizon Airlines Pty Ltd early 1999 and noted in store Kathmandu without engines 27Apr99. Regd as **VH-IMJ** to Horizon Airlines Pty Ltd 30Jun00. Ferried Bankstown, Sydney 12Jul00 with an all white fuselage with small 'Horizon' titles and red/yellow diagonal stripes on fin. Painted at RAAF Richmond in full new Horizon Airlines c/s for operation in a 44 seat pax config Oct00. Last flew 28Jul03 when ferried Bankstown and stored. Horizon Airlines placed in Administration 14Oct03 and later ceased operations. Returned lessor. Regn cld 31Aug04 and regd as **4R-SER** to IAP Group Australia (Pvt) Ltd the same date. Lsd Aero Lanka, (Pvt) Ltd and del as 4R-SER ex Bankstown via Broken Hill and Charleville to Darwin (nightstop) 17Sep04. Continued to Denpasar and Jakarta-Halim 18Sep04. Aircraft painted with Aero Lanka titles and fin motif and c/o five days of crew training before aircraft continued ferry via Medan, Phuket (nightstop), Yangon (nightstop), Kolkata, Hyderabad, Colombo-Bandaranaike and finally Ratmalana, Sri Lanka where it arrived 30Sep04. Entered service 05Oct04. WFU by summer 2010 and stored Ratmalana. Noted still present Feb11 with faded paintwork. Lsd Ivoirienne de Transports Aériens late Dec11 for sub-lse to East Horizon Airlines of Afghanistan. Ferried via Colombo-Katunayake and Mumbai. Noted Kabul painted as **TU-PAD** in full East Horizon Airlines c/s 09Jan12 (also has Airlinkers LLC titles on nose). Reportedly WFU. Noted stored Kabul Jun16.

TT in excess of 14,947 hrs, 21,034 ldgs (figures at 17Sep04)

1800 (281) Srs.2B/424

Regd as **G-BLGJ** to British Aerospace plc Aircraft Group 02Apr84 (CofR G-BLGJ/R1). First production Super 748. F/f 30Jul84. Demonstrated at Farnborough Air Show 1984 in British Aerospace c/s. Regn cld 17Dec84 as transferred Antigua. Del LIAT (1974) Ltd as **V2-LCQ** 18Dec84 arriving Antigua 20Dec84. After several days of crew training entered service 29Dec84. Lsd British Aerospace plc from 21Nov85 to 07Dec85 for demonstrations in Ecuador. Overran runway on landing Dominica 01Aug90 and nose gear collapsed. Repaired. WFU Antigua by Aug95. Sold Holter Leasing Inc Sep96. Regd as **C-GBCN** to Dellair Trading Inc 10Jul97. Noted Thunder Bay, Ontario 24Dec97 painted as **VT-DOA**. Seen again in full Bengal Air c/s with dual regns C-GBCN/VT-BAA 26Sep98. Ferried via Liverpool to Exeter 19Nov98. Departed for Calcutta via Nice 20Nov98. Canadian regn cld 07Dec98. Regd to Bengal Air Services Ltd as **VT-BAA** 01Jan99. Stored Calcutta/Kolkata, India since arrival due problems with Indian certification. Regn cld 01Dec05. Noted derelict at Kolkata 27Feb14.

TT in excess of 18,525 hrs, 29,140 ldgs (figures at 10Jul97)

1801 (282) Srs.2B/424

F/f 13Dec84 as **G-11-4**. F/f as **V2-LCR** 20Dec84. Del LIAT (1974) Ltd 21Dec84 arriving Antigua 23Dec84. In service 03Jan85. WFU Antigua by Aug95. Sold Holter Leasing Inc Sep96. Regd as **C-GBCS** to Dellair Trading Inc 09Dec97. Noted Thunder Bay 07Oct98 in full Bengal Air c/s with dual regns C-GBCS/**VT-BAB**. Later stored Winnipeg. Noted with small 'Flightcraft' titles on fin Mar02. Lsd Atlantic Airlines de Honduras S de RL and ferried La Ceiba, Honduras 16Aug02. Regn cld 05Sep02. Restored as **C-GBCS** to Dellair Trading Inc 09Dec02 but aircraft remained in store at La Ceiba not having flown for Atlantic Airlines. Regn cld 10Mar03 as sold as **HR-ATC**. Noted at Grand Cayman 22Apr03 painted as HR-ATC in Bengal Airways c/s with Atlantic Airlines titles and tail logo. Carried additional 'DONDE VOLAR ES UN PLACER' titles. Impounded by local authorities in an ownership dispute. Later returned to use with Atlantic Airlines as HR-ATC and noted in service at Tegucigalpa 14Dec04. Became stuck in mud off runway at Guanaja Island, Honduras when doing a U-turn 02Jan07. Recovered the same day. Noted still operational on 26Sep08 at La Ceiba, Honduras. Company ceased operations Oct08 and aircraft advertised for sale by Airtec S. de R.L. 18Jul09. Noted still stored La Ceiba 03Mar11. Again advertised for sale by Asispo of Tegucigalpa, Honduras on 18Jun12 for 90,000$ with only one engine and propeller. Still present La Ceiba 16Oct13.

TT 22,669 hrs, 35,070 ldgs

1802 (283) Srs.2B/424

F/f 18Apr85 as **G-11-5**. Regd as **G-BLYL** to British Aerospace plc 07May85 (CofR G-BLYL/R1). Del LIAT (1974) Ltd as G-BLYL 07May85 arriving Antigua 10May85. Regn cld 24May85 as transferred Antigua and regd **V2-LCS**. In service 24May85. WFU Antigua by Aug95. Sold Holter Leasing Inc Sep96. Regn **VT-BAC** rsvd for Bengal Air but ntu. Stored Saulte Ste. Marie, Canada. Sold Wasaya Airways Ltd for reduction to spares at Saulte Ste. Marie, Ontario, Canada but aircraft still intact Feb07.

TT in excess of 19,132 hrs, 30,023 ldgs (figures at 30Apr95)

1803 (284) Srs.2B/424

F/f 19Jun85 as **G-11-9**. Del LIAT (1974) Ltd as **V2-LCT** 28Jun85 and ferried ex Woodford the following day arriving Antigua 04Jul85. In service 08Jul85. WFU Antigua by Aug95. Sold Holter Leasing Inc Sep96. Regn **VT-BAD** rsvd for Bengal Air but ntu. Painted in full Bengal Air c/s as **C-GBCY** (though not officially regd as such) and stored Winnipeg. Noted Winnipeg 20Mar02 in basic Bengal Air c/s but with small 'Flightcraft' titles on fin. Was due to be the second aircraft for Atlantic Airlines de Honduras S de RL. Regd as C-GBCY to Wasaya Airways Limited

Partnership 01Sep05 on sale to them and ferried from Winnipeg to Thunder Bay, Ontario, Canada 02Sep05 for reduction to spares. Regn cld 30Sep05 but aircraft still intact Feb07. Still present 19Sep09 but with numerous parts missing. Aircraft removed from register 21Aug13.

TT 19,448 hrs, 30,587 ldgs

1804   (285)   Srs.2B/435

F/f 11Oct85 as **G-11-10**. Del Cameroon Airlines as **TJ-CCF** 30Oct85. Named "Kadei". W/o Yaoundé, Cameroun 28Jun89. Overran on landing in poor visibility and hit embankment. 2 crew and 1 pax killed, 44 survived.

TT 5,569 hrs, 7,150 ldgs

1805   (286)   Srs.2B/435

F/f 12Nov85 as **G-11-11**. Del Cameroon Airlines as **TJ-CCG** 22Nov85 and ferried ex Woodford the following day. Named "Menchum". WFU and stored Douala, Cameroun by Aug97.

TT in excess of 7,592 hrs, 9,775 ldgs (figures at 23Feb94)

1806   (287)   Srs.2B/501

F/f 29Jul88 as **G-11-1** direct to East Midlands for completion. Regd to British Aerospace plc Civil Aircraft Division as **G-BPEP** 14Oct88 (CofR G-BPEP/R1). Painted in full Makung Airlines Co Ltd c/s after sale to them. Del ex East Midlands as G-BPEP 17Nov88. Regn cld 21Nov88 as transferred Republic of Taiwan and regd **B-1771**. Company renamed UNI Airways Corporation 12Mar96. Sold Necon Air Ltd as **9N-AEG** with del Kathmandu 30Nov97. Entered service 03Dec97. W/o Ramkot 11 miles southwest of Kathmandu, Nepal while on approach on flight B7128 from Pokhara 05Sep99 after port wing sliced through a telecommunications tower. 5 crew and 10 pax killed.

TT in excess of 12,596 hrs, 20,971 ldgs (figures at 30Jun95)

1807   (288)   Srs.2B/501

F/f 02Dec88 as **G-11-2** direct to East Midlands for completion. Regd to British Aerospace plc Civil Aircraft Division as **G-BPIW** 25Nov88 (CofR G-BPIW/R1). Painted in full Makung Airlines Co Ltd c/s after sale to them. F/f after completion 24Jan89. Del ex East Midlands as G-BPIW 01Feb89. Regn cld 09Feb89 as transferred Republic of Taiwan and regd **B-1773**, first flying as such 18Feb89. Company renamed UNI Airways Corporation

12Mar96. Sold Necon Air Ltd as **9N-AEH** with del Kathmandu 14Dec97. Entered service 19Dec97. After departing Kathmandu for Biratnagar 03Mar98, the nose undercarriage failed to fully retract. On returning Kathmandu and landing on foam, the nose leg collapsed. Repaired. W/d from regular service 18Apr01. Sold Executive Aerospace (Pty) Ltd and del ex Kathmandu 30Aug01 via Hyderabad, Trivandrum, Male, Gan, Mahé and Mayotte arriving Johannesburg International 07Sep01. Stripped to bare metal. Regd to Aerospace Express (Pty) Ltd as **ZS-AGB** 19Nov01. Painted overall white with Executive Aerospace titles and regn ZS-AGB applied (in honour of the company's Contracts Director **A**nthony **G**erald **B**ustin). Noted as such in hangar Johannesburg International 20Nov01 with fin scheme still to be applied. Lsd Lion Air (Pvt) Ltd of Sri Lanka in full c/s with del ex Johannesburg 07Sep02 named "Lanka's Pride in the Sky". Regn cld 27Sep02 and regd **4R-AGB**. Re-regd **4R-LPV** 25Mar03. Withdrawn from Sri Lanka 10Jul04 and operated on behalf of Island Aviation Services Ltd of the Maldives still as 4R-LPV. Ferried ex Male via Seychelles to Moroni 08Sep04 after an initial air-test on the same date. Ferried to Johannesburg 10Sep04. Restored as **ZS-AGB** to Aerospace Express (Pty) Ltd 06Oct04. Noted operational Johannesburg 13Oct04 painted overall white without titles. Lsd Comores Aviation 10Feb05 to 22Jul05. Extended maint lay-up with effect from this last date. Executive Aerospace liquidated on 27Feb08. Noted in external storage Johannesburg O.R. Tambo Airport, South Africa engineless and with several parts missing Sep09. B/U by Aug12.

TT 21,178 hrs, 32,961 ldgs

1808   (289)

Not completed. Fuselage to Hatfield, U.K. 27Apr89 for open rotor noise trial rig static tests. Forward fuselage to Chester, Hawarden U.K. 1993. Remains b/u Hatfield, U.K. Jul95.

1809   (290)

Not completed. Fuselage used for structure work in Flight Shed at Woodford from 1989. Moved to Irvine, Strathclyde, Scotland by Sep94.

An unidentified 748 is regd as 9Q-CMU to SOZACA of Lubumbashi, DRC.

C-GBCY c/n 1803 of Wasaya Airways Ltd, seen at Thunder Bay, Ontario, on 19th September 2009. The aircraft was Canadian registered only for a one-off ferry flight for spares recovery.

(Fred Barnes)

ANDOVER
INDIVIDUAL AIRCRAFT HISTORIES

(1572)   Set 1

F/f 09Jul65 as **XS594** unpainted. Del to A & AEE at Boscombe Down 02Dec65. Returned Hawker Siddeley Aviation Ltd at Woodford 11Feb66 to 13May66 and again from 28Sep66. Reflown 05May67 and returned to A & AEE at Boscombe Down 17May67 for 'heavy weight' trials. Returned Woodford a third time 09Aug67 and flew on trials Sep67. Brought up to production standard and reflown 21Oct68. To 15 MU (Wroughton) 25Nov68. Air-drop trials with A&AEE 03Jun69. To 5 MU (Kemble) 04Sep69. Empire Test Pilots' School preview with the A&AEE 28Oct69 and released to the Ministry of Defence 25Nov69. To 46 Squadron (Abingdon) 15Aug70. To 5 MU (Kemble) 1970 for storage. SOC 24Jan80 and used as an instructional airframe. To SAS Regiment Ewyas Harold, Herefordshire 1981. To Otterburn weapons range 22Feb82. Scrapped at Otterburn Ranges, Northumberland, U.K. 1994.

TT 1,981 hrs

(1573)   Set 2

F/f 06Oct65 as **XS595** unpainted. Del to A & AEE at Boscombe Down 25Jan66. Returned to Hawker Siddeley Aviation Ltd 11Feb66. Used for hot weather and rough field trials in the Radfan area of Aden by Hawker Siddeley/A & AEE from 01Mar66 to 22Mar66 before returning Woodford. Returned to A & AEE at Boscombe Down 20Apr66 for radio, navigation and reliability trials. Shown at both Hanover Air Show 03/04May66 and Farnborough Air Show from 02Sep to 12Sep66 when returned Woodford. Tested with ferry tanks. Brought up to production standard and reflown 25Jan67. To RAF charge and del Abingdon 19Sep67. To 46 Squadron (Abingdon) 01Oct67. To 84 Squadron (Sharjah) 03Nov67 coded 'A' and used by the Search and Rescue Flight from 10Jul69 to 01Aug69 and from 09Sep69. To 5 MU (Kemble) 14Dec70 for storage. SOC 28Jan80. To Brize Norton fire dump, Oxfordshire, U.K. 1981.

TT 891 hrs

(1574)   Set 3

F/f 16Dec65 as **XS596** unpainted. Del to A & AEE at Boscombe Down 01Jun66 for airfield criteria trials. Returned to Hawker Siddeley Aviation Ltd 19Jan68. Del Royal Air Force 27Jan69 and to 5 MU (Kemble) 27Jan69. To 60 MU (Leconfield) 23Apr69. Allotted to 46 Squadron (Abingdon) 20Jun69 and del 04Jul69. To Air Training Sqn 24Apr70 and to Station Flight Abingdon 15Jun70. To Station Flight Thorney Island 01Sep70. To 46 Sqn (Thorney Island) 01Oct73. Cat.3R Disposal Account 25Oct73 and to 46 Sqn (Thorney Island) 23Nov73. To 5 MU (Kemble) 30Jul75 for storage. To 115 Squadron (Brize Norton) 14Apr80. Squadron moved to Benson 04Jan83. Stored RAF Northolt 26Nov84 and at RAF Benson 01Jul85. To 115 Sqn (Benson) 22Oct85. Ferried Woodford 26Jan87 for conversion to C.Mk.1 (PR) and repaint in transport c/s. F/f as such 20Jul89. Del RAF Benson 30Jul89. To 60 Squadron (Wildenrath) 31Jan90. Unit markings applied 08Feb90 with f/f with unit 14Feb90. To Shawbury for storage 16Mar92. Squadron disbanded 31Mar92. To DRA (Boscombe Down) Jun92 and used for exercising British rights under the 'Open Skies Policy'. Initially operated by the DRA. Operator renamed the DERA from 01Apr97 and as QinetiQ from 02Jul01. Noted flying Fairford 17Jul06 (RIAT) and again at Yeovilton 07Jul07 with 'UNITED KINGDOM OPEN SKIES' titling. Stored after last flight Riga-Aalborg-Boscombe Down 16Oct07. Used to provide parts to keep QinetiQ's other two Andovers flying. Moved to scrapping area after removal of all useful parts 19Dec11 and still present 24Sep12.

TT 7,187 hrs, 6,189 ldgs

(1575)   Set 4

F/f 07Feb66 as **XS597**. Del to A & AEE at Boscombe Down 01Apr66 for paratroop and supply dropping trials. Fitted with nose boom and rear fuselage painted white. Returned Hawker Siddeley Aviation Ltd at Woodford 26May67 for refurbishment and to bring up to production standards. Del to 15 MU (Wroughton) 25May68. To Station Flight Abingdon 01Jun70. To Station Flight Thorney Island 01Sep70. To 46 Squadron (Thorney Island) 01Oct73. To 32 Squadron (Northolt) 06Nov73, and painted in grey and white transport c/s. Noted 13Dec79 painted with 'Burand Airways' titles for a film. To Station Flight Brize Norton 12Nov80. To 32 Squadron (Northolt) 17Feb81. To ASF Benson 11Jul84 for major check, and again 17Oct85 for minor check, returning 12Sep84 and 13Nov85, respectively. To Hurn 20Jan86 for repaint by Lovaux Ltd, returning to 32 Sqn (Northolt) 14Apr86. To ASF Benson 15Jan87 and to 115 Sqn (Benson) 20Feb87. To 60 Sqn (Wildenrath) 05Mar87 and to ASF Benson 11Jul88. To 60 Squadron (Wildenrath) 09Aug88. Stored Shawbury from 25Mar92. SOC 08Jul93, the same date as sold at auction for £86,000. Ferried Southend 11Nov93. Regd as **G-BVNJ** to Flightline Ltd 19May94 (CofR G-BVNJ/R1). Regn cld 21Nov94 as transferred South Africa and painted as **3D-ATS** on sale to Balmoral Central Contracts Ltd. Del ex Southend 04Dec94 via Cyprus, Nairobi and Maputo. First seen Lanseria 09Dec94 and again 28Dec95 with 'WFP' (World Food Programme) titles at Lanseria. Seen Lanseria 03Feb95, 04Jul95 and 01Dec95. Noted Lanseria with no regn 13Aug96 and by 16Aug96 with regn **9Q-CMJ** applied. Departed Lanseria Sep96. Still active Jan01 with Aid Air. By 10Jun05 regn 9Q-CMJ was carried by a Cessna 182F and the Andover presumably WFU.

Set 5

F/f 22Mar66 as **XS598**. Del to Handling Station Flight Boscombe Down 01Jul66 and to Station Flight Abingdon 13Jul66. To RAF Andover Operational Conversion Unit (Abingdon) 14Sep66 coded 'E'. Aborted take-off and overran runway Abingdon 05Jul67. SOC 01Aug67. Fuselage used for loading and centre of gravity training at the Air Movements School, Brize Norton by May75. To Moreton-in-Marsh, Gloucestershire. U.K. for emergency training Feb94. Fuselage still there Jun01.

TT 612 hrs, 1,321 ldgs

Set 6

F/f 11May66 as **XS599**. Del to Station Flight Abingdon/Andover Operational Conversion Unit 01Jul66 coded 'A'. Shown at Paris Le Bourget Air Show with show number L471 in two tone brown camouflage c/s with 'Royal Air Force Air Support Command' titles and now uncoded 07Jun69. To Air Training Squadron (Thorney Island) 01Aug70. To 242 Operational Conversion Unit (Thorney Island) 01Nov70. To 46 Squadron (Thorney Island) 01Dec74. To 5 MU (Kemble) 18Apr75 for storage. Test flown 28Sep76 & again 21Feb77. SOC and sold Royal New Zealand Air Force as **NZ7620** 16Mar77. Ferried to Brize Norton the same day. Del ex Brize Norton 20Mar77 arriving Whenuapai 02Apr77. To 1 Squadron (Whenuapai) 18Apr77. Squadron deactivated 07Dec84. Transferred to 42 Squadron (Whenuapai) Dec84. Retired from service 96 and stored Ardmore. Sold Eureka Aviation as **9Q-CYG** 28Nov96. Del via Brisbane 08Feb97 en route Wevelgem, Belgium. Lsd Bazair and noted Nairobi Aug97 in full c/s named "Ville de Nazareth". Del Antwerp for storage without titles 16Dec97. Ferried Liège 27Jan98. Sold South African organisation 'Church Alive' and painted as **EL-VDD** by

02May98. Del ex Antwerp 05May98 and noted Lanseria 20May98 unpainted. Re-regd **3C-JJX** and first noted as such at Lanseria 07Aug98 painted in J.A.M. Air c/s (Jesus Alive Ministries International) named "LIFE Angel". Departed for Rwanda 08Aug98. Seen Lanseria 18Oct02 repainted in overall white c/s with pale blue cheatline and no titles (was in Jam Air c/s on 14Oct02). Sold 748 Air Services Ltd Oct02 and regd as

5Y-SFE. Belly landed at Lokichoggio, Kenya on 10Jun05 after operating a round trip from Lokichoggio to Boma airstrip, Torit airfield and Natinga airfield in Southern Sudan and w/o. Later the same day struck by Lockheed L-100-30 Hercules S9-BAS c/n 4472 of TRANSAFRIK International Ltd and suffered further fin damage.

TT 14,434 hrs, 21,550 ldgs

3C-JJX Set 6 of JAM Air at Lanseria, South Africa, on 21st October 1998. *(Keith Gaskell)*

NZ7621 Set 7 of the Royal New Zealand Air Force. *(WHC)*

XS602 Set 9 of the Royal Air Force Air Support Command, wearing titles which were only carried during 1967-69. *(WHC)*

XS603 Set 10 of 115 Squadron at Brize Norton, Oxfordshire, on 18th March 1978. (Keith Gaskell)

Set 7

F/f 08Jun66 as **XS600**. Del to Station Flight Abingdon/Andover Operational Conversion Unit 15Jul66 coded 'B'. To Air Training Squadron (Thorney Island) 01Aug70. To 242 Operational Conversion Unit (Thorney Island) 01Nov70. To 46 Squadron (Thorney Island) 19Feb75. To 5 MU (Kemble) 11Apr75 for storage. SOC and sold Royal New Zealand Air Force as **NZ7621** 20Apr77. Del ex Brize Norton 04May77 arriving with 1 Squadron (Whenuapai) 24May77. To 42 Squadron (Ohakea) 09Sep77. To 1 Squadron (Whenuapai) 10Jan78. To 42 Squadron (Ohakea) 10Feb78. To 1 Squadron (Whenuapai) 02Oct78. Squadron deactivated 07Dec84. Transferred to 42 Squadron (Whenuapai). WFU Jun96. Donated to RNZAF Museum Wigram, New Zealand 28Jun96. Stored outside a/o 2007.

TT 10,528 hrs

Set 8

F/f 24Jun66 as **XS601**. Del to Station Flight Abingdon/Andover Operational Conversion Unit 11Aug66 coded 'C'. To 46 Squadron (Abingdon) Jan67. Displayed at Farnborough Air Show Sep68 with Air Support Command titles. To Woodford from A & AEE Boscombe Down for mods 19Aug70. Reflown and del 46 Squadron (Thorney Island) 17Sep70. To 5 MU (Kemble) 28May75 for storage. To Otterburn weapons range, Northumberland, U.K. 22Mar82. SOC 29Mar83 and reportedly scrapped 1994.

Set 9

F/f 08Jul66 as **XS602**. Del to Station Flight Abingdon/Andover Operational Conversion Unit 19Aug66 coded 'D'. Ground accident Abingdon 13Oct67. Repaired on site. To 46 Squadron (Abingdon) 18Jan68. Minor accident 15Jun70. Repaired on site. Squadron moved to Thorney Island 11Sep70. To 5 MU (Kemble) 09Apr75 for storage. Air-tested 16Nov76 & ferried to Brize Norton 18Nov76. SOC and sold Royal New Zealand Air Force as **NZ7622** 19Nov76 and used by the RAF/RNZAF for conversion training with 241 Operational Conversion Unit. Del ex Brize Norton 25Jan77 arriving Whenuapai 05Feb77. To 42 Squadron (Ohakea) 08Feb77 but remained Whenuapai until ferried Woodbourne 13Feb77. Converted to a VIP configuration at No.1 Repair Depot at Woodbourne before returning to 42 Squadron (Ohakea) 26Jun78. At one time named 'Rangi Tahu' (Chief of the Skies). Squadron moved to Whenuapai 10Dec84. Retired from service 30Jun98. Regd to 748 Air Services as **3C-KKB** and ferried via Brisbane 21Sep98 and Darwin 22Sep98 arriving Southend 30Sep98. Del ex Southend 03Oct98 on sale to 748 Air Services Ltd of Kenya. Seen Rand 12Mar99 & 08Apr00. Noted Nairobi 14Mar03. W/o landing Rumbek airstrip in Southern Sudan on 15Aug03 after nose leg collapse. Hulk still present Oct04.

TT 17,428 hrs, 19,087 ldgs

Set 10

F/F 09Aug66 as **XS603**. Del to Station Flight Abingdon/Andover Operational Conversion Unit 21Sep66 coded 'F'. To 46 Squadron (Abingdon) 31Dec66. Noted with 46 Squadron marks and no code letter 08May67. To OCU Abingdon 10May67. To 46 Sqn (Abingdon) 23May68. To Operational Conversion Unit (Thorney Island) 1969. To 46 Squadron (Thorney Island) Sep70. Loaned to Electronic Warfare and Avionics Unit (Wyton) 19Aug75. Squadron disbanded 31Aug75 and aircraft to 5 MU (Kemble) for storage 17Oct75. Del Fairford 17Dec75 for conversion to E.Mk.3. Del 241 Operational Conversion Unit (Brize Norton) 24Jun76 for preparation for 115 Squadron. To A&AEE 05Aug77 for CA release trials. To 115 Squadron (Brize Norton) 16Dec77 named 'Guy Devas'. Loaned to EWAU (Wyton) 28Jun79. To 115 Sqn (Brize Norton) 19Nov79. To St Athan 25Mar80 and back to 115 Sqn (Brize Norton) 12May80. Squadron moved to Benson 07Jan83. To Ministry of Defence (Procurement Executive) 17Oct84 for IRFIS modifications by British Aerospace plc with del to Woodford 15Oct84. F/f after IRFIS mods 17Apr85. Del ex Woodford 25Apr85 back to 115 Squadron (Benson). To ASF Benson for major check 19Nov85, returning to 115 Sqn (Benson) 06Feb86. To ASF Benson 14May87 and back, returning to 115 Sqn (Benson) 02Jun87. To ASF Benson 01Nov88 and back to 115 Sqn (Benson) 06Dec88. Operation of aircraft transferred to Hunting Aviation Ltd 12Oct93 when calibration task contracted out. Squadron disbanded 19Oct93. Operation of aircraft transferred to Hunting Aviation Ltd 12Oct93 when calibration task contracted out. Del East Midlands 20Oct93. Retired from service 19Oct96 at end of Hunting contract and del to East Midlands 20Oct93. Painted as **P4-PVS** and ferried from East Midlands to Charleroi 26Oct96. Re-regd **9Q-CVS** on sale to the Air Transport Office and noted Rand 01Jun97. Regd **EL-WCP** by Jul97 and noted Rand as such 04Nov97. The 'EL' prefix was WFU in 2002. Subsequently reported stored Kinshasa-N'djili, DRC. Current status unknown.

Set 11

F/f 22Aug66 as **XS604**. Del to Station Flight Abingdon/Andover Operational Conversion Unit 29Sep66. To 46 Squadron (Abingdon) 01Dec66. Squadron moved to Thorney Island 11Sep70. Cat 3 damage 08May74. Repaired on site and reissued 11Jun74. To 5 MU (Kemble) 23Apr75 for storage. SOC and sold Royal New Zealand Air Force as **NZ7623** 26Jan77. Del ex Brize Norton 26Jan77 arriving Whenuapai 10Feb77. To 42 Squadron (Ohakea) 11Feb77. To 1 Squadron (Whenuapai) 26Jan79. To 42 Squadron (Ohakea) 09Mar79. To 1 Squadron (Whenuapai) 10May79. Squadron deactivated 07Dec84. Transferred to 42 Squadron (Whenuapai) Dec84. Retired from service 96 and stored Ardmore. Sold Eureka Aviation as **9Q-CDY** 28Nov96. Del via Brisbane 08Feb97 en route Wevelgem, Belgium. Lsd Bazair and noted Nairobi Aug97 in full c/s named "Ville de Bethlehem". Noted stored Liège Jan98 without titles. Stored Antwerp by 31May98 and still present Apr03. Fin, tailplane & wings removed at root and fuselage trucked to the Provinciaal Instituut voor Brandweer - en Ambulanciersopleiding at Ranst, Belgium overnight 14/15Sep06 with 'Lombaerst Industries – Industrial assembly & installation works' titles.

Set 12

F/f 09Sep66 as **XS605**. To Station Flight Abingdon 17Oct66. Loaned to Ministry of Aviation, ferried from Abingdon to A&AEE 02Nov66 for STOL checks. Del to Station Flight Abingdon/Andover Operational Conversion Unit 17Oct66. To 46 Squadron (Abingdon) 31Dec66. To 242 Operational Conversion Unit (Thorney Island) 04Oct71. To 46 Squadron (Thorney Island) 15Dec71. Squadron disbanded 31Aug75 and aircraft to 5 MU (Kemble) 25Sep75 for storage. To Fairford for conversion to E.Mk.3 17Dec75. To 115 Squadron (Brize Norton) 18Jul77. Squadron moved to Benson 07Jan83. Ferried 28Jul78 to Manchester from West Freugh for repaint and to Farnborough 09Aug78 on completion. Del to 115 Sqn (Brize Norton) 11Dec78. Squadron moved to Benson 04Jan83. To St Athan 09Feb83, returning to Benson 17Mar83. Loaned to Ministry of Defence (Procurement Executive) for IRFIS modifications by British Aerospace plc with del to Woodford 09Jan84. F/f after IRFIS mods 25Oct84. Del ex Woodford to A & AEE 17Nov84 before returning 22Nov84 to 115 Squadron (Benson). To ASF Benson 02Apr85, returning to Benson 02May85. To ASF Benson 14Aug86 for minor check returning to 115 Sqn (Benson) 17Oct86. To Luton 18Nov86 for repaint by McAlpine Aviation, back to 115 Sqn 27Jan87. To ASF Benson 07Jan88 for maintenance, back to 115 Sqn 25Mar88. Painted in 75th anniversary marks. Squadron disbanded 19Oct93. Operation of aircraft transferred to Hunting Aviation Ltd 12Oct93 when calibration task contracted out. Retired from service and ferried Northolt, Middlesex, U.K. for storage Feb95. Noted 31Oct97 with wings and tail removed and finally B/u Nov97.

Set 13

F/f 05Oct66 as **XS606**. Del to Station Flight Abingdon/Andover Operational Conversion Unit 03Nov66. Issued to Far East Air Force 15Dec66. To 52 Squadron (Seletar) 23Dec66. 52 Squadron moved to Changi 17Feb69. Squadron disbanded 31Dec69. To Station Flight Abingdon 15Jan70 and carried 46 Squadron markings Mar70. To Station Flight Thorney Island 04Sep70. To 5 MU (Kemble) 16Dec70 for storage. Loaned to Ministry of Defence (Procurement Executive) 04Aug72 having ferried to Farnborough two days before. Loaned to Ministry of Defence (Procurement) Executive 04Aug72. To Royal Aircraft Establish-

ment Farnborough and repainted in their grey, blue and white c/s. To RAE Bedford Aero Flight for STOL Steep Approach trials from 09May to 13Sep73 when returned RAE Farnborough and later used for parachute drop trials. Transferred to Ministry of Defence (Procurement Executive) 01Aug75 and ferried to Boscombe Down 24Sep75 for use by the Empire Test Pilots' School (ETPS) as a flying classroom for STOL, autopilot and asymmetric flight exercises. ETPS came under the control of QinetiQ from 02Jul01. 'QinetiQ' titles added beneath cockpit windows by Oct09. Took part in Jersey International display 23Aug11. Flew last flight at Boscombe Down 31Aug12 and the last operational flight of a UK military Andover. Ferried to Hurn 19Dec12 in full ETPS c/s for preparation for a ferry to Kenya. ETPS c/s removed by 21Dec12. Painted as **TL-AEW** 06Apr13, the marks **TL-DON** having been originally reserved but not used. Ferried Hurn-Algiers 16Apr13 on sale to Westwind Aviation Ltd of Kenya. Ferried Algiers-Tamanrasset-N'Djamena for a two night stop 17Apr13. Ferried from N'Djamena to Nairobi-Wilson via Juba 19Apr13. After removal of ferry equipment positioned to Juba 07May13. Later painted overall white without titles, and noted as such at Nairobi-Wilson 14Oct13. W/o 10Nov15 after take-off from Malakal Airport, South Sudan. No fatalities.

TT 11,262 hrs, 12,266 ldgs

Set 14

F/f 20Oct66 as **XS607**. Del to Station Flight Abingdon/Andover Operational Conversion Unit 12Nov66. Issued to Far East Air Force 15Dec66. To 52 Squadron (Seletar) 23Dec66. 52 Squadron moved to Changi 17Feb69. Squadron disbanded 31Dec69. To 5 MU (Kemble) 14Jan70. To 46 Squadron (Thorney Island) 14Apr71. To 5 MU (Kemble) 26May71. To Station Flight Thorney Island 03Aug71. To 46 Squadron (Thorney Island) 29Sep71. Loaned to Ministry of Defence (Procurement Executive) 15Oct71 and operated by the A & AEE. Returned to 46 Squadron (Thorney Island) 1972. Transferred to Ministry of

XS605 Set 12 Andover E.Mk.3 of 115 Squadron at Brize Norton, Oxfordshire, on 5th June 1993 in 75th Anniversary colours and showing evidence of the APU fitting. (Keith Gaskell)

9Q-CPW Set 14 in store at Johannesburg-Rand on 18th January 2000. (Keith Gaskell)

Defence (Procurement Executive) 01Apr76 for operation by the A & AEE. Regd as **G-BEBY** to Hawker Siddeley Aviation Ltd 23Jul76 (CofR G-BEBY/E1). Del Bitteswell 23Jul76 as XS607. F/f as G-BEBY 02Aug76 and CofA issued 10Aug76, the date aircraft positioned Bitteswell to Manchester. Departed Manchester 11Aug76 for a demonstration tour of India. Del via Gatwick at end of tour 31Aug76. Regn cld 06Sep76 as transferred to military marks. Returned to A & AEE as **XS607** 13Sep76. Del to Royal Aircraft Establishment 16Sep76 and frequently based at West Freugh for sonobuoy research. Painted in RAE c/s at Dan-Air Engineering Ltd Ringway 28Jul78-09Aug78. Used as a large flying laboratory. Later fitted with Anti-Radar Missile Airborne Data Analysis System (ARMADAS) and used for towed decoy trials. RAE absorbed into the Defence Research Agency 01Apr91. Based Boscombe Down with effect from 15Aug94. Last DRA flight at Boscombe Down 15Sep95 and WFU being SOC the same date. Ferried Hurn regd as **9Q-CPW** 28Aug96. Departed Hurn for Ostend 02Oct96 on sale to Waltair S.P.R.L. Noted Kinshasa 27Feb98 in service and later in store at Rand 19Jan00. Seen Kinshasa 15Mar01 and by Sep03 at the same location stored with Waltair Aviation titles. Noted being prepared for Trans Air Cargo Services at Kinshasa-N'djili Aug07.

Set 15

F/f 04Nov66 as **XS608**. Del to Station Flight Abingdon/Andover Operational Conversion Unit 06Dec66. Issued to Far East Air Force 15Dec66. To 52 Squadron (Seletar) 23Dec66. 52 Squadron moved to Changi 17Feb69. Squadron disbanded 31Dec69. To 5 MU (Kemble) 13Jan70 for storage. To Station Flight Thorney Island 10Nov70. Involved in accident 08Mar71. Repaired on site and reissued to 46 Squadron (Thorney Island) 01Dec71. To Station Flight Thorney Island from 12Apr72 until returned 46 Squadron (Thorney Island) 01Oct73. Squadron disbanded 31Aug75. To 5 MU (Kemble) 18Sep75 for storage. Air-tested 16Oct76 and ferried Brize Norton 18Oct76. SOC 18Oct76. Sold Royal New Zealand Air Force as **NZ7624** and used by the RAF/RNZAF for conversion training with 241 Operational Conversion Unit. Del ex Brize Norton 30Nov76 arriving Whenuapai 11Dec76. To 1 Squadron (Whenuapai) 12Dec76. Squadron deactivated 07Dec84. Transferred to 42 Squadron (Whenuapai) Dec84. Withdrawn from use 1992 and noted derelict Ardmore May95. Hulk transferred to Whenuapai Air Base, New Zealand fire school and still present 14Oct11 less wings.

TT 8,395 hrs

Set 16

F/f 18Nov66 as **XS609**. Del to 46 Squadron (Abingdon) 21Dec66. Undercarriage collapsed Fairford 30May68. Repaired and returned to service 19Aug68. 46 Squadron moved Thorney Island Sep70. w/o on take-off from Ampugnano Air Base Siena, Italy en route Pisa 08Apr72. 2 crew and 4 RAF pax killed. Struck off charge 01Jul72.

TT 3,061 hrs, 3,970 ldgs

Set 17

F/f 08Dec66 as **XS610**. Del to 46 Squadron (Abingdon) 24Jan67. Cat.3R Damage 28Jan69, repaired on site by 71 MU. 46 Squadron moved to Thorney Island Sep70. To 242 Operational Conversion Unit (Thorney Island) 12Dec74. To 46 Squadron (Thorney Island) 08May75. To 5 MU (Kemble) for storage 11Sep75 following disbandment of 46 Squadron on 31Aug75. Del Brize Norton 08Feb77 and converted to E.Mk.3 by 13Jan78. To 115 Squadron (Brize Norton) 20Jan78. To St Athan 29Sep79 returning to 115 Sqn (Brize Norton) 11Dec79. Squadron moved to Benson 04Jan83. To ASF Benson 12Sep83, to 115 Sqn (Benson) 10Oct83. To ASF Benson 12Apr84 for major check, returning to 115Sqn 01May84. To ASF Benson 17Jul85, returning to 115 Sqn 29Jul85. To Ministry of Defence (Procurement Executive) for IRFIS modifications by British Aerospace plc with del to Woodford 19Aug85. F/f after IRFIS mods

10Feb86. Del back to 115 Squadron (Benson) 17Feb86. Displayed at Farnborough Air Show Sep86. To ASF Benson 13Feb87 for major check, returning to 115 Sqn 30Apr87. To ASF Benson for maintenance 27Jun88, back to 115 Sqn 15Jul82. Squadron disbanded 19Oct93. Operation of aircraft transferred to Hunting Aviation Ltd 12Oct93 when calibration task contracted out. Retired from service 19Oct96 at end of Hunting contract. Painted as **P4-BLL** and ferried from East Midlands to Charleroi 26Oct96. Regd **9Q-CVK** on sale to the Air Transport Office and noted as such Rand 18Jun97. Damaged landing Thonyor, Southern Sudan c.2003. Returned to service after eight months. Diverted to Kapoeta, Southern Sudan after an engine failure approx Feb05. On ferry flight to Lokichoggio suffered a further engine failure soon after t/o and crash landed short of the runway when returning Kapoeta, Sudan Jun05. No fatalities.

Set 18

F/f 23Dec66 as **XS611**. Del to 46 Squadron (Abingdon) 02Feb67. To 21 Squadron (Khormaksar) 15Feb67. To Middle East Communications Squadron (Muharraq) 17Jul67 as a VIP aircraft. To 84 Squadron (Muharraq) 20Dec70. To 46 Squadron (Thorney Island) 29Sep71. Loaned to the Ministry of Defence (Procurement Executive) 01Nov73 for use with the A & AEE and later to Royal Aircraft Establishment 04Mar74 and in Aug74 for 'Mod 201' handling trials. Allotted back to the RAF 17Sep74 and to Thorney Island 11Dec74. To 5 MU (Kemble) 27Feb75 for storage. SOC and sold to Royal New Zealand Air Force as **NZ7625** 16Mar77. Del ex Brize Norton 19Mar77 arriving Whenuapai 02Apr77. To 1 Squadron (Whenuapai) 18Apr77. To 42 Squadron (Ohakea) 31Aug77. To 1 Squadron (Whenuapai) 13Feb78. To 42 Squadron (Ohakea) 25Jan79. Squadron moved to Whenuapai 10Dec84. Retired from service 20Jun98. Regd as **3C-KKC** to 748 Air Services and ferried via Brisbane 21Sep98 and Darwin 22Sep98 arriving Southend via Rome 29Sep98. Del ex Southend 03Oct98 on sale to 748 Air Services Ltd of Kenya. Noted Nairobi 11Mar00. Stored Lokichoggio, Kenya after last flight 14Jul01 and remained on ramp until finally b/u Mar07.

TT 15,218 hrs, 21,638 ldgs

Set 19

F/f 13Jan67 as **XS612**. Del to 46 Squadron (Abingdon) 17Feb67. To 52 Squadron (Seletar) 29Mar67. 52 Squadron moved to Changi 17Feb69. Squadron disbanded 31Dec69. To Station Flight Abingdon 14Jan70 and noted with 46 Squadron marks by 21Mar70. Cat 3 damage 11May70. To 5 MU (Kemble) 07Jul70 for storage. To 46 Squadron (Thorney Island) 29Jun73. To 5 MU (Kemble) 16Apr75 for storage. SOC 26Jan77. Sold to Royal New Zealand Air Force as **NZ7626** and del ex Brize Norton 28Jan77 arriving Whenuapai 08Feb77. To 1 Squadron (Whenuapai) 11Feb77. Squadron deactivated 07Dec84. Transferred to 42 Squadron (Whenuapai) Dec84. Retired from service 1996 and stored Ardmore. Sold Eureka Aviation NV as **9Q-CJR** 28Nov96. Ferried from Auckland 17Apr97 via Brisbane, Darwin, Bali, Medan, Colombo, Karachi, Bahrain, Larnaca and Naples en route Wevelgem where it arrived 24Apr97. Noted Wevelgem 30Apr97 painted overall white with 'Eureka Aviation' titles. Regd as **EL-AFY** to Analinda Financial Corp and f/f as such at Ostend 30May97. Lsd Eastern Congo Airlines and noted as such at Goma 18Aug97. Ferried Rand by 04Sep97 painted overall white without titles. Operated for Société de Fret et de Transport – SAFT out of Libreville 1998 and seen Rand 25Jan98 & 10Feb98. Sold Gabon Express as **3C-CPX** and ferried from Rand to Libreville 31May98 by Bob Sobek. Entered service 26Oct98 from Libreville to Port Gentil. Visited Rand 03Jul99, 08Apr00 and 28Aug00. Repainted at Rand 13Sep00. Noted Rand 16Oct02 regd as **3D-MKX** with evidence of former Gabon Express titles. Reportedly for sale. Departed Rand for Kinshasa, DRC 01Mar03 for operation by Malu Aviation. Seen at Kinshasa, DRC, 28Feb06 and subsequently w/o at Bandundu, DRC, date unknown. 2 crew survived.

NZ7627 Set 20 of the Royal New Zealand Air Force in the unusual overall all-white scheme carried during the 1990s. *(George Jenks/WHC)*

XS637 Set 21 Andover C.Mk.1 of 60 Squadron at Brize Norton, Oxfordshire, on 7th September 1991 with 75th Anniversary markings '1916-1991' on the top of the fin. *(Keith Gaskell)*

Set 20

F/f 26Jan67 as **XS613**. Del to 46 Squadron (Abingdon) 17Feb67. To 52 Squadron (Seletar) 29Mar67. 52 Squadron moved to Changi 17Feb69. Squadron disbanded 31Dec69. To 5 MU (Kemble) 16Jan70 for storage. To 46 Squadron (Thorney Island) 25Feb71. To Station Flight Thorney Island 18Mar71. To A&AEE investigating cowling ice-up 22Mar71, returning to Station Flight Thorney Island 24Mar71. To 46 Squadron (Thorney Island) 27May71. To 242 Operational Conversion Unit Thorney Island 14Mar72. To 46 Squadron (Thorney Island) 11Apr72. To 5 MU (Kemble) 12Jun74 for storage. SOC 22Apr77. Sold Royal New Zealand Air Force as **NZ7627** with del ex Brize Norton 25Apr77 arriving Whenuapai 06May77. To 42 Squadron (Ohakea) 20May77. Squadron moved to Whenuapai 10Dec84. Shown at Australian International Air Show at Avalon, Victoria Oct92 painted overall white. Retired from service 20Jun98 and stored Ardmore. Painted as **3C-KKS** and ferried via Darwin 24Apr99 and Bastia-Southend 26Apr99 painted overall white. Painted with Air Katanga titles as **9Q-COE** 30Apr99. Regn **3C-KKS** taped back on and ferried Ostend 19May99. Ferried Ostend-Malaga-Las Palmas 23/24May99. Seen Lanseria in full Air Katanga gold/white c/s as **9Q-COE** 02Sep99 (although not officially regd as such until 10May00), 20Sep01, 29Jan02 and 19Apr02. Noted still active Manono, DRC without titles 18Jun05. Sold 748 Air Services Ltd of Kenya and regd **5Y-BSX** 29Jul06. WFU Lokichoggio, Kenya 01Jun07 and put in store. Still present 19Sep09.

TT 14,706 hrs, 17,859 ldgs

Set 21

F/f 14Feb67 as **XS637**. Del to 46 Squadron (Abingdon) 15Mar67. To 52 Squadron (Seletar) 29Mar67. 52 Squadron moved to Changi 17Feb69. Squadron disbanded 31Dec69. To Station Flight

Abingdon 15Jan70. To Station Flight Thorney Island 01Sep70. To Commander Air Forces Northern Europe (NATO) and based Fornebu, Oslo late 1970 in desert camouflage. Later painted with white top and staggered blue cheatline after Mar75. To 32 Squadron (Northolt) 13Nov75. To Station Flight Brize Norton 16Nov78. To St Athan 15Feb80 for repaint, returned to Station Flight Brize Norton 11Feb81. To Commander Air Forces Northern Europe (NATO) at Benson 04Jan83. To 115 Sqn (Benson) 14Jul83. To Commander Air Forces Northern Europe (NATO) 09Aug83. To ASF Benson for major check 17Oct84. To Commander Northern Air Forces Europe (NATO) at Benson 26Nov84, and then Northolt from 01May85. To ASF Benson for modifications 10Jun85, returning to 32 Sqn (Northolt) 10Jul85. To ASF Benson 29Apr86, returning to 32 Sqn 15May86. To ASF Benson for major check 03Nov86. To 60 Sqn (Wildenrath) 16Mar87. Squadron disbanded 31Mar92. Stored Shawbury from 02Apr92. SOC 08Jul93 and sold at auction the same date for £80,000. Ferried Southend 01Nov93 for civil conversion. Regd as **G-BVNK** to Flightline Ltd 19May94 (CofR G-BVNK/R1) but remained stored at Southend unmarked. R/o Southend in full ITAB Cargo c/s as **9Q-CJJ** 07Apr95 named "Fatima". UK regn cld 19Apr95 as transferred Zaire. Del Southend-Ostend 20Apr95 with call sign Shabair 903. Re-regd **9Q-CLL** 24Apr95. Noted as such at Lanseria, South Africa 13Oct95. Noted active at Rand 02Jun97 but reportedly wfu by Jun98 and regn cld 01Jun98. Possibly the airframe noted derelict at Lubumbashi in 2003 in ITAB Cargo c/s. (See HS748 c/n 1561 with same regn).

Set 22

F/f 08Mar67 as **XS638**. Del to 46 Squadron (Abingdon) 03Apr67. Cat 3 damage 11May70. To 46 Squadron (Thorney Island) 29Jun73. To 242 Operational Conversion Unit (Thorney Island) 19Feb75. To 46 Squadron (Thorney Island) 02May75. To 5 MU (Kemble) 08May75 for storage. SOC 30Dec76. Sold Royal New

Zealand Air Force as **NZ7628** and del ex Brize Norton 27Jan77 arriving Whenuapai 08Feb77. To 42 Squadron (Ohakea) 10Feb77 but remained Whenuapai until ferried Woodbourne 13Feb77. Converted to VIP configuration at No.1 Repair Depot, Woodbourne and returned to 42 Squadron (Ohakea) 02Nov77. Squadron moved to Whenuapai 10Dec84. Retired from service 96 and stored Ardmore. Sold Eureka Aviation as **9Q-CYB** 28Nov96. Ferried via Brisbane 18Apr97 en route Wevelgem, Belgium. Sold International Transair Business - ITAB Cargo Apr97. Noted active Lanseria 10Feb02. Repainted Lanseria Jun02 with white top, grey undersides and blue cheatline. Noted still active Manono, DRC without titles 18Jun05. Status unknown.

Set 23

F/f 29Mar67 as **XS639**. Del to 46 Squadron (Abingdon) 01May67. To 60 MU Leconfield for modifications 01Nov68, retd to 46 Sqn (Abingdon) 06Feb69. 46 Squadron moved to Thorney Island 09Sep70. 46 Squadron disbanded 31Aug75. To 32 Squadron (Northolt) 11Nov75. Del Fairford 17Dec75 for preparation for 115 Squadron. To 115 Squadron (Brize Norton) 29Jul76. Converted to E.Mk.3A 1978. To RAF Kemble 29Jun79. To 115 Sqn (Brize Norton) 15Aug79 and then loaned to Electronic Warfare and Avionics Unit (Wyton) 18Apr80. To 115 Sqn (Brize Norton) 24Oct80, moving with the squadron to Benson 04Jan83. To ASF Benson 31Aug83, and retd to 115 Sqn 11Nov83. To Hurn 15Apr86 for repaint by Lovaux Ltd 15Apr86, retd to 115 Sqn 29May86. To ASF Benson 02Jun86, returning to 115 Sqn (Benson) 01Jul86. To ASF Benson 20Aug87, returning to 115 Sqn (Benson) 11Sep86. To ASF Benson 29Nov88. To 32 Squadron (Northolt) 01Apr92. Ferried to the RAF Museum, Cosford, Shropshire, U.K. for preservation 13Jul94 with serial **9241M** allotted. Displayed in Hangar 1 at Cosford (Aug15).

Set 24

F/f 14Apr67 as **XS640**. Del to 46 Squadron (Abingdon) 04May67. To 60 MU 01Dec67. Del to Ministry of Technology 02Feb68 for use of A&AEE for speech broadcast trials. Cat.3R Damage 20Oct71, repaired on site by 71 MU. Returned to 46 Squadron (Abingdon) 01Apr68. Loaned to Ministry of Defence (Procurement Executive) 04Jul74 to 17Oct74 for Mod.201 trials at Thorney Island. Returned to 46 Squadron (Abingdon) 17Oct74. Squadron disbanded 31Aug75 and aircraft to 5 MU (Kemble) for

storage. Del Fairford 17Dec75 for preparation for service with 115 Squadron. To 5 MU (Kemble) 24Aug76. To 115 Squadron (Brize Norton) 01Oct78, to 5 MU (Kemble) 08Nov78. Converted to E.Mk.3 Dec78-29Jun79. To 115 Sqn (Brize Norton) 29Jun79. Squadron moved to Benson 04Jan83. To Ministry of Defence (Procurement Executive) for IRFIS modifications by British Aerospace plc with del to Woodford 21Mar85. F/f after IRFIS mods 16Sep85. Del back to 115 Squadron (Benson) 24Sep85. To ASF Benson 17Oct88, returning to 115 Sqn (Benson) 03Nocv88. Squadron disbanded 19Oct93. Operation of aircraft transferred to Hunting Aviation Ltd 19Oct93 when calibration task contracted out. Del East Midlands 19Oct93. Retired from service 19Oct96 at end of Hunting contract. Painted as **P4-TBL** and ferried from East Midlands to Charleroi 26Oct96. Seen Rand 18Nov96, 03Dec96, 06Feb97, 20Feb97 and again 09May97 (with Hunting Aviation logo on nose). Painted as **9Q-CVC** with ITAB Cargo titles and noted as such Lanseria 04Feb99. Damaged beyond repair landing at a bush strip in Katanga, DRC Apr99. B/u for spares. (See Set 29 with same regn)

Set 25

F/f 05May67 as **XS641**. Del to RAF Leconfield 25May67 and later Abingdon. To 15 MU (Wroughton) 05Jul67. To 84 Squadron (Sharjah) 22Aug67 coded 'B'. Occasionally used by the Search and Rescue Flight from 08Oct68. Squadron moved to Muharraq Dec70 and later disbanded 31Oct71. To 46 Squadron (Thorney Island) 01Oct71. Cat.3R ground incident 23Sep74, repaired on site by 71 MU. To 5 MU (Kemble) for storage 17Sep75 before 46 Squadron disbanded 31Aug75. Del Fairford 17Dec75. To 115 Squadron (Brize Norton) 07Jan77. To 5 MU (Kemble) 09Nov78. To 115 Sqn (Brize Norton) 14Dec78. Squadron moved to Benson 04Jan83. To 60 Squadron (Wildenrath) 03Nov87. To 115 Sqn (Brize Norton) 04Dec87. Painted in hemp c/s 17Dec87. Del Woodford 17Feb88 for conversion by British Aerospace PLC to C.Mk.1 (PR). F/f as such 26Mar90. To 60 Squadron (Wildenrath) 27Apr90 as Ascot 8009. Flown to Shawbury for storage 18Feb92 prior to Squadron disbanding 31Mar92. Used as an instructional airframe at the School of Technical Training (Cosford) from Jun93 as **9198M** (allotted 14Jun93), coded 'Z'. Dismantled and roaded to Sandbach Car & Commercial Dismantlers Ltd of Sandbach, Cheshire, U.K. 30Nov05. Fuselage displayed at the Glastonbury Festival in Jun08 and Jul09. Last noted Sandbach 20Sep09.

One of the Royal New Zealand Air Force Andovers in the attractive light blue colour-scheme carried by 42 Squadron aircraft.

Set 26

F/f 23May67 as **XS642**. Del to 15 MU (Wroughton) 15Jun67. To 84 Squadron (Sharjah) 17Aug67 coded 'C' in desert camouflage with orange spinners. Occasionally used by the Search and Rescue Flight. Squadron moved to Muharraq Dec70 and later disbanded 31Oct71. To 5 MU (Kemble) for storage 23Dec70. Declared a Non-effective Aircraft 18May76. Allotted serial **8785M** 13Mar83 and used as an instructional airframe at Benson for crash/rescue training. Struck off charge 18Jan83. Remains still present on fire dump 15Sep91. B/U Benson, Oxfordshire, UK Jun/Jul94.

Set 27

F/f 14Jun67 as **XS643**. Del to 15 MU (Wroughton) 04Jul67. To 84 Squadron (Sharjah) 04Sep67 coded 'D'. Squadron moved to Muharraq Dec70. To 5 MU (Kemble) 27Sep71 for storage. Declared a Non-effective Aircraft 01May75. To 115 Squadron (Brize Norton) 09Feb78. To 5 MU (Kemble) 18Apr78, then 115 Sqn (Brize Norton) 05Jun78 and 5 MU (Kemble) 17Aug78. To 115 Sqn (Brize Norton) 10 Oct78. Converted to E.Mk.3 Aug80. Converted to E.Mk.3A Feb82. To 115 Sqn (Brize Norton) 09Mar82. Squadron moved to Benson 04Jan83. To ASF Benson 29Apr87. To Luton for repaint by McAlpine Aviation Ltd 18May87, and back to 115 Sqn 22Jul87. To 32 Squadron (Northolt) early 1992. Painted in overall grey c/s with thin light blue cheatline below windows Sep92 and noted as such at Düsseldorf 03Mar93. To DRA Boscombe Down 06Jun94. WFU Boscombe Down Aug96. Transported to Manston, Kent, U.K. on three low loaders 18Mar98 for the use of the Defence Fire Services Civilian Training School with serial **9278M** allocated. Sold as scrap by 2001 to Hanningfield Metals, Stock, Essex. Nose section noted Mar16 in Masons Metal scrapyard, Dudley, West Midlands, UK.

Set 28

F/f 14Jul67 as **XS644**. Del to Royal Air Force Operational Conversion Unit at Abingdon 15Aug67. Unit re-titled Air Training Squadron (also known as Andover Training Squadron) 30Apr68. To Air Training Sqn (Thorney Island) 01Aug70. To 242 Operational Conversion Unit Thorney Island 01Nov70. To 5 MU (Kemble) 17Jun74 for storage. To 242 Operational Conversion Unit Thorney Island 23Jul74. To 46 Squadron (Thorney Island) 01May75. Squadron disbanded 31Aug75 and aircraft to 5 MU (Kemble). Del RAF Wyton 15Oct75 for the Electronic Warfare Evaluation and Trials Unit later renamed Electronic Warfare and Avionics Unit. To A & AEE early 1977 for flight trials of SRIM 3730. To Ministry of Defence (Procurement Executive) 17Feb77 and del to Hawker Siddeley Aviation Ltd at Hawarden 26Apr77 for tests by HSA and modifications to an earlier fitted under fuselage radar pod. To A & AEE 18May77 before return to Electronic Warfare and Avionics Unit at RAF Wyton 30May77. Carried 51 Squadron markings in 1978. Radar pod removed by 1981. To 115 Squadron (Brize Norton) 10Jun81 but still operated by the Electronic Warfare and Avionics Unit at Wyton. To 115 Sqn (Benson) 06Jan83 but still operated by the Electronic Warfare and Avionics Unit at Wyton, to whom it was transferred 18Feb83. Allotted to A&AEE from Wyton for CA trials 23.Mar83. Converted to E.Mk.3A Apr83. Released to RAF 06May83, and to 115Sqn (Benson) 09May83. To Electronic Warfare and Avionics Unit (Wyton) 19Jul83. Returned to 115 Sqn (Benson) 08Nov83. To Luton for repaint by McAlpine Aviation Ltd 10Mar87, returning to 115 Sqn (Benson) 06May87. To ASF Benson 25Jul88, then 115 Sqn (Benson) 01Nov88. To 32 Squadron (Northolt) early 1992 and painted in overall grey c/s with thin blue cheatline below windows from 22Feb93 to 31Mar93. Sold Air Aid Limited. Regd as **VR-BOI** 14Jun94 and del 21Jun94. Noted as such at Entebbe 26Aug96. Re-regd **9Q-COE** and noted on repaint in ITAB c/s Lanseria 16Nov96 (although not officially regd as such until 15Jan98). Noted Rand 02Jun97. Damaged beyond repair landing at the same strip in Katanga, DRC

Apr99 at which Set 24 was w/o. It was recovering spares from the first aircraft when the nose leg broke off causing cracking of the fuselage. Regn cld 01Jun99. (See Set 20 with same regn).

Set 29

F/f 21Sep67 as **XS645**. Del to 46 Squadron (Abingdon) 05Oct67. To 84 Squadron (Sharjah) 06Nov67 coded 'E'. Squadron moved to Muharraq Dec70. To Station Flight Thorney Island 29Sep71. To 46 Squadron (Thorney Island) 05Nov71. Operated by 242 Operational Conversion Unit Thorney Island from Feb to May72 before return to 46 Squadron (Thorney Island) May72. To 5 MU (Kemble) 19Jun74 for storage. SOC 28Apr77. Sold to Royal New Zealand Air Force as **NZ7629** and del ex Brize Norton 04Oct77 arriving with 1 Squadron (Whenuapai) 20Oct77. Trials aircraft for additional wing fuel tank modification (later incorporated into all RNZAF Andovers). To 42 Squadron (Ohakea) 23Jan79. To 1 Squadron (Whenuapai) 18Feb79. To 42 Squadron (Ohakea) 16May79. To 1 Squadron (Whenuapai) 31Jul79. Squadron deactivated 07Dec84. To 42 Squadron (Whenuapai) Dec84.

Operated on behalf of the United Nations for use with the Middle East peace keeping force based in Teheran from late Sep88 until Dec90. Painted all white with United Nations titles. Noted 20May89 at Honiara, Solomon Islands, all white w/o titles. Retired from service 20Jun98 and stored Ardmore. Painted as **3C-KKT** and del ex New Zealand 31Mar99 arriving Southend 04Apr99. R/o in Air Katanga c/s as **9Q-CVC** 08Apr99. Regn **3C-KKT** taped over 9Q-CVC 03May99 and Air Katanga titles removed. Departed Southend for Ostend 21Jun99 and onwards to Malaga 24Jun99. Noted Lanseria 13Sep00 & 21Nov01 in full Air Katanga c/s painted as **9Q-CVC**. Noted still active Manono, DRC without titles 18Jun05 and again Lanseria 10Mar06. Noted active at Manono, DRC, w/o titles 18Jun05 and at Lanseria 10Mar06. (See Set 24 with same regn). Status unknown.

Set 30

F/f 19Oct67 as **XS646**. Del to 46 Squadron (Abingdon) 06Nov67. To 84 Squadron (Sharjah) 01Dec67 coded 'F'. Used by the Search and Rescue Flight from 27Apr69 to 09May69. Squadron moved to Muharraq Dec70. To 5 MU (Kemble) 30Sep71 for storage. Loaned to Ministry of Defence (Procurement Executive) and ferried to Farnborough via Bedford 26Jan73 for use by the Royal Aircraft Establishment at Farnborough. Used as a large flying laboratory. Transferred to MoD(PE) for use by RAE 01Aug75. Carried out trial investigation into problems encountered when making automatic approaches in poor visibility using the later abandoned Doppler Microwave Landing System during 1976. Infra-red cameras were mounted in a re-profiled nose in 1982 for trials with electro-optic sensors. The aircraft was also fitted with an under floor pylon that carried a Vinten camera pod. RAE absorbed into Defence Research Agency 01Apr91. In early 1994 it was fitted with an FLIR installation that was integrated with the aircraft's navigation system. Based Boscombe Down from 11Jul94. Operator renamed the DERA from 01Apr97 and as QinetiQ from 02Jul01. Fitted with an extended radar nose cone by Aug10. Last flew 06Apr11 and noted in external storage at Boscombe Down 24Sep12. Sold to Westwind Aviation Ltd of Kenya and robbed of all useful parts at Boscombe Down Nov13. Nose section removed Mar14 and transported elsewhere by military vehicles.

TT 6,600 hrs, 5,081 ldgs

Set 31

F/f 15Jan68 as **XS647**. Del to RAF at 15 MU (Wroughton) 22Feb68. Loaned to Ministry of Technology from 22Mar68 and del to A & AEE at Boscombe Down until 31Dec68. To 5 MU (Kemble) 27Jan69 for storage. Operated by 84 Squadron (Sharjah) early 1970 until Jul70. Struck off charge Jan81. Sold to British Aerospace plc 28Jan81. Arrived Woodford by road

25Mar81. Fuselage used as a design rig for the Advanced Turbo-prop Aircraft. By early 1985 the complete fuselage had become the basis of the Advanced Turboprop fuselage and cockpit mock-up with a new fibreglass fin and rear fuselage. Mock-up used for trial installation of seating, interior furnishings and cockpit layouts. ATP mock-up to BAe Hatfield Customer Centre by road

15Aug88. To Wales Aircraft Museum after closure of Hatfield 1994. To Enstone airfield Oxfordshire, U.K. by Feb96.

Two Andovers have been noted in Democratic Republic of Congo Air Force colours recently with serials 9T-TCO and 9T-TCP with unconfirmed Set numbers.

XS641 Set 25 Royal Air Force immediately after its conversion to its photographic rôle as a C.Mk.1 (PR) on 27th April 1990. (WHC)

9Q-CVC Set 29 of Air Katanga at Lanseria, South Africa, on 21st November 2001. This was the second Andover to carry this registration after the first 9Q-CVC was damaged beyond repair. (Richard J. Church)

VT-DUO c/n HAL/K/506 while on its visit to Woodford in 1966/7 prior to delivery to Indian Airlines Corporation.

HAL 748
INDIVIDUAL AIRCRAFT HISTORIES

C/n   Set No   Series

HAL/K/500 (2) Srs.1/103

F/f 01Nov61 as **BH572** from Hindustan Aeronautics Kanpur airfield. Named "Subroto" 26Nov61 in honour of a former Chief of Air Staff of the Indian Air Force, Air Marshall Subroto Mukerjee. As the Indian prototype, the aircraft was used for development work. It departed Kanpur on 04Aug62 on a promotional tour via Barrackpore (north of Calcutta) to Rangoon, Bangkok, Butterworth, Singapore, Jakarta, Singkep, Baranti and back to Jakarta on 11Aug62. On 16Aug62 it flew back to Singapore before departing for Medan on 20Aug62 and later visited Kuala Lumpur and Phnom Penh before returning Bangkok via Siem Reap on 26Aug62. The following day it flew to Rangoon before returning to Barrackpore on 31Aug62. It finally returned to Kanpur on 01Sep62 having flown 50 hrs and 05 mins on the tour of which 7 hrs 30 mins was display flying and experience flights. Regd **VT-DRF** early in 1964.

Del Indian Air Force as BH572 17Apr64, the first del to the military. Later permanently loaned to the Chairman of Hindustan Aeronautics Ltd as a personal transport and subsequently used as a company corporate aircraft. Noted active Delhi 22Nov07 in white c/s uncoded and Banglore 2011.

HAL/K/501 (8) Srs.1/104

F/f 13Mar63 as **BH573**. Converted to Srs.2/104. Del Indian Air Force 13Oct64 named "Jumbo" after the late Wing Commander K.K. (Jumbo) Majumdar. VIP. Status unknown.

HAL/K/502 (9) Srs.1/104

F/f 12Sep63 as **BH574**. Converted to Srs.2/104. Del Indian Air Force 23Feb65. VIP. Last noted Yelahanka Dec93. Status unknown.

HAL/K/503 (11) Srs.1/104

Originally wrongly painted as **BH575** and f/f as such Jan64. Converted to Srs.2/104 and repainted with correct serial as **BH-1047**. Del Indian Air Force 27Jun66. VIP. Last seen Palam Mar92. Reportedly WFU by early 2008 location unknown.

HAL/K/504 (31) Srs.2/203

Originally wrongly painted as **BH576**. First Indian production Series 2. F/f 28Jan64 as BH576. Repainted with correct serial as **BH-1048**. Loaned Indian Airlines Corporation Jan65 for evaluation. Del Indian Air Force 19Nov65. VIP. Coded 'L'. Noted Mumbai 12Nov10 in white top c/s uncoded.

HAL/K/505 (32) Srs.2/203

F/f 21Jan65 as **BH-1010**. Regd to Hindustan Aeronautics Ltd as **VT-DTR** 1965. Del Indian Air Force as **BH-1010** 14Dec65. VIP. Coded 'Y'. Seen Yelahanka Dec98 named "Jyoti". Noted Delhi 02Feb11 in white top c/s uncoded, and again at Bangalore, Yelahanka 09Feb13.

HAL/K/506 (33) Srs.2/224

F/f 11Feb66 as **VT-DUO**. Del Hawker Siddeley Aviation Ltd at Woodford 19Mar66 in natural metal finish for fitting out painting and preparation for commercial use. F/f after this 06Apr67 and c/o performance trials until 28Apr67. Del ex Woodford 10May67 on return to Hindustan Aeronautics Ltd. Loaned Indian Airlines Corporation 22Jun67 before official handover to the airline on 28Jun67 at Chakeri. Named "Taj Mahal". Entered service 08Aug67. W/o Hyderabad, India while crew training 05Mar84 at which time the aircraft was the world lead 748 for total hours flown. Overran runway into boundary wall on take-off during simulated No.2 engine failure. No fatalities among 3 crew on board. Regn cld 28Mar06.

TT 37,603 hrs, 36,369 ldgs

BH576 c/n HAL/K/504 of the Indian Air Force at Kanpur in January 1964. Even though the full serial is not clear in the photograph, it was wrongly painted as BH576 and later revised to BH-1048.
(George Jenks/WHC)

HAL/K/507   (41)   Srs.2/203

F/f Oct66 as **BH-1011**. Del Indian Air Force 06Dec66. VIP. Coded 'A' and later 'H'. Noted active Bangalore 22Sep09 in white top c/s uncoded and again at Bangalore 08Feb11.

HAL/K/508   (42)   Srs.2/203

F/f Jan67 as **BH-1012**. Del Indian Air Force 17Mar67. VIP. Coded 'K'. WFU Palam, New Delhi, India Feb01.

HAL/K/509   (43)   Srs.2/203

F/f May67 as **BH-1013**. Del Indian Air Force 17Jun67. VIP. Noted active Delhi 12Mar08 in white top c/s uncoded.

HAL/K/510   (51)   Srs.2/203

F/f Aug67 as **H-913**. Del Indian Air Force 27Sep67. VIP. Coded 'A'. Noted active Delhi 14Sep07 in white top c/s now coded 'D' and again Bangalore 08Feb11 uncoded.

HAL/K/511   (52)   Srs.2/224

F/f 07Nov67 as **VT-DXF**. Del Indian Airlines Corporation 25Nov67 named "Ajanta". W/o landing Mangalore, India 19Aug81 while operating flight IC557 from Bangalore. Overshot runway into valley in bad weather. No fatalities among 4 crew and 22 pax on board.

TT 33,093 hrs, 30,858 ldgs

HAL/K/512   (53)   Srs.2/224

F/f 02Jan68 as **VT-DXG**. Del Indian Airlines Corporation 19Jan68 named "Sauchi". W/o fifty miles south west of Madurai, India 09Dec71 when en route Trivandrum-Madurai. Crashed into hillside at Chinnamanur. 4 crew and 17 pax killed. 10 pax survived.

TT 7,108 hrs, 6,862 ldgs

HAL/K/513   (65)   Srs.2/224

F/f 04Mar68 as **VT-DXH**. Del Indian Airlines Corporation 22Mar68 named "Somnath". Trans-ferred Vayudoot Ltd 15Apr89. Company merger into Indian Airlines Corp completed Mar94 and aircraft put in storage. Transferred Indian Border Security Force, Ministry of Home Affairs by Oct94. Stored Delhi, India from Sep98 and still present Dec07.

TT in excess of 48,942 hrs, 45,159 ldgs

HAL/K/514   (67)   Srs.2/224

F/f 23Apr68 as **VT-DXI** (15May68 has also been quoted). Del Indian Airlines Corporation 30May68 named "Amber". W/o on take-off Tirupati, India 16Jun81 while operating flight IC519 to Hyderabad. Failed to gain height in heavy rain. No fatalities among 4 crew and 24 pax on board.

TT 31,279 hrs, 28,926 ldgs

HAL/K/515   (69)   Srs.2/224

F/f 21Jun68 as **VT-DXJ**. Del Indian Airlines Corporation 17Jul68 named "Rameshwaram". Damaged Belgaum 09Jul72 after overrunning runway. Repaired. W/o on approach Bombay, India when flying from Pune 04Aug79. Crashed into Kiroli Hills, Panvel. 5 crew and 40 pax killed.

TT 24,911 hrs, 21,908 ldgs

HAL/K/516   (78)   Srs.2/218

F/f Nov68 as **H-914**. Del Indian Air Force 05Dec68. VIP. Coded 'D'. Last seen Palam Mar92. Status unknown.

HAL/K/517   (79)   Srs.2/218

F/f Dec68 as **H-915**. Del Indian Air Force 14Jan69. VIP. Noted active Delhi 25Apr08 in white top c/s coded 'G' and again at HAL Bangalore uncoded 08Feb11 and again at Bangalore, Yelahanka Feb15.

HAL/K/518   (80)   Srs.2/224

F/f 03Jan69 as **VT-DXK**. Del Indian Airlines Corporation 22Jan69 named "Ellora". Lsd Vayudoot Ltd in full c/s by 17Apr83. Transferred Vayudoot Ltd 07Jul86 & regd to them 08Jul87. Company merger into Indian Airlines Corp completed Mar94 and aircraft put in storage. Sold International Air Parts Pty Ltd Oct96 & reduced to spares Hyderabad 1996/7. Regn cld 10Dec04.

TT 53,033 hrs, 50,556 ldgs

HAL/K/519   (84)   Srs.2/224

F/f 19Feb69 as **VT-DXL**. Del Indian Airlines Corporation 29Mar69 named "Konark". Trans-ferred Vayudoot Ltd 07Jul86 & regd to them 08Jul86. Company merger into Indian Airlines Corp completed Mar94 and aircraft put in storage. Sold International Air Parts Pty Ltd Oct96 & reduced to spares Hyderabad, India 1996/7. Regn cld 10Dec04.

TT 51,849 hrs, 49,093 ldgs

HAL/K/520   (85)   Srs.2/224

F/f 14Apr69 as **VT-DXM**. Del Indian Airlines Corporation 28Apr69 named "Khajuraho". Transferred Vayudoot Ltd & regd to them 21Dec86. Company merger into Indian Airlines Corp completed Mar94 and aircraft put in storage. Sold International Air Parts Pty Ltd Oct96 & reduced to spares Hyderabad, India 1996/7. Regn cld 10Dec04.

TT 50,117 hrs, 47,054 ldgs

HAL/K/521   (86)   Srs.2/224

F/f 29May69 as **VT-DXN**. Del Indian Airlines Corporation 17Jun69 named "Sarnath". Transferred Vayudoot Ltd 31Mar88 & regd to them 05May88. Company merger into Indian Airlines Corp completed Mar94 and aircraft put in storage. Sold International Air Parts Pty Ltd Oct96 & reduced to spares Hyderabad, India 1996/7. Regn cld 10Dec04.

TT 48,730 hrs, 44,711 ldgs

HAL/K/522   (94)   Srs.2/224

F/f 18Jul69 as **VT-DXO**. Del Indian Airlines Corporation 09Aug69 named "Martand". Damaged in heavy landing Trivandrum 17Dec71. Repaired. Transferred Vayudoot Ltd 31Dec88 & regd to them 05Jan89. Company merger into Indian Airlines Corp completed Mar94 and aircraft put in storage. Sold International Air Parts Pty Ltd Oct96 & reduced to spares Hyderabad, India 1996/7. Regn cld 10Dec04.

TT 43,964 hrs, 41,360 ldgs

HAL/K/523   (95)   Srs.2/224

F/f 08Sep69 as **VT-DXP**. Del Indian Airlines Corporation 03Dec69 named "Pratapgarh". Lsd Vayudoot Ltd and then returned lessor. Transferred Vayudoot Ltd & regd to them 21Dec86. Company merger into Indian Airlines Corp completed Mar94 and aircraft put in storage. Sold International Air Parts Pty Ltd Oct96 & reduced to spares Hyderabad, India 1996/7. Regn cld 10Dec04.

TT 49,263 hrs, 45,404 ldgs

HAL/K/524   (96)   Srs.2/224

F/f 08Nov69 as **VT-DXQ**. Del Indian Airlines Corporation 12Feb70 named "Pushkar". Lsd Vayudoot Ltd in full c/s by 1982. Returned lessor and repainted in Indian Airlines c/s. Transferred

VT-DXN c/n HAL/K/521 of Indian Airlines in the airline's orange and white colour-scheme. (WHC)

Vayudoot Ltd 01Apr89 & regd to them 04Apr89. Company merger into Indian Airlines Corp completed Mar94 and aircraft put in storage. Sold International Air Parts Pty Ltd Oct96 & reduced to spares Hyderabad, India 1996/7. Regn cld 10Dec04.

TT 50,217 hrs, 46,754 ldgs

HAL/K/525 (97) Srs.2/224

F/f 21Jan70 as **VT-DXR**. Del Indian Airlines Corporation 26Feb70 named "Mahabali Puram". Transferred Vayudoot Ltd 03Dec88 & regd to them 17Dec88. Company merger into Indian Airlines Corp completed Mar94 and aircraft put in storage. Sold International Air Parts Pty Ltd Oct96 & reduced to spares Hyderabad, India 1996/7. Regn cld 10Dec04.

TT 48,144 hrs, 45,083 ldgs

HAL/K/526 (98) Srs.2/219

F/f Sep70 as **H-1030**. Del Indian Air Force 21Oct70. Navigation Trainer. Coded 'A'. Noted active Hyderabad 19Nov05 in grey c/s uncoded. On overhaul Kanpur Oct07. Noted Hyderabad 04Mar10.

HAL/K/527 (99) Srs.2/219

F/f Dec70 as **H-1031**. Del Indian Air Force 12Jan71. Navigation Trainer. Noted Hyderabad 04Mar10.

HAL/K/528 Srs.2/219

F/f Jan71 as **H-1032**. Del Indian Air Force 30Jan71. Navigation Trainer. Coded 'C'. W/o Dubagunta, Andhra Pradesh, India 24Dec96 while en route Tambaran-Hyderabad. Port engine and wing separated. 4 crew and 18 pax killed.

HAL/K/529 Srs.2/219

F/f Feb71 as **H-1033**. Del Indian Air Force 23Mar71. Navigation Trainer. Coded 'D'. Reportedly converted to transport config. Noted Hyderabad 04Mar10 in grey c/s uncoded.

HAL/K/530 Srs.2/219

F/f Feb71 as **H-1034**. Del Indian Air Force 30Mar71. Navigation Trainer. Noted Hyderabad 04Mar10 in grey c/s uncoded.

HAL/K/531 Srs.2/219

F/f Sep71 as **H-1175**. Del Indian Air Force 18Oct71 (18Dec71 also quoted). Navigation Trainer. Noted Mumbai 09Nov09 in grey c/s uncoded and again at Hyderabad 04Mar10 now in white top c/s uncoded.

HAL/K/532 Srs.2/219

F/f Feb71 as **H-1176**. Del Indian Air Force 30Mar71. Navigation Trainer. Prototype Indian large rear freight door aircraft. Converted Srs.2M Freighter. On overhaul Kanpur Oct07. Noted at Yelahanka Aero India 2011 in grey c/s uncoded 14Feb11.

HAL/K/533 Srs.2/218

F/f Jan71 as **H-1177**. Del Indian Air Force 04Mar71. VIP. Noted active Delhi 13Mar05 coded 'E'. Noted active Delhi 26Jan11 in white top c/s uncoded, and again at Bangalore, Yelahanka Feb13 Noted active at Trivandrum, Kerala 13Oct15 in overall grey c/s, uncoded.

HAL/K/534 Srs.2/218

F/f Mar71 as **H-1178**. Del Indian Air Force 30Mar71. VIP. Noted active at the Aero India aviation show at Bangalore 04-09Feb03 coded 'F'. Noted active Delhi 16Oct07 in white top c/s now coded 'B'. Noted at Bangalore 2009.

HAL/K/535 Srs.2/218

F/f Jun71 as **H-1179**. Del Indian Air Force 09Jul71. VIP. Coded 'I'. Noted active Delhi 18Jan08 in white top c/s now coded 'K' and again at Delhi 02Feb11 now uncoded.

HAL/K/536 Srs.2/220

F/f Feb72 as **H-1180**. Del Indian Air Force 31Mar72. Signal Trainer. Noted active Delhi 20Jan10 in grey c/s uncoded.

HAL/K/537 Srs.2/220

F/f Jan72 as **H-1181**. Del Indian Air Force 01Feb72. Signal Trainer. Coded 'B' in white top c/s. Later coded 'E'. Noted active Delhi 10Jun09 in grey c/s now coded 'H'.

HAL/K/538 Srs.2/220

F/f Jan72 as **H-1182**. Del Indian Air Force 17Feb72. Signal Trainer. Noted Mumbai 06Sep09 in grey c/s uncoded.

HAL/K/539   Srs.2/220

F/f Apr72 as **H-1386**. Del Indian Air Force 17May72. Signal Trainer. Noted on overhaul at HAL Kanpur 05Nov15.

HAL/K/540   Srs.2/224

F/f 25Feb72 as **VT-EAT**. Del Indian Airlines Corporation 21Apr72 named "Lalqila". Damaged Cochin after overrunning runway and colliding with boundary fence 12May72. Repaired. Nose wheel collapsed Indore 23Oct86. Repaired. Lsd Vayudoot Ltd in their c/s. Transferred Indian Border Security Force, Ministry of Home Affairs and regd to them 29May91. On overhaul Kanpur Oct07. Noted active Jaipur 19Mar09 looking pristine in new c/s with white top and fin with thin red/blue cheat lines below window line and large Indian flag on fin and again Delhi 12Jun10. Seen active Delhi in full Indian Border Security c/s 10Sep15.

HAL/K/541   Srs.2/224

F/f 20Mar72 as **VT-EAU**. Del Indian Airlines Corporation 30May72 named "Qutb Minar". W/o Hyderabad, India 15Mar73 on a training flight. Crashed during a single engined circuit. 3 crew killed.   *TT 2,463 hrs, 2,400 ldgs*

HAL/K/542   Srs.2/224

F/f 29May72 as **VT-EAV**. Del Indian Airlines Corporation 15Jun72 named "Armanath". Transferred Vayudoot Ltd 15Apr89. Transferred Indian Border Security Force, Ministry of Home Affairs and regd to them 10Jul91. Noted in service Delhi 18Jan09. Reportedly wfu by Jun12. Noted in external storage at Delhi without engines or titles May13.
TT 44,780 hrs, in excess of 37,387 ldgs

HAL/K/543   Srs.2/224

Originally built for Indian Airlines Corporation as **VT-EAW** but not del and stored Kanpur. F/f 21Jan77 as **H-2064**. Del Indian Air Force 22Mar79. ASR. Coded 'G' and later 'B'. Noted at Agra with 106 Sqn modified for use in the photo reconnaissance rôle, coded 'B'. Retired from use in this rôle Dec13. Noted at HAL Kanpur 05Nov15 in grey c/s after overhaul.

HAL/K/544   Srs.2/224

Originally built for Indian Airlines Corporation as **VT-EAX** named "Chittaurgarh". F/f Dec72. Del Woodford 11Jan73 for performance trials by Rolls Royce and Hawker Siddeley Aviation Ltd as VT-EAX in full Indian Airlines c/s. Departed Woodford 19Apr73 on return to Hindustan Aeronautics Ltd and stored at Kanpur. F/f 20Sep76 as **H-2065**. Del Indian Air Force 29Mar78. ASR. Coded 'H'. Noted active Yelahanka 11Feb11 in grey c/s uncoded. Noted at Agra with 106 Sqn modified for use in the photo reconnaissance rôle, coded 'H'. Retired from use in this rôle Dec13.

HAL/K/545   Srs.2/224

Originally built for Indian Airlines Corporation as **VT-EAY** but not del and stored Kanpur. F/f 09Nov78 as **H-2066** and del Indian Air Force 30Nov78. ASR. Coded 'P'. Noted active Delhi 29Feb08 in grey c/s uncoded and again Delhi 12Jun10. Possible conversion to PR rôle.

HAL/K/546   Srs.2/224

Originally built for Indian Airlines Corporation as **VT-EAZ** but not del and stored Kanpur. F/f 24Nov72. Del Civil Aviation Department National Airports Authority as **VT-EFQ** 28Feb78 and immediately lsd to Indian Airlines Corporation until 30Sep80. Restored to Civil Aviation Department, National Airports Authority as a Flight Inspection Aircraft. WFU Delhi by 24Sep00. Positioned Bangalore, Yelahanka, India Aug07 for use as an instructional airframe by the VSM Aerospace School.
TT 10,417 hrs, in excess of 8,370 ldgs

HAL/K/547   Srs.2/224

Originally built for Indian Airlines Corporation as **VT-EBA** but not del and stored Kanpur. F/f unknown. Del Civil Aviation Department, National Airports Authority as **VT-EFR** 29Sep78 as a Flight Inspection aircraft. WFU Delhi by 24Sep00. Noted still present Delhi, India 19Sep07 but was removed during 2010.
TT 5,071 hrs, in excess of 2,621 ldgs

HAL/K/548   Srs.2/224

Originally built for Indian Airlines Corporation as **VT-EBB** but not del and stored Kanpur. F/f 09Feb73. Del National Remote Sensing Agency as **VT-EFN** 12Oct77. Believed WFU. Regn cld 02Sep96.
TT 3,434 hrs, in excess of 1,445 ldgs

HAL/K/549   Srs.2/224

Originally built for Indian Airlines Corporation as **VT-EBC** but not del and stored Kanpur. F/f unknown. Del Indian Border Security Force, Ministry of Home Affairs as **VT-EHL** 08Mar82, not being regd until 14Jun82. Noted active Delhi 14Nov09 looking spotless in similar colours to c/n HAL/K/540 VT-EAT above and again operational at Delhi 03Oct12.

HAL/K/550   Srs.2/218

F/f 30Mar73 as **H-1512**. Del Indian Air Force 26Mar74. VIP. Noted active Delhi 23Apr08 in white top c/s now coded 'J' and again at Aero India 2011 show at Bangalore, Yelahanka uncoded 10Feb11 and again at Aero India show 20Feb15 at the same location.

VT-EFQ c/n HAL/K/546 after withdrawal from flight inspection duties for the National Airports Authority, in storage at Delhi.   (Simon Watson)

HAL/K/551   Srs.2/247

F/f 12Jul73 as **H-1513**. Del Indian Air Force 30Mar74 as a multi-engine pilot trainer. Later converted to Srs.2M Freighter with a large rear freight door. W/o Yelahanka, Bangalore, India 25Mar91. Crashed soon after take-off and burnt out. 2 crew and 28 pax (pilot officers training as engineers) killed.

HAL/K/552   Srs.2/247

F/f 01Sep73 as **H-1514**. Del Indian Air Force 29Mar74 as a multi-engine pilot trainer. Later converted to Srs.2M Freighter with a large rear freight door. Coded 'A'. Later Coded 'B'. Noted active Delhi 03Nov07 in grey c/s uncoded and again at Hyderabad in 2009.

HAL/K/553   Srs.2/247

F/f 23Oct73 as **II-1515**. Del Indian Air Force 14May74 as a multi-engine pilot trainer. Coded 'B'. Noted active Kolkata 16Feb05 and again at Gwalior, Madhya Pradesh on 07Dec12.

HAL/K/554   Srs.2/247

F/f 05Dec73 as **H-1516**. Del Indian Air Force 29May74 as a multi-engine pilot trainer. Coded 'F' and later 'C'. Noted Yelahanka 11Feb11 in grey c/s uncoded. Noted active at Bangalore, Yelahanka 19Feb15 in grey c/s, uncoded.

HAL/K/555   Srs.2/247

F/f 09Jan74 as **H-1517**. Del Indian Air Force 27Aug74 as a multi-engine pilot trainer. Later converted to Srs.2M Freighter with a large rear freight door. In 2003 carried titles 'Aircraft and Systems Testing Establishment'. Noted active Delhi 10Aug07 in grey c/s uncoded.

HAL/K/556   Srs.2/247

F/f 09Feb74 as **H-1518**. Del Indian Air Force 30Aug74 as a multi-engine pilot trainer. Coded 'B'. Noted active Delhi 08Nov07 in grey c/s uncoded. Noted at Uttarlai Air Base, Rajasthan Feb13.

HAL/K/557   Srs.2/247

F/f 29Mar74 as **H-1519**. Del Indian Air Force 24Sep74 as a multi-engine pilot trainer. Coded 'G'. Noted active Bangalore, Yelahanka 11Feb05 and again in 2007.

HAL/K/558   Srs.2/247

F/f 31Mar74 as **H-1520**. Del Indian Air Force 04Jan75 as a multi-engine pilot trainer. W/o Yelahanka, Bangalore, India while crew training 27Apr75. No fatalities or injuries.

TT 119 hrs, 160 ldgs

HAL/K/559   Srs.2/247

F/f 22Aug74 as **H-1521**. Del Indian Air Force 08Nov74 as a multi-engine pilot trainer. Later converted to Srs.2M Freighter with a large rear freight door. Noted Delhi 02Feb11 in grey c/s uncoded and again at Bangalore, Yelahanka in Feb15.

HAL/K/560   Srs.2/247

F/f 16Jan75 as **H-1522**. Del Indian Air Force 25Feb75 as a multi-engine pilot trainer. Later converted to Srs.2M Freighter with a large rear freight door. Coded 'H'. Seen Yelahanka Feb07 and flying at Mumbai, 17Nov15 in grey c/s, uncoded.

HAL/K/561   Srs.2/247

F/f 03Mar75 as **H-1523**. Del Indian Air Force 26Mar75 as a multi-engine pilot trainer. Later converted to Srs.2M Freighter with a large rear freight door. Coded 'E'. Noted Delhi 23Jan11 in grey c/s uncoded.

HAL/K/562   Srs.2/247

F/f 03Jun75 as **H-1524**. Del Indian Air Force 03Jul75 as a multi-engine pilot trainer. Later converted to Srs.2M Freighter with a large rear freight door. Noted active Delhi 29Feb08 in grey c/s uncoded and again at HAL Bangalore 10Feb11 engineless on maintenance.

HAL/K/563   Srs.2/247

F/f 14Aug75 as **H-1525**. Del Indian Air Force 13Sep75 as a multi-engine pilot trainer. Later converted to Srs.2M Freighter with a large rear freight door. Coded 'D' and later 'C'. Noted Delhi 08May10 in grey c/s uncoded.

HAL/K/564   Srs.2/247

F/f 30Oct75 as **H-1526**. Del Indian Air Force 27Nov75 as a multi-engine pilot trainer. Coded 'E'. Noted Baroda/Vadodara, Gujarat 29Nov09 in grey c/s uncoded.

HAL/K/565   Srs.2/247

F/f 26Dec75 as **H-1527**. Del Indian Air Force 25Jan76 as a multi-engine pilot trainer. Later converted to Srs.2M Freighter with a large rear freight door. Noted Baroda/Vadodara, Gujarat 22Aug10 in grey c/s uncoded.

HAL/K/566   Srs.2/247

F/f 17Feb76 as **H-1528**. Del Indian Air Force 31Mar76 as a multi-engine pilot trainer. Coded 'G'. Noted Delhi 20Jan10 in grey c/s uncoded and again flying at Hindon Airport, Uttar Pradesh 07Oct12.

HAL/K/567   Srs.2/247

F/f 12Mar76 as **H-1529**. Del Indian Air Force 31Mar76 as a multi-engine pilot trainer. Later converted to Srs.2M Freighter with a large rear freight door. Coded 'A'. Noted Delhi 22Oct08 in grey c/s uncoded and again at Hyderabad in 2009.

HAL/K/568   Srs.2/247

F/f 28Aug76 as **H-1530**. Del Indian Air Force 23Nov76 as a multi-engine pilot trainer. Later converted to Srs.2M Freighter with a large rear freight door. Coded 'J'. Noted Delhi 14Nov09 in grey c/s uncoded.

HAL/K/569   Srs.2M LFD

F/f 13Feb78 as **H-2175**. Del Indian Air Force 20Apr78 as a Freighter. Loaned to the Defence Research & Development Organisation (DRDO) and converted to the ASP (Airborne Surveillance Platform) prototype and F/f with pylons only fitted from Kanpur on 24May89.

Ferried to Bangalore for fitment of large rotodome by the DRDO. F/f with rotodome fitted 05Nov89. Public debut at Aero India Show Dec96. W/o 11Jan99 2.5 km from 'INS Rajali' the Arakkonam Naval Air Station near Chennai, India. Rotodome allegedly became detached from the support pylons and collapsed onto aircraft taking away the top of the fin and rudder and causing loss of control. Crashed into dense forest killing 2 IAF test pilots, 2 IAF flight test engineers and 4 senior DRDO scientists.

H-2175 c/n HAL/K/569 of the Indian Defence Research & Development Organisation (DRDO) with its rotodome fitted. This aircraft was sadly written-off on 11th January 1999.

(Simon Watson)

H-1528 c/n HAL/K/566 of the Indian Air Force carrying code 'G' on the fin. (Simon Watson)

HAL/K/570 Srs.2M LFD

F/f 20Mar78 as **H-2176**. Del Indian Air Force 04May78 as a Freighter. Loaned DRDO and was due to be the second ASP. The pylons had already been fitted but not the rotodome when H-2175 was written-off and the programme cld. Pylons removed and aircraft fitted with an extended nose to house the Indian Light Combat Aircraft (LCA) multi-mode radar system. Used as flying testbed for many LCA systems including radar and avionics and fitted with an APU. Noted at the Aero India Show early 2001.

Currently used by 'Centre for Airborne Systems' – CABS with HAL at Bangalore as a flying test bed for the ELTA Systems Ltd Airborne Warning Radar for the Embraer 145 in a joint India/Israeli programme. Shown at the Aero India show Bangalore, Yelahanka Feb03.

HAL/K/571 Srs.2M LFD

F/f 06Sep78 as **H-2177**. Del Indian Air Force 30Sep78 as a Freighter. Coded 'A' and later 'I'. On overhaul Kanpur Oct07. Noted Mumbai 08Oct09 in grey c/c uncoded.

HAL/K/572 Srs.2M LFD

F/f 11Nov78 as **H-2178**. Del Indian Air Force 26Dec78 as a Freighter. W/o Leh, Kashmir, India 07Jun79. 27 killed.
TT 121 hrs, 77 ldgs

HAL/K/573 Srs.2M LFD

F/f 17Jan79 as **H-2179**. Del Indian Air Force 22Feb79 as a Freighter. Coded 'D'. One time named "Garud". On overhaul Kanpur Oct07. Noted Baroda/Vadodara, Gujarat 22Aug10 in grey c/s uncoded, at Mumbai 09Mar11, at Aero India show 2013 at Bangalore, Yelahanka, and again there Oct14.

HAL/K/574 Srs.2M LFD

F/f 09Mar79 as **H-2180**. Del Indian Air Force 28Mar79 as a Freighter. Noted active Delhi 05Mar08 in grey c/s uncoded and again at Aero India 2011 at Yelahanka 10Feb11. Noted flying at Mumbai 10Oct14.

HAL/K/575 Srs.2M LFD

F/f 17Jul79 as **H-2181**. Del Indian Air Force 12Sep79 as a Freighter. On overhaul Kanpur Oct07. Noted Kolkata 21Apr09 in grey c/s uncoded and flying at Mumbai 23Feb13.

HAL/K/576 Srs.2M LFD

F/f 13Nov79 as **H-2182**. Del Indian Air Force 10Dec79 as a Freighter. Coded 'G'. Noted Baroda/Vadodara, Gujarat 29Nov09 in grey c/s uncoded.

HAL/K/577 Srs.2M LFD

F/f 21Jan80 as **H-2183**. Del Indian Air Force 22Mar80 as a Freighter. Noted active Delhi 19Dec07 in grey c/s uncoded and again at HAL Bangalore 08Feb11. Seen active at Bangalore, Yelahanka 20Feb15.

HAL/K/578 Srs.2M LFD

F/f 07Mar80 as **H-2184**. Del Indian Air Force 29Mar80 (24Mar80 also quoted) as a Freighter. Noted Baroda/Vadodara, Gujarat 29Nov09 in grey c/s uncoded.

HAL/K/579 Srs.2M LFD

F/f 20Nov81 as **H-2372**. Del Indian Air Force 29Dec81 as a Freighter. Coded 'F'. Noted Delhi 21Oct08 in grey c/s uncoded and active at Bangalore, Yelahanka 06Feb13.

Right: H-2176 c/n HAL/K/570 used as a radar test bed. The aircraft's conversion to carry a rotodome was abandoned after the crash of c/n HAL/K/569 in January 1999. (Simon Watson)

HAL/K/580   Srs.2M LFD

F/f 22Feb82 as **H-2373**. Del Indian Air Force 30Mar82 as a Freighter. Noted Delhi 29Nov09 in grey scheme uncoded. Seen active at the Aero India show at Bangalore, Yelahanka 21Feb15 and again at Bangkok, Don Mueang Airport, Thailand 30Aug15.

HAL/K/581   Srs.2M LFD

F/f 19Mar82 as **H-2374**. Del Indian Air Force 31Mar82 as a Freighter. Noted still active at the Aero India exhibition at Bangalore 12Feb07. Noted active Delhi 24Apr08 in grey c/s uncoded and again at Aero India 2011 at Bangalore, Yelahanka 09Feb11.

HAL/K/582   Srs.2M LFD

F/f 02Sep82 as **H-2375**. Del Indian Air Force 13Jan83 as a Freighter. Coded 'C'. Noted active Delhi 13Sep07 in grey c/s uncoded and again at Kolkata 21Apr09.

HAL/K/583   Srs.2M LFD

F/f 19Nov82 as **H-2376**. Del Indian Air Force 23Mar83 as a Freighter. Noted Delhi 18Jul09 in grey c/s uncoded.

HAL/K/584   Srs.2M LFD

F/f 31Jan83 as **H-2377**. Del Indian Air Force 25Mar83 as a Freighter. Coded 'K'. Noted Yelahanka with a white top and thin pale blue cheat line 11Feb05 uncoded. Noted active Delhi 24Apr08 in grey c/s uncoded and again in mid Mar11.

HAL/K/585   Srs.2M LFD

F/f 10Mar83 as **H-2378**. Del Indian Air Force 17Aug84 as a Freighter. Coded 'Q'. Noted active Ahmedabad 27Mar09 in grey c/s uncoded. Noted in service at Bangkok 29Sep14.

HAL/K/586   Srs.2M LFD

F/f 21Oct83 as **H-2379**. Del Indian Air Force 30Nov85 as a Freighter. Coded 'R'. Noted Delhi 09Feb06 named "Sarathi" with white top and grey underside. Noted Mumbai 09Mar10 in grey c/s uncoded, and again at Bangalore, Yelahanka Mar15.

HAL/K/587   Srs.2M LFD

Regd as **VT-EIR** to Hindustan Aeronautics Ltd 07Apr84. F/f as VT-EIR. Del Indian Border Security Force, Ministry of Home Affairs 12Sep84 having previously been allocated to the Indian Air Force as **H-2380**. Stored Delhi, India from Sep98 and still present engineless 19Sep07.

TT 4,442 hrs, in excess of 2,299 ldgs

HAL/K/588   Srs.2M LFD

F/f 05Mar84 as **H-2381**. Del Indian Air Force 13Sep84 as a Freighter. Coded 'A'. Last noted active Mumbai 30Mar11 in grey c/s uncoded.

Military serials are applied to aircraft in some cases with '-' between letter and numerals and sometimes without while it is reported that serials have appeared on the same aircraft in both forms on occasions.

PRESERVED AIRCRAFT

The following aircraft are known to be preserved in museums and other locations around the world:

C/n	Regn	Location
		748s
1543	G-BEJD	Awaiting re-assembly by the Speke Aerodrome Heritage Group at Liverpool
1552	C-91 2502	Preserved as a gate guardian at the Força Aérea Brasileira Galeão main base entrance
1554	C-91 2504	Museu Aeroespacial – MUSAL, Campo dos Afonsos, Rio de Janeiro
1587	CR-831	Sri Lanka Air Force Museum, Ratmalana, Colombo, Sri Lanka
1601	A10-601	RAAF Museum, Point Cook, Victoria, Australia
1684	FAE684	Museo Aeronáutica de la Fuerza Aérea Ecuatoriana, Quito
1691	SCM-3101	In front of Koggala Lake airstrip, Sri Lanka
1709	3C-QQP	Australian Aviation Museum, Bankstown, Sydney
1715	60302	HRH Crown Prince Maha Vajiralongkorn's private collection, Taweewattana Palace, Bangkok, Thailand
1738	FAE738	Museo Aeronáutica del Éspace, Quito
1746	CR-833	Opposite Weerawila Airfield, Sri Lanka
1792	C-FQVE	Private near Saskatoon, Canada
		Andovers
C/n	Regn	Location
Set07	NZ7621	RNZAF Museum, Wigram
Set23	XS639	RAF Museum, Cosford

Chapter 5A
748 and Andover
Registration and Constructor's
Number Cross References

NB: Registrations marked in brackets were either carried or allocated but not taken up officially.

CIVIL REGISTRATIONS

BOTSWANA

A2-ABA	1611
A2-ABB	1612
A2-ABC	1681
A2-ZFT	1691
A2-ZGF	1706

TONGA

A3-MCA	1712

UNITED ARAB EMIRATES

A6-ABM	1799
A6-GRM	1798

CHINA - TAIWAN

B-1771	1806
B-1773	1807

CANADA

C-FAGI	1699
C-FAMO	1669
C-FBNW	1759
C-FCSE	1679
C-FDOX	1749
C-FFFS	1663
C-FGET	1724
C-FGGE	1589
C-FINE	1611
C-FKTL(1)	1613
C-FKTL(2)	1778
C-FLIY	1723
C-FLJC	1596

C-FMAK	1668
C-FPJR	1725
C-FQPE	1761
C-FQVE	1792
C-FTTW	1681
C-FYDU	1694
C-FYDY	1661
C-GANA	1758
C-GΛPC	1599
C-GBCN	1800
C-GBCS	1801
C-GBCY	1803
C-GBFA	1781
C-GCUK	1762
C-GCZY	1587
C-GDOP	1745
C-GDOV	1582
C-GDTD	1779
C-GDUI	1577
C-GDUL	1578

C-GDUN	1581
C-GEGJ	1711
C-GEPB	1686
C-GEPH	1635
C-GEPI	1594
C-GFFA	1789
C-GFFU	1579
C-GFNW	1758
C-GGNZ	1690
C-GGOB	1691
C-GGOO	1692
C-GHSC	1790
C-GHSF	1782
C-GJVN	1640
C-GLTC	1656
C-GMAA	1576
C-GOUT	1621
C-GPAA	1675
C-GQSV	1618
C-GQTG	1619

Note: Some aircraft in the Canadian C-F sequence also carried CF- marks earlier.

Heading picture: G-BVOU c/n 1721 of Emerald Airlines in Lynx (Parcels) colours. (WHC)

C-GQTH	1617
C-GQWO	1597
C-GRCU	1697
C-GRXE	1783
C-GSBF	1662
C-GSXS	1674
C-GTAD	1750
C-GTLD	1722
C-GYMX	1665

CHILE

CC-CEC	1614
CC-CED	1615
CC-CEE	1616
CC-CEF	1617
CC-CEG	1618
CC-CEH	1619
CC-CEI	1620
CC-CEJ	1621
CC-CEK	1622

CANADA

CF-AGI	1699
CF-AMO	1669
CF-CSE	1679
CF-INE	1611
CF-MAK	1668
CF-MAL	1587
CF-TAG	1664
CF-TAX	1586
CF-TAZ	1663
CF-YQD	1635

ERRONEOUSLY PAINTED

CG-TLD	1722

CAPE VERDE ISLANDS
(see also D4-)

CR-CAV	1719
CR-CAW	1720
CR-CAX	1720

PORTUGAL

CS-TAF	1681
CS-TAG	1687
CS-TAH	1721
CS-TAO	1777
CS-TAP	1782
CS-TAQ	1790
CS-TAR	1797
CS-TAU	1750
CS-TAV	1588

BAHAMAS
(see also VP-Bxx)

C6-BEA(1)	1746
C6-BEA(2)	1761
C6-BEB	1761
C6-BEC	1763
C6-BED	1763
(C6-BED)	1764
C6-BEE	1764
(C6-BEE)	1765
C6-BEF	1765

GERMANY

D-AFSD	1656
D-AFSE	1711
D-AFSF	1723
D-AFSG	1724
D-AFSH	1725
D-AFSI	1726
D-AFSJ	1727
D-AHSA	1784
D-AHSB	1785
D-AHSC	1786
D-AHSD	1791
D-AHSE	1792
D-AHSF	1797

FIJI

DQ-FAL	1613
DQ-FBH	1661
DQ-FBK	1665

ANGOLA

D2-MAF	1566
D2-MAG	1561

CAPE VERDE ISLANDS
(see also CR-Cxx)

D4-CAV	1719
D4-CAW	1720

SPAIN

EC-DTP	1544

EIRE

EI-BSE	1549
EI-BSF	1544

FALSE IDENTITY

EX-DLT	1630

LIBERIA

EL-AFY	Set 19
EL-AIF	1565
EL-AIH	1755
EL-VDD	Set 06
EL-WCP	Set 10

FRANCE
(including Overseas Territories)

F-BSRA	1678
F-BSRU	1681
F-BUTR	1717
F-GFYM	1717
F-GHKA	1680
F-GHKL	1677
(F-GMHT)	1717
F-GODD	1658
F-GPDC	1612
F-ODQQ	1745
F-ODTX	1764
F-OSPM	1611

UNITED KINGDOM

G-APZV	1534
G-ARAY	1535
G-ARMV	1536
G-ARMW	1537
G-ARMX	1538
G-ARRV	1548
G-ARRW	1549
G-ASJT	1559
G-ASPL	1560
G-ATAM	1576
G-ATEH	1585
G-ATEI	1586
G-ATEJ	1587
G-ATEK	1588
G-ATMI	1592
G-ATMJ	1593
G-AVRR	1635
G-AVXI	1623
G-AVXJ	1624
G-AVZD	1601
G-AXVG	1589
G-AXVZ	1671
G-AYDH	1678
G-AYFL	1679
G-AYIM	1687
G-AYIR	1681
G-AYVR	1700
G-AYYG	1697
G-AYYH	1701
G-AZAE	1695
G-AZJH	1698
G-AZSU	1612
G-BABJ	1718
G-BAFY	1716
G-BASZ	1717
G-BBGY	1713
G-BBLN	1719
G-BBPT	1720
G-BBTA	1722
G-BCDM	1735
G-BCDZ	1662
G-BCOE	1736
G-BCOF	1737
G-BDVH	1746
G-BEBA	1613
G-BEBY	Set 14
G-BEEM	1743
G-BEJD	1543
G-BEJE	1556
G-BEKC	1541
G-BEKD	1544
G-BEKE	1545
G-BEKF	1542
G-BEKG	1557
G-BETX	1753
G-BETY	1752
G-BETZ	1751
G-BFLL	1658
(G-BFUA)	1599
G-BFVR	1760
G-BGJV	1768
G-BGMN	1766
G-BGMO	1767
G-BGPR	1770
G-BHCJ	1663
(G-BHRG)	1676
G-BICK	1782
(G-BIOV)	1591
G-BIRF	1781
G-BIUV	1701
G-BJGI	1789
G-BJTL	1790
G-BJTM	1792
G-BKAL	1791
G-BKIG	1796
G-BKLD	1774
G-BKLE	1787
G-BKLF	1788
G-BKLG	1793
G-BKLH	1794
G-BKLI	1795
G-BLGJ	1800
G-BLYL	1802
G-BMFT	1714
G-BMJU	1783
G-BNJK	1594
G-BOHY	1784
G-BOHZ	1785
G-BORM	1670
G-BPDA	1756
G-BPEP	1806
G-BPFU	1757
G-BPIW	1807
G-BPNJ	1680
G-BPNK(1)	1677
G-BPNK(2)	1667
G-BPNW	1584
G-BURJ	1667
G-BVNJ	Set 4
G-BVNK	Set 21
G-BVOU	1721
G-BVOV	1777
G-BVZS	1564
G-DAAL	1557
G-EDIN	1757
G-EMRD	1797
G-ERMV	1537
G-FBMV	1537
G-GLAS	1756
G-HDBA	1798
G-HDBB	1799
G-HDBC	1786
G-HDBD	1797
G-JIILN	1750
G-MRRV	1549
G-OJEM	1791
G-OMDS	1757
G-OPFW	1714
G-ORAL	1756
G-ORCP	1647
G-OSOE	1697
G-OTBA	1712
G-SOEI	1689
G-SSFS	1792
G-VAJK	1557

ECUADOR

HC-AUD	1682
HC-AUE	1683
HC-AUK	1684
HC-BAZ	1738
HC-BEY	1739

COLOMBIA

HK-1408	1657
HK-1409	1658
HK-1698X	1620

PANAMÁ

HP-416	1585
HP-432	1594
HP-484	1662

HONDURAS

HR-AQV	1764
HR-ATC	1801

THAILAND

HS-RTAF(1)	1570
HS-RTAF(2)	1715
HS-TAF(1)	1570
HS-TAF(2)	1715
HS-THA	1567
HS-THB	1568
HS-THC	1569
HS-THD	1644
HS-THE	1645
HS-THF	1646
HS-THG	1693
HS-THH	1707
HS-THI	1708

GUINEA-BISSAU

J5-GAT	1760

ERRONEOUSLY PAINTED

LF-INE	1611

NORWAY

LN-FOM	1631

ARGENTINA

LV-HGW	1539
LV-HHB	1540
LV-HHC	1541
LV-HHD	1542
LV-HHE	1543
LV-HHF	1544
LV-HHG	1545
LV-HHH	1546
LV-HHI	1547

LV-IDV	1556
LV-IEE	1557
LV-IEV	1558
(LV-PGG)	1597
LV-PIZ	1539
LV-PJA	1540
LV-PJR	1541
LV-PRJ	1541
LV-PUC	1542
LV-PUF	1543
LV-PUM	1544
LV-PUP	1545
LV-PVF	1547
LV-PVH	1546
LV-PXD	1556
LV-PXH	1557
LV-PXP	1558

MARSHALL ISLANDS
(see also VT-)

MI-GJV	1768
MI-8203	1796

UNITED STATES OF AMERICA

N43AZ	1583
N117CA	1781
N118CA	1789
(N119CA)	1791
N339C	1720
(N666)	1716
N687AP	1687
N743LA	1689
N743MZ	1697
N748AV	1782
N748BA	1783
N748D(1)	1559
N748D(2)	1689
N748LL	1716
N749AV	1790
N749LL	1783
(N750AV)	1792
N57910	1656

AUSTRIA

OE-LHS	1589
OE-LHT	1590

DENMARK

OY-APT	1621
OY-DFS	1576
OY-DFV	1535
OY-MBH	1617
OY-MBY	1618

PHILIPPINES
(see also RP-)

PI-C784	1535
PI-C1014	1636
PI-C1015	1637
PI-C1016	1638
PI-C1017	1639

PI-C1018	1640
PI-C1019	1641
PI-C1020	1576
PI-C1021	1642
PI-C1022	1643
PI-C1023	1659
PI-C1024	1660
PI-C1025	1663
PI-C1026	1664
PI-C1027	1609
PI-C1028	1590
PI-C1029	1586

INDONESIA

PK-IHA	1614
PK-IHB	1615
PK-IHC	1616
PK-IHD	1700
PK-IHE	1620
PK-IHF	1622
PK-IHG	1627
PK-IHH	1629
PK-IHI	1626
PK-IHJ	1630
PK-IHK	1633
(PK-IHL)	1735
PK-IHM	1634
PK-IHN	1794
PK-IHO	1774
PK-IHP	1787
PK-IHR	1722
PK-IHS	1615
PK-IHT	1793
PK-IHV	1795
PK-IHW	1788
PK-KHL	1735
PK-MHD	1695
PK-MHM	1695
PK-MHR	1696
PK-OBQ	1638
PK-OBV	1585
PK-OBW	1567
PK-OCH	1766
PK-RHQ	1610
PK-RHS	1610

BRAZIL

PP-VDN	1625
PP-VDO	1626
PP-VDP	1627
PP-VDQ	1628
PP-VDR	1629
PP-VDS	1630
PP-VDT	1631
PP-VDU	1632
PP-VDV	1633
PP-VDX	1634
PP-VJQ	1535

ARUBA

P4-BLL	Set 17
P4-PVS	Set 10
P4-TBL	Set 24

PHILIPPINES
(see also PI-)

RP-C1014	1636
RP-C1015	1637
RP-C1016	1638
RP-C1017	1639
RP-C1018	1640
RP-C1019	1641
RP-C1021	1642
RP-C1023	1659
RP-C1024	1660
RP C1025	1663
RP-C1026	1664
RP-C1028	1590
RP-C1029	1586
RP-C1030	1663
RP-C1031	1589
RP-C1032	1613
RP-C1041	1588
RP-C1042	1584
RP-C1043	1670
RP-122	1641
RP-211	1641
(RP-2000)	1641
RP-2001	1641

SWEDEN

SE-LEG	1723
SE-LEK	1725
SE-LEO	1726
SE-LEX	1727
SE-LEY	1631
(SE-LIA)	1736
SE-LIA	1717
(SE-LIB)	1737
SE-LIB	1776
(SE-LIC)	1703
SE-LIC	1778
SE-LID	1760
SE-LIE	1595
SE-LIF	1596

BANGLADESH

S2-AAT	1770
S2-AAX	1767
S2-ABE	1658
S2-ADL	1773
S2-ADW	1766
S2-AEE	1647
S2-AXX	1767

ICELAND

TF-GMB	1711

GUATEMALA

TG-MAL	1587

CAMEROON

TJ-AAN	1749
TJ-AAO	1750

TJ-CCD	1749	VP-LIU	1592	VT-EAU	541	**VENEZUELA**	
TJ-CCE	1750	VP-LIV	1588	VT-EAV	542		
TJ-CCF	1804	VP-LIW	1585	VT-EAW	543	YV-C-AMC	1535
TJ-CCG	1805			VT-EAX	544	YV-C-AMC	1582
TJ-XAF	1749			VT-EAY	545	YV-C-AME	1577
TJ-XAH	1750	**BRITISH VIRGIN**		VT-EAZ	546	YV-C-AMF	1581
		ISLANDS		VT-EBA	547	YV-C-AMI	1578
				VT-EBB	548	YV-C-AMO	1579
CENTRAL AFRICAN		VP-LVN	1538	VT-EBC	549	YV-C-AMY	1580
REPUBLIC		VP-LVO	1537	VT-EFN	548	YV-04C	1577
		VP-LVQ	1666	VT-EFQ	546	YV-05C	1578
TL-DON	Set 13			VT-EFR	547	YV-06C	1579
TL-AEW	Set 13			VT-EHL	549	YV-07C	1581
		FIJI		VT-EIR	587	YV-08C	1582
				(VT-GOA)	1786	(YV-09C)	1744
CONGO		VQ-FAL	1613	(VT-WAY)	1785	(YV-10C)	1745
BRAZZAVILLE		VQ-FBH	1661			YV-39C	1591
		VQ-FBK	1665			YV-45C	1744
TN-AFI	1764			**ANTIGUA &**		YV-46C	1745
TN-AGA	1611			**BARBUDA**			
		ADEN				**NEW ZEALAND**	
				V2-LAA	1670		
GABON		(VR-AAU)	1550	V2-LAZ	1762	ZK-CWJ	1647
		(VR-AAV)	1551	V2-LCG	1757	ZK-DES	1689
TR-LFW	1611	(VR-AAW)	1552	V2-LCQ	1800	ZK-MCA	1712
TR-LQJ	1635			V2-LCR	1801	ZK-MCB	1767
TR-LQY	1576			V2-LCS	1802	ZK-MCF	1697
		BERMUDA		V2-LCT	1803	ZK-MCH	1791
				V2-LDA	1783	ZK-MCJ	1661
IVORY COAST		VR-BFT	1714	V2-LDB	1767	ZK-MCP	1694
		VR-BOI	Set 28	V2-LDK	1791		
TU-PAD	1799			V2-LIK	1583	**SOUTH AFRICA**	
				V2-LIP	1584		
		CAYMAN ISLANDS		V2-LIV	1588	ZS-AGB	1807
AUSTRALIA						"ZS-AGB"	1707
		VR-CBH	1557			ZS-DBL	1737
VH-AHL	1606			**MARSHALL**		ZS-DBM	1736
VH-AMQ(1)	1605			**ISLANDS**		ZS-HSA	1576
VH-AMQ(2)	1603	**BRUNEI**		*(see also MI-)*		ZS-HSI	1635
VH-AYS	1608					ZS-IGI	1635
VH-DQY	1773	VR-UEH	1694	V7-8203	1796	ZS-JAY	1717
VH-IMG	1604					(ZS-KLC)	1784
VH-IMI	1736					ZS-LHN	1681
VH-IMJ(1)	1720	**BRUNEI**		**BRUNEI**		ZS-LSO	1783
VH-IMJ(2)	1799	*(see also V8-)*				ZS-NNW	1785
VH-IMK	1737			V8-UEH	1694	ZS-NWW	1786
VH-IPA	1772	VS-UEH	1694			ZS-OCF	1647
VH-IPB	1773					ZS-ODJ	1680
VH-POZ	1602			**MÉXICO**		(ZS-OEO)	1737
		INDIA				(ZS-OJU)	1796
				XA-SAB	1673	ZS-OJU	1782
BAHAMAS		VT-BAA	1800	XA-SAC	1674	ZS-OLE	1796
(see also C6-)		VT-BAB	1801	XA-SAF	1675	(ZS-PLO)	1747
		(VT-BAC)	1802	XA-SEI	1576	ZS-PLO	1797
VP-BCJ	1609	(VT-BAD)	1803	XA-SEV	1598	ZS-SBU	1690
VP-BCK	1610	VT-DOA	1800	XA-SEY	1599	ZS-SBV	1692
VP-BCL	1611	VT-DRF	500			ZS-SBW	1691
VP-BCM	1612	VT-DTR	505			ZS-TPW	1784
VP-BFT	1714	VT-DUO	506	**BURKINO FASO**		ZS-XGE	1770
		VT-DXF	511			ZS-XGY	1764
		VT-DXG	512	XT-MAL	1754	ZS-XGZ	1740
ANTIGUA		VT-DXH	513	XT-MAN	1775		
		VT-DXI	514			**EQUATORIAL GUINEA**	
VP-LAA	1670	VT-DXJ	515				
VP-LAJ	1593	VT-DXK	518	**CAMBODIA**		3C-CPX	Set 19
VP-LAX	1581	VT-DXL	519			(3C-JJJ)	Set 6
VP-LAZ	1762	VT-DXM	520	(XU-???)	1782	3C-JJX	Set 6
VP-LCG	1757	VT-DXN	521	(XU-???)	1790	3C-KKB	Set 9
VP-LII	1537	VT-DXO	522			3C-KKC	Set 18
VP-LIK	1583	VT-DXP	523			3C-KKP	1565
VP-LIN	1586	VT-DXQ	524	**LAOS**		3C-KKS	Set 20
VP-LIO	1535	VT-DXR	525			3C-KKT	Set 29
VP-LIP	1584	VT-EAT	540	XW-PNA	164?	3C-QQP	1709

SWAZILAND

3D-ATS	Set 04
3D-BAE	1611
3D-MKX	Set 19
3D-POZ	1602

REPUBLIQUE DE GUINEE

3X-GEE	1602
3X-GEW	1701

CEYLON/ SRI LANKA

4R-ACJ	1571
4R-ACR	1587
4R-AGB	1807
4R-HVA	1768
4R-HVB	1757
4R-LPV	1807
4R-SER	1799

TANZANIA

5H-MPG	1728
5H-RJN	1728
5H-STZ	1728
5H-WDL	1740

NIGERIA

5N-ARJ	1750

MADAGASCAR

5R-MJA	1772
5R-MJB	1773
5R-MJS	1746
5R-MTI	1780
5R-MUT	1780

NIGER

5U-BAR	1779
5U-BAS	1778

SAMOA

5W-FAN	1701
5W-FAO	1714

KENYA

5Y-BSX	Set 20
5Y-BVQ	1778
5Y-BXT	1701
5Y-BZR	1737
5Y-CBI	1784
5Y-HAJ	1776
5Y-HVS	1736
5Y-IAK	1564
5Y-PFA	1736
5Y-SAL	1764
5Y-SFE	Set 6

5Y-TCA	1740
5Y-TCO	1772
5Y-YKM	1779
(5Y-YKN)	1776
(5Y-YKO)	1778
5Y-???	1736
5Y-???	1687
5Y-???	1689
5Y-???	1697

SÉNÉGAL

6V-AEO	1769
6V-AET	1676
6V-AFX	1588

JAMAICA

6Y-JFJ	1593

LESOTHO

7P-LAI	1681

MALAWI

7Q-YKA	1666
7Q-YKB	1667

GUYANA

8R-GEU	1747
8R-GEV	1748

GHANA

9G-ABV	1576
9G-ABW	1685
9G-ABX	1686
9G-MKV	1736

ZAMBIA

9J-ABJ	1676
9J-ABK	1677
9J-ABL	1576
9J-ABM	1635
9J-ABW	1680
9J-ADM	1706

SIERRA LEONE

9L-LBE	????
9L-LBF	1561
9L-LBG	1566
9L-LBH	1611

NEPAL

9N-AAU	1671
9N-AAV	1672
9N-ABR	1771
9N-ACH	1537
9N-ACM	1549

9N-ACN	1736
9N-ACP	1667
9N-ACW	1798
9N-ACX	1799
9N-ADE	1784
9N-ADF	1791
9N-AEG	1806
9N-AEH	1807
9N-RAC	1698

DEMOCRATIC REPUBLIC OF CONGO/ZAIRE

9Q-CDY	Set 11
9Q-CJJ	Set 21
9Q-CJR	Set 19
9Q-CLL(1)	Set 21
9Q-CLL(2)	1561
9Q-CMJ	Set 4
9Q-CMU	????
9Q-COE(1)	Set 28
9Q-COE(2)	Set 20
9Q-CPW	Set 14
9Q-CSR	1664
9Q-CST	1642
9Q-CVC(1)	Set 24
9Q-CVC(2)	Set 29
9Q-CVK	Set 17
9Q-CVS	Set 10
9Q-CYB	Set 22
9Q-CYG	Set 6

RWANDA

9XR-AB	1564

TRINIDAD & TOBAGO

9Y-TDH	1670
9Y-TFS	1756
9Y-TFT	1757
9Y-TFX	1758
9Y-TGD	1759
9Y-TGH	1766
9Y-TGI	1767

UNITED KINGDOM CLASS 'B' CONDITIONS

G11	1598
G11-1	1718
G11-2	1719
G11-3	1716
G11-4	1720
G11-5	1700
G11-6 (1)	1721
G11-6 (2)	1722
G11-7	1712
G11-8	1713
G11-9 (1)	1717
G11-9 (2)	1760
G11-10	1714
G11-11	1769
G-11 (1)	1599
G-11 (2)	1535
G-11 (3)	1668
G-11 (4)	1672

G-11 (5)	1679
G-11-1 (1)	1679
G-11-1 (2)	1702
G-11-1 (3)	1783
G-11-1 (4)	1806
G-11-1 (5)	1797
G-11-2 (1)	1678
G-11-2 (2)	1703
G-11-2 (3)	1797
G-11-2 (4)	1750
G-11-2 (5)	1807
G-11-3 (1)	1681
G-11-3 (2)	1704
G-11-3 (3)	1662
G-11-3 (4)	1782
G-11-4 (1)	1680
G-11-4 (2)	1705
G-11-4 (3)	1801
G-11-4 (4)	1584
G-11-5 (1)	1687
G-11-5 (2)	1706
G-11-5 (3)	1802
G-11-6 (1)	1699
G-11-6 (2)	1707
G-11-6 (3)	1790
G-11-7 (1)	1700
G-11-7 (2)	1735
G-11-8 (1)	1701
G-11-8 (2)	1756
G-11-9 (1)	1697
G-11-9 (2)	1717
G-11-9 (3)	1803
G-11-10(1)	1695
G-11-10(2)	1761
G-11-10(3)	1783
G-11-10(4)	1804
G-11-11(1)	1769
G-11-11(2)	1805
G-11-12	1774
G-11-13	1775
G-11-14	1776
G-11-15	1781
G-11-16	1780
G-11-17	1785
G-11-18	1786
G-11-19	1779
G-11-20	1778
G-11-22	1787
G-11-23	1793
G-11-24	1794
G-11-687	1687
G-11-782	1782
G-11-790	1790
G-11-797	1797

MILITARY SERIALS

ARGENTINA

T-01	1597
T-02	1597
T-03	1597
(TC-71)	1648
(TC-72)	1649
(TC-73)	1650
(TC-74)	1651
(TC-75)	1652
(TC-76)	1653
(TC-77)	1654
(TC-78)	1655

AUSTRALIA

A10-595	1595
A10-596	1596
A10-601	1601
A10-602	1602
A10-603	1603
A10-604	1604
A10-605	1605
A10-606	1606
A10-607	1607
A10-608	1608
N15-709	1709
N15-710	1710

BELGIUM

CS-01	1741
CS-02	1742
CS-03	1743

BENIN

TY-21A	1741
TY-22A	1742

BRAZIL

C-91 2500	1550
C-91 2501	1551
C-91 2502	1552
C-91 2503	1553
C-91 2504	1554
C-91 2505	1555
C-91 2506	1729
C-91 2507	1730
C-91 2508	1731
C-91 2509	1732
C-91 2510	1733
C-91 2511	1734

BRUNEI

AMB-110	1694
AMDB-110	1694

COLUMBIA

FAC-1101	1702
FAC-1102	1703
FAC-1103	1704
FAC-1104	1705
FAC-1108	1776

DEMOCRATIC REPUBLIC OF CONGO

9T-TCO	Set ??
9T-TCP	Set ??

ECUADOR

FAE001	1684
FAE682	1682

FAE683	1683
FAE684	1684
FAE738	1738
FAE739	1739
FAE740	1734
FAE741	1731
FAE742	1733
FAE743	1729
FAE744	1730

INDIA

BH572	500
BH573	501
BH574	502
BH575	503
BH576	504
BH-1010	505
BH-1011	507
BH-1012	508
BH-1013	509
BH-1047	503
BH-1048	504
H-913	510
H-914	516
H-915	517
H-1030	526
H-1031	527
H-1032	528
H-1033	529
H-1034	530
H-1175	531
H-1176	532
H-1177	533
H-1178	534
H-1179	535
H-1180	536
H-1181	537
H-1182	538
H-1386	539
H-1512	550
H-1513	551
H-1514	552
H-1515	553
H-1516	554
H-1517	555
H-1518	556
H-1519	557
H-1520	558
H-1521	559
H-1522	560
H-1523	561
H-1524	562
H-1525	563
H-1526	564
H-1527	565
H-1528	566
H-1529	567
H-1530	568
H-2064	543
H-2065	544
H-2066	545
H-2175	569
H-2176	570
H-2177	571
H-2178	572
H-2179	573
H-2180	574
H-2181	575
H-2182	576
H-2183	577
H-2184	578

H-2372	579
H-2373	580
H-2374	581
H-2375	582
H-2376	583
H-2377	584
H-2378	585
H-2379	586
H-2380	587
H-2381	588

NEPAL

NA-020	1698
RAN-20	1698

NEW ZEALAND

NZ7620	Set 6
NZ7621	Set 7
NZ7622	Set 9
NZ7623	Set 11
NZ7624	Set 15
NZ7625	Set 18
NZ7626	Set 19
NZ7627	Set 20
NZ7628	Set 22
NZ7629	Set 29

SOUTH KOREA

1713	1713
1718	1718

SOVIET UNION

"57"	1548

SRI LANKA

CR-830	1691
CR-831	1587
CR-833	1746
CR-834	176
CR-835	1757
SCM-3101	1691
SCM-3102	1746

TANZANIA

JW9008	1751
JW9009	1752
JW9010	1753

THAILAND

11-111	1570
99-999	1715
60203	1569
60204	1644
60205	1646
60206	1645
60301	1570
60302	1715

60303	1569
60304	1644
60305	1646
60306	1645

UNITED KINGDOM

XS594	Set 1	1572
XS595	Set 2	1573
XS596	Set 3	1574
XS597	Set 4	1575
XS598		Set 5
XS599		Set 6
XS600		Set 7
XS601		Set 8
XS602		Set 9
XS603		Set 10
XS604		Set 11
XS605		Set 12
XS606		Set 13
XS607		Set 14
XS608		Set 15
XS609		Set 16
XS637		Set 21
XS638		Set 22
XS639		Set 23
XS640		Set 24
XS641		Set 25
XS642		Set 26
XS643		Set 27
XS644		Set 28
XS645		Set 29
XS646		Set 30
XS647		Set 31
XS789		1561
XS790		1562
XS791		1563
XS792		1564
XS793		1565
XS794		1566
XW750		1559
8669M		1548
8785M		Set 26
9178M		1565
9198M		Set 25
9241M		Set 23
9278M		Set 27

UNITED STATES OF AMERICA

"208"	1707

VENEZUELA

TR-0203	1579
0111	1591
6201	1578

ZAMBIA

AF601	1600
AF602	1688

Chapter 5B
Current Status Reports for Avro/HS/BAe 748,
HS Andover & HAL 748

Avro/HS/BAe 748

1543	1 /105 F	G-BEJD	ex Emerald	Display Speke, UK
1552	2 /205	C-91 2502	FAB	Display Galeão, Brazil
1554	2 /205	C-91 2504	FAB	Display MUSAL, Rio
1561	**2A/206**	**9Q-CLL**	**Stellavia**	**Active?**
1565	2A/206	3C-KKP	Gabon Express	Status unknown
1569	2 /207	60303	RThAF	Stored Takhli AF Base
1570	2 /208	60301	RThAF	Stored Don Mueang
1576	**2A/214LFD**	**C-GMAA**	**Wasaya**	**Active**
1587	2 /222	CR-831	Sri Lanka AF	Display Ratmalana
1601	2 /228	A10-601	RAAF	Display Point Cook
1640	2A/209	C-GJVN	Bradley A/S	Stored Trois Rivières
1642	2 /209	9Q-CST	Trans Service	Status unknown
1644	2 /243	60304	RThAF	Stored Don Mueang
1645	2 /243LFD	60306	RThAF	Stored Don Mueang
1646	2 /243LFD	60305	RThAF	Stored Don Mueang
1647	2A/242	S2-AEE	Bismillah	Status unknown
1656	**2A/244**	**C-GLTC**	**Wasaya**	**Active**
1663	2A/209LFD	C-FFFS	Wasaya	Stored Pickle Lake
1664	2 /209	9Q-CSR	Trans Service	Status unknown
1669	2A/258LFD	C-FAMO	Calm Air Int	Stored Thompson
1679	**2A/269**	**C-FCSE**	**Air North**	**Active**
1684	2A/267	FAE684	FAE	Display Quito
1687	2A/270	N687AP		Stored Southend
1688	2A/265	AF602	Zambia AF	Stored Rand, SA
1689	2A/242	N753LA	Zone 4 Int	Stored Southend
1691	2A/272	SCM-3101	Sri Lanka AF	Display Koggala Lake
1694	**2A/273**	**C-FYDU**	**Air North**	**Active**
1697	2A/275	N743MZ	Zone 4 Int	Stored Southend
1698	2A/271LFD	NA-020	Nepal Army	Stored Kathmandu
1699	**2A/276**	**C-FAGI**	**Air North**	**Active**
1701	**2A/266LFD**	**5Y-BXT**	**Avro Express**	**Active**
1707	2 /243	None	-	Used as hotel Cha Am
1708	2 /243	None	-	Display Pattaya
1709	2 /268	3C-QQP	ex RAN	Museum Bankstown
1713	**2A/248**	**1713**	**RKAF**	**Active**
1715	2 /208	60302	RThAF	Museum Bangkok
1718	**2A/248**	**1718**	**RKAF**	**Active**
1722	2A/216	C-GTLD	Bradley AS	Stored Trois Rivières
1723	**2A/244LFD**	**C-FLIY**	**Air Creebec**	**Active**
1724	2A/244	C-FGET	ex Air Inuit	Stored Sault Ste Marie
1725	**2A/244**	**C-FPJR**	**Air Creebec**	**Active**
1729	2A/281LFD	FAE743	FAE	Stored Eloy Alfaro A/P
1736	**2B/287LFD**	**5Y-PFA**	**Planes for Africa**	**Active**
1739	2A/285LFD	FAE739	FAE	Stored Cotopaxi A.P
1741	2A/288LFD	TY-21A	Benin Air Force	Status unknown
1742	2A/288LFD	TY-22A	Benin Air Force	Stored Cotonou
1745	2A/283	C-GDOP	Calm Air	Stored Thompson
1746	2A/301LFD	CR-833	Sri Lanka AF	Display Weerawila

1749	2A/310LFD	C-FDOX	Air Inuit	Active
1754	2A/320LFD	XT-MAL	Burkina Faso AF	Status unknown
1758	2A/335LFD	C-GANA	Air North	In work
1766	2A/347	S2-ADW	Bismillah A/L	Active
1767	2A/347	S2-AAX	Bismillah A/L	Active
1770	2A/351	S2-AAT	ex Best Aviation	Status unknown
1772	2B/360LFD	5Y-TCO	Safe Air Co	Active
1784	2B/378	5Y-CBI	Planes for Africa	Active
1786	2B/378	ZS-NWW	Exec Aerospace	Status unknown
1790	2B/FAA	C-GHSC	Calm Air	Stored Thompson
1799	2B/426	TU-PAD	East Horizon	Stored Kabul
1801	2B/424	HR-ATC	Atlantic A/L	Stored La Ceiba

HS Andover

Set 7 C.Mk.1	NZ7621	RNZAF		Museum Wigram
Set 10 E.Mk.3	EL-WCP	ATO		Status unknown
Set 14 C.Mk.1	9Q-CPW	Air Kasai		Status unknown
Set 20 C.Mk.1	5Y-BSX	748 A/S		Stored Lokichoggio
Set 22 C.Mk.1	9Q-CYB	ITAB Cargo		Status unknown
Set 23 E.Mk.3A	XS639	RAF		Musuem Cosford
Set 29 C.Mk.1	9Q-CVC	Air Katanga		Status unknown

HAL 748

500	1 /103	BH572	HAL	Active
501	2 /104	BH573	Indian A/F	Status unknown
502	2 /204	BH574	Indian A/F	Status unknown
504	2 /203	BH-1048	Indian A/F	Active
505	2 /203	BH-1010	Indian A/F	Active
507	2 /203	BH-1011	Indian A/F	Active
509	2 /203	BH-1013	Indian A/F	Active
510	2 /203	H-913	Indian A/F	Active
516	2 /218	H-914	Indian A/F	Status unknown
517	2 /218	H-915	Indian A/F	Active
526	2 /219	H-1030	Indian A/F	Active
527	2 /219	H-1031	Indian A/F	Active
529	2 /219	H-1033	Indian A/F	Active
530	2 /219	H-1034	Indian A/F	Active
531	2 /219	H-1175	Indian A/F	Active

532	2M LFD	H-1176	Indian A/F	Active
533	2 /218	H-1177	Indian A/F	Active
534	2 /218	H-1178	Indian A/F	Active
535	2 /218	H-1179	Indian A/F	Active
536	2 /220	H-1180	Indian A/F	Active
537	2 /220	H-1181	Indian A/F	Active
538	2 /220	H-1182	Indian A/F	Active
539	2 /220	H-1386	Indian A/F	Active
540	2 /224	VT-EAT	Border S/F	Active
543	2 /224	H-2064	Indian A/F	Active
544	2 /224	H-2065	Indian A/F	Active
545	2 /224	H-2066	Indian A/F	Active
546	2 /224	VT-EFQ	VSM School	Bangalore
549	2 /224	VT-EHL	Border S/F	Active
550	2 /218	H-1512	Indian A/F	Active
552	2M LFD	H-1514	Indian A/F	Active
553	2 /247	H-1515	Indian A/F	Active
554	2 /247	H-1516	Indian A/F	Active
555	2M LFD	H-1517	Indian A/F	Active
556	2 /247	H-1518	Indian A/F	Active
557	2 /247	H-1519	Indian A/F	Active
559	2M LFD	H-1521	Indian A/F	Active
560	2M LFD	H-1522	Indian A/F	Active
561	2M LFD	H-1523	Indian A/F	Active
562	2M-LFD	H-1524	Indian A/F	Active
563	2M LFD	H-1525	Indian A/F	Active
564	2 /247	H-1526	Indian A/F	Active
565	2M LFD	H-1527	Indian A/F	Active
566	2 /247	H-1528	Indian A/F	Active
567	2M LFD	H-1529	Indian A/F	Active
568	2M LFD	H-1530	Indian A/F	Active
570	2M LFD	H-2176	Indian CABS	Active
571	2M LFD	H-2177	Indian A/F	Active
573	2M LFD	H-2179	Indian A/F	Active
574	2M LFD	H-2180	Indian A/F	Active
575	2M LFD	H-2181	Indian A/F	Active
576	2M LFD	H-2182	Indian A/F	Active
577	2M LFD	H-2183	Indian A/F	Active
578	2M LFD	H-2184	Indian A/F	Active
579	2M LFD	H-2372	Indian A/F	Active
580	2M LFD	H-2373	Indian A/F	Active
581	2M LFD	H-2374	Indian A/F	Active
582	2M LFD	H-2375	Indian A/F	Active
583	2M LFD	H-2376	Indian A/F	Active
584	2M LFD	H-2377	Indian A/F	Active
585	2M LFD	H-2378	Indian A/F	Active
586	2M LFD	H-2379	Indian A/F	Active
588	2M LFD	H-2381	Indian A/F	Active

BAe ATP

This evocative sunset photograph shows an ATP departing for an evening flight. *(Christian Lindberg)*

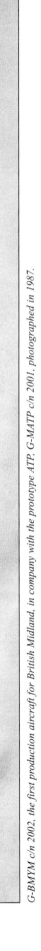

(WHC/BAe)

G-BMYM c/n 2002, the first production aircraft for British Midland, in company with the prototype ATP, G-MATP c/n 2001, photographed in 1987.

Chapter 6
General History

By the early 1980s, British Aerospace had become aware of the fact that many operators of jet airliners had been forced to withdraw from very short haul routes due to rapidly increasing fuel prices. Their aircraft were being redirected to more profitable longer sectors. British Aerospace saw that there was an opportunity to fill this void with a new type of turbo-propeller airliner of somewhat higher capacity than the 748. Although the Rolls-Royce Dart was a well proven, reliable and relatively fuel-efficient engine, more modern power plants had vastly improved fuel consumption, were of simpler design and somewhat quieter in operation. Similarly, the latest multi-bladed, composite and slow turning propellers were much quieter in operation and contributed to the improved economics and environmental acceptability of the latest industry offerings. BAe and its predecessors had built over half of the world's turbo-propeller airliners at this time and with its many years of experience, took up the challenge of developing a new type to replace the 748 on the Manchester assembly lines. It was thought that the type would also complement the company's 146 and Jetstream range of aircraft. First details of the proposed ATP were revealed at the SBAC Farnborough Air Show in September 1982.

BAe took advantage of the increased power output available from the initially selected Pratt and Whitney PW124 and later PW126 engines to increase the passenger capacity of its new proposal by 50% over the BAe 748, which was at the time still in production. At this time, the up to 72 passenger capacity offered by this project was by far the highest of the twin turbo-propeller airliners then on offer or proposed by the world's manufacturers.

PRODUCTION GO AHEAD

The company launched its new Advanced Turbo-Propeller airliner on the 1st March 1984 as the "ATP". It was decided to carry over elements of the successful 748 design and combine these with the latest technology. The same fuselage cross section as the 748 was retained but stretched by 18ft 4in (5.59m) and incorporated two passenger entrance doors to port, one forward and one aft of the wing, to facilitate quick turnaround times. The maximum internal cabin width was increased over that of the 748 by 1½in (3.81cm) by utilising sculptured sidewall panels while the constant cross section passenger cabin length was increased to 54ft (16.5m). Cabin windows were reduced in size and increased in number to allow each seat row to have its own window. To assist with development of the type, the last produced Andover C.Mk.1 (set 31) was obtained in January 1981. The airframe was used as a design rig for the new aircraft. With the new multi-bladed propellers of greater diameter it was decided to adopt the inner wing and basic centre section of the C.Mk.1 Andover mated to the outer wings of the Series 2B version of the 748. This same Andover C.Mk.1 fuselage was later fitted with a slightly swept fin similar in shape to that finally adopted for the ATP. The same airframe was also used as a mock-up for trial installation of seating, interior furnishings and cockpit layouts. The first order for the ATP was placed in December 1985 when British Midland Airways ordered three aircraft for use on its scheduled network.

As with the 748, all major airframe components would be manufactured at Chadderton and transported by road to Woodford

---

One of the two Magic Bird Cargo aircraft, seen in 2006 – one of several airlines that operated the ATP for a short period only.

for final assembly with the prototype fuselage making this journey in December 1984. In the case of the later Jetstream 61 version, these components would be transported by road to Prestwick for final assembly.

The prototype, G-MATP, first flew from Woodford on 6th August 1986 returning two hours forty minutes later landing in a 24 knot crosswind. The crew comprised J.A. Robinson (the company's Chief Test Pilot), A.J. Hawkes (Project Pilot) and B. Lomas (Flight Test Engineer). It made its public debut at the Farnborough Air Show after the issue of a Permit to Fly on 28th August 1986 returning to Woodford on 8th September. Cold weather and icing trials were conducted in Finland, Norway and Iceland in February, March and April 1987. The first production aircraft G-BMYM, destined for British Midland Airways, took to the air on 20th February 1987 and was flown to Spain for noise and performance trials in Granada and Almeria in the following March and April. This airframe was the first to be fitted with the optional Auxiliary Power Unit (APU). The Garret GTCP36-150J APU was fitted in the port wing root on a trial basis prior to the aircraft being flown to Yuma and Mojave in the United States for hot weather and high altitude tests in late July 1987. The blue British Midland fuselage top was also temporarily painted white in order to reflect heat. On completion of these trials the aircraft returned to Woodford in late September. In the meantime, the second production aircraft had flown on 9th June 1987 in time to be shown statically at the Paris Air Show in the same month. In October 1987 it was announced that Wings West Airlines Inc of California, USA had ordered ten aircraft with an option on a further two for delivery in the spring of 1988. With further orders rumoured to be in prospect the future of the ATP was now looking much brighter. For four weeks in November and December 1997 British Midland Airways in association with British Aerospace flew G-BMYK on an intensive pre-certification 200 hour programme of typical operational flying to eighteen European destinations without any technical delays. It also proved that the aircraft could dock on standard airport jetways.

CERTIFICATION

Following type certification to the European Joint Airworthiness Requirements (JAR) in March, British Midland Airways took delivery of its first aircraft, G-BMYL, on 20th April 1988 and the type entered service on 9th May on the Birmingham to Brussels route. British Midland's other two aircraft were delivered in late May and mid June. The first aircraft for Wings West was first flown in full American Eagle colours on 11th February 1988 but parent company American Airlines did not approve of the order and it was later cancelled. This left several aircraft on the production line with no orders. However, in July 1988 the Airlines of Britain group (which included British Midland Airways) placed an order for five aircraft with an option on a further two for operation by Loganair Ltd and Manx Airlines Ltd. This was followed later in the same month by an order for eight aircraft for British Airways with an option on a further eight.

The first of the Manx Airlines' aircraft, which had been the second destined for Wings West, was delivered to them on 26th August. Another order placed during the year was from Ligaçoes Aéreas Regionais – LAR of Portugal for three aircraft with an option on a fourth. This was in effect the first export order to be received following the Wings West cancellation. The first two aircraft for Portugal were delivered in October and December 1988. Following its display at Farnborough in September, British Airways accepted its first aircraft, G-BTPA, in December 1988. The honour of flying the first revenue flight by a British Airways' ATP went to G-BTPC when it flew from Glasgow to Benbecula as the BA5814 on 7th January 1989. Internal German Services were inaugurated with the type soon after on 20th February and all eight aircraft of the initial order had been received by mid July 1989. With both LAR and British Airways, the ATPs were replacing previously used HS748s.

Manx Airlines' second aircraft, which had been the first destined for Wings West, was delivered to them in March 1989 after it had

Detail of the six-bladed propeller used on the ATP, on an Atlantic Airlines aircraft at Coventry.

G-BZWW c/n 2005 in American Eagle/Wings West colours and showing evidence of its proposed US registration N375AE on the nosewheel doors. The photograph was taken during a test flight in 1988. (WHC/BAe)

G-BRTG c/n 2019 of SATA Air Açores, in a photograph taken prior to delivery in late 1989. The aircraft would later adopt the registration CS-TGL. (WHC/BAe)

ATP production at Chadderton, where major airframe components were built before transportation by road to Woodford for final assembly. (WHC)

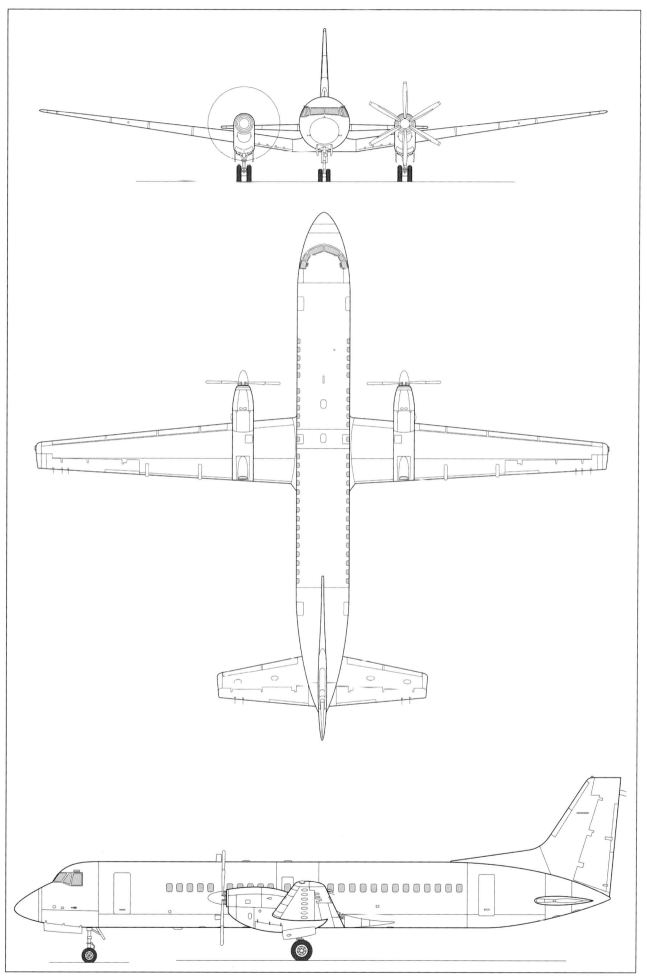

British Aerospace ATP.

The British Aerospace P132 Maritime Patrol Aircraft, which did not proceed beyond design work.

completed certification trials of the new PW126A engines in Spain late in 1988. On the 28th March 1989, Air Wisconsin Inc ordered fourteen aircraft with options on a further six while SATA Air Açores ordered three aircraft to replace HS748s on schedules within the Azores Islands. Two of the SATA aircraft were fitted with the optional wider forward baggage door and were the only ATPs to be built with this feature. The door width was increased to 4ft 2in (1.27m) from the standard 2ft 9in (0.84m) and was reportedly ordered to enable the easy carriage of coffins. Aircraft incorporating this modification had one less cabin window on the starboard side. Loganair Ltd accepted its first two aircraft in October 1989.

FAA CERTIFICATION

FAA type certification had been granted in early September 1988 in anticipation of the Wings West deliveries but the initial delivery to a United States customer was to Air Wisconsin in January 1990. This company was to take delivery of two further ATPs in the spring and another two aircraft in October and November 1990 for a network of scheduled services from their hub at Chicago, O'Hare. Air Wisconsin was one of only two customers to take up the APU option, though the first three aircraft were delivered without the APU fitted and returned to Woodford the following year for subsequent modifications. Manx Airlines and LAR each received their third aircraft in May and June 1990 respectively while a new customer was Bangladesh Biman Airlines which took delivery in September 1990 of the first two of three aircraft ordered. The last aircraft to be handed over in 1990 were SATA's second and third machines in December.

On 19th August 1990, G-BRLY (c/n 2025) was first flown with a shorter nose leg. This aircraft was to become a company demonstrator and was shown at Farnborough the following month before departing on sales tours of the USA and Canada in October and November and to Eastern Europe in early December 1990. Meanwhile the first prototype, after carrying out certification tests with the upgraded PW126A engines during 1988, was fitted with an APU and carried out cold weather trials in Greenland in March 1990. It was later fitted with the new shorter nose leg in time to appear at the Farnborough Air Show in September 1990 where it was shown in the United Express colour scheme.

BAe P132
MARITIME PATROL AIRCRAFT

Around this time British Aerospace proposed a Maritime Patrol Aircraft based on the ATP which was named the P132. In association with GEC Avionics and Thorn EMI Electronics, the P132 was designed as an affordable, highly effective anti-submarine warfare (ASW) and anti-surface unit warfare platform (ASUW). The aircraft would have carried the Thorn EMI Searchwater 2 Radar in a bulbous housing beneath the fuselage just forward of the wing giving a full 360° radar coverage. The radar would have additionally incorporated an IFF Interrogator to enable identification of radar contacts. The radar was to be supported by a RACAL Kestrel Mk.II Electronic Support Measures (ESM) system. A GEC TICM II Thermal Imaging System was proposed mounted under the nose for short range surveillance and identification. A GEC AQS 902/920 Central Tactical System (CTS) and a CAE AN/ASQ-504(V) Magnetic Anomaly Detector (MAD) were also proposed. Also to be fitted was a GEC Avionics' AQS928 Acoustic Processing System to handle data from a wide range of passive and active sonobuoys. Both rotary and single sonobuoy launchers were to be located in the rear fuselage. Four underwing hard points were added for the carriage of weapons such as Stingray torpedoes or long range Harpoon air-to-surface missiles and/or stores. Apart from the two cockpit crew, six additional crew members would have comprised a Tactical Coordinator, a Radar Operator, an Acoustic Operator, an ESM Operator and two observers. Of the last two,

one would have been a sonobuoy operator when required. With its large cabin, a sizeable crew rest area was also proposed. To provide additional electrical power an optional APU would have been mounted aft of the rear pressure bulkhead which would have been run in flight. With an endurance of over nine hours with full tanks, the P132 would have been a formidable MPA platform but after a considerable amount of design work, it was not proceeded with.

FURTHER DELIVERIES

Air Wisconsin took delivery of its second batch of five aircraft between January and June 1991 having earlier reduced its total order to ten. A new customer was Turk Hava Tasimaciligi – THT, a subsidiary of Turkish Airlines, which took delivery of four aircraft. The first two were delivered in September and October 1991, the third in February 1992 and the last in September 1992 after earlier leasing the BAe company demonstrator from July 1992 until the fourth aircraft was received. These APU equipped aircraft were used on Turkish domestic schedules. British Airways' fleet was increased to twelve with the addition of four new aircraft between November and December 1991. The Airlines of Britain group ordered two additional aircraft that were delivered to Loganair in November 1991 and February 1992. A new customer was Merpati Nusantara Airlines (another HS748 user) that ordered five aircraft that were delivered between February and July 1992 for use on inter-island schedules within Indonesia. British Midland Airways transferred its three aircraft to its partner airlines with the first going to Loganair in October 1991 and the remaining two to Manx Airlines in October 1992. British Airways took delivery of its thirteenth ATP in July 1992 followed by its final aircraft in August 1993. A major sales tour was made to Saudi Arabia, India and the Far East over a forty day period commencing on 26th April 1963 using G-JATP c/n 2055. During this tour the aircraft visited thirteen countries, flew 118.40 hours and carried out 54 landings but sadly no new sales resulted. Air Malta leased one of SATA – Air Açores' aircraft in full Air Malta colour scheme from October 1992 until April 1994, the aircraft being used on the short sector schedules to North Africa and Sicily. To cover for the shortfall in its fleet in 1993, SATA leased an additional aircraft from BAe from May to December. This last aircraft was one of three aircraft repossessed by BAe from LAR of Portugal in January and February. Of the other two, one was leased to Manx Airlines from August 1993 to July 1994 and the other was sold to Manx Airlines in May 1994.

Other aircraft to return to BAe during this period were the four aircraft of THT of Turkey. These were traded in for new BAe RJ100s which were delivered to Turkish Airlines. The four Turkish ATPs were returned in September and October 1993 and after removal of their APUs were operated by the short lived Euro Direct Airlines from July and August 1994 until the company ceased trading in February 1995. A fifth aircraft used by Euro Direct was the former LAR aeroplane that had been leased to Manx Airlines.

An artist's impression of the BAe P132 Maritime Patrol Aircraft.
(WHC/BAe)

G-JATP c/n 2055 in Jetstream Aircraft colours and with the short-lived Jetstream ATP titles in 1993.   *(WHC)*

PRODUCTION MOVED TO PRESTWICK

There was a dearth of sales following the Merpati Nusantara deal and BAe was forced to ferry all but one of the last eleven Woodford assembled ATPs to Teesside, Waddington and/or Prestwick in primer for storage from January 1993 until customers could be found for them. Final assembly was transferred to Prestwick with the last Woodford assembled aircraft, c/n 2063, making its first flight on 25th May 1993. This enabled Woodford to devote all of its commercial aircraft production capacity to assembly of the RJ Series of airliners following the closure of the Hatfield line some one and a half years earlier. The Airlines of Britain group took three more aircraft from the stored airframes, two going to Loganair in October and September 1993 and one to Manx Airlines in March 1994.

With all of BAe's propeller engined airliner production now at Prestwick, the division was renamed Jetstream Aircraft Ltd. The division's separate design and development departments set about looking at their long-term future. In the shorter term it was decided to upgrade the ATP with the more powerful Pratt and Whitney PW127D engines of 2,750 shp (2,051kW), for improved hot and high performance and with increased operating weights. On 26th April 1993 it was announced that the new version would be renamed the Jetstream 61. All Prestwick assembled aircraft would be built to the new standard. Looking to the future, the company announced two further developments of the aircraft to be launched during 1994. These were named the Jetstreams 51 and 71, the first of which would have had an overall length of 80ft 5in (24.51m) and seated 52 passengers in seats with a pitch of 32in (81cm). The Jetstream 71 was to have had an overall length of 101ft 9in (31.01m). These two new aircraft would have been somewhat faster in operation than the Jetstream 61, had 4,000 shp (2,983kW) engines and would have had a high set tailplane. The

first of the Jetstream 61s and the first Prestwick assembled aircraft took to the air on 10th May 1994. Later in the year, it was shown at the Farnborough Air Show together with the first ATP prototype which had been re-engined with the uprated PW126D engines.

Two operators withdrew their ATPs in 1994. A major change in the structure of the Airlines of Britain group took place in March when Loganair Ltd relinquished all their ATP routes to Manx Airlines Ltd together with their ATP fleet and were left to concentrate on their Highlands and Islands routes with smaller aircraft. September 1993 saw Air Wisconsin Inc in the United States transfer its ATP fleet to United Feeder Services Inc (UFS) and concentrate on its BAe 146 operations. The new ATP carrier continued to fly its ATPs on schedules centred on Chicago-O'Hare.

In 1995 two of the stored ATPs were sold to Seoul Air International of Korea, one of which was the last Woodford assembled aircraft. Both aircraft were delivered in March and were employed on ad hoc charter work throughout the Far East.

In January 1995 Manx Airlines commenced operating as a British Airways franchise carrier and the aircraft started appearing in British Airways colours. However, three aircraft continued to operate in Manx Airlines colours on the Isle of Man routes which were not part of this new arrangement. EuroDirect Airlines ceased trading in February 1995 and all five of its aircraft were repossessed by BAe and put into storage apart from one that was leased to Manx Airlines from April to November. Air Ostrava Ltd of the Czech Republic leased two aircraft from Manx Airlines Ltd from May 1995 to January 1996 for use on its international scheduled routes. British Midland Airways re-introduced two aircraft to service from January 1995 to March 1997 on lease from Manx Airlines Ltd.

AERO INTERNATIONAL REGIONAL – AIR

It was announced on 26th January 1995 that all commercial airliner activity within British Aerospace was to be merged with Avions de Transport Regional. In yet another change of direction by BAe, Avro International and Jetstream Aircraft were to become part of a new organisation named Aero International Regional – AIR with headquarters at Toulouse. With the Jetstream 61 now in direct competition with the ATR 72 of similar capacity, it was decided to abandon production and development of the Jetstream 51/61/71 in favour of the more successful ATR 42/72 range of aeroplanes. Although this new company was to be very short lived, the decision to abandon aircraft production at Prestwick had been made. Even with all these changes, certification of the Jetstream 61 was completed with the type certificate being granted on 15th June 1995. It was still hoped to complete approximately six aeroplanes at Prestwick and sell them with little additional cost. In common with other Jetstream aircraft, it was proposed that the basic Jetstream 61 would carry the model number 6100 and those built to United Kingdom build standard as model number 6102. However, the company failed to sell any of the Prestwick assembled Jetstream 61s. Those that were completed were broken-up and many new fuselages distributed among airport fire services throughout the United Kingdom for training purposes.

NEW CUSTOMERS

In October and November 1996 Canarias Regional Air took delivery of three former EuroDirect Airlines' aircraft for operation on Air Europa Express domestic schedules based on Palma in the Spanish Balearic Islands. A further four aircraft were added by the same carrier between January and April 1997 with some of them based on a new hub at Tenerife in the Canary Islands. The last four ATPs were former British Airways' aircraft that had been returned to BAe between September and December 1996 after British Airways had handed over its Highland and Islands services to British Airways Express carriers at the end of the summer season in October 1996. On 1st September 1996 Loganair and Manx Airlines were merged to form British Regional Airlines Ltd. In September 1996 the sale of five new aircraft to LAPA of Argentina was at an advanced stage of negotiation. This led to the last five aircraft stored at Teesside being ferried to Prestwick for preparation. Unfortunately the deal was not concluded and the aircraft were then put into storage at Prestwick, joining one of the UFS aircraft, which was returned to BAe in the same month.

In March 1997 Canarias Regional Air took delivery of an eighth aircraft that had been in store since the demise of EuroDirect. A new customer was found for two of the new aircraft stored in Prestwick in the shape of British World Airlines. These were delivered in September and December 1997. In yet another change Loganair Ltd broke away from British Regional Airlines following a management buy out in March 1997. Another of the Prestwick aircraft was prepared for Ireland Airways in September but the company's Air Operators Certificate was revoked in February 1998 and the aircraft was not delivered. SUN-AIR of Scandinavia based in Denmark took delivery of Seoul Air International's two aircraft in November 1997 and January 1998 to operate on scheduled services in the British Airways Express name. These two aircraft had been returned to BAe in September and November 1996.

In May 1998 the operations of Canarias Regional Air were split in two with three aircraft going to a new Canarias Regional Air operation in the Canary Islands and the remaining five transferred to a new Air Europa Express operation based in Palma where they were joined by a sixth used aircraft in June of the same year. This last aircraft had been used as a BAc corporate shuttle aircraft until the ex UFS aircraft replaced it in March 1998.

British Airways withdrew its last ten ATPs between June 1998 and January 1999, flying its last revenue service with the type on 26th January. Four of these aircraft joined an expanded Air Europa Express operation between October and December 1998. British World Airlines doubled its fleet to four aircraft in December 1998 with the addition of two new aeroplanes from storage at Prestwick. This company was finding plenty of work for the ATPs on short-term leases both in the United Kingdom and Europe. December 1998 saw SUN-AIR taking a third aircraft on strength, this being the last of the new ATPs remaining in storage.

Air Europa Express took delivery of another four ex British Airways' aircraft between May and July 1999 together with a fifth and sixth aircraft which had earlier seen service with Canarias Regional Air (which had ceased operations in February 1999), enabling them to establish a second hub at Madrid. The last two ex British Airways aircraft joined British World Airlines in December 1999, raising their fleet to six aircraft.

British Airways took over British Regional Airlines in March 2001 after its earlier conversion to a public limited company in June 1999. The company was then renamed British Airways CitiExpress and at the same time was merged with Brymon Airways, another British Airways owned company. Merpati Nusantara Airlines had retired its remaining four ATPs after the loss of one of its aircraft and by April 2001 all had been returned to Woodford, while the nine UFS ATPs were all in store at Kingman, Arizona after the last had been withdrawn from service in February 2000. SATA Air Açores leased two additional aircraft from BAE Systems' Asset Management organisation with delivery in May and August 2000, raising their fleet to four (one aircraft was written-off in December 1999). One of these was the former company demonstrator while the second was the first of the former Merpati Nusantara aeroplanes to be re-marketed. Air Europa Express accepted its seventeenth ATP in May 2000 and was then flying the largest ATP fleet of any carrier up to that time.

ATP FREIGHTER

Early in the year 2000 it was announced that West Air Sweden AB and BAE Systems were to jointly develop a freighter conversion programme for the ATP which BAE Systems would promote as the 'ATPF'. This would later incorporate a large freight door aft of the wing on the port side within the parallel section of the fuselage. The door aperture measures 5ft 8in (1.73m) high x 8ft 8in (2.64m) wide and the door opens outwards and slides to the rear flush with the fuselage on rails. The weight of the door is 256 lbs (117 kgs) and with the additional door frame structure, top and bottom sills and the pneumatically operated door seals a total of 440 lbs (200 kgs) is added to the basic operating weight of the aircraft, a small penalty for the advantages the large door provides for the operator. With the large door fitted the aircraft can accept up to seven standard LD3 containers (eight if the forward vestibule is removed) or five standard LD4 containers (with an additional two half LD4 containers with the forward vestibule removed). With a system of ceiling- and floor-fixed straps and restraint nets the payload of the aircraft is just over 8 tonnes. The constraint nets are attached to six newly fitted rails, four in the side walls, and two in the ceiling while two attachment points are at floor level. The rails run the full length of the cabin except when interrupted by emergency windows or doors allowing variable settings for the restraint nets. The forward starboard baggage door is mechanically locked closed and the operating mechanism removed while the rear passenger and service doors and frames are removed and the area sealed over. All but one of the cabin windows aft of the over-wing emergency exit to port is removed and the area sealed over in order to strengthen the structure. All non-essential equipment is removed in an effort to reduce the aircraft weight and increase payload. The first aircraft was fitted with a floor roller system attached to the seat rails, with a permanent rollermat system to be fitted later. West Air took delivery of six of the former UFS aircraft between April 2000 and May 2001. The first five aircraft entered service between September 2000 and August 2001 initially without the large main deck cargo doors and with a payload of over 8.4 tonnes. They had all been converted into an all freight rôle with a complete reconfiguration of the interior into an E-class cargo compartment. The aircraft were modified to conform to JAA regulations rather than FAA rules to which the aircraft had been originally certificated and were fitted with a new avionics package which included a Universal Avionics UNS-1K Flight Management System. This new system includes an interface between the flight deck displays and the autopilot and has achieved Precision RNAV approval and meets the basic RNAV rules made mandatory in 2001. All aircraft have the sidewall panels replaced by protective panels and a seven unit smoke detection system is fitted together with a fire door to the cockpit with smoke seals. Ten cabin lights are fitted together with nine 9G cargo separation nets. The landing gear lock release is relocated to the cockpit area from the main cabin due to its inaccessibility when the cabin is full of freight. At the same time TCAS (Traffic Collision and Avoidance System) and GPWS (Ground Proximity Warning System) are incorporated. BAE Systems also approved, as an option, the higher operating weights for the ATP that had already been approved for the abandoned Jetstream 61 programme. Work commenced in the summer of 2001 preparing

G-JEMF c/n 2015 at Bucharest-Băneasa on 13th April 2005, showing details of its recently-installed Large Freight Door. Although painted in full Emerald Airways colours, this aircraft would never serve with them.
(Keith Gaskell)

the sixth aircraft for the complete cargo door conversion programme which was completed in July 2002. Design of the new cargo door was undertaken by BAE System's Aircraft Services Group at Prestwick, which holds the design authority, while West Air developed a tailor-made container to maximise use of the available cabin volume. The interior conversion kits are supplied by ACS of Canada. The first aircraft to incorporate the large door was displayed statically at the Farnborough Air Show in late July 2002 by BAE Systems. It had first flown from Lidköping on 10th July crewed by West Air's Chief Pilot Mikael Heed and Johan Karlson together with technician Anders Nilsson.

The ATP freighter enjoys considerable advantages over its 748 predecessor with a 33% increase in payload, a 36% increase in volumetric payload and a 50% increase in range. Costs are approximately 10-15% higher than the 748, which overall gives the ATP a much higher profit potential for its operator. It is also considerably quieter in operation than the 748 and has lower emission levels, making it more environmentally friendly, especially with its mainly overnight operations in this rôle.

SECOND-HAND SALES IN THE 21ST CENTURY

Air Europa Express was put into voluntary liquidation on 29th October 2001, while British World Airlines went the same way soon afterwards on 13th December. This brought twenty-three additional aircraft onto the already overcrowded stored fleet of aircraft around the world. Disposal of British World's fleet started in February 2002 with the sale of two aircraft to European Executive Express of Sweden, though these aircraft were destined never to enter service but were soon sold on to West Air Sweden AB where they would become this operator's tenth and eleventh ATPs after conversion to freighters. Two further aircraft had been earlier added to West Air Sweden fleet in March and April 2002, raising their fleet of freighter ATPs to eight while a ninth was leased in September 2002 for operation as a passenger aircraft.

From September 2002 Manx Airline's identity was finally lost when it was fully absorbed into British Airways CitiExpress and the company's three ATPs were repainted in British Airways colours.

G-BTTO c/n 2033 of Atlantic Airlines with its Large Freight Door open.

West Atlantic Sweden's SE-MAF c/n 2002 is shown stored at Malmö on 31st August 2016, still in its West Air Europe livery.

(Hakan Frylen)

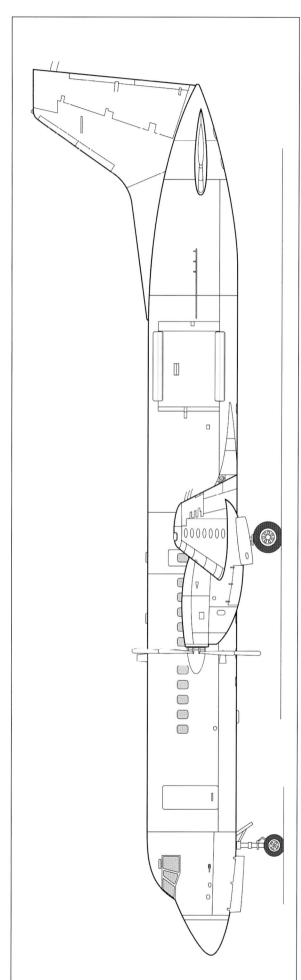

Romaero completed twenty-two Large Freight Door conversions of ATPs at their Baneasa plant in Romania, in a programme than ran from 2003 to 2008. The first conversion was done by West Air at Lidkoping, making twenty-three LFD conversions in all.
(Drawing by Mike Zoeller)

On 17th March 2003 it was announced that BAE Systems had reached agreement with British European Aviation Services at Exeter to design an E-Class freighter interior for the ATP. This would give prospective customers a second option when selecting conversion work. The new version was to have UK CAA approval.

Three months later, on 17th June 2003, it was announced that BAE Systems Regional Aircraft and Romaero SA had agreed a programme for the production of ten Large Freight Door kits to be manufactured at their Băneasa plant in Bucharest for subsequent fitment to ATPs. At the same time it was announced that a number of hail damaged ATPs would be ferried to Băneasa from Zaragoza in Spain for repair work. Romaero was also contracted to fit large cargo doors to five ATPs during 2004 of which two were completed on behalf of West Air Sweden. The first of these was rolled out on 22nd June 2004 and was ferried to West Air on the 7th July for completion of the interior freight conversion. On 23rd September 2008 the last of twenty-one Large Freight Door conversions completed by Romaero was ferried out of Băneasa.

Romaero SA had already been associated with British Aerospace in earlier years. The company completed nine One-Eleven airliners under licence at their Băneasa plant and also produced tailplanes for late production British built One-Elevens. Until recently it had built Britten-Norman Islanders to order on behalf of the Isle of Wight based company and built over five hundred examples. It also builds major sections of Canadair water bombers, Lear Jets, the rear sections of IAI executive jets and tail booms of Agusta helicopters as well as carrying out heavy maintenance on many airliner types and military transports for customers around the world.

In late December 2003 the first of three used aircraft was ferried to Blackpool from storage in the USA for preparation for passenger use by Emerald Airways Ltd. These aircraft were followed by two former Bangladesh Biman ATPs in late January 2004 and were expected to be joined by up to seven Large Freight Door equipped aircraft where they would have supplemented/ replaced existing 748 aircraft in the pure freight rôle. Passenger services were re-launched on the Liverpool to Isle of Man route on 10th May 2004 with two of the former American aircraft while the third entered service as a pure freighter in January 2005 after conversion at Blackpool.

The two Bangladeshi ATPs were ferried to Băneasa for fitment of large cargo doors in July and August 2004 but although one was ferried to Blackpool on completion, it had not entered service when the company's AOC was suspended on 4th May 2006. The company was later put in the hands of administrators on 11th May.

British Airways CitiExpress retired the last of its ATPs on 28th March 2004, although four had already been withdrawn during 2003. Loganair Ltd leased three of the ATPs with effect from 1st March 2004 until 31st May 2005 to operate over former British Airways CitiExpress routes which required the higher capacity of the ATPs. One of these retired ATPs was leased and later sold by BAE Asset Management to Asian Spirit Airlines of the Philippines for scheduled passenger use from December 2003. It was withdrawn in May 2007.

In early September 2004 an ATP was leased to EuroAir Ltd of Athens for evaluation prior to taking delivery of the first of three aircraft in November of the same year. These passenger configured aircraft were expected to be used on ad hoc charter work before establishing a new network of scheduled passenger services, but the deal later stalled.

Magic Blue Airlines of Holland was expected to take up to six aircraft, but although three aircraft were painted in their colour scheme, the company collapsed before any were delivered.

A view of the interior of an ATP Freighter, showing a pallet and the roller floor.

Atlantic Airlines in the United Kingdom took delivery of two Large Freight Door equipped freighter aircraft in 2005, a third in May 2006, a fourth in August of the same year and a fifth former Emerald Airways aircraft in February 2007. The last was their first and only freighter not to be fitted with a Large Freight Door and was operated on lease from April 2007 to September 2010. August 2007 saw the addition of the company's fifth aircraft with a large freight door and the sixth aircraft in the fleet. After E-Class freight conversion at Coventry the first of these entered service on contract cargo work in January and February 2006. The company was now committed to taking a total of ten Large Freight Door equipped ATPs bringing its fleet up to eleven aircraft by the end of 2008. However, with a decline in business due to the worldwide recession the last two aircraft were put in store at Coventry on receipt from Băneasa pending an upturn in business. This company's aircraft were fitted with a cabin rollermat system with a rollerball unit adjacent to the Large Freight Door.

In late January 2006 it was announced that First Flight Couriers Pvt Ltd of India were to lease three freighter ATPs. These were delivered in June, August and October 2006 for use on a domestic parcel/package delivery network after conversion by West Air's engineering department at Lidköping. However, following an accident with one of the aircraft in June 2007 the fleet was withdrawn from use.

In April 2006 it was confirmed that West Air Sweden had purchased the three strong fleet of SUN-AIR. The first two of these were quickly converted into E-class freighters and entered service in late August and early October 2006. The third aircraft continued in service with SUN-AIR until the end of July 2006 before delivery to Lidköping for conversion. The West Air group also took delivery of two Large Freight Door equipped aircraft on lease from BAE Systems, the first entering service in September 2006 and the second ferrying to Lidköping for E Class modifications in early October 2006. West Air Sweden also contracted to take delivery of a further ten ATPs for conversion to E-Class freighters with delivery of the first three in August and September 2006. By January 2008 the West Air group had twenty-five operational ATP freighters of which ten had Large Freight Doors. Two further passenger configured aircraft were leased to NEX Time Jet AB of Sweden by West Air from October 2008 with a third aircraft coming from West Air after lease from BAE Systems Asset Management. One of West Air's Large Freight Door equipped aircraft was leased to Air Go Airlines of Greece in August 2008.

Another new operator was MagicBird Airlines NV of Amsterdam which took delivery of its two freight configured aircraft on lease from BAE Asset Management Turboprops in April and May 2006 though both had been withdrawn from use late in May 2007.

An interior view of a Large Freight Door fitted pure freighter ATP with the roller ball at the door and the roller floor to the front and rear of it. No restraining nets are fitted at this time.

Enimex Ltd of Estonia contracted to take two passenger configured aircraft with the first delivered in mid July 2006. The second aircraft was never delivered and there is some doubt as to whether the first aircraft ever became operational before it was returned to BAE Systems in mid August 2007.

In late January 2007 BAE Systems announced that they had increased their order for Romaero produced Large Freight Doors from ten to twenty-five due to demand for the aircraft.

SATA Air Açores took delivery of a fifth aircraft in June 2007 to operate a new route in Madeira, the first time the ATPs had operated outside of the Azores in SATA's own name. However the fleet was gradually withdrawn from use starting in October 2009 with the final two being retired on 28th May 2010. This marked the end of over forty-one years of continual operation of Woodford produced airliners by this operator.

On 29th October 2008 it was announced that the West Air Sweden AB group and Atlantic Airlines Ltd were to merge as West Atlantic AB but that all three carriers involved would continue to operate individually with aircraft painted in a common colour scheme. The intention was to take advantage of the economies that could be made by merging various sections within the new carrier over a period of time. A long time stored aircraft entered service with West Air Sweden in December 2009 after purchase from BAE Asset Management while two ex West Air Luxembourg aircraft returned to West Air Sweden service in

December 2009 after periods of storage. It was confirmed on 8th February 2010 that the West Air Group had obtained three cargo configured aircraft from BAE Asset Management in December 2009. It was expected that all West Air Sweden's freighter configured ATPs would transfer to the Luxembourg and UK registers, though West Atlantic later reversed this policy.

With the addition of two former SATA passenger configured aircraft in October and November 2010 for operation by NEX Time Jet AB, the West Air group had a total of forty-five ATPs of which nine were in storage and awaiting entry into service. The first was leased to NEX Time Jet in April 2011 while in September 2013 another ex SATA aircraft was leased to the same operator. Later several aircraft were transferred to West Air Luxembourg and Atlantic Airlines, leaving West Air Sweden with just seven operational ATPs, none of which had Large Freight Doors, and four passenger configured aircraft operating for Next Jet. It was expected that no freighter ATPs would remain on the Swedish register, but these plans were later cancelled and the first of the Luxembourg registered aircraft returned to the Swedish register in mid May 2013 with the last aircraft transferring at the end of February 2015. All West Air Luxembourg ATP operations reverted to Swedish control after the sale of the company to FAST Logistics Luxembourg SARL on 25th October 2013. West Air Sweden officially became renamed as West Atlantic AB on 9th August 2013 and as West Atlantic Sweden AB on 10th November 2015. The Atlantic Airlines fleet of operational BAe ATPs are transferring to West Air/Atlantic Sweden AB, with the first ten moving across in September, October and November 2015 and February, March, May and June 2016.

A new airline named Air Aceh, based in northern Sumatra, was awaiting delivery of a former Asian Spirit passenger configured ATP in mid 2009 but although painted in their colour scheme it was never delivered. This aircraft had been purchased on Air Aceh's behalf by Regional One, Inc of Miami. This same organisation purchased three passenger configured aircraft in June 2009 from BAE Asset Management and continued their lease to SATA Air Açores while it obtained a cargo configured aircraft from the same source in late December 2009. Regional One specialises in leasing and sales of commuter type aircraft but it is not known what the plans are for all these aircraft. Jakarta based PT Deraya took delivery of two freight configured aircraft with Large Freight Doors in July and August 2009 which had earlier been intended for use by Emerald Airways Ltd and after one of these was written-off in May 2013, took delivery of a third example in March 2014. All three of these aircraft were/are leased from PTB (Emerald) Pty Ltd. A further freighter without a Large Freight Door was delivered in January 2015 from the same source.

A large pallet being loaded through the Large Freight Door of an ATP.

Highest recorded flown aircraft

Type	c/n	Regn	Operator	Figures
ATP	2019	SE-MEE	NEX Time Jet AB	30,794 hours
	2019	SE-MEE	NEX Time Jet AB	57,413 landings

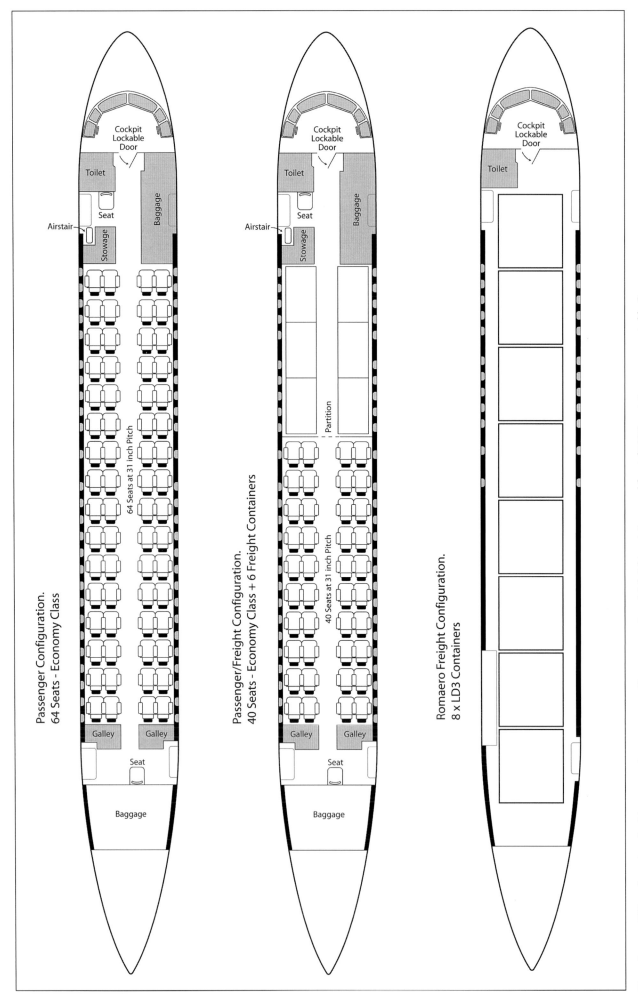

Chapter 7
Technical Description

WING

The wings are generally a composite of the outer section of the HS748 Series 2B and the inner section of the Andover C.Mk.1. They are of cantilever construction and have a two spar fail-safe structure. Horn balanced ailerons are fitted with a geared tab in each together with Fowler trailing edge flaps. Wing top skins are made from aluminium-zinc alloy while the bottom wing skins are made from copper, magnesium and manganese aluminium alloy. Pneumatic de-icing boots are fitted to the wing leading edges outboard of the engine nacelles.

FUSELAGE

The fuselage consists of an all-metal circular section semi-monocoque fail-safe structure similar to that of the 748 but lengthened by 18ft 4in (5.59m) and fitted with a re-contoured nose section. Two passenger entry doors are provided, both on the port side, with hydraulically-powered airstairs at the forward door. There are two service doors, one to the rear and one forwards, both to starboard. Both passenger doors and the rear service door open outwards and forwards and rest with the interior trim against the fuselage, protecting them from the elements. The forward service door slides upwards and inwards. Twenty-six cabin windows are provided on each side of the cabin measuring 1ft 2in (35.56cm) high x 10in (25.40cm) wide with corner radii of 4in (10.16cm). In a later modification Kevlar panels were fitted to the outside of the fuselage adjacent to the propellers, to protect the fuselage from damage caused by ice dislodged from the propellers.

TAIL UNIT

The tail unit is of a cantilever all-metal structure, with slightly swept vertical and non-swept horizontal surfaces. The aircraft has a power-assisted rudder fitted with spring and trim tabs. There is a trim tab in each elevator. Pneumatic de-icing boots are fitted to the leading edges of both the fin and the tailplane.

Heading picture: The ATP cockpit at night.

LANDING GEAR

A Dowty Rotol-designed hydraulically-operated retractable tricycle type undercarriage is fitted. All three units are twin wheeled and retract forwards. The main units are fully interchangeable and are fitted with telescopic, single stage, oleo-pneumatic shock absorbers, employ 34 x 11.75-14 tubeless tyres and retract into the bottom of the engine nacelles. Powered nosewheel steering through angles up to ± 47° is permitted while ± 90° can be obtained with automatic disconnection and reconnection of the steering rack. The nosewheels are fitted with 22 x 6.75-10 tyres. All landing gear doors are operated mechanically and the forward doors of the main undercarriage are sequenced to retract after lowering the wheels. Oleo units can be replaced without removal of the legs while oleo seals can be replaced without removal of the shock absorbers. Carbon brakes are fitted as standard with a heat pack life of 4,000 landings. Although fitted with three independent hydraulic power sources, the undercarriage can be set to free-fall with gravitational effect after the manual uplock has been released if required in an emergency.

Tyre Pressures	Mainwheels	Nosewheels
All versions	95lb/in²	73lb/in²
	6.65kg/cm²	5.13kg/cm²

DOORS AND EMERGENCY EXITS

The two passenger doors and the rear service door are Class 1 emergency exits and are fitted with automatic inflatable chutes. Additionally, single overwing emergency exits size 3ft (0.92m) x 1ft 8in (0.51m) are provided either side of the aircraft with Type III plug doors. Emergency evacuation from the cockpit area is identical to that of the 748.

FLYING CONTROLS

The flying control system consists of conventional manually operated ailerons, elevators and rudder with geared tabs on the ailerons and elevators and a spring tab on the rudder. Direct linkage to the flying controls is provided through a system of rods and cables. There are five settings on the Fowler flaps, these being 0°, 7°, 15°, 20° and 29°. Take-off settings are 7°, 15° or 20°,

approach settings are 15° and 20° and landing settings are 20° and 29°. Flap control linkage is similar to that of the 748. Should a control surface jam in either the aileron or elevator circuit, one pilot can retain control of the surfaces on his side of the aircraft, mechanically to port or electrically to starboard via the autopilot servos. A standby control system utilising the autopilot servos is engaged automatically should an uncontained engine disc burst disrupt the controls. A double-sided pneumatic ram driven by engine bleed air assists the flight crew with rudder control should an engine fail. Ailerons and elevators have control locks and the rudder is fitted with a gust damper. As with the 748, a stall warning system is fitted operating a control column stick shaker.

FLIGHT DECK LAYOUT

Dual flying controls are fitted for the normal two-pilot crew. The IPECO seats with kidney pads and thigh supports are fully adjustable, including seat back height and tilt. A third crew seat is mounted on the flight deck door with an oxygen socket and headset jack plug socket adjacent to it.

Windscreen panels are similar to those of the 748 with electric heating provided to the two main and side panels with a choice of two heating levels to disperse either condensation or ice. Independent two speed windscreen wiper systems are fitted to the two main windows with wipers operating over an 82° arc. Washer fluid is fed from reservoirs by duplicated pumps through a nozzle beneath each main panel.

Instruments on the forward panels and side and central consoles are lit integrally and the roof panels edge lit. Two variable intensity wander lights are provided with variable red-white filters. Fixed intensity fluorescent floodlights are located under the glareshield while there is an overall flight deck light mounted in the roof.

ACCOMMODATION

The aircraft has a crew of two on the flight deck and two cabin attendants (one seat adjacent to the forward passenger door and one at the rear of the cabin) in the passenger-configured version. Passenger accommodation can be variable according to the operator's individual requirements. Standard passenger seat layouts range from 60 at 34in (86cm) pitch to 72 at 30in (76cm)

ATP cabin interior view.   *(WHC/BAe)*

This Vickers Viscount V.757 testbed, C-FTID-X c/n 384, was used to flight test the ATP engine/propeller combination by Pratt & Whitney Aircraft of Canada.

pitch in paired seats either side of a central gangway. In both cases a forward toilet and a rear galley are standard. With lower seating levels a more comprehensive galley with ovens can be fitted. By keeping the toilets and galleys at opposite ends of the cabin, meal services can be provided with less interruption from passenger movement.

Large overhead baggage bins run the full length of the cabin on both sides. In the standard 64-seat configuration these offer 1.5ft³ (0.042m³) of stowage space for each passenger. Each of the eighteen bins is 4ft 6in (1.37m) long and 1ft 4½in (0.42m) deep and provides stowage for 80lb (36kg) of carry-on luggage. In this same standard configuration additional wardrobe space of 70ft³ (1.98m³) is provided for hanging coats etc. and for stowing oversize hand luggage. This is in addition to the 96ft³ (2.72m³) of overhead bin volume. The checked baggage holds include the standard rear hold of 180ft³ (5.09m³) and the forward hold which can vary from 155ft³ (4.39m³) to 94ft³ (2.66m³) depending on the configuration of the aircraft.

POWERPLANT

The ATP is powered by two Pratt and Whitney Canada PW 100 Series engines driving six-bladed slow turning British Aerospace/Hamilton Standard propellers offering high fuel efficiency, high power-to-weight ratio, low noise output and a high climb and cruise efficiency. The engine is a triple shaft free turbine consisting of two modules, the reduction gearbox and the turbomachine, the latter based on a three concentric shaft design. The low and high-pressure compressors are of advanced centrifugal design with an overall pressure ratio of 14.7 to 1. The third concentric shaft is driven by a power turbine of two stage axial design and drives the propeller through the reduction gearbox. This gearbox produces an overall reduction ratio of 16.6 to 1 giving a propeller speed of 1,200 rpm when the turbine is rotating at 20,000 rpm. Accurate power scheduling is achieved by an electronic control system which signals a mechanical fuel controller to govern the fuel flow to the engine. The engine/ six-bladed propeller combination was flight-tested by Pratt & Whitney Aircraft of Canada in Viscount 757 c/n 384.

Maintenance costs are kept to a minimum due to the simplicity of the basic design which has only six major rotating components and no inter-shaft bearings. An optional engine health monitoring system is available which can reduce greatly or even eliminate the need for hot end inspections. Initially the ATP was fitted with the PW124 engine with a power rating of 2,400shp (1,790kW). Later versions were fitted with PW126 and PW126A engines of 2,653shp (1,978.3kW) and 2,662shp (1,985kW) respectively. The Specific Fuel Consumption of the PW126A engine is 0.484 lb/shp/hr (294.4 g/kW/hr) at take-off. The Jetstream 61 was powered by PW126D engines of 2,750shp (2,050.7kW). The dry weight of each engine is only 1,060lb (480.8kg).

Each Hamilton Standard 6/5500/F-1 propeller consists of a hub assembly and six blades. The propellers are of a simple lightweight composite design, each blade comprising a central aluminium spar with a urethane foam filled contoured glass fibre shell. Each blade is electrically de-iced and a nickel sheath protects the outer leading edge. The propellers operate at relatively low speeds, thus adding to the quietness of the aircraft. The speeds are 1,200 rpm at take-off and between 960 and 1,020rpm in climb and cruise. Cabin noise is reduced by a solid-state syncrophase control system. The propeller is fitted with a sensitive pitch control system that enables it to deliver up to 6,500lb (2,950kg) of reverse thrust for use during the landing run. Due to the slow turning nature of the propellers, they can also be used to power the aircraft backwards from airport gates saving time and towing charges.

SYSTEMS

FUEL

Fuel types Jet A, A-1, JP4 or JP5 are certificated while AVGAS can be used in an emergency (maximum period of use 150 hours between engine overhauls).

Integral tanks of 1,400Imp Gals (1,681US Gals, 6,364litres) are located in the wings outboard of the engines with collector tanks inboard of the engine nacelles. Fuel gauging is by means of a capacitance system with twin indicators on the flight deck.

A single pressure refuelling point is located under the starboard wing just outboard of the engine and incorporates an illuminated refuelling panel. The fuel required in each tank can be pre-selected and the refuel/defuel valve in each wing is closed electrically when the selected levels have been reached. Maximum refuelling rate is 140Imp Gals (168US Gals, 636litres) per minute enabling full tanks to be achieved within ten minutes. Overwing refuelling can also be undertaken through points located above each tank.

Twin AC fuel pumps in each collector tank supply fuel to hydro-mechanical fuel control units. Should there be an engine failure, the live engine can be fed from both tanks via a cross-feed system. Any single pump can supply the fuel demanded by both engines.

HYDRAULICS

Hydraulic power is supplied by two Abex engine-driven variable delivery pumps with a normal working pressure of 2,450lb/in² (169bars). The system operates the landing gear, nosewheel steering, brakes and forward airstairs. Either pump can still supply the full system load should one fail. Standby hydraulic power is supplied by a 28 Volt DC auxiliary pump and completely separate system and reservoir. This can be used for emergency operation of the landing gear, airstairs and brakes. The main system has a flow rate of 9Imp Gals (11US Gals, 41litres) per minute controlled to 2,450lb/in² (169bars) while the emergency system has a flow rate of 0.5Imp Gals (0.6US Gals, 2.25litres) per minute controlled to 2,500lb/in² (172.4bars).

The hydraulic system servicing bay is located in the starboard wing root fillet and incorporates quick release self-sealing couplings to assist rapid servicing. By utilising the DC auxiliary pump, the need for ground servicing rigs is eliminated.

ELECTRICS

AC electrical power is provided by two Lucas three phase 200Volt, 30/45Kva variable frequency alternators, one mounted on each engine. A 28Volt DC sub-system comes from two 250amp Transformer Rectifier Units (TRUs). Should a single TRU fail, the remaining unit is capable of supplying all essential DC loads after shedding some non-essential items. Emergency power is supplied from two 37Ah nickel-cadmium batteries. A second sub-system provides 1.5Kva 200/115 V constant frequency power from two solid-state static inverters fed from the 28V DC bus-bars. The power enables the engines to be started from either internal batteries, a Ground Power Unit or from an optionally fitted Garret Model GTCP36-150 Auxiliary Power Unit. This last unit can also provide cabin air conditioning and heating on the ground and is located in the port wing/fuselage fillet. It is housed in a fireproof enclosure and can only be used when the aircraft is stationary or taxiing.

AIR CONDITIONING AND PRESSURISATION

Cabin pressurisation and air conditioning are supplied from a twin pack Hamilton Standard Environmental Control System (ECS) offering sub-zero delivery temperature capability. A differential pressure of 5.5lb/in² (0.387kg/cm²) maintains sea level conditions up to 12,300ft (3,749m) with an 8,000ft (2,438m) cabin altitude at 25,000ft (7,620m). The system is controlled automatically through duplicated discharge valves with manual reversion. Cabin and flight deck temperatures are controlled independently between 15° and 30°C. Output from the ECS packs is a mixture of 60% fresh air and 40% re-circulated air providing 20ft³ (0.57m³) per minute of conditioned air per passenger. Air enters the cabin both from the overhead Passenger Service Units and through floor level grills. Should a pack failure occur, the remaining pack output can be boosted to still provide the full cabin differential pressure.

OXYGEN

The aircraft is equipped with an integral high-pressure oxygen system for use by the flight crew. This comprises a lightweight cylinder containing 1,132 litres of gaseous oxygen at a pressure of 1,850lb/in² (126bars) when fully charged. The pressure is reduced to 72lb/in² above ambient via a pressure relief valve. Each crew member has a quick-don oxygen mask incorporating a microphone and oxygen regulator together with a pair of smoke goggles. Two portable breathing sets with face masks are provided for the flight attendants. Each of these is fitted with a shoulder harness, an intercom and a lightweight cylinder of 310 litres capacity at 1,800lb/in². Nine portable oxygen therapy sets are provided for the passengers. Each of these has a carrying strap and a cylinder of 120 litres capacity at 1,800lb/in².

WATER SYSTEM

Potable water is supplied from a 12Imp Gals (60litres) storage tank located below the cabin floor aft of the wing. The system is pressurised by air tapped from the de-icing system. Waste water from the galley and sink is piped overboard via a heated drain mast. The system is replenished through a filling point in the lower rear right wing fillet.

The toilet servicing panel is located in the lower fuselage ahead of the forward passenger door.

ICE PROTECTION

The wing, tailplane and fin leading edges are de-iced pneumatically using inflatable rubber boots. Two settings are provided to overcome normal and heavy icing conditions. The system operates automatically with manual reversion. Nacelle mounted lights illuminate the leading edges when required.

Engine nacelles, propellers, windscreens, pitot heads, the stall warning vane and waste water drain mast are all heated electrically. An independent two-speed windscreen wiper system is fitted to each main windscreen panel augmented by independent windscreen washers. Cockpit side windows are demisted using engine bleed air.

AVIONICS

The standard fit is as follows but could be varied to suit individual customer requirements: -

01	Electronic Flight Instrumentation System	(Four Tube Smiths Industries SDS-201)
02	Digital Air Data System	(Dual Smiths Industries)
03	Attitude & Heading Reference System	(Dual LITTON LTR-81-01)
04	Weather Radar	(Bendix RDS-86)
05	Communications/Navigation & Identification Plug units including: -	(Bendix Series 111 back)
		(Twin VHF Comm VCS-40B)
		(Twin VHF Nav VNS-41B)
		(Single ADF DFS-43B)
		(Single DME DMS-44B)
		(Single ATC Transponder TRS-42B)
06	Autopilot/Flight Director	(Duplex Bendix FCS-60B)
07	Radio Altimeter	(Single TRT AHV-16)
08	Communications Control System	(Dowty Electronics UA-50)
09	Passenger Address System	(Single Collins 346-2B)
10	Tape Replay Unit	(Sunstrand CAS801)
11	Cockpit Voice Recorder	(Single Fairchild A100A)
12	Ground Proximity Warning System	(Single Sunstrand GPWS Mk.V)
13	Flight Data Recorder	(Single Plessey PV1584F)

SPECIFICATION DATA

OVERALL DIMENSIONS

	Imperial	Metric	Notes
Wing span	100ft 6in	30.63m	
Wing aspect ratio		11.984	
Sweepback at quarter chord		2.92°	
Dihedral		7°	
Overall length	85ft 4in	26.01m	
Maximum fuselage diameter	8ft 9in	2.67m	
Overall height	23ft 5in	7.14m	(1)
	24ft 2in	7.37m	(2)
Tailplane span	36ft 0in	10.97m	
Fuselage ground clearance	3ft 10in	1.16m	
Wheelbase	31ft 9¾in	9.70m	
Wheeltrack	27ft 9in	8.46m	
Main wheel turning circle radius	32ft 0in	9.75m	
Propeller diameter	13ft 9in	4.19m	
Propeller ground clearance	1ft 11¾in	0.60m	
Propeller fuselage clearance	2ft 7½in	0.80m	
Passenger door (port forward)			
Height	5ft 8in	1.73m	
Width	2ft 4in	0.71m	
Height to sill	6ft 10in	2.09m	(1)
	6ft 7in	2.00m	(2)
Passenger door (port rear)			
Height	5ft 8in	1.73m	
Width	2ft 4in	0.71m	
Height to sill			
	5ft 7½in	1.71m	(1)
	6ft 0in	1.83m	(2)
Forward baggage door			
Height	3ft 7in	1.09m	
Width	2ft 9in	0.84m	
	4ft 2in	1.27m	(3)
Height to sill	6ft 10in	2.09m	(1)
	6ft 7in	2.00m	(2)
Rear service door			
Height	5ft 2in	1.58m	
Width	2ft 4in	0.71m	
Height to sill	5ft 7½in	1.71m	(1)
	6ft 0in	1.83m	(2)
Large Rear Freight Door			
Height	5ft 8in	1.73m	
Width	8ft 8in	2.64m	
Height to sill	6ft	1.83m	
Overwing Emergency Exits			
Height	3ft	0.92m	
Width	1ft 8in	0.51m	

(1) With long nose leg at mid-centre of gravity position
(2) With short nose leg at mid-centre of gravity position
(3) Optional

EXTERNAL AREAS

	Imperial	Metric	Note
Gross wing area	842.83ft²	78.30m²	
Fin and rudder area	148ft²	13.75m²	
Tailplane area	243ft²	22.57m²	

INTERNAL DIMENSIONS

	Imperial	Metric	Note
Maximum cabin length	63ft 0in	19.20m	
Constant section cabin length	54ft 0in	16.50m	
Maximum cabin height	6ft 4in	1.92m	
Maximum cabin width	8ft 2½in	2.50m	
Maximum floor width	6ft 9in	2.06m	
Useable cabin volume	2,652ft³	75.10m³	
Rear freight hold volume	180ft³	5.11m³	
Main forward freight hold volume			
Option A	155ft³	4.38m³	
Option B	128ft³	3.62m³	
Second forward freight hold volume			
Option A	45ft³	1.26m³	
Option B	16ft³	0.45m³	
Bulk 'E' Class Freighter			
Maximum cabin volumetric capacity	2,474ft³	70m³	(4)
	2,615ft³	74m³	(5)
Maximum density	6.35lb/ft³	102kg/m³	(5)
	6.8lb/ft³	109 kg/m³	(2)

WEIGHTS AND LOADINGS

	Imperial	Metric	Note
Basic operating weight empty	31,400lb	13,242kg	(1)
	31,800lb	14,424kg	(2)
Typical operating weight empty	29,652lb	13,450kg	(4)
	29,432lb	13,350kg	(5)
	30,446lb	13,810kg	(6)
	30,225lb	13,710kg	(7)
Maximum fuel	11,200lb	5,080kg	(3)
Maximum payload	15,800lb	7,166kg	(1)
	16,430lb	7,452kg	(2)
	18,347lb	8,322kg	(4)
	18,567lb	8,422kg	(5)
	17,553lb	7,962kg	(6)
	17,775lb	8,062kg	(7)
Maximum ramp weight	50,700lb	22,997kg	(1)
	52,350lb	23,745kg	(3)
Maximum take-off weight	50,550lb	22,930kg	(1)
	52,200lb	23,678kg	(3)
Maximum landing weight	49,052lb	22,250kg	(1)
	51,000lb	23,133kg	(3)
Maximum zero-fuel weight	46,804lb	21,230kg	(1)
	47,200lb	21,409kg	(1)
	48,000lb	21,772kg	(2)
Maximum wing loading	61.92lb/ft²	302.3kg/m²	
Maximum power loading	9.49lb/s.h.p.	5.78kg/kW	

(1) ATP initial CAA and FAA approved
(2) Jetstream 61 and later ATP Freighter (optional increase) CAA approved
(3) ATP Freighter, Pax aircraft (optional increased weight) & Jetstream 61
(4) Bulk cargo 'E' class freighter (with forward vestibule)
(5) Bulk cargo 'E' class freighter (without forward vestibule)
(6) As (4) with Large Freight Door
(7) As (5) with Large Freight Door

PERFORMANCE

Cruising speed	312mph (271kt, 502km/h)	High Speed	(1)
	272mph (236kt, 437km/h)	Cost economic	(2)
Airspeed Limitations			
Never exceed speed V_{NE}	227kt IAS	At sea level	
Increasing linearly to	230kt IAS	Up to 15,000ft	
Increasing linearly to	220kt IAS	Above 15,000ft	
Decreasing linearly to	221kt IAS	At 22,000ft	
	208kt IAS	At 25,000ft	
Never exceed speed V_{FE}	180kt IAS	7° or 15° flap	
flaps extended	150kt IAS	20° flap	
	140kt IAS	29° flap	
Never exceed speed V_{LE}	180kt IAS		
landing gear extended			
Never exceed speed V_{LO}	180kt	For lowering	
landing gear	150kt	For retraction	
operating speed			
Manoeuvring rough V_A	170kt	At all	
air speed		altitudes	
(1) At 13,000ft (3,960m)			
(2) At 18,000ft (5,485m)			

Service ceiling at MTOW	25,000ft, 7,620m	
Take-off field length at MTOW	4,410ft, 1,345m	(1)
	4,360ft, 1,329m	(2)
Landing field length at MLW	3,818ft, 1,164m	
Maximum payload range	712 miles (619nm, 1,146km)	(3)
Maximum ferry range	2,670 miles (2,320nm, 4,296km)	
(1) Standard ATP		
(2) Jetstream 61		
(3) With reserves for 115miles (100nm, 185km) diversion and 45 minutes hold at 10,000ft (3,050m)		

OPERATIONAL NOISE LEVELS
ICAO ANNEX 16 /
FAR PART 36 CHAPTER 3

Flight phase	**Chapter 3 Limit**	**BAE Systems ATP**
Flyover	89 EPNdB	79.5 EPNdB
Approach	98 EPNdB	95.8 EPNdB
Sideline	94 EPNdB	82.7 EPNdB*
* 29° Approach flap		

6) **'C' Check.**
To be completed at intervals not exceeding 2,500 flight hours.

The '½C' and 'C' Check lives were increased later to 1,500 and 3,000 hours respectively while in January 2006 the Service Check life was increased to 70 flight hours, the 'A' Check life was increased to 400 flight hours, the '½ C' Check to 2000 flight hours and the 'C' Check to 4000 flight hours.

MAINTENANCE PROGRAMME

As with the 748, the maintenance programme for the ATP was designed to be flexible and could be adapted to suit individual operator requirements. However the standard programme laid down was initially as follows:-

1) **Pre-flight check.**
2) **Daily Check.**
   To be actioned every 24 hours.
3) **Service Check.**
   To be completed at intervals not exceeding 50 flight hours.
4) **'A' Check.**
   To be completed at intervals not exceeding 250 flight hours.
5) **'½ C' Check.**
   To be completed at intervals not exceeding 1,250 flight hours.

CUSTOMER SUPPORT

This is covered by the similar section on the 748 and can be found in Part 1.

AIRCRAFT DELIVERIES BY YEAR

Year	Total	Year	Total	Year	Total
1988	7	1992	9	1996	0
1989	11	1993	3	1997	2
1990	11	1994	1	1998	3
1991	13*	1995	2	**Total**	62
* Includes one demonstrator aircraft on long-term lease					

Three examples from later ATP production are shown on this page: G-MANB c/n 2055 (above) of Manx Airlines, taken at Manchester in October 1997 (Tom Singfield); G-11-060 c/n 2060 (below) was rolled out at Prestwick in Ireland Airways livery on 18th December 1997, but this operator's AOC was revoked in February the following year and the aircraft was repainted white before its sale to British World Airways as G-OBWO (Tom Singfield collection); c/n 2052 (bottom) illustrates the colourful history of some ATPs with use by operators in Turkey, Spain, the Netherlands, Indonesia and for eight months by EuroDirect Airlines as G-OEDF in the United Kingdom, with whom it is shown at Berne in September 1994 (Tom Singfield).

Chapter 8
ATP Operators

Air Aceh, PT ( )
Banda Aceh, Sumatra, Indonesia

Owned jointly by Able Sky Sdn Bhd of Malaysia and the Aceh Government, this carrier was due start operations with a single ex Philippino ATP in Dec08. However, by early Jul09 the airline had still not commenced operations. The company was due to take a second passenger-configured aircraft later in 2009 with a third expected to follow. Projected scheduled destinations from its home base on the northern tip of Sumatra were Batam, Jakarta, Lekhseumawe, Medan, Padang, Pekanbaru and Semeleu while internationally Kuala Lumpur and Penang were due to be served. The initial route due to be flown was from Banda Aceh to Medan.

PK-   2055

Air Europa Express, Líneas Aéreas SA (UX/PMI)
Palma de Mallorca, Spain

After initially operating as a division of Canarias Regional Air SA from Oct96, this organisation broke away from the former company and commenced operating in its own right with effect from 11May98 using five aircraft with a sixth added the following month. Eight additional aircraft were ordered in Sep98 for a new Madrid hub operation. By May00 the fleet had increased to seventeen aircraft. Schedules were flown from Palma to Alicante, Barcelona, Ibiza, Menorca, Rome, Salamanca, Valencia and Zaragoza, from Barcelona to Bilbao, Granada, Ibiza, Menorca and Valladolid and from Ibiza to Madrid. The new Madrid hub

saw schedules to Alicante, Asturias, Badajoz, Bilbao, Jerez, Lá Coruña, Málaga and Santiago de Compostela together with Oporto in Portugal. Charter flights were also flown. The company ceased operations at midnight on 29Oct01 and the company was put into voluntary liquidation.

EC-GJU	2033	EC-GSG	2041	EC-HEH	2014
EC-GKI	2039	EC-GSH	2043	EC-HES	2042
EC-GKJ	2038	EC GSI	2044	EC-HFM	2015
EC-GLC	2041	EC-GUX	2024	EC-HFR	2016
EC-GLD	2052	EC-GYE	2007	EC-HGB	2010
EC-GLH	2042	EC-GYF	2010	EC-HGC	2007
EC-GNI	2043	EC-GYR	2011	EC-HGD	2011
EC-GNJ	2044	EC-GZH	2012	EC-HGE	2012
EC-GSE	2038	EC-HCO	2052	EC-HNA	2033
EC-GSF	2039	EC-HCY	2013		

Air Go Airlines SA (4A/AGS)
Athens, Greece

This company took delivery of a Large Freight Door fitted cargo-configured ATP sub-leased from West Air Sweden AB in Aug08. The aircraft was employed on ad hoc cargo flights from Greece to Albania, Bulgaria, Cyprus, Romania, Turkey and Yugoslavia and flew for the Swedish Postal Service during the Christmas period in 2008. This operator relocated to Bulgaria in Aug10 (see below).

SX-BPS   2005

Heading picture: G-BTPD c/n 2011 of British Airways, seen during test flying, presumably in 1989, in the older colour-scheme.   *(WHC/BAe)*

Air Go Airlines Bulgaria EAD (4A/AGE)
Sofia, Bulgaria

Air Go Airlines SA was reformed as a Bulgarian carrier with effect from Aug10. Its Large Freight Door fitted cargo configured aircraft was initially based in Marseilles flying on behalf of West Air Sweden AB and adopted Bulgarian marks in early Jan11. The aircrat was withdrawn from use on 28Oct11.

LZ-BPS   2005   SX-BPS   2005

Air Malta plc (KM/AMC)
Malta

Air Malta leased an aircraft from SATA - Air Açores from late Oct92 to late Apr94. The aircraft was operated on schedules from Malta to Catania, Monastir, Palermo and Tunis after entering service on 25Oct92. The lease ended on 01May94 and the aircraft returned to the lessor on 03May94.

CS-TGL   2019

Air Ostrava Ltd (8K/VTR)
Ostrava, Czech Republic

This company leased two aircraft from Manx Airlines Ltd from May95. Scheduled services were operated between Ostrava, Prague and Amsterdam until the type was withdrawn in Jan96.

OK-TFN   2006   OK-TFO   2023

Air Wisconsin Inc (ZW,UA/AWI)
Appleton, Wisconsin, USA

Air Wisconsin ordered fourteen aircraft, with an option on a further six. Only ten aircraft were accepted, between Jan90 and May91. The aircraft were employed on United Express schedules from Chicago to points including Appleton, Fort Wayne, Green Bay, Kalamazoo, Lansing, Madison, Milwaukee, Moline, Oshkosh, Peoria, South Bend, Toledo and Wausau. The aircraft were transferred to the newly created United Feeder Service Inc, a division of Trans States Airlines Inc, on 07Sep93 when Air Wisconsin became an all BAe 146 operator.

N851AW	2020	N855AW	2029	N858AW	2035
N852AW	2021	N856AW	2032	N859AW	2036
N853AW	2022	N857AW	2034	N860AW	2037
N854AW	2028				

Asian Spirit (6K/RIT)
Manila, Philippines

On 19Nov02 it was announced that this carrier was to take two aircraft on long-term lease in a 68-seat passenger configuration. The first was delivered in early Dec03 with the type being used initially on routes from Manila to Calbayog, Catarman, Tagbilaran and Virac. With effect from Feb05 the aircraft flew schedules from Manila to Antique, Ormoc and San Jose. From Jun05 Antique was dropped from the ATP schedule while Basco was an added destination both direct from Manila and via Tuguegarao while later in the same year Masbate replaced San Jose as a destination. The second aircraft was not taken up, after the company took delivery of a leased BAe 146-100. The aircraft was withdrawn from use in early May07 and sold in Jul08 prior to the company name being changed to Zest Air in Sep08.

RP-C2786 2055   (RP-C)   2054

Atlantic Airlines Ltd (NPT)
Coventry, West Midlands, UK

This company advertised for flight crew and engineering staff in Jul05 for a fleet of ATP freighters fitted with Large Freight Doors. The first two were delivered to Coventry for interior modifications in early July and early Oct05 with a third in May06 and a fourth in mid Aug06. The only ATP freighter operated without a Large Freight Door was leased from early Feb07 until early Sep10 while a sixth aircraft with a Large Freight Door was added in Aug07, a seventh in Oct07, an eighth in Jan08, a ninth in Apr08, a tenth in early Jul08 and an eleventh in Sep08. By mid Nov11 only one aircraft was still awaiting completion of its E Class modifications and this entered service in Sep13.

The aircraft were initially flown on behalf of DHL linking Jersey, Guernsey, Luton and Brussels and on behalf of Business Post/Parcel Force linking Aberdeen and Coventry via Edinburgh after introduction to service on 29Jan06. One of MagicBird's ATPs was used to fly a regular service between Rome-Fiumicino and Lamezia on behalf of Atlantic Airlines in the summer of 2006.

More recently the aircraft have been flown under contract to DHL from Ljubljana in Slovenia and from Luxembourg to the organisation's new hub at Leipzig in Germany, the above route to Brussels, from Cork to Amsterdam via East Midlands, from Basel to East Midlands and from East Midlands to Tallinn via Stockholm-Arlanda. Two aircraft currently fly on behalf of Royal Mail, one from Guernsey to Edinburgh via Hurn and the other links East Midlands with the Isle of Man and Belfast. On 29Oct08 it was announced that Atlantic Airlines and the West Air Sweden group were to merge as West Atlantic but that all three airlines in

Air Wisconsin's penultimate ATP, N859AW c/n 2036, in United Express livery. Note the additional outer fuselage panels in line with the propeller.

the group would continue to operate as separate entities. Coventry schedules were moved to Birmingham from Dec09 to Nov11 while the airfield was unlicensed. All the operational BAe ATPs were transferred to the Swedish register with the first ten transferring in Sep, Oct and Nov15 and Feb, Mar, May and Jun16. The last UK registered ATP flight took place on 28May16.

G-BTPA	2007	G-BTPJ	2016	G-MANH	2017
G-BTPC	2010	G-BTTO	2033	G-MANM	2005
G-BTPE	2012	G-BUKJ	2052	G-MANO	2006
G-BTPF	2013	G-BUUP	2008	G-OAAF	2029
G-BTPG	2014	G-BUUR	2024		
G-BTPH	2015	G-JEMB	2029		

Biman Bangladesh Airlines (BG/BBC)
Dhaka, Bangladesh

Three aircraft were ordered, of which only two were delivered in Aug and Sep90. The type was used on routes from Dhaka to Calcutta, Chittagong, Cox's Bazar, Ishurdi, Jessore, Rajshahi, Saidpur and Sylhet. The aircraft were withdrawn from use and sold to Emerald Airways Ltd in Jan04.

| S2-ACX | 2026 | S2-ACY | 2027 | (S2-ACZ) | 2033 |

British Airways CitiExpress Ltd
(BA,TH/BAW/BRT)
Ronaldsway Airport, Isle of Man, UK

Following British Airways' purchase of the British Regional Airlines Group Ltd early in 2001, it was merged with Brymon Airways Ltd to form the above company on 31Mar02. At the time thirteen ATPs were in operation of which three operated in Manx Airlines colours (see separate listing for details). For the initial summer season the ATPs were employed on schedules linking Glasgow with Aberdeen and Shetland, Belfast Harbour, Benbecula, Manchester and Stornoway, Manchester with Aberdeen, Belfast Harbour, Edinburgh, Jersey, Connaught-Knock and Southampton and Edinburgh with Belfast Harbour. Weekend charters were also flown from Jersey to Liverpool, Norwich and London-Stansted. Manx Airlines Ltd was absorbed fully on 01Sep02 adding additional schedules from the Isle of Man to Birmingham, Dublin, Glasgow, Liverpool and Manchester. By Oct02 British Airways Regional Division had also become part of this group. During 2003 three ATPs were withdrawn from use as their leases expired. This took place in March, August and September while an additional aircraft was withdrawn in Feb04. Three aircraft were leased to Loganair Ltd with effect from 01Mar04 until 31May05 when the routes from Glasgow to Aberdeen, Benbecula and Stornoway, from Aberdeen to Shetland and from Edinburgh to Belfast City were transferred to them. The final CitiExpress ATP revenue service was flown on 28Mar04 and the remainder of the fleet was put in storage.

G-MANA	2056	G-MANG	2018	G-MANM	2005
G-MANB	2055	G-MANH	2017	G-MANO	2006
G-MANC	2054	G-MANJ	2004	G-MANP	2023
G-MANE	2045	G-MANL	2003	G-MAUD	2002
G-MANF	2040				

British Airways plc (BA/BAW)
Glasgow, Scotland

This airline ordered eight aircraft to replace HS748 aircraft on German internal services and to expand service both within Germany and the United Kingdom. Later six additional aircraft were ordered in batches of four, one and one. The first batch of aircraft was delivered between Dec88 and Jul89, the second batch in Nov and Dec91 and the individual aircraft in Jul92 and after initial lease from the manufacturer from Aug93. The final aircraft was purchased in Jun94. Additional aircraft were leased from

Manx Airlines Ltd and BAe at various times. Details of these can be found in the individual aircraft histories section. The type entered service on 07Jan89 between Glasgow and Benbecula and on the internal German services on 20Feb89. Points served within Germany from Berlin-Tegel were Bremen, Hannover and Münster together with Westerland/Sylt from the start of the summer schedules in the same year. At the start of the winter schedules in Oct89 a Monday to Friday service was introduced between Manchester and Tegel via Hannover. Nuremburg was added to the network in late Oct89.

The type was withdrawn from the Internal German Service network in 1991, from which time it replaced HS748s on the Highland Division network. Points served within Scotland included Aberdeen, Benbecula, Edinburgh, Glasgow, Inverness, Kirkwall, Sumburgh and Stornoway. Belfast International was served from Manchester and Glasgow, while Birmingham was linked with Glasgow, Edinburgh and Aberdeen. With effect from 27Oct96 British Airways withdrew from internal Scottish services and ceased serving Benbecula, Kirkwall, Lerwick and Stornoway. These routes were transferred to British Airways Express carriers, leading to the withdrawal of four ATPs by the end of 1996. Further aircraft were withdrawn gradually until the last revenue flight took place on 26Jan99 from Edinburgh to Manchester as BA1865. See also British Airways CitiExpress Ltd, Loganair Ltd, Manx Airlines Ltd and Sun-Air of Scandinavia A/S.

G-BRLY	2025	G-BTPG	2014	G-BTPN	2044
G-BTPA	2007	G-BTPH	2015	G-BTPO	2051
G-BTPC	2010	G-BTPJ	2016	G-BUWP	2053
G-BTPD	2011	G-BTPK	2041	G-PEEL	2023
G-BTPE	2012	G-BTPL	2042	G-UIET	2006
G-BTPF	2013	G-BTPM	2043		

British Midland Airways Ltd (BD/BMA)
East Midlands Airport, Nottinghamshire, UK

British Midland Airways ordered three aircraft with delivery in Apr, May and Jun88. The type entered service on 09May88 between Birmingham and Brussels, this the first revenue flight by any operator. The type was employed on routes from Birmingham to Brussels, Guernsey and Jersey and from East Midlands to Belfast, Glasgow, Guernsey and Jersey in summer 1988 while weekend services were flown from Heathrow to Leeds/Bradford and Teesside. At the start of the winter programme in 1988 two aircraft were deployed to Heathrow to cover the schedules to Birmingham and East Midlands, replacing Shorts 360s. The third aircraft was flown on Channel Islands routes to Birmingham and East Midlands and from East Midlands to Amsterdam.

One aircraft was transferred to Loganair in Oct91 and the other two to Manx Airlines Ltd at the end of Oct92. These last two aircraft were returned to British Midland in Jan95 and returned to service on routes from East Midlands to Belfast, Brussels, Guernsey and Jersey. The last aircraft was withdrawn on 14Mar97 but the final ATP service was flown with a leased British Regional Airlines Ltd aircraft on 28Mar97.

| G-BMYK | 2003 | G-BMYM | 2002 | G-MANL | 2003 |
| G-BMYL | 2004 | G-BRLY | 2025 | G-MAUD | 2002 |

British Regional Airlines Ltd - BRAL
See Manx Airlines Ltd

British World Airlines Ltd (VF/BWL)
Southend, Essex, UK

British World Airlines leased four new aircraft from BAe Asset Management Turboprops for ad hoc passenger and cargo charters with delivery in Sep and Dec97 and Jun and Dec98. Aircraft were leased to numerous operators in both the United Kingdom and Europe. A further two aircraft were delivered in Dec99. One of the aircraft was operated with a quick-change conversion kit from a passenger to freight rôle retaining the forward vestibule. Contracts were signed in early Jan00 to operate three aircraft on oil industry support work based in Aberdeen. The company ceased operations on 14Dec01.

G-OBWL	2057	G-OBWN	2059	G-OBWP	2051
G-OBWM	2058	G-OBWO	2060	G-OBWR	2053

Canarias Regional Air (UX,CW,FW/CNM)
Las Palmas de Gran Canaria, Spain

Canarias Regional Air leased eight aircraft from BAe Asset Management Turboprops with delivery between Oct96 and Apr97. The aircraft were operated on scheduled services on behalf of Air Europa Express, based on hubs at Palma, Barcelona and Tenerife. However, from 11May98 the Canaries-based operations became independent of those of Air Europa Express. Arrecife (Lanzarote), El Hierro (Valverde), Fuertaventura, Las Palmas de Gran Canaria, Santa Cruz de La Palma and Santa Cruz de Tenerife were connected on a scheduled basis with three ATP aircraft until all scheduled services ceased on 31Jan99 and the aircraft were returned to BAe.

EC-GJU	2033	EC-GLC	2041	EC-GNI	2043
EC-GKI	2039	EC-GLD	2052	EC-GNJ	2044
EC-GKJ	2038	EC-GLH	2042		

CityJet Ltd (WX/BCY)
Dublin, Eire

CityJet Ltd leased a British World Airline's aircraft with effect from 27Mar99 to operate three daily rotations between Dublin and East Midlands. From 04Apr99 an aircraft in full CityJet colours was used until the contract ended on 30Sep99.

G-OBWL	2057	G-OBWM	2058

Deraya PT (DRY)
Halim Airport, Jakarta, Indonesia

Deraya took delivery of two cargo-configured aircraft with Large Freight Doors in late Jul and early Aug09. Following an accident with one of these aircraft on 31May13, a third Large Freight Door equipped aircraft was prepared for this carrier at Bucharest-Băneasa with effect from early Sep13 and delivered in Mar14. A fourth cargo configured aircraft without the Large Freight Door was delivered in Jan15. They primarily operate between Jayapura and Wamena in Western Papua. The first two aircraft had been intended for use by Emerald Airways Ltd but had never entered service with them when that company ceased operations. All aircraft are leased from International Air Parts Pty Ltd through their subsidiary PTB (Emerald) Pty Ltd.

PK-DGA	2026	PK-DGC	2052	PK-DGI	2027
PK-DGB	2029				

Emerald Airways Ltd (G3/JEM)
Liverpool Airport, Merseyside, UK

In Oct03 this operator advertised for ATP-qualified staff for a fleet of three used ATPs purchased in the USA. The first aircraft was delivered in late Dec03, the second in mid-Jan04 and the third in Mar04. The type entered scheduled passenger service on 10May04 on the Liverpool-Isle of Man route (which was operated five times per day from Monday to Friday and four times per day at weekends) until the company once again withdrew from

G-JEMF c/n 2015 at Băneasa on 13th April 2005 in storage. The ATP was never officially registered as such, nor delivered to Emerald Airways Ltd. (Keith Gaskell)

operating its own scheduled passenger services on 12Jun05. One aircraft was, however, wet leased to continue operating the Isle of Man to Liverpool and Manchester routes on behalf of EuroManx Ltd with effect from 13Jun05. The company also carried out ad hoc charters both domestically and internationally.

Both of Bangladesh Biman's aircraft were also purchased for subsequent freighter conversion and delivered in late Jan04. The two ex Bangladeshi aircraft were fitted with Large Freight Doors by Romaero S.A. at Bucharest-Băneasa while a similarly-converted aircraft was due to be leased from BAE Systems but was not accepted. The third of the original ex-USA aircraft was converted to a pure freighter but without the Large Freight Door at the company's engineering base at Blackpool. It was anticipated that up to ten ATP freighters would have been operated and that Large Freight Doors would have been fitted to several of them. The company's fleet was grounded when their AOC was suspended on 04May06. Administrators were appointed on 11May06.

G-JEMA	2028	G-JEMC	2032	G-JEME	2027
G-JEMB	2029	G-JEMD	2026	(G-JEMF)	2015

Enimex Ltd (ENI)
Tallinn, Estonia

This company took delivery of its first passenger-configured ATP in early Jul06 with a second aircraft due to follow later. There is some doubt as to whether the first aircraft ever entered service before it was returned to BAE Systems in mid-Aug07. The second aircraft was never received. They were due to be employed on ad hoc charter work.

ES-NBA	2023	(ES-NBB)	2018

Estonia Air (OV/ELL)
Tallinn, Estonia

Two NextJet passenger configured ATPs commenced flying scheduled services on this company's behalf with effect from 25Oct15 from Tallinn to Copenhagen, Oslo, Stockholm and Vilnius. However, Estonia Air ceased all operations on 07Nov15.

SE-LLO	2023	SE-MAL	2045	SE-MEX	2018

EuroAir Ltd (6M/EUP)
Athens, Greece

Euroair Ltd leased one aircraft for evaluation in early Sep04 prior to leasing three aircraft from BAE Asset Management. The first aircraft was delivered on 01Nov04 in a 64-seat passenger configuration. A network of scheduled services was due to be operated but the only aircraft delivered was returned on 20Mar05 reportedly without use.

G-MANM	2005	SX-	2006	SX-	2018
SX-BTK	2005				

EuroDirect Airlines Ltd (9R)

Hurn Airport, Dorset, UK

This operator introduced the first of five leased aircraft into service on 04Jul94 on a scheduled route from Gatwick to Berne. The second aircraft followed two days later on Hurn to Amsterdam schedules. The three other aircraft were all delivered in Aug94. The ATPs were flown additionally on schedules from Hurn to Paris and Humberside and from Exeter to Paris.

A second hub at Humberside saw schedules to Aberdeen, Brussels and Dublin and to Hamburg via Stansted. The company ceased operations on 26Feb95 and all aircraft were returned to BAe.

G-BTTO	2033	G-OEDF	2052	G-OEDI	2038
G-BUKJ	2052	G-OEDH	2039	G-OEDJ	2024
G-OEDE	2033				

EuroManx Ltd (3W/EMX)

Ronaldsway Airport, Isle of Man, UK

With effect from 13Jun05, Emerald Airways Ltd withdrew from operating scheduled passenger services from Liverpool to the Isle of Man leaving EuroManx Ltd as the sole operator. However, an ATP was wet leased from Emerald Airways Ltd from the same date to operate over the same route and to other destinations on behalf of EuroManx Ltd. Either of the passenger-configured aircraft was used for this contract until Emerald Airways Ltd had its AOC suspended on 04May06.

| G-JEMA | 2028 | G-JEMC | 2032 |

European Air Transport (QY/BCS)

Brussels National, Belgium

With effect from 19Dec14, an Atlantic Airlines freighter fitted with a Large Freight Door has been employed on this company's regular five-times-a-week schedule between Brussels, Nantes and, at one time, Poitiers. A second similarly-configured aircraft has also been leased from West Atlantic Airlines linking Brussels with Luton and Stansted and with Jersey and Guernsey with effect from 27Apr15.

| G-BTPF | 2013 | G-BTPH | 2015 | G-BUUR | 2024 |

European Executive Express AB (RY/EXC)

Karlstad, Sweden

This airline took delivery of two former British World Airlines' aircraft in Feb02 for use on scheduled passenger work. The aircraft were not used and were subsequently sold to West Air Sweden AB later in the same year.

| (SE-LNX) | 2057 | SE-LNY | 2058 | SE-LNZ | 2060 |

First Flight Couriers Pvt Ltd ( )

Mumbai, India

It was announced on 25Jan06 that this start-up airline was to be set up by an established Indian express parcels/document delivery company with an initial fleet of three ATP freighters leased from BAE Regional. The aircraft were delivered in early Jun, early Aug and late Oct06 and commenced operations on 01Sep06. The aircraft had been fitted earlier with West Air Sweden's E-Class freight mods, TAWS, HF and had increased AUW mods. They initially linked the cities of Bangalore, Chennai, Delhi and Mumbai. One of the aircraft was written off in Jun07 and the remaining two aircraft were withdrawn from service in Aug07.

| (VT-FFA) | 2051 | VT-FFB | 2039 | VT-FFC | 2051 |
| VT-FFA | 2054 | | | | |

Flysmåland AB (DC,TF)

Växjö, Sweden

With effect from 01Feb12 a Next Jet ATP in a 68-seat passenger configuration was leased to operate over the Växjö-Småland to Stockholm-Bromma route by this carrier under the Sverigeflyg Service AB group programme with SE-LLO being painted in their full colours. The route is code shared with both Golden Air Flyg AB and Malmö Aviation AB, but is no longer operated. Other ATPs of NEX Time Jet AB operated this route for short periods as well.

| SE-LLO | 2023 | SE-MAK | 2040 | SE-MAL | 2045 |

Golden Air Flyg AB (DC/GAO)

Trollhättan, Sweden

This company leased an ATP from NEX Time Jet AB from 16 to 24Jan11 to operate over the route Örnsköldsvik to Stockholm-Arlanda. See also Flysmåland AB.

| SE-MAL | 2045 |

G-MANC c/n 2054 in First Flight Couriers colours. This aircraft was later registered VT-FFA, but saw service for a few months only before being withdrawn.

International Air Parts Pty Ltd
Sydney, Australia

This organisation took over the assets of the failed Emerald Airways Ltd on 16Oct06 which included five ATPs, two in passenger configuration, one in freight configuration and two aircraft that had been fitted with Large Freight Doors at Bucharest-Băneasa but which had not had the E Class freight modifications completed when the airline collapsed. The single freighter was leased to Atlantic Airlines Ltd from Feb07 until Sep10 and after the fitment of a Large Freight Door in Bucharest, to Deraya PT in Mar14. The two Large Freight Door equipped freighters were earlier leased to Deraya PT in Jul and Aug09. A sixth freight configured aircraft was obtained from Regional One Inc in Jan14 and after maintenance was ferried out on lease to Deraya PT in Jan15. Of the two ex passenger configured ex Emerald aircraft, one was broken-up for spares in Jun14 and the other in Jun15 at Coventry. All aircraft were registered to associate company, PTB (Emerald) Pty Ltd.

(G-BTUE)	2039	G-JEMC	2032	PK-DGB	2029
G-BUKJ	2052	G-JEMD	2026	PK-DGC	2052
G-JEMA	2028	G-JEME	2027	PK-DGI	2027
G-JEMB	2029	PK-DGA	2026		

Ireland Airways Ltd (2E/EIX)
Dublin, Eire

Ireland Airways was due to take delivery of two ATPs, one of which was fully painted in the company's colour scheme, with delivery due in early 1998, but the operator's AOC was revoked on 13Feb98 and the contract was cancelled. Schedules from Dublin to Donegal and Sligo were due to be operated.

(EI-)	2059	EI-COS	2060

Jersey European Airlines Ltd (JY/JEA)
Exeter, Devon, UK

This airline leased two aircraft from British World Airlines Ltd to operate schedules between Southampton and Guernsey and between Glasgow and Birmingham from Mar and Apr99. Short-term leases also took place prior to this. Aircraft were operated in full British World colours until the leases ended in Oct99.

G-OBWL	2057	G-OBWN	2059	G-OBWO	2060
G-OBWM	2058				

Kullaflyg AB (2N)
Halmstad, Sweden

A 68-passenger ATP of NEX Time Jet AB commenced flying over the Halmstad-Stockholm-Arlanda route on 02May12. This is the second Sverigeflyg Service AB group operation with NEX Time Jet ATPs.

SE-MAL	2045

Ligações Aéreas Regionais SA
See Linhas Aéreas Regionais SA

Líneas Aéreas Privadas Argentinas SA - LAPA (MJ/LPR)
Buenos Aires, Argentina

An order for five aircraft for this carrier failed to materialise although the previously-stored aircraft were ferried to Prestwick for preparation in Sep96 with delivery planned for between Dec96 and Mar97.

Linhas Aéreas Regionais, SA - LAR (TH,TP/PDF)
Lisbon, Portugal

This company, which was known as Ligações Aéreas Regionais S.A. until 30Dec88, ordered three aircraft with the first two being delivered in Oct and Dec88 and the third in Jun90. ATPs replaced HS748s on routes from Lisbon to Faro and Oporto. The type was withdrawn from service and the aircraft returned to BAe in Jan and Feb93.

CS-TGA	2008	CS-TGB	2009	CS-TGC	2024

Lionair Inc ( )
Manila, Philippines

This company obtained a passenger-configured aircraft from Asian Spirit in Jul08. It was not operated by them but was due for lease to Air Aceh of Indonesia through Regional One Inc.

RP-C2786	2055

Loganair Ltd (BA,LC/LOG)
Glasgow, Scotland

After initially ordering two aircraft, Loganair eventually ordered eight of which seven were accepted. The first two were delivered in Aug and Oct89, the third and fourth in Oct/Nov91, the fifth in Feb92 and the final two in Sep/Oct93. Two additional aircraft were leased from Manx Airlines Ltd, one in Nov/Dec91 and the other from Dec91 to Mar92. They were based initially in Manchester operating schedules to Belfast City, Connaught, Edinburgh, Guernsey and Jersey. From 28Mar94 all the ATPs and the routes they flew were transferred to Manx Airlines Ltd.

The company leased three ATPs from British Airways CitiExpress Ltd with effect from 01Mar04 to operate over the routes from Glasgow to Aberdeen, Benbecula and Stornoway and from Aberdeen to Shetland under a British Airways franchise agreement. A fourth aircraft was leased from the end of Jun to early Sep04 to cover maintenance inputs on the company's ATPs. The aircraft were also used to cover shortfalls in the British Airways CityExpress programme on several occasions. The last revenue service was flown on 31May05. From 27Feb12 until 03Mar12 an Atlantic Airlines aircraft was leased to cover one rotation per day over the Aberdeen to Stornoway and Aberdeen to Shetland routes.

G-BUUP	2008	G-LOGF	2054	G-MAUD	2002
G-LOGA	2040	G-LOGG	2055	G-OLCC	2017
G-LOGB	2045	(G-LOGH)	2056	G-OLCD	2018
G-LOGC	2017	G-MANF	2040	G-PEEL	2023
G-LOGD	2018	G-MANJ	2004	G-UIET	2006
G-LOGE	2004	G-MANL	2003		

MagicBird Airlines BV ( )
Amsterdam, Netherlands

MagicBird Airlines took delivery of one cargo-configured aircraft to operate a Swedish Postal contract flying five nights per week between Stockholm-Arlanda and Sundsvall from 13Apr06. A second aircraft entered service later in the summer of 2006 operating an Alitalia freight schedule from Rome-Fiumicino to Lamezia on behalf of Atlantic Airlines Ltd. Both aircraft were withdrawn from service after last flying on 24May07.

G-BTPL	2042	(PH-MGB)	2042	(PH-MGC)	2052
G-BUKJ	2052				

G-OLCC c/n 2017 of Loganair on a pre-delivery flight over Brixham, Devon, UK in August 1989. The aircraft was later registered G-LOGC before being passed on to Manx Airlines. *(WHC/BAe)*

MagicBlue Airlincs BV (MJB)
Rotterdam, Netherlands

This company planned to take delivery of up to six ATP freighters and passenger-configured aircraft from December 2005, at least two of which were expected to be fitted with Large Freight Doors. On 16Dec05 it was reported that the company had collapsed before any of its aircraft had been delivered.

(PH-MJF)	2033	(PH-MJK)	2042	PH-MJP	2023
(PH-MJG)	2038	(PH-MJL)	2052		

Malmö Aviation AB (TF)
Malmö-Sturup, Sweden

See Flysmåland AB

Manx Airlines Ltd (BA,TH,JE/MNX)
Ronaldsway Airport, Isle of Man, UK

Manx Airlines initially ordered three aircraft with delivery in Sep88, Mar89 and May90. One aircraft was leased from BAe for two and a half weeks in Jan91 and again from Nov92 to Apr93 while a second aircraft came from the same source from Jun93 to Aug94. Additionally an aircraft was leased from Loganair from Oct92 to Jun93. Two aircraft were obtained from British Midland Airways Ltd in Oct93. The aircraft were flown on schedules from the Isle of Man to Belfast International and City, Birmingham, Cardiff, Dublin, Glasgow, Jersey, Liverpool, London Heathrow and Luton and to Manchester. Other schedules were flown from Dublin to Cardiff, Jersey and Liverpool and from Belfast to Liverpool. From 25Mar91 the carrier was officially split into the two companies Manx Airlines (IOM) Ltd and Manx Airlines (Europe) Ltd, the second company registered in the UK in order to comply with European Union regulations and allow international operations from the UK mainland. This however had no immediate operational effect on the company's ATP operations. From 28Mar94 the seven ATPs of Loganair Ltd were added together with the routes of that carrier that were not contained solely within Scotland. Routes new to Manx Airlines included ATP schedules from Belfast City to East Midlands, Edinburgh, Glasgow, Luton and Manchester and from Manchester to Connaught, Dublin, Edinburgh, Guernsey, Jersey and Southampton, from Glasgow to Dublin and from Jersey to Cardiff and Dublin. Two new aircraft were also added in Mar and May94.

With effect from 09Jan95 all Manx Airlines (Europe) Ltd schedules became part of a British Airways franchise agreement to operate under the British Airways Express scheme. All but three of the ATP fleet were painted in British Airways colours. On 13Aug96 British Airways announced that it was withdrawing from its Scottish internal services and was handing over the routes to Manx Airlines (Europe) Ltd with effect from 27Oct96. On 01Sep96 Manx Airlines (Europe) Ltd and Loganair Ltd had earlier amalgamated as British Regional Airlines Ltd, usually abbreviated to 'BRAL'.

New ATP routes inherited from British Airways included those from Aberdeen to Birmingham, Glasgow, Manchester and Lerwick, from Glasgow to Benbecula and Stornoway and from Stornoway to Inverness. Later changes saw the severance of the company's ties with the Airlines of Britain Group in early 1997 allowing the two companies to form closer links with British Airways. In March 1997 Loganair Ltd once again became independent of BRAL following a management buy-out but continued to operate as a British Airways franchise carrier using smaller aircraft than the ATP. BRAL became a Public Limited Company with effect from 18Jun99. British Airways announced on 08Mar01 that it was taking over BRAL and would merge it with Brymon Airways Ltd and rename the group British Airways CitiExpress (see separate listing). The company has also leased aircraft to other carriers. British Midland Airways took two aircraft, one from Jan to Oct95 and the other from Jan95 to Mar97. Two aircraft were leased to Air Ostrava from May95 to Jan96 while single aircraft have been leased to British Airways for one week in Jan90, from Sep90 to Mar91, from Oct to Dec92 and from Dec92 to Apr93. Single aircraft were also leased to Loganair Ltd in Nov/Dec91 and Dec91 to Mar92. From January 1995 three ATPs continued to fly some of Manx Airlines' own schedules from the Isle of Man together with some Channel Islands routes in full Manx Airlines colours. Despite all the changes, Manx Airlines continued to be promoted as a separate company with its own colour scheme and flight identity until 31Aug02. From 01Sep02 the company's separate identity was lost finally and all operations were merged into those of British Airways CitiExpress Ltd.

G-BMYK	2003	G-LOGE	2004	G-MANL	2003
G-BMYM	2002	G-LOGF	2054	G-MANM	2005
G-BRLY	2025	G-LOGG	2055	G-MANO	2006
G-BTTO	2033	G-MANA	2056	G-MANP	2023
G-BUUP	2008	G-MANB	2055	G-MANU	2008
G-BUUR	2024	G-MANC	2054	G-MAUD	2002
G-ERIN	2003	G-MANE	2045	G-OATP	2005
G-LOGA	2040	G-MANF	2040	G-OEDJ	2024
G-LOGB	2045	G-MANG	2018	G-PEEL	2023
G-LOGC	2017	G-MANH	2017	G-UIET	2006
G-LOGD	2018	G-MANJ	2004		

Merpati Nusantara Airlines PT (MZ/MNA)
Jakarta, Indonesia

Merpati Nusantara Airlines ordered five aircraft with delivery between Feb and Jul92. The fleet was employed on a scheduled network linking Jakarta, Bengkulu, Pangkalpinang, Pekanbaru, Tanjung Pandan and Tanjung Pinan. Following the write-off of one of the aircraft in Apr97 the type was withdrawn and put in store.

PK-MTV	2046	PK-MTX	2048	PK-MTZ	2050
PK-MTW	2047	PK-MTY	2049		

NEX Time Jet AB
See Next Jet

NextJet - (NEX Time Jet AB) (2N/NTJ)
Stockholm, Sweden

This company announced in early Jun08 that it was due to take delivery of three passenger configured ATPs on lease from West Air Sweden. Fitted out with 68 passenger seats, the first aircraft entered revenue service on 08Oct08 between Stockholm-Arlanda and Gällivare. The other two aircraft entered service on the routes linking Stockholm-Arlanda with Hemavan/Tärnaby via Vilhelmina with effect from 26Oct08 and Arvidsjaur via Lycksele with effect from 02Nov08. Pending delivery of their own aircraft, with effect from 02Jun08 to 22Aug08 this company temporarily

G-BUUR c/n 2024 in basic Linhas Aéreas Regionais SA colours with 'Manx' titles. The aircraft flew as such from August 1993 until July 1994.
(WHC)

flew two West Air Sweden AB freighter ATPs on West Air's behalf in order to gain experience with the type. By autumn 2010 the Gällivare route was operated via Kramfors-Sollefteå but was taken over by another aircraft type in Feb12 although ATP operations later returned. The first of the two ex SATA aircraft was taken on strength in early Apr11, since when passenger charters have been undertaken throughout Europe. With effect from 01Feb12 many of the flights were code shared with SAS (Scandinavian Airlines System) and are shown with both 2N and SK flight numbers. From 01Feb12 one aircraft was operated on behalf of Flysmåland AB between Växjö and Stockholm-Bromma in Sverigeflyg colours. From 02May12 a new route from Halmstad to Stockholm-Arlanda was flown in co-operation with Kullaflyg AB. A fifth aircraft entered service in Sep13 which had formerly operated with SATA. Other destinations served from Arlanda have included Borlänge, Halmstad (on behalf of Braathens Regional), Jönköping, Kiruna, Luleå, Örebro, Örnsköldsvik, Ronneby, Skelleftea, Sundsvall, Trollhatan, Umea and Visby. With effect from 25Oct15 two of the aircraft commenced operations on behalf of Estonia Air with a third joining them on 04Nov15. The last operations for this carrier ended on 07Nov15. From the following day, Nextjet ATPs started flying from Tallinn to Oslo, Stockholm and Vilnius on behalf of Nordic Aviation Group AS, but ended on 05Feb16. Flights were resumed ten days later until 24Mar16 with two daily roundtrips between Tallinn and Stockholm and again from 15Apr-08Jul16 with up to three daily roundtrips between Tallinn and Stockholm, a Sunday service between Tallinn and Oslo and occasional schedules to Vilnius. Tallinn to Arlanda flights started again on 30Aug16 until the last flight took place on 30Sep16. Occasional international charters were also flown with Jyvaskyla in Finland visited once from Stockholm-Vasteras. Eighteen flights a week were scheduled to be operated between Vasteras and Helsinki from 15Sep16 with ATPs in co-operation with Finnair though SAAB 340As have been used at first. One aircraft was permanently wfu on 31Oct15, leaving four operational aircraft in the fleet.

SE-LGY	2035	SE-MAK	2040	SE-MEG	2031
SE-LGZ	2021	SE-MAL	2045	SE-MEX	2018
SE-LLO	2023	SE-MEE	2019			

Nordic Aviation Group, AS (JP/ADR)
Tallinn, Estonia

The Estonian Government set up this group to commence operating schedules on 08Nov15 to some destinations previously served by Estonia Air utilising leased aircraft. NextJet ATPs were employed on routes to Stockholm (up to four daily) and Vilnius (twice daily Monday to Friday) while the type was also flown on a single rotation to Oslo on Sundays. The Stockholm service was reduced to three times daily from Monday to Friday and twice on Saturdays and Sundays with effect from 30Nov15. The last flight took place on 05Feb16, but flights were re-instated on 15Feb16 twice daily between Tallinn and Stockholm and continued until 24Mar16 and resumed up to thrice daily together with a Sunday rotation between Tallinn and Oslo on 15Apr16 until 28Jly16. From 30Aug16 schedules were once again flown between Tallinn and Stockholm-Arlanda until the last revenue flight by an ATP (SE-MAL) was flown as JP7002 from Tallinn-Arlanda on 13Sep16. Flights were operated under Adria Airways AOC. All four operational NextJet passenger configured ATPs at the time were used on these services on different occasions.

Olympic Airways, Ltd (OPA/OAL)
Athens, Greece

This operator used a demonstrator for three days of trials beginning 04Mar88.

G-BZWW   2005

PGA - Portugália - Companhia Portuguesa de Transportes Aéreos SA (NI/PGA)
Lisbon, Portugal

Portugália leased one aircraft from SATA - Air Açores from 01Oct96 to 30Mar97 to operate on the company's schedules between Lisbon and Faro in full company colours. The aircraft was used additionally on routes to Bilbao, Faro and Madrid.

CS-TGL   2019

PTB (Emerald) Pty Ltd
See International Air Parts Pty Ltd

Regional One Inc ( )
Miami, Florida, USA

This organisation, which specialises in leasing and selling aircraft to airlines worldwide, obtained its first aircraft in Apr09 in the Philippines. This was painted fully for a new airline in Indonesia called Air Aceh PT, but has failed to move from Manila at the time of writing. Regional One later acquired three further passenger-configured aircraft from BAE Asset Management and continued their lease to SATA Air Açores, though the first was returned to the lessor in Oct09. One of these aircraft was subsequently leased to NextJet AB from Aug13 and the other two in May and Jun10. The final acquisition has been a cargo-configured aircraft that was obtained from BAE Asset Management at the end of Dec09. This last aircraft was sold to PTB (Emerald) Pty Ltd in Jan14. The other two ex-SATA aircraft remain in store at Southend.

CS-TFJ	2018	CS-TGY	2049	RP-C2786	2025
CS-TGX	2025	G-BUKJ	2052			

SATA Air Açores
See Serviço Acoriano de Transportes Aéreos, E.P.

Scandinavian Airlines System – SAS (SK/SAS)
Stockholm, Sweden

With effect from 01Feb12 NEX Time Jet flights between Stockholm-Arlanda and Arvidsjaur, Hemavan, Lycksele and Vilhelmina operated with BAe ATPs were code shared with SAS and marketed with both company's flight numbers. Örnsköldsvik was a later added destination. With effect from 25Oct15, Estonia Air code shared with SAS on ATP flights from Tallinn to Copenhagen, Oslo, Stockholm and Vilnius until Estonia Air ceased operations on 07Nov15.

Seoul Air International Ltd (SHI)
Seoul, Republic of Korea

Seoul Air International obtained two aircraft with delivery in Mar95. The aircraft were used on ad hoc charter work throughout the Far East until returned to BAe in Sep and Nov96.

HL5227	2061	HL5228	2063

Serviço Açoreano de Transportes Aéreos, E.P. - SATA (SP/SAT)
Ponta Delgada, Azores

OY-SVI c/n 2061 of Sun-Air of Scandinavia A/S in British Airways 'Mountain of the Birds/Benyhone' colours.   *(WHC/BAe)*

Marketing itself as SATA Air Açores, this company ordered three aircraft with delivery in Dec89 and Nov and Dec90. A fourth aircraft was leased from BAe from May to Dec93 and another from British World Airlines for two weeks in May00. Following the loss of one of its aircraft in Dec99 the company arranged the lease of two further aircraft from the manufacturer with delivery in May and Aug00. A fifth aircraft was leased from BAE Systems with delivery in Jun07 after the award of a new route in Madeira from Funchal to Pôrto Santo which was flown up to four times daily while a new route from Funchal to Las Palmas was flown twice weekly with effect from Jun08. Points served within the Azores included Flores Island, Graciosa Island, Horta, Pico Island, Ponta Delgada, Santa Maria, São Jorge Island and Terceira.

One of the aircraft was leased to Air Malta from Oct92 to May94 and to PGA - Portugália from Oct96 to Mar97. The start of the gradual retirement of the fleet began in Oct09 with the last two being withdrawn from use on 28May10 and later sold to the West Atlantic group.

CS-TFJ	2018	CS-TGM	2030	CS-TGY	2049
CS-TGB	2009	CS-TGN	2031	G-OBWR	2053
CS-TGL	2019	CS-TGX	2025		

Sun-Air of Scandinavia A/S (EZ,BA/SUS)
Billund, Denmark

Sun-Air leased two used aircraft from BAe Asset Management Turboprops with delivery in Nov97 and Jan98. A third new aircraft was delivered in Dec98. The aircraft were used on scheduled services from Billund to Bergen, Manchester and Oslo and on charter flights throughout Europe. Scheduled flights were operated as British Airways Express.

From summer 2003 new scheduled destinations from Billund were Dublin and Edinburgh, while a twice daily Billund to Brussels schedule was started in Oct04. All three aircraft were sold to West Air Sweden AB with delivery in Apr, Jun and early

Aug06 after operating the last revenue service on 30Jul06.

OY-SVI	2061	OY-SVT	2062	OY-SVU	2063

Sverigeflyg Service AB
See Flysmåland AB and Kullaflyg AB

TAP Air Portugal
(Transportes Aéreos Portugueses, E.P) (TP/TAP)
Lisbon, Portugal

The ATPs of LAR Transregional were used to operate international scheduled services from both Lisbon and Porto to destinations including Bilbao, Bordeaux, Málaga, Santiago de Compostela and Seville at various times between Apr91 and Dec92.

Trans States Airlines Inc
See United Feeder Services Inc

Türk Hava Tasimaciligi - THT (ZH/TK/THT)
Ankara, Turkey

This subsidiary of Turkish Airlines leased four aircraft from BAe with delivery in Sep91, Oct91, Feb92 and Sep92. A fifth aircraft was leased from BAe from Jul to Sep92. Domestic scheduled services were operated from Ankara and Istanbul to points that included Adana, Antalya, Batman, Bursa, Denizli, Diyarbakir, Elazig, Erzincan, Izmir, Kars, Kayseri, Konya, Malatya, Mus, Samsun, Sanliurfa and Trabzon. The aircraft were returned to the lessor in Sep and Oct93 when the company's routes were absorbed into that of the parent company and BAe RJ100s were introduced into service.

TC-THP	2025	TC-THU	2038	TC-THZ	2052
TC-THT	2039	TC-THV	2033		

(WHC/BAe)

G-11-20 c/n 2020 in of Air Wisconsin/United Express, later to become N851AW of Air Wisconsin Inc, and seen here after painting in December 1989.

United Feeder Service Inc (UA/U2/UFS)
Chicago, Illinois, USA

With effect from 07Sep93 this company, a division of Trans States Airlines Inc, took over the Air Wisconsin Inc fleet of ten ATPs and continued to operate them on United Express services from Chicago O'Hare to destinations including Akron, Fort Wayne, Green Bay, Kalamazoo, Peoria, South Bend, Wausau and Youngstown. One of the aircraft was returned to BAe in Sep96, and by 19Feb00 the last of the fleet had been retired from service.

N851AW	2020	N855AW	2029	N858AW	2035
N852AW	2021	N856AW	2032	N859AW	2036
N853AW	2022	N857AW	2034	N860AW	2037
N854AW	2028				

West Air Europe
See West Atlantic Sweden AB

West Air Luxembourg SA (WLX)
Luxembourg

A subsidiary of West Air Sweden AB, this company was set up in 2001. It became operational in Dec03 with a single ATP, initially operating on behalf of Federal Express on the Düsseldorf–Paris route. A second aircraft was added in Jun04, a third in Sep04 while a fourth was transferred from the West Air Sweden fleet in Jan05, this having a Large Freight Door. A fifth and a sixth aircraft were added in May05 and Sep07 while a seventh, eighth and ninth aircraft with Large Freight Doors were added in Jan08, late May08 and Jan09. The aircraft are primarily employed on Federal Express services from Paris-Charles de Gaulle to Amsterdam, Budapest, Düsseldorf, Lyons, Munich and Stuttgart, from Amsterdam to Stansted and from Lyons to Marseille together with ad hoc charter work. Regular flights have also been flown on behalf of Twin Jet Airlines of France between Marseille and Tunis and Swiftair SA of Spain. The company also utilises West Air Sweden ATPs to cover maintenance downtime on its fleet. On 29Oct08 it was announced that Atlantic Airlines and the West Air Sweden group were to merge as West Atlantic but that all three airlines in the group would continue to operate as separate entities. Two of the aircraft were put in temporary storage at the end of May and Sep09 and later returned to service with West Air Sweden in Dec09. A third aircraft was transferred back to West Air Sweden in Mar10 but had returned to West Air Luxembourg in early Jul11 while seven other ex West Air Sweden aircraft were added in late Jul11, mid Aug11, Nov11 (two), mid Jan12, Mar12 and mid Apr12. A further five aircraft were due to

transfer but these plans were later cancelled and all but one of the aircraft had reverted to Swedish registry by mid November 2013. The company was sold to FAST Logistics Luxembourg SARL on 25Oct13 and all ATP operations reverted to Swedish control. The last aircraft was returned to West Air Sweden on 28Feb15.

LX-WAD	2038	LX-WAK	2061	LX-WAT	2011
LX-WAE	2037	LX-WAL	2059	LX-WAV	2041
LX-WAF	2056	LX-WAM	2060	LX-WAW	2021
LX-WAG	2053	LX-WAN	2020	LX-WAX	2063
LX-WAH	2004	LX-WAO	2043	LX-WAZ	2035
LX-WAI	2002	LX-WAP	2057		
LX-WAJ	2062	LX-WAS	2058		

West Air Sweden AB (PT/SWN)
See West Atlantic Sweden AB

West Atlantic AB ( )
See West Atlantic Sweden AB

West Atlantic Sweden AB ( )
Göteborg, Malmö & Lidköping, Sweden

West Air Sweden obtained six former United Feeder Service Inc aircraft with delivery to Lidköping between Apr00 and May01. Three more used aircraft were obtained in Mar, Apr and Sep02, the last aircraft leased for use in the passenger rôle for ad hoc charter work. After being converted to freighter configuration, the first ATP entered service on overnight Swedish Postal contract flights on 05Sep00, supplementing the earlier used HS748s. Two further aircraft were obtained in late summer 2002 and after conversion to freighters entered service in Apr and Jul03. One of the initial six aircraft (SE-LGZ, c/n 2021) was converted into the first Large Freight Door (LFD) version by West Air's Engineering Department at Lidköping. This was completed and first flew on 10Jul02, was shown at Farnborough Air Show later that month and entered service in Aug02. From Apr03 it was operated on behalf of DHL initially linking Copenhagen and Stockholm with Vaasa and Oulu in Finland. See the 'ATP General History' section for details of the specialised conversion work to cargo configuration and the large cargo door modifications carried out by this carrier.

On 02Oct03 it was announced that a second large rear freight door equipped aircraft was to be leased from BAE Systems after door fitment by Romaero in Bucharest while the passenger rôle

SE-LGU c/n 2022 in the later colour-scheme of West Air Sweden, which was first introduced on the HS748s. Note that, although the aircraft is configured as a freighter, it is not fitted with the Large Freight Door.

aircraft was ferried to Băneasa to be similarly converted in Jan04. These last two aircraft entered service in Oct and Dec04. It is understood that most of the ATPs added to the fleet have been certificated at the higher maximum take-off weight and fitted with TAWS (Terrain Awareness Warning System) and enhanced Mode S transponders by early 2004. An eleventh aircraft, fitted with a large freight door, was delivered in Jun05. More recently, the three strong fleet of SUN-AIR of Scandinavia was purchased with delivery in Apr, Jun and early Aug06. These entered service in Aug and Oct06 after E Class freight modifications were completed. Two further LFD fitted aircraft were taken on strength with the first entering service in Aug06 and the second in Feb07. A further seven aircraft entered service in Dec06, in Apr, May, July, two in Sep07 and one in Jan08 of which four were fitted with LFDs bringing the West Air Sweden/Luxembourg fleet of ATPs up to twenty-five aircraft. Of three additional aircraft in storage at Lidköping, two were leased to Next Jet AB as passenger configured aircraft in Oct08 and the third is expected to be reduced to spares. A third passenger configured aircraft was leased from BAE AMO for sub-lease to Next Jet AB in Nov08. All operational cargo configured ATPs are now fitted with short nose legs to facilitate loading. Initial points served included Stockholm-Arlanda, Sundsvall and Växjo before an extensive domestic network was flown on behalf of the Swedish Postal service with a hub at Stockholm-Arlanda. Today Gällivare, Jönköping, Kiruna, Luleå and Umeå are served. These destinations are currently served under contract to Amapola Flyg AB who would appear to have taken over the Swedish Post contract from West Air Sweden recently. However, from Jun12 a new contract commenced operating with Swedish Post direct utilising six aircraft. The aircraft are also used on overnight and daytime parcels services for Ciblex between Paris and Marseille and for DHL from Copenhagen to Bergen, Malmö, Stockholm and Stavanger, from Stockholm to Vaasa in Finland and from Helsinki to Tallinn in Estonia. Aircraft are also flown on behalf of Federal Express from Helsinki to Copenhagen, while UPS have used the aircraft in the past. Ad hoc charter work is also performed within Europe.

A subsidiary company, West Air Luxembourg S.A. was set up to operate ATP aircraft and commenced operations in Dec03 and by Jan09 was operating nine aircraft transferred from the parent company though two were returned in late May and Sep09 and a third in Mar10. With effect from Jul03 aircraft started appearing with 'West Air Europe' titles and by summer 2006 all aircraft, with the exception of SE-LGU, were so marked. With effect from 28Oct06 the Norwegian Postal Service contracted for the use of initially four West Air ATPs linking at various times Ålesund, Bergen, Bodö, Evenes, Molde, Stavanger, Torp, Tromsö and Trondheim through an Oslo hub. The last 748 flew for the Swedish Postal Service on 24May07 from which time only West Air ATPs operated the domestic flight schedules apart from a daily Malmö-Arlanda schedule which was briefly flown by a BAe 146-200QT in West Air Europe colours. In Nov05 the first of several ATPs was ferried to Lidköping for modification to E-class freight and JAA version standards on behalf of BAE Systems by West Air's Engineering Department. West Air Sweden's ATP fleet also provides standby cover for West Air Luxembourg's ATP fleet. One Large Freight Door fitted aircraft was sub-leased to Air Go of Greece in Aug08 and from Aug20 was operating West Air Sweden/Atlantic Airlines flights. This was due to be replaced in early 2009 in West Air service by another aircraft on lease from BAE Systems but without a Large Freight Door fitted. However, due to the drop off in demand, the completion of this aircraft's conversion was put on temporary hold until completed in early Dec09.

On 29Oct08 it was announced that Atlantic Airlines and the West Air Sweden group were to be merged as West Atlantic but that all three airlines in the group would continue to operate as separate entities. The new company headquarters were set up at Göteborg in Sweden. Currently the West Atlantic group has forty-seven ATPs of which four are passenger configured and leased to

NextJet of Sweden. The remaining thirty-seven aircraft are all cargo configured while twenty of these are fitted with Large Freight Doors. One of the latter was leased to Air Go of Greece and later Bulgaria from Aug08 until Oct11. One of the Large Cargo Door fitted aircraft was still to have its E Class freight mods completed at the time of writing. The first aircraft to be repainted in the new West Atlantic colours was rolled out in early Apr09. A forty-first aircraft was used for trial installation of cockpit instrumentation but by Nov09 was being reduced to spares. For details of routes flown see Atlantic Airlines, West Air Luxembourg, West Air Sweden, NextJet and Air Go. In Dec09 three further cargo configured aircraft without Large Freight Doors were obtained from BAE Asset Management but it is not known with which carrier within the group will fly them or if they will be used for spares. Two passenger configured ATPs were added in Oct/Nov10, one of which joined the NextJet fleet in Apr11 and the second later in the year. Later several aircraft were transferred to West Air Luxembourg and Atlantic Airlines leaving West Air Sweden with just seven operational ATPs none of which had Large Freight Doors and four passenger configured aircraft operating for Next Jet. It was expected that no freighter ATPs would remain on the Swedish register but these plans were later cancelled and the first of the Luxembourg registered aircraft was returned to the Swedish register in mid May13 with the penultimate aircraft transferring in mid November 2013. All West Air Luxembourg ATP operations reverted to Swedish control after the sale of the company to FAST Logistics Luxembourg SARL on 25Oct13. West Air Sweden officially became renamed as West Atlantic AB on 09Aug13. In March 2015 the entire operational fleet of ATPs with this carrier had Swedish registrations reserved for them.

G-BTPA	2007	LX-WAO	2043	SE-LPU	2060
G-BTPC	2010	LX-WAP	2057	SE-LPV	2041
G-BTPE	2012	LX-WAS	2058	SE-LPX	2063
G-BTPF	2013	LX-WAT	2011	SE-MAF	2002
G-BTPG	2014	LX-WAV	2041	(SE-MAG)	2003
G-BTPH	2015	LX-WAW	2021	SE-MAH	2004
G-BTPJ	2016	LX-WAX	2063	SE-MAI	2010
G-BTPL	2042	LX-WAZ	2035	SE-MAJ	2038
G-BTTO	2033	LZ-BPS	2005	SE-MAK	2040
G-BUUP	2008	(SE-KXO)	2054	SE-MAL	2045
G-BUUR	2024	SE-KXP	2056	SE-MAM	2005
G-MANC	2054	SE-LGU	2022	SE-MAN	2006
G-MANH	2017	SE-LGV	2034	SE-MAO	2011
G-MANM	2005	SE-LGX	2036	SE-MAP	2037
G-MANO	2006	SE-LGY	2035	SE-MAR	2052
G-OAAF	2029	SE-LGZ	2021	SE-MAY	2044
G-ORWP	2051	(SE-LHX)	2026	SE-MEE	2019
LX-WAD	2038	SE-LHX	2020	SE-MEG	2031
LX-WAE	2037	(SE-LHY)	2027	SE-MHC	2007
LX-WAF	2056	SE-LHZ	2059	SE-MHD	2008
LX-WAG	2053	SE-LLO	2023	SE-MHE	2012
LX-WAH	2004	SE-LNX	2061	SE-MHF	2013
LX-WAI	2002	SE-LNY	2062	SE-MHG	2014
LX-WAJ	2062	(SE-LNZ)	2063	SE-MHI	2017
LX-WAK	2061	SE-LPR	2057	SE-MHJ	2024
LX-WAL	2059	SE-LPS	2043	SE-MIIK	2033
LX-WAM	2060	SE-LPT	2058	SX-BPS	2005
LX-WAN	2020				

Wings West Airlines Inc (AA,RM/WWM)
San Luis Obispo, California, USA

This airline ordered ten aircraft with options placed on a further two in Oct98 for operation on the American Eagle network but the order was cancelled after the first aircraft had flown following objections to the deal by American Airlines Inc.

(N375AE)	2005	(N379AE)	2009	(N382AE)	2012
(N376AE)	2006	(N380AE)	2010	(N383AE)	2013
(N377AE)	2007	(N381AE)	2011	(N384AE)	2014
(N378AE)	2008				

Chapter 9
Individual Aircraft Histories

Note: The figures in brackets next to the Construction Number denote the Set Number

FTS 2

Fatigue test specimen comprising fuselage, tail and stub wings. B/U Woodford between Jan and 13Feb03.

2001   (1)

Regn **G-OATP** reportedly rsvd but not used. Regd to British Aerospace plc as **G-MATP** 15Jan86 (CofR G-MATP/R1). First prototype. F/f 06Aug86 in BAe house c/s, Permit to Fly issued 28Aug86 and flown Farnborough the same day for the SBAC Show. Returned Woodford 08Sep86. Flown to Rovaniemi, Finland for cold weather trials 27Feb87 returning Woodford 03Mar87 having also visited Tromsö in Norway. To Reykjavik for icing trials from 26Mar87 to 16Apr87. Used for trials and certification tests with PW126A engines 1988. Fitted with an APU Feb90 and used for cold weather trials in Greenland 09-16Mar90. Fitted with prototype shorter nose leg later in 1990. Painted in United Express c/s Aug90 for SBAC Air Show. Titles removed after show. Repainted in United Express c/s for Farnborough Air Show 1992. Titles once again removed after show. Flown with various drag reduction mods. F/f with PW127D engines 18Jun93. Departed Woodford for Roswell, New Mexico, USA for hot weather trials 03Aug93. Returned Woodford 10Sep93. C/o icing trials in Iceland 22-25Apr and 29Apr to 12May94. Ferried East Midlands 23Aug94 for repaint in Jetstream 61 c/s. Regd as **G-PLXI** to Jetstream Aircraft Ltd 26Aug94 (CofR G-PLXI/1) and f/f as such 01Sep94. Shown at Farnborough Air Show Sep94. Based Prestwick Flight Test centre with effect from 16Sep94. WFU by 21Jan97. Regd British

Aerospace (Operations) Ltd 18Jun97. Ferried Prestwick-Woodford 28Oct97 and stored. Regd BAE Systems (Operations) Ltd 02Mar00 (CofR G-PLXI/2). Stripped of parts Feb03 and returned to storage. Was due to be donated to the 'Jetstream Club', an independent section of the 'The Wirral Aviation Society' (TWAS), for preservation at Liverpool Airport and to be moved by road from Woodford in Sep05 but the airframe was found to be unsuitable. Scrapped 13Aug08. Regn cld as PWFU 09Jun09.

TT 2,475 hrs, 1,851 ldgs

2002   (2)

Regd to British Aerospace plc Civil Aircraft Division as G-BMYM 18Sep86 (CofR G-BMYM/R1). F/f 20Feb87 in British Midland c/s, CofA issued 23Mar87. Ferried Granada, Spain 24Mar87 for noise trials and then to Almeria for performance trials before returning Woodford 24Apr87. Demonstrated at Paris Air Show with show no.'206' Jun87. Departed Woodford for Goose Bay, Yuma and Mojave with a night stop at Reykjavik en route for hot weather trials 29Jul87 after fitment of an APU in the port wing root and repaint with a white fuselage top and British Aerospace titles. Returned Woodford 22Sep87 and returned to production line for refurbishment, repaint of cabin roof and removal of APU. Del British Midland Airways Ltd 17Jun88. Entered service from East Midlands to Glasgow 22Jun88. Returned Woodford for mods Nov88 to 15Dec88 and 09-15Mar89. Regd to British Midland Airways Ltd 10Jul89 (CofR G-BMYM/R2). Transferred to Manx Airlines Ltd 31Oct93 and del Isle of Man 01Nov93. Repainted at Hurn 01-12Dec93.

The first of the ATPs, c/n 2001, being rolled out of the assembly hangar at Woodford. It would become G-MATP for its first flight in August 1986.

(WHC/BAe)

Regd as **G-MAUD** to Manx Airlines (Europe) Ltd 14Dec93 (CofR G-MAUD/R1). Regn **G-MANK** reportedly rsvd 1994 but not used. Transferred British Midland Airways Ltd and entered service as BD271 from East Midlands to Belfast International 16Jan95 in Manx c/s. Ferried Teesside as BD9551 20Jan95 for repaint in British Midland c/s. Returned East Midlands as BD9521 24Jan95. Returned to service as BD233 from East Midlands to Brussels 25Jan95. Last service Belfast to East Midlands 14Mar97. Returned British Regional Airlines Ltd and ferried Hurn as BD9561 15Mar97 for repaint in British Airways interim new c/s. Returned East Midlands as JE7901 25Mar97. Ferried Manchester as BA9562P 29Mar97 and entered service as BA7783 from Manchester to Belfast 31Mar97. Painted in British Airways 'Blue Poole' c/s 08-10Jun97. Operator renamed British Airways CitiExpress Ltd from 31Mar02. Rear fuselage damaged by baggage vehicle Manchester 07Jul02. Repaired and re-flown 26Sep02. Returned to service 05Oct02. Regd British Airways CitiExpress Ltd 14Jan03 (CofR G-MAUD/R2). Flew final service for British Airways CityExpress as BA4423 from Isle of Man to Glasgow 28Feb04. Lsd Loganair Ltd and entered service as BA8776 from Glasgow to Aberdeen 29Feb04. Flew last flight as BA8824 from Stornoway to Glasgow 03Jul04 before ferrying to Southend as TH091P the following day for maintenance. Returned Glasgow as TH001P 19Jul04 and returned to service as BA8821 from Glasgow to Stornoway 20Jul04. Flew Loganair's last revenue ATP service on behalf of British Airways as BA8810 from Benbecula to Glasgow 31May05. Ferried Southend as TH001P 02Jun05 at end of lse for storage. Regd WestLB AG 28Oct05 (CofR G-MAUD/R3). Regn **SE-MAF** rsvd to West Air Sweden AB 13Jul06. Ferried Southend-Lidköping 25Aug06 for conversion E-class freight & JAA version for lse West Air Sweden AB and regn cld the same date as transferred Sweden. Noted in hangar in West Air Europe c/s painted as SE-MAF 05Dec06. Regd as SE-MAF to Siemens Financial Services AB 14Dec06. Air-tested the same day and entered service 18Dec06. Regd Erik Thun AB 10Jan12. Proposed transfer to West Air Luxembourg as LX-WAI abandoned. Regd European Turboprop Management AB 11Jun13. Ferried Arlanda-Malmö 10Jan16 for storage, noted engineless Aug16.   ***TT 30,267 hrs, 38,429 ldgs***

2003   (3)

Regd to British Aerospace plc Civil Aircraft Division as **G-BMYK** 18Sep86 (CofR G-BMYK/R1). F/f 09Jun87 in British Midland c/s, CofA issued 10Jun87. Shown statically at Paris Air Show with show no.'207' 10-22Jun87. C/o route proving trials in the certification programme based at East Midlands from 23Nov to 20Dec87. Returned Woodford 21Dec87 and brought up to full production standard. Del British Midland Airways Ltd 31May88. Entered service from Birmingham to Brussels 01Jun88. Mods carried out at Woodford from 07Jan to 02Feb89 and in Apr89. Regd to British Midland Airways Ltd 10Jul89 (CofR G-BMYK/R2). While en route East Midlands-Jersey on 11Aug91 with 4 crew and 59 pax on board the aircraft entered cloud at 15,600 ft. Following, later established, ice build up on the leading edge of the wings, propellers and flying control surfaces, the aircraft suffered from severe vibration followed by the left wing dropping and the aircraft entering a stall. After leaving cloud at 13,000 ft the ice dispersed, the vibration subsided and the aircraft was recovered at 12,000 ft with no injuries to crew or pax and the aircraft continued to Jersey without further incident. Transferred to Manx Airlines Ltd 27Oct93 and del Hurn for repaint 06-14Nov93. Regd as **G-ERIN** to Manx Airlines (Europe) Ltd 14Dec93 (CofR G-ERIN/R1). Re-regd **G-MANL** to British Regional Airlines Ltd 03Oct94 (CofR G-MANL/R1). Transferred to British Midland Airways Ltd at East Midlands 09Jan95. Ferried Teesside 14Jan95 and repainted in British Midland c/s. Returned East Midlands as BD9531 18Jan95 and entered service as BD271 from East Midlands to Belfast International 19Jan95. Returned to British Regional Airlines Ltd and repainted in British Airways Express c/s by 22Oct95 when noted at Woodford. Operator renamed British Airways CitiExpress Ltd from 31Mar02. Regd British Airways CitiExpress Ltd 14Jan03 (CofR

G-MANL/R2). Flew final service for British Airways CityExpress as BA7626 from Belfast Harbour to Glasgow 29Feb04. Lsd Loganair Ltd and entered service as BA8821 from Glasgow to Stornoway 01Mar04. Ferried from Glasgow to Southend as TH001P 24Jul04 and air-tested at Southend as TH001E 03Aug04. Air-tested as TH001A and returned to Glasgow as TH002P 02Sep04. Returned to service as BA8776 from Glasgow to Aberdeen and Lerwick 03Sep04. Flew last revenue flight as BA8775 from Aberdeen to Glasgow 21Apr05. Ferried to Southend as TH001P 11May05 at end of lse for storage. Regd WestLB AG 28Oct05 (CofR G-MANL/R3). Regn **SE-MAG** rsvd to West Air Sweden AB 13Jul06. Lsd West Air Sweden AB and ferried Southend-Lidköping 29Sep06 for conversion E-class freight & JAA version. Noted stored awaiting hangar input 05Dec06 but later reduced to spares without use apart from EFIS cockpit trial installation. UK regn cld 21Dec07 as transferred Sweden. By Nov09 outer wings and tailplane removed and many parts missing at start of B/U process still marked as G-MANL.   ***TT 25,515 hrs, 33,328 ldgs***

2004   (4)

Regd to British Aerospace plc Civil Aircraft Division as **G-BMYL** 18Sep86 (CofR G-BMYL/R1). F/f 17Jan88, CofA issued 15Apr88. Del British Midland Airways Ltd 20Apr88. Entered service from Birmingham to Brussels 09May88. Mods programme carried out Woodford 12Feb to 08Mar89. Regd to British Midland Airways Ltd 10Jul89 (CofR G-BMYL/R2). Del Teesside 21Oct91 and painted in Loganair c/s. Regd as **G-LOGE** to Loganair Ltd 25Oct91 (CofR G-LOGE/R1). Ferried ex Teesside 30Oct91. Regd to Manx Airlines (Europe) Ltd 29Mar94 (CofR G-LOGE/R2). Re-regd **G-MANJ** 06Sep94 (CofR G-MANJ/R1). R/o Southend in British Airways Express c/s 10Mar95. Made emergency landing Liverpool with port main landing gear locked up 16May00. Repaired and ferried Isle of Man 26Jul00. Ferried Eindhoven for repaint in British Airways Union Flag c/s 27Jul00. Returned to service 11Aug00. Operator renamed British Airways CitiExpress Ltd from 31Mar02. Regd British Airways CitiExpress Ltd 14Jan03 (CofR G-MANJ/R2). Flew final service for British Airways CityExpress as BA4429 from Isle of Man to Glasgow 29Feb04. Lsd Loganair Ltd and entered service as BA8821 from Glasgow to Stornoway 02Mar04. Flew last flight as BA8824 from Stornoway to Glasgow 28Jun04 and ferried Southend the following day as TH001P for maintenance. Returned Glasgow as TH092P 04Jul04. Flew last revenue flight as BA8824 from Stornoway to Glasgow 19Jul04 and ferried to Southend for maintenance as TH002P 20Jul04. Returned to Glasgow as TH001P 10Aug04 and returned to service as BA8823 from Glasgow to Stornoway 11Aug04. Flew last revenue service as BA8812 from Isle of Man to Glasgow 30May05. Ferried Southend as TH001P 01Jun05 at end of lse for storage. Regd WestLB AG 28Oct05 (CofR G-MANJ/R3). Regn **SE-MAH** rsvd to West Air Sweden AB 13Jul06. Regn cld 06Sep06 as exported Sweden. Ferried Southend-Lidköping for lse West Air Sweden AB and conversion E-class freight & JAA version 15Sep06 using G-MANJ as the radio call sign. Noted in hangar undergoing mods and fuselage skin repair 05Dec06. Regd as SE-MAH to Siemens Financial Services AB 12Apr07. Entered service 16Apr07 in white top c/s. Transfer to West Air Luxembourg as **LX-WAH** abandoned and ferried Oslo-Malmö 30Dec15 for storage, noted engineless Aug16.   ***TT 30,177 hrs, 38,007 ldgs***

2005   (5)

Regd to British Aerospace plc Civil Aircraft Division as **G-BZWW** 22Jan88 (CofR G-BZWW/R1). F/f 11Feb88 in full American Eagle c/s for Wings West as G-BZWW but with fleet number 375 carried on nose undercarriage doors. Regn **N375AE** allocated and originally applied to aircraft prior to f/f (noted at Woodford 03Feb88). Demonstrated to Olympic Airways 4/7Mar88. American Eagle titles removed 31May88 and British Aerospace ATP titles applied after order cld. Aircraft retained by BAe for development purposes. C/o certification trials with

PW126A engines in Almeria 28Oct to 15Nov88. Re-regd **G-OATP** 20Dec88 (CofR G-OATP/R1). F/f as G-OATP in Manx Airlines c/s 19Mar89. CofA issued 21Mar89 . Del Manx Airlines Ltd 22Mar89. Regd to Manx Airlines Ltd 23Mar89 (CofR G-OATP/R2). Named "King Godred Crovan 1079-1095". Nosewheel collapsed on landing Isle of Man in a strong crosswind on 23Dec90 when operating flight JE884 from Luton with 4 crew & 69 pax on board. No injuries to pax or crew. Repaired. Re-regd as **G-MANM** to British Airways CityExpress (IOM) Ltd 17Oct94 (CofR G-MANM/R1). Ferried Southend 18Apr95. R/o Southend in British Airways Express c/s 25Apr95. Named "Elaine Griffiths" by 23Sep95. Ferried Isle of Man to Southend as TH091 12Apr01. R/o in Union Flag c/s and ferried to Manchester as TH091E 26Apr01. Returned to service as BA7734 from Manchester to Southampton the same day. Operator renamed British Airways CitiExpress Ltd from 31Mar02. Flew last revenue flight as BA8808 from Benbecula to Glasgow 14Feb04 and ferried Glasgow to Southend for handback check and storage as TH003P the same date. Air-tested as TH001E 17Mar04. Regd BAE Systems (Operations) Ltd 20May04 (CofR G-MANM/R2). Painted overall white with blue engines and departed Southend for Athens 03Sep04 on lease to EuroAir Ltd for evaluation returning Southend 09Sep04. Air-tested 27Oct04. Regn cld 28Oct04 as transferred Greece and lsd EuroAir Ltd with del from Southend to Athens as **SX-BTK** 01Nov04. Returned Southend 20Mar05 and put in storage. Restored as **G-MANM** to Trident Aviation Leasing Services (Jersey) Ltd 19May06 (CofR G-MANM/R3) and noted marked as such 29May06. Ferried Southend to Bucharest-Băneasa 10Jun06

for fitment of LFD. Regn **SE-MAM** rsvd to West Air Sweden AB 16Aug06. Ferried Băneasa-Lidköping 06Mar07 for conversion E-class freight & JAA version. UK regn cld 04May07 as transferred Sweden. Regd as SE-MAM to Trident Aviation Leasing Services (Jersey) Ltd 14Jun07. Entered service 02Jul07 painted overall white and without titles. Ferried Lidköping 08Jul08 and sub-lsd Air Go Airlines SA of Greece. Regn cld 16Jul08. Del Lidköping to Athens as **SX-BPS** 20Aug08 and named "Eleonora" by 23Aug08. Seen Stockholm-Arlanda 16Dec08 operating Swedish Post flights. Arrived Isle of Man for maintenance 14Jun10. Completed 01Jul10 and put in temporary storage. Engine cowlings painted blue by 14Jul10. Noted crew training Prestwick 16Aug10 prior to re-entering service and operating on behalf of West Air Luxembourg SA between Malta and Marseilles sub-lsd by AirGo Airlines Bulgaria EAD. Ferried Malmö-Marseilles 05Jan11 and re-entered service after being regd **LZ-BPS**. Flew last service as NPT461 from Lille to Birmingham on 28Oct11 before ferrying to Coventry the same day. WFU and put into storage. Noted with one engine missing 15Feb12. Restored as **G-MANM** to Atlantic Airlines Ltd 04Sep13 (CofR G-MANM/R4). Noted painted as G-MANM painted overall white with West Atlantic titles and emblems 04Oct13. Air tested as NPT62E 22Oct13. Ferried from Coventry to East Midlands as NPT423P 23Oct13. Entered service as NPT423 to Jersey 24Oct13. Regn **SE-MAM** reserved to West Air Sweden AB 06Mar15. Regn G-MANM cld 24Sep15 as transferred Sweden. Restored as SE-MAM to West Atlantic Aircraft Management AB 30Sep15 for ops by West Air Sweden AB.

G-OATP c/n 2005 in the original Manx Airlines' ATP colour-scheme, photographed in 1989.   *(WHC/BAe)*

G-MANO c/n 2006 of British Airways CitiExpress Ltd in 'Rendezvous' colours at Southampton on 9th April 2002.   *(Keith Gaskell)*

2006 (6)

F/f 20Jul88 as **G-11-5** in American Eagle c/s. Originally allocated to Wings West as **N376AE** and painted as such before order cld. Reportedly carried G-5-376 prior to f/f. Regd to Manx Airlines Ltd as **G-UIET** 26Aug88 (CofR G-UIET/R1) and flown as such the same day in full Manx c/s. CofA issued 22Sep88. Handed over 29Sep88. Del Liverpool 11Oct88. Flown with Loganair titles Nov88. Mods programme c/o Woodford May89. Lsd British Airways plc 09Jan90 to 16Jan90 (last flight as BA1388 from Brussels to Tegel) for operation on German internal and international schedules based on Tegel. Named "King Reginald 1187 - 1228" 1990. Lsd Loganair Ltd 06Dec91 to 31Mar92. Lsd British Airways plc 26Oct92 to 15Dec92. Re-regd **G-MANO** 28Nov94 (CofR G-MANO/R1). Ferried Woodford 27Apr95 for painting in Air Ostrava c/s as **OK-TFN**. Departed Woodford 07May95. UK regn cld 17May95 as transferred Czech Republic and del ex East Midlands the same day as OK-TFN on lse to Air Ostrava. Ferried Southend at end of lse 09Jan96. Restored as **G-MANO** to Manx Airlines Ltd 10Jan96 (CofR G-MANO/R2). R/o all white 12Jan96. Ferried Hurn 29Nov97 and repainted in British Airways c/s with 'Rendezvous' fin scheme. Departed Hurn 12Dec97. Operator renamed British Airways CitiExpress Ltd from 31Mar02. Flew last revenue flight as BA4388 from Birmingham to Isle of Man 04Sep03. Ferried from Isle of Man to Southend as BA1004P 05Sep03 for handback to lessor checks. Returned lessor 11Oct03 and air-tested 19Oct03. Regd BAE Systems (Operations) Ltd 14Nov03 (CofR G-MANO/R3). Due for lse EuroAir Ltd but ntu. Painted overall white by 10Sep04. Ferried Southend to Bucharest-Băneasa 13Jun06 for fitment of LFD. Regn **SE-MAN** rsvd to West Air Sweden AB 16Aug06. Ferried Băneasa-Lidköping 30Apr07 for conversion E-class freight & JAA version. UK regn cld 07Sep07 as transferred Sweden. Regd as SE-MAN to Trident Aviation Leasing Services (Jersey) Ltd 11Sep07. Air-tested 12Sep07. Ferried to Southend for painting in West Air Europe c/s 14Sep07. Ferried to Malmö on completion 28Sep06 and entered service 30Sep07 on a Norwegian Post flight from Bergen. Last flew as SE-MAN 29Apr11 and regn cld 11May11 as exported UK. Restored as **G-MANO** to Atlantic Airlines Ltd 12May11 (CofR G-MANO/R4). Regn **SE-MAN** reserved to West Air Sweden AB 06Mar15. Last revenue flight Dublin-East Midlands as NPT421 06Feb16 and positioned to Coventry. UK marks cld 18Feb16 and restored as SE-MAN to West Atlantic Aircraft Management AB 23Feb16. Ferried Coventry-Stansted 10Mar16 as SWN023Y and entered service Stansted-Jersey the same day as SWN023J.

2007 (7)

Originally allocated to Wings West as **N377AE** before order cld and fin actually painted in American Eagle c/s. Regd to British Airways plc as **G-BTPA** 19Aug88 (CofR G-BTPA/R1). F/f 25Aug88 in British Airways c/s. Shown at SBAC Show Farnborough Sep88. CofA issued 18Nov88. Del Glasgow as BA8971P 22Dec88. Entered service from Glasgow to Manchester as BA5731 09Jan89. Named "Strathallan". Flew last revenue flight as BA1661 from Manchester to Glasgow 07May98. Air tested 22Jun98. Ferried Glasgow to Woodford as BA1570E 30Jun98 at end of lse with British Airways titles and logo removed. Regd to British Aerospace (Operations) Ltd 07Aug98 (CofR G-BTPA/R2). Painted in Air Europa Express c/s and regn cld 02Oct98 as transferred Spain. Lsd Air Europa Express Líneas Aéreas SA as **EC-GYE** with del 03Oct98 from Woodford to Palma. Ferried Woodford by 22Jun99. Restored as **G-BTPA** to British Aerospace (Operations) Ltd 15Jul99 (CofR G-BTPA/R3) but not painted as such. Regn cld 26Aug99 as transferred Spain and del as EC-HGC on renewed lse to Air Europa Express Líneas Aéreas SA. Company ceased operations and was put into voluntary liquidation 29Oct01. Stored Palma. Restored as G-BTPA to Capital Bank Leasing 12 Ltd 24Jan02 (CofR G-BTPA/R4). Had been ferried Zaragoza for further storage by 04Feb02. Damaged by hailstorm and further damaged by tractor 08Jul02. Ferried Bucharest-Băneasa for hail damage repair and fitment of LFD 01Feb06 in old Air Europa Express c/s. Being

worked in hangar at Băneasa 30Oct07. Lsd Atlantic Airlines Ltd. Ferried Băneasa-Coventry 09Apr08 for conversion E-class freight & JAA version. CofA issued 06Oct08. Ferried Hurn and entered service Hurn-Jersey 10Oct08. Regd Atlantic Airlines Ltd 19Jan09 (CofR G-BTPA/R5). Regn **SE-MHC** reserved to West Air Sweden AB 06Mar15. Last revenue flight Bastia-Marseille 26Mar16 as PT404. Ferried Marseille-Coventry as SWN902 30Mar16 for storage, noted engineless Aug16.

2008 (8)

Originally allocated to Wings West as **N378AE** before order cld. F/f as **G-11-8** 11Oct88 in Ligações Aéreas Regionais c/s. Del Ligações Aéreas Regionais SA as **CS-TGA** 25Oct88 named "Douro". Entered service from Lisbon to Toulouse 26Oct88. Mods programme c/o Prestwick 28Jan to 08Mar90. Returned BAe with del Woodford 21Jan93. Regd as **G-BUUP** to British Aerospace plc - Regional Aircraft 18Feb93 (CofR G-BUUP/R1). Ferried from Woodford to East Midlands 27Apr93 for storage. Ferried from East Midlands to Isle of Man 13Jul93 for further storage. Regd to Manx Airlines Ltd 12May94 (CofR G-BUUP/R2) and operated in LAR c/s with Manx Airlines titles. Ferried Hurn 19Jun95 and painted white with Manx titles, returning Isle of Man 23Jun95.

Flown in 1997 still all white with additional "Manx Airlines 50 years of service" fin logo. Port main undercarriage collapsed on returning Manchester as BA7725 03Aug97. Regd as **G-MANU** to British Regional Airlines Ltd 20Aug97 (CofR G-MANU/R1) and painted as such by 10Nov97. After repair ferried Manchester to Isle of Man 19Nov97 still painted overall white with black British Airways titling and returned to service. Ferried Isle of Man to Woodford as TH091P 31Jan01 on return BAE Systems. Regd Trident Aviation Leasing Services (Jersey) Ltd 21Feb01 (CofR G-MANU/R2). Restored as **G-BUUP** 30Mar01 (CofR G-BUUP/R3). Ferried Woodford-Southend as WDF01 13May02 and then to Zaragoza 24May02 for storage. Damaged by hailstorm 08Jul02. Ferried Zaragoza to Bucharest-Băneasa 22Feb06 for hail damage repair and fitment of LFD after an aborted attempt the previous day. As at 30Oct07 being worked in hangar at Băneasa. Lsd Atlantic Airlines Ltd. Ferried Băneasa-Coventry 22Jan08 for conversion E-class freight & JAA version. CofA issued 27May08 and ferried East Midlands 29May08 and entered service the same day from East Midlands to Cork. Regd Atlantic Airlines Ltd 01Jul08 (CofR G-BUUP/R4). Ferried Birmingham-Aberdeen as LC781P 26Feb02 for lse Loganair Ltd. Entered service as LC781 from Aberdeen to Stornoway 27Feb12. Returned lessor as LC772P 03Mar12. Regn **SE-MHD** reserved to West Air Sweden AB 06Mar15. Last flight as G-BUUP 07Mar16 Maastricht-Coventry as NPT 572. UK marks cld 18Mar16 and regd SE-MHD to West Atlantic Aircraft Management AB 21Mar16 for ops by West Atlantic Sweden, entering service 31Mar16 as SWN420 Coventry-Dublin.

2009 (9)

Originally allocated to Wings West as **N379AE** before order cld. F/f 01Dec88 as **G-11-9** in LAR c/s. Del Ligações Aéreas Regionais SA as **CS-TGB** 11Dec88 named "Tejo". Entered service 15Dec88. Mods programme c/o Prestwick Oct89 to 20Nov89. Returned BAe and del Oporto-Woodford 21Jan93. Ferried East Midlands for storage 28Feb93. Regd as **G-BUWM** to British Aerospace plc - Regional Aircraft 19Apr93 (CofR G-BUWM/R1). R/o East Midlands 22Apr93 all white. SATA Air Açores titles applied and r/o as G-BUWM 09May93. Lsd SATA and ferried to Ponta Delgada as G-BUWM 13May93. Regn cld 14May93 as transferred Portugal and restored as **CS-TGB**. Returned Isle of Man at end of lse 08Dec93. Restored as **G-BUWM** to Jetstream Aircraft Ltd 10Dec93 (CofR G-BUWM/R2). Ferried Glasgow 12Apr95 in SATA Air Açores c/s. Ferried Woodford 11Oct95 and put in store. Regd British Aerospace (Operations) Ltd 12Jun97 (CofR G-BUWM/R3). Regd BAE Systems (Operations) Ltd 02Mar00. Aircraft blown into c/n 2001 by high winds 20Mar04. Sold Atlantic Airlines Ltd spring 2008 for spares removal. Regn cld as PWFU 01Jul08. Nose section removed and despatched to Coventry 22Jul08. B/u 11Aug08.   *TT 9,346 hrs, 11,959 ldgs*

2010   (10)

Originally allocated to Wings West as **N380AE** before order cld. Regd to British Airways plc as **G-BTPC** 01Sep88 (CofR G-BTPC/R1). F/f 16Dec88 as G-11-10 in British Airways c/s, CofA issued 30Dec88. F/f as G-BTPC 04Jan89 and del Glasgow via Manchester as BA8976T the same day. Entered service from Glasgow to Benbecula as BA5814 07Jan89. Later named "Strathblane". Flew last revenue flight as BA1858 from Birmingham to Aberdeen 07Jun98 before positioning Glasgow as BA1858P the same day. Air tested 24Jul98. Ferried Glasgow to Woodford as BA1573E 03Aug98 at end lse. Regd British Aerospace (Operations) Ltd 13Aug98 (CofR G-BTPC/R2). Painted in Air Europa Express c/s Sep98. UK regn cld 20Oct98 as transferred Spain. Lsd Air Europa Express Líneas Aéreas SA as **EC-GYF** with del Palma 20Oct98. Ferried Southend 03Aug99 as AEA002 and restored as **G-BTPC** to British Aerospace (Operations) Ltd 13Aug99 (CofR G-BTPC/R3). Noted in hangar Southend painted as **EC-HGB** 09Sep99. UK regn cld 20Oct99 as transferred Spain. Del ex Southend 20Oct99 for renewed lse to Air Europa Express Líneas Aéreas SA. Company ceased operations and was put into voluntary liquidation 29Oct01. Stored Palma. Had been ferried Zaragoza for further storage by 11Jan02. Restored as **G-BTPC** to Capital Bank Leasing 1 Ltd 24Jan02 (CofR G-BTPC/R4). Damaged by hailstorm 08Jul02. Ferried Bucharest-Băneasa for hail damage repair and fitment of LFD 03Aug05 in old Air Europa Express c/s. Regn **SE-MAI** rsvd to West Air Sweden AB 13Jul06. Ferried Băneasa-Lidköping 11Oct06 in hybrid Air Europa/primer c/s for conversion E-class freight & JAA version. Regn cld 31Jan07 as transferred Sweden. Regd as SE-MAI to Capital Bank Leasing 1 Ltd 09Feb07 and painted overall white without titles or logos. Entered service 19Feb07. Ferried Malmö-Southend as PT900 13Jun07. Painted in full West Air Europe c/s and ferried Southend-Malmö 02Jul07. Regn cld 30Aug10. Restored as **G-BTPC** to Atlantic Airlines Ltd 31Aug10 (CofR G-BTPC/R5) but retains full West Air Europe c/s. Entered hangar in Isle of Man 15Jun14. R/O 18Jun14 engineless for external storage. Returned to service by 19Sep14. Regn **SE-MAI** reserved to West Air Sweden AB 06Mar15. Restored as SE-MAI to West Atlantic Aircraft Management AB for operation by West Air Sweden AB 04Sep15.

2011   (11)

Originally allocated to Wings West as **N381AE** before order cld. Regd to British Airways plc as **G-BTPD** 01Sep88 (CofR G-BTPD/R1). F/f 01Feb89, CofA issued 07Feb89. Del Manchester as BA8967P 08Feb89. Entered service from Manchester to Glasgow as BA5731 08Feb89. Later named "Strathconan". Landed Aberdeen with brakes locked and veered off runway 22Feb95. Repaired. Flew last revenue flight as BA1783 from Birmingham to Glasgow 10Jul98. Ferried Glasgow to Woodford as BA1578E 08Sep98 at end lse. Painted in Air Europa Express c/s as **EC-GYR** Sep98. Regd as **G-BTPD** to BAe (Operations) Ltd 26Oct98 (CofR G-BTPD/R2). UK regn cld 20Nov98 as transferred Spain. Lsd Air Europa Express Líneas Aéreas SA as **EC–GYR** with del Palma 20Nov98. Ferried Southend by 10Aug99 and noted in hangar Southend still painted as EC-GYR 09Sep99. Restored as **G-BTPD** to BAe (Operations) Ltd 13Oct99 (CofR G-BTPD/R3) but had already been painted as **EC-HGD** by 25Sep99. UK regn cld 03Nov99 as transferred Spain for renewed lse to Air Europa Express Líneas Aéreas SA as EC-HGD. Del ex Southend 05Nov99. Company ceased operations and was put into voluntary liquidation 29Oct01. Stored Madrid. Had been ferried Zaragoza for further storage by 11Jan02. Restored as **G-BTPD** to Seaforth Maritime (JARL) Ltd., Flexifly Ltd 24Jan02 (CofR G-BTPD/R4). Damaged by hailstorm 08Jul02. Ferried Bucharest-Băneasa for hail damage repair and fitment of LFD 24May05 in old Air Europa Express

c/s. Regn **SE-MAO** rsvd to West Air Sweden AB 16Aug06. Ferried Băneasa-Lidköping 08Mar07 for conversion E-class freight & JAA version. UK regn cld 28Jun07 as transferred Sweden. Ferried Lidköping-Southend for paint in West Air Europe c/s 17Aug07 as SE-MAO. Del Southend-Malmö as PT900 29Aug07 on completion. Regd as **SE-MAO** to NWS2 11Sep07. Entered Service 18Sep07. Regn cld 14Jan08 and regd as **LX-WAT** to West Air Luxembourg SA. Restored as **SE-MAO** to European Turboprop Management AB 25Sep13 for ops by West Air Sweden AB.

2012   (12)

Originally allocated to Wings West as **N382AE** before order cld. Regd to British Airways plc as **G-BTPE** 01Sep88 (CofR G-BTPE/R1). F/f 08Mar89, CofA issued 12Mar89. Del Glasgow as BA8962P 16Mar89. Entered service from Stornoway to Inverness as BA5835 20Mar89. Named "Strathdon". Damaged on take-off Sumburgh 23Dec91 after port wing tip hit ground in high winds. Diverted Kinloss. Ferried Glasgow 05Jan92. Returned to service 20Jan92. Flew last revenue flight as BA1903 from Glasgow to Birmingham before positioning back to Glasgow as BA1801P both on 08Oct98. Air tested and then ferried Glasgow to Woodford as BA1335E both on 15Oct98 at end lse. Painted in Air Europa Express c/s and ferried Woodford to Southend 05Nov98. Regd BAe (Operations) Ltd 06Nov98 (CofR G-BTPE/R2). R/o Southend as **EC-GZH** 17Dec98. Regn cld 18Dec98 as transferred Spain on lse to Air Europa Express Líneas Aéreas SA. Returned Woodford at end lse 28Jul99. Restored as **G-BTPE** to British Aerospace (Operations) Ltd 30Jul99 (CofR G-BTPE/R3). Painted as G-BTPE 03Aug99. Regn cld 10Sep99 as transferred Spain and regd **EC-HGE** for renewed lsd to Air Europa Express Líneas Aéreas SA with del the same date. Company ceased operations and was put into voluntary liquidation 29Oct01. Stored Palma. Ferried Zaragoza by 11Jan02 for storage. Restored as **G-BTPE** to Capital Bank Leasing 3 Ltd 05Feb02 (CofR G-BTPE/R4). Damaged by hailstorm 08Jul02. Ferried Zaragoza to Bucharest-Băneasa 20Jul05 for hail damage repair and fitment of LFD in old Air Europa Express c/s. Lsd Atlantic Airlines Ltd and ferried Băneasa-Coventry 26Oct07 for conversion E-class freight & JAA version. CofA issued 29Feb08. Ferried Coventry-East Midlands 01Mar08 and entered service. Regd Atlantic Airlines Ltd 29Oct08 (CofR G-BTPE/R5). Noted at Hurn in West Atlantic's new overall white c/s with black/red/yellow emblem on fin and forward fuselage 19Jan14. Regn **SE-MHE** reserved to West Air Sweden AB 06Mar15. UK marks cld 01Feb16 and regd SE-MHE 02Feb16 to West Atlantic Aircraft Management AB for ops by West Atlantic Sweden. Ferried Coventry-Stansted 09Feb16 and entered service Stansted-Guernsey.

2013   (13)

Originally allocated to Wings West as **N383AE** before order cld. Regd to British Airways plc as **G-BTPF** 02Sep88 (CofR G-BTPF/R1). F/f 12Apr89, CofA issued 18Apr89. Del Glasgow as BA8986P 05May89. After crew training entered service from Glasgow to Belfast as BA5842 08May89. Named "Strathearn". Flew last revenue flight as BA1661 from Manchester to Glasgow 29Oct98. Air tested as BA1553E 11Dec98. Ferried from Glasgow to Woodford as BA1554P 18Dec98 at end lse. Regd BAe (Operations) Ltd 05Feb99 (CofR G-BTPF/R2). Painted in Air Europa Express c/s and became **G-11-013** before reverting to G-BTPF by 27Apr99. Lsd Air Europa Express Líneas Aéreas SA with del Palma 14May99. Regn cld 17May99 as transferred Spain and regd **EC-HCY**. Company ceased operations and was put into voluntary liquidation 29Oct01. Stored Barcelona. Ferried Zaragoza for further storage by 11Jan02. Restored as **G-BTPF** to Capital Bank Leasing 5 Ltd 24Jan02 (CofR G-BTPF/R3). Damaged by hailstorm 08Jul02. Ferried Bucharest-Băneasa for hail damage repair and fitment of LFD 14Jun05 in basic new Air Europa Express c/s. Painted overall white & lsd Atlantic Airlines Ltd. Ferried Băneasa-Coventry 21Aug07 for conversion E-class freight & JAA version. CofA issued 09Nov07. Entered service 12Nov07 all white with Atlantic Airlines titles in green and full fin c/s. Regd Atlantic Airlines Ltd 29Oct08 (CofR G-BTPF/R4). Regn **SE-MHF** reserved to West Air Sweden AB 06Mar15. Last revenue flight 28May16 Jersey-Coventry as NPT558. UK marks cld 21Jun16 and regd as SE-MHF to WAAM AB for ops by West Atlantic Sweden. Ferried Coventry-Aberdeen 04Jly16 as SWN028P and entered service Aberdeen-East Midlands as SWN028E.

2014　(14)

Originally allocated to Wings West as **N384AE** before order cld. Regd to British Airways plc as **G-BTPG** 02Sep88 (CofR G-BTPG/R1). F/f 13May89, CofA issued 22May89. Del Glasgow as BA8945P 26May89 and after several crew training details entered service from Glasgow to Benbecula as BA5814 30May89. Named "Strathfillan". Flew last revenue flight as BA1640 from Glasgow to Manchester 14Nov98. Air tested as BA1553E 11Dec98. Ferried from Manchester to Woodford as BA1555P 18Dec98 at end lse. Regd BAe (Operations) Ltd 05Feb99 (CofR G-BTPG/R2). Painted in Air Europa Express c/s by 27Apr99. Lsd Air Europa Express Líneas Aéreas SA with del ex Woodford 11Jun99. Regn cld 11Jun99 as transferred Spain where regd **EC-HEH**. Company ceased operations and was put into voluntary liquidation 29Oct01. Stored Madrid. Ferried Madrid-Woodford 20Dec01. Restored as **G-BTPG** to Capital Bank Leasing 5 Ltd 24Jan02 (CofR G-BTPG/R3). Ferried Woodford-Southend 18Apr02 in full Air Europa Express c/s and parked. Ferried Southend-Zaragoza for storage 07Jun02. Damaged by hailstorm 08Jul02. Ferried Bucharest-Băneasa for hail damage repair and fitment of LFD 16Dec05 in old Air Europa Express c/s. Lsd Atlantic Airlines Ltd. Ferried Băneasa-Coventry 02Jul08 painted overall white for storage pending conversion E-class freight & JAA version. Regd Trident Aviation Leasing Services (Jersey) Ltd 29May09 (CofR G-BTPG/R4). Regd Siemens Financial Services AB 08Jun09 (CofR G-BTPG/R5). Regd Atlantic Airlines Ltd 11Oct11 (CofR G-BTPG/R6). Following completion of E-class freight & JAA version mods a shakedown air test was flown 09Nov11 and a full CofA Air Test 10Nov11 as NPT61T. CofA issued 12Nov11 and entered service as NPT420 16Nov11. Noted i/s Coventry in full Atlantic Airlines c/s 15Feb12. Noted at Luton in West Atlantic's new overall white c/s with black/red/yellow emblem on fin and forward fuselage 19Jan14. Regn **SE-MHG** reserved to West Air Sweden AB 06Mar15 and entered service Coventry-Dublin as PT420 08Jan16, regd as SE-MHG.

2015　(15)

Regd to British Airways plc as **G-BTPH** 02Sep88 (CofR G-BTPH/R1). F/f 01Jun89, CofA issued 11Jun89. Del Glasgow as BA8903P 15Jun89. Entered service from Glasgow to Manchester as BA5731 16Jun89. Named "Strathnaver". Demonstrated Norwich with Air UK titles added 21Nov91. Flew last revenue flight as BA1865 from Edinburgh to Manchester 05Dec98. Air tested as BA1553E 14Jan99. Ferried from Manchester to Woodford as BA1551P 22Jan99 at end lse. Regd BAe (Operations) Ltd 26Feb99 (CofR G-BTPH/R2). Painted in Air Europa Express c/s by Jun99. Regn cld 23Jul99 as transferred Spain and regd **EC-HFM** on lse Air Europa Express Líneas Aéreas SA. Ferried Southend for maintenance 08Oct01. Company ceased operations and was put into voluntary liquidation 29Oct01. Stored Southend. Restored as **G-BTPH** to Capital Bank Leasing 6 Ltd 24Jan02 (CofR G-BTPH/R3). Ferried Southend-Zaragoza 13May02 for storage. Damaged by hailstorm 08Jul02. Ferried from Zaragoza to Bucharest-Băneasa 02Sep03 for repair and fitting of an LFD. Prior to LFD being fitted, painted in Emerald Airways c/s and noted painted as **G-JEMF** 10Nov04. Noted Băneasa 13Apr05 stored in full Emerald Airways c/s with door mod completed. Painted overall white and repainted as **G-BTPH**. Ferried Coventry 01Jul05 on lease to Atlantic Airlines Ltd. Converted to E-class freight & JAA version. Ferried East

Midlands 09Jan06 and repainted with Atlantic Airlines fin scheme and fuselage titles in black. Returned Coventry 24Jan06 and entered service 29Jan06. Regd Atlantic Airlines Ltd 29Oct08 (CofR G-BTPH/R4). Noted Coventry with grey top and dark blue underside, engines and fin without titles 19Mar09 and in full West Atlantic c/s after titles and logos had been applied 07Apr09. Regn **SE-MHH** regd to West Air Sweden AB 06Mar15. Ferried as NPT770P East Midlands-Coventry still as G-BTPH and UK marks cld 07Jun16. Regd as SE-MHH to JAHGBTPH, LLC 08Jun16 for ops by West Atlantic Sweden AB. Ferried Coventry-East Midlands Jly16 and entered service 05Jul16 East Midlands-Jersey as SWN423.

2016　(16)

Regd to British Airways plc as **G-BTPJ** 02Sep88 (CofR G-BTPJ/R1). F/f 06Jun89. Ferried Le Bourget 07Jun89 for display at the Paris Air Show with show No.'210'. Returned Woodford 16Jun89. CofA issued 09Jul89. Del Glasgow 14Jul89. Entered service from Glasgow to Belfast as BA5844 16Jul89. Named "Strathpeffer". Flew British Airways last own operated revenue ATP flight as BA1865 from Edinburgh to Manchester 26Jan99. Ferried Manchester-Woodford as BA1552P 16Mar99. Regd BAe (Operations) Ltd 19May99 (CofR G-BTPJ/R2). R/o Woodford in Air Europa Express c/s 29Jun99. Del ex Woodford 30Jul99. Regn cld 30Jul99 as transferred Spain and regd **EC-HFR** on lse Air Europa Express Líneas Aéreas SA. Seen Southend 21Aug01 with additional 'Viajes Ecuador' & 'La Agencia de sus Vacaciones' titles. Company ceased operations and was put into voluntary liquidation 29Oct01. Stored Madrid. Ferried Zaragoza by 11Jan02 for further storage. Restored as **G-BTPJ** to Capital Bank Leasing 7 Ltd 24Jan02 (CofR G-BTPJ/R3). Damaged by hailstorm 08Jul02. Ferried Bucharest-Băneasa 04Oct05 for hail damage repair and fitment of LFD in old Air Europa Express c/s. Lsd Atlantic Airlines Ltd. Ferried Băneasa-Coventry 23Sep08 painted overall white for storage pending conversion E-class freight & JAA version. Regd Trident Aviation Leasing Services (Jersey) Ltd 03Jun09 (CofR G-BTPJ/R4). Regd Deutsche Leasing Sverige AB 30Sep09 (CofR G-BTPJ/R5). Regd to European Turboprop Management AB 12Sep13.

TT 19,337 hrs, 21,368 ldgs

2017　(17)

Regd to Loganair Ltd as **G-OLCC** 05Dec88 (CofR G-OLCC/R1). F/f 16Aug89, CofA issued 22Aug89. Del Glasgow 25Aug89 and entered service the same day. Re-regd **G-LOGC** to Loganair Ltd 15Apr92 (CofR G-LOGC/R1). Ferried Hurn for painting in Manx Airlines c/s 07Apr94. Returned East Midlands as MNX100P 16Apr94. Regd Manx Airlines (Europe) Ltd 03Jun94 (CofR G-LOGC/R2). Re-regd **G-MANH** 16Nov94 (CofR G-MANH/R1). Ferried Woodford 17Mar95 for painting in British Airways Express c/s. Del ex Woodford 25Mar95. Painted in Union Flag c/s and ferried Southend-Manchester as TH091E 29Mar01. Operator renamed British Airways CitiExpress Ltd from 31Mar02. Regd British Airways CitiExpress Ltd 14Jan03 (CofR G-MANH/R2). Ferried Blackpool for repair 28Mar03. Returned Isle of Man as BRT003P 02May03. Flew last revenue British Airways CitiExpress ATP service as BA4410 from Manchester to Isle of Man 28Mar04 and put in storage. Air tested as TH001E 18Aug04 & ferried Isle of Man to Bucharest-Băneasa as TH001P 20Aug04 on return to BAE Asset Management for storage. Regd BAE Systems (Operations) Ltd 21Sep04 (CofR G-MANH/R3). Fitted with an LFD by Romaero SA. Regd Trident Aviation Leasing Services (Jersey) Ltd 19Sep05 (CofR G-MANH/R4). Ferried Băneasa to Coventry 06Oct05 on lse Atlantic Airlines Ltd painted overall white. Converted E-class freight & JAA version. CofA issued 22Feb06. Entered service 25Feb06 and noted Luton in full Atlantic Airlines c/s 04Mar06 with fuselage titles in green. Regd Atlantic Airlines Ltd 26Aug08 (CofR G-MANH/R5). Noted at Ronaldsway in West Atlantic's new overall white c/s with black/red/yellow emblem on fin and forward fuselabge 20Apr14. Regn **SE-MHI** reserved to West Air Sweden AB 06Mar15.

2018   (18)

Regd to Loganair Ltd as **G-OLCD** 05Dec88 (CofR G-OLCD/R1). F/f 18Sep89, CofA issued 29Sep89. Del Glasgow 02Oct89. Re-regd **G-LOGD** to Loganair Ltd 27Apr92 (CofR G-LOGD/R1). Lsd Manx Airlines Ltd with del Isle of Man 23Oct92. Regd Manx Airlines Ltd 13Apr93 (CofR G-LOGD/R2). Regd Loganair Ltd 24Jun93 (CofR G-LOGD/R3). Ferried Hurn for painting in Manx Airlines c/s 18Mar94. Del ex Hurn 26Mar94. Regd Manx Airlines (Europe) Ltd 03Jun94 (CofR G-LOGD/R4). Re-regd **G-MANG** 22Aug94 (CofR G-MANG/R1). Ferried from Manchester to Teesside 28Dec94. Painted in British Airways Express c/s and returned Manchester 07Jan95. Nosewheel collapsed on landing Manchester while inbound from Southampton as BA7783 18Mar98. Repaired and ferried Manchester to Isle of Man as JE100P 07Jun98. Returned to service 15Jun98. Painted in Union Flag c/s by 15Dec00. Operator renamed British Airways CitiExpress Ltd from 31Mar02. Regd British Airways CitiExpress Ltd 14Jan03 (CofR G-MANG/R2). Flew last revenue service as BA7622 from Belfast Harbour to Glasgow 24Mar04 and ferried Isle of Man as TH001P the same day for storage. Air tested as TH001E 21Sep04 and ferried Southend as TH007P the same day on return BAE Assett Management for storage. Regd BAE Systems (Operations) Ltd 19Oct04 (CofR G-MANG/R3). Due for lse EuroAir Ltd but ntu. Regd Trident Aviation Leasing Services (Jersey) Ltd 28Nov05 (CofR G-MANG/R4). R/o painted overall white 12Jun06. Noted Southend with regn **ES-NBB** overtaped with G-MANG Jul06 being prepared for Enimex Ltd. Air-tested 04 and 20Sep06 and again 12Oct06. Del to Enimex Ltd never took place. R/o in full SATA Air Açores c/s at Southend 20May07. Air-tested 07Jun07 with marks **CS-TFJ** overtaped. Regn cld 07Jun07 as transferred Portugal. Lsd SATA Air Açores and del via Lisbon 09Jun07. Named "Açores". Sold Regional One Inc of Miami, FL, USA Jun09 and lse to SATA Air Açores continued until 29May10, when ferried Ponta Delgada-Oporto-Norwich as SP001P for all white paint. Ferried Southend for storage 08Jun10 on completion. Noted carrying out engine runs 17Apr13. Noted in hangar with NextJet titles 19May13. Registered as **SE-MEX** to Regional One Inc 18Jun13. Ferried to Stockholm-Arlanda on lease to NextJet AB 23Aug13. Entered service as NTJ891 from Arlanda to Visby.

2019   (19)

F/f 10Nov89 as **G-11-19** painted in full SATA - Air Açores c/s after initially being painted as **CS-TGL**. Regd to British Aerospace (Commercial Aircraft) Ltd Airlines Division as **G-BRTG** 20Nov89 (CofR G-BRTG/R1) and f/f as such the same day. Regn cld 08Dec89 as transferred Portugal. Del Serviço Açoreano de Transportes Aéreos EP as **CS-TGL** 13Dec89. Entered service 17Dec89. Named "Santa Maria" after del. Lsd Air Malta with del from Faro 22Oct92 in full Air Malta c/s. Entered service from Malta to Palermo 25Oct92. Lse ended 01May94 and returned SATA Air Açores 03May94. Lsd PGA - Portugália (Companhia Portuguesa de Transportes Aéreos, S.A) 01Oct96 to 30Mar97 in full company c/s with 'Sun Liner/Rota do Sol' titles. Suffered rudder damage at Funchal 18Feb10. Repaired and returned to service 13May10. Regn **SE-MEE** rsvd to West Air Sweden AB 13Aug10. Sold West Air Sweden, AB 15Oct10 when ferried from Ponta Delgada to Malmö for later sub-lse to NEX Time Jet AB. Regd Erik Thun AB as SE-MEE 12Jan11. H/o to Next Jet – (NEX Time Jet, AB) on lse 04Apr11 and noted Arlanda with all white fuselage, SATA fin colours and 'NextJet' titles the following day. Noted Arlanda 23Feb12 with 'The best way to enter Lapland' and 'enterlapland.se' titles. Noted at Arlanda with an all navy blue fin 05Apr13. Permanently wfu 30Oct15. CofA expired 15Sep16.

2020   (20)

Regd to British Aerospace (Commercial Aircraft) Ltd Airlines Division as **G-WISS** 12Jun89 (CofR G-WISS/R1). F/f 05Dec89 as G-WISS in primer. Regn cld 12Dec89 as transferred USA having been painted as **G-11-20** and flown as such the previous day. Ferried Woodford to Shannon as G-11-20 22Dec89 for painting in United Express c/s. Restored as **G-WISS** 29Dec89 (CofR G-WISS/R2) but cld 03Jan90 as transferred USA with UK marks not used. Returned Woodford 03Jan90. Del Air Wisconsin Inc as **N851AW** 14Jan90. Del Woodford for systems update and fitment of APU and short nose leg 15Apr91. Re-del Air Wisconsin Inc 05Jul91. Sold United Feeder Service Inc 07Sep93. WFU & stored Kingman from 19Feb00. Regn **SE-LHX** rsvd for West Air Sweden AB 16Oct00. US regn cld Jan01. Ferried ex Kingman arriving Lidköping as SE-LHX 31Mar01 for conversion to a pure freighter. Conversion to E-class freight and JAA version completed 08Aug01. Regd to West Air Sweden AB 08Aug01. Ferried Woodford 12Aug01 in United Express c/s. R/o in West Air Sweden c/s 21Aug01, ferried Prestwick 27Aug01 and returned to service. Regd European Turboprop Management AB 27Sep01. Regn cld 03Sep04 and transferred to West Air Luxembourg SA as **LX-WAN**. Noted Düsseldorf as such 14Sep04 with West Air Europe titles. Ferried Düsseldorf-Southend 05Nov05 for hail damage assessment. Ferried Southend-Lidköping for repair 25Nov05. Repair carried out and returned to service 30Jun06. Temporarily stored Malmö from 29May09. Restored as **SE-LHX** to European Turboprop Management AB 11Dec09. Air tested 12Dec09 and entered service the following day. Ferried Isle of Man 10Jun11 for maintenance. Regn cld as transferred Luxembourg 01Jul11. Departed Isle of Man as **LX-WAN** 08Jul11 for West Air Luxembourg SA. Restored as **SE-LHX** to European Turboprop Management AB 30Aug13 for ops by West Air Sweden AB. CofA expired 17Jun16.

2021   (21)

Regd to British Aerospace (Commercial Aircraft) Ltd Airlines Division as **G-BRKM** 07Sep89 (CofR G-BRKM/R1). F/f 27Jan90 as **G-11-21** in primer to Hurn for painting in United Express c/s 27Jan90. Regn cld 29Jan90 as transferred USA and UK marks not used. Returned Woodford 09Feb90. Flown as G-11-021 07Mar90. Flown as **N852AW** 09Mar90 but damaged in heavy icing. Repaired and del Air Wisconsin Inc as N852AW 15Mar90. Del Woodford for systems update and fitment of APU and short nose leg 28Sep91. Re-del Air Wisconsin 19Nov91. Sold United Feeder Service Inc 07Sep93. WFU & stored Kingman by 05Feb00. Regn **SE-LGZ** rsvd for West Air Sweden AB Oct00. US regn cld Jan01. Ferried ex Kingman arriving Lidköping 23May01 for conversion to a pure freighter. Converted to E-class freight and JAA version and as the prototype Large Freight Door (LFD) version of the ATP Freighter. F/f as such from Lidköping 10Jul02. Regd European Turboprop Management AB 11Jul02. Ferried from Lidköping to Prestwick 19Jul02 and shown to the design team before continuing to Farnborough later in the day as PT900. Shown statically at Farnborough Air Show before ferrying back to West Air 29Jul02. Entered revenue service Aug02. Port wing struck from behind by high loader destroying inner half of aileron and most of the outboard section of flap at Helsinki 31Jan07. After temporary repair ferried to Lidköping 14Feb07. Returned to service 17Feb07. Temporarily transferred NEX Time Jet AB 02Jun/22Aug08 to gain experience with the type. Regn cld 22Jan09 and regd as **LX-WAW** to West Air Luxembourg SA. Restored as **SE-LGZ** to European Turboprop Management AB 30Aug13 for ops by West Air Sweden AB. Last flew before conversion to 'Universal Avionics EFIS' cockpit at Malmö (like SE-LGX c/n 2036) 04Mar14. Returned to service 18May14. Stored at Isle of Man since 19Jun15.

2022   (22)

F/f 27Mar90 as **G-11-022** in primer. Ferried East Midlands for paint in United Express c/s 03Apr90. Del Air Wisconsin Inc as **N853AW** 09Apr90. Del Woodford for systems update and fitment of APU and short nose leg 16Jul91. Re-del Air Wisconsin 20Sep91. Sold United Feeder Service Inc 07Sep93. WFU & stored Kingman by 19Feb00. Sold West Air Sweden AB with del ex Kingman arriving Lidköping as **SE-LGU** 07Apr00 in full new

CS-TGL c/n 2019 of SATA Air Açores on the ramp at Ponta Delgada in the Azores. (WHC/BAe)

United Express c/s. C/o type acceptance approval flight 05May00. Noted in hangar Lidköping 27Jul00 in hybrid United Express/West Air c/s being converted to freighter config-uration. Conversion to E-class freight and JAA version completed 23Aug00. Regd to West Air Sweden AB 24Aug00. Entered service 05Sep00. Regd European Turboprop Management AB 27Sep01. This is the only ATP to retain West Air Sweden titles. Severe wing damage at Malmö during refuelling 23Oct09. CofA expired 31Aug10. Repair started mid Oct10 with completion scheduled for end Jan11. Regd European Turboprop Management AB 30Aug13. Still stored Malmö Aug16.

TT 22,451 hrs, 30,162 ldgs

2023   (23)

Regd to British Aerospace (Commercial Aircraft) Ltd Airlines Division as **G-PEEL** 06Oct89 (CofR G-PEEL/R1). F/f 01May90 in Manx Airlines c/s, CofA issued 08May90. Del Manx Airlines Ltd 12May90 named "King Somerled (1158-1164)". Lsd British Airways plc with del from the Isle of Man to Tegel as BA8833P 03Sep90. Entered service from Tegel to Nuremburg as BA3211 03Sep90. Regd to British Aerospace plc Airlines Division 20Sep90 (CofR G-PEEL/R2). Regd Manx Airlines Ltd 13Nov90 (CofR G-PEEL/R3). Flew last service for British Airways 22Mar91 and returned Manx Airlines Ltd. Lsd Loganair Ltd 01Nov to 06Dec91. Damaged Liverpool landing with nosewheel partly retracted 19Apr92. Repaired. Lsd British Airways 15Dec92. Regd British Airways plc 23Feb93 (CofR G-PEEL/R4). Returned Manx Airlines Ltd 01Apr93. Regd Manx Airlines Ltd 26May93 (CofR G-PEEL/R5). Re-regd **G-MANP** 28Oct94 (CofR G-MANP/R1). Ferried Woodford for paint in Air Ostrava c/s 18Apr95. Returned Woodford to East Midlands 27Apr95 in full Air Ostrava c/s. Painted as **OK-VFO**. UK regn cld 17May95 as transferred Czech Republic and del ex East Midlands the same day on lease to Air Ostrava. Ferried Southend at end of lease 10Jan96 and restored to Manx Airlines Ltd as **G-MANP** 15Jan96 (CofR G-MANP/R2). R/o all white 17Jan96 and returned to service with Manx Airlines Ltd. Painted in Union Flag c/s Jan01. Operator renamed British Airways CitiExpress Ltd from 31Mar02. Flew last revenue service as BA7626 from Belfast Harbour to Glasgow 17Mar04. Ferried to Isle Man as TH001P 26Mar for storage. Ferried to Southend for further storage as TH001E 27Sep04. Air-tested 16May05. Into paint 29May05. R/o Southend in full MagicBlue c/s 05Jun05 with regn G-MANP taped over. Air tested Southend 17Jun05 with regn PH-MJP concealed. Regd Lombard Manx Leasing Ltd 05Jul05 (CofR G-MANP/R3). Regn PH-MJP reserved to Lombard Manx Leasing Ltd 07Jul05. Noted Southend marked as **PH-MJP** 01Oct05. Painted overall white and r/o marked as **ES-NBA** 27May06. Air-tested as **G-MANP** 31May and 03Jun06. Regd Trident Aviation Leasing Services (Jersey) Ltd 19Jun06 (CofR G-MANP/R4). Lsd Enimex Ltd and ferried Tallinn 18Jul06 as G-MANP. Regn cld as transferred Estonia 19Jul06 and regd **ES-NBA** and noted as such at Tallinn 05Aug06. Ferried Tallinn to Lidköping 17Aug07 for prospective conversion E-class freight & JAA version and increased AUW mods on behalf of BAE Systems but not c/o. Restored as **G-MANP** to Trident Aviation Leasing Services (Jersey) Ltd 28Aug07 (CofR G-MANP/R5). Stored after arrival Lidköping in pax configuration. Regn **SE-LLO** rsvd to West Air Sweden AB 30Apr08. UK regn cld 03Oct08 as transferred Sweden. Regd as SE-LLO to Trident Aviation Leasing Services (Jersey) Ltd 30Oct08 for lse West Air Sweden AB for sub-lse NEX Time Jet AB. Entered service as 2N556 from Stockholm-Arlanda to Gällivare 02Nov08 painted overall white with Next Jet titles. Regd Arafart AB c/o Erik Thun AB 18Dec08. By 24Jun09 noted still all white but with large additional 'bring EXPRESS' titles. WEF 01Feb12 commenced operations from Stockholm-Bromma to Växjö with Flysmåland. Carries 'Sverigeflyg.se' titles and by 02Mar12 was carrying the company's Stockholm silouette fin scheme in green and white. Returned to NEX Time Jet AB after last flight 09Mar12 but returned to the Flysmåland route on 19Mar12. Returned to NEX Time Jet AB again 04Apr12 but returned to the Flysmåland route

on 11Apr12. Returned to NEX Time Jet AB again 25Apr12 but returned to operate the Flysmåland route on 02May12. Regd European Turboprop Management AB 26Sep13. Ferried from Arlanda to Ronaldsway as NTJ 9708 now devoid of all titles with a green and white fin 08Nov13. Noted flying overall white without titles 01Dec13. Noted flying in new NextJet fuselage c/s 30Mar14.

2024   (24)

F/f 21May90 as **G-11-024** in primer to Hurn for painting. Returned Woodford in LAR c/s 01Jun90. Export CofA issued 09Jun90. Del Linhas Aéreas Regionais SA as **CS-TGC** as PDF019P 20Jun90 named "Guadiana" having been earlier painted with the name "Mondego". Returned BAe with del Oporto-Woodford 21Jan93. Regd as **G-BUUR** to British Aerospace - Regional Aircraft 18Feb93 (CofR G-BUUR/R1). Ferried from Woodford to East Midlands for storage 28Apr93. Ferried to Isle of Man 24Jun93 still in LAR c/s. CofA issued 05Aug93. Regd to Manx Airlines Ltd 20Aug93 (CofR G-BUUR/R2). Operated in LAR c/s with Manx titles. Arrived Woodford 21Jul94. To Hurn from 08-18Aug94 for Euro Direct crew training. Regd as **G-OEDJ** to Jetstream Aircraft Ltd 01Sep94 (CofR G-OEDJ/R1). Painted in Euro Direct c/s by 28Oct94. Del Euro Direct Airlines Ltd 15Nov94. Company ceased trading 26Feb95. Returned BAe at Woodford 27Feb95 and used as a company shuttle aircraft, being painted all white by 06Jun95. Regd British Aerospace (Operations) Ltd 12Jun97 (CofR G-OEDJ/R2). Painted with British Airways titles in black. Ferried Woodford to Isle of Man for lease British Regional Airlines Ltd 16Aug97. Regd British Regional Airlines Ltd 08Sep97 (CofR G-OEDJ/R3). Returned Manchester-Woodford at end lse 24Nov97. Used as BAe Warton company shuttle aircraft from 30Nov97. Regd BAe (Operations) Ltd 14Jan98 (CofR G-OEDJ/R4). Corporate shuttle use ceased Mar98. Regn cld 01Jun98 as transferred Spain. Lsd Air Europa Express Líneas Aéreas SA as **EC-GUX** with del ex Woodford 02Jun98. Company ceased operations and was put into voluntary liquidation 29Oct01. Stored Madrid. Had been ferried Zaragoza for further storage by 11Jan02. Restored as **G-BUUR** to Trident Aviation Leasing Services (Jersey) Ltd 18Jan02 (CofR G-BUUR/R3). Damaged by hailstorm 08Jul02. Ferried Bucharest-Băneasa for hail damage repair and fitment of an LFD 16Apr05 in old Air Europa Express c/s. Ferried Băneasa-Coventry 09May06 as third aircraft for Atlantic Airlines Ltd. Converted E-class freight & JAA version and entered service from Aberdeen on 30Sep06 in full Atlantic Airlines c/s. Regd Atlantic Airlines Ltd 26Aug08 (CofR G-BUUR/R4). Noted at Cologne in West Atlantic's new overall white c/s with black/red/yellow emblem on fin and forward fuselage 19Aug14. Commenced operating regular five times weekly flights between Brussels and Nantes on behalf of European Air Transport as QY1541/2 19Dec14. Registration **SE-MHJ** reserved to West Air Sweden AB 06Mar15. Last revenue flight 19Mar16 as QY2694 Brussels-Luton and to Coventry as NPT770P the same day for storage. Noted 19Jly16 painted as SE-MHJ, UK marks cld 22Sep16, and regd 23Sep16 to JAHGBUUR, LLC for ops by West Atlantic Sweden AB. Still stored Coventry 26Oct16, engineless.

TT 21,632 hrs, 23,287 ldgs

2025   (25)

Regd to British Aerospace (Commercial Aircraft) Ltd Airlines Division as **G-BRLY** 22Sep89 (CofR G-BRLY/R1). First production aircraft with short nose leg. F/f 19Aug90 as G-BRLY in primer direct to Hurn for painting. Painted in full British Airways c/s and flown to Farnborough Air Show 01Sep90. Returned Woodford 10Sep90. Regd to British Aerospace plc Airlines Division 20Sep90 (CofR G-BRLY/R2). CofA issued 30Oct90. Carried out demonstration tour to the USA and Canada from 29Oct to 23Nov90 and to Eastern Europe and Sweden from 02-12Dec90. Regd to Manx Airlines Ltd 04Jan91 (CofR

G-BRLY/R3). Lsd Manx Airlines Ltd 04Jan91 to 23Jan91. Regd to British Aerospace (Commercial Aircraft) Ltd Airlines Division 13Feb91 (CofR G-BRLY/R4). Departed Woodford on a Far East, Australia and New Zealand demonstration tour 21Feb91 after removal of British Airways titles and tail logo. Flown in New Zealand with 'Mount Cook Airline' titles and tail logo. Returned Woodford 14Apr91. Lsd British Airways plc in full c/s with del Glasgow 17Apr91. Regd to British Airways plc 10May91 (CofR G-BRLY/R5). Flew last service from Manchester to Glasgow as BA5732 02Oct91 and returned Woodford 23Oct91. Regd British Aerospace (Commercial Aircraft) Ltd Airlines Division 27Nov91 (CofR G-BRLY/R6). Carried out demonstration tours to Iran and UAE from 12-20Dec91 and to South America and the Caribbean from 23Jan to 29Feb92. Lsd British Airways plc again with del to Glasgow 02Mar92. Regd British Airways plc 09Apr92 (CofR G-BRLY/R7). Flew last service as BA5849 from Belfast to Glasgow 07Jun92 and ferried Hurn 09Jun92. Painted in THT c/s before ferry Woodford 22Jun92. Regn cld 02Jul92 as transferred Turkey. Del Turk Hava Tasimaciligi - THT 03Jul92 as **TC-THP**. Restored as **G-BRLY** to Trident Aviation Leasing Services (Jersey) Ltd 25Sep92 (CofR G-BRLY/R8) on return East Midlands.

Regd Manx Airlines Ltd 20Oct92 (CofR G-BRLY/R9). Lsd Manx Airlines Ltd 01Nov92 in THT c/s with Manx titles. Lsd British Airways plc with all white fuselage and British Airways titles in black with a blue fin with a white circle superimposed and del from Isle of Man to Glasgow 28Apr93. Entered service from Glasgow to Stornoway 01May93. Regd to British Airways plc 23Jun93 (CofR G-BRLY/R10). Flew last service as BA5835 from Stornoway to Glasgow via Inverness 09Dec93. Air tested Glasgow as BA5671E and returned BAe 17Dec93. Ferried Prestwick 21Dec93. Ferried Prestwick to Isle of Man for storage 06Jan94. Regd Trident Aviation Leasing Services (Jersey) Ltd 28Feb94 (CofR G-BRLY/R11). Lsd British Airways plc yet again and entered service as BA5737 from Glasgow to Manchester 24Aug94. Regd British Airways plc 05Sep94 (CofR G-BRLY/R12). Flew last service as BA5892 from Birmingham to Glasgow 09Nov94. Ferried Isle of Man as BA5657P for srorage 20Nov94. Lsd British Airways again with del from Isle of Man to Glasgow as BA5616E 30Nov94. Entered service as BA5360 from Glasgow to Birmingham 01Dec94. Lse completed 01Jul95. Lsd British Regional Airlines Ltd with British Airways Express titles 17Jul95. Regd Jetstream Aircraft Ltd 14Jul95 (CofR G-BRLY/R13). Regd Manx Airlines (Europe) Ltd 18Jul95 (CofR G-BRLY/R14). Lsd British Midland Airways Ltd 14-28Mar97. Returned Isle of Man to Woodford 12Jan99 at end lse. Regd Trident Aviation Leasing Services (Jersey) Ltd 05May99 (CofR G-BRLY/R15). Ferried from Woodford to Aberdeen 15Feb00 for major overhaul. Regn removed 31Mar00 on preparation for lse to SATA Air Açores. UK regn cld 23May00 as transferred Portugal and lsd SATA Air Açores as **CS-TGX** in full c/s named "Faial" with del 24May00. Ferried Southend 02Feb04 for repaint in new SATA c/s. Ferried Southend-Oporto 12Feb04 on completion. Sold Regional One Inc of Miami, FL, USA Jun09 and lse to SATA Air Açores continued until 19Oct09 when ferried Ponta Delgada to Norwich via Oporto for painting overall white as SP001P. Ferried Southend as SP002P 26Oct09. Breaking up began 09Feb16.

TT in excess of 21,560 hrs, 37,340 ldgs (figures at 30Jun09)

G-BRLY c/n 2025 of BAe with temporary Mount Cook Airline titles while on demonstration to them in February-March 1991. (WHC/BAe)

The same aircraft in Turk Hava Tasimaciligi - THT colours where it would serve as TC-THP for approximately eleven weeks from early July 1992. Note wing root APU exhaust. (WHC)

S2-ACX c/n 2026 of Bangladesh Biman Airways seen in a photograph taken during test flying (or possibly crew training) prior to delivery in 1990.
(WHC/BAe)

2026   (26)

F/f 24Jul90 as **G-11-026** in Bangladesh Biman c/s after earlier being painted as **S2-ACX**. H/o Bangladesh Biman Airways as S2-ACX 09Aug90, first flying as such 16Aug90. Remained at Woodford for crew training. Ferried ex Woodford 19Sep90 via Crete, Luxor, Djibouti, Seeb and Delhi to Dhaka. Grounded Dec90 to Aug91. Skidded off runway Chittagong 02Jul97 with propeller and undercarriage damage. Repaired. Regn **SE-LHX** rsvd for West Air Sweden AB 16Oct00 but ntu. Stored Dhaka 2001. Returned to service 23Apr03. Sold Emerald Airways Ltd. Ferried from Dhaka 21Jan04 via Karachi, Teheran, Bucharest and Prague arriving Blackpool 25Jan04 in full Bangladesh Airlines c/s as S2-ACX. Regd as **G-JEMD** to Emerald Airways Ltd 03Feb04 (CofR G-JEMD/R1) but remained in store still painted as S2-ACX. R/o as G-JEMD for engine runs in Bangladeshi c/s without titles 30Jun04. Ferried to Bucharest-Băneasa as JEM007E for fitment of LFD 08Jul04. On completion, ferried ex Băneasa 08Jan05 and diverted Norwich with engine shut down. Ferry to Blackpool continued following day as JEM007P. Company's AOC suspended 04May06. Never entered service with Emerald Airways Ltd. Regd PTB (Emerald) Pty Ltd 12Dec06 (CofR G-JEMD/R2). R/o overall white 26Jun08. Ferried to Kemble for short term storage 19Sep08. Ferried Coventry 09Apr09. Air-tested 27May06. Lsd Deraya PT with del from Coventry via Malta & Sharm El Sheikh 28/29Jul09 arriving Jakarta-Halim 01Aug09. Regn cld 05Aug09 as exported Indonesia and regd **PK-DGA** 10Aug09. Painted with thin light/dark blue cheatlines and red 'Deraya' titles. Ferried from Merauke to Townsville, Queensland, Australia for a routine engine change 22Feb11.

2027   (27)

F/f 23Aug90 as **G-11-027** in Bangladesh Biman c/s after earlier being painted as **S2-ACY**. F/f as **S2-ACY** 15Sep90. Del Bangladesh Biman Airways as S2-ACY 20Sep90. Grounded Dec90 to Aug91. Regn **SE-LHY** rsvd for West Air Sweden AB 16Oct00 but ntu. Stored Dhaka 2001. Returned to service 23Apr03. Sold Emerald Airways Ltd. Ferried from Dhaka 21Jan04 via Karachi, Teheran, Bucharest and Prague arriving Blackpool 25Jan04 in full Bangladesh Airlines c/s as S2-ACY. Regd as **G-JEME** to Emerald Airways Ltd 03Feb04 (CofR G-JEME/R1) but remained in store still painted as S2-ACY. R/o as G-JEME for engine runs 30Jun04. After air-test ferried to Bucharest-Băneasa as JEM75E for fitment of LFD 09Aug04. Company's AOC suspended 04May06. Remained in store

Băneasa after fitment LFD. Regd PTB (Emerald) Pty Ltd 12Dec06 (CofR G-JEME/R2). Ferried Băneasa to Blackpool 09Oct07 painted overall white without titles for interior freight mods. Ferried to Kemble for short term storage 19Sep08. Ferried Coventry 09Apr09. Lsd Deraya PT with del from Coventry via Malta & Sharm El Sheikh 06/07Aug09 arriving Jakarta-Halim 11Aug09. Regn cld 13Aug09 as transferred Indonesia and regd **PK-DGI** 13Aug09. Painted with thin light/dark blue cheatlines and red 'Deraya' titles. Arrived at Cairns from Timika 10Feb13. Ferried Sydney-Bankstown for maintenance with Skyforce 11Feb13. Ferried Bankstown-Cairns-Jayapura 18Feb13. Veered off runway in a heavy landing at Wamena, Indonesia after a flight from Jayapura 31May13. Nose leg detached and propellers and underbelly damaged as the aircraft stuck in soft ground. Declared a write-off by Mar14.

TT 15,785 hrs, 25,475 ldgs

2028   (28)

F/f 18Sep90 as **G-11-028** in primer direct to Hurn for painting. Returned Woodford in United Express c/s 29Sep90. Del Air Wisconsin Inc as **N854AW** 09Oct90. Regd to Wilmington Trust Co Oct90. Sold United Feeder Service Inc 07Sep93. WFU & stored Kingman by 19Feb00. Regd Wachovia Bank of Delaware 27Oct03. Regd Wells Fargo Bank Northwest NA 05Dec03. Sold Emerald Airways Ltd and ferried ex Kingman 10Jan04 via Duluth, Goose Bay and Keflavik arriving Blackpool 12Jan04 in full old United Express c/s. Regd as **G-JEMA** to Emerald Airways Ltd 24Feb04 (CofR G-JEMA/R1). Painted as G-JEMA and ferried to Filton as JEM70E 25Mar04 for repaint. Returned Blackpool as JEM70E in new Emerald Airways c/s 03Apr04. Carried out two air-tests as JEM04T 07May04. CofA issued 07May04. Ferried Liverpool as JEM70E 09May04. Operated on behalf of Euromanx Ltd from 13Jun05. Company's AOC suspended 04May06 and stored Liverpool from the same date. Ferried Liverpool-Blackpool 17Nov06 for further storage. Regd PTB (Emerald) Pty Ltd 11Dec06 (CofR G-JEMA/R2). Regn canx as PWFU 09Jun14. B/u for spares.

TT 18,153 hrs, 27,267 ldgs

2029   (29)

F/f 13Oct90 as **G-11-029** in primer direct to Hurn for painting. Returned Woodford in United Express c/s 22Oct90. Regd as **N855AW** to British Aerospace Inc Oct90. Del Air Wisconsin Inc as N855AW 06Nov90. Sold United Feeder Service Inc 07Sep93.

WFU & stored Kingman by 05Feb00. Regd Wachovia Bank of Delaware 21Oct03. Regd Wells Fargo Bank Northwest NA 05Dec03. Sold Emerald Airways Ltd. Following air-test ferried ex Kingman to Duluth 20Feb04 where aircraft went technical. Ferried ex Duluth to Goose Bay 16Mar04 and via Keflavik to Blackpool 17Mar04. Regd as **G-JEMB** to Emerald Airways Ltd 29Mar04 (CofR G-JEMB/R1). Ferried Southend as JEM71E 11Jun04 for repaint in Emerald Airways c/s returning Blackpool as JEM70E 25Jun04. CofA issued 12Jul04. Converted to E-class freight and JAA version and r/o as such 08Dec04. Ferried from Blackpool to Paris-Le Bourget as JEM70E 13Jan05 prior to entering service. Company's AOC suspended 04May06 and aircraft ferried from Marseilles to Blackpool 05May06 as JEM888Q for storage. Regd PTB (Emerald) Pty Ltd 12Dec06 (CofR G-JEMB/R2). Lsd Atlantic Airlines Ltd and ferried from Blackpool to Coventry as NPT61E 07Feb07. Regd as **G-OAAF** to Atlantic Airlines Ltd 27Feb07 (CofR G-OAAF/R1). Noted Coventry in full Atlantic Airlines c/s 15Apr07. Entered service 18Apr07 between East Midlands and Belfast. Ferried Coventry as NPT61P 07Sep10 and WFU. Returned lessor. Taxied to centre of airfield for full power engine runs 15Feb12 still in full Atlantic Airlines c/s. CofA re-issued 06Sep13. Ferried from Coventry to Băneasa as NPT64Y 07Sep13 for fitment of a Large Freight Door prior to lease to Deraya PT. Regd to PTB (Emerald) Pty Ltd 16Sep13 (CofR G-OAAF/R2). Regn canx 28Feb13 as transferred Indonesia. Del to Deraya PT from Băneasa as **PK-DGB** via Trabzon and Kuwait 12Mar14. Skidded off runway in heavy rain at Wamena, Indonesia, after a flight from Jayapura 04Mar15. Nose and port main undercarriage collapsed and No.1 engine and propeller severely damaged. W/O; dismantled and shipped to Sydney.

TT in excess of 19,295 hrs, 25,830 ldgs (figures at 16Sep13)

2030 (30)

F/f 25Nov90 as **G-11-030** with large forward freight door in primer direct to Hurn for painting. Returned Woodford in SATA - Air Açores c/s 04Dec90 as **G-11-30**. Del SATA - Air Açores as **CS-TGM** 15Dec90. Named "Graciosa" after del. W/o 11Dec99 on approach Horta operating SP530 from Ponta Delgada after hitting Pico de Esperança mountain near São Jorge. 4 crew and 31 pax killed.

TT 11,299 hrs, 23,572 ldgs

2031 (31)

F/f 14Nov90 as **G-11-031** with large forward freight door in primer direct to Hurn for painting. Returned Woodford in SATA - Air Açores c/s 25Nov90. Del SATA - Air Açores as **CS-TGN** 06Dec90. Named "Flores". Flew last regular scheduled flight from Terceira to Ponta Delgada 28May10. Sold Sold West Air Sweden, AB and ferried Ponta Delgada to Malmö direct in 8 hrs 5 mins 03Nov10 for later sub-lse NEX Time Jet AB. Regd as **SE-MEG** to European Turboprop Management AB 22Jul11. Noted Malmö still marked as CS-TGN engineless and with doors and windows sealed 06Jan12.

TT 26,305 hrs, 51,288 ldgs

2032 (32)

F/f 30Nov90 as **G-11-032** in primer. Ferried Hurn for painting 03Dec90. Returned Woodford in United Express c/s without titles as G-11-32 13Dec90. Regd as **N856AW** to British Aerospace Inc Dec90. Painted as such and del Air Wisconsin Inc 04Jan91. Sold United Feeder Service Inc 07Sep93. WFU & stored Kingman by 19Feb00. Regd Wachovia Bank of Delaware 27Oct03. Regd Wells Fargo Bank Northwest NA 05Dec03. Sold Emerald Airways Ltd and del ex Kingman 20Dec03 via Duluth, Goose Bay and Keflavik arriving Blackpool 21Dec03 in full United Express new c/s. Regn cld 24Dec03 and regd as **G-JEMC** to Emerald Airways Ltd 29Dec03 (CofR G-JEMC/R1). Ferried to Southend as JEM70E for repaint in Emerald Airways new c/s 01Mar04. Returned Blackpool as JEM71E 15Mar04. CofA issued 16Apr04. Commenced crew training 17/18Apr04 with visits to Liverpool and the Isle of Man. Ferried Liverpool as JEM01T

21Apr04. Operated on behalf of Euromanx Ltd from 13Jun05. Flew last revenue service as 3W412 from Liverpool to Isle of Man on 04May06 and stored following Emerald Airways AOC being suspended on the same date. Ferried Blackpool 21Nov06 for continued storage. Regd PTB (Emerald) Pty Ltd 11Dec06 (CofR G-JEMC/R2). Ferried Coventry as Neptune 62P 20Mar09 for storage and painted overall white by 15Aug10. Parting out commenced early Jun15 and by 16Jun15 outer wings removed and rear fuselage and fin cut off. Regn cld 10Aug16 as PWFU.

TT 17,158 hrs, 25,669 ldgs

2033 (33)

F/f 10Dec90 as **G-11-033** in primer. Painted in Bangladesh Biman c/s with regn **S2-ACZ** taped over. Reverted to G-11-033 and stored Woodford. Order cld and regd as **G-BTTO** to British Aerospace plc – Air-lines Division 16Aug91 (CofR G-BTTO/R1). CofA issued 23Aug91. F/f as G-BTTO 28Aug91 with Biman titles removed for demonstration trip to the Czech Republic. Returned Woodford 30Aug91. Fitted with APU. Ferried Hurn 02Oct91 for painting in THT c/s. Returned Woodford 03Nov91. Regd Trident Aviation Leasing Services (Jersey) Ltd 09Jan92 (CofR G-BTTO/R2). Demonstrated at London City Airport 05Feb92. Regn cld 28Feb92 as transferred Turkey. Del Turk Hava Tasimaciligi - THT as **TC-THV** 29Feb92 named "Isparta". Returned BAe and ferried Istanbul - Prestwick 03Sep93 for storage. Restored as **G-BTTO** to Jetstream Aircraft Ltd 29Sep93 (CofR G-BTTO/R3). Noted Isle of Man still painted as TC-THV 16Oct93. By 31Oct93 was painted as G-BTTO with Manx Airlines titles. Regd Trident Aviation Leasing Services (Jersey) Ltd 30Nov93 (CofR G-BTTO/R4). Ferried Prestwick 01Mar94. Ferried Woodford 14Mar94. Painted in EuroDirect c/s as **G-OEDE** for publicity purposes 27Mar94. Positioned Hurn 07Apr84 as **G-BTTO** for launch of new airline (with marks G-OEDE uncovered) before returning Woodford the following day. Ferried Prestwick 21Apr94. Re-regd as **G-OEDE** to EuroDirect Airlines Ltd 28Jun94 (CofR G-OEDE/R1). Del 06Jul94 and entered service the same day between Hurn and Amsterdam. Named "Spirit of the Humber" 16Aug94. Returned BAe at Woodford 27Feb95 after EuroDirect ceased trading the previous day. Regd Trident Aviation Leasing Services (Jersey) Ltd 28Mar95 (CofR G-OEDE/R2). Regd Trident Aviation Leasing Services (Jersey) Ltd as **G-BTTO** 07Apr95 (CofR G-BTTO/R5). Painted all white with British Airways Express titles. Regd as G-BTTO to Manx Airlines (Europe) Ltd 13Apr95 (CofR G-BTTO/R6). Lsd Manx Airlines (Europe) Ltd and entered service 14Apr95. Damaged Belfast City airport 12Nov95 and wfs. Regd Trident Aviation Leasing Services (Jersey) Ltd 01Jul96 (CofR G-BTTO/R7) and after repair stored Prestwick. Ferried Woodford by 02Jul96. Painted in Air Europa Express c/s. Lsd Canarias Regional Air SA with del Woodford-Palma 24Oct96. Regn cld 25Oct96 as transferred Spain and regd **EC-GJU**. Ferried Palma-Woodford for mods 21Apr97. Ferried Woodford-Malaga 12May97 on return Canarias Regional SA. Painted in new Canarias Regional c/s 1998. Ferried Woodford at end lse 19Feb99. Restored as **G-BTTO** to BAe Systems (Operations) Ltd 10Mar99 (CofR G-BTTO/R8) but remained stored as EC-GJU 12May99. Regd BAE Systems (Operations) Ltd 02Mar00. Lsd Air Europa Express Líneas Aéreas SA and del ex Woodford 16May00. Regn cld 17May00 as transferred Spain and regd **EC-HNA**. Seen Palma 05Sep01 with additional 'Diario de Mallorca' titles to starboard, 'Diario de Ibiza' titles to port and 'Mallorca Zeitung' titles. Company ceased operations and was put into voluntary liquidation 29Oct01. Stored Palma. Had been ferried Zaragoza for further storage by 11Jan02. Restored as **G-BTTO** to Trident Aviation Leasing Services (Jersey) Ltd 18Jan02 (CofR G-BTTO/R9). Damaged by hailstorm 08Jul02. Ferried to Bucharest-Băneasa for repair and fitment of LFD 11Aug04. Regn **PH-MJF** rsvd to MagicBlue Airlines NV 19Jul04 but ntu. Lsd Atlantic Airlines Ltd and del Băneasa-Coventry 16Aug06 painted overall white for conversion E-class freight & JAA version. CofA issued 08Dec06 to **G-BTTO**. Ferried Hurn as NPT543P 31Dec06 all white with Atlantic

G-BTTO c/n 2033 in Euro Direct colours in March 1994. The aircraft was re-registered as G-OEDE prior to delivery to the airline.　　　*(WHC)*

Airlines titles in green and Atlantic fin emblem. Regd Atlantic Airlines Ltd 26Aug08 (CofR G-BTTO/R10). Noted at Aberdeen in West Atlantic's new overall white c/s with black/red/yellow emblem on fin and forward fuselage 11Jan14. Entered hangar at Coventry for conversion to 'Universal Avionics' EFIS cockpit (like c/n 2036 SE-LGX) 08May14. Air tested as NPT061E 18Nov14. Air tested again 12Feb15 and put into storage at Coventry. Registration **SE-MHK** reserved to West Air Sweden AB 06Mar15. UK regn cld 29Apr16. Regd 11May16 as SE-MHK to JAHGBTTO, LLC and dep Coventry for Malmö 24Aug16. Air-tested 30Aug16 and ferried to Jonkoping 31Oct16 as SWN807P, entering service to Oslo 01Nov16 as SWN8007.

TT 16,851 hrs, 17,377 ldgs

2034　(34)

F/f 24Feb91 as **G-11-034** in full United Express c/s. Regd as **N857AW** to British Aerospace Inc Mar91. Del Air Wisconsin Inc 06Apr91. Regd Air Wisconsin Inc Jun91. Sold United Feeder Service Inc 07Sep93. WFU & stored Kingman by 05Feb00. Regn cld May00. Sold West Air Sweden AB and del ex Kingman 04Jun00 via Winnipeg, Iqaluit and Keflavik arriving Lidköping as **SE-LGV** 06Jun00 in full new United Express c/s. Conversion to E-class freight and JAA version completed 13Feb01. Regd to West Air Sweden AB 28Feb01. Entered service 09Mar01. Regd European Turboprop Management AB 27Sep01. Ferried Lidköping-Southend as PT900 30Mar07 for maintenance. Ferried Southend-Paris Charles de Gaulle as PT392 23Apr07 on completion. Ferried Isle of Man 28Feb10 with Norwegian 'posten' titles, robbed of its engines and put in long term storage. CofA expired 28Feb10.

TT 20,931 hrs, 27,551 ldgs

2035　(35)

F/f 04Apr91 as **G-11-035** in primer. Regd to British Aerospace Inc as **N858AW** Apr91. Painted in United Express c/s as N858AW at Woodford. H/o Air Wisconsin Inc 01May91. F/f as N858AW 06May91. Ferried ex Woodford 08May91. Regd Air Wisconsin Inc Jun91. Wing damage during refuelling Dec91. Returned to service 17Mar92. Sold United Feeder Service Inc 07Sep93. WFU & stored Kingman by 19Feb00. Regn **SE-LGY** rsvd for West Air Sweden AB Oct00. Sold West Air Sweden AB

and del ex Kingman via Winnipeg, Iqaluit and Keflavik arriving Lidköping as SE-LGY 15Jan01 in old United Express c/s. Conversion to E-class freight and JAA version completed 16May01. Regd to West Air Sweden AB 17May01. Entered service 21May01. Ferried Woodford 21Aug01 in United Express c/s. R/o in West Air Sweden c/s 29Aug01. Regd European Turboprop Management AB 27Sep01. Temporarily transferred NEX Time Jet AB 02Jun-22Aug08 to gain experience with the type. Planned transfer to West Air Luxembourg as **LX-WAZ** abandoned. Stored Malmö 30Dec15. CofA expired 31May16, still stored Malmö Aug16.

TT 23,624 hrs, 30,659 ldgs

2036　(36)

F/f 04May91 as **G-11-036** in primer. Regd British Aerospace Inc as N859AW May91. Painted in United Express c/s as **N859AW** at Woodford. F/f as such 24May91. Del Air Wisconsin Inc 26May91. Regd Air Wisconsin Inc Jun91. Sold United Feeder Service Inc 07Sep93. Sold United Airlines Inc 29Dec94. WFU & stored Kingman by 05Feb00. Regn cld May00. Sold West Air Sweden AB and del ex Kingman 04Jun00 via Winnipeg, Iqaluit and Keflavik arriving Lidköping as **SE-LGX** 06Jun00 in full old United Express c/s. Noted on engine runs Lidköping 27Jul00.

Conversion to E-class freight and JAA version completed 31Oct00. Regd West Air Sweden AB 13Nov00. Entered service 16Nov00. Regd European Turboprop Management AB 27Sep01. Trial installation at Malmö of new cockpit layout utilising 'Universal Avionics' EFI-890R EFIS equipment, UNS-1L FMS and TAWS using a Vision1 Synthetic Display System commenced mid Sep09 and f/f after mods on 15Feb10. Carried out further air tests on 16Feb10, 14/15Apr10, 04May10, 20May10, 16Aug10 and 24Sep10 and put in store. Two further air tests on 12Mar13. Returned to service by 26Aug13.

2037　(37)

Regd as **G-BTNK** to British Aerospace plc - Airlines Division 31May91 (CofR G-BTNK/R1). F/f 07Jun91 as **G-11-037** in full United Express c/s with Paris Air Show number '262'. Regd Trident Aviation Leasing Services (Jersey) Ltd 11Jun91 (CofR G-BTNK/R2). Flown to Le Bourget as **G-BTNK** 13Jun91 and shown statically at the Paris Air Show. Returned Woodford 19Jun91. Regn cld 20Jun91 as transferred USA and reverted to **G-11-037**. Regd as **N860AW** to Tracey Leasing Corp Jun91. Del Air Wisconsin Inc 29Jun91 on lse until 01Jan93. Regd First Security Bank of Utah Dec91. Returned Trident Aviation Leasing Services (Jersey) Ltd 31Jan93 and stored. Sold United Feeder Service Inc 07Sep93. Del United Feeder Service Inc 01Oct93 and noted Chicago without titles 28Oct93. Ferried Goose Bay to Reykjavik 13Sep96 and onwards to Prestwick the following day on return BAe. Regn cld Sep96 and put in storage. Restored as **G-BTNK** to Trident Aviation Leasing Services (Ireland) Ltd 01Oct96 (CofR G-BTNK/R3). Regd to Trident Aviation Leasing Services (Jersey) Ltd 10Oct96 (CofR G-BTNK/R4). Noted Prestwick stored still painted as N860AW 30Jul97. Ferried Prestwick-Woodford 20Oct97 in basic United Express c/s for further storage. Regd as **G-CORP** to BAe (Operations) Ltd 02Mar98 (CofR G-CORP/R1) and painted in BAe house c/s. F/f as G-CORP 23Mar98. Used as a BAe corporate shuttle aircraft based at BAe Warton from 29Mar98, the same date CofA issued. Regd BAE Systems (Operations) Ltd 02Mar00. Flew last shuttle flight 17Jan03 and ferried Warton-Southend as BAE301P 22Jan03. Air tested as WFD11 18Feb03 and put in storage. Regd Trident Aviation Leasing Services (Jersey) Ltd 14Aug03 (CofR G-CORP/R2). Regn **SE-MAP** rsvd to West Air Sweden AB 16Aug06. R/o in West Air Europe c/s 11Oct06. Ferried Southend to Băneasa for fitment of Large Freight Door 27Mar07. Ferried Băneasa-Lidköping 25Sep07 for conversion E-class freight & JAA version in full West Air Europe c/s. UK regn cld 19Nov07 as transferred Sweden. Regd as SE-MAP to Trident Aviation Leasing Services (Jersey) Ltd 07Dec07. Entered service 02Jan08. R/o Isle of Man as **LX-WAE** 25Nov11 and noted on engine runs 01Dec11, the same date Swedish regn cld as exported Luxembourg. Ferried Isle of Man to Coventry as WLX516 06Dec11. Regd to Smart Cargo SA and continues ops for West Air Luxembourg SA. Ferried to Ronaldsway on return to West Air Sweden for storage 28Feb15 at TT 17,252 hrs, 18,932 landings.

Restored as **SE-MAP** to West Atlantic Aircraft Management AB 31Aug15 for operation by West Air Sweden AB. Final ATP to fly in Luxembourg marks.

2038   (38)

Regd as **G-SLAM** to British Aerospace plc - Airlines Division 24Apr91 (CofR G-SLAM/R1). Painted as G-SLAM but not flown as such. Re-regd **G-BTNI** 29May91 (CofR G-BTNI/R1). F/f 19Jun91 as G-BTNI all white. Regd to Trident Aviation Leasing Services (Jersey) Ltd 13Sep91 (CofR G-BTNI/R2). Painted in THT c/s with G-BTNI taped on. Regn cld 02Oct91 as transferred Turkey. Del Turk Hava Tasimaciligi - THT as **TC-THU** 02Oct91 named "Rize". Returned BAe and ferried Istanbul - Isle of Man 14Oct93 for storage all white. Ferried Prestwick 31Mar94. Restored as **G-BTNI** to Trident Aviation Leasing Services (Jersey) Ltd 05Apr94 (CofR G-BTNI/R3). Ferried Hurn 17Jun94 where painted with United Express titles and tail fin logo. Ferried Hurn-Prestwick 20Jun94. Regn **N238JX** allocated for lse UFS after mod to FAA PW126A standard but not del. Del Manchester for painting overall white 12Aug94. Ferried Manchester-Prestwick 14Aug94. Regd as **G-OEDI** to Trident Aviation Leasing Services (Jersey) Ltd 15Aug94 (CofR G-OEDI/R1). Del EuroDirect Airlines Ltd 19Aug94. R/o Southend in EuroDirect c/s 08Nov94. Regd EuroDirect Airlines Ltd 28Nov94 (CofR G-OEDI/R2). Returned BAe at Woodford for storage 27Feb95 after EuroDirect ceased trading the previous day. Regd Trident Aviation Leasing Services (Jersey) Ltd 07Apr95 (CofR G-OEDI/R3). Painted overall white by 07Jun95. Painted with Air Europa Express titles by 23Oct96 without fin marks. Ferried Southend 25Oct96 for painting in full Air Europa Express c/s. R/o 29Oct96 and ferried Woodford the same day. Lsd Canarias Regional Air SA with del Woodford-Palma 21Nov96. Regn cld 22Nov96 as transferred Spain and regd **EC-GKJ**. Lse transferred to Air Europa Express Líneas Aéreas SA and re-regd **EC-GSE** by 25Jan98. Company ceased operations and was put

G-BTNI c/n 2038 and G-JEME c/n 2027 undergoing hail damage repair and the fitment of Large Freight Doors in the hangar at Bucharest-Băneasa on 13th April 2005,

(Keith Gaskell)

into voluntary liquidation 29Oct01. Stored Palma. Had been ferried Zaragoza for further storage by 11Jan02. Restored as **G-BTNI** to Trident Aviation Leasing Services (Jersey) Ltd 18Jan02 (CofR G-BTNI/R4). Damaged by hailstorm 08Jul02. Ferried from Zaragoza 16Nov03 and diverted Nice technical. Arrived Bucharest-Băneasa for repair and fitment of LFD 14Jan04. Regn **PH-MJG** rsvd to MagicBlue Airlines NV 19Jul04 but ntu. Ferried from Băneasa to Lidköping 08Dec05 for E-class freight & JAA version mods by West Air Sweden on behalf of BAE Systems. Regn cld 15Aug06 as transferred Sweden. Regd as **SE-MAJ** to Trident Aviation Leasing Services (Jersey) Ltd 17Aug06 for operation by West Air Sweden AB. Ferried Lidköping-Southend in hybrid primer/Air Europa Express c/s for repaint 24Aug06. R/o in full West Air Europe c/s 01Sep06 and ferried Southend-Lidköping the same day. Entered service 05Sep06. Regn cld as transferred Luxembourg 17Jan12. In service as **LX-WAD** from Copenhagen to Helsinki 24Jan12. Restored as **SE-MAJ** to European Turboprop Management AB for ops by West Air Sweden AB 09Oct13.

2039   (39)

F/f 08Jul91 as **G-11-039** in primer. Painted in THT c/s and flown as **G-BTUE** 04Sep91. Regd as **G-BTUE** to British Aerospace Plc - Airlines Division 05Sep91 (CofR G-BTUE/R1). Regn cld 09Sep91 as transferred Turkey as sold as **TC-THT** but reverted to **G-11-039** 11Sep91. Restored as **G-BTUE** to British Aerospace plc - Airlines Division 12Sep91 (CofR G-BTUE/R2). Regd to Trident Aviation Leasing Services (Jersey) Ltd 13Sep91 (CofR G-BTUE/R3) with regn cld the same date as transferred Turkey. Del Turk Hava Tasimaciligi - THT as **TC-THT** 14Sep91 named "Sanliurfa". Returned BAe and ferried Istanbul-Isle of Man 19Oct93 for storage all white. Restored as **G-BTUE** to Trident Aviation Leasing Services (Jersey) Ltd 03Nov93 (CofR G-BTUE/R4). Ferried Woodford 27May94 overall white. Regd as **G-OEDH** to Trident Aviation Leasing Services (Jersey) Ltd 04Aug94 (CofR G-OEDH/R1). Painted in EuroDirect c/s at Woodford and f/f as such 22Aug94. Regd to EuroDirect Airlines Ltd 22Aug94 (CofR G-OEDH/R2). Del EuroDirect Airlines at Humberside 25Aug94. Ferried from Hurn to Glasgow 12Feb95 for storage prior to EuroDirect ceasing ops 26Feb95. Regd Trident Aviation Leasing Services (Jersey) Ltd 07Apr95 (CofR G-OEDH/R3). Ferried Woodford 21Apr95. Painted overall white by 11May95. Painted as **G-OGVA** by 10Apr96 but had reverted to **G-OEDH** by 27Sep96. Painted with European Regional Airlines Association titles for Farnborough Air Show Sep96 with additional "50,000,000 passengers means good business" titles. Ferried Southend 04Oct96 for repaint in Air Europa Express c/s. Returned Woodford 10Oct96. Lsd Canarias Regional Air SA with del Woodford-Palma 08Nov96. Regn cld 11Nov96 as transferred Spain and regd **EC-GKI**. Ferried Palma-Woodford for mods 17May97. Ferried Woodford-Palma 23Jun97 on return Canarias Regional SA. Lse transferred to Air Europa Express Líneas Aéreas SA and re-regd **EC-GSF** by 08Feb98. Company ceased operations and was put into voluntary liquidation 29Oct01. Stored Madrid. Had been ferried Zaragoza for further storage by 11Jan02. Restored as **G-BTUE** to Trident Aviation Leasing Services (Jersey) Ltd 18Jan02 (CofR G-BTUE/R5). Damaged by hailstorm 08Jul02. Ferried Zaragoza-Southend for repair 03Oct03. Completed by 05May04 and painted overall white by 08Jun04. Ferried Southend-Lidköping 14Mar06 for E-class freight and increased AUW mods. Painted in First Flight Couriers c/s by napsab. Export CofA issued 09Jun06. Lsd First Flight Couriers Pvt Ltd of India and del Lidköping-Southend 12Jul06. Del ex Southend via Brindisi 03Aug06. Regn cld 11Aug06 as transferred India. Regd as **VT-FFB** to Trident Aviation Leasing Services (Jersey) Ltd 18Aug06. On landing Chennai from Mumbai and Bangalore on 15Jun07 the nose gear collapsed rearwards and sheared off together with the mountings. Came to rest on nose where a small fire was quickly extinguished. There was further damage to the nosewheel doors, forward underbelly and the propellers. The aircraft was later declared as beyond economic repair. Regn cld 04Jul08. Restored as **G-BTUE** to

Aircraft Maintenance Services Ltd of Blackpool, UK 22Jul08 (CofR G-BTUE/R6) but had been reduced to spares at Chennai in Jun08. Regn cld as PWFU 23Jun09.

TT 14,905 hrs, 14,599 ldgs

2040   (40)

F/f 14Aug91 as **G-LOGA** in primer. Regd as **G-LOGA** to British Aerospace plc - Airlines Division 19Aug91 (CofR G-LOGA/R1). R/o Woodford in Loganair c/s 30Aug91. CofA issued 06Nov91. Del Loganair Ltd 07Nov91. Regd Loganair Ltd 08Nov91 (CofR G-LOGA/R2). Regd Manx Airlines (Europe) Ltd 29Mar94 (CofR G-LOGA/R3). Regd as **G-MANF** to British Regional Airlines Ltd 19Sep94 (CofR G-MANF/R1) and operated in Loganair c/s with Manx titles. R/o Southend 01Mar95 in British Airways Express c/s. Operator renamed British Airways CitiExpress Ltd from 31Mar02. Regd British Airways CitiExpress Ltd 14Jan03/FlyBe Leasing Ltd (CofR G-MANF/R2). Ferried Shannon-Isle of Man as TH001E after repaint in Union Flag c/s 23Aug03. Flew last revenue flight as BA8808 from Benbecula to Glasgow 27Mar04 and ferried Southend as TH003P the following day for storage. Lsd Loganair Ltd to cover for maintenace inputs on their ATP fleet. Ferried Southend to Glasgow as TH002P 29Jun04 and entered service as BA8821 from Glasgow to Stornoway 30Jun04. Flew last service as BA8824 from Stornoway to Glasgow 02Sep04 and ferried to Southend as TH006P 07Sep04 for further storage. Regd BA Connect Ltd 07Feb06. Regn **SE-MAK** rsvd to West Air Sweden AB 13Jul06. Lsd West Air Sweden and ferried Southend-Lidköping 14Dec06 for storage and eventual conversion E-class freight & JAA version but conversion not c/o. Regd Flybe Leasing Ltd 11Jul07. UK regn cld by the CAA 16Jul07. Regd European Turboprop Management AB as SE-MAK 10Jul08. Ferried Southend 21Jul08 for repaint in Next Jet c/s without titles or logo and returned Southend-Lidköping 19Aug08 as 2N700. Lsd NEX Time Jet AB and entered service as a pax aircraft as 2N554 from Arlanda to Gällivare 08Oct08. Regd Erik Thun AB 13Oct08. Noted Stockholm-Arlanda in full c/s with additional FLYG TILL FJÄLLEN I SOMMAR! titles 26Mar09. Operated on behalf of Flysmåland AB 01/02May12.

2041   (41)

F/f 12Sep91 as **G-11-041** in primer. Regd as **G-BTPK** to British Aerospace plc - Airlines Division 03Oct91 (CofR G-BTPK/R1). Painted in British Airways c/s as G-BTPK and f/f as such 31Oct91. CofA issued 06Nov91. Del British Airways plc at Glasgow as BA8920P 07Nov91. Named "Strathrannoch". Entered service from Glasgow to Belfast as BA5844 08Nov91. Regd Trident Aviation Leasing Services (Jersey) Ltd and again to British Airways plc 08Jan92 (CofR G-BTPK/R2). Flew last service as BA5383 from Birmingham to Glasgow 29Sep96. Ferried Glasgow-Woodford as BA5644E 07Nov96 on return BAe. Regd Trident Aviation Leasing Services (Jersey) Ltd 19Nov96 (CofR G-BTPK/R3). Painted in Air Europa Express c/s Nov96. Regn cld 17Jan97 as transferred Spain and del on lse to Canarias Regional Air SA as **EC-GLC** the same day from Woodford to Palma. Ferried Zaragoza-Woodford for maintenance 29Sep97. Returned Woodford-Palma 17Oct97. Lse transferred to Air Europa Express Líneas Aéreas SA and re-regd **EC-GSG** by 26Jan98. Company ceased operations and was put into voluntary liquidation 29Oct01. Stored Barcelona. Had been ferried Zaragoza for further storage by 11Jan02. Restored as **G-BTPK** to Trident Aviation Leasing Services (Jersey) Ltd 18Jan02 (CofR G-BTPK/R4). Damaged by hailstorm 08Jul02. Ferried Băneasa 15Jul03 for repair. Fitted with a Large Rear Freight Door for lse to West Air Sweden AB and r/o fully painted in West Air c/s 22Jun04 (the first Romaero conversion). Ferried to Lidköping as G-BTPK 07Jul04 for conversion to an E-class freight and JAA version. UK regn cld 19Jul04 as transferred Sweden. Regd as **SE-LPV** to Trident Aviation Leasing Services (Jersey) Ltd 04Oct04 for operation by West Air Sweden AB. Entered service 13Oct04. Regn cld 28May08 and transferred West Air

Luxembourg SA as **LX-WAV**. Restored as **SE-LPV** to JAHLXWAV, LLC for ops by West Air Sweden AB 04Oct13. Ferried Billund-Malmö 04Jan16 for external storage, engineless. CofA expired 13Sep16.

TT 24,961 hrs, 26,331 ldgs

2042 (42)

Regd as **G-BTPL** to British Aerospace plc - Airlines Division 03Oct91 (CofR G-BTPL/R1). F/f 11Oct91 as **G-11-042** in primer. Painted in British Airways c/s and f/f as **G-BTPL** 13Nov91. CofA issued 22Nov91. Del Manchester as BA8944P 22Nov91. Entered service as BA5288 from Manchester to Belfast the same date. Named "Strathspey". Regd to Trident Aviation Leasing Services (Jersey) Ltd 08Jan92 and to British Airways plc the same day (CofR G-BTPL/R2). Flew last service as BA5401 from Birmingham to Glasgow 30Oct96. Ferried Glasgow-East Midlands as BA5647E 22Nov96 on return BAe. Painted in Air Europa Express c/s. Ferried Woodford 17Dec96. Regd Trident Aviation Leasing Services (Jersey) Ltd 20Dec96 (CofR G-BTPL/R3). Lsd Canarias Regional Air SA with del Woodford-Palma 07Mar97 after air-test 05Mar97. Regn cld 10Mar97 as transferred Spain and regd **EC-GLH**. Ferried Palma-Woodford for maintenance 03Nov97. Returned Woodford-Palma 18Nov97. Ferried Southend at end lse 19Nov98. Restored as **G-BTPL** to BAe (Operations) Ltd 10Mar99 (CofR G-BTPL/R4). R/o Southend in Air Europa Express c/s still as EC-GLH 27Mar99. Painted as G-BTPL by 06Jul99. Regn cld 16Jul99 as transferred Spain and regd **EC-HES** for lse Air Europa Express Líneas Aéreas SA. Company ceased operations and was put into voluntary liquidation 29Oct01. Stored Madrid. Had been ferried Zaragoza for further storage by 11Jan02. Restored as **G-BTPL** to Trident Aviation Leasing Services (Jersey) Ltd 18Jan02 (CofR G-BTPL/R5). Damaged by hailstorm 08Jul02. Ferried Southend 03Dec02 as G-BTPL for repair. Repair completed and entered paint shop 30Sep03 where painted overall white. Ferried Exeter 29Oct04 for conversion to E-class freight & JAA version. Regn **PH-MJK** rsvd to MagicBlue Airlines NV 01Oct04. Noted painted in full MagicBlue c/s at Exeter 03Apr05 with regn G-BTPL taped on. Ferried Exeter-Southend 24Aug05. Air-tested Southend 23Sep05 and again 22Mar06. Ferried Southend-Coventry 02May06 still in Magic Blue c/s for preparation for MagicBird Ailines NV. By 09Jun06 named "Brandon". Regn **PH-MGB** rsvd to Magic Bird Airlines NV 07Sep06. Last flew 24May07 and stored Coventry. Sold European Turboprop Management AB for operation by West Atlantic AB Dec09. Regd European Turboprop Management AB as **G-BTPL** 18Jan11 (CofR G-BTPL/R6) but remains in store Coventry. Moved to the 'Airbase' compound for static display mid Jan15, intact but without engines or propellers.

TT 16,170 hrs, 19,000 ldgs

2043 (43)

Regd as **G-BTPM** to British Aerospace plc - Airlines Division 19Nov91 (CofR G-BTPM/R1). F/f 29Nov91 in British Airways c/s. CofA issued 11Dec91. Del Glasgow as BA8972P 13Dec91. Entered service as BA5731 from Glasgow to Manchester 16Dec91. Regd British Airways plc 22Jun92 (CofR G-BTPM/R2). Named "Strathrory". Flew last service as BA5730 from Manchester to Glasgow 26Nov96. Ferried Glasgow-East Midlands as BA5653E 13Dec96 on return BAe. Ferried Woodford as **G-11-2043** 23Jan97. Regd to Trident Aviation Leasing Services (Jersey) Ltd 12Feb97 (CofR G-BTPM/R3). Painted in Air Europa Express c/s. Lsd Canarias Regional Air SA with del ex Woodford 06Apr97. Regn cld 07Apr97 as transferred Spain and regd **EC-GNI**. Lse transferred Air Europa Express Líneas Aéreas SA and re-regd **EC-GSH** 23Jan98. Damaged Palma 06Apr98 after diversion when nosewheel failed to fully retract after taking off from Barcelona for Bilbao. Repaired by 26Jun98. Rear fuselage damaged after struck by GPU at Madrid 25Jul01. Company ceased operations and was put into voluntary liquidation 29Oct01. Stored Madrid. Ferried Madrid-Woodford

20Dec01. Restored as **G-BTPM** to Trident Aviation Leasing Services (Jersey) Ltd 18Jan02 (CofR G-BTPM/R4). Regn **SE-LPS** rsvd to Trident Aviation Leasing Services Ltd 25Feb02. Ferried Woodford-Southend as **G-BTPM** in full Air Europa Express c/s and parked 25Apr02. Painted overall white by 25Sep02. Air tested as WFD11 26Sep02 and ferried Lidköping the same day. Regn cld 27Sep02 as transferred Sweden. Regd as **SE-LPS** to Trident Aviation Leasing Services (Jersey) Ltd 11Oct02. Lsd West Air Sweden AB for operation as a pax aircraft. Entered service 15Nov02. Ferried Bucharest-Băneasa 20Jan04 for fitment of a Large Rear Freight Door. On completion, ferried from Băneasa to Malmö-Sturup 20Aug04 and onwards to Lidköping 25Aug04 for conversion to an E-class freight and JAA version. Entered service 13Dec04. Regn cld 14Jan05. Transferred West Air Luxembourg SA as **LX-WAO** and del 18Jan05. Restored as **SE-LPS** to JAHLXWAO, LLC for operation by West Air Sweden AB 14Nov13.

2044 (44)

Regd as **G-BTPN** to British Aerospace plc - Airlines Division 19Nov91 (CofR G-BTPN/R1). F/f 13Dec91 in British Airways c/s, CofA issued 20Dec91. Del Manchester as BA8979P 23Dec91 and entered service as BA5611 from Manchester to Glasgow the same day. Regd British Airways plc 22Jun92 (CofR G-BTPN/R2). Named "Strathbrora". Flew last service as BA5892 from Birmingham to Glasgow 06Dec96. Ferried Glasgow-East Midlands 17Jan97 on return BAe. Ferried East Midlands-Woodford 03Feb97 in Air Europa Express c/s. Regd to Trident Aviation Leasing Services (Jersey) Ltd 12Feb97 (CofR G-BTPN/R3). Lsd Canarias Regional Air SA with del from Woodford to Palma 18Apr97. Regn cld 18Apr97 as transferred Spain and regd **EC-GNJ**. Lse transferred Air Europa Express Líneas Aéreas SA and re-regd **EC-GSI** by 05Feb98. Painted with additional "EXTREMADURA, Naturalmente" titles. Ferried Southend for maintenance 24Oct01. Company ceased operations and was put into voluntary liquidation 29Oct01. Stored Southend. Restored as **G-BTPN** to Trident Aviation Leasing Services (Jersey) Ltd 18Jan02 (CofR G-BTPN/R4). Ferried Southend-Zaragoza for storage 21May02. Damaged by hailstorm 08Jul02. Ferried Exeter 21Mar03 for repair. Entered hangar 15Nov03. Work completed 01May04 and returned to storage with repaired sections in primer. Ferried Southend 29Oct04 and ferried Norwich 04Nov04. R/o after repaint overall white 13Nov04. Ferried Norwich-Kemble for long term storage 19Nov04. Ferried Southend 16Feb07 for maintenance. Ferried Southend-Lidköping 15Jun07 for conversion E-class freight & JAA version and increased AUW mods on behalf of BAE Systems. Completed and stored by Nov07. Regn **SE-MAY** rsvd to West Air Sweden AB 14Mar08. UK regn cld 17Dec08 as transferred Sweden. Regd as **SE-MAY** to Trident Aviation Leasing Services (Jersey) Ltd 10Dec09 after air test the same day. Entered service 11Dec09. Regd European Turboprop Management AB 17Nov11. Regd Erik Thun AB 09Jan12. Regd European Turboprop Management AB 12Jun13. Stored Malmö 30Dec15 and engineless by 28Feb16.

TT 19,659 hrs, 21,932 ldgs

2045 (45)

Regd as **G-LOGB** to British Aerospace plc - Airlines Division 11Dec91 (CofR G-LOGB/R1). F/f 18Dec91 as **G-11-045** in primer. R/o Woodford in Loganair c/s 22Jan92 and f/f as such 10Feb92. CofA issued 27Feb92. Del Manchester 28Feb92. Regd Loganair Ltd 20Mar92 (CofR G-LOGB/R2). Regd Manx Airlines (Europe) Ltd 29Mar94 (CofR G-LOGB/R3). Re-regd as **G-MANE** 07Jun94 (CofR G-MANE/R1). Painted in Manx Airlines c/s at Woodford 29Jun/01Jul94. Painted in British Airways Express c/s at Woodford 25Mar to 02Apr95. Operator renamed British Airways CitiExpress Ltd from 31Mar02. Regd FlyBe Leasing Ltd 14Jan03 (CofR G-MANE/R2). Ferried Manchester-Shannon as TH001P 27Jul03 for repaint in Union Flag c/s. Ferried Shannon-Isle of Man as TH001P 04Aug03 on completion. Flew last revenue flight as BA4410 from Manchester to the Isle of Man 26Mar04. Ferried Isle of Man to Southend as TH002P 28Mar04 for storage. Regd BA Connect Ltd 07Feb06. Regn **SE-MAL** rsvd to West Air Sweden AB 13Jul06. Lsd West Air Sweden and ferried Southend-Lidköping 15Dec06 for storage. UK regn cld by the CAA 16Jul07. Regd European Turboprop Management AB as SE-MAL 09Oct08 for operation by NEX Time Jet AB as a pax aircraft. Ferried Lidkoping-Southend for repaint 11Oct08. Painted in same colours as c/n 2040 and ferried back to Lidkoping 20Oct08 for completion of interior refit. Ferried Arlanda 26Oct08 and entered service the same day as 2N778 from Arlanda to Hemevan via Vilhelmina. Regd Erik Thun AB 21Nov08. Noted Arlanda 12Dec08 in full Next Jet c/s with additional 'Arvidsjaurs Idol Kevin' titles to promote a TV programme entitled "Idol 2008". Lsd Golden Air Flyg AB 16/24Jan11. Operated on behalf of Flysmåland AB from 11Mar12 to 19Mar12, from 04Apr12 to 11Apr12 and again from 25/30Apr12. Inaugurated service on the Halmstad-Arlanda route on 02May12 on behalf of Kullaflyg AB.

2046   (46)

Regd as **G-BTZG** to British Aerospace plc - Airlines Division 11Dec91 (G-BTZG/R1). Regn **PK-MAA** reportedly rsvd. Initially painted in Merpati c/s as **PK-MTV**. F/f 14Feb92 as **G-BTZG**. Regn cld 24Feb92 as transferred Indonesia. Del Merpati Nusantara Airlines PT as **PK-MTV** 25Feb92 named "Sipora". Displayed at Asian Aerospace Show Singapore Feb92. H/o 28Feb92. In service 04Mar92. Stored Jakarta by 04Dec97. Ferried Woodford 14Sep99 on return BAe. Restored to Trident Aviation Leasing Services (Jersey) Ltd as **G-BTZG** 03Dec99 (G-BTZG/R2) but remained in store Woodford still painted as PK-MTV. Painted as G-BTZG by 02Jul04. Sold West Air Sweden AB Apr08 for recovery of spares. Break-up started week ending 18Jul08 with removal nose section. Scrapped 11/12Aug08. Regn cld as PWFU 27Mar09.   ***TT 8,372 hrs, 7,456 ldgs***

2047   (47)

Regd as **G-BTZH** to British Aerospace plc - Airlines Division 11Dec91 (G-BTZH/R1). Regn **PK-MAC** reportedly rsvd. Initially painted in Merpati c/s with regn **PK-MTW** Feb92. F/f 13Mar92 as **G-BTZH**. Regn cld 30Mar92 as transferred Indonesia. Del Merpati Nusantara Airlines PT as **PK-MTW** 31Mar92 named "Pulau Laut". Struck GPU at Palembang 16Dec92. Repaired. Stored Jakarta by 04Dec97. Ferried through Muscat arriving East Midlands 02Apr01. Ferried Woodford for storage 03Apr01. Restored to Trident Aviation Leasing Services (Jersey) Ltd as **G-BTZH** 02May01 (G-BTZH/R2) but remained in store Woodford still painted as PK-MTW. Painted as G-BTZH by 02Jul04. Sold West Air Sweden AB Apr08 for recovery of spares. Nose section removed and finally scrapped 12Aug08. Regn cld as PWFU 02Sep08.   ***TT 6,690 hrs, 6,039 ldgs***

2048   (48)

Regd as **G-BTZI** to British Aerospace plc - Airlines Division 11Dec91 (G-BTZI/R1). Reg **PK-MAD** reportedly rsvd. F/f 04Apr92 as G-BTZI in primer. Painted in Merpati c/s as **PK-MTX** by 20Apr92. **G-BTZI** painted over for testing. Regn cld 29Apr92 as transferred Indonesia. Del Merpati Nusantara Airlines PT as **PK-MTX** 30Apr92 named "Sangeang". W/o 19Apr97 6km short of Buluh Tumbang Airport, Belitung. 4 crew and 11 pax killed, 1 crew and 37 pax survived.
          TT 9,082 hrs, 8,895 ldgs

2049   (49)

Regd as **G-BTZJ** to British Aerospace plc - Airlines Division 11Dec91 (G-BTZJ/R1). Regn **PK-MAE** reportedly rsvd. F/f 01May92 as G-BTZJ in primer. Painted in Merpati c/s as **PK-MTY** by 13May92. Marked as **G-BTZJ** for testing. Regn cld 01Jun92 as transferred Indonesia. Del Merpati Nusantara Airlines

PT as **PK-MTY** 02Jun92 named "Selayar". Stored Jakarta by 04Dec97. Ferried Woodford on return BAe 11Aug99. Restored to British Aerospace (Operations) Ltd as **G-BTZJ** 25Aug99 (G-BTZJ/R2) but remained in store Woodford as PK-MTY. Regd BAE Systems (Operations) Ltd 02Mar00. Regd Trident Aviation Leasing Services (Jersey) Ltd 31May00 (G-BTZJ/R3). F/f in SATA Air Açores c/s 06Jul00. Regn cld 31Jul00 as transferred Portugal. Lsd SATA Air Açores as **CS-TGY** with del ex Woodford 01Aug00. Ferried Southend for repaint in SATA's new c/s 20Mar05. R/o 28Mar05 and returned SATA. Sold Regional One Inc of Miami, FL, USA Jun09 and lse to SATA Air Açores continued until ferried from Ponta del Garda to Norwich via Oporto as SP001P 23Apr10. Painted overall white and ferried Southend 06May10 as SP001P for storage. Engines removed by 17Mar16 and moved to AERS scrapping area 04Apr16 after sale to West Atlantic for reduction to spares.
          TT 18,513 hrs, 32,907 ldgs

2050   (50)

Regd as **G-BTZK** to British Aerospace plc - Airlines Division 11Dec91 (G-DTZK/R1). Regn **PK-MAF** reportedly rsvd. F/f 28May92 as G-BTZK in primer. Painted in Merpati c/s and flown 10Jun92. Shown statically at ILA '92 Berlin Air Show with show No.'88S' 12-21Jun92. Flown at Woodford Air Show 27Jun92. Regn cld 06Jul92 as transferred Indonesia. H/o Merpati Nusantara Airlines PT as **PK-MTZ** 06Jul92 named "Numfoor". Del 07Jul92. Stored Jakarta by 04Dec97. Ferried Woodford 25Apr00 and put in store. Restored as **G-BTZK** to Trident Aviation Leasing Services (Jersey) Ltd 16Aug01 (G-BTZK/R2) but remained in store Woodford still painted as PK-MTZ. Painted as G-BTZK by 02Jul04. Sold West Air Sweden AB Apr08 for recovery of spares. Nose section removed by 08Aug08 and finally scrapped 12-13Aug08. Regn cld as PWFU 02Sep08.
          TT 6,838 hrs, 5,958 ldgs

2051   (51)

Regd as **G-BTPO** to British Aerospace plc Airlines Division 10Jun92 (CofR G-BTPO/R1). Regd to British Airways plc 22Jun92 (G-BTPO/R2). F/f 22Jul92 in British Airways c/s, CofA issued 29Jul92. Del Glasgow as BA8930P 30Jul92. Entered service as BA5848 from Glasgow to Belfast 31Jul92. Named "Strathclyde". Flew last revenue flight as BA1661 from Manchester to Glasgow 01Dec98. Ferried Glasgow-Woodford as BA1551P 16Mar99 at end lse. Regd Trident Aviation Leasing Services (Jersey) Ltd 08Jun99 (G-BTPO/R3). Painted as **G-OBWP** in British World Airlines c/s and noted Woodford 31Aug99. Re-regd G-OBWP 08Oct99 (G-OBWP/R1). Del British World Airlines Ltd at Southend 03Dec99. Regd British World Airlines Ltd 12Jan00 (G-OBWP/R2). Lsd Brit Air 20Apr to 01May00. Lsd Binter Canarias S.A summer 2001. Flew last service from Stornoway to Aberdeen as BWL3493 13Dec01. Company ceased operations 13Dec01. Ferried Aberdeen-Woodford 21Dec01 for storage. Regd Trident Aviation Leasing Services (Jersey) Ltd 05Feb02 (G-OBWP/R3). Ferried Zaragoza for storage in full British World c/s 01Mar02. Damaged by hailstorm 08Jul02. Ferried Exeter 07Feb03 for further storage. Into hangar for repair mid Aug04. Ferried Exeter-Southend 02Feb06. R/o Southend in First Flight Couriers Pvt Ltd c/s 16Feb06 with incorrect Indian marks **VT-FFA** taped over. Ferried Southend-Lidköping 29Mar06 for conversion to E-class freight and JAA version and increased A.U.W mods on behalf of BAE Systems. Ferried Lidköping-Southend 23Aug06. Air tested 21Sep06 and lsd First Flight Couriers Pvt Ltd with del Southend-Brindisi 19Oct06 en route India. Regn cld 25Oct06 as transferred India and regd as **VT-FFC** to Trident Aviation Leasing Services (Jersey) Ltd 31Oct06. WFU 31Aug07 and stored Bangalore. Restored as **G-OBWP** to Trident Aviation Leasing Services (Jersey) Ltd 20Feb09 (G-OBWP/R4). Ferried ex Bangalore-Hosur via Muscat, Sharm el-Sheikh and Dubrovnik arriving Southend 12Mar09 in full FFC c/s. Ferried Coventry 28Mar09 for care and maintenance. Sold European

G-BTZG c/n 2046 of Merpati lAirlines PT in February 1992. The aircraft would become PK-MTV for delivery later that month. (WHC/BAe)

Turboprop Management AB for possible future operation by West Atlantic AB Dec09. Regd European Turboprop Management AB 09Jan12 (G-OBWP/R5).

TT 12,522 Hrs, 13,407 ldgs

2052   (52)

Regd as **G-BUKJ** to British Aerospace plc - Regional Aircraft 05Aug92 (CofR G-BUKJ/R1). F/f 24Aug92 in THT c/s. Regd Trident Aviation Leasing Services (Jersey) Ltd 01Sep92 (CofR G-BUKJ/R2). Shown at Farnborough Air Show 04/11Sep92. Regn cld 16Sep92 as transferred Turkey. Del Turk Hava Tasimaciligi - THT as **TC-THZ** 17Sep92 named "Elazig". Ferried from Istanbul to Isle of Man 24Sep93 all white for storage on return to BAe. Restored as **G-BUKJ** to Jetstream Aircraft Ltd 12Oct93 (CofR G-BUKJ/R3) though still painted as TC-THZ 31Oct93. Regd to Trident Aviation Leasing services (Jersey) Ltd 03Nov93 (CofR G-BUKJ/R4). Ferried Woodford all white as G-BUKJ 06Apr94. Painted in EuroDirect c/s as **G-OEDF** by 21Apr94. Reverted to **G-BUKJ** for flight testing. Del EuroDircct Airlines Ltd 28Jun94. Regd as **G-OEDF** to EuroDirect Airlines Ltd 30Jun94 (CofR G-OEDF/R1). Inaugurated Berne to Gatwick service as EUD357 04Jul94. Returned BAc at Woodford for storage 27Feb95 after EuroDirect ceased trading 26Feb95. Regd Trident Aviation Leasing Services (Jersey) Ltd 28Mar95 (CofR G-OEDF/R2). R/o all white at Woodford 13May95. Painted in Air Europa Express c/s by 20Dec96. Regn cld 28Feb97 as transferred Spain. Lsd Canarias Regional Air SA as **EC-GLD** with del Woodford-Palma 01Mar97. Ferried Palma-Woodford for maintenance 16Oct97. Returned Woodford-Palma 30Oct97. Painted in new Canarias Regional c/s 1998. Ferried Woodford at end lse 16Feb99. Restored as **G-BUKJ** to BAe (Operations) Ltd 10Mar99 (CofR G-BUKJ/R5). Painted in Air Europa Express c/s Apr99. Regn cld 08May99 as transferred Spain and regd **EC-HCO**. Del Air Europa Express Líneas Aéreas SA 08May99. Later named "Rafael Alberti". Company ceased operations and was put into voluntary liquidation 29Oct01. Stored Palma. Had been ferried Zaragoza for further storage by 11Jan02. Restored as **G-BUKJ** to Trident Aviation Leasing Services (Jersey) Ltd 18Jan02 (CofR G-BUKJ/R6). Damaged by hailstorm 08Jul02. Ferried Southend 28Apr04 and noted on hail damage repair 01Oct04 still in Air Europa Express c/s. R/o 10Dec04 and ferried Southcnd-Exeter 13Dec04 for conversion to E-class freight & JAA version. Regn **PH-MJL** rsvd to MagicBlue Airlines NV 01Oct04. Returned Exeter-Southend 26Aug05 in Air Europa Express/primer c/s. Moved into Air Livery hangar for repaint in MagicBlue c/s 07Sep05. R/o 12Sep05. Air-tested in full MagicBlue Airlines c/s 29Sep05 with UK regn taped on. MagicBlue titles removed and flown from Southend to Stockholm-Arlanda and back for cargo loading trials 21Feb06. Ferried Southend-Coventry 03Mar06 for pre-service maintenance. Lsd MagicBird Airlines NV and entered service 13Apr06 from Stockholm-Arlanda with MagicBird Cargo titles. By 09Jun06 named "Fabian". Regn **PH-MGC** rsvd to Magic Bird Airlines NV 07Sep06. Flying controls damaged by storm on ground East Midlands 18Jan07. Repaired and returned to service 16Apr07. Last flew 24May07 and stored Marseille. Ferried from Marseille to Băncasa 14Sep07 where seen in external storage 30Oct07. Sold Regional One Inc of Miami, USA late Dec09. Regn cld as transferred USA 21Dec10. Still present at Băneasa 31Oct13. Sold to PTB (Emerald) Pty Ltd and restored to them as **G-BUKJ** 07Jan14 (CofR G-BUKJ/R7). Air tested 09Dec14. Regn cld as transferred Indonesia 09Jan15. Noted painted overall white as **PK-DGC** 19Jan15. Del Deraya PT from Băneasa via Trabzon and Kuwait 22Jan15.

TT in excess of 11,282 hrs, 11,678 ldgs (figures at 24May07)

2053   (53)

F/f 09Sep92 as **G-11-053** in primer. Del Teesside 13Jan93 for storage. Returned Woodford 17Mar93. Regd as **G-BUWP** to British Aerospace plc - Jetstream Aircraft 30Mar93 (CofR G-BUWP/R1). F/f as G-BUWP 14Apr93 painted all white with British Airways titles. Ferried Waddington 23Apr93. Ferried Woodford 30Jul93. Lsd British Airways and h/o 13Aug93 with del Glasgow as BA8944P the same day painted overall white with British Airways titles. Entered service as BA5708 from Glasgow to Aberdeen 13Aug93. Regd to British Airways plc 17Aug93 (CofR G-BUWP/R2). Operated BA5815 from Benbecula to Glasgow 04Jun94 prior to ferry Heathrow for painting in full British Airways c/s as BA5646E 29Jun94. R/o 04Jul94 and ferried Glasgow as BA5648E 05Jul94. Ferried Glasgow-Inverness as BA5690P and re-entered service as BA5830 from Inverness to Stornoway 11Jul94. Named "Strathisla" by Jun95. Flew last revenue flight as BA1560A from Manchester to Glasgow 25Jan99. Air tested Glasgow as BA1558E 15Apr99 and ferried Woodford as BA1550P the same date at end lse. Regd Trident Jet (Jersey) Ltd 08Jun99 (CofR G-BUWP/R3). Painted as **G-OBWR** in full British World Airlines c/s and noted Woodford 05Oct99. Re-regd G-OBWR 08Oct99 (CofR G-OBWR/R1). Del British World Airlines Ltd at Southend 08Dec99. Regd British World Airlines Ltd 12Jan00 (CofR G-OBWR/R2). Operated for Crossair 31Jan to 21Mar00, Valkanair 07/13Apr00 and European Regions Air 27Apr to 03May00. Lsd SATA Air Açores 14-28May01. Flew last service as BWL506 from Scatsta to Abcrdeen 06Dec01. Company ceased operations 13Dec01. Regd Trident Jet (Jersey) Ltd 05Feb02 (CofR G-OBWR/R3). Ferried Aberdeen-Zaragoza for storage 13Feb02. Damaged by hailstorm 08Jul02. Ferried Zaragoza-Southend 18Dec02 for hail damage repair. Repair completed, painted overall white and stored. Regn **SE-MAR** rsvd to West Air Sweden AB 16Aug06. Lsd West Air Sweden and ferried Southend-Lidköping 02Jan07 for conversion E-class freight & JAA version. Regn cld 26Apr07 as transferred Sweden. Regd as SE-MAR to Trident Jet (Jersey) Ltd 27Apr07. Entered service 02May07 painted overall white without titles. Due for fitment of LFD at some future date. Planned transfer to West Air Luxembourg as **LX-WAG** abandoned. Regd European Turboprop Management AB 20Jun13.

2054   (54)

F/f 08Oct92 as **G-11-054** in primer and used for flight testing with new rudder settings and stall warning system. Ferried Teesside 13Jan93 for storage. Ferried Waddington 10Mar93 for further storage. Ferried Prestwick 30Mar93. Positioned Woodford 27Aug93. Regd as **G-LOGF** to British Aerospace plc - Jetstream Aircraft 31Aug93 (CofR G-LOGF/R1). Painted in Loganair c/s at Woodford Sep93. F/f as G-LOGF 14Oct93. CofA issued 21Oct93. Del Loganair Ltd 21Oct93. Regd Loganair Ltd 21Oct93 (CofR G-LOGF/R2). Transferred Manx Airlines and regd Manx Airlines (Europe) Ltd 29Mar94 (CofR G-LOGF/R3). Ferried Woodford 27Jun94 and painted in interim Manx Airlines c/s. Ferried Woodford - Belfast as MNX101P 29Jun94. Regd as **G-MANC** to British Regional Airlines Ltd 07Nov94 (CofR G-MANC/R1). Ferried East Midlands 07Dec94. Painted in Manx Airlines full c/s and departed East Midlands 11Dec94. Ferried Southend 02Dec98. R/o Southend in Manx Airlines new c/s 08Dec98. Operator renamed British Airways CitiExpress Ltd from 31Mar02. Ferried Glasgow-Southend for repaint in Union Flag c/s 09Jul02. Ferried Southend-Isle of Man 25Aug02 as BRT062 and returned to service 26Aug02 as JE329 from Isle of Man to Manchester. Regd to British Airways CitiExpress Ltd 24Dec02 (CofR G-MANC/R2). Flew last revenue service as BA7822 from Stansted to Manchester 28Mar03. Ferried Southend as TH005P 29Mar03 and put in storage. Air tested Southend as WFD001 25Aug03. Returned lessor 01Sep03. Regd Trident Aviation Leasing Services (Jersey) Ltd 24Nov03 (CofR G-MANC/R3). Was due to be the second aircraft for Asian Spirit but ntu. Regn **SE-KXO** rsvd for West Air Sweden AB 10Dec04 but ntu. Painted overall white 22-27Sep05. Ferried Southend-Lidköping 14Nov05 for conversion to E-class freight, JAA version and increased A.U.W mods on behalf of BAE Systems. Due for lease to First Flight Couriers Pvt Ltd of India. Painted in First Flight c/s by 20Mar06 at Lidköping by Northern Aircraft Painting Services AB (napsab) but without titles. By the same date had carried out two air-tests for its Export CofA which was issued on 29Mar06. H/o BAE on completion 24Apr06. Ferried

Lidköping-Southend 24May06 as G-MANC taped over VT-FFA. Del ex Southend via Brindisi 02Jun06. Regn cld 07Jun06 as transferred India and regd as **VT-FFA** to Trident Aviation Leasing Services (Jersey) Ltd 09Jun06 for operation by First Flight Couriers Pvt Ltd. WFU 31Aug07 and stored Bangalore. Restored as **G-MANC** to Trident Aviation Leasing Services (Jersey) Ltd 20Feb09 (CofR G-MANC/R4). Ferried ex Bangalore-Hosur via Muscat, Sharm el-Sheikh and Dubrovnik arriving Southend 14Mar09 for further storage in full FFC c/s. Ferried Coventry 27Mar09 for care and maintenance. Sold European Turboprop Management AB for operation by West Atlantic AB Dec09. Regd European Turboprop Management AB 09Jan12 (G-MANC/R5) but remains in store.

TT 15,491 hrs, 22,803 ldgs

2055 (55)

F/f 30Oct92 as **G-11-055** in primer. R/o 15Mar93 as **G-JATP** in Jetstream Aircraft demonstrator c/s. Later had Jetstream ATP titles added. Regd as G-JATP to British Aerospace plc - Jetstream Aircraft 30Mar93 (CofR G-JATP/R1). F/f as G-JATP 16Apr93 after fitment of an APU. C/o Middle and Far East sales tour from 26Apr to 05Jun93. Shown Paris Air Show Jun93 with show No.'227'. APU removed. Painted in Loganair c/s at Woodford Aug93. Re-regd **G-LOGG** 08Sep93 (CofR G-LOGG/R1) and f/f as such 21Sep93. CofA issued 27Sep93. Regd to Loganair Ltd 27Sep93 (CofR G-LOGG/R2) with del the same day. Noted flying with Manx Airlines titles 19Mar94. Transferred Manx Airlines and regd Manx Airlines (Europe) Ltd 29Mar94 (CofR G-LOGG/R3). Painted in Manx Airlines c/s at Woodford 23-25May94. Re-regd **G-MANB** 14Sep94 (CofR G-MANB/R1). Painted in Manx Airlines new c/s at Southend 07-15Feb99. Operator renamed British Airways CitiExpress Ltd from 31Mar02. Flew last service in Manx c/s as JE305 from Isle of Man to Gatwick 22May02. Ferried Southend the same day as TH061P. R/o in British Airways Union Flag c/s 02Jun02 and ferried Manchester as TH061P the same day. Returned to service as BA4145 from Manchester to Aberdeen 03Jun02. Regd to British Airways CitiExpress Ltd 24Dec02 (CofR G-MANB/R2). Flew last revenue service as BA4346 from Liverpool to the Isle of Man 08Aug03. Ferried Southend as TH004P 10Aug03 for storage. Air tested as TH001T 23Sep03. Returned lessor 01Oct03. Regd Trident Aviation Leasing Services (Jersey) Ltd 19Nov03 (CofR G-MANB/R3). Painted in Asian Spirit c/s with regn RP-C2786 for publicity 24Nov03. Lsd Asian Spirit Airlines and del ex Southend via Heraklion 02Dec03 with G-MANB taped over Philippine regn. UK regn cld 08Dec03 as transferred Philippines and regd **RP-C2786**. WFU early May07. Regd Lionair Inc 08Jul08. Due for lse Air Aceh of Indonesia through Regional One Inc of Miami, FL, USA Apr09 and painted in Air Aceh's full c/s and stored Manila. Still present 11Feb13 but without titles.

TT 19,507 hrs, 27,687 ldgs

2056 (56)

F/f 23Nov92 as **G-11-056** in primer. Ferried Teesside 23Dec92 for storage. Ferried Waddington 11Feb93 for further storage. Regd as **G-LOGH** to British Aerospace plc - Jetstream Aircraft 31Aug93 (CofR G-LOGH/R1). Ferried Woodford 28Sep93 as **G-11-056**. Ferried Prestwick 17Jan94. Returned Woodford for paint. Re-regd as G-MANA to Jetstream Aircraft Ltd 21Feb94 (CofR G-MANA/R1). Ferried to Prestwick in Loganair c/s with Manx titles as G-MANA 25Feb94. CofA issued 22Mar94. Del 23Mar94. Regd Manx Airlines (Europe) Ltd 23Mar94 (CofR G-MANA/R2). Painted in Manx Airlines new c/s at Southend ??/07Feb99. Operator renamed British Airways CitiExpress Ltd from 31Mar02. Ferried Southend 06May02 as TH061P. R/o in British Airways Union Flag c/s 20May02 and ferried Manchester the same day. Regd to British Airways CitiExpress Ltd 24Dec02 (CofR G-MANA/R3). Flew last revenue service as BA4382 from Birmingham to Isle of Man 31Oct03 and ferried Southend as TH001E the same date for storage. Air tested as BRT081E 02Dec03. Regd Trident Aviation Leasing Services (Jersey) Ltd

15Jan04 (CofR G-MANA/R4). Regn **SE-KXP** rsvd for West Air Sweden AB 10Dec04. Ferried Southend to Bucharest-Băneasa 11Dec04 for fitment of Large Freight Door for lse to West Air Sweden AB. Noted Băneasa 13Apr05 with Large Freight Door fitted and rear service door removed and area sealed over in British Airways c/s. Ferried Băneasa-Southend 06May05 for repaint. R/o in full West Air Europe c/s 25May05 with G-MANA taped over Swedish marks. Ferried Southend-Lidköping 06Jun05 for conversion to an E-class freight and JAA version and have the increased MTOW mods carried out. UK regn cld 06Jul05 as transferred Sweden. Regd as **SE-KXP** to Trident Aviation Leasing Services (Jersey) Ltd 26Sep05. In service 02Oct05. Ferried Oslo to Isle of Man 27Jul11 for maintenance. Noted painted as **LX-WAF** 19Aug11 after r/o Isle of Man. Swedish regn cld as exported Luxembourg 25Aug11. Ferried Isle of Man to Luxembourg as WLX428B 31Aug11 for operation by West Air Luxembourg SA. Restored as **SE-KXP** to Eric Thun AB 15May13 for operations by West Air Sweden AB. Regd European Turboprop Management AB 30May13.

2057 (57)

F/f 15Dec92 as **G-11-057** in primer. Ferried Teesside 23Dec92 for storage. Ferried Waddington 11Feb93 for further storage. Ferried Prestwick-Teesside as PWK11 for further storage 27Sep95. Ferried Prestwick as PWK03 09Sep96 with wheels down for preparation for frustrated sale to Líneas Aéreas Privadas Argentinas (LAPA). Ferried Prestwick-Woodford 03Jul97 for painting in British World c/s as **G-OBWL** and noted as such 22Jul97. Reverted to **G-11-057** and returned Prestwick 24Jul97. CofA issued 26Sep97. Del Southend for crew training 26Sep97 the same day as regd as **G-OBWL** to British World Airlines Ltd (CofR G-OBWL/R1). Lsd Air Nostrum 25Oct-21Dec97. Lsd KLM exel 15Mar to 03Apr98. Lsd Debonair Ltd 12-19Apr98. Lsd Air France 20Apr98 to 01Jun98 and 05-30Jun98. Lsd Jersey European Airways Ltd 05-11Jul98. Lsd Binter Mediterraneo SA 02Dec98 to 10Jan99. R/o Southend 01Apr99 in full CityJet c/s with "Midland Cities Express" titles. Ferried Southend-East Midlands 04Apr99 on lse CityJet Ltd. Returned British World 30Sep99 and based Aberdeen from 04Oct99 still in full CityJet c/s on oil related charter work. Ferried Southend 31Oct99 for repaint. R/o in full British World Airlines Ltd c/s 04Nov99. Flew last service as BWL510 from Scatsta to Aberdeen 13Dec01. Company ceased operations 13Dec01. Ferried Aberdeen-Southend 14Feb02 for maintenance. Sold West Air Sweden AB and ferried Southend-Lidköping 26Apr02 for conversion to E-class freighter. Regn cld 05Jun02 as transferred Sweden with regn **SE-LPR** rsvd although **SE-LNX** had been earlier rsvd to European Executive Express AB 19Apr02. Regd as SE-LPR to European Turboprop Management (Bermuda) Ltd 12Sep02. Conversion to E-class freight and JAA version completed 13Sep02. Entered service 16Sep02 in British World c/s without titles. Ferried Skövde-Southend as PT900 30Jul03 for repaint in full West Air c/s. On completion ferried to Lidköping as PT901 06Aug03 with West Air Europe titles. Transferred West Air Luxembourg SA 27May05 when Swedish regn cld. Noted Amsterdam as **LX-WAP** the following day. Ferried Glasgow-Southend as WLX503 09Feb07 for 'C' Check with Inflite. Ferried Southend to Paris-Charles de Gaulle as WXP491 on 02Mar07 on completion of maintenance. Restored as **SE-LPR** to JAHLXWAP, LLC for ops by West Air Sweden AB 04Oct13.

2058 (58)

F/f 29Jan93 as **G-11-058** in primer. Ferried Waddington 03Mar93 for storage. Ferried Prestwick 30Mar93. Ferried Prestwick-Teesside as PWK11 for further storage 25Sep95. Ferried Prestwick as PWK01 11Sep96 for preparation for frustrated sale to Líneas Aéreas Privadas Argentinas (LAPA). Ferried Prestwick-Woodford 29Sep97. Into paint shop 06Oct97. Painted in British World c/s and noted painted as **G-OBWM** 13Oct97. Ferried Prestwick as G-11-058 28Oct97. Returned Woodford 19Dec97. Regd as G-OBWM to British World Airlines Ltd 22Dec97 (CofR

G-OBWM/R1) with CofA issued the same date. Del Southend 23Dec97 on lse. Lsd Air France 28Mar to 05Apr98. Lsd KLM exel 05-24Apr98. Lsd Debonair Ltd 29Apr to 12Jun98 and 19-22Jun98. Lsd Air Nostrum 23Jun to 16Jul98. Lsd Swiftair SA of Spain 06Dec98 to 31Jan99. Lsd Air Baltic 28Feb99 to 06Mar99. Lsd CityJet Ltd 27Mar to 04Apr99. Lsd Jersey European Airlines Ltd with del Southend-Guernsey 06Apr99. Flew last service as BWL512 from Scatsta to Aberdeen 13Dec01. Company ceased operations 13Dec01. Ferried from Aberdeen to Västerås, Sweden 27Feb02 on sale European Executive Express. Regn **SE-LNY** rsvd to European Executive Express AB 19Apr02 but ntu. Sold West Air Sweden AB with regn **SE-LPT** rsvd. Ferried from Västerås to Lidköping 12Dec02 for E-class freight and JAA version mods. UK regn cld 17Dec02 as transferred Sweden. Conversion completed 09Jul03 when regd to Gladsheim Aviation Finance AB as SE-LPT. Ferried Southend 13Jul03 for repaint in West Air c/s. On completion ferried Southend-Lidköping as PT901 21Jul03 with West Air Europe titles and entered service the same day. Ferried Malmö-Southend as PT994 for C Check 09Mar07. Ferried Southend-Lidköping as PT900 16May07 on completion. Regn cld 04Sep07. Transferred West Air Luxembourg SA as **LX-WAS** and noted Glasgow as such 20Sep07. Restored as **SE-LPT** to European Turboprop Management AB for ops by West Air Sweden AB 18Oct13.

2059   (59)

F/f 19Feb93 as **G-11-059** in primer. Used for development tests at Woodford. Regd as **G-BVEO** to British Aerospace plc - Jetstream Aircraft 12Oct93 (CofR G-BVEO/R1). Ferried ex Prestwick to Iceland for icing trials 30Oct93 to 01Nov93 and 17Jan94 before returning Woodford 15Feb94. To Prestwick 25Mar94. Regd to Jetstream Aircraft Ltd 02Dec94 (CofR G-BVEO/R2). Ferried Prestwick-Teesside as PWK11 for storage 02Oct95. Ferried Prestwick as PWK06 17Sep96 for preparation for frustrated sale to Líneas Aéreas Privadas Argentinas (LAPA). Regn cld as PWFU 09Jun97 but restored to Jetstream Aircraft Ltd 12Jun97 (CofR BVEO/R3). Regn cld as PWFU 30Jul97. Storage continued Prestwick. Ferried Woodford 16Dec97 for further storage still painted as G-BVEO. Reportedly the second aircraft for Ireland Airways Ltd but ntu. R/o Woodford in full British World c/s as **G-11-059** 15Sep98. Del British World Airways Ltd as BWL01P from Woodford to Southend 22Dec98 as **G-OBWN**, being regd as such to British World Airlines Ltd the same date (CofR G-OBWN/R1). Lsd Jersey European Airlines Ltd 27Mar99. Op for Valkanair 06-12Apr00. Company ceased operations 13Dec01. Stored Southend. Ferried Southend-Lidköping 08Mar02 on sale West Air Sweden AB for E-class freight and JAA version mods. Regn cld 13Mar02 as transferred Sweden with regn **SE-LHZ** rsvd. Regd as SE-LHZ to ABB Credit Finans AB 26Apr02 for operation by West Air Sweden AB. Ferried Southend as SE-LHZ 26Apr02 for painting in West Air Sweden c/s. R/o in full West Air Sweden Cargo c/s 02May02. Returned Lidköping 03May02. Entered service 06May02. Regd Gladsheim Aviation Finance AB 01Nov02. Regn **LX-WAL** rsvd for West Air Luxembourg SA. Swedish regn cld 19Dec03 and regd LX-WAL and operated with West Air Luxembourg titles. Ferried Paris, Charles de Gaulle to Southend as WLX593 for maintenance 20Apr07. After an aborted attempt to ferry to Paris-Charles de Gaulle on 14May07 on completion of check, finally ferried Paris as WLX491 15May07. Flew last flight as LX-WAL 05Feb10. Restored as **SE-LHZ** to Siemens Financial Services AB 09Mar10. Regn cld 23Mar12 as exported Luxembourg. Restored as **LX-WAL**. Restored as **SE-LHZ** to European Turboprop Management AB for ops by West Air Sweden AB 24Sep13.

2060   (60)

F/f 24Mar93 as **G-11-060** in primer. Ferried Prestwick for storage 08Apr93. Ferried Teesside in primer for storage 18Sep95. Ferried Prestwick as PWK05 16Sep96 for preparation for frustrated sale to Líneas Aéreas Privadas Argentinas (LAPA). Ferried from Prestwick to Woodford 21Aug97 returning 15Sep97. Returned

Woodford 15Dec97. R/o in Ireland Airways c/s 18Dec97. Regn **EI-COS** rsvd. Ireland Airways AOC revoked 13Feb98 and aircraft not del. Painted overall white and noted Woodford 03Jun98 painted as **G-OBWO**. F/f as such 09Jun98. Regd as G-OBWO to British World Airlines Ltd 16Jun98 (CofR G-OBWO/R1) with CofA issued the same date. Del 19Jun98 still overall white. Lsd Jersey European Airways Ltd 12-26Jul98. R/o Southend in full British World c/s 25Sep98. Lsd Binter Mediterraneo 14Feb to 14Mar99. Lsd Jersey European Airways Ltd 27Mar to 06Apr99 and again from ??99 to 30Sep99. Lsd CityFlyer Express and ferried Southend to Gatwick as CFE001P 15Nov99. Entered service as CFE8047 from Gatwick to Jersey the same day. Flew last service as CFE8157 from Cork to Gatwick and returned to Southend as CFE002P 21Nov99. Operated for Crossair 04Feb to 12Mar00 and 22-25Mar00. Flew last service as BWL510 from Scatsta to Aberdeen 13Dec01. Company ceased operations 13Dec01. Ferried from Aberdeen to Västerås, Sweden 15Feb02 on sale to European Executive Express.

Regn **SE-LNZ** rsvd to European Executive Express AB 19Apr02 but ntu. UK regn cld by the CAA 04Dec02. Sold West Air Sweden AB with regn **SE-LPU** rsvd. Ferried from Västerås to Lidköping 09Dec02 for E-class freight and JAA version mods. Regd as SE-LPU to Nordea Finans Sverige AB 31Mar03. Entered service 07Apr03 in British World c/s. Ferried Malmö-Southend as PT900 21Jul03 for repaint in full West Air c/s. After completion ferried to Lidköping as PT901 30Jul03 with West Air Europe titles. Regn cld 21Jun04 and transferred to West Air Luxembourg SA as **LX-WAM** with CofA issued 25Jun04. Temporarily stored Malmö from 29Sep09. Restored as **SE-LPU** to Siemens Financial Services AB 09Dec09. Air tested 11Dec09 and entered service the following day. Regn cld 19Apr12 as exported Luxembourg and restored as **LX-WAM**. Restored as **SE-LPU** to European Turboprop Management AB for ops by West Air Sweden AB 18Oct13. Stored at Coventry 09Sep15 and still present 17Apr16, by then engineless. CofA expired 14Jan16.

TT 10,897 hrs, 11,207 ldgs

2061   (61)

F/f 06Apr93 as **G-11-061** in primer (07Apr93 also quoted). Used for development tests at Woodford. Regd as **G-BUYW** to British Aerospace plc - Jetstream Aircraft 11Jun93 (CofR G-BUYW/R1). F/f as G-BUYW 11Jun93. Icing trials in Iceland 21-23Sep93. Flown to Iceland, Greenland and the USA for further icing trials ex Woodford 28Sep93 returning 09Dec93. Returned Prestwick 31Jan94. Regd to Jetstream Aircraft Ltd 02Dec94 (CofR G-BUYW/R2). Ferried Woodford 09Jan95 and painted in Seoul Air c/s. R/o 24Jan95. Regn cld 07Mar95 as transferred South Korea and painted as **HL5227**. H/o 16Mar95. Noted crew training Woodford 29Mar95. 'Travel Bug' titles by Sep95. Returned Prestwick 11Oct96 and put in store. Restored as **G-BUYW** to Jetstream Aircraft Ltd 18Nov96 (CofR G-BUYW/R3) but remained painted as HL5227. Regd to British Aerospace (Operations) Ltd 12Jun97 (CofR G-BUYW/R4). Noted Prestwick still in store 30Jul97. Ferried Southend 12Sep97 as G-BUYW. Painted in new British Airways "Mountain of the Birds/Benyhone" c/s and r/o 19Sep97. Regn cld 23Jan98 as transferred Denmark. Del Southend-Århus 26Jan98 as OY-SVI on lse SUN-AIR of Scandinavia although not regd as such until 03Feb98.

Lsd BA CitiFlyer Express 19-22Aug02. Repainted in 'Union Flag' c/s and noted as such at Cologne 17Jan06. Last service on behalf of British Airways as BA8268 from Oslo to Billund 19Feb06 and wfu. Noted Billund 04Apr white tailed and without titles. Sold West Air Sweden AB and ferried Billund-Lidköping 24Apr06 for E-class freight and JAA version mods. Regn **SE-LNX** rsvd to West Air Sweden AB 04Jul06. Painted in same c/s as 2063 below. Regd as SE-LNX to Siemens Financial Services AB 30Aug06. Entered service 31Aug06. Regn cld as exported Luxembourg 10Nov11. Re-regd **LX-WAK**. Restored as

Seoul Air's two aircraft, HL5227 c/n 2061 and HL5228 c/n 2063, formate with each other prior to delivery from Woodford in April 1995. (WHC/BAe)

(WHC/BAe)

G-BWYT c/n 2053 of Sun-Air of Scandinavia A/S in British Airways 'Wings/Denmark' colour-scheme in November 1997. It was delivered as OY-SVU later that month.

SE-LNX to European Turboprop Management AB for ops by West Air Sweden AB 12Sep13. Arrived Isle of Man 14Feb14 and rolled our engineless on 13Mar14 for storage. Returned to hangar beginning Jun14 and returned to service mid Jun14. Ferried to Malmö as PT900 09Apr15 prior to return to service.

2062   (62)
F/f 06May93 as **G-11-062** in primer. Ferried Prestwick for storage 11Jun93. Ferried Teesside for storage 20Sep95. Ferried Prestwick as PWK06 16Sep96 for preparation for frustrated sale to Líneas Aéreas Privadas Argentinas (LAPA). Ferried Woodford for further storage 25Nov97. Moved into hangar 03Jun98. Noted flying Woodford in British Airways "Dove/Colum" c/s 11Dec98 still as G-11-062. Del SUN-AIR of Scandinavia as **OY-SVT** 16Dec98 as EZ001 although not regd as such until 28Dec98. Noted in 'Union Flag' c/s at Billund by 22Apr96. Regn **SE-LNY** rsvd to West Air Sweden AB 09May06. Operated last British Airways/Sun-Air flight as BA8242 from Edinburgh to Billund 30Jul06. Sold West Air Sweden AB and ferried Billund-Lidköping as EZ006 01Aug06 for E-class freight & JAA version mods. Regd as SE-LNY to European Turboprop Management AB 20Oct06. Entered service 30Oct06. Planned transfer to West Air Luxembourg as **LX-WAJ** abandoned. Regd to GCC Capital AB 30Apr14.

2063   (63)
F/f 25May93 as **G-11-063** in primer. Last Woodford assembled ATP. Del Biggin Hill for interior fit 11Nov93 before returning Prestwick for storage. Ferried Woodford for painting in Seoul Air c/s 20Jan95. Returned Prestwick 06Feb95. H/o Seoul Air 16Mar95. Noted crew training at Woodford 29Mar95 as **HL5228**. Del ex Woodford 07Apr95. Returned BAe at Prestwick 07Nov96. Regd as **G-BWYT** to Jetstream Aircraft Ltd 18Nov96 (CofR G-BWYT/R1) but remained stored still painted as HL5228. Regd British Aerospace (Operations) Ltd 12Jun97 (CofR G-BWYT/R2). Ferried Woodford 04Sep97 as G-BWYT still in Seoul Air c/s. Painted in new British Airways "Wings/Denmark" c/s and r/o as such 29Oct97. Regn cld 19Nov97 as transferred Denmark. Painted as **OY-SVU** and f/f as such 20Nov97. Lsd SUN-AIR of Scandinavia with del Woodford-Billund 20Nov97. Regd as OY-SVU 28Nov97. I/s 03Dec97 Billund to Oslo. Lsd BA CitiExpress 12-16Aug02. Repainted in 'Union Flag' c/s and noted as such at Hannover 09Mar06. Last service on behalf British Airways BA8268 from Oslo to Billund 29Mar06. Noted Billund 04Apr being masked up for painting on sale to West Air Sweden AB. Regn **SE-LNZ** rsvd to West Air Sweden AB 09May06 but NTU.

Ferried Billund-Lidköping 01Jun06 for E-class freight and JAA version mods. Regn **SE-LPX** rsvd to West Air Sweden AB 04Jul06. Noted Lidköping 22Sep06 in full West Air Europe c/s with white top and fin rather than the normal dark grey and with silver spinners painted as SE-LPX. Regd as SE-LPX to Siemens Financial Services AB 25Sep06. Entered service 09Oct06. R/o Isle of Man for engine runs painted as **LX-WAX** 26Jul11. Swedish regn cld as exported Luxembourg 27Jul11. Ferried Isle of Man to Oslo as LX-WAX 02Aug11. Restored as **SE-LPX** to European Turboprop Management AB for ops by West Air Sweden AB 17Sep13.

2064   (64)
Regd as **G-JLXI** to Jetstream Aircraft Ltd as a Jetstream 61 03Mar94 (CofR G-JLXI/R1). Components del Prestwick by road 25Oct92. First Prestwick assembled aircraft. F/f 10May94. Ferried East Midlands in primer for painting in Jetstream 61 c/s 18Jul94. Returned Prestwick 23Aug94. Shown at Farnborough Air Show 05-11Sep94. Dismantling commenced 19Aug96 and completed at Prestwick 12Apr97. Regn cld as PWFU 12Jun97. Nose to BAe Flying College as a flight simulator.
TT 179 hrs, 119 ldgs

2065   (65)
Fuselage del Prestwick 30Jan94 by road from Woodford for final assembly reportedly after systems installation completed. F/f 26Jul95 as **G-11-065** in primer. Dismantling commenced 12Aug96 and completed at Prestwick Mar97.

2066   (66)
Fuselage del Prestwick 01May93 by road from Woodford for final assembly. **G-11-066**. Completed up to engine installation in primer. Scrapped Prestwick between Sep96 and Mar97.

2067   (67)
Fuselage del Prestwick 23May93 by road from Woodford for final assembly. **G-11-067**. Not completed. Noted Prestwick 16Sep96 without engines, doors or leading edges. Scrapped Mar97.

2068   (68)
Fuselage del Prestwick 28Feb93 by road from Chadderton for final assembly. **G-11-068**. Not completed. Fuselage donated to Prestwick Fire Service 09Sep96.

2069   (69)
Fuselage del Prestwick 12Sep93 by road from Chadderton for final assembly. Not completed. Fuselage donated to Prestwick Fire Service 09Sep96. Rear section reported burnt by Jan99. Finally burnt & B/U by Feb04.

2070   (70)
Not completed. Fuselage to Chorley International Fire Training Centre at Astley near Chorley, UK by 19Mar96. Still present 02Apr09.

2071   (71)
Not completed. Fuselage to Woodford Airport Fire Department where converted to RFFS Smoke Training Facility by 28Feb96. Marked as **"N-ORAK"**. Moved to Manchester International Airport 08Aug11.

2072   (72)
Not completed. Fuselage to Manchester Airport Fire Service 07Mar96.

2073   (73)
Not completed. Fuselage to Blackpool Airport Fire service Mar96.

2074   (74)
Not completed. Fuselage stored Chadderton and later scrapped.

2075   (75)
Not completed. Forward and centre fuselage sections to Hawarden Airport Fire Service 23Apr96.

2076   (76)
Not completed. Scrapped Chadderton.

2077   (77)
Not completed. Scrapped Chadderton.

2078   (78)
Not completed. Nose only built - scrapped at Chadderton.

Chapter 10A
Registration and Constructor's
Number Cross-References

PORTUGAL			EC-GSG	2041	ESTONIA			G-BTPM	2043
			EC-GSH	2043				G-BTPN	2044
CS-TFJ	2018		EC-GSI	2044	ES-NBA	2023		G-BTPO	2051
CS-TGA	2008		EC-GUX	2024	ES-NBB	2018		G-BTTO	2033
CS-TGB	2009		EC-GYE	2007				G-BTUE	2039
CS-TGC	2024		EC-GYF	2010	UNITED KINGDOM			G-BTZG	2046
CS-TGL	2019		EC-GYR	2011				G-BTZH	2047
CS-TGM	2030		EC-GZH	2012	G-BMYK	2003		G-BTZI	2048
CS TGN	2031		EC-HCO	2052	G-BMYL	2004		G-BTZJ	2049
CS-TGX	2025		EC-HCY	2013	G-BMYM	2002		G-BTZK	2050
CS-TGY	2049		EC-HEH	2014	(G-BRKM)	2021		G-BUKJ	2052
			EC-HES	2042	G-BRLY	2025		G-BUUP	2008
			EC-HFM	2015	G-BRTG	2019		G-BUUR	2024
SPAIN			EC-HFR	2016	G-BTNI	2038		G-BUWM	2009
			EC-HGB	2010	G-BTNK	2037		G-BUWP	2053
EC-GJU	2033		EC-HGC	2007	G-BTPA	2007		G-BUYW	2061
EC-GKI	2039		EC-HGD	2011	G-BTPC	2010		G-BVEO	2059
EC-GKJ	2038		EC-HGE	2012	G-BTPD	2011		G-BWYT	2063
EC-GLC	2041		EC-HNA	2033	G-BTPE	2012		G-BZWW	2005
EC-GLD	2052				G-BTPF	2013		G-CORP	2037
EC-GLH	2042				G-BTPG	2014		G-ERIN	2003
EC-GNI	2043		EIRE		G-BTPH	2015		G-JATP	2055
EC-GNJ	2044				G-BTPJ	2016		G-JEMA	2028
EC-GSE	2038		(EI-COS)	2060	G-BTPK	2041		G-JEMB	2029
EC-GSF	2039		(EI-)	2059	G-BTPL	2042		G-JEMC	2032

CS-TGA c/n 2008 of Ligações Aéreas Regionais SA - LAR at Lisbon, Portugal.   *(WHC/BAe)*

Reg	C/n
G-JEMD	2026
G-JEME	2027
G-JEMF	2015
G-JLXI	2064
G-LOGA	2040
G-LOGB	2045
G-LOGC	2017
G-LOGD	2018
G-LOGE	2004
G-LOGF	2054
G-LOGG	2055
(G-LOGH)	2056
G-MANA	2056
G-MANB	2055
G-MANC	2054
G-MANE	2045
G-MANF	2040
G-MANG	2018
G-MANH	2017
G-MANJ	2004
(G-MANK)	2002
G-MANL	2003
G-MANM	2005
G-MANO	2006
G-MANP	2023
G-MANU	2008
G-MATP	2001
G-MAUD	2002
G-OAAF	2029
(G-OATP)	2001
G-OATP	2005
G-OBWL	2057
G-OBWM	2058
G-OBWN	2059
G-OBWO	2060
G-OBWP	2051
G-OBWR	2053
G-OEDE	2033
G-OEDF	2052
G-OEDH	2039
G-OEDI	2038
G-OEDJ	2024
G-OGVA	2039
G-OLCC	2017
G-OLCD	2018
G-PEEL	2023
G-PLXI	2001
G-SLAM	2038
G-UIET	2006
G-WISS	2020

SOUTH KOREA

Reg	C/n
HL5227	2061
HL5228	2063

LUXEMBOURG

Reg	C/n
LX-WAD	2038
LX-WAE	2037
LX-WAF	2056
(LX-WAG)	2053
(LX-WAH)	2004
(LX-WAI)	2002
(LX-WAJ	2062
LX-WAK	2061
LX-WAL	2059
LX-WAM	2060
LX-WAN	2020
LX-WAO	2043
LX-WAP	2057
LX-WAS	2058
LX-WAT	2011
LX-WAV	2041
LX-WAW	2021
LX-WAX	2063
(LX-WAZ)	2035

BULGARIA

Reg	C/n
LZ-BPS	2005

UNITED STATES

Reg	C/n
(N238JX)	2038
N375AE	2005
N376AE	2006
(N377AE)	2007
(N378AE)	2008
(N379AE)	2009
(N380AE)	2010
(N381AE)	2011
(N382AE)	2012
(N383AE)	2013
(N384AE)	2014
N851AW	2020
N852AW	2021
N853AW	2022
N854AW	2028
N855AW	2029
N856AW	2032
N857AW	2034
N858AW	2035
N859AW	2036
N860AW	2037

CZECH REPUBLIC

Reg	C/n
OK-TFN	2006
OK-VFO	2023

DENMARK

Reg	C/n
OY-SVI	2061
OY-SVT	2062
OY-SVU	2063

NETHERLANDS

Reg	C/n
PH-MGB	2042
PH-MGC	2052
(PH-MJF)	2033
(PH-MJG)	2038
(PH-MJK)	2042
(PH-MJL)	2052
PH-MJP	2023

INDONESIA

Reg	C/n
PK-DGA	2026
PK-DGB	2029
PK-DGC	2052
PK-DGI	2027
PK-MTV	2046
PK-MTW	2047
PK-MTX	2048
PK-MTY	2049
PK-MTZ	2050
PK-	2055

PHILIPPINES

Reg	C/n
RP-C2786	2055

SWEDEN

Reg	C/n
(SE-KXO)	2054
SE-KXP	2056
SE-LGU	2022
SE-LGV	2034
SE-LGX	2036
SE-LGY	2035
SE-LGZ	2021
(SE-LHX)	2026
SE-LHX	2020
(SE-LHZ)	2027
SE-LHZ	2059
SE-LLO	2023
(SE-LNX)	2057
SE-LNX	2061
(SE-LNY)	2058
SE-LNY	2062
(SE-LNZ)	2060
(SE-LNZ)	2063
SE-LPR	2057
SE-LPS	2043
SE-LPT	2058
SE-LPU	2060
SE-LPV	2041
SE-LPX	2063
SE-MAF	2002
SE-MAG	2003
SE-MAH	2004
SE-MAI	2010
SE-MAJ	2038
SE-MAK	2040
SE-MAL	2045
SE-MAM	2005
SE-MAN	2006
SE-MAO	2011
SE-MAP	2037
SE-MAR	2053
SE-MAY	2044
SE-MEE	2019
SE-MEG	2031
SE-MEX	2018
SE-MHC	2007
SE-MHD	2008
SE-MHE	2012
SE-MHF	2013
SE-MHG	2014
SE-MHI	2017
SE-MHJ	2024
SE-MHK	2033

GREECE

Reg	C/n
SX-BPS	2005
SX-BTK	2005

BANGLADESH

Reg	C/n
S2-ACX	2026
S2-ACY	2027
S2-ACZ	2033

TURKEY

Reg	C/n
TC-THP	2025
TC-TIIT	2039
TC-THU	2038
TC-THV	2033
TC-THZ	2052

INDIA

Reg	C/n
(VT-FFA)	2051
VT-FFA	2054
VT-FFB	2039
VT-FFC	2051

UNITED KINGDOM CLASS 'B' IDENTITIES

Reg	C/n
G-5-376	2006
G-11-5	2006
G-11-8	2008
G-11-9	2009
G-11-10	2010
G-11-19	2019
G-11-20	2020
G-11-21	2021
G-11-30	2030
G-11-32	2032
G-11-013	2013
G-11-021	2021
G-11-022	2022
G-11-024	2024
G-11-026	2026
G-11-027	2027
G-11-028	2028
G-11-029	2029
G-11-030	2030
G-11-031	2031
G-11-032	2032
G-11-033	2033
G-11-034	2034
G-11-035	2035
G-11-036	2036
G-11-037	2037
G-11-039	2039
G-11-041	2041
G-11-042	2042
G-11-045	2045
G-11-053	2053
G-11-054	2054
G-11-055	2055
G-11-056	2056
G-11-057	2057
G-11-058	2058
G-11-059	2059
G-11-060	2060
G-11-061	2061
G-11-062	2062
G-11-063	2063
G-11-065	2065
G-11-2043	2043

The first ATP to be painted in West Atlantic livery was c/n 2015, shown here in 2009 as G-BTPH before entering service. The West Air/West Atlantic group of companies have owned more ATPs than any other operator.   *(BAE Systems)*

Chapter 10B
BAe ATP Current Status Report

2002	F		SE-MAF	West Atlantic	Stored Malmö	2034	F		SE-LGV	West Atlantic	Stored Isle of Man
2004	F		SE-MAH	West Atlantic	Stored Malmö	2035	F		SE-LGY	West Atlantic	Stored Malmö
2005	**F LFD**		**SE-MAM**	**West Atlantic**	**Active**	**2036**	**F**		**SE-LGX**	**West Atlantic**	**Active**
2006	**F LFD**		**SE-MAN**	**West Atlantic**	**Active**	**2037**	**F LFD**		**SE-MAP**	**West Atlantic**	**Active**
2007	F LFD		SE-MHC	West Atlantic	Stored Coventry	**2038**	**F LFD**		**SE-MAJ**	**West Atlantic**	**Active**
						2040	**Pax**		**SE-MAK**	**NextJet**	**Active**
2008	**F LFD**		**SE-MHD**	**West Atlantic**	**Active**	2041	F LFD		SE-LPV	West Atlantic	Stored Malmö
2010	**F LFD**		**SE-MAI**	**West Atlantic**	**Active**						
2011	**F LFD**		**SE-MAO**	**West Atlantic**	**Active**	2042	F		G-BTPL	West Atlantic	Stored Coventry
2012	**F LFD**		**SE-MHE**	**West Atlantic**	**Active**						
2013	**F LFD**		**SE-MHF**	**West Atlantic**	**Active**	**2043**	**F LFD**		**SE-LPS**	**West Atlantic**	**Active**
2014	**F LFD**		**SE-MHG**	**West Atlantic**	**Active**	2044	F		SE-MAY	West Atlantic	Stored Malmö
2015	**F LFD**		**SE-MHH**	**West Atlantic**	**Active**						
2016	F LFD		G-BTPJ	West Atlantic	Stored Coventry	**2045**	**Pax**		**SE-MAL**	**NextJet**	**Active**
						2051	F		G-OBWP	West Atlantic	Stored Coventry
2017	**F LFD**		**SE-MHI**	**West Atlantic**	**Active**						
2018	**Pax**		**SE-MEX**	**NextJet**	**Active**	**2052**	**F**		**PK-DGC**	**Deraya**	**Active**
2019	Pax		SE-MEE	NextJet	Stored Malmö	**2053**	**F**		**SE-MAR**	**West Atlantic**	**Active**
2020	F		SE-LHX	West Atlantic	Stored Isle of Man	2054	F		G-MANC	West Atlantic	Stored Coventry
2021	**F LFD**		**SE-LGZ**	**West Atlantic**	**Active**	2055	Pax		RP-C2786	Regional One	Stored Manila
2022	F		SE-LGU	West Atlantic	Stored Malmö						
						2056	**F LFD**		**SE-KXP**	**West Atlantic**	**Active**
2023	**Pax**		**SE-LLO**	**NextJet**	**Active**	**2057**	**F**		**SE-LPR**	**West Atlantic**	**Active**
2024	F LFD		SE-MHJ	West Atlantic	Stored Coventry	**2058**	**F**		**SE-LPT**	**West Atlantic**	**Active**
						2059	**F**		**SE-LHZ**	**West Atlantic**	**Active**
2026	**F LFD**		**PK-DGA**	**Deraya**	**Active**	2060	F		SE-LPU	West Atlantic	Stored Coventry
2031	Pax		CS-TGN	West Atlantic	Stored Malmö						
						2061	**F**		**SE-LNX**	**West Atlantic**	**Active**
2033	F LFD		SE-MHK	West Atlantic	Stored Malmö	**2062**	**F**		**SE-LNY**	**West Atlantic**	**Active**
						2063	**F**		**SE-LPX**	**West Atlantic**	**Active**